MATTHEW TO ACTS

TEACHER
GENESIS TO REVELATION SERIES
VOLUME 3

ABINGDON PRESS

Nashville

ISBN 0-687-07228-X
ISBN 978-0-687-07228-6
Manufactured in the United States of America

This book is printed on acid-free paper.

09 10 11—14 13 12 11

GENESIS TO REVELATION SERIES, VOLUME 3
Table of Contents

HOW TO TEACH GENESIS TO REVELATION

Unique Features of This Bible Study

In Genesis to Revelation, you and your class will study the Bible in three steps. Each step provides a different level of understanding of the Scripture. We call these steps Dimension One, Dimension Two, and Dimension Three.

Dimension One concerns what the Bible actually says. You do not interpret the Scripture at this point; you merely take account of what it says. Your main goal for this dimension is to get the content of the passage clear in your mind. What does the Bible say?

Dimension One is in workbook form. The members of the class will write the answers to questions about the passage in the space provided in the student book. All the questions in Dimension One can be answered by reading the Bible itself. Be sure the class finishes Dimension One before going on to Dimensions Two and Three.

Dimension Two concerns information that will shed light on the Scripture under consideration. Dimension Two will answer such questions as

- What are the original meanings of some of the words used in the passage?
- What is the original background of the passage?
- Why was the passage most likely written?
- What are the relationships between the persons mentioned in the passage?
- What geographical and cultural factors affect the meaning of the passage?

The question for Dimension Two is, What information do we need in order to understand the meaning of the passage? In Dimension One the class members will discover what the Bible says. In Dimension Two they will discover what the Bible means.

Dimension Three focuses on interpreting the Scripture and applying it to life situations. The questions here are

- What is the meaning of the passage for my life?
- What response does the passage require of me as a Christian?
- What response does this passage require of us as a group?

Dimension Three questions have no easy answers. The task of applying the Scripture to life situations is up to you and the class.

Aside from the three-dimensional approach, another unique feature of this study is the organization of the series as a whole. Classes that choose to study the Genesis to Revelation Series will be able to study all the books of the Bible in their biblical order. This method will give the class continuity that is not present in most other Bible studies. The class will read and study virtually every verse of the Bible, from Genesis straight through to Revelation.

How many times have you stumbled over a biblical name or maybe even avoided discussing a person or place because you could not pronounce the word? While you are

using the Genesis to Revelation Series, you may find a good Bible pronunciation guide helpful. These are available from any Christian bookstore. The *Harper's Bible Pronunciation Guide* (The Society of Biblical Literature, 1989, ISBN 0-06-068951-X) is one such guide.

An excellent additional resource is *Bible Teacher Kit* (Abingdon, 1994, ISBN 0-687-78006-3). It has both Bible maps and a glossary of terms.

Weekly Preparation

Begin planning for each session early in the week. Read the passage that the lesson covers, and write the answers to Dimension One questions in the student book. Then read Dimensions Two and Three in the student book. Make a note of any questions or comments you have. Finally, study the material in the teacher book carefully. Decide how you want to organize your class session.

Organizing the Class Session

Since Genesis to Revelation involves three steps in studying the Scripture, you will want to organize your class sessions around these three dimensions. Each lesson in the student book and this teacher book consists of three parts.

The first part of each lesson in the teacher book is the same as the Dimension One section in the student book, except that the teacher book includes the answers to Dimension One questions. These questions and answers are taken from the New International Version of the Bible.

You might use Dimension One in several ways:

1. Ask the group members to read the Scripture and to write the answers to all the Dimension One questions before coming to class. This method will require that the class covenant to spend the necessary amount of study time outside of class. When the class session begins, read through the Dimension One questions, asking for responses from the group members. If anyone needs help with any of the answers, look at the biblical reference together.

2. Or, if you have enough class time, you might spend the first part of the session working through the Dimension One questions together as a group. Locate the Scripture references, ask the questions one at a time, and invite the class members to find the answers and to read them aloud. Then allow enough time for them to write the answers in the student book.

3. Or, take some time at the beginning of the class session for group members to work individually. Have them read the Dimension One questions and the Scripture references and then write their answers to the questions in the spaces provided in the student book. Discuss together any questions or answers in Dimension One that do not

seem clear. This approach may take longer than the others, but it provides a good change of pace from time to time.

You do not have to organize your class sessions the same way every week. Ask the class members what they prefer. Experiment! You may find ways to study the Dimension One material other than the ones listed above.

The second part of each lesson in this teacher book corresponds to the second part of the student book lessons. The Dimension Two section of the student book provides background information to help the students understand the Scripture. Become familiar with the information in the student book.

Dimension Two of this teacher book contains additional information on the passage. The teacher book goes into more depth with some parts of the passage than the student book does. You will want to share this information with the group in whatever way seems appropriate. For example, if someone raises a question about a particular verse, share any additional background information from the teacher book.

You might raise a simple question such as, What words or phrases gave you trouble in understanding the passage? or, Having grasped the content of the passage, what questions remain in your mind? Encourage the group members to share confusing points, troublesome words or phrases, or lingering questions. Write these problems on poster paper or chalkboard. This list of concerns will form the outline for the second portion of the session.

These concerns may also stimulate some research on the part of the group members. If your study group is large enough, divide the class into three groups. Then divide the passage for the following week into three parts. Assign a portion of the passage to each group. Using Bible commentaries and Bible dictionaries, direct each group to discover as much as it can about this portion of the passage before the class meets again. Each group will then report its findings during the class session.

The third part of each lesson in this teacher book relates to Dimension Three in the student book. This section helps class members discover how to apply the Scripture to their own lives. Here you will find one or more interpretations of the passage—whether traditional, historical, or contemporary. Use these interpretations when appropriate to illumine the passage for the group members.

Dimension Three in the student book points out some of the issues in the passage that are relevant to our lives. For each of these issues, the student book raises questions to help the students assess the meaning of the Scripture for their lives. The information in Dimension Three of the teacher book is designed to help you lead the class in discussing these issues. Usually, you will find a more in-depth discussion of portions of the Scripture.

The discussion in the teacher book will give you a better perspective on the Scripture and its interpretation before you begin to assess its meaning for today. You will probably want to share this Dimension Three information with the class to open the discussion. For each life situation, the teacher book contains suggestions on facilitating the class discussion. You, as the teacher, are responsible for group discussions of Dimension Three issues.

Assembling Your Materials

You will need at least three items to prepare for and conduct each class session:
• A teacher book
• A student book
• A Bible—you may use any translation or several; the answers in this teacher book are taken from the New International Version.

One advantage of the Genesis to Revelation Series is that the study is self-contained. That is, all you need to teach this Bible study is provided for you in the student and teacher books. Occasionally, or perhaps on a regular basis, you might want to consult other sources for additional information.

HOW TO LEAD A DISCUSSION

The Teacher as Discussion Leader

As the teacher of this series or a part of this series, one of your main responsibilities during each class period will be to lead the class discussion. Some teachers are apprehensive about leading a discussion. In many ways, it is easier to lecture to the class. But remember that the class members will surely benefit more from the class sessions when they actively participate in a discussion of the material.

Leading a discussion is a skill that any teacher can master with practice. And keep in mind—especially if your class is not used to discussion—that the members of your group will also be learning through practice. The following are some pointers on how to lead interesting and thought-provoking discussions in the study group.

Preparing for a Discussion—Where Do I Start?

1. Focus on the subject that will be discussed and on the goal you want to achieve through that discussion.

2. Prepare by collecting information and data that you will need; jot down these ideas, facts, and questions so that you will have them when you need them.

3. Begin organizing your ideas; stop often to review your work. Keep in mind the climate within the group—attitudes, feelings, eagerness to participate and learn.

4. Consider possible alternative group procedures. Be prepared for the unexpected.

5. Having reached your goal, think through several ways to bring the discussion to a close.

As the teacher, do not feel that your responsibility is to give a full account or report of the assigned material. This practice promotes dependency. Instead, through stimulating questions and discussion, the participants will read the material—not because you tell them to but because they want to read and prepare.

How Do I Establish a Climate for Learning?

The teacher's readiness and preparation quickly establish a climate in which the group can proceed and its members learn and grow. The anxiety and fear of an unprepared teacher are contagious but so are the positive vibrations coming from a teacher who is prepared to move into a learning enterprise.

An attitude of shared ownership is also basic. Group members need to perceive themselves as part of the learning experience. Persons establish ownership by working on goals, sharing concerns, and accepting major responsibility for learning.

Here are several ways the teacher can foster a positive climate for learning and growth.

1. *Readiness.* A teacher who is always fully prepared can promote, in turn, the group's readiness to learn.

2. *Exploration.* When the teacher encourages group members to freely explore new ideas, persons will know they are in a group whose primary function is learning.

3. *Exposure.* A teacher who is open, honest, and willing to reveal himself or herself to the group will encourage students to discuss their feelings and opinions.

4. *Confidentiality.* A teacher can create a climate for learning when he or she respects the confidentiality of group members and encourages the group members to respect one another's confidentiality.

5. *Acceptance.* When a teacher shows a high degree of acceptance, students can likewise accept one another honestly.

How Can I Deal With Conflict?

What if conflict or strong disagreement arises in your group? What do you do? Think about the effective and ineffective ways you have dealt with conflict in the past.

Group conflict may come from one of several sources. One common source of conflict involves personality clashes. Any group is almost certain to contain at least two persons whose personalities clash. If you break your class into smaller groups for discussion, be sure these persons are in separate groups.

Another common source of group conflict is subject matter. The Bible can be a very controversial subject. Remember the difference between discussion or disagreement and conflict. As a teacher you will have to decide when to encourage discussion and when to discourage conflict that is destructive to the group process.

Group conflict may also come from a general atmosphere conducive to expression of ideas and opinions. Try to discourage persons in the group from being judgmental toward others and their ideas. Keep reminding the class that each person is entitled to his or her own opinions and that no one opinion is more valid than another.

How Much Should I Contribute to the Discussion?

Many teachers are unsure about how much they should contribute to the class discussions. Below are several pitfalls to avoid.

1. The teacher should remain neutral on a question until the group has had adequate time to discuss it. At the proper time in the discussion the teacher can offer his or her opinion. The teacher can direct the questions to the group at large, rechanneling those questions that come to him or her.

At times when the members need to grapple with a question or issue, the most untimely response a teacher can make is answering the question. Do not fall into the trap of doing the group members' work for them. Let them struggle with the question.

However, if the teacher has asked the group members to reveal thoughts and feelings, then group members have the right to expect the same of the teacher. A teacher has no right to ask others to reveal something he or she is unwilling to reveal. A teacher can reveal thoughts and feelings, but at the appropriate time.

The refusal to respond immediately to a question often takes self-discipline. The teacher has spent time thinking, reading, and preparing. Thus the teacher usually does have a point of view and waiting for others to respond calls for restraint.

2. Another pitfall is the teacher's making a speech or extended comments in expressing an opinion or summarizing what has been said. For example, in an attempt to persuade others, a teacher may speak, repeat, or strongly emphasize what someone says concerning a question.

3. Finally, the pitfall of believing the teacher must know "the answers" to the questions is always apparent. The teacher need not know all the answers. Many questions that should be raised are ultimate and unanswerable; other questions are open-ended; and still others have several answers.

BIBLE TEACHER KIT (Abingdon Press, 1994, ISBN 0-687-78006-3)

This essential tool kit for teachers of Bible study classes is full of resources to enhance the learning process. The three-ring binder contains 160 resource pages featuring

• background articles
• charts
• a timeline
• a glossary of biblical terms
• eight 20" x 32" full-color maps of Bible lands
• ten one-color maps of Bible lands then and now
• a full-color video of Bible lands

Many of the resource pages include photocopying privileges, so you can distribute additional copies to members of the class or photocopy onto transparencies.

The kit also includes

• eight 20" x 32" full-color maps of Bible lands
• a full-color video of Bible lands

MATTHEW
Table of Contents

About the Writers

Robert E. Luccock is a retired minister. He was professor of worship and preaching, Boston University School of Theology, Boston, Massachusetts. David Kueker is pastor of Pawnee United Methodist Church, Pawnee, Illinois.

INTRODUCTION TO MATTHEW

by David Kueker

The meaning of Christianity rests upon the meaning of the Christ, Jesus of Nazareth, and the meaning of his life, his deeds, his teachings, his death, and his resurrection. The first four books of the New Testament, known as Gospels, tell us the story of the life of Jesus. The word *gospel* means "good news." *The Gospel According to Matthew* means "the good news of Jesus Christ from Matthew's viewpoint."

Where Did the Gospels Come From?

The Bible contains four Gospels, known as Matthew, Mark, Luke, and John. Tradition assigns their authorship to the disciples Matthew and John, Peter's travel companion John Mark, and Paul's travel companion, the physician Luke. The early church thought that the Gospels were only trustworthy if written by eyewitnesses or those close to eyewitnesses.

In fact, the Gospels themselves are anonymous works. Nowhere do the authors name themselves, except the author of John who describes himself as "the beloved disciple" and says no more. For the sake of convenience, however, we continue to use the names that history has given the Gospels: Matthew, Mark, Luke, and John.

Many different people had input to the developing understanding of Jesus' life. Modern scholarship sees several levels to the development of the Gospels. The first level is the historical event of what Jesus said or did before eyewitnesses.

The second level is the retelling of what Jesus said or did, again and again. Both Jewish-Christians and Gentile-Christians passed on what Jesus said or did according to their vital needs. Scholars call this the *verbal tradition*. The words and deeds of Jesus lived on in this way for at least thirty years.

As these bits of Jesus' words and deeds were being told and retold, each began to take on a form. Some lost their historical context and became brief sayings, almost proverbs. In the process of being told and retold, the parables of Jesus were translated into the practical needs of the first-century Christian churches. Therefore some parables are very short, while others are long and complicated. Other bits of the tradition held on to details of where they happened in the life of Jesus. In time these bits began to be connected by the early church into small informal collections that were told together.

And then someone decided to gather these unwritten bits of history, put them in an order, and write them down. Now one could read a complete statement about Jesus from the beginning of his life to the events after his death. A scholar would call this person a *redactor*, a word that means "editor." These editors gathered the stories of Jesus from every source they could find and put them together in an order like pearls on a string.

The three levels can be seen in Luke's explanation of the origin of his own Gospel (Luke 1:1-4).

1. *Historical Events:* "Many have undertaken to draw up an account of the things that have been fulfilled among us. . . ."

2. *Verbal Tradition:* ". . . just as they were handed down to us by those who from the first were eyewitnesses and servants of the word. . . ."

3. *Redactor:* ". . . it seemed good also to me to write an orderly account for you. . . ."

The layers move from what Jesus actually said, through the memories of eyewitnesses and the early church, up to the editor who brought all the material together. Remember that persons at each level heard Jesus speaking to them in the story on a personal level. The story meant something to them. As they passed it on in their own words, we also receive their perspective along with the words of Jesus.

That this perspective has been passed along is not negative. The translations of the various versions of the Bible available today also add their perspective as they translate. They cannot help it. These additions are not harmful as long as we are aware of them.

As we read Matthew, then, we need to keep the following three sets of questions in our mind:

1. Why is this passage important to Matthew, the editor? What point is Matthew trying to make?

2. Why is this passage important to the disciples and the early church? What problems might they have faced that made this saying of Jesus especially meaningful to them?

3. What was the intent and purpose of Jesus? What was he trying to say to the people he spoke to? Jesus was a Jew speaking to other Jews. The Gospels are writings of the early church, which was made up mostly of non-Jewish Christians.

For example, the early church quickly fastened upon the words of Jesus in the Sermon on the Mount as highly important teachings of Jesus in contrast with the teaching of the Pharisees.

In Matthew 5:28-29a, Jesus says: "But I tell you that anyone who looks at a woman lustfully has already committed adultery with her in his heart. If your right eye causes you to sin, gauge it out and throw it away. . . ."

The early church took this advice at face value. For this reason, and because of the mood of the times, men and women secluded themselves in cloistered monasteries. For years people took those phrases literally.

A careful reading and a concern for the purpose of Jesus, however, may lead us to decide that his words are not a pronouncement that "lust is the same as adultery." We may see that his intention was to knock the props out from under the self-righteousness of any of his hearers. "Underneath you are all the same," Jesus could have been saying, "and you all stand in need of God's forgiveness." This stance outraged the Pharisees and is consistent with the context.

Keeping these three sets of questions in mind helps us understand the point that Matthew is trying to make to the readers of his generation. But it can also lead us into a deeper understanding of what the Bible means. These questions are particularly important when a particular section of Matthew is difficult to understand.

How Is Matthew Related to the Other Gospels?

The first three Gospels, Matthew, Mark, and Luke, also known as the *Synoptic Gospels,* are very closely related. (John's material is so different that it appears to be unrelated.) Because of this, early scholars began to wonder if one of the first three Gospels was a "parent" to the other two. Two of the three might be adaptations of the other. This question became known as the *synoptic problem.*

Certain evidence suggests a parent Gospel. Matthew, Mark, and Luke all share quite a lot of material that is worded almost exactly alike. Most of the rest of Matthew and Luke that does not appear in Mark is strikingly similar. Each Gospel also has portions that appear only in that Gospel.

The most widely accepted theory is that Mark's Gospel, the shortest, was the first to be written. Mark was a resource for the writing of Matthew and Luke. Matthew and Luke have some material in common that is not found in Mark. To account for this, scholars believe that they may have had another written source. This source was a collection of Jesus' sayings and parables that scholars called "Q," short for the German word for source, *Quelle.* This theory is called the *two-sources theory.* Matthew and Luke might have written their Gospels with Mark and "Q" in front of them. They were seeking to provide a more complete account of Jesus' life. In this theory, "M" and "L" stand for material that appears only in Matthew and Luke.

Another theory is based on the fact that where Matthew and Mark disagree on passages they have in common, Luke agrees with Matthew. Therefore Matthew or Luke would have been first. Mark's Gospel then would be a very carefully constructed condensation of Matthew. The tradition of the early church, well established less than a century after Jesus' death, is that Matthew was the first Gospel.

Who Was the Author of Matthew?

The author of the Gospel According to Matthew remains a shadowy figure. His book shows him to be well acquainted with Judaism and probably a trained scribe and teacher. While he is critical of the Judaism of Jesus' time, he is careful to show Jesus as emerging from the traditions of the Old Testament. The Gospel is intended to present Jesus either to people of Jewish background or to a people very familiar with Judaism.

The author of Matthew's Gospel writes after the destruction of Jerusalem (Matthew 22:7). Therefore a dating before about A.D. 70 is excluded. Some time has probably elapsed since the composition of Mark's Gospel. Therefore Matthew could have been written in A.D. 85. The critical attitude toward Judaism suggests an origin outside Israel but close enough to Israel to be within the Jewish sphere of influence. Most scholars suggest the author came from Syria or Northern Palestine. Some think the author came from Antioch, one of the largest and most important cities in the Roman Empire. Antioch was located in Syria, north of Galilee. As an important trading center and the Roman provincial capital, Antioch had a large Jewish community and was an early stronghold of the Christian community.

Matthew's Gospel spread quickly and soon became very important in the early church. Passages from Matthew are more frequently quoted in the writings of early Christians than any of the other Gospels. Matthew's importance then and now is as a teaching Gospel. Matthew's intention is to teach us how to be disciples of Christ. Matthew is carefully organized so that it lends itself easily to teaching, preaching, and being read in worship. Its passages are beautifully and meaningfully rendered. Matthew's Gospel also answers questions. Written with an eye toward disputes in the early church, Matthew attempts to give an authoritative "last word" on a subject. Many questions that are raised by Mark's rougher version of Jesus' life are smoothed over and answered neatly in Matthew.

What Is the Structure of Matthew's Gospel?

Matthew's intentions as a teaching Gospel can particularly be seen in how he structures his Gospel. Sections of Jesus' teaching are alternated with the ongoing story of Jesus' life and death, which is called *the narrative.* Five times during the story of the life of Jesus, Matthew stops the narrative to give whole chapters of the teachings of Jesus on a subject. Matthew, then, is made up of six narratives (historical) sections, with five teaching sections between them.

Chapters 1–4 (Historical): Birth and Appearance
Chapters 5–7 (Teaching): Righteous Living
Chapters 8–9 (Historical): Mighty Works
Chapter 10 (Teaching): How to Be a Missionary
Chapters 11–12 (Historical): Jesus Rejected by His People
Chapter 13 (Teaching): The Kingdom of God
Chapters 14–17 (Historical): The Messiah Corrects the Pharisees
Chapter 18 (Teaching): Loving Those With No Status
Chapters 19–23 (Historical): The Final Confrontation in Jerusalem
Chapters 24–25 (Teaching): The Second Coming
Chapters 26–28 (Historical): Passion, Death, Resurrection

What Is the Theology of Matthew?

Jesus fulfills the faith of the Old Testament.

Matthew wanted his readers to see that Jesus not only emerged out of orthodox Jewish tradition, but also fulfills many ancient prophecies. Matthew uses a style that echoes Old Testament phrases and commonly used words and uses over sixty quotes from the Old Testament. Matthew thereby establishes Jesus as the Messiah through the Old Testament. Thus Jesus emerged from Judaism, but Matthew shows clearly the contrast between Jesus' teaching and that of normal Judaism as taught by the scribes and Pharisees. Matthew advises a balance between the tradition of the Old Testament and the tendency of the new emerging non-Jewish early church to ignore the Jewish tradition as irrelevant. " 'Every teacher of the law who has been instructed about kingdom of heaven is like the owner of a house who brings out of his storeroom new treasures as well as old' " (13:52).

Discipleship and the church are important.

Matthew's Gospel is the "how to" manual for the individual disciple and the early church. High standards are set for both. It instructs the individual, for example, in how to be a good person (Chapters 5–7) and how to be a missionary (Chapter 10). Chapter 18 instructs the church not to be haughty or proud. Persons are to love those with little status, such as the children, who should be sought as "lost sheep." Those who fall short of the requirements of discipleship are to be forgiven and given another chance.

The Gospel also reflects Matthew's concern that discipleship is submission to authority, first to Jesus and then to the church's leaders. Matthew, for example, is the only Gospel to contain Jesus' speech where Peter is given "the keys of the kingdom of heaven."

The kingdom of God will reign in the present and future.

The reign of Christ as Lord over the souls of his followers in the present will be followed by a gathering of the faithful disciples into a real kingdom of God in the near future. Many of the Kingdom passages relate to the high ethical conduct required of the disciples as they are exhorted to prepare for the coming of the Kingdom. And so the kingdom of God is shown to be present, as the reign of King Jesus has begun in their hearts. Yet Matthew's Gospel is also apocalyptic, for Matthew's church serves and waits for the second coming of the King (Chapters 24–25). The Kingdom in Matthew seems primarily to be a heavenly rather than an earthly place, contrary to current popular interpretation.

Matthew, following Jewish custom with only five exceptions, substitutes the phrase "kingdom of heaven" for "kingdom of God" used in the other Gospels. The name of God was sacred and not used lightly in everyday conversation, so Matthew politely substitutes *heaven.*

They will call him Immanuel—which means, "God with us" (1:23).

— 1 —

Jesus' Birth, Infancy, and Baptism

Matthew 1–3

DIMENSION ONE:
WHAT DOES THE BIBLE SAY?

Answer these questions by reading Matthew 1

1. With whom does the genealogy of Jesus begin? (1:2)

    The genealogy begins with Abraham.

2. What five women are included? (1:3, 5, 6, 16)

    Tamar, Rahab, Ruth, the wife of Uriah (Bathsheba), and Mary are included.

3. Is the ancestry traced to Joseph or Mary? (1:16)

    The ancestry is traced to Joseph.

4. How many generations are reported? (1:17)

    Forty-two generations are reported, in three groups of fourteen each.

5. What are the major divisions in the ancestry? (1:17)

    The ancestry is divided from Abraham to David, from David to the Babylonian Exile, from the Exile to the Christ.

6. Why does Joseph first want to divorce Mary? (1:18)

    Mary is with child before they come together.

7. What does the name *Jesus* signify? (1:21)

    He will save his people from their sins.

Answer these questions by reading Matthew 2

8. Who is the king of Judea when Jesus is born? (2:1)

    Herod is the king.

9. How do the Magi (wise men) know that Jesus is to be born in Bethlehem? (2:5-6)

    It is written by the prophet (Micah).

10. Why don't the wise men return to Herod? (2:12)

    They are warned in a dream not to return to Herod.

11. Why does Joseph take the family to Egypt? (2:13)

    Joseph is warned in a dream that Herod is about to search for the child and kill him.

12. Whom does Herod kill in Bethlehem? (2:16)

    He kills all boys in Bethlehem and its vicinity who are two years old and under.

13. Where does Joseph take Jesus and Mary when they return from Egypt? (2:21-23)

    They went to Israel first, then to Galilee.

Answer these questions by reading Matthew 3

14. What message does John the Baptist preach? (3:2)

    John preaches for the people to "Repent, for the kingdom of heaven is near."

15. Who foretells that a preacher will "prepare the way for the Lord"? (3:3)

    Isaiah foretells this (Isaiah 40:3).

16. Where do the people come from who want to be baptized by John? (3:5)

    They come from Jerusalem, Judea, and the whole region of the Jordan.

17. Whom does John call a "brood of vipers"? (3:7)

John calls the Pharisees and Sadducees vipers.

18. What does John tell them to do? (3:8)

They are to "produce fruit in keeping with repentance."

19. Why does John first refuse to baptize Jesus? (3:14)

He says that Jesus should baptize him.

20. Why does Jesus say it is fitting for John to baptize him? (3:15)

Jesus says it is proper "to fulfill all righteousness."

21. What does Jesus see when he is baptized? (3:16)

Jesus sees the Spirit of God descending like a dove and lighting on him.

22. What does the voice from heaven say? (3:17)

"This is my Son, whom I love; with him I am well pleased."

DIMENSION TWO:
WHAT DOES THE BIBLE MEAN?

A familiar saying is "Don't judge a book by its cover." We could sometimes say, "Don't judge a book by its title." The Gospel According to Matthew may be such a book. It would not be altogether accurate to describe this as a book by Matthew. He compiled it, he edited it, but he did not *write* it, as Thomas Carlyle wrote *A History of the French Revolution.* Matthew incorporated extended passages of earlier works in his book. But it would be equally misleading to say that Matthew merely compiled and edited more original work. Matthew brought all the material together in an original way to make a statement about Jesus that had not been made in this particular way. His Gospel is one of the most original books ever published.

Scholars have devoted lifetimes to identifying the sources of Matthew's Gospel. In a few bold strokes we can only suggest the outlines of scholars' work. Matthew contains almost the entire Gospel According to Mark (600 of the 661 verses) with remarkably few changes. Two hundred and thirty-five verses, out of the 1,068 in Matthew, come from a source known as "Q." This source is found in Luke but is seemingly unknown to Mark. The remaining 230 verses are peculiar to Matthew alone, coming from written and oral traditions. The importance of such source analysis for students should be that Matthew's Gospel is a proclamation of the faith of the first-century Christian church, a gathering together of the common tradition concerning Jesus the Christ. The Gospels emerged from the church, not the other way around. And not by the writing of just three men called Evangelists.

Matthew 1:16, 21, 23. Three names (Christ, Jesus, and Immanuel) are given to Jesus in Chapter 1. They are probably more important than anything else in the chapter. We shall discuss the titles *Christ* and *Immanuel* and the name *Jesus* later at points where the name and titles are associated with Jesus' activity (9:1-8; 16:13-20; 28:16-20).

The student book does not go into a discussion of the names and titles at this time. This seems better left to the times when the meaning of the names can be seen in the activity of Jesus' life. In this first unit of study it is important for students to recognize how revealing the names and titles are. They should focus their attention elsewhere, though. You may want to make sure everyone understands that *Christ* is not Jesus' last name. *Christ* means the "chosen or anointed one."

Matthew 1:1-17. These verses are the genealogy for Jesus. For centuries the Jews had hoped that a messiah would come with salvation and deliverance for Israel. The Messiah was to be a "Son of David." In Jesus, one had come who promised salvation from sin, one whom God raised victorious even over death. The genealogy confirms the hope of many in Israel that Jesus is the Son of David. Again and again throughout the Gospel, Jesus is addressed as "Son of David" (12:23; 15:22; 20:30-31; 21:9, 15).

The students may want to compare the genealogies of Matthew and Luke (Luke 3:23-38). The main difference is that Luke goes all the way back to Adam, while Matthew stops with Abraham. Matthew concerns himself only with Jesus' descent in the line of the covenant with Israel. Luke sees Jesus as a universal Savior, tracing his line back to human beginnings.

You may want to discuss the four women who appear on the list before it comes to Mary. Tamar, a widow, slept with her father-in-law (Genesis 38). Ruth was an alien (Ruth 1:4). Rahab was a prostitute in Jericho (Joshua 2:1-7). Bathsheba (Uriah's wife) was seduced by David (2 Samuel 11–12). Matthew's listing of these women helps show how God uses ordinary people to carry out the divine purpose. Most of the names on the list are ordinary people, with their own sins and their own faithfulness. God does not restrict the agents of holy purpose to the people of Israel.

Matthew does not hide the problem of how Jesus could be born of the virgin Mary, yet be descended from David through Joseph. He does not solve it, either. As suggested in the student book, trying to explain this discrepancy serves little purpose. Whether or not Jesus is the Christ does not depend on a solution to this riddle.

Matthew 1:18-25. These verses announce Jesus' birth. How could Joseph plan to divorce a woman he had not yet married? In those days parents sometimes arranged for even their very young children to be married later in life. When they became old enough, the engagement was then ratified. The couple are now betrothed and must remain so for one year. In every way except conjugal love they are recognized as husband and wife. The relationship is so binding one can break it only by divorce. Mary and Joseph are at this stage when she becomes pregnant. A divorced woman was helpless and almost hopeless in those days. Our story reflects Joseph's torn feelings of shame at Mary's discovery and tender concern for what would happen to her.

Matthew 1:23. The class may wish to discuss the question of the virgin birth. However, the discussion should not take time and attention from matters more central to New Testament faith. Only Matthew and Luke mention the virgin birth. Mark, John, and Paul say nothing about it. The virgin birth apparently is not essential to the idea of Jesus the Christ for some persons. Above all, the class should respect and affirm the faith of each student whatever he or she believes about this matter. Verse 20 is the affirmation none can afford to miss: "What is conceived in her is from the Holy Spirit." We can hear this as much more than a clinical report. Whatever the nature of Jesus' conception in Mary's body, that he is a child of the Holy Spirit determines his mind, spirit, and destiny.

Matthew 2. The wise men were probably astrologers (Magi) from Persia to the east of Israel. The story does not call them kings (as does the Christian hymn). Nor does it tell us that there were three of them. This number comes from the number of gifts they presented. That they came "from the East" is more than a passing detail. Even in the manger, Israel has not exclusive possession of Jesus.

Matthew 2:16. Herod had five wives during his life. He murdered one of these women. Of his seven children, he killed three sons. The remaining sons were guilty of incest with each other's daughters. Herod Antipas, Herod's son, had John the Baptist beheaded. At the time, he was married to his half-brother's wife, Herodias. This was the same Herod who mocked Jesus at his trial. An appalling family to be kings in Israel!

Matthew 2:15. Matthew repeatedly mentions Old Testament prophecies and predictions to account for what happens in Jesus' life. In this way, he affirms that the salvation history of the Jews is preparation for the fulfillment in Christ. If we try to take it all literally it may make Jesus seem almost like a puppet simply going through the pre-programmed action prescribed in ancient Scripture. In the prophet Hosea's mind (Hosea 11:1), the words "out of Egypt I called my son" refer to Israel's deliverance from slavery in Egypt. Matthew turns these words into a prediction of the child Jesus taking refuge in Egypt. But Matthew's implausible reinterpretation of Scripture should not trouble us. He was following a well-understood course familiar to early Christian apologists. Whether they shape the story to fit the Scripture, or reach for quotations to support the story, the fulfilling purpose of God stands quite independent of Old Testament "predictions."

Matthew 1:20; 2:12, 13, 19, 22. Much of what is crucial in these events happens because of dreams. People in the ancient world put great stock in the interpretation of dreams. They trusted that God might speak to them through their dreams. We need not rationalize such an expectation as intuition, the subconscious mind at work, or extrasensory perception. Whatever happens, however it comes about, we see God moving "in mysterious ways." God used dreams such as the ones that came to Joseph and the wise men to protect the young child.

Matthew 3. To move from Chapter 2 to Chapter 3 is to cross three important dividing lines. Students of the Gospel should be aware of these divisions. The first line makes a thirty-year leap through time. Herod died in what we now call 4 B.C. Soon after that, Joseph, Mary, and the infant Jesus went to Nazareth. At the second line, when next we see him, Jesus is a thirty-year-old man beginning his public ministry. Matthew shows us nothing of his life behind that intervening curtain of history. (Luke gives us one picture of the twelve-year-old Jesus in the Jerusalem Temple. See Luke 2:41-51.)

With Chapter 3 we also begin reading a quite different kind of literature. From here on, we have in hand the record of Jesus' life and ministry, his healings and teachings. These lead at last to the account of his trial and crucifixion. Much of this record is attested by other ancient sources. Matthew's first two chapters contain stories told to show the wonder and glory of Jesus' birth. They also show the darkness and tragedy that stalked his nativity. These chapters are more like the great paintings of Raphael or the music of Bach. Greater truth comes from the nativity story as Matthew tells it than anything we could discover if we had a clinical account of Mary's confinement and her delivery. Truth is here in the birth and infancy stories but it comes to us through a different kind of literature.

The third line we cross on entering Chapter 3 is the beginning of Matthew's Book I (Chapters 3–7). Five of these books lie ahead of us. They set forth in a carefully ordered and sequential way the account of Jesus' life and teaching. Chapter 3 is accordingly the commencement of God's disclosure of what is to become the new covenant or New Testament.

Matthew 3:1-12. When this passage was written, it had been four hundred years since a true prophet had prophesied in Israel. Moreover, this was a feverish time. Messianic expectations ran high. So when John appeared preaching repentance, calling the whole nation to be baptized, people saw it as a sign. Some scholars believe that John was strongly influenced by, if not actually a member of, a community of Essenes. The Essenes were a sect of Jews dwelling at Qumran. They believed in ritual washing for purification, a rite they regularly repeated. The Dead Sea

Scrolls found at Qumran provide evidence of such cultic practice. The Essenes believed that the time of the Messiah was approaching. John's messianic expectations conceivably were fired and heightened beyond even what those at Qumran believed.

Both John and Jesus begin their ministries with the identical announcement, "Repent for the kingdom of heaven is near" (4:17). Jesus will later link John's coming with Elijah (11:14), one of the expected signs of the Messiah's appearing.

Matthew 3:13-17. It seems odd that Jesus would submit to a baptism of repentance. "To fulfill all righteousness"—what does that mean? Other translations are more helpful. *The Revised English Bible* reads, "It is right for us to do all that God requires." As the student book points out, the whole nation is called to John's baptism. Never in all of Israel's history has such a thing happened. Jesus obeys God's call in going with the others. His righteousness must exceed that of the scribes and Pharisees (5:20). We readily recognize a principle of credibility and ministry here.

Christian baptism traces its origin back to Jesus' own baptism. Seeing him baptized in the Jordan puts us in mind of our own baptism, though many of us were baptized quite differently. But Jesus' baptism and ours are not the same in several important aspects. Jesus was not baptized into a church. No church existed. He was already a member of the covenant people of God. John spoke no formula words, "In the name of the Father, and of the Son, and of the Holy Spirit." Christians since the first century have been baptized "into Christ." (See Romans 6:1-4 for a theology of Christian baptism.) Jesus was not baptized "into John." Most distinctive, Christian baptism is a sacrament of grace. Infant baptism is a sign of God's loving us even before we have faith to love God. John's baptism was singularly for repentance.

DIMENSION THREE: WHAT DOES THE BIBLE MEAN TO ME?

The Bible may speak to us more clearly if we think of it as a book written to call forth a personal reply from the reader. Unlike many books we can read while remaining essentially unchanged, the Bible is a book we see ourselves reflected in, confronted by life and death decisions. We can, and often do, read the Bible without any response. But that in itself is a life and death decision. Remember, the Bible gives us an invitation. The Bible does not serve us with a conscription. A good question to keep in mind as we reach Dimension Three in each lesson of this study might be, What is the R.S.V.P. of this passage to me?

Matthew 1:1-17—Genealogy From Abraham to Jesus

Our response to Matthew's genealogy is thanksgiving for all the generations that connect Abraham to Jesus. And appreciation of the promises of God carried over that line! Although the names are not written down anywhere, eighty generations form a line coming down to us from the time of Jesus. Every twenty-five years since that time, another person (new generation) has been added. The promises declared in all that has gone before now come down to us. Someone in every generation, whether our particular ancestor or not, transmitted God's promises that now have come to us. All these promises call for personal response.

Perhaps class members would like to share what they remember, or what has been told to them, of one person whose name would be in the line of seventy-nine. Reflect on how "ordinary people" become the instruments and bearers of God's good news.

Matthew 2:16-18—Murder

Whenever innocent people suffer, are we not called on to respond in some way? One cannot imagine Jesus remaining unaffected when he learned later in his life that children had died because he had been born. Neither can we just stand by unaffected. Someone may suggest that the whole event was part of "God's plan" and therefore that the death of the innocents is not what it seems. That argument will not do. If every human life is precious in God's sight, how can we think of God planning for these precious children to be killed? Until we have explained the whole burden of evil in the world, we will never know how this terrible murder fits into God's plans, if indeed it does.

Our children have been blessed with more than they need, while other children are disadvantaged. Slaughter of the innocents recurs not always in the form of physical murder. Opportunities denied and necessities withheld also kill. We think of the children in our own world who suffered because by accident of birth they live in abject poverty, or war, or deprivation, or abusive situations. We think of children uneducated and undereducated who may suffer those consequences throughout their lives. We think of children wiped out without concern by genocide.

Matthew 3:2, 8—Fruit That Befits Repentance

One way of getting to the heart of what these verses mean (in fact the whole episode of John's preaching) would be to ask the students how they respond to this: When it comes to the Christian gospel, we have to hear the bad news before we get the good news. The word of the gospel is not "hallelujah" or "praise God," but "Repent!" Repentance not only hurts, it upsets. More often than not, turning one's life around (the literal meaning of repent) calls for major psychological and/or spiritual surgery. Not always. Sometimes our sins so overwhelm us that we joyfully embrace any turning around by which we can be free. But John the Baptist is preaching about sin that clings so closely that we neither want nor are able to give it up. In making changes, often the best we can do is to want to want to.

Ask the class members, How do people frequently show repentance? Some of the following ways may be suggested: giving up something for Lent, saying prayers more faithfully, going to church more regularly, apologizing, and so forth. Nothing is wrong with any of these answers. But is this the fruit that befits what is repented? You might then want to consider some of the sins of which we stand convicted by the Christian gospel. Some of these sins are hardheartedness, fearfulness and lack of faith, self-indulgence at the expense of others, idolizing things of our own making, lust, and so forth. You will have no trouble compiling quite a list. Now comes the crucial question: What specific thing must be done (what fruit) in penitence for each of these sins? for our own particular sins? The more the students are willing and able to share of their own falling short and missing the mark, the closer you will come to reaching the core of the problem. Both John the Baptist and Jesus recognized the human condition. We have to turn around before we can receive forgiveness and the gifts of the Spirit. For many of us this requirement that we turn around comes as bad news. The frightening truth is, however, that until we really hear the bad news about ourselves, the *good news* of a new life in Christ has no meaning. We see no reason for it.

Matthew 1:20, 2:13, 19, 22—Dreams

If the frequent direction of events through dreams prompts students to discuss this idea further, two observations seem in order. The first is that we understand more about dreams than did the ancients, even though they were wiser than we in taking dreams seriously. We know, for example, that dreams come from the subconscious mind. Material buried below the level of our awareness appears in dreams, almost always in disguised, symbolic form. Our fears, our hatreds, our repressed desires take form in our dreams; and dream analysis has become a method of resolving emotional problems.

The other observation is that while no scientific demonstration has yet shown that dreams can reliably and accurately go forward in time, philosophers, mystics, artists, and poets have thought that the human mind can transcend the present moment in time by going in either direction. Is it possible that signs from the future come to us in dreams?

We should acknowledge how open Joseph was to God's leading. However the signs and warnings came to him, and as astonishing as the messages were, he listened and obeyed. How has God said surprising things to us? Did we obey or refuse?

Jesus began to preach, "Repent, for the kingdom of heaven is near" (4:17).

2

Temptations; The Sermon on the Mount

Matthew 4–5

DIMENSION ONE:
WHAT DOES THE BIBLE SAY?

Answer these questions by reading Matthew 4

1. Where do the temptations of Jesus occur? (4:1)

   Jesus is tempted in the desert.

2. How long do the temptations last? (4:2)

   Jesus is tempted for forty days and forty nights.

3. What is the first temptation? (4:3)

   Jesus is tempted to turn stones into bread.

4. Why does Jesus resist the first temptation? (4:4)

   It is written that man does not live on bread alone but by God's every word.

5. What is the second temptation? (4:5-6)

   Jesus is tempted to throw himself down from the Temple to test God's promise that angels will lift him up.

6. Why does Jesus resist the second temptation? (4:7)

   Jesus resists the second temptation because it is written that the Lord is not to be tested.

7. What does the devil promise Jesus with the third temptation? (4:9)

   The devil promises Jesus all the kingdoms of the world and their splendor.

8. What is the third temptation? (4:8-9)

   Jesus is tempted to worship the devil.

9. Why does Jesus resist the third temptation? (4:10)

   It is written, "Worship the Lord your God, and serve him only."

10. When does Jesus return to Galilee? (4:12)

    Jesus returns when he hears John has been put in prison.

11. Where does Jesus go to live in Galilee? (4:13)

    Jesus goes to live in Capernaum.

12. How does Jesus begin his preaching? (4:17)

    Jesus begins his preaching by calling for repentance, for the kingdom of heaven is near.

13. What two sets of brothers does Jesus call? (4:18-21)

    Jesus calls Simon (Peter) and Andrew, and James and John.

14. What does Jesus do as he goes about Galilee? (4:23)

    As he goes about Galilee Jesus teaches, preaches, and heals.

Answer these questions by reading Matthew 5

15. Where is Jesus when he gives this sermon, and to whom is he speaking? (5:1)

    Jesus teaches his disciples on the mountain.

16. How many beatitudes does he speak? (5:1-11)

    Jesus speaks nine beatitudes on this occasion.

17. Which beatitude does Jesus address to the disciples? (5:11)

    "Blessed are you when people insult you, persecute you and falsely say all kinds of evil against you because of me."

18. Why are the disciples told to let their light shine? (5:16)

They are to let their light shine so people may see their good deeds and praise God.

19. What inner attitude does Jesus say makes a person subject to judgment? (5:22)

One who is angry with his brother is subject to judgment.

20. How does Jesus say one can commit adultery? (5:28)

One can commit adultery by looking at another with lust.

21. According to Matthew, does Jesus permit divorce on any grounds? (5:32)

Divorce is permitted on the ground of unfaithfulness.

22. How are Jesus' followers to be? (5:48)

"Be perfect, therefore, as your heavenly Father is perfect."

DIMENSION TWO: WHAT DOES THE BIBLE MEAN?

Matthew 4:1-11. Jesus being tempted by the devil is one of the most dramatic scenes in Matthew. Three things should be noted. The first is that the temptation was a solitary experience for Jesus. The second is that it was an inner experience within Jesus' own heart, mind, and soul. The third thing we need to note is that it was nonetheless a real encounter with evil.

Obviously, Jesus must have told his disciples what happened in the desert. Matthew includes this temptation story in order to present Jesus' whole life as an example of the perfect doing of the will of God. In this way Matthew prepares for teaching true discipleship. A true disciple approaches any desert where the command of the Spirit leads him or her into battle and temptation. (You may wish to compare Matthew's account with Luke 4:1-13, where the order of the second and third temptations is reversed.)

The meaning of what happened on that mountain becomes clear when we put away the sense we have of the word *temptation.* In common speech, to *tempt* someone is to seduce, lure, or entice that person to do an evil act. In the New Testament, the Greek word *peirazo,* which we translate "to tempt," means "to try, prove, or test a person." The devil did challenge Jesus to do things that would have been wrong. But the testing or determination as to whether Jesus had the faith and commitment to be obedient to God's will is what is important. Another way to see it would be as a test of how Jesus would use the power given him by God when the Spirit descended upon him at his baptism.

With this in mind, it becomes easier to see how and why the Holy Spirit immediately led Jesus from baptism into temptation.

God does not ask for shortcuts to either plenty or faith, or bargains for political power. God asks of Jesus only unwavering obedience to God's will. In the desert of the Exodus, God tested Israel's faith and Israel failed. They demanded food, they demanded a sign, and they bowed down before an idol. Jesus is the Son of God. Contrary to the enticement of the devil, Jesus must not fail his testing. And this is a real contest. When you come to think of it, a new covenant is being forged here on the desert mountain. God made the old covenant with Israel. Matthew believes that with Jesus, God makes a new covenant. The pattern of Israel's testing in Deuteronomy is pointedly repeated here.

Matthew 4:12. Herod had John arrested because he wanted to silence the prophet's denunciation of Herod's unlawful and immoral marriage. But Herod did infinitely more than silence John. Jesus saw in that arrest the signal for him to come from obscurity and begin his ministry. Events were set in motion that moved surely toward Calvary, the Resurrection, the Christian church, and the New Testament. What made Jesus choose that moment to begin his ministry? Who can know for certain? Jesus probably saw in this violent defiance of justice and morality the point beyond which he could no longer remain silent. John had announced the approach of the kingdom of God. John had baptized Jesus. Jesus believed that in John, Elijah had appeared heralding the Messiah, as tradition promised (11:13-15). The difference in the proclamation between John the Baptist and Jesus is not in the message but in the one who proclaims it. John's preparation for the way of the Lord is fulfilled in the ministry of Jesus.

Matthew 4:12. We might think the place for Jesus to begin his ministry would be Jerusalem or somewhere else in Judea. Poetry and paintings of Galilee make it seem an idyllic place of beauty and retreat, not the arena for travail and confrontation. We would be mistaken. In this region, north and west of the Lake of Galilee, twenty-five miles west to east and fifty miles from south to north, lived around three million people. Galilee had 204 villages with a population of at least fifteen thousand each. Two principal highways passed through the region. Jesus saw the traffic of his world, from Egypt to Syria, from the Mediterranean to the eastern empires, passing his front door, so to speak. Moreover, Galilee was a world heavily Gentile in character.

One of the reasons Matthew wrote his Gospel was to send the power of the good news of the Christ to the world beyond Israel, because Israel did not receive it. Several times Matthew tells of Jesus pointing to the faith of Gentiles in responding to his message. Jesus probably did not begin preaching in Galilee only because that was his home and he happened to be there when news of John's arrest arrived. If that is the case, though, then we can only observe that Galilee proved a most fertile soil for his sowing. Someone once said, "Judea is on the way to nowhere; Galilee is on the way to everywhere."

The quotation in Matthew 4:15-16 is from Isaiah 9:1-2. As it was originally written, this quotation foretells of the Messiah and what his coming will mean to the whole world. Isaiah may not have foreseen the Christ as he finally came to the world. But Matthew understood how the Christ's coming gave light to all who sit in darkness. According to Matthew, Jesus appears as fulfillment of that promise. Jesus' preaching will have effect even beyond the borders of Israel.

Matthew 4:17. More than one listener to Jesus' first words might have said, "Hold on a minute. The face and the voice is Jesus. The words are John's." Jesus began his preaching with John's declaration and call. This ties Jesus even more strongly to the need of repentance and serves Matthew's fulfillment purpose. (See in Mark 1:14-15 a fuller announcement and invitation.) The words "the kingdom of heaven" *is near* need to be underlined and emphasized when reading and thinking about this chapter. Because they are the first words spoken in Jesus' preaching, they call for attention and remembrance. Matthew did not place them there by accident. Before you focus on them in teaching you might ask the students, "What message, of all the things Jesus said, do you believe was first and foremost in his mind?" To carry the exercise very far would be an exercise in futility. But as a probe to stimulate thought it could be provocative. We could make a good case for saying that the announcement of the near approach of God's kingdom comes first in importance for Jesus. In a way the whole Gospel comes from that statement.

Matthew 4:23-25. Teaching, preaching, and healing are the activities to which Jesus devoted his ministry. In these verses Matthew gives us a summary of what we will see and hear in the chapters to come.

Any trained person could speak and teach in the synagogues of that day, as Jesus was asked to do in Nazareth, described in Luke 4:16-21. Healing was considered a revelation from God. The healing that Jesus did, even more than his teaching and preaching, aroused misunderstanding and controversy.

Matthew, throughout his Gospel, focuses on two groups: disciples and crowds. He pays close attention to those in close companionship and those farther away. He speaks first of the crowds, Jews first and, in all probability, Syria afterward. He turns to the disciples in Chapter 5.

Matthew 5. This chapter contains the Sermon on the Mount. We cannot know why Matthew located this sermon here. But certain parallels to Moses and the covenant of Sinai are quite persuasive. Moses went up on a mountain and received the tablets of the law there. Jesus takes his disciples to a mountain and calls them to a higher righteousness as the condition of entrance into the kingdom of God. Matthew not only presents Jesus as the one who teaches with authority but also as the Lord who fulfills the law. At Sinai, God established the covenant with Israel. Matthew may be saying here that God enters a new covenant with Israel through the Christ. We do not know whether Matthew intended such a comparison. But at least the apparent analogy helps our understanding of the Gospel.

Matthew 5:2-12. These verses are called *the Beatitudes.* This sermon, together with three or four parables, are the most treasured of all Jesus' teachings. Calling these verses a discourse on the morality of faith might be better. But no one quarrels with the title *sermon* after all this time. It does bear some resemblance to the pattern of Paul's letters. His letters usually begin with a thanksgiving and blessing, then move on to address the issues at hand. So Matthew puts the blessings first in the discourse. The blessings are wonderful promises, good news. Then in the light of what has been promised and bestowed, Jesus goes on to talk of morality. However you decide to teach this lesson, one thing must be emphatically stressed. The Beatitudes have little or no meaning apart from the gospel (good news) that we find in the Christ, Immanuel, God with us. In fact, without the gospel, the Beatitudes may well become counsel leading to despair. As Paul asks, "And who is equal to such a task?" (2 Corinthians 2:16).

The parallel to Matthew 5–7 is found in Luke 6:17-49. There we will discover some divergence from Matthew. Luke's sermon is spoken on a plain, not on a mountain. Luke includes four beatitudes, not nine, and in Luke, Jesus speaks to the crowds as well as the disciples. He speaks to them in direct address: "Blessed are *you.* . . ." Matthew uses this form of speech only in the ninth beatitude. Matthew gathers into this extended discourse a great deal of material that appears elsewhere in Mark and Luke. How well it all fits together!

The students may like to know that the four Gospels contain sixteen beatitudes in all. Seven are not included here in Matthew 5. Four of these are found elsewhere in Matthew (11:6; 13:16; 16:17; 24:46). Two are peculiar to Luke (Luke 11:28; 14:13-14). John's Gospel records one beatitude (John 20:29). You might want the students to look up these others and compare them with the Beatitudes we know so well.

Matthew 5:17-48. These passages are enormously difficult. We, as teachers, are challenged to enter deeply into those difficulties without watering down the teachings to accommodate our own dispositions and inclinations. In these passages Jesus holds up for his disciples a higher measure of morality. He does not abolish the law (5:17-20), but expects the disciples to fulfill all the law, and then some. He looks beyond the letter to the Spirit. He looks beyond murder to anger, beyond adultery to lust. Murder and adultery come out of the poison wells of anger and lust. These requirements are staggering.

Matthew 5:22. "Anyone who is angry . . . will be subject to judgment." A murderer is subject to the judgment of a court. But what court can convict a person of anger? Anger is an inner attitude, not subject to judicial review. It may be in verse 22 that *judgment* means God's judgment.

The words "anyone who says to his brother, 'Raca' " should be understood to mean "whoever holds another person in contempt." To speak contemptuously to or of another was forbidden under penalty by the Sanhedrin, the Jewish high court.

To call anyone *fool* was far more serious in those days than we understand the word. When we use the word, we are apt to mean a foolish person. The word *fool* has sometimes been understood, very likely in this instance, as *rebel against God.* When spoken against another in public such denunciation warranted the worst punishment, burning in hell. *Gehenna,* the word we translate "hell," was the Valley of Hinnom, southwest of Jerusalem where refuse was burned. In Canaanite days human sacrifices were carried out there.

Matthew 5:27-33. Interpretation of Jewish law at the time of Jesus strictly prohibited looking at a woman, or touching her unnecessarily, or whatever might be suspected of erotic interest. Jesus uses a hyperbole, that is, he greatly exaggerates when he states his example. If the eye offends, gouge it out. His suggestions are harsh measures. Perhaps they are not meant to be taken literally. But these measures go to the sources of sin.

Matthew 5:31-32. Regarding marriage and divorce, Mark and Luke are unequivocal. They allow no exceptions. Matthew alone allows the traditional ground of unfaithfulness. (See Dimension Three for a discussion of what this means to us.)

Matthew 5:38-42. The greatest insult one could give another was to strike that person's right cheek with the back of the hand. It was an insult fit for a heretic. It has been suggested that Jesus has the disciples in mind here. They will probably be struck numerous times on the right cheek by people who consider them heretics because of Jesus. Even so they are not to retaliate.

Matthew 5:48. This verse is translated in Luke, "Be merciful, just as your Father is merciful."

DIMENSION THREE: WHAT DOES THE BIBLE MEAN TO ME?

Matthew 4:1-11—Temptation

Dorothy Söelle, a modern theologian, has written a book entitled *Death by Bread Alone.* She turns around what Jesus said and looks at it from that perspective. "Man does not live on bread alone" becomes, "By bread alone you shall die." Ask the class to reflect on this forceful way of warning. People are hungry; bread is a necessity. What does

bread mean to us? It means a great deal more than food. Couldn't we truthfully say that many other things are the bread we try to live alone by? What about the technology, the material goods, the diversions that capture our physical and psychological senses and with which we try to feed our needs? Don't we try to substitute these for commitment to God's peaceable kingdom of persons living together in harmony and justice?

People have doubts and a convincing sign could support their faith. What are we tempted to do that may be similar to the jump from the Temple? Is it tempting to take prosperity and good fortune as a sign that God looks after us with favor? Anything that puts it up to God to prove divine love is an enticement of the devil. Jesus made it painfully clear—no signs, only faith!

The third temptation might lead you and the students to wrestle with the question of ends and means. Does the end (all the kingdoms of the world) ever justify the means (bow down and worship the devil)? Or is the end foreshadowed in the means? That is, if we worship the devil how will even the tiny kingdoms in which we have influence ever serve God?

Matthew 5:3-11—The Beatitudes

The Greek word we translate "blessed" or "happy" is *makarios. Makarios* is an exclamatory cry, "What joy there is in God's promise!" Joy that can never be taken from us. Recall that in his final discourses to his disciples reported in John's Gospel (John 16:22) Jesus said, "No one will take away your joy." One way to get at what this statement means for us is to use our imaginations.

Compare the person who mourns for the world's sin and suffering without any assurance of God's presence and care with one who mourns within the embrace of God's promise. What difference does it make? But above all be sure that no one tries to evade the pain by embracing God. To receive God's blessing is not to avoid pain and the agonizing struggle for faith. The Beatitudes do not promise anyone a rose garden.

The class may discuss this topic if time allows.

Matthew 5:21-47—The Higher Righteousness

Jesus' formula, "You have heard that it was said . . . but I tell you" teaches us that our faith challenges "old" thinking. He has already affirmed his disciples by telling them that they are the salt of the earth, light of the world, that they have something exciting to share, that they are capable of going good deeds. No more can the adherent of Jesus take a conventional, easy way because Jesus has represented the old law with a new interpretation that goes beyond that to strike at the center, or spirit, of the law.

What are the ways we try to circumvent what we know to be right, or good, or true? How do we recast attitudes, beliefs, and behaviors to suit ourselves? to realize that more or better is expected of us?

Seek first his kingdom and his righteousness (6:33).

— 3 —

The Sermon on the Mount

Matthew 6–7

DIMENSION ONE:
WHAT DOES THE BIBLE SAY?

Answer these questions by reading Matthew 6

1. What does Jesus warn his disciples against? (6:1)

   Jesus warns the disciples against doing their "acts of right-eousness" as to be seen by others.

2. Of what three forms of piety does Jesus speak? (6:2, 5, 16)

   Jesus speaks of giving to the needy, prayer, and fasting.

3. What does Jesus call people who make a show of their religion? (6:2, 5, 16)

   He calls them hypocrites.

4. What does Jesus say these people receive? (6:2, 5, 16)

   He says, "They have received their reward in full."

5. With what three petitions about God does Jesus' prayer begin? (6:9-10)

   The petitions are "hallowed be your name; your kingdom come; your will be done on earth as it is in heaven."

6. What three things does Jesus ask for? (6:11-13)

   Jesus asks God to give us our daily bread, forgive our debts, and keep us from temptation.

7. Where does Jesus say our treasures are? (6:21)

   Jesus says that our hearts are where our treasures are.

8. Why does Jesus say we cannot serve God and money? (6:24)

   Jesus says we cannot serve God and money because no one can serve two masters.

9. What three things does Jesus warn us not to worry about? (6:25, 31)

   Jesus says not to be anxious about eating, drinking, and clothing.

10. Why does Jesus say we should look at the birds? (6:26)

    We should look at the birds because they do not sow or reap or store away food, yet God feeds them.

11. Why does Jesus tell us to consider the lilies? (6:28)

    The lilies do not labor nor spin, yet their splendor is greater than Solomon's.

12. Instead of worrying, what does Jesus say we are to do? (6:33)

    We are to seek first the kingdom of God and God's righteousness.

Answer these questions by reading Matthew 7

13. If we who are evil know how to give good gifts to our children, what does God do? (7:11)

    God in heaven will give good gifts to those who ask.

14. How should we treat others? (7:12)

    We should treat others the way we would like to be treated ourselves.

15. How will the disciples know the true prophets from false prophets? (7:16)

They will know them by their fruits.

16. Who will enter the kingdom of heaven? (7:21)

Those who do the will of God will enter the kingdom of heaven.

17. What is the person like who hears Jesus' words and puts them into practice? (7:24)

That person is like a wise man who built his house on a rock.

18. What is a person like who hears Jesus' words and does not put them into practice? (7:26)

That person is like a foolish man who built his house on sand.

19. Why were the crowds amazed at Jesus' teaching? (7:29)

He taught them as one who had authority and not as one of their teachers of the law.

DIMENSION TWO: WHAT DOES THE BIBLE MEAN?

Chapter 6 is the middle chapter of the Sermon on the Mount. This chapter compels us to examine our motives. It leads to the disturbing conclusion that mixed motives and divided purposes are unacceptable in the Christian life. In the way we practice our piety, view our property, and seek inner peace for ourselves, Jesus calls for uncompromising commitment to God's purposes, uncontaminated by self-serving intentions.

Matthew 6:2-4, 5-6, 16-18. The three-verse poem in verses 2-4, 5-6, and 16-18 contains striking parallelism. Each verse begins, "When you give to the needy . . . When you pray . . . When you fast . . ." Then, in each case, the identical caution follows to not be like the hypocrites. The reason is given in the next line. The hypocrites sound trumpets, stand in the synagogues, and disfigure their faces. Why do they do these things? They do these things so they may be seen and praised. Each of the three parts of the poem is the same all the way to the end. With the third verse (verses 16-18) the poem has become memorable and the truth is inescapable. In the practice of devotion it is all for God or nothing.

A hypocrite is a person who pretends to be someone or something he or she is not. Hypocrites wear masks. The J. B. Phillips translation uses the word *playactors* to speak of people who practice their piety so they can be seen and praised. They are acting a part in public they do not really believe. It may be that the word we translate *hypocrite* had a somewhat different sense for Jesus and for Matthew. Wil-

liam Albright's translation in *The Anchor Bible* calls such people *overscrupulous.* They parade their piety pretentiously. The difference between a hypocrite and an overscrupulous practitioner is important. The first is a pious fraud. The other has mixed up sincere devotion with playing to the gallery. Being an overscrupulous practitioner may be even more dangerous than being a hypocrite. We may more readily unmask an outright fraud. We shall know them by their fruits. The grandstanders, on the other hand, with their hearts set both on pleasing God and winning the plaudits of the public, may never realize that such double-hearted piety is unacceptable to God.

Matthew 6:7-13. This prayer contains the most widely known words Jesus ever spoke. Careful study of this prayer rewards the student, if in nothing else, by getting the prayer priorities straight. We should look first at the setting in Luke 11:1-4. We see here that Jesus gave this prayer as an answer to the disciples' request that he teach them to pray. All Christian prayer has this prayer as a model. When studying this prayer, a useful exercise might be to ask each member of the class to write a prayer following the model of Jesus' prayer. These prayers might be either single sentences, petitions, or more extended expositions of the Lord's Prayer supplications. Putting the words Jesus used into our own words in today's setting helps us to understand better what these words that we often say by rote really mean.

"May your name be held in honor" is a way of asking that God's name be honored by faithfulness to the covenant established with the community of Israel. In Chapter 7, near the conclusion of the Sermon on the Mount, Jesus tells his disciples how God's name is to be hallowed. "Not everyone who says to me, 'Lord, Lord,' shall enter the kingdom of heaven, but only he who does the will of my Father who is in heaven" (7:21).

"Let your kingdom come, let your will be done, as in heaven, so also on earth" (*Matthew, The Anchor Bible,* by W. F. Albright and C. S. Mann; Doubleday and Company, Inc., 1971; page 74). Such a prayer could only be spoken in trust and faith that when the time has come, God will establish the divine reign. Even now, as the Kingdom approaches, God's will may be done in our midst.

These first three petitions have to do with hallowing God's name, and doing God's will, on earth as in heaven. Then follow three petitions for personal needs.

We cannot be sure what "daily bread" meant to Matthew or Jesus. Matthew uses a word, *artos,* that until recently was unknown in the whole of Greek literature. But a papyrus fragment has been found on which the word occurs on what must be a shopping list. So the phrase very likely should be translated, "Give us the food we need for the coming day." Two thoughts appear in this petition. One is the recollection of the Exodus where the Israelites were given food for each day. They could not keep a supply during the long trek. They needed daily faith as well as daily bread. The other thought comes from the words shortly to follow about anxiety for tomorrow's food and clothes. One day's needs should be met one day at a time.

The word of entreaty for forgiveness is *debts*. None can claim to have given God all that he or she owes. The disciples ask God to forgive or cancel what they still owe, just as they are to remit any debts others may owe to them. Of course, Jesus is not speaking of money. He is referring to the transgression of the covenant, disobedience to God's will.

Why would God lead anyone into temptation? This question has baffled Christians from the beginning. The word *temptation* can mean either "testing or tribulation." In either case, one will ask to be delivered. The disciples might fail the trial. They might be done in by the ordeal of persecution, even crucifixion. We may be helped by considering Jesus' own experience in his passion. Jesus asks God to allow "this cup [to] be taken from me" (26:39). Even Jesus asked to be spared such testing and trauma. We pray to be delivered from the power of evil (or the Evil One). Jesus had met the Evil One in his own testing.

Matthew 6:25-34. Hearing these terribly difficult words in their original context would help us understand them better. Jesus would soon be sending his disciples on their mission (Chapter 10) as sheep among wolves. The prospect must have been frightening. At first Jesus' words do seem an impossible expectation, enough to drive the disciples to despair. Do not be anxious? How can we help it? But study the passage carefully. Note verses 26, 30, and 32. Jesus assures the disciples that God knows their needs, cares for what happens to them, and will provide their necessities.

The final verse says in effect not to borrow tomorrow's worries today. Nothing in this whole chapter makes much sense apart from the good news that God is with us, both today and tomorrow.

Matthew 7:1-5. This passage is one of the most easily misunderstood of Jesus' teachings. He does not mean that we should refrain from judging in the everyday sense. Try to imagine even a single day when a person makes no judgments, especially no moral judgments. Such a person would come to the end of that day swamped by moral chaos and indecisiveness. What Jesus is cautioning against is the censorious hypocrite.

Moreover, we need a sense of humor to get the full impact of what Jesus says here. Verses 3-5 provide a beautiful scenario for a cartoon. A man is pointing to a tiny speck in someone's eye, while all the time a great plank protrudes out of his own eye, obstructing his vision and knocking down things that are in the way. We see that hypocrisy, as well as beauty, is in the eye of the beholder. Of course, we have to judge, but judgment becomes us only when done with compassion. And isn't it human nature that people judge others for the very things they fail to handle well themselves?

Twice now in the Sermon on the Mount we have heard Jesus rebuke the hypocrites. Much more is to come later in the Gospel. He condemns hypocrisy almost above any other sin. Hypocrites pretend to a righteousness they do not have. They are a treacherous breed, spreading guilt and self-contempt all over the place. Jesus' picture of them with planks sticking out of their eyes is devastating. The very act of condemning others puts the logs in the hypocrite's eyes.

Matthew 7:7-11. Here is another troublesome passage. What do you make of the promise that everyone who asks receives? Is this true? Ask the students and see what responses you get. Did you ever ask and not receive? Maybe you did not ask hard enough. (But does God have to be bullied?) Maybe you asked for the wrong thing. (But how are we to know?)

Read carefully what Jesus says. He does not say you will get everything you ask for. Rather the promise is that God will answer your prayer. If you keep on asking, seeking, and knocking, God will open a way. The emphasis in the passage is on persistence. Jesus encourages the disciples not to be disheartened in their praying. God knows their needs. God will not mock them, even when they do not receive what they ask for.

John gives us a word of Jesus, not found in Matthew, that helps us here. "And I will do whatever you ask in my name, so that the Son may bring glory to the Father" (John 14:13). This does not remove all the difficulty, but like a fine compass it points to the true North of our praying. In Christ's name our prayers must be uttered. Whatever we ask must be in the Spirit (name) of Christ. A word of caution to the teacher is in order here. We had better be careful how we handle this difficult problem. You may have a student who will tell of a prayer that surely was offered in Christ's name, yet was not answered. We must not declare that someone did not receive because he or she did not pray in Christ's name. The mystery of how prayers are answered is profound. The best that we can do, perhaps the only thing we can do, is to try to pray always in the Spirit of Jesus. We must keep on praying even when we do not receive. We should have confidence that God hears.

Matthew 7:12. Something like the Golden Rule is widely found among most of the religions of the world. It makes good worldly sense for harmonious living. In fact, who could fault the Golden Rule? Important as it is, however, none should mistake it for an adequate summary of the gospel. Standing by itself, it says nothing of God's action and response to the needs of humankind (the things Chapter 1 is all about). It says nothing about the cross, about forgiveness, about discipleship, or about the Kingdom.

But the Golden Rule does not stand by itself. Matthew places it directly after the assurance that God in heaven gives good things to those who ask. The disciples are to be merciful, kind, and forgiving, as God is. This is the context of the so-called Golden Rule. To see it in action, turn to

25:31-40, the Last Judgment, and to Luke 10:30-37, the good Samaritan.

Matthew 7:13-14. One might title this short two-verse passage "The Lure of the Easy Way." Jesus is preparing his disciples and all who will ever follow them for what they will find when they take their mission to the world. In Chapter 10, we will read more of the life-endangering threats that await them. Here Jesus warns them not of fearful hazards. The consequences of these ways are indeed fearful. But Jesus is warning them of the popular ways that so many find so easy. Faith can so easily be deceived and seduced by the promise of ease.

Of what easy way does Jesus speak? Our first thought may be of carnal pleasures that attract so many. Money and all that it can buy is an enticement. So are success or popularity. But the easy way also runs through the life of faith and through the church. The Christian life is sometimes made to seem easy. "Come to Jesus and be saved." Nothing is said about the narrow, hard way required of any who would follow Jesus. People who try to lure others into the life of faith by any of these promises are false prophets. Jeremiah denounced such deceivers who cried, "'Peace, Peace' . . . when there is no peace" (Jeremiah 8:11). In the Gospel of John we read that after some particularly hard saying many of his disciples (not the Twelve) drew back and no longer went about with Jesus (John 6:66).

For students interested in history, you might suggest that they reflect on what have been the great ages of Christian history. Were they the times of prosperity when everything went well for the church? Or have they been the hard times of torment when the church was under attack, as under Roman persecution, with the Puritans in England, or the Quakers in England and America? Jesus was right, "The gate is wide and the road is broad." Beware!

Matthew 7:15-20. "By their fruit you will recognize them." This theme is a favorite of Jesus. He comes back to it several times in Matthew's account. (The parable in Chapter 21 about the son who told his father he would not go and work in his vineyard, but later went is one example of how Jesus used this theme. Another example is the parable of the Last Judgment in Chapter 25.) Jesus points out to his disciples that one of the quickest ways to recognize a ravenous wolf in sheep's clothing is to look at the fruit in the wolf's life! What has he or she done? What has he or she to show for all the fancy words spoken? Jesus' picture is suggestive. All the fancy foliage on a fruit tree means nothing if the harvest is skimpy. (We can anticipate the severe judgment of the fig tree that bore no fruit described in Matthew 21:18-19.)

Matthew 7:21-23. In a way, these verses are yet another attack on hypocrisy. The person to watch out for is the one with the piously glib tongue who actually does little of God's will. The people who protest "Lord, Lord" are like the hypocrites (6:5-7) who think they will be heard for their many words, especially their pious words.

Matthew 7:24-28. Jesus' metaphor of the house built on sand has become a common saying in our culture. One is apt to hear it used by persons who have no idea that it forms the conclusion to the Sermon on the Mount. The meaning stands out in verses 24 and 26—"Everyone who hears these words of mine and puts them into practice . . . everyone who hears these words of mine and does not put them into practice." The emphasis is once again on *doing*. One may wonder at this point if the picture Matthew gives us of Jesus does not imply a kind of works theology. One is saved by doing good works. The words taken out of context might suggest that. But the truth is closer to the words of the apostle James, "Faith without deeds is dead" (James 2:26). But all of this stops short of the profound truth. One will hardly do the works that are implicit in the Sermon on the Mount without faith in the gospel itself.

Matthew 7:28-29. With these verses you should remind the students of the structure of this Gospel. Remind them of how it is divided into five sections, each consisting of a narrative portion and a teaching discourse. Each discourse ends with a formula transition: "After Jesus had finished . . ." (You will find these words repeated in some form in 11:1; 13:53; 19:1; 26:1.) The Sermon on the Mount is an important block of Jesus' teaching and comes near the beginning of his ministry. Because of this, it would be well to pause long enough at this transition to look back. Have the students try to sum up the essence of Chapters 5–7. As they do this, you keep certain guidelines clear within which to think and summarize.

Sometimes it helps to focus more quickly on the essentials of a question if we can be sure of what something does not mean. We may save ourselves guessing and groping if we can rule out some widely held misconceptions.

● *The Sermon on the Mount is not a counsel of perfection.* Jesus is not asking us to be perfect. (Review the discussion under Matthew 5:48.) He does not expect his followers to rise so far above their human nature that they will be able to do what the Sermon calls for.

● *The Sermon on the Mount is not an impossible ideal designed to convict people of their sin and impel them to the cross.* That has been a common interpretation among some people. But it sounds more like the atonement theology of a later day than anything Jesus might have said, meant, or understood. Jesus did not manipulate people in any such way. His "yea" was "yea" and his "nay" was "nay."

When Jesus told his disciples that they were to take up their crosses and follow him he said exactly that. People have come to see the cross as a sacrifice through which men and women have been led to God's love and forgiveness. But the Sermon on the Mount is not a ploy or bait to bring people to despair and so lead them to the cross.

● *The Sermon on the Mount is not a so-called interim ethic.* That is, according to early Christians, the world will soon end, inaugurating the age to come. In the short interim before this day, we are to live the way Jesus described in the Sermon on the Mount. Human nature being what it is, people could not be expected to live this way over the long haul. But if we lie on history's deathbed, surely we can be perfect while we wait. If that is what the Sermon on the Mount really means, then what relevance can it have for us now after nearly two thousand years? Besides, if this is what Jesus meant he would have said so. He talked enough about the close of the age so that if he meant the Sermon on the Mount to be the ethic until that time he would not have hidden such an intention.

So then, how do we understand this remarkable proclamation? Most scholars believe that these chapters bear witness to the new life that draws near with the approach of the Kingdom. Life is like this in the kingdom of heaven. Here and there the Kingdom has already come in sight. Wherever it has materialized, this is the way people live their faith. These are the dangers to which people should be alert. These are the blessings that they find; these are the values that they serve. This is the confidence that they manifest. And these are the stumbling blocks and disqualifications we need to heed. It is of these things that Jesus speaks. He speaks both of this world and the world to come. These are the promises of God. This is what God offers even now.

DIMENSION THREE: WHAT DOES THE BIBLE MEAN TO ME?

Matthew 6:25-34—Worry and Seeking the Kingdom

The time in which we live is full of care and anxiety. Human beings are ever confronted by a future and are accordingly always inspired by the questions: What will the future bring? Will I pull through? Will my work be successful?

Hence how can Jesus exhort us: "Do not worry"? Plants and animals do not need to care like we do about food and clothing. They live and grow according to natural instinct. They do not have to bear responsibility like we do for others. Hence, how can Jesus compare our life with the birds of the air and the lilies of the field? Can we survive without sowing, reaping, and storing away in barns? Are not labor and spinning a part of life? What does it mean to seek first his kingdom and his righteousness? What does it mean to live one day at a time?

Matthew 6:20, 24—God and Money

One may believe that treasures in heaven are promissory notes redeemable in some age to come. They may well be. But the treasures Jesus loved are closer than that. The mourners and the poor, the homeless and the hungry, the peacemakers and the children, these are the treasures Jesus loved. If the Sermon on the Mount does nothing else it should cause us to wonder (and maybe to tremble) at where our treasures really are.

The Scripture speaks often about money and the love of money. Matthew rightly tells us that our hearts are where our treasure is. What we find most valuable has our full passion behind it; where our greatest passions lie, there we are usually willing to spend our treasure. And we do this to the point of idolatry. Money becomes an end, or a god, in itself.

Often we think that if we had more, we would be able to give more, but one of the insidious effects of money (and of human nature) is that the more we have, often the more we want to keep. And that, Matthew tells us, leads to enslavement.

What is our orientation to money? to debt? Is our conception of money tied to our concept of our self-worth? to our notions of power? to how we show love?

The Son of Man has authority on earth to forgive sins (9:6).

4

The Healings

Matthew 8–9

DIMENSION ONE:
WHAT DOES THE BIBLE SAY?

Answer these questions by reading Matthew 8

1. What does the leper say when he kneels before Jesus? (8:2)

   "Lord, if you are willing, you can make me clean."

2. What does Jesus tell the man with leprosy after healing him? (8:4)

   Jesus tells the man not to tell anyone, but to show himself to the priest and offer the gift that Moses commanded.

3. Why does the Roman centurion come to Jesus? (8:5-6)

   The centurion comes to Jesus because his servant is lying at home paralyzed and in terrible suffering.

4. What does the centurion ask Jesus to do? (8:8)

   The centurion asks Jesus to say the word and his servant will be healed.

5. What does Jesus say about the centurion? (8:10)

   He says that he has not found such faith even in Israel.

6. What does Jesus then do? (8:13)

   He tells the centurion to go and it will be done for him as he believed it would.

7. Who in Peter's family is sick? (8:14)

   Peter's mother-in-law is sick with a fever.

8. What prophecy does Matthew say Jesus fulfilled by this healing? (8:17)

   This healing fulfills what was spoken by Isaiah.

9. What does the teacher of the law who came up to Jesus say to him? (8:19)

   The teacher of the law tells Jesus that he will follow him wherever Jesus goes.

10. What does Jesus reply? (8:20)

    Jesus tells him that foxes and birds have homes, but the Son of Man has no place to lay his head.

11. What does Jesus tell the man who wants to bury his father first? (8:22)

    He tells the man to follow him and leave the dead to bury their own dead.

12. When Jesus has quieted the storm, what do the men in the boat say? (8:27)

    The men were amazed and asked each other what kind of man can make the winds and the waves obey him.

13. What do the two demon-possessed men in the region of the Gadarenes say when they see Jesus? (8:29)

    They want to know what Jesus has to do with them. Has Jesus come to torture them before the appointed time?

14. What does Jesus do to the demons in the two men? (8:32)

    He sends them into a herd of pigs who then rush down a steep bank and die in the lake.

15. What do the people who hear about it want Jesus to do? (8:34)

The people who hear about it plead with him to leave their region.

Answer these questions by reading Matthew 9

16. What does Jesus tell the man who is paralyzed? (9:2)

Jesus tells the man who is paralyzed that his sins are forgiven.

17. Why does Jesus tell the man to get up and walk? (9:6)

He tells the man to walk so that the teachers of the law may know that the Son of Man has authority on earth to forgive sins.

18. Why does Jesus say that he eats with sinners? (9:12-13)

He says that it is not healthy persons who need a doctor, but the sick. He came not to call the righteous, but sinners.

19. Why do people not put new wine in old wineskins? (9:17)

If new wine is put in old wineskins, the skins burst. The wine runs out and the skin is ruined.

20. What does the ruler want Jesus to do? (9:18)

The ruler wants Jesus to come and put his hand on his daughter who has just died.

21. What does the woman with the bleeding do? (9:20)

The woman touches the edge of his cloak in the hope that she will be healed.

22. When Jesus restores the sight of the two blind men, what does he warn them not to do? (9:30)

Jesus sternly tells them to "see that no one knows about this."

23. When the crowds marvel at Jesus' healing, what do the Pharisees say? (9:34)

They say, "It is by the prince of demons that he drives out demons."

DIMENSION TWO:
WHAT DOES THE BIBLE MEAN?

In Chapters 5–7, Matthew reported that Jesus taught them as "one who had authority." Now in Chapters 8–9,

Matthew gives us a demonstration of that authority. Matthew has gathered ten episodes of healing from various sources. He brings them together in this sequence to serve two purposes. By these miracles, the authority of the Sermon on the Mount is confirmed. And, by the wonders of these healings, we recognize beyond any doubt "what kind of man is this" (8:27). He is the Son of Man, the Messiah. These chapters are of first importance to us on that account, but also for three other reasons. For the first time in the Gospel, Jesus refers to himself as the Son of Man. This raises the question of what Jesus thinks of himself. These chapters also are the most appropriate place to face the problem of the miracles. And here we see for the first time that the Gospel may bring a greater response of faith among Gentiles than it does among Jews.

These chapters build through a dramatic sequence. (See the "The Ten Wonders" on page 33.) Part one (8:1-17) contains three incidents of healing. Jesus heals the leper, the centurion's servant, and Peter's mother-in-law. A brief interlude follows (8:18-22). In the interlude, it seems as though Matthew (and Jesus) intends to show that being a disciple of this wonderful healer is not to be what we might call a picnic.

Three demonstrations of power make up part two (8:23–9:8). Jesus shows a power over the winds and waves, over demons, and over sin. Another interlude reveals more about what life with this miracle worker will be like. It will mean association with nonobservant Jews (sinners) and tax collectors. The final part of the sequence shows us four more healings. In these healings the daughter of the ruler, the woman with the bleeding, two blind men, and the demon-possessed man who could not talk are healed. The climax of the two chapters comes in the charge, "It is by the prince of demons that he casts out demons." This accusation will hound Jesus all the way to Calvary.

Matthew 8:1-4. Leprosy is now called Hansen's disease. It was a frightful affliction. When a person was afflicted with leprosy, the disease would begin with the appearance of little nodules. These would then begin to ulcerate. The ulcers would develop a discharge with a foul odor. The hair around the ulcers would fall out. The eyes would become staring. Gradually the vocal chords would become ulcerated and the person's voice would become hoarse. The person's hands and feet would always become ulcerated. The person slowly would become covered with ulcerated growths. Because of these growths the muscles of the sufferer would waste away. This would cause the tendons of the hands to contract until the person's hands looked like claws. Since this disease also affects the nerve endings and can cause numbness, the fingers and toes were especially subject to injury, sometimes even to the point of falling off. From contracting the disease until death could take twenty or thirty years. Leprosy is a slow, progressive death.

The social stigma of the leper may have been even more devastating. Lepers were ostracized from society in Jesus' day. They could look forward to no human contact for as long as they lived. Theirs was a living death. How extreme, then, for Jesus to touch a leper.

Jesus knows what charges will be brought against him for this radical behavior. So he emphasizes how essential it is for the healed man to observe the ritual prescribed in Leviticus 14. Both Mark and Matthew stress that Jesus does not want publicity on account of the healings. People would acclaim him as a miracle worker. They would not see him as the one who comes in the name of the Lord to call men and women to repentance and faith.

Matthew 8:5-13. Do not fail to point out to students the compassion of the Roman centurion as well as his faith. For an officer to be so concerned for one of his slaves must have been unusual. In that society, slaves were of no human value at all. A dead slave was replaceable, like a worn-out tool. But here was a man who cared enough about his slave to seek help. And he sought help from a healer of the despised Jewish people. Jesus expected to find this kind of faith in Israel. He does not find it. Yet here comes one of the hated Romans with faith that Jesus can help his slave.

Jesus is able to heal the servant. Even more remarkable is that he is able to do it at a distance. He does not need to be at the man's side. Of course, this underscores his authority to which no demonic powers of disease or destruction are equal.

Matthew 8:14-15. In Mark 1:29-31, you will read a more detailed account of this healing. Mark's Gospel is thought to contain firsthand recollections of Peter himself. We might expect Jesus to make Peter's home his headquarters for the Capernaum ministry in Galilee.

Matthew 8:18-22. Students should be encouraged to look up the passage in Daniel 7:13-14. In Daniel we find the image of Jewish apocalyptic hopes (that is, expectation of final heavenly victory). These hopes center on the figure of the Son of Man (also called the Ancient of Days) coming with the clouds of heaven. This Son of Man will be given "authority, glory, and sovereign power." This image is what the title *Son of Man* meant to those who heard Matthew's Gospel. What a shock, then, to hear Jesus say, "The Son of Man has no place to lay his head." How could anyone even imagine such a thing? The heavenly redeemer, homeless among the people he comes to redeem? At this point, Jesus does not seem concerned about changing the image of the Messiah. It appears that he is emphasizing to these would-be followers that they will have nowhere to lay their heads.

"Let the dead bury their own dead" makes sober sense in at least one possible way. This could be better expressed, "Let the dying bury their dead." In Aramaic (the language Jesus spoke) and Hebrew, the word for *dead* can also mean "dying." If "dying" is the proper meaning, Jesus may be calling those who would follow him to embrace the future, not to linger or yearn for the past. Perhaps Jesus refers to the old covenant, perhaps to the prophet John the Baptist. But now the emphasis is no longer on those teachings but on the heavenly kingdom that has come near in Jesus. Jesus is not dismissing grief in a harsh and hurtful way. Instead, he may be using his answer to call people away from the past to a new future. Those who do not have the courage, the faith, or the vision to go toward that new day can remain behind and bury the past.

It has also been suggested that "Lord, let me first go and bury my father" was a commonly used excuse for not doing something. A man's father might be young and healthy with many years ahead of him. "Let me bury my father" would then imply that the person wanted to wait twenty or thirty years until his or her father dies to be called for discipleship. Delayed discipleship Jesus neither wants nor needs.

Matthew 8:23-34. The student book postpones the extended reflection on the miracles until Dimension Three ("What Has God Done for You Lately?") You, as teacher, may not agree with what the students believe. People have understood the miracles in many ways. The miracle stories do not form the basis of faith. They are an expression of faith already arrived at on other grounds.

Most interpretations of the miracles fall into one of three possible views.

• *A literal reading.* According to this understanding, everything happened just as it has been recorded. If television cameras had been there, we would have seen the event exactly as the Gospels report it. The event would be explained in the same way today.

• *The naturalistic explanation.* Those who understand the miracles in this way believe things may have happened as the Gospel tells us. These people find natural explanations of what happened, though. The people in the story were unaware of the natural phenomena. To the person who received the miracle, Jesus' power seemed beyond all accounting except as an epiphany of God's power. According to the naturalistic view, if we knew all the factors we could explain what happened by citing the so-called natural causes.

• *The hiddenness understanding.* In this way of looking at things, the true nature of miracles lies mostly hidden in mystery. Some of them can be accounted for by explanations that we know. For example, a psychosomatic illness may be suddenly cured by the spiritual force of one such as Jesus. Other miracles are still beyond our understanding, such as this calming of the storm on Galilee. By whatever intervention this event occurred, the effect was to call forth wonder and praise. The explanation of how it happened is forever lost. But knowing how the miracles happened is not as important as the faith that they inspired.

The Pharisees interpreted the miracles in one other way. They believed that the prince of demons gave Jesus his power (9:34). Anyone who acts in defiance of Jewish law and tradition must be an agent of the devil.

THE HEALINGS

The important truth that you will want to emerge from any discussion of miracles is that we see the miracles as sacramental of God's power. A sacrament is an action, using "outward and visible signs," to communicate "inward and spiritual" reality. For example, a friendly smile or embrace is sacramental of friendship. Touching the leper transcended all known bounds of relationship with such a diseased person. This act of Jesus then, became sacramental of love. Later in the Gospel of Matthew we will apply this general truth to two particular sacraments of the church, baptism and Communion.

You must be careful when you discuss this issue. The *literalist* may be in danger of emphasizing the magic in miracles. This person may forget that in and of themselves miracles are no more than signs pointing to God. If Jesus Christ himself is the great Miracle, in fact God's supreme Sacrament, then it may be needlessly futile to strain after explanations of these lesser miracles.

The *naturalist*, in explaining the miracles, frequently explains them away. Such a person may unintentionally turn Jesus into a sort of Wizard of Oz. He or she may have Jesus doing things that appear wonderful but are really no more than natural cause and effect. Explanations may enhance wonder for some. But explanations can also blight our wonder and wrap God's glory in a shroud of presumptive knowledge. Because we live in an age of science, we are prone to make quick judgments about what could or could not happen. We prejudge the whole matter of miracles. In effect we make ourselves arbiters of what God is able to do. There is much about our world that Jesus and the people of his day did not know. But they did know something that we may have lost. They knew that "The earth is the LORD'S . . . , /the world, and all who live in it" (Psalm 24:1). On that account we do well to take the miracles seriously, if not literally. Seriously, that is, in terms of the purposes for which the Gospel intends them.

Matthew 8:23-27. While Jesus was in the boat, a violent storm suddenly swept down on the lake. In just a few minutes, the lake was churning into a terrifying turbulence. Such storms are a common occurrence on the Sea of Galilee. The configuration of mountains and a narrow valley funnels the winds down to the Sea of Galilee. The Sea of Galilee is more than six hundred feet below the level of the Mediterranean.

In one of Rembrandt's most dramatic paintings, he pictures for us a small fishing boat riding up the steep slope of a huge wave. The boat is about to be slammed down in a trough between waves, deeper than the height of the mast. Sails and lines are ripped and torn, whipping in the wind. Five of the disciples try desperately to reef the sail and keep the mast from snapping. One disciple is seasick over the side. The others hover over Jesus asleep in the stern of the boat. The painting catches the scene just as the disciples scream, "Lord, we're going to drown!" (Matthew leaves out Mark's more likely detail, "Teacher, don't you care if we drown?") The painting is terrifyingly real and honest.

Jesus' first words upon waking are most unexpected. He asks them why they are afraid. He accuses them of having little faith. It should be obvious why anyone would be afraid in that storm. At the height of the storm they cry, "Lord, save us!" In the calm that followed they ask what sort of man can get even the winds and waves to obey him. One of the great epiphanies of Jesus' ministry took place in the aftermath of that storm on the Sea of Galilee. Matthew's reason for telling the story is to report what happened to the disciples, not what happened to the weather. If the disciples really trusted God with the faith Jesus had, and they should have, they could face a fisherman's death. They should have calm confidence in the God who made the storm as well as the sunshine. God loves them far beyond death.

Matthew 8:28-34. Someone may raise the question about the man who owned the swine. The loss of his pigs would have wiped him out. Even though Jesus is the Messiah, does this give him the right to come onto another man's property and destroy his herd of pigs while restoring two persons with mental illness to sanity? The story has all the characteristics of an "acted parable." A parable makes *one* point. We should not try to analyze all of its details. The point here is that Jesus demonstrated his authority over evil spirits.

Matthew 9:1-8. This passage contains the key episode in these two chapters of Matthew's Gospel. The forgiveness of sin is the major theme of the Gospel. Forgiveness comes as God's response to our greatest need. From the Annunciation in Matthew 1:21 to Peter's assurance at Pentecost (Acts 2:38), this forgiveness comes from God. In the forgiveness and healing of this man who is paralyzed, the good news finds incarnation.

The story also reflects the close relationship between our physical and spiritual health. Not all illness is due to sin. The Book of Job challenged the notion that righteousness prevents suffering and that sufferers have sinned, although this doctrine of retributive justice was prevalent. But unforgiven sin can hinder wholeness of body and spirit.

Equally important for Matthew in this passage is the hostility that Jesus' action aroused among the scribes. The teachers of the law were the keepers of morality. They looked after conformity to the ritual codes of cleanliness and sacred duty. They understood that according to the Jewish tradition, none but the Messiah could forgive sin. The charge that Jesus is blaspheming is the indictment that will lead to the showdown before Caiaphas and Pilate. In this story we see two important things. We see God's tender compassion reaching out to a paralyzed man enabling him to walk. And we see God's unqualified mercy challenging the tightly controlled and constricted clerical power of priests and scribes.

Matthew 9:10-13. As Jesus demonstrates more and more of his authority and compassion, he arouses the anger and jealousy of the religious guardians of Israel—the Pharisees. Later on we shall look more closely at this often misunderstood group who condemned Jesus so. The essence of their opposition appears in this first recorded controversy. They feel Jesus is breaking the code concerning ritual cleanliness. They also disapprove of the physician going to the sick, whoever they were and wherever he found them.

Matthew 9:14-17. The word *bridegroom* is a commonly used figure of speech referring to the Messiah. Jesus uses it again in the parable of the wedding banquet (25:1-13). Matthew clearly implies that Jesus regards himself as the bridegroom. Jesus reminds them that the bridegroom will one day be "taken from them"—a forewarning of the Passion.

Matthew 9:18-34. Several more healings occur. Jesus brought back to life the daughter of a ruler. Even while he was on his way, a woman who had a longstanding problem came to be healed. There is some contrast between the two stories. In one, the ruler, a person of authority, came in person to request Jesus' presence at his home to heal his little girl. The woman, due to her gender and to her illness, was on the social fringe and did not approach Jesus directly, but believed that just being near Jesus would be enough. In both cases, their faith was rewarded in that just a touch by Jesus' hand or of his cloak was sufficient for healing.

Faith enters the third healing as well. In yet another petition, the two blind men asked Jesus for mercy and healing. When questioned, they affirmed their belief in Jesus's power to heal. And so it was accomplished.

No details are offered in the cure of the man who was demon-possessed, except that the crowd continued in their amazement and the Pharisees became more entrenched in their suspicion.

Matthew 9:35-37. The scene shifts here, as Matthew moves from the specific stories of healings in one community to the general comment about multiple healings, sermons, and lessons accomplished throughout the towns and villages. It is as if this interlude summarizes Jesus' ministry to that point and sets the stage for him to teach and empower his disciples to do as they have seen him do.

DIMENSION THREE: WHAT DOES THE BIBLE MEAN TO ME?

Matthew 8:1-17—Miracles

This section records several healings, all of which are performed with the touch of the hand or the utterance of a word. In short, we have no medical way to explain these occurrences; they are miracles.

While we continue to have representatives for God claim the gift of healing, many persons of faith regard them with great skepticism. Many of the persons who seem to have this gift are quiet and unobtrusive about it, and are successful as well. Have the class discuss miracles in general and faith healing in particular. Do they believe these things are possible any longer? Have they ever seen a healer at work? In what scientifically unexplainable ways have they seen God at work in the world?

Matthew 8–9—What Has God Done for You Lately?

It will help to fulfill the purpose of the Gospel to consider together what God has done for us lately. So Jesus performed miracles long ago. What wonderful thing has he performed in you? Think about the things in these two chapters that Matthew tells us Jesus did. A person with leprosy is cleansed. A paralyzed man walks. The daughter of a ruler is raised from death. Outcasts and sinners receive good news when Jesus joins them at table. Jesus did these things and empowered his disciples to continue to do them. Jesus still does these things. Encourage the students to tell from their own experience how Jesus gives new sight, how Jesus sets men and women free from paralysis of will or purpose. Some of the stories may be of how Jesus washed people's imaginations clean of anger, lust, and greed. But all of the stories will be of how Jesus has raised us out of a living death into new life.

The Ten Wonders

8:1-4	Healing the man with leprosy
8:5-13	Healing the centurion's servant
8:14-17	Healing Peter's mother-in-law
	Interlude: Inquiries of Jesus
8:23-27	Calming the storm
8:28-34	Exorcising demons from two possessed men
9:1-8	Healing and forgiving the paralyzed man
	Interlude: Calling of Matthew
	Interlude: Inquiries of Jesus
9:18-26	Restoring the ruler's daughter
9:20-22	Healing the woman with the bleeding
9:27-31	Giving sight to two men who are blind
9:32-34	Exorcising a demon from a man without speech

Whoever loses his life for my sake will find it (10:39).

5

The Conditions of Discipleship

Matthew 10–11

DIMENSION ONE:
WHAT DOES THE BIBLE SAY?

Answer these questions by reading Matthew 10

1. Who were the two sets of brothers mentioned first among the twelve disciples? (10:2)

   Simon Peter and Andrew were brothers. James and John, sons of Zebedee, were brothers.

2. Where did Jesus tell the disciples not to go, and where did he send them? (10:5-6)

   They were not to go among the Gentiles or to any Samaritan towns. He sent them to the lost sheep of Israel.

3. What five things did Jesus tell them to do? (10:7-8)

   He told them to preach, heal, raise the dead, cleanse those who have leprosy, and drive out demons.

4. What did Jesus tell the disciples not to take on their mission? (10:9)

   They are not to take any gold, silver, or copper and no bag or extra tunic, sandals, and staff.

5. How would the disciples live while on their mission? (10:10)

   They are to earn their food as laborers.

6. What were the disciples to do when anyone would not receive them? (10:14)

   They were to shake the dust from their feet when they left an unreceptive home or town.

7. When they were persecuted in a town, what were the disciples to do? (10:23)

   When they were persecuted in one town they were to flee to the next town.

8. Would the Son of Man come before they had completed their mission? (10:23)

   The Son of Man would come before they had gone through all the cities of Israel.

9. Why would the disciples be treated as Jesus would be treated? (10:24)

   They are to be treated as Jesus because a student is not above his teacher.

10. What does Jesus say about the person who refuses to take the cross and follow him? (10:38)

    He says that the person who refuses to follow him "is not worthy of me."

11. What does Jesus say about losing and finding life? (10:39)

    Jesus says that the one who loses life for Jesus' sake will find it.

Answer these questions by reading Matthew 11

12. What do John's disciples ask Jesus? (11:3)

    They ask if Jesus is the one to come or should they expect someone else.

13. What does Jesus tell John's disciples to tell him? (11:5)

    They should tell John that "the blind receive sight, the lame walk, those who have leprosy are cured, the deaf hear, the dead are raised, and the good news is preached to the poor."

14. How does John compare with the least in the kingdom of heaven? (11:11)

   Though John is the greatest of all persons "born of woman," one who is least in the kingdom of heaven is greater than John.

15. Who does Jesus say John is if people will accept it? (11:14)

   Jesus says that John is the Elijah who was to come.

16. What do people say about John? (11:18)

   They say he has a demon.

17. What do people say about Jesus? (11:19)

   They say Jesus is a glutton and a drunkard, a friend of tax collectors and sinners.

18. Why does Jesus denounce Korazin and Bethsaida? (11:20)

   He denounces them because they did not repent.

19. What does Jesus say will happen at Capernaum on the Day of Judgment? (11:23)

   Capernaum will go down to the depths (Hades).

20. What does Jesus say to those who are weary and burdened? (11:28)

   Jesus says if they come to him he will give them rest.

21. How does Jesus describe his yoke and his burden? (11:30)

   He says his yoke is easy and his burden is light.

DIMENSION TWO: WHAT DOES THE BIBLE MEAN?

What we read in Chapter 10 is not the sort of thing an army recruiting sergeant will tell a prospective enlistee who walks in off the street and asks if he can join the army. One hardly gets enthusiastic volunteers by telling them about the physical and emotional pain of war, the boredom of military discipline, and the high risk of combat. Nor did Jesus tell his prospective disciples of all the risks and consequences when he said, "Follow me." But before they go out on their first mission, Jesus lays it all out for them. He tells them that they must expect and be prepared to face the cross, which is the price of discipleship.

Matthew 10:2. Nowhere else in his Gospel does Matthew use the word *apostle.* The word means, literally, "one who is sent." By the end of the first century it was commonly held that the twelve disciples were the first apostles. They had been sent out by Jesus to proclaim the Kingdom. The mantle later fell on others such as Paul and Barnabas. The apostles were also said to be those who had seen the risen Lord. Matthew prefers the word *disciple* to refer to followers gathered round a teacher.

Matthew 10:8. "Raise the dead" could also be translated "raise the dying." In both Hebrew and Aramaic (the language Jesus spoke), the word is the same. Jesus could as well mean raise the dying back to life, new life.

Matthew 10:10. Christian disciples or missionaries, both in Jesus' time and later, worked their way on the journey. Members of a synagogue would readily accept the responsibility to feed and otherwise sustain a traveling teacher.

Matthew 10:14. Shaking off the dust is a ritual, symbolic action. This action indicates that the place that would not receive the disciples is henceforth corrupted. One must not carry even its dust to another place, lest corruption be spread. Rejecting a disciple is here treated as rejecting the Christ himself.

Matthew 10:16-33. These verses are a prophecy by Jesus of what will happen to him. These verses also tell what was happening to Jewish Christians in Matthew's time. Followers of Jesus were hounded and persecuted as conflict with the Jews mounted. Verse 23 offers encouragement to the threatened disciples. Verse 23 states that the persecutions will be bearable because the Son of Man will come before the mission to all Israel is completed. As Matthew reports these words of Jesus, the reference may be to the coming of the resurrected Son of Man. The risen Lord did appear before the mission to Israel had been fulfilled.

Matthew 10:25. "The house of Beelzebub" refers to the charge by the Pharisees that Jesus casts out demons by the prince of demons (9:34). Beelzebub was the chief of devils, Satan.

Matthew 10:26-33. These verses contain good news. The disciples are not to fear. (Three times Jesus encourages them, verses 26, 28, and 31.) And why not? Jesus' answer comes across the long time and distance to disciples in this much later day.

First, because ultimately the truth will come to light and be revealed, the believer can proclaim the truth upon the housetops. Second, the disciples can put off their fears, because Jesus assures them that they are of more value than sparrows. Finally, Jesus assures them, if they acknowledge him, he will testify for them before his Father who is in heaven.

Now you may need to take a deeper look at what is being said here. Someone may point out that this seems calculating. "You do this for me, and I'll do that for you." Does that sound like Jesus? It helps to remember that, when Matthew compiled his Gospel, Christian disciples were being delivered to councils, flogged in synagogues, and betrayed by their own families. They faced a cold, lonely, threatening world. They needed a word of reassurance that they had a defender in the Christ. But an even more profound truth lies behind the "you-for-me and I-for-you" terms of the promise. A so-called disciple who will not stand up for Jesus will find nothing offered by God in heaven that he or she ever cares to stand for.

Matthew 10:34-39. As though to illustrate how hard discipleship is, Jesus goes on to speak in hyperbole. One cannot fully appreciate the sayings of Jesus without understanding hyperbole. Hyperbole is a statement that is exaggerated fancifully. One example might be "I could eat a horse."

Jesus frequently put things in the most extreme images. He did this so people would realize the real meaning of the truth. For example, Jesus says, "It is easier for a camel to go through the eye of a needle than for a rich man to enter the kingdom of God" (19:24). That statement is hyperbole about how hard it will be to get to heaven. The hyperbole does away with the notion that we can manage it without too much difficulty.

The hyperbole in verses 37-39 stings even more when we read it in Luke 14:26. "If anyone comes to me and does not hate his father and mother, his wife and children . . . he cannot be my disciple." One can scarcely imagine Jesus' meaning what that statement says literally. How can anyone be a disciple of Jesus with all that hate in his or her heart? What he means is, being my disciple cannot be second to anything else. That hardly makes the demand much easier, but we can at least see that Jesus is not encouraging anyone to hate someone else.

Matthew 10:38. Here for the first time Jesus speaks of the cross. So sensitive to everyone and everything around him, Jesus could not have failed to imagine where the road he had set out to travel would take him. And anyone who refused to walk that road with him "is not worthy of me." He says it three times. Later he is to say in some way "The Son of man must suffer many things and be killed" three times (Matthew 16:21; 17:22; 20:18-19).

The disciples all know what the cross is. The cross is the price of discipleship. Jesus is here trying to tell them. But they do not really understand. Peter will later be angry when Jesus tells him what is going to happen (16:22). Jesus then has to tell Peter, "Out of my sight, Satan!"

Matthew 11:1. Once again we come upon the ending to a book within the Gospel. We know that Matthew ends Book II of his Gospel at this place because Jesus had finished this particular teaching. He now goes on to the next development in his life. Here we begin Book III.

Matthew 11. We come upon at least three haunting verses in Chapter 11. These verses do not lose their grip on the mind and the imagination of the faithful reader after the Bible is closed. Dimension Three in the student book points to verses 6, 21, and 30. Little more need be said about them here. You will recall that when we considered the nine Beatitudes in the Sermon on the Mount (5:3-11) it was pointed out that Matthew also included four further beatitudes. Matthew 11:6 is the first of these. "Blessed is the man who does not fall away on account of me." You might want to think with the students about whether this beatitude is comparable to the nine in the Sermon on the Mount.

And speaking of blessings, we would indeed be blessed if the woes that befell Korazin and Bethsaida prompted us to consider some of the mighty works that God is doing in our own cities that our eyes fail to see.

The "easy yoke" and the "light burden" almost certainly do not mean what we first assume. After Chapter 10, how could they? Nothing about persecution, flogging, and betrayal is easy. Maybe Jesus speaks again in hyperbole. But a more likely reading is to be found in the use of the image of the yoke. A yoke is used on a beast of burden, enabling the ox to pull or carry great weight because the harness is fitted so well to the animal's body. To be in the service of Jesus the Christ, to shape our living to the Beatitudes, gives lifting power beyond what we could otherwise handle.

Matthew 11:12. This verse has many problems of language. Even highly competent linguistic scholars cannot unravel the meaning with certainty. This verse is not one of the verses students need to linger over. But just in case anyone may want to discuss it, you can suggest some ways to understand the verse.

You do not misread the Gospel if you see a double meaning here. The first part of the verse, "From the days of John the Baptist until now . . ." seems to mean, according to one interpretation, "from John's day until now" people have violently ravaged the Kingdom proclaimed by Jesus. The "until now" means that these words were spoken by Jesus some time after John's disappearance and death. The other interpretation of the first part of the verse is that, from the days of John the Baptist until now, the kingdom of heaven has been coming violently. In either case, just what Jesus meant is not altogether clear. Up to that point in his life there had been no overt violence.

At the same time, the second part of the verse seems clearly to mean that people have tried to storm their way into the Kingdom—with violence! This may well be hyperbole. The difficulty is that nothing in Jesus' life suggests that the Kingdom can be taken by violent clashing of swords. It might be better if Matthew 11:12 were not here. Yet when all is said and done the verse may serve as a powerful reminder that the coming of the Kingdom may be more of a violent disturbance than a walk through the fields to consider the lilies.

Matthew 11:25-27. Verse 25 is a none-too-subtle comment about the "wise and learned" teachers of the law—Pharisees and priests. They have closed minds and hard hearts and cannot see what Jesus reveals. Yet "little children," the child-like common people, gladly recognize what God discloses.

DIMENSION THREE:
WHAT DOES THE BIBLE MEAN TO ME?

Matthew 11:6, 21, 30
The Meaning of Being Jesus' People

Whether we are enlisting in an army, signing on to a whaling expedition, or choosing to be Jesus' people, we will want to know three things. We will want to know what are the conditions of enlistment, what will it cost, and what will we get out of it or what the consequences will be. Chapter 10 spells out these conditions, and not in small footnotes to be read after we have been sworn in.

The conditions of discipleship are that the disciples put their heads, their hands, and their hearts to the work that Jesus does (10:7-8). This means proclaiming the kingdom of heaven. It means healing and raising the dead or dying. It means cleansing what is unclean and casting out demonic powers wherever we find them.

What is the appropriate way for us to do these things today? Can we read Jesus' word, not literally in all cases, but truthfully? We do not need to become faith healers to help people back to health. Think of how many ways there are for people to be healed. We do not need to revive someone who has died in order to call others out of a living death.

Where are the demonic powers in our world that we might help exorcise? physical addictions? social ills? How is Jesus, through the risen and living Christ, doing these things in our time? What institutions are head, hands, and heart for Christ in our midst? How many disciples join the Christ now as he seeks entrance into our common life? These are all questions to be raised by persons who seriously seek to know the conditions of discipleship.

The cost of discipleship entails facing what the Teacher or Master faced (10:17-18, 23-25, 34-38). The consequences come in what is promised, life and blessing (10:32, 39).

Matthew 10:26, 28, 31—Do Not Fear

Jesus gave the disciples four reasons why they need not be afraid. Ask the students to dig out these reasons from the passage.

1. "Nothing is concealed," which means, "the truth will come out." The world will one day discover that what Jesus said is true.

2. "Those who kill the body" these days are growing more numerous. Our society is not nearly as safe as it used to be. But a higher purpose is at work here because those persons cannot kill the soul, if we trust in God.

3. The disciples are "worth more than many sparrows." God knows and cares what happens to us. God notices when we fall.

4. Jesus will acknowledge the disciples who bear witness faithfully.

Do these reasons calm our fears as they were intended to encourage the first disciples? It will be interesting to learn from the students how they find courage to meet the conditions and pay the cost of being Jesus' disciples. This, after all, is the bottom line of the chapter for us.

Still other seed fell on good soil, where it produced a crop (13:8).

— 6 —
Parables of the Kingdom
Matthew 12–13

DIMENSION ONE:
WHAT DOES THE BIBLE SAY?

Answer these questions by reading Matthew 12

1. Why did the Pharisees rebuke Jesus in the grain fields? (12:2)

   When they picked heads of grain and ate them, they did what was unlawful on the sabbath.

2. What did Jesus say David and the priests did? (12:4-5)

   David and the priests broke ritual laws. David ate the consecrated bread; the priests desecrated the sabbath.

3. What did the Pharisees ask Jesus when he entered the synagogue? (12:10)

   The Pharisees asked if it is lawful to heal on the sabbath.

4. What did Jesus do for the man with the shriveled hand? (12:13)

   He completely restored it, as sound as the other.

5. What did the Pharisees do when they witnessed Jesus' act? (12:14)

   They plotted against Jesus for how they might kill him.

6. What order does Jesus give the people he heals? (12:16)

   Jesus tells the people he heals not to tell who he is.

7. What do the Pharisees say about Jesus when he heals the man who was blind and mute? (12:24)

   They say Jesus drives out demons by Beelzebub, the prince of demons.

8. How does Jesus answer this charge? (12:25)

   He tells them that no city or household divided against itself will stand.

9. What sin does Jesus say will not be forgiven? (12:32)

   Whoever speaks against the Holy Spirit will not be forgiven.

10. What three things does Jesus say he is greater than? (12:6, 41, 42)

    Jesus says he is greater than the Temple, Jonah, and Solomon.

11. What does an evil spirit do when he finds his house empty, swept, and in order? (12:45)

    The evil spirit brings seven other evil spirits more wicked than itself to go and live there.

12. Who does Jesus say his mother, brothers, and sisters are? (12:50)

    Whoever does the will of God is Jesus' mother, brother, and sister.

Answer these questions by reading Matthew 13

13. To whom does Jesus speak beside the sea? (13:1-2)

    Jesus speaks to large crowds.

14. From where does Jesus speak? (13:2)

    Jesus speaks from a boat.

15. Where do the seeds fall in Jesus' parable? (13:4-8)

    The seeds fall on a path, rocky places, among thorns, and on good soil.

16. Why does Jesus say that he speaks to the crowds in parables? (13:13)

Jesus speaks in parables because "though seeing, they do not see; / though hearing, they do not hear or understand."

17. What does Jesus say to his disciples about prophets and righteous men? (13:17)

They longed to see and hear what the disciples see and hear, but did not.

18. What is the meaning of the seed falling among thorns? (13:22)

The person hears the word, but the worries of life and the deceitfulness of wealth choke it, making it unfruitful.

19. What did the owner say to the servants who wanted to pull the weeds from his wheat? (13:29-32)

He told them to wait until the harvest.

20. After the first two parables, what five similes (statements of likeness) does Jesus use for the kingdom of heaven? (13:31, 33, 44, 46, 47)

The kingdom of heaven is like a mustard seed, yeast mixed in flour, hidden treasure, a pearl of great value, and a fishing net.

21. In the parables of the weeds and the net what will happen at the close of the age? (13:41-43, 49-50)

Angels will weed out everything that causes sin and all who do evil and separate the wicked from the righteous. The evil will be thrown in the fiery furnace, and the righteous will shine like the sun in the Kingdom.

DIMENSION TWO:
WHAT DOES THE BIBLE MEAN?

The storm gathering against Jesus intensifies through the events reported in Chapter 12, the second half of the narrative portion of Matthew's Book III. In Chapter 11, Matthew has further established the messiahship of Jesus. Does he not do the things the long-expected Christ would do (11:5)? Among the little children (11:25) this is good news, and they "listened to him with delight" (Mark 12:37). But the revelation is hidden from the wise (Matthew 11:25). Instead of rejoicing at what they see and hear, the teachers of the law and the Pharisees take offense. For the first time, those who are offended at the blasphemy of Jesus secretly meet to discuss how to destroy him (12:14).

Jesus declares that the Kingdom has come upon us (12:28). In Chapter 13, Matthew gathers seven parables of the Kingdom. These stories tell how the Kingdom will come and the amazing effect of its appearance.

Matthew 12:1-8. Two incidents provoke bitter controversy regarding the sabbath. Putting in perspective this conflict between Jesus and the Pharisees is important. To many people today, this may seem like a petty issue. You might ask the class, presumably made up of Christians, which of the Ten Commandments (Exodus 20:1-17) they consider the least important. They probably will admit that setting priorities among the commandments is inappropriate. Chances are they will say the third (you shall not take the name of the Lord in vain) or the fourth (remember the sabbath day to keep it holy) is the least important. On the whole, we are not Sabbatarians. Anger over picking a few heads of grain to eat on the sabbath seems like much ado about nothing. The disciples were not stealing. By custom they were allowed this courtesy as they passed through the fields.

But for the moment, let's see the issue from the Pharisees' point of view. Strict observance of the sabbath was part of the survival mode for Israel. The paganism of the Gentile world enveloped the Jews. It permeated even the towns and cities of their own land.

Paganism and secularism permeate the climate in which we live too; and Christians have to nurture their families in the Judeo-Christian values. For the Jews, institutions like the sabbath observance, the dietary code, and laws for socializing (whom to eat with, what house to enter) were the marks of being faithful Jews. To ignore those things might be to lose their identity as people of the covenant.

Jesus never disregarded any of the commandments, not even this one. He said he had not come to abolish the law, but to fulfill the law. "Anyone who breaks one of the least of these commandments and teaches others to do the same will be called least in the kingdom of heaven" (5:17, 19). The issue was never whether to be lax in observing the sabbath. The issue was what the sabbath observance may have excluded. It was really the same issue that Jesus challenged when he condemned the Pharisees for tithing while they neglected "the more important matters of the law, justice—mercy and faithfulness" (23:23). Observing sabbath laws (no work on the sabbath, and picking grain was work) prevented response to hunger and healing. The issue was: Keep the sabbath laws, but remember, mercy takes precedence over sacrifice.

Matthew 12:9-13. As the student book suggests, Jesus could have postponed the healing until the sabbath ended. If a person's life were in danger, one could heal without breaking the sabbath law. But the man with the shriveled hand was not in danger of dying. Why did Jesus not avoid the confrontation with the Pharisees? Was it not to keep the priority of mercy from being suffocated by a tangle of constricting rules? Jesus knew that the way to force the issue was to do the merciful thing and then point to it as proper observance of the sabbath.

Matthew 12:15-21. Here we have one more example of Matthew quoting from the Scripture to prove that Jesus is the Messiah. He chooses the first of the servant songs of second Isaiah, the prophet of the Babylonian Exile (Isaiah 42:1-4). In this case, the connection is farfetched. The servant songs picture either the nation of Israel or a messianic figure who serves the nation as a wounded healer. Isaiah's servant suffers in order to redeem people and nations from their sins. Jesus was to become this Savior. Matthew, in this quotation, has seized upon one line in the song, "No one will hear his voice in the streets," (12:19) and applied it to Jesus' request that persons he had healed not make him known (12:16). It seems that Jesus did not want to associate the approach of the Kingdom with his healing miracles. That men and women repent and believe the gospel is far more important.

Matthew 12:22-23. This next controversy breaks out, not over the sabbath, but over the source of Jesus' authority. Having already made up their minds to destroy Jesus, the Pharisees looked for charges to bring against him. Accusing Jesus of being in league with Satan is not new (9:34). But they are making this into the big lie. Repeat the charge often enough and maybe it will stick. Jesus cleverly turns their design against them with his familiar retort about a house divided. If Satan is casting out his own demonic demons, the satanic kingdom is in disarray. How will it stand? Jesus silences the Pharisees for the moment by asking them by whom their people cast out demons. If Jesus exorcises evil spirits by the power of the devil, what about their own people? If Jesus does this by the power of the Spirit of God, then "the kingdom of God has come upon you." Jesus' forensic skill in debate is sharp. Either they concede his claims for the Kingdom or they condemn their own people.

Matthew 12:31-32. In Dimension Three we shall consider this troublesome verse about the sin that cannot be forgiven. (See the student book.)

Matthew 12:38-42. It looks as though Matthew, not Jesus, uses the Jonah parable as an allegory of the Resurrection. Such a reference, however memorable, is beside the point in this place. The sign Jesus reminds his hearers of is that Nineveh repented when Jonah preached there. Many in Israel have not repented, even though "one greater than Jonah" has arrived. Jesus follows the Jonah sign immediately with a recollection of the Queen of Sheba's visit to Solomon (1 Kings 10:1-10). The Queen of Sheba, a Gentile, listened to the wisdom of the wisest of Israel's kings. Now, says Jesus, someone greater than Solomon has come. Are they listening?

Notice the three announcements, "someone greater than . . . is here." The Pharisees asked for a sign, a healing, an exorcism, or whatever Jesus would do. He condemns the evil and adulterous generation always looking for a sign. He then gives the Pharisees an astounding blasphemy

of their beliefs. He tells them that his authority is greater than the Temple, the sign of his preaching is greater than Jonah, and his wisdom is greater than Solomon. Matthew does not report their reaction or response. They must have been speechless.

Matthew 12:43-45. We find nothing obscure in these verses. What we find is a disconcerting picture that somehow turns into a mirror into which we would rather not look. (See Dimension Three.)

Matthew 12:46-50. Those who know the Gospel story find it difficult to disassociate this episode from the statement in John's Gospel that "even his brothers did not believe in him" (John 7:5). Matthew says nothing to agree with what John writes. We do sense, though, in the way Matthew describes what happens, that Jesus dismisses his family almost in a cavalier way, without feeling. That Jesus' family failed to understand him or appreciate his ministry may well have been true, but that is not the point of these verses. Their only purpose is to include in Jesus' family all who do God's will.

Matthew 13. We may well call this the teacher's chapter. Jesus speaks these words primarily to give encouragement to his disciples. He is preparing them to teach and preach in his name. Along with the storm warnings of persecution and trial, these "teachers of the law who [have] been instructed about the kingdom" (13:52) need the assurance that the word they have been given to deliver is like a good seed. When planted in good soil it will bring forth a bountiful harvest. Even though their planting will grow entangled with evil, at the end time God's harvest will gather the grain into "the kingdom of their Father" (13:43). Such promises must have been the sustaining hope of the teachers and leaders of the early Christian congregations.

Is such assurance any less important in our day? Don't we who teach need to hear and believe the same promises? Don't we expect to hear that God's word that we sow will produce a harvest, often beyond where we can now see? In God's time, and at God's reaping, evil will be overcome.

The positive note of hope in the parables of the Kingdom has frequently been muted or missed altogether. The emphasis has usually been upon the poor soils in the parable of the sower and the wicked deed of the enemy sowing weeds in the farmer's field. The accent in the two longer parables in Chapter 13 is on harvest, the abundant reaping at the close of the age. It will be important for you to stress the good news, even above the caution about rocky soil, thorns, and noxious weeds.

You might bring the parables within the experience of the students by asking the following questions:

• What evidence do we have that good teaching (nurturing) produces good harvests? As in all Christian living, we live by faith, not by sight (2 Corinthians 5:7). But have we ever seen "good seed yielding good grain"? Where? When?

• What do we do about weeds growing amid wheat? What balance can we strike between patience and zeal? This parable speaks to us of the church, the family, the community, the world. When shall we tolerate evil in anticipation of a future reckoning or harvest, and when shall we pull the weeds from among the grain?

Matthew 13:3-9, 18-23. This parable is told twice. It is told once as a simple parable, once as allegory. Jesus rarely, if ever, allegorizes his teaching. Later interpreters have often turned parables, stories told to make a single moral point, into allegories, in which all the details are freighted with meaning. Perhaps verses 18-23 are such an instance. Whoever allegorized the sower, if indeed Jesus did not do it himself, did not change the inner logic and meaning of the story.

Seed was usually broadcasted by the sower. If the wind blew, some would land outside the plowed area. A right-of-way always passed between the long narrow strips of field. Seed falling on the right-of-way could not sprout before the birds got it. Rocky ground was the thin skin of soil covering the hard ledge of rock beneath. No roots could develop to sustain grain there.

Matthew 13:10-17. These verses are troublesome, especially when we compare Matthew's quotation with the Isaiah verses (Isaiah 6:9-10). These verses were used repeatedly in the early church to explain the stubborn rejection of the Christian message by many Jews. It sounds as though God deliberately made the heart of the people calloused so they would not see and hear and turn. That idea hardly squares with the Old Testament faith that God would redeem Israel. It says something to us of the bewilderment and despair of the prophet.

Matthew, quoting the Greek translation of the original Hebrew, softens the verses. Because of their dullness of heart the people no longer see and hear. The people are responsible for their own close-mindedness, not God. When we move from Isaiah to Jesus and Matthew, according to the older translation, Jesus spoke in parables so that people would not understand. This statement disagrees with everything we know about Jesus and his purpose. That simply won't do. Jesus means that he speaks in parables so they will understand. To the disciples "the knowledge of the secrets of the kingdom of heaven [have] been given" (13:11). To the others Jesus must speak in parables so they too may know. This passage is understood only by those who are willing to follow Jesus the full distance of suffering and self-sacrifice.

Of the twenty parables in the Gospel of Matthew, six appear also in both Mark and Luke. Three are found in Luke but not in Mark. Two of the best known parables, the parables of the good Samaritan and the prodigal son, do not appear in Matthew. They very likely come from a source available only to Luke.

Seven of these twenty parables in the Bible pertain to the kingdom of heaven. Matthew gathers them in this place for people to hear as Jesus' response to all the charges of blasphemy and being in league with the devil that the Pharisees have leveled against Jesus. And they serve as assurance and encouragement to the disciples.

Matthew 13:31-35. The first two of the five similes Matthew closes the chapter with talk of God's power to bring the kingdom of heaven into being. These are not similes for gradual growth. The idea of the Kingdom gradually evolving from a tiny seed is alien to Jewish hopes. They believed that at the close of the age the Kingdom would suddenly appear. Among the Jews, leavening is associated with evil. Fermentation is an evil process. The Jews prepared for Passover by removing all old yeast from the house. A new leaven is introduced for the new baking (1 Corinthians 5:6-8). It must have surprised his listeners when Jesus compared the kingdom of heaven to leaven. Jesus proclaimed the power to transform the old relationships into a new covenant.

Matthew 13:44-46. The next two similes are chosen to picture the discipline and sacrifice required of any who would enter the Kingdom. In Jesus' day people buried their coins or their gold. Houses might be destroyed in war or ransacked by thieves (6:19). There were no banks for ordinary people. The man who bought the field did nothing fraudulent. By custom and by law the treasure was his for the finding. Says Jesus, the Kingdom is worth the sacrifice of all that one has. Presumably the treasure could transform the man's life. So, too, can the Kingdom.

Both the treasure and the pearl of great value could have been found by chance or as the result of ardent search. How it was found is hardly the point. Either one is worth more than everything else in a person's life.

The final simile of the net emphasizes the truth of God's promised harvest. When men fished in the Sea of Galilee they dropped weighted nets into the water. When the nets were drawn they stretched out in the shape of a wide-mouth funnel. The fish swam into that closed net and were hauled ashore. Then the good fish were separated from the useless fish. All people will be separated at God's final hauling of the nets of history.

Ask students to group these seven parables by pairs with one parable standing by itself. What do these seven parables teach us?
• One parable, the parable of the sower, declares that good seed in good soil will produce good grain.
• The two parables about the mustard seed and the leaven speak of God's power and intention to establish the Kingdom.
• The two parables about the wheat and the weeds and the net give the promise of a harvest at the close of the age. At this harvest the righteous will be gathered into God's

kingdom and the unrighteous will be cast into the furnace of fire.

- The two parables about the hidden treasure and the pearl of great value tell of the price and sacrifice that the Kingdom is worth.

DIMENSION THREE: WHAT DOES THE BIBLE MEAN TO ME?

Matthew 13:3-9—Even Good Seed Needs Good Soil

The original purpose of this parable—to encourage the disciples by the promise of power in God's word—has frequently been obscured by attention to the soils. Nevertheless, truth speaks with force from the image of the four kinds of soil.

How does a person's life get so caked up that seed is devoured almost as soon as it lands? Maybe one problem for many of us is that we have no tillable ground in our lives. Everything falls along the path.

Why do some people have only a thin skin of soil covering a rocky ledge beneath mind, heart, and imagination? Their soil is so shallow that nothing survives. Are we just tasters and samplers of life, not cultivating deep enough to allow roots to grow?

What are the thorns among which good seed is choked in our lives?

These images act somewhat as a scanner by which we can see the true shape of our lives. Fortunately the parable does not leave us without the assurance that good seed brings forth abundantly from good soil. What makes good soil?

Matthew 13:24-30 Letting Wheat and Weeds Grow Together

Isn't this one of the hardest things we have to do in trying to be Christian? Our first impulse on seeing what we believe to be evil is to pull it out, by the roots if at all possible. Yet the parable reminds us that we can not always tell the potentially good from what may turn out to be bad. And in tearing out the evil, how much good may be destroyed? Consider this truth as it applies to family life, to young people growing up, to social problems in the community. When do we do greater harm by rushing in to uproot than by letting things come to a natural harvest? Of course, the parable speaks not of a natural harvest, but of God's harvest. Still, does not God harvest many fields along the way?

Paradoxically, we dare not deny the danger of letting the weeds take over and stifle the wheat. Do not some things need to be nipped in the bud? How much simpler would it be if we have a neat rule to tell us when to be patient and when to be zealous? Alas, we have none. We must live by faith, not by sight. It would be helpful to work at discovering guidelines for such walking.

Who do you say I am? . . . You are the Christ, the Son of the living God (16:15-16).

7

You Are the Christ

Matthew 14–16

DIMENSION ONE:
WHAT DOES THE BIBLE SAY?

Answer these questions by reading Matthew 14

1. Why did Herod throw John the Baptist into prison? (14:3-4)

   John had told Herod it was unlawful for him to have his brother's wife.

2. Why did Herod promise the daughter of Herodias whatever she desired? (14:6-7)

   He was pleased with her dancing.

3. What did the daughter ask for? (14:8)

   She asked for John the Baptist's head on a platter.

4. What does Jesus do when he hears about John's death? (14:13)

   Jesus withdraws by boat privately to a solitary place.

5. What does Jesus say to the disciples when they tell him to send the crowds away? (14:16)

   He tells them to give the people something to eat.

6. When Jesus took the five loaves and two fish in his hands, what did he do? (14:19)

   He gave thanks, broke the loaves, and gave the bread to the disciples.

7. Where was Jesus when the storm arose on the Sea of Galilee? (14:23)

   He was up in the hills praying.

8. What does Peter say when he sees Jesus walking on the water? (14:28)

   He says, "Lord, if it's you, tell me to come to you on the water."

9. What do the disciples do and say when the wind stops? (14:33)

   They worship Jesus, saying, "Truly you are the Son of God."

Answer these questions by reading Matthew 15

10. What does Jesus say makes a person "unclean"? (15:11, 18)

    What a person says makes a person "unclean."

11. What kind of guides are the Pharisees? (15:14)

    Jesus says that the Pharisees are blind guides.

12. Who comes to see Jesus in the region of Tyre and Sidon? (15:21-22)

    A Canaanite woman comes to see Jesus.

13. What does she want? (15:22)

    She wants Jesus to have mercy on her, for her daughter is suffering terribly from demon-possession.

14. What is Jesus' first response to the woman? (15:24)

    He says he was sent only for the lost sheep of Israel.

15. Why does he finally heal her daughter? (15:28)

    He heals the daughter because the woman's faith is great.

16. What does Jesus warn the disciples about the Pharisees? (16:6)

    He warns them of the yeast of the Pharisees.

17. What does he mean by "the yeast of the Pharisees"? (16:12)

    It refers to the teaching of the Pharisees.

18. Who do the disciples tell Jesus that people say he is? (16:14)

    People say he is John the Baptist, Elijah, the prophet Jeremiah, or another of the prophets.

19. Who does Simon Peter say that Jesus is? (16:16)

    Peter says that Jesus is the Christ, the Son of the living God.

20. What does Jesus say to Peter? (16:18-19)

    Jesus tells Peter that Peter is the rock on which Jesus will build his church.

21. What does Jesus tell his disciples that he must endure? (16:21)

    He tells them that he must suffer many things at the hands of the elders, chief priests, and teachers of the law and be killed.

DIMENSION TWO: WHAT DOES THE BIBLE MEAN?

Chapters 14–17 constitute the narrative portion of Matthew's Book IV (messiahship, suffering, the life of the church). We find here a series of pictures marking the end of the Galilean ministry as well as a foreshadowing of the Jerusalem Passion story. One of the peaks of Matthew's Gospel comes in Chapter 16 when Peter confesses Jesus to be "the Christ, the Son of the living God." For Matthew this moment signals the beginning of the Christian church.

Matthew 14:1-12. The name of Herod is written in blood across the pages of the New Testament. He was responsible for murdering the children of Bethlehem when Jesus was born, imprisoning and murdering John the Baptist, and mocking Jesus at his trial. The Herods were an example of despotic cruelty in the world that made no place for Jesus.

A tetrarch was a petty ruler, originally over one-quarter of a region's political division. He was lower than a true king (although the Gospel refers to King Herod). A tetrarch was always limited by and dependent on his overlord. In the case of the Herods, they were dependent on the Roman emperor. The Herods were Jews but were hated by the whole nation for collaborating with the Romans. Remembering the details of this appalling family history are of small consequences to the whole study of Matthew. That the students get some sense of the evil the Herods directed against John and Jesus is enough.

We have already learned how closely the lives and voices of Jesus and John were linked. The report of John's execution must have hurt Jesus deeply. After all, John had prepared the way for Jesus, baptized him, and announced that the kingdom of heaven is near. The report of John's death also cast a heavy shadow of events to come over Jesus. The death of John must have been the catalyst for the revelations of Chapters 16 and 17.

Matthew 14:13-21. First, Matthew tells us the story of the feeding of the multitude. Probably because of the threat to him implied by John's death, Jesus withdrew "privately to a solitary place." Wherever it was it became the scene for one of the most important and memorable events in Jesus' life. The importance in this story is seen in the sacramental meaning of the bread. That the loaves were enough to feed so many is seen as a miracle, but that is not its only importance. A good way to get at the significance of the episode would be for you as teacher to read carefully Chapter 6 of John, one of the longest chapters in all the four Gospels.

The event held exceptional importance for John. John contains no account of an upper room dinner from which our Communion is in part derived. Instead John sees in this event on a lonely hillside the foreshadowing of the Eucharist. (*Eucharist*, meaning "thanksgiving," will be discussed when we come to the Last Supper in Matthew 26.) Jesus, according to John, and as the early church already confessed, is the Bread of Life. When he broke the loaves and distributed the bread to the multitude, he was giving them the symbol of himself. Matthew does not use such an image in his account of the feeding. But in the upper room, Jesus says of the bread, "This is my body" (26:26). Matthew's use of the formula of taking bread, giving thanks, breaking it, and giving it to the disciples indicates a sacramental reference.

We shall never know whether Jesus miraculously produced enough bread to satisfy the physical hunger of everyone there, or whether people had their own bread and shared it to make it go around. Each person might have been given a communion-size morsel, for all we know. However the bread was divided, people were satisfied. Perhaps they were satisfied as we are satisfied at the Lord's Table though we eat but a tiny bit of the consecrated loaf. Jesus is saying, "In me you will be given enough and some to spare."

Matthew 14:22-36. This storm scene differs in two ways from the one in Chapter 8. For one thing, Jesus is not in the boat this time when the storm blows up. He sent his disciples on ahead. We are permitted at least the suspicion that the boat represents the church. The storm possibly symbolizes the tempest in which Christians are and will be caught. Perhaps, then, Chapter 8 shows us a storm where Jesus is physically present with his disciples. In other words, it depicts his earthly ministry now going on. In the Chapter 14 storm, Jesus is no longer there. The disciples are without him in the boat. This could have the meaning of a post-resurrection encounter, somehow transposed to an earlier time. If the two storms have no such symbolic connection, at least the meaning is clear that the church needs Christ to face all storms. He comes across the water to uphold the faithful, but fearful, followers and to quiet the elements that beat upon and rage against them. Reading the stories in this way is reading them as proclamation rather than history. Such an event surely must have happened when Jesus was with the disciples. But Matthew compiled his Gospel for just such a purpose of proclamation.

Matthew 15:1-20. Matthew deliberately reports this controversy in a way to put the Jerusalem Pharisees in a most unfavorable light. It seems to imply that they consider ceremonial hand washing more important than refraining from evil thoughts of sexual immorality, false testimony, and slander. And so they may have done. The codes concerning ritual and diet were indispensable to the faithful Jews dwelling in the midst of pagan peoples. It is like the dispute over sabbath observance in Chapter 12. We must not dismiss ceremonial practice as fussy trivia in itself. As with the sabbath issue, the heart of the matter is what people exclude on account of traditional observance. Jesus is emphatic about this. He came not to destroy but to fulfill the law. He directs his condemnation against those who put tradition (worthy as it may be in itself) above God's commandment.

Matthew 15:21-28. See Dimension Three.

Matthew 15:32-39. This episode differs in no essential detail from the earlier feeding in Chapter 14. A thousand fewer were here, if the exact count has any meaning at all. These four thousand (plus the women and children) were reportedly with Jesus for three days. Seven loaves are available here. Seven baskets of unused bread are gathered here, as opposed to twelve in the earlier incident where only five loaves were multiplied. All of these numbers have sacred connotations.

You may want to stress what is probably the principal difference. This second feeding seems to have been for a gathering of Gentiles. Jesus' itinerary takes him at this time into largely non-Jewish regions. If Matthew had breaking bread for non-Jews in mind, this compounds even further the offense already given by Jesus' eating with non-Jews and mingling with tax collectors.

Matthew 16:1-4. If this passage has a familiar ring, it is not your imagination. Look back at Chapter 12:38-41. These verses originally must have been a block of material that circulated independently. Matthew has used it twice as a judgment against the Pharisees. We must always keep in mind that, at the time when Matthew wrote his Gospel, the church for which he wrote and the Jerusalem Pharisees were in bitter conflict. The conflict between the early church and the Pharisees was probably more intense than the differences between Jesus and the Pharisees of his day. So we should not be surprised at the condemnation of the Pharisees that Matthew places in his Gospel.

Matthew uses the placement of the warning against signs as an introduction to an important exchange between Jesus and the disciples. As they so often do in Matthew's Gospel, the disciples misunderstand Jesus when he speaks of the yeast of the Pharisees and Sadducees. They think he is talking about bread. They are embarrassed because they forgot to bring bread with them when they crossed the lake. And not only did they forget to bring bread, Jesus reminds them that they seem to have forgotten how, on two previous occasions when there was no bread, that Jesus satisfied their hunger. Jesus is not talking about bread. He is talking about the teaching of the Pharisees and Sadducees. It would be imperative for Matthew's young Christian congregation to have the reinforcement of Jesus' own word of authority in their dispute with the Pharisees of their day.

Yeast involves the process of fermentation that Jews believed was evil. Except for the simile in Chapter 13, leavening is everywhere spoken of as corrupting.

Matthew 16:13-20. As the student book emphasizes, these are among the most important verses in the New Testament. From the genealogy at the beginning of his Gospel, Matthew has consistently proclaimed Jesus as Messiah. Here he brings new force to the faith by having the first disciple, Simon Peter, declare that Jesus is the Christ.

If this event did take place prior to the Resurrection, as Matthew and Mark have it, then Mark's terse report is more likely the authentic account (Mark 8:27-30). At this stage in Jesus' ministry we find it hard to imagine him speaking in detail about Peter's role in a future church. He has not even revealed for the first time what lies immediately ahead of them. The disciples would surely have been bewildered by such futuristic talk. Their heads were already filled with false ideas about the power and glory of the Messiah.

In some ways these words to Peter have all the earmarks of a post-resurrection promise. It probably was somehow transposed into an earlier sequence. We will probably never know exactly what was said. However that may be, neither Mark nor Luke include any word about Peter as the foundation of the church. They do not include his role with the keys of the Kingdom either.

Peter did become the dominant figure in the early Jerusalem church. (Recall the importance of his visit to Cornelius in Acts 10 and the controversy over the mission to the Gentiles in Acts 11.) Matthew knew this history when he wrote. He may have had Jesus speak these words in order to ratify the authority of Peter.

Matthew 16:21-28. What you must not allow students to overlook here is the sequence of revelations. Peter's confession of Jesus as the Christ is followed at once by Jesus' incredible announcement that he must "suffer many things at the hands of the elders, chief priests, and teachers of the law, and that he must be killed." From this point on, the purpose of the Gospel will be to put together the two ideas of Messiah and suffering. But, for the disciples and all Christians who follow them, this can never be an exercise in historical search and theological construction. Because if they are to follow him they must deny themselves. First they must take up the cross, then they will know.

DIMENSION THREE:
WHAT DOES THE BIBLE MEAN TO ME?

Matthew 16:21—Christ and Suffering

One of faith's most severe challenges is still, How do you reconcile the Chosen One (Christ) being put to death in shame? And what about all who follow him? The Gospel poses no question more critical. And it won't do simply to retreat behind the claim that it is God's will. Why? What kind of will is it that asks these things? If you do not face this question with the class now, the time will come later. Who can avoid it? Many answers may be suggested by different class members. Let them all be spoken and respected. But your great help as a teacher will be to stir the imagination of your students to realize that this is not a question permitting intellectual answers. Suffering cannot be fully explained. But we can join Christ wherever he suffers for people, and so by the grace of God suffering may be redeemed.

The class may discuss the following topics or use the optional material in the student book as time allows.

Matthew 14:20; 15:37—Bread That Satisfies

We marvel that Jesus could take five or seven loaves and feed a multitude of thousands. But that does little to satisfy my hunger here and now. What this miraculous story really says, however, is that Jesus can take even the little bit that anyone offers him in faith, even now, and multiply it so that deep hungers within us are satisfied. We can read these episodes primarily as the account of a miraculous baker or fish monger in Galilee long ago. But the best I could wish for is that I had been one of the four or five thousand who were present on that day. If we read the reports as the account of one who gives even to us the bread of life, the living bread that is able to sustain us in all our needs, then this is good news indeed. How does Jesus satisfy our hungers when he gives himself? How is our hunger satisfied in Communion? in any other encounters we may have with Jesus?

Matthew 14:22-33—Lord of the Fearful

Here we all are, huddled and afraid, in a small craft beaten by wind and wave. Maybe the craft is a church, perhaps it is a family. It could be a whole community or even a nation. In Matthew's story, the boat may have represented the young church, frightened by the peril threatening to take them down.

The Gospel story says "during the fourth watch," the worst of all stretches of time in the dark hours between midnight and first light. Jesus came walking on the water. Although the disciples were far from land, the Master knew their peril. He understood their fears. He came, and he comes, as Lord of the fearful. How does he come? What does he do? The disciples are so human here in their fear, that somehow their fear seems a comfort to us in our fears. And lovable, impulsive, reckless Peter left the boat and started across the water. He sank, but Jesus upheld him. What is the model here for us? In the midst of what gales now beating upon us could we stand up and launch out across the deep?

Matthew 15:21-28—Lord, Help Me!

It has been suggested that there should be a statue or icon of this woman, whose name we do not even know, at every exit from every church in Christendom. She represents the outsider. She represents all who cry for help beyond the doors of the church. This Canaanite woman cried out to Jesus across the barriers of race, nationality, and religion. Ask the class: What voices do we hear crying beyond our doors? Are there desperate people who no longer cry to the church because they have no confidence the church will either hear or help, but whose cries we still must hear? In the name of Jesus, how can we listen, and then reach out?

But many who are first will be last, and many who are last will be first (19:30).

— 8 —

Transfiguration and Church Discipline

Matthew 17–19

DIMENSION ONE:
WHAT DOES THE BIBLE SAY?

Answer these questions by reading Matthew 17

1. Who does Jesus take with him to the high mountain? (17:1)

   He takes Peter, James, and John.

2. Who appears to them when Jesus is transfigured? (17:3)

   Moses and Elijah appear to them.

3. What does Peter offer to do? (17:4)

   Peter offers to build three shelters, one each for Moses, Elijah, and Jesus.

4. What does the voice from the cloud say? (17:5)

   The voice from the cloud says, "This is my Son, whom I love; with him I am well pleased. Listen to him!"

5. Whom does Jesus say was Elijah? (17:12-13)

   He says that John the Baptist was Elijah.

6. What happens when the distraught father brings the boy suffering from seizures to the disciples? (17:16)

   The disciples cannot heal the boy.

7. Why can the disciples not heal the boy? (17:20)

   They cannot heal the boy because of their little faith.

Answer these questions by reading Matthew 18

8. How can persons be the greatest in the kingdom of heaven? (18:4)

   Persons should humble themselves like a child.

9. What should happen to ones who cause a little one to sin? (18:6)

   It would be better for them to have a millstone hung around their neck and be drowned.

10. What is God's will regarding these little ones? (18:14)

    God's will is for none of them to be lost.

11. If a brother who sins against you will not listen when you show him his fault, what do you do? (18:16)

    Take one or two others to establish their testimony as witnesses.

12. If he still refuses to listen, what then? (18:17)

    Then you should tell it to the church.

13. What if he will not listen even to the church? (18:17)

    Then let him be treated as the church would treat a pagan or a tax collector.

14. How often should you forgive a brother who sins against you? (18:22)

    You should forgive him seventy-seven times (or seventy times seven).

15. How much does the servant owe the king in Jesus' story? (18:24)

    The servant owes ten thousand talents.

16. How much does the servant's fellow servant owe him? (18:28)

The fellow servant owes one hundred denarii.

Answer these questions by reading Matthew 19

17. What does Jesus say about divorce? (19:9)

Jesus says that whoever divorces his wife, except for marital unfaithfulness, and marries another woman, commits adultery.

18. What does Jesus tell the disciples about the children who are brought to him? (19:14)

Jesus tells the disciples that the kingdom of heaven belongs to children such as these.

19. What question does the young man ask Jesus? (19:16)

He asks what Jesus thinks he must do to get eternal life.

20. What does Jesus tell him to do when he says he has kept all the commandments? (19:21)

Jesus tells him to sell what he possesses, give to the poor, and follow him.

DIMENSION TWO: WHAT DOES THE BIBLE MEAN?

Chapter 17 completes the long narrative portion of Matthew's Book IV (Chapters 14–17.) The chapter takes us to a high mountain where a previously unseen glory shines around Jesus and the two figures who join him. The chapter then brings Jesus and his disciples back to Galilee from regions around Caesarea Philippi, Tyre, and Sidon.

Matthew 17:1-8. Mount Hermon towers in majesty above all of Syria, Phoenicia, and Galilee. Snow covers its 9,100 foot summit for most of the year. Mount Hermon is the highest mountain anywhere around. It is near where Jesus travels outside Galilee at this time. For these reasons and because Mount Hermon has been a sacred mountain as far back as prehistory, scholars for the most part locate the Transfiguration on Mount Hermon's slopes.

The Transfiguration is not easy to interpret. Mystical experiences usually translate poorly into verbal, linear language. Do not dismiss it as a hallucination. Give full play to your sense of wonder and awe at the extraordinary events taking place on the mountain. Help the students move beyond the *what* and *how* of the physical events to the *when* and *why* of Matthew's purpose and the meaning it had for Jesus. This may be one of those events whose meaning became more clear to Jesus' followers after his death and resurrection than it was when it happened.

Transfiguration means "to see something or someone in a new way." Transfiguration lifts our vision to a new order of reality. We become aware of a glory surrounding what we thought was something common and everyday. You will doubtless think of transfigurations that have come to you to help illustrate what happened to the disciples. In the experience, whose exact nature we cannot know, they saw Jesus in a new light.

The transfiguration of Jesus to his three disciples (and through them to all who heard their gospel) was God's endorsement of all that had gone before that luminous moment on the mountain. In some way, through this event, God says of God's son, "With him I am well pleased. Listen to him!"

The student book points out some of the Old Testament imagery. Matthew, following the oral tradition, uses this imagery so people will see it as part of the divine pattern of revelation from the beginning. The three booths that Peter wants to build refer to the Feast of Booths, or Tabernacles, one of Israel's three great annual festivals. The Feast of Booths is an autumn-harvest celebration.

Matthew 17:14-21. The Italian painter Raphael pictures the Transfiguration in one of his finest paintings. You may find it a useful, visual enhancement to your teaching. Showing the contrast between the glory on the mountain and the scene of frustration and anguish that Jesus descended to at the foot of the mountain is especially helpful. Most libraries have collections of reproductions of great paintings.

"If you have faith . . . nothing will be impossible for you." Verse 20 has frequently discouraged readers who have prayed with all the faith they possessed but felt their prayers were not answered. The whole problem of unanswered prayer is too great to discuss here, unless some person in your class suffers acutely from this distress. For such a person, this episode offers little help. You will find much more comfort in the Gethsemane story (Matthew 26:36-75) and in Paul's Letter to the Romans (Chapter 8).

We have learned enough about psychosomatic medicine (the influence of the mind on the body) to know that without a strong sense of faith and hope, healing is impeded or may not occur at all. You probably should stress this positive dimension with the students. Do not leave any feeling that their prayers were not answered because they were not heard. Also try to keep any of the class members from feeling that their faith is inferior. Jesus never says that anywhere in any of the Gospels. He is saying to his disciples and church leaders who would come after them that they can never heal in his name without faith in God's power.

Matthew 17:22-23. The placement of this prediction of death immediately following the Transfiguration is hardly arbitrary. The glory of the epiphany must not obscure the certainty of the cross. Jesus is God's beloved Son. Nevertheless he will be delivered into the hands of men who will kill him. The Transfiguration has outshone this foreboding prediction. But the dark promise remains.

Matthew 17:24-27. This strange story seems rather out of place in the midst of such overwhelming moments of glory and darkening words of distress. It deals with what in Matthew's time must have been a baffling question of whether or not a Christian should pay the two-drachma (Temple) tax. Jesus would hardly counsel such tax delinquency. All faithful Jews supported the Temple. But by Matthew's time the Temple had been destroyed by the Romans (in A.D. 70). What could be the reason for the tax after the Temple's destruction?

The issue was really civil disobedience. Jesus dealt with this issue in a far more strategic setting in Jerusalem (22:15-29.) Here in Capernaum, Jesus is telling Peter that although Christians are indebted to no political state or ruler, in order not to give offense (scandalize people who would observe such refusal) Christians should pay the required tax. Literally the phrase *not offend* means "so that your behavior does not cause others to stumble." This does not mean that Jesus condemns all civil disobedience, or that he supports compliance with every Roman demand. He was well aware that some things we cannot render to God if we have already rendered them to Caesar.

How or whether Jesus accurately predicted Peter would catch a fish with a coin in its mouth is an irrelevant detail. Such fish were not unheard of. But Jesus has no interest in clairvoyance or magic tricks.

Matthew 18. With Chapter 18, the teaching discourse, we come to the conclusion of Matthew's Book IV. Earlier Jesus had announced the near approach of the Kingdom (4:17). Matthew's first purpose after the announcement is to reveal what life will be like in the Kingdom. Matthew has gathered the sayings of Jesus into a sermon unified around the theme of the kingdom of heaven (Chapters 5–7, the Sermon on the Mount). Then Matthew makes clear what it will cost and require of all who will enter (Chapter 10). How the Kingdom will come and what it will be like are shown in the seven parables of Chapter 13. Now Christians must learn a discipline for their life in the congregation. They must live in humility, with forgiveness and special care for the little ones in the faith.

Matthew 18:1-4. Again Mark (Mark 9:33-37) is more frank about the very human disciples. He has them arguing about who among them is the greatest. He paints them—warts and all. Matthew points out the human blemishes in these verses. In Matthew they ask the question in general. They ask, Who is the greatest? A child in the midst answers their question, not by saying anything, but by being a child. Humility becomes the first of seven marks of their life together.

If we look at the whole chapter, we discover the following seven distinguishing marks of the common life of the congregation:

1. *living together in humility toward one another*
   "Whoever humbles himself [herself] like this child. . . ." (18:4)
2. *seeing the Christ in one another*
   "Whoever welcomes a little child like this in my name welcomes me. . . ." (18:5)
3. *living so as to give no offense to anyone*
   "Woe to the man through whom they [sins] come. . . ." (18:7)
4. *caring for the weak little ones*
   "See that you do not look down on one of these little ones. . . ." (18:10)
5. *accepting moral/spiritual discipline by the church*
   "Tell it to the church . . . treat him as you would a pagan or a tax collector." (18:17)
6. *praying together in the congregation*
   "Where two or three come together in my name, there am I. . . ." (18:20)
7. *forgiving one another without limit*
   "Not seven times but seventy-seven times you shall forgive your brother." (18:21-22)

Matthew 18:7. Jesus acknowledges that, being who we are and living as we do, occasions for stumbling will come. Just don't you be the one to offend! In this instance Jesus speaks not of someone deliberately enticing or seducing another to sin. Rather he speaks of behavior that appeals to a weakness that another person cannot control. We might speak of it as unknowingly setting up another person to sin. But if we really cared for the little ones we ought to know what we do. The apostle Paul confronts this problem in 1 Corinthians 9:19-23. Apparently it was a problem in the Greek Christian as well as the Jewish Christian world. Is it still a problem?

Matthew 18:10. A good dictionary (Oxford, Webster's, Random House) or *Roget's Thesaurus* will help you get inside the word *despise.* It means, in its most common sense, "to treat with contempt." Let no one be at ease, thinking Jesus' words here are not for him or her.

The phrase *little ones* is widely used to speak of newcomers to the faith, whatever their age.

Matthew 18:12-14. If we read this parable in Luke 15, we understand it as part of a triad of stories about God's search for the lost. The lost are represented by a sheep, a coin, and a boy (actually two boys, for the elder brother was also a prodigal from the father's love, and the father "went out and pleaded with him"). Matthew introduces the parable of the lost sheep to remind the congregation that it is the Father's will that not one of these little ones should perish. The people are the shepherds in Christ's name in the new community.

Matthew 18:17. Of interest here is the role of the congregation in discipline. The discipline is not priestly or formal judicial discipline and sanction, as it was later to become.

Here the people are counseled to judge. They are to expel a member, after exhausting all avenues of reconciliation, if it is for the good of all.

Matthew 18:23-35. No parable is more forceful than this story of the unmerciful servant that appears only in Matthew. Ten thousand talents would be a fortune in today's rate of exchange; far more than the servant could ever hope to have borrowed, much less repaid. A denarius was a day's wage for a laborer (not much, and even less by contrast with the debt of the first servant). Jesus doubtless uses hyperbole again to dramatize the incomprehensible chasm between the amount of debt of these two servants, and thus, the extent of forgiveness the first servant was readily accorded.

Matthew 19:1-2. The Gospel provides no exact itinerary of Jesus' ministry. Nor can we always identify the sayings of Jesus with particular places and times. Notwithstanding, a broad course of travels and seasons does appear.

In 3:12–16:12, Jesus spent most of the early times of his ministry in Galilee, around Capernaum and across the lake.

In Chapters 16:13–17:21, Jesus withdraws to the north, outside Israel, in Phoenicia and Caesarea Philippi.

Chapters 16:22–18:35 find the disciples gathering again in Galilee and returning to Capernaum.

Jesus then enters Judea, east of the Jordan (19:1–20:16). (John 4:4 speaks of Jesus passing through Samaria, west of the Jordan, along the mountain top. Matthew has no report of such a journey.)

Chapter 20:17-34 records Jesus' journey to Jerusalem through Jericho.

Jesus is in Jerusalem from Chapter 21 through the end of Matthew.

Matthew 19:1. Jesus leaves Galilee, never to see it again.

Matthew 19:3-12. See the student book and Dimension Three in the teacher book for guidance in dealing with this troublesome question.

Matthew 19:13-15. These verses are frequently read at the sacrament of baptism. They are appropriate words to use at that time. Jesus loved children. More than that, he saw in a child's humility, receptivity, and trusting nature a model for the kingdom of heaven. But let us not mistake this episode for baptism. Jesus did not baptize anyone. Christian baptism began in the early church, originally for adult believers. The essential meaning of baptism we find not here, but in Romans 6:1-6.

Matthew 19:16-22. Luke calls the young man who came to Jesus with a question about inheriting eternal life a ruler (Luke 18:18-30). The name has stuck. By that title the scene is indelibly etched in our imagination. Whoever he was, or

whatever he ruled, he gave Jesus an excellent opportunity to show the danger to which great possessions expose a person.

Two dimensions of this encounter might be overlooked. The first is Jesus' immediate answer to the man's inquiry. The man seems to think there is some extra credit one can earn to insure eternal life. Jesus dismisses such self-advancement. Jesus reminds the man that he knows what is good. The man should keep the commandments. Mark reports at this point that Jesus loved him (Mark 10:21). Matthew makes no comment about Jesus' feelings toward the man. But eternal life is not gained just by keeping commandments. One enters eternal life by doing—going, selling, giving, following. All of these words are active verbs. They spell a lifetime of commitment. We learn from this meeting the danger of great possessions. We also learn the truth that no one enters eternal life by being a perfect rule keeper.

Matthew 19:27-30. These verses come as a consolation to all who have left family and possessions to follow Jesus. In this life such persons rarely if ever receive reward comparable to the rich and powerful. In the new world, says Jesus, they will receive a hundred times as much.

DIMENSION THREE:
WHAT DOES THE BIBLE MEAN TO ME?

Matthew 19:3-12—Marriage After Divorce

Almost half the marriages in the United States end in divorce. Well over half the people who divorce remarry. The church is no sanctuary from this relentless social pattern. Christian people, like all others, divorce and re-marry. Jesus' sweeping prohibition troubles and embarrasses many. These people, though they acknowledge the pain and failure of divorce, welcome it as the least destructive of the evils they must choose from.

The student book tries to suggest some grounds on which we can come to terms with Jesus' teaching in principle. Matthew, if not Jesus, recognizes unchastity as justification for divorce. Sexual infidelity has almost universally been accepted as grounds for breaking the marriage covenant. Many people say that a person can be unfaithful to his or her marriage partner in many different ways. They argue that the focus is too narrow when we limit the permission to divorce only to those whose partners have committed adultery. Harassment, humiliation, mental cruelty, child abuse, alcoholism, and neglect all violate the sacred vows of a Christian marriage. In principle, do they not meet the same qualification as Jesus' "except for marital unfaithfulness"?

We will not resolve the problem in any short class discussion. Moreover we must recognize that marriage is only one of many covenants less honored today than in Jesus' day. Is it realistic to think that we can restore the marriage covenant to the biblical ideal while the rest of our social life unravels and goes through profound changes? Jesus, nevertheless, says something here that many still hold as ideal. Marriage is a sacred covenant. To that covenant they will be true, God being their helper, so long as both partners shall live.

Would it help to resolve the problem if a marriage ritual of a civil contract were required of everyone, as it is in some European countries? Couples who then wanted to pledge marriage vows each to the other in covenant with God could have a consecration or commitment of vows in the church. For centuries of Christian history this was the practice. Under this system the church would no longer act as deputy for the state in "pronouncing two people as husband and wife." This might not answer all the questions about divorce. Marriages consecrated before God might still break down. But such an arrangement might reinforce the special nature of marriage in Christ's name, differentiating it from marriage in general. It is not likely to come about. But to discuss it might focus some of the issues more sharply.

The class may discuss the following topic or use the optional material in the student book as time allows.

Matthew 19:27-30—A Hundredfold in the New World

Too often these verses have been used to justify people saying, "Pie in the sky, by and by." In other words, never mind poverty and inequity in the here and now. We will all get our reward in the world to come. This sanctimonious shoving people aside, usually done by those with great possessions, is self-serving. Jesus would dispatch such comforters in a moment by telling them to go, sell, give, and follow.

But a truth is here. To follow Jesus is to find a reward in another realm or order of life. The reward is in a new world of the age to come but already present for any who will enter it now. Such persons seek not the chief seats in the present time. They do not want big bank accounts and all the wealth of those who "have it made." Their joy and fulfillment is in doing and following. They seem last in the pecking order of the world. They find, on the contrary, that they are first in being blessed, as they had never imagined. They do not want to be first in line, ahead of everyone else, or anyone else. That would be to exchange their blessing for the same old rewards. But they are first in having found the pearl of truly great value. People who make that discovery will tell us that they already have a hundredfold of what life is really all about.

The Son of Man will be . . . mocked and flogged and crucified (20:18-19).

9

Journey to Jerusalem

Matthew 20–21

DIMENSION ONE:
WHAT DOES THE BIBLE SAY?

Answer these questions by reading Matthew 20

1. With whom does the landowner make the agreement to work and for how much? (20:1-2)

   The landowner makes an agreement with the laborers early in the morning to pay a denarius for a day's work.

2. At what later times after that does he hire more workers? (20:3, 5, 6)

   He hires more workers at the third, sixth, ninth, and eleventh hours.

3. Who is paid first, and how much do they receive? (20:9)

   Those who were hired last receive a denarius.

4. How much are those who worked longer paid? (20:10)

   They are paid the same, a denarius.

5. What complaint do the workers make who have worked all day? (20:12)

   They complain because everyone is paid the same.

6. How does the landholder answer this complaint? (20:13-14)

   The workers agreed to work for a denarius. Is not the landholder allowed to do what he chooses with his own money?

7. Who comes to Jesus asking a special favor? (20:20)

   The mother of the sons of Zebedee comes and asks for a favor.

8. What does she want? (20:21)

   She wants Jesus to grant that her two sons may sit on Jesus' right and left in his kingdom.

9. What does Jesus say in answer to her request? (20:23)

   Jesus tells the brothers that it is not his to grant who sits at his right or left hand.

10. Why did the Son of Man come? (20:28)

    The Son of Man did not come to be served, but to serve, and to give his life as a ransom for many.

11. What do the two blind men cry to Jesus as he leaves Jericho? (20:29-30)

    They cry out, "Lord, Son of David, have mercy on us!"

12. What do they say to Jesus when he asks them, "What do you want me to do for you?" (20:33)

    The two blind men ask Jesus to restore their sight.

Answer these questions by reading Matthew 21

13. Where are the two disciples Jesus sends on an errand? (21:1)

    They are in Bethphage.

14. What does he ask them to bring to him? (21:2)

    He tells them to bring him a donkey and the colt tied by her.

15. Why does Jesus want to do this? (21:4)

    He does this to fulfill what was spoken through the prophet.

16. As Jesus rides into the city, what do the crowds do? (21:9)

   They shout "Hosanna" and bless the name of Jesus.

17. What is the first thing Jesus does when he enters the city? (21:12)

   He drives out of the Temple those who were buying and selling there. He overturns the tables of the money changers and the benches of those selling doves.

18. Where does Jesus go when he leaves the city? (21:17)

   Jesus goes to Bethany.

19. What does Jesus do on his way into the city the next morning? (21:18-19)

   He curses a fig tree because it had nothing on it but leaves.

20. What do the chief priests and the elders ask Jesus when he enters the Temple? (21:23)

   They ask him by what authority he is doing these things and who gave him the authority.

21. What does Jesus ask the priests and elders in response? (21:25)

   He asks whether the baptism of John was from heaven or from men.

22. In Jesus' story, what is the difference between the two sons? (21:29-30)

   One says he will refuse to work as his father had asked, but did go; the other says he will go, but he does not.

23. What will the owner of the vineyard do to the wicked tenants? (21:41)

   He will bring the wretched tenants to a wretched end and will rent the vineyard to other tenants who will give him his share of the crop at harvest.

24. What do the chief priests and Pharisees think when they hear these parables? (21:45)

   They think that Jesus is speaking about them.

DIMENSION TWO:
WHAT DOES THE BIBLE MEAN?

As Matthew tells it, three things stand out to explain what is happening in Chapters 20–21. These three things also help explain why subsequent events take the course we now call Holy Week. The four parables Jesus told, his triumphal entry into the city, and his cleansing of the Temple are part of the central purpose for which Jesus comes to Jerusalem. Each event in its particular way asserts that Jesus is the Messiah, Son of David. Each event also asserts that Israel is judged for her failure to believe what God is doing.

In teaching this lesson it will help students to get to the meaning of the gospel if they read with the following two questions in mind: What statement does Jesus make by what he says and does? What response do the Pharisees, chief priests, and elders make to what they see and hear? The key passages to keep in mind include the parables (the laborers in the vineyard, 20:1-16; the fig tree incident, 21:18-22; the two sons, 21:28-32; and the wicked tenants, 21:33-44). The two other key passages are the entry into Jerusalem (21:1-11) and the cleansing of the Temple (21:12-17). If we understand the importance of what is said and done from Jericho to the disturbance in the Temple precincts, nothing should surprise us in the events that follow.

Matthew 20:1-16. Probably none of Jesus' other parables produces such contradictory feelings. The student book suggests that our response to the parable depends on who we identify with in the story. Quite a few of Jesus' parables end with surprises we are unprepared for. Who would suppose, for example, that a Samaritan (a person from a hated group of people) would help the wounded victim while a priest and Levite (honored persons) walk right by (Luke 10:30-37)? Who would suppose that a father would kill the fatted calf for the younger son when the older brother has been a dutiful son all his life (Luke 15:11-32)? Jesus uses the device of surprise and reversal of expectations to jolt the listener's easy assumptions. Nowhere is the surprise greater than in this story of the vineyard.

Most people disapprove of what the landholder does because subconsciously they identify with the workers who have worked all day. We do not mind if the landholder wants to give a denarius to the one-hour fellows. But we who have borne the heat and burden of the day can expect more. Then comes the shocker!

When we try to make an economic theory out of the parable it falls apart. Trying to read the parable that way is missing the point entirely.

The landholder did not deceive anyone. The grumbling of the daylong workers came because of their expectations, not the landowner broken agreement. Many people have tried to embellish the parable by imagining why the men in the marketplace were still idle at five o'clock. There could be many reasons. They could be marginal workers. The landowner could have made a miscalculation as to how many men would be needed. The weather could have changed. Such speculation adds nothing to Jesus' point. The landowner needed their help at the end of the day.

He generously paid them a denarius. All else is superfluous.

So keep in mind how this story would be heard by the Pharisees. Theirs was a kingdom of meticulous rule keeping, not overflowing grace. Jesus here takes his stand on the opposite ground.

Matthew 20:17-19. Jesus' third prediction of the Passion is spoken just before they start up for Jerusalem. He is warning the disciples not to approach the Holy City with ideas of political messianism in mind. The large crowd (20:29) that followed Jesus must have frightened him. It was a time of feverish messianic hope. Jesus is a compassionate healer, a stirring prophet, and a teacher of good news. The people would try to acclaim just such a person king. Jesus wanted no such kingship. His authority must be that of a servant (20:26).

Matthew 20:26-28. In these three verses Jesus voices the unmistakable norm for all who will be teachers, ministers, deacons, or missioners in his name in the days to follow his death. The word *ransom* rises from the page and marches through the New Testament. That we were "bought with a price" (1 Corinthians 6:20) and "justified by his blood" (Romans 5:9) became from earliest times a cardinal tenet of Christian belief.

Jesus wanted the disciples to know that it would cost a great deal in suffering and humiliation for them to learn the full measure of God's love. When Jesus says "for many" (20:28), the words echo the suffering servant song in Isaiah 53:10-12. In that context, the prophet of the Exile saw the community of the covenant people made righteous by the servant in his suffering. Doubtless Jesus saw the new community of Israel gathered in his name healed by the suffering of the Son of Man.

Matthew 20:29-34. In Mark 10:46-52, one blind man named Bartimaeus cries out to Jesus, "Son of David, have mercy on me." Matthew gives no clue as to why two men accost Jesus. The change from one to two men placed here at Jericho is irrelevant to the main purpose of the incident. More than anything else, Jesus needed followers who would see and understand. Would this drama of Jesus opening blind eyes by the Jericho roadside speak to the disciples? Does it say, in effect, "Follow me. . . . Drink the cup I am going to drink (20:23), and you will see?"

Matthew 21:1-11. Here we watch one of the highest moments of drama in the entire Gospel. This event is heavy with consequences for all time to come. We may never be able to sort out with certainty what was in Jesus' mind or in the mind of the crowd that greeted him with *Hosannas.* Neither do we know what was in the mind of those who remembered the event and passed on the tradition. Matthew wrote for a church maybe fifty years after the event. We do not know what was on his mind either.

Some things seem clear. The entry into Jerusalem must have been carefully planned. The animals Jesus needed were easily provided. A code word by which the accomplice would release the animals (21:3) was even taken care of. Matthew must have had in mind the prophecy of Zechariah that the king would come riding on a donkey, and on a colt, the foal of a donkey. Matthew has always shown that Jesus fulfilled prophecy, even prophecy that has a king riding on two animals, apparently at the same time. (Mark 11:7 places him only on the colt.)

Even before the story reached Matthew's hand, imagery from Old Testament history had been recognized in the event. For example, in 2 Kings 9:13, the people acclaim Jehu by placing their garments on the road. The "branches from the trees" goes back to the palm branches mentioned in 1 Maccabees 13:51 in the Apocrypha. (The Apocrypha contains books that many Protestants do not hold equal to the canonical Scriptures but are considered useful and good to read.) The crowds reenacted that historic scene welcoming a conqueror who had delivered Israel from the oppression of an enemy. This indicates how the crowds, and probably the disciples, thought about Jesus' entry into Jerusalem.

What Jesus thought is harder to know. If he regarded himself as Messiah, Son of David, it was never in terms of a political savior or revolutionary conqueror.

Matthew 21:12-13. According to Mark, Jesus merely looks around at the Temple scene on this day. He then returns to Bethany on the Mount of Olives across the Kidron Valley. Matthew does not agree with Mark. Jesus moves right into the Temple precincts. His outrage erupts at what he sees, and he turns the courtyard into a shambles.

Understanding what is meant by "the Temple" is important. Measurements can only be approximate. Archaeological evidence suggests that the entire Temple precincts were nearly five hundred feet long and two hundred and fifty feet wide. The money changers were in the Court of the Gentiles. All pilgrims had to go to the money changers to secure coins with which to pay the Temple tax. The exchange could cost nearly a day's wage on top of the tax itself, altogether two day's wages. Also in this huge surrounding court were those who sold doves for the sacrifice. A pair of doves bought in the Temple could cost over a week's wages. Doves purchased for less outside the Temple would usually be declared unsuitable for the sacrifice. No wonder Jesus was outraged at this extortion from the poor. He denounced the whole, ugly business in the words of Jeremiah and drove them all out. The priests and elders were infuriated. This was the last straw! Who could predict what this traveling teacher would do next? And the crowd was acclaiming him as the Son of David! It had become a matter, not of whether, but of when and how they would do away with him.

Matthew 21:18-22, 28-32, 33-44. First, the priests had to deal with the blasphemy of "Hosanna to the Son of David." Next, they watch the lawless assault on the business of the

Temple tax and traffic in sacrificial offerings. Now come the arrogant implications of Jesus' parables.

In Luke 13:6-9, we will read what is probably the original tradition concerning the fig tree without fruit. Luke does not tell it as a parable about faith. Rather Luke tells it as a warning that one who produces no fruit shall be cut down. Mark and Matthew introduce an incident that closely resembles the Luke parable. Mark just mentions that the fig tree is without fruit (Mark 11:13-14). Matthew goes off in another direction, one he has already covered (17:20), that of faith and prayer. But Matthew places it with the next two parables. Then the more pointed implication that Jesus accuses Israel of failure to bring forth fruit is clear. This charge goes all the way back to the preaching of John the Baptist (3:10).

The parable of the two sons is less ambiguous. One son, Israel, says yes, but does not obey. Those who said no, but then obey, are the tax collectors and harlots.

Finally, we see the most direct implication of all. The wicked tenants, Israel, to whom God has entrusted the vineyard, kill the prophets and finally the son. Jesus condemns them by quoting from Psalm 118:22-23. That inference, that Israel is the stone that God rejects, the Pharisees and priests find intolerable.

"They knew he was talking about them" (21:45). What Jesus did is reason enough to take action against him. But now his impudence in condemning them drives them to make quick work of it.

Matthew 21:46. Apparently they tried immediately to dispose of Jesus. But they dared not face the uprising of the people. It would have to be done with stealth, under secret cover.

DIMENSION THREE:
WHAT DOES THE BIBLE MEAN TO ME?

Matthew 20:1-16—Begrudging God's Generosity

This story is not a blueprint on how to run a vineyard. This story is really about God's grace. But is it much easier to accept such an absurd economy of grace? Some persons have been faithful a long time. They have endured affliction without complaint, resisted temptation, and remembered others with compassion. Why should these not receive grace commensurate with their good works? How can someone who has idled through life and then comes at the eleventh hour get as much when wages are paid? (See if the students see a resemblance between the elder brother in the parable of the prodigal son and these grumbling laborers.) There is no way that this kind of economy can be made to fit our system of rewards and merits. The question the landowner asks is still the question to us, Can God not be generous? Who are we to impose a pay scale for God's grace?

Someone may make the point that we need a system of incentives. Otherwise, people may become lazy and indolent. Why not take the easy way out and only work for one hour? In the world of commerce that may well be true. But ask the class, Does receiving the grace of God make one spiritually slothful? When a person has received the blessing of God's limitless generosity, does that person not become more, rather than less, faithful?

The class may discuss these topics if time allows.

Matthew 20:20—Who Paid a Price For Us?

Jesus paid a price for us, of course, in more ways than one. By the stripes of his forgiveness we are healed of the burden of sin. By his death and resurrection we are healed of the fear of death. By his Spirit that gathers the community of the church we have been given a spiritual home in a dry and weary land. And so on. You might have the class count the ways Christ's death has set them free.

But take the exercise one step further. Have others paid a price, in the same spirit, that we could be free of whatever may have held us captive? A parent, a child, a brother or sister, a friend or teacher? More often than not, such freedom is purchased at a very high price, some counterpart to death on a cross in which a person may give up the best that he or she has for our sake.

How can we save such a price from being wasted?

Write Your Own Parable

Chances are a few of your students might find writing a parable of their own an interesting project. It is not as easy as it seems. But it can be quite instructive to take a Christian truth and translate it into story form with a different setting. Good examples of stories with one setting whose truth applies in another are the wheat and the weeds (13:24-30) and the wicked tenants (21:33-41).

You can help the students understand the nature of parables. A parable is a comparison or a similitude. A parable is a fictitious saying or narrative in which something is expressed in terms of something else. The narrative is usually of something that might naturally occur and teaches a moral. Parables are similar to allegories, except that in an allegory all the details represent truths corresponding to the realm to which the allegory points. John Bunyan's *Pilgrim's Progress* comes to mind as a familiar allegory. A parable, on the other hand, makes one point; and its details are not significant in themselves except as they point to the principal truth. That is to say, in the most familiar parable of the good Samaritan, the truth of the story is that the Samaritan is the good neighbor. All the details of the inn to which the Samaritan took the wounded victim, the inn keeper, and how he was paid are of no real importance or significance. The best parables are not lush with details.

With most of Jesus' parables we have to make the connection between the sphere in which Jesus sets his story and the sphere of life Jesus really speaks about. The design is deliberate. The notable exception is the parable of the good Samaritan. That story concerns men acting in the very domain where we are to apply the truth, namely being a neighbor on the roads where we travel.

A parable can illustrate a truth that the author has found in his or her own life. Or it can point to a truth about life in the world, a disclosure, a judgment, or warning. Of one thing you may be sure. Persons who try writing parables of their own will come to a new appreciation of Jesus. They will not only appreciate his teachings and his prophetic perception, but they also will appreciate his awareness of how we take in truth through imagination. Imagination simply means using mental images. Try some!

Chapter 10 of the teacher book contains one suggested exercise for the students as they read Chapters 22 and 23. You might want to look ahead to *Woes and Blessings* in Dimension Three of Chapter 10 and share the reading guide a week ahead of time. The students who want to do this exercise will find themselves reading at a deeper level.

Give to Caesar what is Caesar's, and to God what is God's (22:21).

— 10 —
Conflict in Jerusalem

Matthew 22–23

DIMENSION ONE:
WHAT DOES THE BIBLE SAY?

Answer these questions by reading Matthew 22

1. What does Jesus compare the kingdom of heaven to in the parable? (22:2)

   He compares the kingdom of heaven to a king who prepared a wedding banquet for his son.

2. What do the invited guests do when they receive the invitation? (22:5-6)

   Some pay no attention and go off. The rest seize his servants who bring the invitation, mistreat them, and kill them.

3. What does the king then do? (22:7)

   He destroys those murderers and burns their city.

4. What does he do after the destruction? (22:9)

   He sends his servants to the street corners to invite anyone they find.

5. What does the king see when he looks at the guests? (22:11)

   He notices a man who was not wearing wedding clothes.

6. What does the king do to that man? (22:13)

   He has the man thrown out into the darkness.

7. How many are invited and chosen? (22:14)

   Many are invited, but few are chosen.

8. What does Jesus say when the Pharisees ask him, "Is it right to pay taxes to Caesar or not?" (22:21)

   He tells them to give to Caesar what is Caesar's, and to God what is God's.

9. What do the Sadducees ask Jesus? (22:28)

   They ask whose wife in the resurrection will a woman be who is widowed by seven brothers.

10. What is Jesus' answer? (22:30)

   In the resurrection, people will neither marry nor be given in marriage.

11. What does Jesus say is the great commandment in the law? (22:37-39)

   "Love the Lord your God with all your heart and with all your soul and with all your mind" is the first and greatest commandment.

Answer these questions by reading Matthew 23

12. What does Jesus say people should do about the Pharisees? (23:3)

   They should obey them and do everything the Pharisees tell them, but should not do what the Pharisees do.

13. Why does Jesus say this? (23:2-3)

   He says this because the teachers of the law and Pharisees sit in Moses' seat, but they do not practice what they preach.

14. What does Jesus call the Pharisees? (23:13, 15, 23, 25, 27, 29)

   He calls the Pharisees hypocrites.

CONFLICT IN JERUSALEM

57

15. What else does Jesus call them? (23:16, 17, 24, 33)

    He calls them blind guides, blind fools, snakes, and a brood of vipers.

16. What does Jesus say is wrong with the Pharisees who give a tenth of their mint, dill, and cummin? (23:23)

    They neglect the more important matters of the law—justice, mercy, and faithfulness.

17. How does Jesus compare the Pharisees to whitewashed tombs? (23:28)

    He says outwardly they appear righteous, but inwardly they are full of hypocrisy and wickedness.

18. What is the hypocrisy of the Pharisees toward the prophets and the righteous? (23:29, 30, 35)

    They build their tombs and decorate the graves of the righteous, but all the righteous blood shed on earth will come upon them.

19. What does Jesus say he would like to do to Jerusalem? (23:37)

    He would like to be as a hen that gathers her chicks under her wings.

20. What does Jesus say regarding Jerusalem? (23:38-39)

    He says their house has left them desolate. They will not see him again till they say, "Blessed is he who comes in the name of the Lord."

DIMENSION TWO:
WHAT DOES THE BIBLE MEAN?

With these two chapters we come to a natural vantage point in Matthew's Gospel. At this point, we can look backward for a review of what we have seen, heard, and learned, and forward to the climax that draws near. Your approach to teaching this lesson might well be to give major emphasis to these assessments, especially if the class has done some reflection on the questions as they read for this chapter. But first a look at some of the details in these chapters that you may wish to clarify for the students.

Matthew 22:1-14. In Jesus' day the custom when a man gave a banquet was to send invitations well in advance. The date, though, was not yet specified. People would then be prepared to attend on short notice (22:3-4). In the student book, you will find a comparison of this parable as told by Matthew and Luke. Only Matthew has the incident about the improper wedding garment. This may well be a veiled

indictment of the Pharisees. The point was not lost on them.

Matthew 22:15-22. You may wish to call special attention to the way Jesus' enemies are trying to trap him. For the Herodians to be allies of the Pharisees is altogether unthinkable. But it happened. The compliment of verse 16 is totally insincere. Jesus understood it for malice.

Since the Pharisees have been the chief enemies of Jesus, we need to understand the issues from their perspective. The Pharisees were keepers of the law. Their immediate rise to a place of importance in Israel comes out of the period of Greek influence. The Hellenistic dominance of culture following Alexander the Great (336–323 B.C.) was so strong that the people of Israel found themselves more and more detached from their unique covenant religion. The Pharisees met this threat by committing themselves to strict observance of the law and all its derivative rules. Israel defined itself by the laws. Should the Mosaic law be abandoned or relaxed the nation would drift away and be lost in a sea of Hellenism. Almost by a caste system the Pharisees kept themselves totally apart from non-Jews and sinners.

Whatever their failures and sins that Jesus condemned, the Pharisees were utterly committed to the nation and faith of Israel. We owe the preservation and transmission of sacred texts and traditions to them. These became heavily overlaid with excess petty regulations. For them the letter of the law finally killed the spirit of the law.

Matthew 22:23-30. The Sadducees were the priestly party. All those who officiated at the Temple worship and sacrifice, including the high priest, were Sadducees. The Sadducees are thought to be descendants of Zadok, the high priest during David's reign. They were educated and usually wealthy. At the point of their power and function, their interests diverged from those of the Pharisees, although both parties were intensely loyal to Israel. Between Pharisee and Sadducee, dissension broke out over who would interpret the law. The Sadducees believed that only what was written in the Scriptures could be law. They did not accept the interpretation of oral law by the Pharisees. The Sadducees also denied all ideas of the resurrection of the body. They did not believe in resurrection because it is not mentioned in the law, the first five books of the Scriptures (what we know today as Genesis through Deuteronomy). The controversy with Jesus broke out over this issue.

Matthew 22:34. "The Pharisees got together" presumably with the Sadducees, who had been silenced rather unceremoniously by Jesus, and with the Herodians (22:15-16), normally a group with which the Pharisees would never associate in any way. Such an alliance, for however brief an interval and limited a purpose, reveals the dynamic that brought the united power of Israel down upon Jesus. Each group tried to hit Jesus at the points where they thought he would be vulnerable against the concerns of their beliefs.

Matthew 22:34-40. The rabbis loved to make sayings to sum up what they thought were the main points of religion. They often discussed which were the weightiest commandments. Jewish tradition has it that one rabbi told how Moses gave 613 commandments, but David reduced them to eleven (Psalm 15:2-5). Isaiah reduced them to six (Isaiah 33:15), Micah to three (Micah 6:8), Amos to two (Amos 5:4), and Habakkuk to one (Habakkuk 2:4). So Jesus is not the first person to have summed up the law.

Matthew 22:41-46. One result of Jesus' declaration is that the Christ is acknowledged as infinitely more than just the lineal descendant of David. People were not to imagine the Christ (Messiah) to be a conquering ruler coming in the image of David.

Matthew 23:2. Moses was the giver of the law. When the Pharisees sit on Moses' chair in the synagogue, they renew the office of lawgiver. All good Jews will practice and observe the law that comes from Moses.

Matthew 23:13. The lawyers surrounded the law with such bounds that they made it impossible for anyone to keep it except a Pharisee. One could say they locked it up and threw away the key.

Matthew 23:15. A convert (proselyte) is a man who becomes a Jew by baptism, circumcision, and making an offering in the Temple. Many proselytes turn out to be more zealous and fanatical than the ones who converted them. These converts could be dogmatic, exclusive, restrictive, and demanding. They were indeed children of hell for the person trying to keep the law.

Matthew 23:16. Jesus forbade all oaths (5:33-37). Notwithstanding, people did take oaths on almost anything of high value. Apparently the Pharisees had a vast scheme of getting around the fulfillment of oaths. They found ways their oaths could be avoided on technicalities. Jesus dismissed the whole sham. Whoever swears by anything sacred swears by the God who made it. One cannot escape such an oath.

Matthew 23:23. Tithing means giving a portion (most commonly a tenth) of one's produce or wealth to the Temple. The Jews tithed many things, including herbs such as mint, dill, and cummin. Jesus regarded these as trifling compared to law, justice, mercy, and faith. He felt many tithers neglected these matters, yet they gave what the law required. They have twisted priorities.

Matthew 23:25. The image Jesus uses here is based on the complex ritual requirements for cleanliness of all utensils. These cleanliness requirements were not just hygiene. They were ritual. Hygiene sometimes lay buried as the reason for the ritual. Certain cups and plates could be clean inside while unclean outside, and vice versa. The laws could be incredibly intimidating to the person trying to stay ritually clean. The Pharisees, says Jesus, were like cups and plates—clean on the outside but contaminated within.

Matthew 23:31. See the section "Those Who Murder the Prophets" in Dimension Three of the student book and of this book.

Matthew 23:37-39. Matthew brings the trail of indictment right down to the present moment. Jesus has traced the path of killing from Abel to Zechariah. (Abel is mentioned in Genesis, the first book of the Hebrew Bible. Zechariah is mentioned in 2 Chronicles, the last book of the Hebrew Bible.) Now he laments over Jerusalem: "You who kill the prophets and stone those sent to you" (verse 37). The line is unbroken: "all this will come upon this generation. . . . Look, your house is left to you desolate" (Matthew 23:36, 38).

DIMENSION THREE: WHAT DOES THE BIBLE MEAN TO ME?

Matthew 23:29-36—Those Who Murder the Prophets

The Epilogue to George Bernard Shaw's play *St. Joan* is really a powerful parable on the seventh of Jesus' woes on the scribes and Pharisees. Joan of Arc was burned at the stake in 1431 for heresy, witchcraft, and sorcery. Nearly five hundred years later she was canonized, made a saint, in the Roman Catholic Church. In Shaw's play, when this happens Joan asks her accusers, "Shall I rise from the dead, and come back to you a living woman?" With great consternation they tell her that heretics are always better dead, that they are not ready for her, nor good enough for her. One by one they ask to be excused. The Inquisitor who had condemned her says he does not see how the Inquisition could possibly be dispensed with under existing circumstances.

Through Shaw's fantasy, we see exactly what Jesus condemned long ago. He condemned adorning the monuments of the righteous, only to kill and crucify, scourge and persecute the prophets and wise men sent to them. Reading part of this Epilogue might be an interesting experience for the class. You should be able to get a copy from your local library. Shaw's play leaves little doubt that Pharisaism has been carried on into Christian history.

The class may discuss the following topics or use the optional material in the student book as time allows.

Matthew 23:13-36—Woes and Blessings

This tirade of woes was spoken by Jesus in an eruption of blazing wrath. Near the end of his ministry. These verses contrast with the Beatitudes that Jesus spoke almost at the beginning. Suppose we put the two lists side by side in the order in which they appear in Chapters 5 and 23.

Blessed are . . .	*Woe to those who . . .*
1. the poor in spirit (5:3)	1. tie up heavy loads on people's shoulders (23:4)
2. those who mourn (5:4)	2. shut the kingdom of heaven against people (23:13)
3. the meek (5:5)	3. make a proselyte a son of hell (23:15)
4. those who hunger and thirst for righteousness (5:6)	4. say to swear by the Temple means nothing (23:16)
5. the merciful (5:7)	5. tithe mint, dill, and cummin (23:23)
6. the pure in heart (5:8)	6. are full of greed and self-indulgence inside the cup (23:25)
7. the peacemakers (5:9)	7. are whitewashed tombs (23:27)
8. those persecuted because of righteous (5:10)	8. decorated the graves of of the righteous (23:29)

As you hold these lists next to each other, does it occur to you that the attitudes and behavior that provoke the woes are really the dark underside of the attitudes and behavior that prompt Jesus' beatitudes? Can the blessings and woes be paired? The class might like to try such an exercise. The following is one reordering of the opposing passages. You might want to try it yourself before you consider what is printed here. At any rate, you want the students to think about it and try it before you show this comparison.

1. You tie up heavy loads on people's shoulders (23:4)
   5. Blessed are the merciful, for they will be shown mercy (5:7)
• The merciful person helps to lift burdens, not lay on greater weight. Could another beatitude be found that might also contrast with laying on heavy loads?

2. You shut the kingdom of heaven against people (23:13)
   2. Blessed are those who mourn, for they will be comforted (5:4)
• You may find these much closer to each other than would first appear. To mourn means more than just the sadness that comes with grief. It means to feel sorrow for God's whole creation, for all who suffer pain, loneliness, remorse, and grief. One who mourns as God mourns will not shut the Kingdom against anyone. From what other blessings might one fall into locking the Kingdom against any who would enter?

3. You make a proselyte a son of hell (23:15)
   3. Blessed are the meek, for they will inherit the earth (5:5)

• Humility, tolerance, and long-suffering patience are hallmarks of meekness, in contrast to the overlording of the fanatical convert. Converts frequently lay their version of newly discovered truth on everyone else with a kind of apocalyptic judgment. Fanatical religious zealots have sometimes inherited much of the earth. But can you imagine a person of true humility deserving of hell?

4. You say to swear by the Temple means nothing (23:16)
   6. Blessed are the pure in heart, for they will see God (5:8)
• The pure in heart have no need to take oaths on this, that, or the other. They neither practice deceit nor give their word with mental reservations. They are to be trusted in what they say. Do you find any other beatitude that may be the opposite of swearing deceitfully?

5. You tithe mint, dill, and cummin (23:23)
   4. Blessed are those who hunger and thirst for righteousness, for they will be filled (5:6)
• How sad that some people should find the summit of their religious experience in tithing these herbs of such little consequence. They never know the blessing of hungering and thirsting for law, justice, mercy, and faith. One might also put the fifth beatitude (5:7) opposite tithing. If human life survives war, terrorism, and genocide, will it be by the blessing of the peacemakers or the consequence of tithing herbs? Be sure the students understand that Jesus does not condemn tithing as such. Jesus finds woe in substituting tithing of herbs for commitment to mercy, justice, law, and faith.

6. You clean the outside of the cup, but are full of greed and self-indulgence inside the cup (23:25)
   1. Blessed are the poor in spirit, for theirs is the kingdom of heaven. (5:3)
• The poor in spirit are those who acknowledged their need for help. They acknowledge their need to learn, and their need for cleansing, both outside and inside. Unless we know these things, of course, we will end up doing in other people by extortion, rapacity, and every trick in the book.

7. You are like whitewashed tombs (23:27)
   6. Blessed are the pure in heart, for they will see God (5:8)
• Tombs are whitewashed so no one would step on them and be contaminated. They look bright and clean. But watch out. They are full of all uncleanness.

8. You decorate the graves of the righteous (23:29)
   8. Blessed are those who are persecuted because of righteousness, for theirs is the kingdom of heaven (5:10)
• We have the choice either to decorate the tombs of the righteous, or to be persecuted for righteousness ourselves. Someone has said, you can either be the victimizer or the victim. What is there in between?

The Indictment of Jesus

At this point in the Gospel, an important exercise will be to have the students review in their minds the issues around which the trial of Jesus will take place. One way to do this would be to have each student prepare the background for the opposition to Jesus and the indictment against him. The students would do this by leafing back through Chapters 3–23. They should note each occasion where something was said and done that broke the law or gave offense by blasphemy or political sedition. What follows is one summary. Others might include additional material. In view of everything else prompted by these two chapters, it would hardly be the best use of time to do this as a class. Students who want to do this should do it on their own time. Their results might be briefly shared as we come to the trial itself.

1. Verbal assaults on the Pharisees and/or Sadducees and giving offense to them.

In 3:7-8, at the baptism by John the Baptist, Jesus calls them a brood of vipers. He then tells them to produce fruit in keeping with repentance.

In 6:2-6, 16-18, in the Sermon on the Mount, Jesus warns against the hypocrites who give to the poor and fast that they may be seen and praised by men.

In 15:8-9, the denunciation by Isaiah is turned against the Pharisees when Jesus tells them that they teach as doctrines the rules of men.

In 16:3, Jesus tells the Pharisees that they cannot interpret the signs of the times when they ask him to show them a sign.

In 20:1-6, Jesus tells the parable of the laborers in the vineyard.

In 21:28-32, Jesus tells the parable of the two sons.

In 21:33-45, Jesus tells the parable of the wicked tenants.

In 22:1-14, Jesus tells the parable of the wedding banquet and the man without proper wedding clothes.

In Chapter 23, Jesus tells the seven woes on the Pharisees.

These nine incidents or verbal assaults infuriated the Pharisees and elders. But such denunciations alone provided no firm ground for indictment. They did harden the resolve of the Pharisees and others to get Jesus.

2. Behavior violating the law.

In 9:10, Jesus eats with sinners and tax collectors.

In 12:1, Jesus picks grain on the sabbath.

In 12:13, Jesus heals the man with the shriveled hand on the sabbath.

In 15:2, the Pharisees ask why Jesus' disciples break the tradition of the elders.

In 21:12-13, Jesus cleanses the Temple.

These were serious offenses, yet they carried no warrant for indictment, even under Jewish law.

3. Blasphemy.

In 9:2, Jesus forgave the sins of the man who was paralyzed.

In 9:34, the Pharisees accuse Jesus of casting out demons by the prince of demons.

In 21:15, Jesus allows the crowds to hail him as the Son of David, a messianic greeting.

Blasphemy, dishonoring, reviling, and showing contempt for God, were punishable by death. This was the charge that had to stick when Jesus came to trial. We will see that it was to bear testimony to the charge of blasphemy that false witnesses were hired. We shall also discover when we get to the trial that the Jews could not execute anyone except as Rome carried out the sentence.

In what ways is it true to say that the very things for which Jesus was indicted, condemned, and crucified have become what we call the good news?

Whatever you did for one of the least of these brothers of mine, you did for me (25:40).

— 11 —
Apocalypse and Judgment
Matthew 24–25

DIMENSION ONE:
WHAT DOES THE BIBLE SAY?

Answer these questions by reading Matthew 24

1. What does Jesus say when the disciples point out the buildings of the Temple? (24:2)

   Jesus tells them not one stone will be left on another; every one will be thrown down.

2. What did Jesus say to his disciples when they asked, "When will this happen?" (24:4)

   He told them to watch out that no one deceives them.

3. What did Jesus say must happen before the end comes? (24:7)

   Nations and kingdoms will rise against each other. There will be famines and earthquakes.

4. Because of wickedness, what will happen to the love of most? (24:12)

   The love of most will grow cold.

5. What else will happen throughout the whole world before the end comes? (24:14)

   The gospel of the Kingdom will be preached.

6. When are the people warned to flee to the mountains? (24:15-16)

   When they see the "abomination that causes desolation" standing in the holy place they are to flee.

7. What are the disciples to do when someone says, "Look, here is the Christ"? (24:23, 26)

   They are not to believe it and not to go out.

8. Will all these things happen before or after "this generation" passes away? (24:34)

   They will happen before this generation is gone.

9. How will the coming of the Son of Man be like the days of Noah? (24:38-39)

   As in the days before the Flood, the people go about their daily activities, knowing nothing about what would happen until the flood took them all away.

10. What will the faithful and wise servant be doing when the master comes? (24:45-46)

    The faithful servant will be giving the household their food at the proper time.

11. What does the wicked servant say and do? (24:48-49)

    He says to himself, "My master is staying away a long time" and will begin to beat the servants and eat and drink with drunkards.

Answer these questions by reading Matthew 25

12. Why were five virgins foolish? (25:3)

    They took their lamps but no oil for them.

13. What happened at midnight? (25:6)

    At midnight they heard the cry that the bridegroom had arrived.

14. What did the wise virgins say when the foolish virgins asked for oil? (25:9)

    They told the foolish virgins to go buy their own because there might not be enough to go around.

15. What did the bridegroom say when the foolish virgins arrived after the door was shut? (25:12)

He said that he did not know them.

16. How did the man going on a journey entrust his property? (25:15)

He gave five talents to one servant, two to another, one to a third, to each according to his ability.

17. What did the servants with two and five talents do with the money they were given? (25:16-17)

They put the money to work to double their money.

18. What did the servant with one talent do? (25:18)

He hid his master's money in the ground.

19. With whom was the master pleased? (25:19-23)

He was pleased with the ones who invested to make more money.

20. What did those on the king's right do? (25:34-36)

They fed the hungry and thirsty king, welcomed him when he was a stranger, clothed him, looked after him when he was sick, and visited him when he was in prison.

21. When had they done these things? (25:40)

They did these things for the king when they did them for one of the least of "these brothers of mine."

DIMENSION TWO: WHAT DOES THE BIBLE MEAN?

Chapter 24 presents the teacher with as great a challenge as any part of the Gospel. In some ways we relate to this chapter of judgment and doom with ready understanding. It seems so contemporary. At the same time, the Jesus we meet here seems less familiar, more frightening than the one we have read about until now. What does this chapter mean to us today?

To answer these questions, we need some tools of biblical language and theology. Three words, *eschaton, apocalypse,* and *parousia* will help us work our way into the hidden meanings in Chapters 24 and 25.

Eschaton is a Greek word for "the last things." The New Testament is primarily a book about the last things in this present age and the beginning of a new age.

Apocalypse is derived from a Greek word for "revelation." An apocalypse is a writing that purports to disclose or reveal the hidden meaning of events taking place in the world. Apocalyptic literature flourished in the ancient religion of Persia. It came into Jewish thought through the Babylonian Exile. In Jewish and later in Christian writings, apocalyptic stories had to do with revelation about the end of the age. These writings told when the end would come, the signs of its coming, and its consequences for people and nations. The Book of Daniel in the Old Testament, and the Revelation to John (The Apocalypse) in the New Testament are the best biblical examples of this literature.

Parousia is a Greek word that refers to the future coming of Christ at the close of this present age.

Chapter 24 is eschatological. It tells about the end time of the present age. It is apocalyptic in its revelation of the signs that must appear prior to the end. And it anticipates the Parousia when the Son of Man will appear. We assume this to be the Christ (on the basis of everything we have read so far in Matthew). This chapter, though, nowhere identifies Jesus as the Son of Man; however, Matthew calls Jesus Son of Man throughout the Gospel.

Did Jesus really say all the things ascribed to him in Chapter 24? What did Jesus believe about the end time and the Parousia? These questions can never be fully answered to everyone's satisfaction. Determining what Jesus said at the time of his crucifixion and what Matthew wanted to say to the church fifty years or so later is difficult. Help students keep from getting stuck on the questions and find ways of living with them faithfully.

Take the second question first. We do not know for sure what Jesus believed about the last things. We do know he lived in a time of feverish excitement over the close of the age and the appearance of the Messiah. It was part of the climate of Jewish faith and expectation. Jesus probably shared his people's anticipation that God would act with decisive power and judgment at the end time. That Jesus was primarily a teacher of hidden revelation does not necessarily flow. The Jesus of Matthew's Gospel is the most apocalyptic Jesus of the four Gospels. But even here Jesus speaks against seeking signs (12:38-39). And in Chapter 24 Jesus warns of people who cry that the Christ is here, in the desert, or in the inner rooms (24:23-26). Followers of Jesus are not to pay these prophecies any attention. Jesus makes the point that no one knows when the end will come. Only God knows the time. Men and women are to be ready whenever it happens (24:42). They are to do what they have been entrusted to do.

What Jesus thought about the coming of the end, whether soon or later, was not the heart of his thought. What people should be most concerned about is feeding the hungry, clothing the naked, welcoming the stranger, visiting the sick, and going to those in prison (25:34-36). These are what will count in the final judgment (the Parousia) "when the Son of Man comes in his glory" (25:31). Jesus himself offers a bypass in Matthew 25:31-46 to the bewilderments of the apocalyptic Chapter 24.

Did Jesus actually say all the things attributed to him in Chapters 24–25? Matthew gathered material from many sources to compose Chapters 24–25. Concluding that some of these words were put in Jesus' mouth by the evangelist gives no reason to question that most of Jesus' teachings reported by Matthew are genuine. We must not be afraid that if we doubt some of the verses in this chapter were spoken by Jesus, then we are in danger of losing the entire Gospel. In no way does that happen. Be sure that students understand this so they will not hesitate to critically analyze this teaching discourse. Whether or not Jesus said it all exactly as Matthew has reported, the chapter has great importance for us in our faith and life today.

One more general comment is in order. Apocalyptic literature has long been a favorite hunting ground for people who want to find predictions in the Bible of judgment and doom for our own day. Reading literal forecasts of what has happened in our lifetime into some verses in Chapter 24 is easy (verses 6, 7, 29). Reading the Bible this way is not responsible. The one who wrote this apocalypse had specific events of his own time in view (the fall of Jerusalem, the destruction of the Temple). To ignore the context of the Scripture and make it a horoscope of desecration and destruction twenty centuries later is to mishandle a writer's testament, and use it for our own interests.

Nevertheless, we can and should draw from what was said and done in the first-century judgment upon ourselves. The kingdom of heaven will appear and will appear at a time when we do not expect it (25:13). So, in a way apocalyptic writing is doing long-range forecasting. But it is not a long-range prediction of specific events, such as the World War II Holocaust in Germany.

Now let's look at some of the questions raised by reading through the text.

Matthew 24:3. Notice the phrase "the sign of your coming." Because we do not find this phrase in either Mark or Luke, it seems clear that Matthew introduced it to further support his faith that Jesus was the Son of Man. Matthew hereby links the return of the Christ (Jesus, Messiah) with the close of the age (*eschaton* and *parousia*).

Matthew 24:5-7, 15-22, 29, 31, 35. These verses belong to the document known as the *Little Apocalypse.* (Compare them with Mark 13:6-8, 14-20, 24-27, 31.) These verses read like a commentary on nineteen hundred years of war. Everything predicted here has happened a hundred times over. It requires no gift of prophecy to realize that these things will happen when people fail to repent of their worship of Caesar above God. War, conquest, famine, and death have been linked together in the metaphor of the four horsemen of the Apocalypse. They had ridden the earth in all the centuries since their prediction in biblical apocalypse.

Matthew 24:9-14. These verses reveal another vision of what we know did come to pass. Matthew was living in a time when those who confessed Jesus as Lord were "handed over to be persecuted" (verse 9). He knew that under duress people did fall away. Under duress most persons' love

grows cold. In the Revelation to John (The Apocalypse), the angel condemns the people of Laodicea for being neither hot nor cold, but lukewarm (Revelation 3:15-16).

Matthew 24:13-14. Observe that apocalyptic literature was not just doomsaying. "He who stands firm to the end will be saved." Also, see in verse 31 that the elect will be gathered at the last trumpet. People enduring war, conquest, famine, and earthquake needed strong confidence in God's will and power to deliver the faithful. Verse 14 is a forecast of preaching the gospel to the whole world.

Matthew 24:15. "The abomination that causes desolation" is one of the key images of the apocalypse. When the prophet Daniel used the term, he referred to the abomination erected in the Temple in 167 B.C. by Antiochus Epiphanes, king of Syria. (Antiochus set up a heathen altar in the Temple and allowed heathen sacrifices.) In A.D. 40, the term was reinterpreted to stand for the Roman emperor Caligula's desecration of the holy place. When Matthew introduced the picture into his vision of the apocalypse, he foresaw the holy places being profaned again by pagan conquerors. The fact that the Temple had been destroyed was not the end of this apocalypse. The end (*eschaton*) was still to come.

Matthew 24:22. The apocalypse is telling people that God has mercifully cut short the time people are to suffer before the close of the age. Martyrs and all those who have been persecuted for righteousness' sake throughout the last two centuries have naturally wondered about this verse.

Matthew 24:28. The hopes of Israel were devastated in A.D. 70 when the Temple was destroyed.

Matthew 24:34-35. Recall that in Matthew 16:28, Jesus had said that "some who are standing here . . . will not taste death before they see the Son of Man coming in his kingdom." And verse 35 seems to be a restatement of Matthew 5:18.

Matthew 24:48; 25:5. The master in the first parable (24:45-51) and the bridegroom in the second (25:1-13) are delayed. In Jesus' original telling of the parable, the delay served only to provide the circumstances under which the foolish maidens would be caught short. Now, with the Son of Man long promised and anticipated still not appearing, the delay may be part of the message in both parables. Yes, the Messiah may be overdue, but he will come!

Matthew 25:1. Look closely at the marginal reading for this verse. A number of ancient manuscripts add the words *and the bride* after *bridegroom.* To read the parable this way makes much more sense. Attendants would not be waiting for the bridegroom alone. This function would be to accompany the bride when the groom comes to take her to his own house, which will be her new home. If Jesus did not allegorize the parable, Matthew surely did. He made the parable a coded way of saying that those who had been chosen to attend Israel as God's bride failed the bride. They fell asleep, and did not provide what would be needed at the day of the Lord. The parable also warns those who attend the church as the bride of Christ to see that it does not happen to you.

Matthew 25:9. See Dimension Three for some thoughts about the refusal of the wise virgins to share the oil.

Matthew 25:13. This parable ends with the warning, "Therefore keep watch, because you do not know the day or the hour." Matthew puts this admonition on the lips of Jesus five times in the twenty-eight verses between 24:36 and 25:14. Despite the delay, that the end of the world would come suddenly and soon was still widely believed. The disciples were to keep awake and be alert. Also because of the delay they may have grown complacent or negligent. The arrival of the Son of Man might find them off guard and not ready.

Matthew 25:14-30. If we did not know the nature of parables, we might well read this story as advice on investing. Let the bankers double your money. Or one might well read it that the world gives more to those who have more and takes away from those who have less. The rich get richer, and the poor get poorer. This may often be true. But the parable is not about banking and wealth. Parables are rarely about what they appear to be about. We transfer their meaning from their story setting to some other realm of life. This parable is really about the stewardship of God's gifts and responsibilities. We are to multiply their returns. In the reckoning at the end, what we were given to look after should yield a return to God. To bury what might be multiplied is to lose whatever we were charged to keep. The word *talent* originally had nothing to do with skill or ability. It was a weight of measure.

Matthew 25:31-46. Many Christians place this parable of the Last Judgment at the very summit of Jesus' teaching. It sums up the meaning and purpose of Jesus' ministry. It has just about everything we have found in the Gospel so far. The Son of Man (Messiah) comes to identify himself with the hungry, the poor, the sick, the homeless, and the prisoner. The Messiah comes to announce a kingdom at the close of the age. He himself will inaugurate this kingdom. He will preside as judge and will separate those who enter from those cast into outer darkness. And the basis of judgment will be how each person responds to the hungry, thirsty, naked, homeless, and imprisoned. A surprise is here. Who could suppose that eternal destiny would depend on how we behaved toward a hungry beggar?

The theme on which the Gospel opens, "Repent, for the kingdom of heaven is near" (3:2), sounds here at the climax. The parable is spoken while there is still time to repent and to minister to the Christ. The Kingdom draws near. Jesus tells us in language even a child can understand what we are to do to enter. Good news, indeed!

DIMENSION THREE: WHAT DOES THE BIBLE MEAN TO ME?

Matthew 24:3-29—Apocalypse Now?

This chapter declares that the end of the present age will come soon. The end will come even before all of "this age" has passed away. Well, two thousand years have come and gone since that warning and prediction. The world is still here. It seems like the "present age" has not yet ended. What happened? Do we need to take this warning seriously anymore?

You might ask the students whether this chapter has any meaning for them now. Do not be surprised if some reply that the chapter seems more relevant than nearly anything else in the whole Gospel. That is because a kind of apocalypse hangs over our world in the threat of explosive world unrest and destruction. What hangs over our world may be more terrible than anything we read in this chapter.

The writer of the apocalypse believed that when they saw the desolating sacrilege in the holy place the end would come. Matthew believed that the destruction of the Jerusalem Temple was a sure sign of the end. He could not have imagined the world going on for nineteen centuries after these dire events.

Can we reinterpret the symbols of the apocalypse? Could it be that "the abomination that causes desolation" (verse 15) is the massive unrest in a world where millions starve to death; where children are orphaned by war and disease; where nations invade other nations? The world's poor are, in the true sense of the parable of the Last Judgment, God's holy temple. Are the nations raising a desolating sacrilege against them?

If the world cannot learn to live in peace, what would be the judgment of God against humankind? That is a tough question to answer. Millions of helpless victims would die. But if you can lead the students to the awareness that we live in a moral universe, and that the immorality of war and poverty brings its own judgment, you may help to understand that the apocalypse is indeed frighteningly relevant to our time.

Do not overlook verses 13 and 30, however. Do we still believe that God will deliver those who "stand firm to the end" when God comes "with power and great glory"? Those words are the heart of apocalyptic writings. The answer, of course, springs from a person's faith. The teacher's business is not to argue with another's faith. Two things may be helpful for you to say. First, nowhere in the apocalypse, nor in the Gospel as a whole, do we find a description of the age to come. So we do not need to base our faith on the literal imagery of "clouds of the sky (or glory.)" It is not for us to know how or when or where. Holding on to the faith that God will do this is hard enough.

The other thing to keep in mind is that the choice of life or death is always before us until the end. Refresh in your own mind the great promise of Ezekiel (Ezekiel 33:14-15). All who will may call upon God's power and purpose to turn the world from darkness to light. The world may yet be saved. But we should not assume we can go on with the same old life, just patched up a bit. It will either be a whole new world, or no world.

Matthew 25:31-46
Bad News and Good News of God's Judgment

One of the appalling things about the Last Judgment is that it all hinges on something so painfully simple, something we could do so easily every day. Giving food to the hungry, a welcome to strangers, visiting the sick and the prisoner. This calls for no special knowledge or power or privilege. Just human kindness and caring for others who hurt. What a dreadful thing to come to a final reckoning of life and realize that we miss out because we did not do the simple, human thing. A team once lost a World Series game because a runner failed to touch second base on what should have been a home run. Any one of us could lose the kingdom of heaven because we fail to touch another life when we could have so easily helped. What are some simple human things we miss out on often?

The class may discuss the following topics or use the optional material in the student book as time allows.

Matthew 25:1-13—Give Us Some of Your Oil

The student book does not include the parable of the wise and foolish virgins in Dimension Three. Someone may ask if the attitude of the bridegroom toward the tardy virgins does not seem unduly harsh. They were foolish to burn their oil wastefully. But should they be shut out from the wedding for which they were the invited attendants? Could the wise virgins not have shared enough of their oil to get them all in?

Ask the students why Jesus did not put something of the spirit of the waiting father in the story of the prodigal son into the bridegroom here. The answer, sad to say, gives sparse comfort. The fact is that each person is responsible for his or her own moral and spiritual reckoning. None can improvise faithfulness at the last moment, any more than they can conjure oil out of nowhere when the moment of need comes. We have to face some tests alone, beyond all help and support that others may give. The foolish virgins were not ready. They were left out. However much God loves us, the test will not be canceled (although allowance will surely be made for those who "never had a chance" or whose lives were twisted by the abuse of others). What tests do students think each of us has to face alone? Are we ready now for God's judgment?

This is my blood of the covenant, which is poured out
for many for the forgiveness of sins (26:28).

12

The Trial of Jesus

Matthew 26

DIMENSION ONE:
WHAT DOES THE BIBLE SAY?

Answer these questions by reading Matthew 26

1. Why do the chief priests and elders not arrest Jesus during the feast? (26:5)

   They want to avoid a riot among the people.

2. What happens in the house of Simon the leper in Bethany? (26:6-7)

   A woman pours a jar of expensive perfume on Jesus' head.

3. Why are the disciples indignant at her sacrifice? (26:8-9)

   They think that the perfume was wasted; it could have been sold so the money could be given to the poor.

4. What does Jesus say? (26:10-11)

   Jesus tells them that she has done a beautiful thing for him. They will always have the poor with them, but they will not always have him.

5. What do the chief priests pay Judas for his betrayal? (26:15)

   They give him thirty silver coins.

6. What meal do the disciples go into Jerusalem to prepare for Jesus? (26:17)

   They prepare for the Feast of Unleavened Bread (the Passover).

7. What does Jesus say as they are eating? (26:21)

   He says that one of them will betray him.

8. What does Judas ask Jesus, and what does Jesus reply? (26:25)

   Judas asks "Surely not I, Rabbi?" Jesus answers, "Yes, it is you."

9. What does Jesus do with the bread? (26:26)

   Jesus takes the bread, gives thanks, and breaks it. He then gives it to the disciples.

10. What does Jesus say when he gives them the bread? (26:26)

    Jesus says, "Take and eat; this is my body."

11. What does Jesus say when he gives the cup? (26:27)

    He tells them to drink from it, for it is his blood of the covenant that is poured out for many for the forgiveness of sins.

12. What does Jesus pray in Gethsemane? (26:39)

    He prays for God to let this cup pass from him, but for God's will to be done.

13. How many of the disciples watched while Jesus made this prayer? (26:40)

    None of the disciples watched while Jesus made this prayer. They all slept.

14. How did Judas betray Jesus to the crowd? (26:49)

    He greeted Jesus with a kiss.

15. What does Jesus say to the man who cut off the servant's ear? (26:52)

    "All who draw the sword will die by the sword."

16. What do the disciples do? (26:56)

They all desert him and flee.

17. Why does the high priest tear his clothes during the trial? (26:65)

He tears his clothes because he thinks Jesus has spoken blasphemy.

18. What is the verdict of the chief priests? (26:66)

They think Jesus is worthy of death.

19. What happens before the cock crows on that night? (26:75)

Peter denies Jesus three times.

DIMENSION TWO: WHAT DOES THE BIBLE MEAN?

From the beginning of the Last Supper, "When evening came" (26:20), to the moment when Jesus died and "gave up his spirit" (27:50) at three o'clock on Friday afternoon is just nineteen hours. Yet in that time, Matthew takes us through the Last Supper, the agony in the garden of Gethsemane, the betrayal, abandonment, and denial of Jesus, the trials before Caiaphas and Pilate, the scourging of Jesus, and the Crucifixion. Within that day, a new faith and a new covenant was born.

With Chapter 26 we begin reading the Passion narrative. The Passion narrative is the earliest part of the Gospel to circulate as the oral tradition. The first Christians regarded this story of Jesus' last day and crucifixion as the most important part of the gospel. A great many questions gather around the three events of the Supper, the garden, and the trial. Every teacher of the Gospel of Matthew would do well to be aware of these questions. They touch on how we understand the New Testament text. Notwithstanding, the great central meanings of the Gospel remain unaltered however these questions are answered. Let's first set those meanings before us in bold strokes so we do not lose them in the confusion of questions. Then we will address the questions.

Matthew 26:26-30—The Last Supper. Jesus ate a last meal with his disciples on the night before he died. During the meal he first took bread, then a cup, giving them new symbolic meaning. By these symbols, followers of Jesus understand that Jesus' death was for them. Verse 26 of Matthew's account does not include the words *which is for you.* These words were recorded by Paul in the First Letter to the Corinthians (1 Corinthians 11:24). But in saying "Take, eat," Jesus gives his body in death for his disciples. And the cup brings the announcement that through his death a new covenant is formed. The covenant is between God and all who turn to God, forgiving and receiving forgiveness. No unanswered questions can change these truths about the Last Supper.

Matthew 26:35-56—Gethsemane. Some of the events of that night were witnessed by the disciples and later by the hired henchmen who came to arrest Jesus. But no one saw or heard the agony of Jesus! He was off by himself. The disciples were asleep. Based on what the disciples did see and hear, and through their consecrated imagination, they were given to understand what they did not see. They understood Jesus' struggle to accept the cup that could not pass. In that scene we see Jesus in all his humanity, yet full of the glory of God.

Matthew 26:57-68—The Trials. Jesus was condemned by the Sanhedrin for blasphemy for saying, "You will see the Son of Man sitting at the right hand of the Mighty One." It was a vision to which the priests and teachers of the law could themselves agree. But Jesus implied that he was the Son of Man. This was arrogant heresy to the high court of Israel. Jesus was condemned by the Sanhedrin. As we shall learn when we get to Chapter 27, Jesus was condemned to death by Pilate for appearing to be the King of the Jews. Rome conceded that title to no one. But no unanswered questions about either trial have changed the fact that Jesus was condemned by the religious authority. They feared his challenge to their tradition. The Roman authorities feared his rebuke to their power.

Let us move now to examine Chapter 26 in greater detail.

Matthew 26:3. At the time of Jesus, Rome occupied and ruled Judea with absolute imperial power. The Jews were free to practice their faith and live their lives only as Rome allowed. The high priest was a puppet of Caesar. He presided in the Temple as long as he did Caesar's bidding and served the interests of Rome. In the 104 years between 37 B.C. and A.D. 67, twenty-eight high priests followed one another to that office. Joseph Caiaphas served from A.D. 18 to A.D. 36. High priests usually did not last that long. Caiaphas must have been very good at cooperating with Rome. He saw Jesus not only as a blasphemer but as a potential troublemaker for Rome. And trouble for Rome spelled trouble for Caiaphas. He had two reasons for wanting Jesus out of the way.

Matthew 26:6-13. What a lovely thing this woman did for Jesus! Unfortunately Jesus' reply to his disciples for their criticism of her has often been taken out of context and quoted to justify indifference to the poor. People who have read the Gospel of Matthew, especially Matthew 25:31-46, should know better.

Matthew 26:14-16. Why did Judas betray Jesus? We will never know for certain why Judas betrayed Jesus. The student book suggests three things that could have triggered Judas' betrayal. He could have been disillusioned. He could have been jealous. Or he might have wanted to manipulate Jesus.

In the rock opera *Jesus Christ Superstar*, by Webber and Rice, we find a mixture of these motives combined in an interesting way. In that drama Judas conspires with the chief priests because Jesus cannot control events like he did before. The situation is getting out of hand as more and more people acclaim Jesus as more than a man. At one point Judas says to Jesus, "You really do believe this talk of God is true." Judas sees their chances weakening with every hour. He cannot believe it, for he sees that it all will lead to disaster for the nation. That explanation may be as plausible as any other. It combines disillusionment with an attempt to control the way events speed toward what Judas perceives as catastrophe. Now if that were the reason it would still be betrayal, not to mention arrogance in Judas assuming to know more than Jesus. But at least such motive has integrity within the mind of Judas. Obviously he wanted to move in a different direction from Jesus.

Matthew 26:23. The Dead Sea scrolls from the Qumran community reveal an eating custom among those Essene Jews. They lived a kind of monastic life in the desert bordering the Dead Sea apart from the rest of Judea. They observed a hierarchic order in reaching out to the bowl. One biblical scholar proposes that the words *with me* in verse 23 indicate that Judas did not wait his turn, thus denying the leadership of Jesus. It is only a speculation, but it would have confirmed to Jesus who the betrayer was. Perhaps he had already read it in the face of Judas.

Matthew 26:17-30. What kind of a meal did Jesus eat with his disciples in the upper room? When was it held? The questions are as old as the New Testament itself. The chronology in John's Gospel differs from that of Mark and Matthew. The day the meal was eaten is decisive as to what meal it was. In this matter John appears to be more reliable.

According to John 19:14 and 31, Jesus died on the "day of Preparation" in the afternoon while the lambs were being slain for the Passover meal. Further evidence supports the belief that it was not the Passover Jesus ate with his disciples in the upper room. The Passover began at sunset on Friday evening. The Crucifixion had taken place by that time. Moreover, many people find it difficult to believe that all the tumult and collaboration with Rome in an execution would have occurred on the holiest day of the year. The evidence here is intuitive, not demonstrated. We may never know. We cannot even prove in what year Jesus died, or when Passover fell in whatever year it was. Most scholars believe that Jesus was crucified in A.D. 30.

If not the Passover, what? Some believe it was a *habhurah* meal. A *habhurah* was a fellowship of disciples who gathered around a teacher or rabbi. Jesus may have thought of his disciples as a *habhurah*. They surely had taken meals together around Capernaum and on their journeys. The one

in this Passover season would have had unusual significance for them, since Jesus had told them he would not eat again with them in this world. He knew that after his death they would gather again to remember all the meals they had taken together. They would remember this one above the others. We do not read it in Matthew's account, but in Paul's report of the upper room Jesus says, "Do this, whenever you drink it, in remembrance of me" (1 Corinthians 11:25). Jesus wanted the disciples to remember the symbols that he invested with the meaning the symbols that he invested with the meaning of his coming death. *Habhurah* meals were taken once a week. Passover came once a year.

The fact is the Last Supper quickly came to be associated with the Passover. And why not? In the first covenant God had delivered the Israelites from Egypt by passing over their houses in the visitation of death (Exodus 12). Now, through the Christ, God gives Israel a new covenant, a new Passover from death to life, confirmed by the Resurrection.

To read the brief account of the Last Supper is to think of the sacrament of the Lord's Supper, Holy Communion, or the Eucharist. The word *eucharist* comes from a Greek word meaning "thanksgiving." At the Last Supper Jesus gave thanks over the bread.

A sacrament is an action done by the church using symbols (water, bread, wine, grape juice) to convey the presence of an invisible reality. In the Holy Communion bread is broken and a cup is poured out. The worshiper eats and drinks trusting that the Spirit of Christ is present at this table. The faithful communicant gives thanks to God for the gift of grace, receives God's forgiveness, and renews the promise made in his or her covenant with God and God's people.

If you look at verse 26, you find four verbs: he *took*, he *gave thanks*, and *broke* it, and he *gave* it to his disciples. These four actions are repeated whenever Communion is given and received. Bread is received, often presented by members of the congregation as the disciples presented the food Jesus was to use in the upper room. Thanks are given in a eucharistic prayer of consecration. Then the loaf is broken, reminding us how Jesus' body was broken for us. Finally the elements are given to the people. This fourfold action, going back to the Last Supper, is the same for all Christians.

Matthew 26:56. No sentence in Matthew leaves us more heavy-hearted than the last sentence of verse 56. They have come so far together, and then Jesus saw his disciples for the last time, running like cowards into the darkness to hide. What a memory it left Jesus to take to the cross. Being abandoned by the ones he had chosen to be his ministers must have troubled Jesus even more than the prospect of his own death. Perhaps Jesus trusted that God would use their cowardice to keep them together for a future no one could possibly have imagined.

Matthew 26:57-68. Many questions surround the first trial before Caiaphas and the Sanhedrin. (The Sanhedrin was the supreme Jewish council of seventy-one teachers of the law, elders, and priests.) Could this court levy capital punishment? Had Jesus committed an offense punishable by death under the Jewish law at that time? If we answer these questions in the affirmative then we have to ask why the high priest involved Pilate at all.

In later times the Sanhedrin was allowed to execute blasphemers, even Gentiles if they entered where they were forbidden in the Temple. But we do not know whether they were allowed to at the time of Jesus' trial. Nor can we be sure what constituted blasphemy at the time of Caiaphas. Earlier in Matthew (9:3) the teachers of the law accuse Jesus of blasphemy because he had the nerve to forgive sin, something only God can do. But the presumption to forgive is not mentioned at the trial.

Perhaps Jesus' claim to be the Christ was considered blasphemy. He further declared that the high priest would see the Son of Man seated at the right hand of the Mighty One, implying that Jesus was that man. With that astounding claim, further witnesses would not be needed.

We might guess that the whole ecclesiastical proceeding would have been in violation of the law. But Caiaphas was too crafty to risk blowing the whole plan by doing something obviously out of order. Nevertheless, the trial was carried out with undue haste. Later in Jewish history, a conviction verdict was not permitted to be carried out until the following day. We do not know if such a restriction prevailed at Jesus' trial. The whole thing could have been hurried up to get it over with before Passover, if John's chronology is correct.

Two traditions are side by side. In verse 57, Jesus is taken directly from Gethsemane to the high priest. Matthew 27:1 refers to a morning meeting as though they had not confronted Jesus in the night (or was this a second appearance?).

These questions have no firm answers. But we see clearly that the Sanhedrin is determined to convict Jesus on the one question over which they have judicial authority—blasphemy against God. That deed was done. If the procedure is within the law, and if what Jesus admits is blasphemy, then Caiaphas acts with what he saw as his duty toward the law of Israel. Where Caiaphas was more culpable from our perspective is in the false charges with which he turns Jesus over to Pilate. Jesus represented no political threat to Rome. The high priest's collusion with Pilate at this point is altogether self-serving. It is the strategy by which he will carry out what he has already determined to do—kill Jesus.

Did the Jews Crucify Christ? To read Matthew 26–27 is to come face to face with the charge that the Jews crucified Christ. This charge is older even than the written Gospels themselves. This charge lies at the root of those shameful chapters of anti-Semitism that have infected the Christian church from the very beginning. Sometimes the Jews have even been charged with *deicide,* the killing of God. Is there some way that we can come to terms with this demon of anti-Semitism and exorcise it?

To say the Jews crucified Christ is like saying the Greeks murdered Socrates or the French burned Joan of Arc at the stake. The Sanhedrin did condemn Jesus to death for reasons we have seen. The reasons do not seem to us, these many generations later, to call for an execution. And behind the charge of blasphemy, Caiaphas had his own reasons for wanting Jesus out of the way. Jesus challenged his ecclesiastical power and his control of the religious life of Israel. But Caiaphas was not "all Jews" even then, and certainly not for two thousand years after. To insist that all people of the Jewish race and faith killed Jesus would be nonsense if it were not shameful and tragic.

We must concede the unmistakable strain of anti-Semitism in the Gospels themselves, especially in John. But we must remember that these Gospels were written in the period roughly A.D. 70 to A.D. 90 when Christians were being expelled from the synagogues and in some cases being killed for heresy. Recall how Stephen was put to death (Acts 6:8-15; 7:54–8:1). Paul consented to the stoning. Naturally the evangelists saw the Jews as enemies of the Christians. They colored the Passion story to reflect most of the guilt on the Jews. Travail, tears, hatred, and fear accompany the birth of a new covenant faith out of the old. That is understandable. But to transmit such prejudice and hostility from one generation to the next and the next and the next is to violate the spirit of Jesus, whose name we supposedly claim.

When we examine the trials we see that the Sanhedrin demanded that Pilate execute Jesus. Caiaphas blackmailed the Roman procurator with threats of civil disorder if the execution were not ordered. Whether or not the Sanhedrin could have put Jesus to death on their own we do not know. It may well have better served their purpose to have the Romans do it. Caiaphas may have feared Jesus would "rock the boat." But Caiaphas intimidated Pilate by charging falsely that Jesus was King of the Jews. As Pilate would have understood the words, this was perjury and false witness.

Pilate, as nearly as we can tell from the accounts in all the Gospels, believed Jesus to be innocent of the charges against him. He tried to find a way of releasing Jesus. He could not satisfy the people. He feared the mob. Overriding his conscience, he gave way to those who demanded Jesus' death and ordered the Crucifixion. Pilate must bear the responsibility of a miscarriage of Roman justice. He could have saved Jesus' life, but perhaps at a higher price than he was willing to pay.

Primary responsibility for Jesus' death must fall on the Sanhedrin. The issue that brought Jesus to the cross was a religious conflict with the Judaism of his day. He was not a political or military challenge to Rome. Rome played a cynical and brutal part in the murder. But having apportioned the guilt in that way, we would do well to consider what we might have done had we been in the Sanhedrin, not knowing Jesus and never having heard of the Resurrection. And then let all who are without sin cast the first stone at the Jews.

DIMENSION THREE: WHAT DOES THE BIBLE MEAN TO ME?

These segments do not appear in the student book. You may want to discuss with the group if you will dig deeper into these activities or will center on the reflective nature of the material in the student book.

Matthew 26:27-28—This Cup Is My Blood of the Covenant

When Jesus and the disciples had finished the Last Supper, Jesus took a cup of wine and said, "This is my blood of the covenant, which is poured out for many for the forgiveness of sins." Forever after the cup of the Lord's Supper has symbolized the death Jesus died in order that we could know we were forgiven. Truly, we have to accept Matthew 26:28 on faith. We may understand a bit more of this verse if we remember how closely Jesus identified himself with the suffering servant of Isaiah. "He bore the sin of many, and made intercession for the transgressors" (Isaiah 53:12). We believe that God was in Jesus the Christ, willingly taking not only the sin of Israel and Rome but our sins as well. For this reason, we find healing in the cup of the Lord's Supper. Ask the students in what ways they would like this kind of healing to be true for them. In what ways has it been true?

Matthew 26:39—Your Will Be Done

Harry Emerson Fosdick once said that it is in Gethsemane that every person faces his or her life's central test. The test comes when we have prayed, "My Father, it if is possible, may this cup be taken from me." Can we go on to pray, "Yet not as I will, but as you will"? Sooner or later everyone comes to some Gethsemane where life offers a bitter cup to drain. We may be facing the loss of something that was everything to us, renunciation of our power or pleasure, even life itself in every way we have ever known for the sake of others. Then can we say, "Not my will but yours be done"?

Can any of the students share their Gethsemanes? Have they ever felt all alone in facing their tests? maybe while those they loved slept? Where did they find courage and faith to drink their cup of suffering and renunciation? These are exceedingly difficult things to talk about and share. If the class has engendered enough trust in the group to share at this level, this could be one of the most helpful sessions of the entire study.

The story of Gethsemane has been a comfort to many Christians who have found reinforcement in remembering how Jesus knelt and prayed as they have had to pray. And God was with them.

Matthew 26:74—Immediately the Cock Crowed

In New England, church spires frequently have a rooster mounted on a weather vane. Altogether fitting that a cock should be seen and imagined to crow atop the steeple. It should remind all who pass by of Peter. After protesting that he would never deny Jesus, even if he had to die, Peter denies his Master three times in one night. "Immediately a rooster crowed" (26:74). Peter wept bitterly for this cowardice in forsaking Jesus.

The final question in the meditation in the student book asks, "Of what denials of Christ would tomorrow's rooster crow remind you?" Maybe the denial was not in words but in something a person failed to do on which Jesus and others depended. If you address this text, first see what the students have remembered from their lives. If appropriate you might ask, Did you ever deny Jesus in consenting to something you should have resisted? Did you ever deny Jesus by burying his gifts to you in the ground out of fear, or disuse, or compromise?

Isn't it good that Matthew included this little episode to remind us that on some morning in the future, maybe tomorrow, a rooster will crow? It would be well if we asked how we will feel when we hear it.

Go and make disciples of all nations, baptizing them . . .
teaching them to obey everything I have commanded you (28:19-20).

— 13 —

Crucified and Risen

Matthew 27–28

DIMENSION ONE:
WHAT DOES THE BIBLE SAY?

Answer these questions by reading Matthew 27

1. What do the chief priests do when morning comes? (27:1-2)

   They come to the decision to put Jesus to death. They take him to Pilate.

2. What does Judas do then? (27:3)

   He is seized with remorse and he returns the thirty silver coins to the chief priests and elders.

3. What do the elders say to Judas? (27:4)

   They tell Judas it is nothing to them and to take responsibility himself.

4. What do the elders do with Judas's money? (27:7)

   They buy a potter's field as a burial place for foreigners.

5. What does Pilate ask Jesus, and what does Jesus reply? (27:11)

   Pilate asks Jesus if he is the King of the Jews. Jesus answers, "Yes, it is as you say."

6. Who was Barabbas? (27:16)

   He was a notorious prisoner.

7. What choice does Pilate give the accusers of Jesus? (27:17)

   He says he will release either Barabbas or Jesus.

8. When the crowd cries for Barabbas to be released, what does Pilate do? (27:24)

   He washes his hands before the crowd, saying, "I am innocent of this man's blood."

9. Who carries Jesus' cross for him? (27:32)

   Simon, a man of Cyrene, carries Jesus' cross.

10. What does the name *Golgotha* mean? (27:33)

    The name means "The Place of the Skull."

11. What charge is fastened over Jesus' head as he hangs on the cross? (27:37)

    "This is Jesus, the King of the Jews."

12. What does Jesus cry from the cross? (27:46)

    Jesus cries and asks why God has forsaken him.

13. What does Matthew say happens when Jesus dies? (27:51-53)

    The curtain of the Temple is torn from top to bottom, the earth shakes, the rocks split, tombs break open, and bodies of the holy peoples are raised to life.

14. Who watches the Crucifixion from afar? (27:55)

    Many women who have followed Jesus watch from afar.

15. Who buries the body of Jesus? (27:57-60)

    A rich man from Arimathea named Joseph buries Jesus.

16. How does Pilate secure the tomb? (27:66)

    He has the tomb sealed with a stone and posts a guard.

Answer these questions by reading Matthew 28

17. Whom do the two Marys meet at the tomb? (28:2, 9)

First they meet an angel of the Lord. Then Jesus meets them.

18. What does Jesus tell the women to say to the disciples? (28:10)

He tells then not to be afraid and to tell the disciples to go to Galilee and they will see him.

19. What does Jesus tell the disciples? (28:19-20)

He tells them to go and make disciples of all nations, to baptize them, and to teach them. He also promises that he is always with them to the very end of the age.

DIMENSION TWO: WHAT DOES THE BIBLE MEAN?

Chapters 27–28 bring the Gospel of Matthew to a close. Included in these final chapters are reports of three principal events. These developments serve as the very heart of the whole Christian gospel. They are the history toward which everything has moved from as far back as Old Testament prophecy: the Crucifixion (27:32-56), the Resurrection (28:1-10), and the Great Commission (28:16-20). You will direct most of the study to these matters. You will also study four related happenings. These are the suicide of Judas (27:3-10), the trial before Pilate (27:11-26), the scourging of Jesus by the Roman soldiers (27:37-41), and the burial of Jesus (27:57-66).

Matthew 27:1-2. From the account in 26:57-66, Jesus is already condemned by the Sanhedrin. This early morning consultation considers only the question of how to execute. We are still left with the question, why Pilate? A great many students of the New Testament have concluded that the Jews were prohibited from carrying out capital punishment at the time of Pilate. If the chief priests and elders are to get rid of Jesus they will have to get the Romans to do it. Also, despite their desperate prosecution of Jesus, the Sanhedrin would rather shift the blame onto Roman heads and hands. In either case, they hustle Jesus off to the governor's palace. They do not waste any time, either. Passover begins at sundown. They want Jesus gone by the commencement of the feast.

Matthew 27:3-10. Only Matthew tells us of Judas's suicide. (Acts 1:15-20 tells of a different violent end to the betrayer.) Matthew almost certainly included the suicide tradition because it fulfilled the Scripture of Zechariah (Zechariah 11:13). (For more information review the study of Zechariah in this series.)

But two things do occur to us when we reflect on this tragic story. Why is Judas filled with such remorse? If he were really a conspirator with the Sanhedrin, would he not now be satisfied? It looks very much as though Judas never intended for events to get so out of hand. When Judas learns that Jesus is delivered over to Pilate, almost surely to be crucified, he is staggered. He rushes to give back the money, as though this could somehow stop the course of events. But what are thirty silver coins (the market price for one Hebrew slave) compared to the death of this Galilean blasphemer?

We also have to wonder whether the chief priests were not secretly unsure of what they had done. Had they believed that sending Jesus to death at Pilate's hands was right, they would not have considered the thirty pieces of silver blood money. They thought Jesus was a blasphemer. But they knew he was not a pretender to Roman power. Was this why they could not cast the money into the treasury? We will never know. We do know that Judas could not live with his guilt and betrayal of Jesus. The Jews regarded suicide as murder. Matthew tells us Judas went to his death doubly condemned as a betrayer and a murderer.

Matthew 27:11-14. Officially Pilate was procurator of Judea. He was responsible directly to the emperor for administration of the province. He had risen up through a chain of command posts to be eligible for such an appointment. He was appointed in A.D. 26, just four years before Jesus was brought to trial in his palace. During these four years the Jews had grown to hate Pilate. He consistently violated their religious and moral sensitivies. His legion had marched into Jerusalem with the emblem of Caesar emblazoned on their pikes. This offended the Jewish prohibition against graven images. To finance the building of a new aqueduct for Jerusalem's water supply, he took funds from the Temple treasury. The Jews threatened to report Pilate to the emperor for his misdeeds. This threat disturbed Pilate. He did not want the emperor to know of his corruption, cruelty, and of his murders. So Pilate was hardly in a position to be cavalier with the Jewish authorities. In a sense they blackmailed him.

Pilate remained at his post for six more years following the Crucifixion. He was finally recalled because he massacred some defenseless Judean villagers.

Matthew 27:15-24. According to Matthew, Pilate now tries to gain Jesus' release. If Matthew's account is accurate, it indicates how out of touch Pilate was with Jewish affairs. Not to be unfair, we have to concede that a Roman governor off in Caesarea would not likely know about a religious controversy originating in Galilee. At any rate, the crowd of hired demonstrators called loudly for Barabbas. Pilate's final strategy gained nothing.

If Pilate cannot stop the execution, he can duck responsibility for it. Or so he thinks (27:24).

CRUCIFIED AND RISEN

73

Matthew 27:32-56. Crucifixion was a Roman method of capital punishment. They copied it from the Phoenicians and the Persians. In the catalogue of sadistic cruelties devised by humans, crucifixion must have few equals. It combines psychological humiliation with slow torture unto exhaustion, sometimes insanity, and death. For crimes of robbery, tumult, and sedition, crucifixion was reserved for punishment of slaves and non-Romans. Thus Jesus could be crucified. Paul, a Roman citizen, could not. Death came comparatively quickly to Jesus. The brutal scourging by the henchmen of the high priest and the savage mockery by the Roman soldiers probably hastened his death. Sometimes prisoners died during the cruel sport that the Roman guards had with them before they were crucified.

The New Testament includes several traditions about the Crucifixion. Luke and John contain details of Jesus' death on Calvary not found in Mark and Matthew. Here we cannot engage in a comparative study. Let it only be pointed out that we should read the Crucifixion story in all four Gospels (Mark 15; Luke 23; John 19). Each of the stories is valuable. The earliest are thought to be in Mark and Matthew.

The inscription placed above Jesus' head, "THIS IS JESUS, THE KING OF THE JEWS," was one of Pilate's cruel jabs at the Jews. Unwittingly he well served the intention of Caiaphas and company. This slogan remained a memento of disgrace with which the early Christian church had to live.

We sometimes feel a kind of horrible fascination with the torture and physical details of the Crucifixion. It is important that these never be forgotten. The center of interest for the reader of the Gospel, however, must always transcend the details to grasp the everlasting meaning of what happened there. This calls for a lifetime of ongoing study, experience, and trust. For this concluding lesson, you may want to ask the students how the cross confirms and validates some of the things already proclaimed in the Gospel. Does the cross mark the commencement of a new age? Or is it more of the same, endlessly repeated? How does the cross open a window into the heart of God—as many have said it does? Into the heart of the God who cares for the least and the lost of the world? What does it reveal about the expected extent of the Christian's commitment to Jesus?

Matthew 27:51-54. The other crucifixion narratives do not tell of most of these phenomena. The symbols are so unmistakable we may believe that Matthew intends them as metaphors. He presents the story so hearers and readers will not miss the spiritual significance of Jesus' death. These are of far greater consequence than any torn curtain, broken rocks, or resuscitated bodies moving about Jerusalem. What all these things tell us is that God acted in an irrefutable way in Jesus' death on the cross and in his resurrection. With Jesus' death on the cross, says the Christian faith, a new way has been opened to the heart of God.

Matthew 27:57-66. Matthew reports this incident in order to counteract the stories that his followers stole Jesus' body from the tomb and made up the tale of the Resurrection. This must have been part of the campaign against the early Christians to discredit their faith.

Matthew 28. No part of the Gospel is more important to Christian faith, nor more difficult to explain. The Resurrection cannot be "explained." The Resurrection only can be experienced. No one saw Jesus rise from the dead. We find many accounts of Jesus appearing and disappearing, now here and now there, now in corporeal form, again in mystical embodiment. These accounts convince us we are dealing with experience beyond the familiar and readily accountable. While the student book does not allude to it directly, you can hardly leave the subject of the resurrected body untouched.

In verse 10 and verses 18-20, Jesus speaks just as he spoke before his death. Many have held to what they find implied here, a physical resurrection. This can neither be demonstrated nor disproved. Such is not necessary. If any hold that belief, they do so on faith, not on sight. But we have to go beyond a resurrected body to a doctrine more satisfactory for all eternity.

Many have held that Jesus was resurrected in the minds, hearts, and faith of the disciples. An important truth is here. Resurrection surely occurs there. If not there, what meaning could it have anywhere else? But that view, exclusive of any other report, is too subjective. It relegates the risen Christ to an inner mystical experience of individuals. The New Testament implies more than that.

Many have believed that Jesus was raised as a spiritual body, released from the flesh. (See 1 Corinthians 15, especially verses 42-58.) In this view Jesus is able on the Galilean mountain to communicate through his spirit with the disciples. He has done this with others across the centuries, important among them the apostle Paul himself (Acts 9:1-9).

Nor can it be overlooked that Jesus spoke of his eternal presence in the company of the faithful, that is to say, in the church. In one sense the church is the resurrected Christ.

Whatever explanations the students may have, it will be important that you move with them from the last chapter of Matthew to the latest chapter of their own lives.

DIMENSION THREE: WHAT DOES THE BIBLE MEAN TO ME?

The class may discuss the following topics or use the ones that appear in the student book.

Matthew 27:24-26—I Wash My Hands of It

Ever since that evening after the Crucifixion, Pilate's washbowl has been haunting us. It is carried by men and women to wherever it is needed. People are forever denouncing their responsibilities by washing their hands in Pilate's washbowl. Politicians ignore their principles, because they might not get reelected. Good citizens will not get involved in politics. Newspaper publishers misrepresent stories to sell papers. Preachers dare not speak up to members of the congregation because those members contribute toward their salaries. Do you hear the splash of the water near you? Where do we try to do as Pilate did—wash off responsibility onto someone else?

Matthew 28:6—He Is Not Here; He Has Risen

The two most profoundly shattering announcements in the Christian gospel are "Today in the town of David a Savior has been born to you" (Luke 2:11), and "He is not here; he has risen." What difference does it make to us, and to our world, that Christ has been raised? Ask the students here at the end of the study what difference it makes. To answer that question is to find a bridge from the days of Jesus' appearing from the dead to the days of our lives.

The following four consequences, at least, should inform the answers of Christian faith. You will find ways of putting these truths in words appropriate to the time, place, and people of *your* teaching.

1. Jesus was "handed over to you by God's set purpose and foreknowledge; and you, with the help of wicked men, put him to death by nailing him to the cross. But God raised him from the dead, freeing him from the agony of death, because it was impossible for death to keep its hold on him" (Acts 2:23-24). Peter spoke those words at Pentecost. Faith has proclaimed this truth from the beginning. God's Spirit in Jesus the Christ was not vanquished by the Sanhedrin, by Pilate, by the cross, or even by death itself. God's love was not destroyed on Golgotha or sealed forever in Joseph's tomb. Instead, through the Resurrection, God "disarmed the powers and authorities, [and] he made a public spectacle of them, triumphing over them by the cross" (Colossians 2:15). We are persuaded that death cannot separate us from the love of God in Christ Jesus.

What difference is this faith going to make in the lives of the class members? Would our lives be different had Jesus not been raised? If so, how different?

2. The new community that gathered, and still gathers in the name of Jesus, is confirmed by his living presence. The Christ is alive and well and living wherever God's people assemble in covenant and commitment. Do you meet the risen Christ in your church? In what ways can such a human, imperfect body as the church be the resurrected Christ? The Resurrection authenticates that promise.

3. The Resurrection clears our vision of where the living Christ will meet us. In the Sermon on the Mount Jesus told the disciples, "Not everyone who says to me, 'Lord, Lord,' shall enter the kingdom of heaven, but only he who does the will of my Father who is in heaven" (Matthew 7:21). And in his parable of the final judgment Jesus summoned those who have cared for the least of his brothers and sisters, "Come . . . take your inheritance, the kingdom prepared for you since the creation of the world" (Matthew 25:34). These declarations now come with the new force of the Resurrection in them. No longer are they just the words of the Teacher, but now they are the mandate of the risen Lord. And he tells us once again that we may join him in doing all that he has commanded (28:20).

4. From the beginning of his Gospel, Matthew has voiced the faith that the present age will end, a new heaven and a new earth will appear. However we may understand that faith, whether in this world or beyond, it tells us that this age will not last forever. Jesus the Christ will be present to the end, for better or worse, through thick and thin. Jesus had promised a kingdom prepared from the creation of the world for those who do God's will. The Resurrection is God's validation of that promise. God's pledges that the divine purpose is being fulfilled in Christ in the present time. That purpose will be consummated in the age to come.

There is no better way to conclude this study of Matthew than to reflect on where you and the class members may see glimpses of the Kingdom of which Jesus speaks.

Perspectives on the Gospel of Matthew

I. Matthew's Portrait of Jesus

1. *Jesus as continuation and fulfillment*

In Jesus a radically new and decisive power has come into the world. Yet he represents a continuation and fulfillment of the promises and the action of God from the beginning.

2. *Jesus as Messiah*

Jesus is the expected Messiah whose challenge cannot be evaded. His principal impact is messianic, not as a human being. His teachings cut across the familiar world and ways to which we are accustomed. Jesus is Immanuel—God with us.

3. *Jesus as an apocalyptic figure*

Jesus is urgent about the end of the world. He expects it soon; but he says that the time and the how of its coming is not the important thing.

4. *Jesus as a man of compassion*

He is a friend of the poor, the dispossessed, a man of unending compassion and sympathy.

5. *Jesus as radical and demanding Lord*

One cannot accommodate the usual ways of life to Jesus. He demands an "all" commitment.

II. The Special Grain in Matthew's Gospel

1. *The center of history lies in the future: the Day of Judgment.* Therefore the teachings of Jesus are of supreme importance for every person. Matthew sees the failure of the disciples to follow Jesus as a failure of faith. This is a warning for the church for which Matthew wrote.

2. *The Gospel is a "law" or manual for church members,* either a Jewish-Christian community or an apostolic

church already "separated." The church is "called out" to practice righteousness.

3. *Matthew is the most Jewish of the Gospels,* despite its intense controversy with the Pharisees. The attacks on Pharisees are against the Pharisaic Jerusalem tradition, not of Jesus' time but of the late first century. Moses and Jesus are seen as closely parallel figures.

4. *The Apocalypse is expected soon.* Matthew writes to encourage and exhort an anxious community.

5. *Matthew is the most systematic teacher of the evangelists.* But neither the Sermon on the Mount nor the parables are to be seen as universal moral teachings apart from the content of faith and the church. The imperative is in the indicative. God has acted in Christ. Therefore we must act.

MARK
Table of Contents

About the Writer

Dr. Orion N. Hutchinson, Jr., was a former Editor of Church School Publications at The United Methodist Publishing House, Nashville, Tennessee.

The beginning of the gospel about Jesus Christ, the Son of God (1:1).

— 1 —

The Beginning of the Gospel

Mark 1

DIMENSION ONE:
WHAT DOES THE BIBLE SAY?

Answer these questions by reading Mark 1

1. What is the task of the messenger as the prophet describes it? (1:2-3)

   The task is to prepare the way for the Lord and make his paths straight.

2. What is the main message of John the Baptist? (1:4, 7)

   John's main message is repentance for the forgiveness of sins and the immediate coming of a great one who is more powerful than he.

3. What clothing does John the Baptist wear? (1:6)

   He wears a garment made out of camel's hair with a leather belt.

4. What food does he eat? (1:6)

   He eats locusts and wild honey.

5. What is the first event in the life of Jesus that Mark records? (1:9)

   The baptism of Jesus in the Jordan is the first event.

6. How does the Spirit appear on this occasion? (1:10)

   The Spirit appears on him "like a dove."

7. What does the voice from heaven say? (1:11)

   "You are my Son, whom I love; with you I am well pleased."

8. Where does Jesus go after this event? (1:12-13)

   Jesus goes into the surrounding desert area.

9. What is the first message of Jesus according to Mark? (1:14-15)

   "The time has come. The kingdom of God is near. Repent and believe the good news!"

10. To whom does Jesus extend his invitation by the Sea of Galilee? (1:16, 19)

    His invitation is extended to Simon and Andrew, James and John.

11. What is the first invitation Jesus extends? (1:17)

    "Come, follow me, and I will make you fishers of men."

12. What is their response? (1:18)

    At once they leave their nets and follow him.

13. What does Jesus do in the synagogue? (1:21)

    He begins teaching.

14. What is the reaction of the people? (1:22, 27)

    They are amazed because he teaches them as one who has authority, not as the teachers of the law. He teaches something new.

15. What disturbance takes place in the synagogue? (1:23-26)

    A person with an evil spirit interrupts Jesus' teaching by shouting questions while recognizing Jesus as the "Holy One of God."

16. What happens next at the house of Simon and Andrew? (1:29-30)

    Jesus ministers to Simon's mother-in-law who was ill with fever. He helps her up and the fever leaves her.

17. What two forms of ministry does Jesus pursue as he goes "throughout Galilee"? (1:39)

Jesus preaches in the synagogues and drives out demons.

18. What type of person does Mark now mention as coming to Jesus? (1:40)

Mark mentions a man who has leprosy.

19. How does Jesus help this man? (1:41)

Jesus, out of compassion, touches him and cleanses him.

20. Then what does Jesus charge this man? (1:43-44)

Jesus warns the healed man not to discuss what has taken place with anyone except the priest. The man is to offer the traditional sacrifices of thanksgiving prescribed in the Jewish law, dating back to the days of Moses.

21. Instead, what does this man do? (1:45a)

He goes out and begins to talk freely about his healing and spreads the news.

22. What is the result for Jesus? (1:45b)

Jesus can no longer openly enter a town but travels in the country; and people come to him from everywhere.

DIMENSION TWO: WHAT DOES THE BIBLE MEAN?

Introducing the Gospel of Mark

This study brings us to a unique account of Jesus' life by an author with some convictions about the life of Jesus. A purpose of the teaching process should be to unveil those convictions that Mark held about the nature of Jesus and to discover how they are expressed and supported in the narrative events the author records.

A common assumption made about the author of this second Gospel account is that he was the companion of Christian emissaries mentioned in Acts (12:12 and 13:5; see also Colossians 4:10; 2 Timothy 4:11; Philemon 24; 1 Peter 5:13) by the name of John Mark. (John was his Jewish name, and Mark was his Roman name.) Of course, nowhere in the account itself is Mark identified as its author. In honesty we must admit that often the names of prominent persons were attached to ancient writings to assure that they would be read. However, that the strength and endurance of the tradition that Mark was the author or editor has not been seriously challenged by research lends support to the presumption that the Gospel has come to us from his influence, if not from his hand. One interesting idea that has some support from Scripture (1 Peter 5:13) and the writings of early church fathers (for example, Papias and Eusebius) is that Mark had a close relationship with Peter. Mark became Peter's secretary, recording what Peter preached concerning Jesus' words and deeds. If this is true, then Mark may well have learned some of the contents of his account from Peter.

Dr. Ernest F. Scott, a distinguished New Testament scholar, described the Gospel of Mark in a lecture as "the most important book ever written." Ask class members to guess why he would make such a bold statement. The reasons they give now may be few. When this study of Mark is completed, the question could be asked again to see if more reasons have become apparent.

The Gospel of Mark stands out as unique among the Gospels for several reasons. First, Mark is the shortest and most concise of the four accounts. Second, Mark is regarded by most scholars as the first Gospel written, probably around A.D. 65–70. One strong evidence for this early dating is that most of Mark's material is included in Matthew and Luke, often word for word. Third, Mark writes against the backdrop of strong skepticism by Jews and non-Jews about Jesus and the Christian gospel and the impending threat of persecution against the Christian community. Many persons were wavering on the brink of belief versus nonbelief. This author, more out of a sense of urgency than literary polish, wanted to affirm widely and reliably the good news that Jesus is the Christ, the Son of God. He accomplished his purpose through using the collected evidence of one or more eyewitnesses.

Mark 1:1-11. Note that the gospel is the "gospel about Jesus Christ." Point out to class members that, technically speaking, we have only one gospel—the gospel of Jesus Christ. The good news is of him. The biographical accounts we have in the New Testament are gospels of Jesus Christ "according to" Matthew, Mark, Luke, and John. A spiritual truth underlies this use of words: the good news is of Jesus' coming, not of our doings or of our ideas about his doings. Although by habit we may speak of the Gospel of Mark, more accurately the title might be the "Gospel of Jesus Christ as Brought to Us by Mark." The writers of these accounts serve as evangelists, bringing us the good news.

The first chapter of Mark gives us not only his theme but also an insight into his methods of presenting that theme. First, largely for the enlightenment of his readers, he begins by placing Jesus in the Old Testament traditions of expectation. Over many generations the belief had arisen, stimulated by the preaching of prophets such as Malachi and Isaiah, that God would enter human history in a special way. Increasingly, it was felt this would be through a person called a "messiah" (anointed one), who would be preceded by a messenger of announcement. Some even taught that Elijah would be returned to earth to serve in this role. Thus Mark introduces Jesus to us as one who, introduced by a spokesman like Elijah, is fulfilling God's promises and who acts with the authority of God.

Mark 1:12-13. Although this reference to Jesus in the desert is brief, it can stimulate many important questions for discussion. For instance, Why, immediately after the exhilarating experience of baptism with God's Spirit hovering near to bless and encourage, does this desolate "dark month of the soul" occur? Does it happen that way to us? What do we encounter after our moments of high inspiration—more inspiration or struggles to endure? Strikingly, in this account Satan seems to be closest just after God has been closest.

Yet also note that ministering spirits were with Jesus to sustain his body and soul in the wilderness. Mark begins the story of Jesus by recalling Jesus' power against Satan. This means that what happens in the life of Jesus is a battle against Satan, not just a mere earthly event.

Mark 1:14-20. Note here that Jesus, when John the Baptist is arrested, in essence picks up John's message to be certain it is heard (1:14-15). The proclamation of the Kingdom's nearness is followed by the invitation to the fishermen. Jesus gives a new task to the fishermen. The new task is doing what Jesus does, traveling with Jesus. We must understand that this new way of life with Jesus will result in new ways of acting.

What interrelation is here that your class members may explore? Also ask the group, What is the nature of this invitation Jesus extends to the fishermen? Is it simply to be his traveling companions? What do you think it meant to these persons to leave their nets and their father in order to follow Jesus?

Mark 1:21-45. To understand these segments properly, you may need to understand some overarching developments that are taking place here. The Gospel of Mark tells us of Jesus' meeting with an evil spirit in a synagogue. For Mark, the miracle is an evidence of the authority of Jesus' teaching (1:21-22). According to Mark, nothing is settled in the miracle itself, so long as we do not accept Jesus who breaks through between evil and good. As you move through Mark shift your focus back and forth between the specific and the general—the specific happening recorded and the general convictions of the author as they are unveiled or supported by the happening.

You may want to begin to place on chalkboard or a large sheet of paper the basic convictions about Jesus, humanity, and God's processes of working that Mark is identifying through the events in his narrative. Then as you move along, the group could identify which conviction is expressed or illustrated through the narrative.

Note, for instance, that Mark identifies Jesus as a person of "authority" (1:22). Mark makes this identification in general ways in this chapter. Jesus is first introduced as one whom John the Baptist says is "more powerful than I" (1:7). Mark then introduces Jesus as one with power or authority over "Satan" and "the wild animals" (1:13), fishermen involved in the important task of pursuing their livelihood (1:16, 19), his synagogue congregation (1:21, 27), evil

spirits (1:26, 32), the diseased (1:30, 34), and the outcast (1:40).

Note also the two sides of the personhood of Jesus as portrayed by Mark. On the one hand is the public person: preaching (1:14), teaching (1:21), traveling (1:38), and immersed in meeting human need (1:30-32, 39, 40). On the other hand is the private person: alone in the wilderness (1:12), in one-to-one dialogues (1:17, 29, 40), going out to "a solitary place" (1:35), and desiring nothing to be said publicly about his ministries (1:44). Invite class members to find the public person and the private person in this chapter.

Jesus is also portrayed as a person with a combination of divine power and human empathy. He is sanctioned by God's Spirit, but he is drawn toward humanity in need—either by the size of the need (1:32, 37, 45) or by bridging the distance from society created by the need (persons with mental illness, 1:23; diseases that are physically repulsive, 1:40).

These are insights about Jesus to which Mark introduces us immediately but that will reappear as we continue the journey with Jesus guided by Mark.

DIMENSION THREE: WHAT DOES THE BIBLE MEAN TO ME?

The class may discuss the following topics or use the material that is in the student book.

Who Is He?

The material in Mark 1 lends itself to a discussion focusing on two very important questions related to Jesus: Who is he? What response shall we make to him?

Mark testifies at the outset to his own conviction about who Jesus is. All of Mark's account will have as its intention to bear witness to that truth. It is "Jesus Christ, the Son of God" who is being introduced and defended to the reader.

Some of your class members may never have wrestled with the question, What do I personally believe about Jesus? Most of us have simply accepted the inherited tradition of Christian conviction with little question. The beginning of the study of Mark affords the teacher an excellent opportunity to raise the question as to one's own convictions about Jesus. The study of Mark can then become a joint pilgrimage toward a faith about Jesus that is personal and lasting.

One way to initiate some discussion about your class members' personal belief in Jesus without being personally threatening is to ask whether they feel persons, even in the church, seriously ponder the question as to who Jesus is or what they personally believe about him. Following this discussion, you might move in the direction of inviting class members to share how their own understanding and convictions about Jesus have changed through the years.

As a teacher, feel free to share at the appropriate time your convictions about Jesus. You have your own witness to make that can help others. However, you will need to be cautious that you do not state your convictions in such a way that others then feel hesitant to express differing views or feel defensive to the point of not sharing their own doubts or uncertainties with class members.

Examples of various ways in which persons have expressed their convictions about Jesus can be found in your hymnal. Scan through the hymns to see the ways in which Jesus is characterized, praised, and prayed to.

What Responses Shall We Make?

Mark's perception is that because of who Jesus is and that because he is the means through which God is coming to humanity, a response should take place on the part of all persons whom Jesus encounters. This perception can become more apparent as you and your class members study Mark 1 and note various persons' responses to Jesus.

The first response is John the Baptist's call for repentance from sin in response to the announcement that the Lord is coming (1:3). This response is symbolized in the act of baptism. God through God's Spirit responds to Jesus' baptism with words of identification and endorsement (1:10-11). Angels respond to meet Jesus' needs in the desolate and dangerous wilderness (1:13).

Jesus echoes John's call for repentance and a new experience of belief (1:14-15). These words imply that, by virtue of who Jesus is and what he says, this response should come about. Two sets of fishermen leave their important work, their fellow workers, and even their father in response to Jesus' invitation (1:18, 20). In a sense the fishermen symbolize or illustrate repentance and belief.

The persons in the synagogue respond with awe and puzzlement (1:27). The "evil spirit" within a man responds with fear (1:24). Simon's mother-in-law responds to her healing by ministering to Jesus and the disciples (1:31). The people of the community respond by seeking Jesus, with the resulting loss of his privacy and anonymity (1:32-34, 37, 45). The man healed of leprosy responds, contrary to the direction of Jesus, by proclaiming widely what Jesus has done for him (1:44-45).

The responses here are primarily of two kinds: words and caring deeds. The words may be those of testimony or of inquisitiveness—affirming or searching, proclamation or growth. The caring deeds are expressions of faith and gratitude through the use of hands and feet. They are acts of love done to meet personal needs. Sometimes, as is true of those in this chapter, these acts are in place of words. In Mark 1 those who offer the response of ministering acts say nothing but do something. Class members might share their own awareness of persons who have responded in these different ways to who Jesus is or to what he did for them.

Mark remembers Jesus as one who demonstrates his response to God in these two ways. Jesus boldly but lovingly affirms. He teaches and heals. He speaks to those who come to him, and he goes to care for those who need him. His is a ministry of words and deeds. As Mark displays Jesus in this manner, he is telling us something about the nature of God, which is a part of what makes the news good. As Son of God Jesus functions in the style of God.

If We Are Not Certain

These responses occur because of who Jesus is and what he does. But what about those who are not certain, as may have been some of those fishermen, some in the synagogue, and some in the community? Mark implies that if we will risk commitment, we will make our discovery as he himself did. Albert Schweitzer sums up this discovery in his life as missionary-physician and also in his famous words at the conclusion of his book, *The Quest of the Historical Jesus* (Macmillan, 1968):

> The names in which men expressed their recognition of Him as such, Messiah, Son of Man, Son of God, have become for us historical parables. We can find no designation which expresses what He is for us.

> He comes to us as One unknown, without a name, as of old, by the lake-side, He came to those men who knew Him not. He speaks to us the same word: "Follow thou me!" and sets us to the tasks which He has to fulfil for our time. He commands. And to those who obey Him, whether they be wise or simple, He will reveal Himself in the toils, the conflicts, the sufferings which they shall pass through in His fellowship, and, as an ineffable mystery, they shall learn in their own experience Who He is.

You might wish to close this lesson with prayer.

*The people heard that he had come home. So many gathered
that there was no room left . . . (2:1-2).*

2

The News Went Around

Mark 2–3

DIMENSION ONE:
WHAT DOES THE BIBLE SAY?

Answer these questions by reading Mark 2

1. Where do these events take place? (2:1)

   These events take place at Capernaum.

2. In what unusual way do persons arrange for the paralyzed man to be brought to Jesus' attention? (2:4)

   They remove the roof above him; and when they have made an opening, they lower "the mat the paralyzed man was lying on."

3. What does Jesus see in the companions of the paralyzed man that brings forth this response? (2:5)

   When Jesus sees their faith, he responds with his healing ministry.

4. What is Jesus' response to the men's faith? (2:5, 11)

   First, he says to the paralyzed victim, "Son, your sins are forgiven." Later Jesus says to him, "I tell you, get up, take your mat and go home."

5. What accusation do the critics of Jesus make against him? (2:7)

   They accuse him of blasphemy because God alone can forgive sins.

6. Of what does Jesus want to convince his critics? (2:10)

   He states that the Son of Man has authority on earth to forgive sins.

7. Where is Levi when Jesus meets him? (2:14)

   Levi is sitting in the tax collector's booth.

8. What invitation does Jesus give to Levi? (2:14)

   Jesus says to Levi, "Follow me."

9. Who are Jesus' companions at the meal in Levi's house? (2:15)

   "Many tax collectors and 'sinners' " as well as his disciples are Jesus' companions at the meal in Levi's house.

10. What question do the Pharisees raise? (2:16)

    "Why does he eat with tax collectors and 'sinners'?"

11. How does Jesus describe his own calling? (2:17)

    Jesus says, "It is not the healthy who need a doctor, but the sick. I have not come to call the righteous, but sinners."

12. What difference is noted between the disciples of John the Baptist and those of Jesus? (2:18)

    John's disciples are fasting but the disciples of Jesus are not fasting.

13. What three figures of speech does Jesus use in his reaction? (2:19-22)

    Jesus speaks of the bridegroom's wedding guests, a new piece of unshrunk cloth on an old garment, and new wine in old wineskins.

14. What new criticism is leveled against Jesus? (2:23-24)

    He and his disciples are accused of violating the sabbath by picking heads of grain.

15. What Old Testament story does Jesus recall in response? (2:25-26)

Jesus recalls 1 Samuel 21:1-6. David and his forces were in hiding, cut off from royal favor. He came to Ahimelech (rather than Abiathar), the priest at Nob, and sought food for his forces. The only food available was the consecrated bread in the tabernacle called "the bread of the Presence." Convinced that David's men were holy in their personal lifestyles and mission, the priest gave David the bread that had been taken from the altar to be replaced by new bread on that day.

16. What does Jesus affirm about the sabbath? (2:28)

"The Son of Man is Lord even of the Sabbath."

Answer these questions by reading Mark 3

17. What question does Jesus ask about the sabbath? (3:4)

He asks, "Which is lawful on the Sabbath: to do good or to do evil, to save life or to kill?"

18. What is the congregation's response? (3:4)

They are silent.

19. Why does Jesus ask for a boat to be prepared for his use? (3:9)

He intends to use the boat as a place for speaking to avoid the crush of the crowd.

20. What direction does Jesus give to the "evil spirits"? (3:12)

He orders them not to tell who he is.

21. What are the tasks of the disciples whom Jesus appoints? (3:14-15)

They are to be with him, to be sent out to preach, and to have authority "to drive out demons."

22. Who are the persons Jesus appoints? (3:16-19)

They are Simon Peter, James, John, Andrew, Philip, Bartholomew, Matthew, Thomas, James (son of Alphaeus), Thaddaeus, Simon, and Judas Iscariot.

23. How do the critics of Jesus explain his actions? (3:22)

"He is possessed by Beelzebub! By the prince of demons he is driving out demons."

24. With what figures of speech does Jesus respond? (3:24-27)

He uses the illustrations of a kingdom divided against itself and of a house divided against itself. Neither the kingdom nor the house can stand if divided. Neither can Satan cast out his own demons without coming to an end.

25. What sin does Jesus indicate cannot be forgiven? (3:29)

Jesus says, "whoever blasphemes against the Holy Spirit will never be forgiven."

DIMENSION TWO: WHAT DOES THE BIBLE MEAN?

Two contrasting attitudes appear in Mark's account of the ministry of Jesus. One is that of popular appeal and the other is that of constant criticism. Note that the two attitudes are often present at the same time and place. Each positive action that increases Jesus' admirers also stimulates and enlarges the number of his negative critics.

Mark 2 brings us into the arena of conflict. In outlining this section of Mark, many biblical scholars use the word *controversies* in their title for this portion. Starting with the healing of the man who was paralyzed (2:1-6), Mark mentions in quick succession five controversies that culminate in a decision by the Pharisees and Herodians to plot to destroy Jesus (3:6).

In the introduction to Dimension Two in the previous lesson (which you may wish to read again to see its relevance for today's lesson), we note that one of the characteristics of Mark is that it was written against the backdrop of strong skepticism by Jews and non-Jews about Jesus, his teachings and his lifestyle. The material studied today clearly unveils the nature and forms of that skepticism. As the class examines Mark 2–3, you might lead into an exploration of the nature of both Jesus' critics and their criticisms. List on poster paper or a chalkboard in two columns these two sets of material. This exploration can be a common thread linking together the study of the various episodes in the two chapters. We will try to note parts of this common thread as we examine the passages.

Mark 2:1. The context for this passage begins with 1:35 when Jesus withdraws to a lonely spot for private prayer. His privacy is interrupted by Simon announcing the increasing and urgent desire of people to see him. From now on Jesus will struggle between the search for privacy and his public ministry. The passage suggests that, in Mark's recollection, almost immediately Jesus is popularly received.

Mark 2:2-12. Although the primary focus here is on the healing compassion of Jesus, also notice the enabling compassion of the four companions who make it possible for their friend to receive Jesus' ministry. Their initiative and determination are remarkable. Yet their names are unknown. Ask class members to share stories of anonymous enablers in their own lives whose unsung efforts resulted in deepening class members' spiritual experiences or in their deeper needs being met.

Also, this passage opens up the large subject of the relationship of spirit, mind, and body in sickness and in healing. This subject by itself could occupy an entire class session. You will have to decide whether it will be profitable for class members to pause here for an extended time in the light of their interests and your timetable. To explore this subject adequately might require supplementary reading. Also you might involve outside resource persons or a panel such as your pastor, a physician, and a psychologist or psychiatrist.

Two basic points should be stressed. This story underlines the interrelatedness of the spiritual and the physical. The story also underlines the fact that Jesus repeatedly conveys—that God works as a partner with us for health, not illness.

This partnership between Jesus and God is troublesome to the Jewish officials. Jesus' assertion that he can forgive sin, which only God can do, is at the heart of the first controversy.

Mark 2:13-22. The calling of Levi is more than just a record of Jesus' invitation to an individual to follow him. The invitation unveils a departure from the standard practices of a religious teacher. Indeed, this departure will itself lead to the second controversy: why Jesus is associating with such unsavory people (2:15-17). A Jewish teacher did not usually seek disciples ("learners"); they sought him. Furthermore, the ones who become disciples of a teacher were usually persons of a similar religious background as the teacher.

Jesus departs from this custom by seeking out disciples, not on the basis of who they were but of what they could become. He invites and selects the unpromising because he sees spiritual possibilities in persons if they become open to his Spirit. Jesus comes to Levi at his place of business and then enters with him into his home, much like Jesus' experience with Zacchaeus as recorded in Luke (19:1-10). The story in Luke enlarges the potential meaning to be found in the story of Levi's calling.

Tax collectors in Jesus' day were unpopular people, not simply because they collected money from the Jews. As a group, the tax collectors were seen to be corrupt and self-seeking. They would collect more taxes than were legally due and keep the extra amount as personal gain. Jesus leaps across the barrier of religious and societal prejudice and even sees the potential of a disciple in such a person. Your class members might suggest what persons in our time are often excluded from typical congregational life but who might have potential for discipleship if the congregation is willing to leap over prejudice and come to

them with understanding and new possibilities. Who are today's tax collectors?

This episode and the resulting criticism lead Jesus to discuss the whole area of relating new to old, and this is the foundation of the third controversy: "old" religion versus "new" religion (3:18-22). He first illustrates by referring to "unshrunk cloth." If this cloth is used to patch a hole in a coat, it will soon shrink and tear loose from the surrounding fabric. If new wine is placed in old wineskins, the wine as it ferments will expand and split the containers. If the new and old are not constructively related to each other, they become destructive.

Mark 2:23–3:6. The primary focus here is on 2:27-28 where the new sabbath principle is announced. The stories preceding and following this statement describe two experiences of human need, for food and for health, that are met by Jesus and his disciples on the sabbath. The fourth controversy centers on Jesus' violation of sabbath law by picking grain and is aggravated by his audacity in comparing himself to King David (2:23-28).

The Jewish attitude toward the sabbath had become very legalistic. (Look up the word *sabbath* in a Bible commentary and notice the various references to it in the Jewish law in the Pentateuch, the first five books of the Old Testament.) This basic attitude is initiated in Genesis 2:3 and Deuteronomy 5:12-15. The real purpose of the sabbath had been lost as time passed.

You might take these two Old Testament passages and re-explore with your class members the initial purpose of the sabbath. Note that the sabbath was to be a remembrance and a celebration. Even the "rest" was for the purpose of remembrance and celebration. The celebration was for a universe designed to meet the needs of God's people and a deliverance that met their deep needs.

The fifth controversy also involves a violation of sabbath law that angers the Jewish leaders even more. Not only does Jesus heal a man who does not have a life-threatening ailment, but he also challenges the leaders' own understanding of the purpose of the sabbath—they who consider themselves the guardians of the sabbath laws. It is at this point, very early in the gospel of Mark, that Jesus' fate seems set. "The Pharisees went out and began to plot with the Herodians [usually grave enemies of the Pharisees] how they might kill Jesus" (3:6).

Mark 3:7-19. Note in verse 7 the attempt of Jesus to get away from the crowds, which is typical of Mark's recollections.

A British Methodist minister, a friend of mine, Kenneth Lawton, rendered the Gospel of Mark in a contemporary form, somewhat like Clarence Jordan's *Cotton-Patch Versions* in our country. Lawton's rendering of this passage brings it to life (from *Mark '71*, Galliard Ltd., 1971):

On arrival, he chose twelve comrades to work with him,
to spread the good news, to counteract false rumours and
to rid people of fear and superstition.

The twelve were a mixed bag. A fish farmer, two brothers, one a quiet religious type, the other a worldly man with a bad temper, a customs official, a member of the Communist Party and others, Pete, Jim and his brother John, Andy, Phil, Bill, Matt, Tom, Jack, Tim, Simon and Jake, who in the end was to betray him.

Mark 3:20-27. Jewish thought of Jesus' day contained a hierarchy of devils, the source of peculiar and/or destructive behavior. Beelzebub was part of that hierarchy. The name *Beelzebub* has roots in the pagan god Baal, always a threat to the purity of Jewish worship after they arrived in the Promised Land. (See Numbers 25:3; 1 Kings 18:18; 2 Kings 10:28; and Jeremiah 23:13.)

Mark 3:28-30. A primary interest of many class members will be verses 28-29 that mention the sin against the Holy Spirit, or the unforgivable sin. The haunting influence of this passage is a tragedy. In counseling I have seen this result in many depressed or guilt-ridden persons who felt they must have committed the sin that "will never be forgiven." Pathetically, I have even known persons hospitalized with emotional illness born out of a fear of falling into this condition. Special care should be taken so as not to create misconceptions or re-enforce sick fears over this issue.

Look carefully at this verse: "Whoever blasphemes against the Holy Spirit will never be forgiven." In other words, forgiveness has not been denied but has never been sought. If one never seeks forgiveness (which is what the Holy Spirit leads us to do), then one may never find it or experience it. It is a matter of plain logic rather than a law of divine retribution.

Mark 3:31-35. Here is a new definition of the Christian family. Chapters 2 and 3 have been marked by repeated examples of inclusion on Jesus' part: the crowds, the man who was paralyzed, the tax collectors and sinners, the needy persons healed on the sabbath, the strange Twelve. The climax is the affirmation and invitation to all who "do the will of God" to be seen as Jesus' family."

DIMENSION THREE:
WHAT DOES THE BIBLE MEAN TO ME?

Invitation to New Possibilities

Because of the length of Mark 2–3 and the number of issues raised within it, it is going to be difficult to cover this material in one class session. If you are not under the pressure of doing this, you may even find two or three sessions would not be too much time to spend on these chapters. Otherwise, you will have to pick and choose where to concentrate and possibly not cover all the verses. One approach would be to assign topics to individuals or

teams for study in advance of the class session and ask them to report their findings to the entire class.

Here are some of the topics and issues arising out of these passages in Mark that lend themselves to discussion and exploration:

The ministries of enablement (2:3-5, 17; 3:9, 14-15);
The interrelationship of spirit, mind, and body (2:5-11; 3:5, 10-11);
The nature of his call (2:13-14, 17; 3:13-19, 33-35);
Christian inclusiveness (2:14-17; 3:11, 13-19, 33-35);
A time to laugh and a time to weep (2:18-20);
The new versus the old (2:6-9, 16-22; 3:2-6, 22-26, 32-35);
The sabbath through Jesus' eyes (2:23–3:6);
The spirits and the Spirit (3:11-12, 22-30);
The sin against the Spirit (3:28-29).

Underneath all these issues is Mark's presentation of Jesus as bringing new life and light to the surface. The church has always had difficulty at this point. By nature the church has been involved in preserving, even defending, the past. Thus the church has a difficult time determining what is the appropriate attitude, ranging from hesitation to fear for confronting the new. Yet we must remember the New Testament reveals the gospel of Christ's coming and of God's grace to us. We are invited into a new covenant. How does your congregation react to the new? How do you as individual Christians react to the new? If we believe God still speaks by the Spirit, are we open to a new word?

After you and your class members have spent as much time as possible studying the passages and topics, it would be well as a summary to list convictions that arise out of the total passages such as

- In God's eyes meeting human need takes precedence over legal customs and society's barriers.
- God sees promise where we feel only prejudice.
- The Christian walk is more of joyous expression than of solemn repression.
- God has new truths that old outlooks may not have.
- Christ's priorities become our sabbath principles.
- Jesus has more confidence in persons than some persons have in others.
- All can be forgiven except the unwillingness to seek or to receive forgiveness.
- Wider and wider God's circle expands beyond ours.

As a follow-up to this last affirmation, William Barclay in his commentary on 3:31-35 states, "Here Jesus lays down the conditions of true kinship" (*The Gospel of Mark*, Daily Study Bible Series, revised edition, Westminster Press, 1975; page 82). Barclay then perceives that true spiritual kinship as lying in a common experience, a common interest, a common obedience, and a common goal. This understanding sums up what these two chapters summon us to have or to find.

He taught them many things by parables (4:2).

3

The Master Teacher

Mark 4:1-34

DIMENSION ONE:
WHAT DOES THE BIBLE SAY?

Answer these questions by reading Mark 4:1-34

1. Where does Jesus begin to teach? (4:1)

   Jesus begins to teach beside the lake.

2. Where does Jesus carry this out? (4:1)

   He gets into a boat because of the size and congestion of the crowd. He teaches from the boat to his hearers who were seated along the shore at the water's edge.

3. How does Jesus communicate with his hearers? (4:2)

   He uses parables.

4. Who is the subject of the first story Jesus tells? (4:3)

   The first parable reported in this chapter is about a farmer sowing seeds.

5. Where do the seeds fall as they are thrown from the sower's hands? (4:4-8)

   Some seeds fall along the path, some on rocky ground, some among thorns, and some fall into good soil.

6. What happened to the seeds in the various places where they fell? (4:4-8)

   The seeds that fell along the path were eaten up by birds. The seeds that fell on rocky places sprouted quickly but died quickly because their roots did not penetrate deeply enough to pick up water to enable the plant to survive under the sun's heat. The seeds that fell among the thorns were choked. The seeds that fell on the good soil grew into fruitful plants with sizable yields.

7. To whom, does Jesus say, has the secret of the kingdom of God been given? (4:11)

   The secret is given to the disciples.

8. How do those outside the kingdom of God react to the parables? (4:12)

   Those who are outside see but do not perceive, hear but do not understand; otherwise they might turn and be forgiven.

9. In the interpretation by Jesus what is the sower represented as sowing? (4:14)

   The sower sows the word.

10. What regrettable things happen in some persons who receive what the sower distributes? (4:15-19)

    When the ones sown along the path hear the word, Satan comes and takes away the word. When the ones sown upon rocky ground hear the word, they receive it with joy, and endure for a while; then, when trouble or persecution arises on account of the word, they fall away. When the ones sown among thorns hears the word, the word is choked by the cares of the world, the delight in riches, and the desire for other things.

11. What hopeful things happen in those persons who are the "good soil"? (4:20)

    They "hear the word, accept it, and produce a crop—thirty, sixty or even a hundred times what is sown."

12. What is the next figure of speech Jesus uses? (4:21)

    The next figure of speech used in his teaching is a lamp.

13. What is supposed to be done with it? (4:21-22)

    A lamp is supposed to be put on a stand to give light to that which is concealed and secret.

14. What lesson does Jesus draw from this parable? (4:22)

The hidden things ultimately come out into the open and the secret things are disclosed.

15. What determines what we receive? (4:24)

The measure we give determines the measure we get.

16. What contrast does Jesus draw between one who has and one who has not? (4:25)

"Whoever has will be given more; whoever does not have, even what he has will be taken from him."

17. What happens to the seed sown in the next parable? (4:26-29)

This seed sprouts and grows through the full cycle of development until it is ready for harvest.

18. What figure of speech does Jesus next use to describe the kingdom of God? (4:31)

Jesus says the kingdom of God is like a mustard seed.

19. What is unusual about this kind of seed? (4:31)

The mustard seed is one of the smallest of all the seeds on earth.

20. How often did Jesus use parables in his public teaching? (4:33-34)

Jesus used parables in all his teaching sessions, and he used many different parables.

21. What did he do privately with his disciples? (4:34)

Privately Jesus explained everything to his disciples.

DIMENSION TWO:
WHAT DOES THE BIBLE MEAN?

Up to this point in Mark, most of the teachings of Jesus that we have encountered have been statements in response to events that have taken place. Often Jesus' teachings have been explanations given in reaction to criticisms. Now we encounter teachings of Jesus that do not appear to be tied to a specific event. Of course, they are related to the whole nature of his ministry and what is happening as a result of it.

This lesson focuses on Jesus in his teaching role. While most of the study period may be spent on these specific passages in Mark, you might also find value in exploring the various methods Jesus uses to inform and guide his hearers. Ask class members: How do you learn from others? What were the means through which your most memorable teachers brought insight to you?

Apparently Jesus had both formal and informal teaching sessions. By formal, we mean certain periods and occasions that were set aside for the purpose of instruction. The set of teachings appearing in this chapter of Mark illustrates one of those sessions. Jewish religious leaders, the rabbis, commonly used this practice. Although today *rabbi* is the formal title of an ordained person in the Jewish ministry, originally it was simply a title of respect meaning "master." *Rabbi* referred to one who was a master of the Jewish law and who could teach the law to others. Disciples ("learners") would cluster around such persons who would then conduct teaching sessions. Jesus was expressing himself in this style and was thus called a rabbi. (See John 1:38, 49; 3:2. See also Jesus' reaction to this title in Matthew 23:8.)

By *informal*, we mean conversations held while walking down the roadways, especially comments or observations made on the journey. *Informal* means casual dialogues with inquirers or chance acquaintants. *Informal* means late evening reflection with a chosen few. *Informal* means question-and-answer sessions. Often teaching was done by lifestyle. Who a teacher was and how he acted taught as much or more than just what the teacher said. Was not the cross the greatest object lesson in all history?

Not only did Jesus use the customary manners of Jewish religious teachers, he also used some of their styles of teaching. The use of parables is a case in point. Parables had been an important vehicle of conveying truth. By using what was familiar to people to introduce them to what was new, teaching became both attractive and understandable. In the Old Testament tradition, parables also had been an important vehicle of conveying truth. A moving illustration of this for you to use is the Twenty-third Psalm. We can almost quote this psalm from memory without having intentionally memorized it. Why is this? The figures of speech are easily understood and remembered. These figures of speech help us remember the spiritual truths the psalmist conveyed through them, which together form a parable.

This method of teaching was used by Old Testament patriarchs (Jacob in Genesis 49:22-25), by the philosophers who wrote the Wisdom Literature (Proverbs 9:1-6; Ecclesiastes 9:13-17), and by the prophets (Isaiah 5:1-7; Hosea 3; 11:1-5). The whole story of Jonah is more than just a biography; it is a parable of Israel's relationship with God. Perhaps the most dramatic use of the parable in the tradition inherited by Jesus is the incident in which the prophet Nathan confronts David with harsh truth by involving David first in sympathy with an exploited character in a parable Nathan told. (See 2 Samuel 12:1-14.)

Thus Jesus does not invent new methods of teaching. Rather, what he does is to use the traditional methods of

THE MASTER TEACHER

teaching. Thus the public tends to identify him as a rabbi or prophet. Yet Jesus does more. He enhances these methods by his skillful use, by the profound nature of the new truths he seeks to convey, and by immersing them into his lifestyle.

Mark 4:1-2, 33-34. Read carefully the explanatory notes on these verses in the student book. They give some important background material.

The English word *parable* comes from a Latin word, *parabola,* which means "comparison." The Greek word, *parabolé,* which literally means to "place beside," is the word Mark, Matthew, and Luke use. Thus a parable is a saying designed to convey meaning by the means of comparison or placing concepts beside pictures. The picture may simply be a figure of speech or a long story. However, parables are not limited to stories. The most famous parables come to us from the Bible and are used to impart spiritual truths.

Mark 4:3-9, 13-20. You might do well to place these two sections together in your study process (as well as verses 26-29 noted later), since they give the parable of the sower and its meaning. The commentary by Jesus that separates the two sections could be considered separately. Point out to your class members that the same parable appears in Matthew 13:2-9, 18-23 and in Luke 8:5-8, 11-15 almost word-for-word. Indeed, these chapters in Matthew and Luke are almost identical in their entirety with Mark 4 and give a good example of how Mark is incorporated into these other two Gospels.

The seeds that fell along the path were picked up and eaten by birds before the seeds sank into the soil. The seeds that fell on the topsoil among rocks sprouted quickly but died quickly because their roots did not penetrate deeply enough to pick up water to enable the plant to survive under the sun's heat. The seeds that fell among the weeds and briars were shut off from sunlight and moisture by the growing tangles of the briar patch. The seeds that fell on the good soil grew into fruitful plants with sizable yields.

This parable is actually not so much a parable of the sower as it is a parable of the soil. The focus is on the various results that occur from the same kind of seed being planted in different places. The result in life or death, growth or struggle, depends on the receptivity of the soil. The soils described are exactly the types of soils you find in Palestine. If, by chance, you have among your class members someone who has visited Israel or Jordan, you might ask that person to share some pictures or slides of the type of terrain found in the rural areas. It is, indeed, rocky soil, some areas having only a thin layer of fertile topsoil. The two burdensome aspects of farming in the Holy Land are clearing the rocks and finding enough water.

In looking for the meanings of this parable you will want to identify the results of the seeds' contact with the earth. Class members may want to recall persons who are described by the various results: (1) Those who are exposed to the word that God communicates but never take it

seriously and give it little heed. The words of others influence them more than the sower's word. (2) Those who know momentary excitement when God sends them his word but develop no permanent allegiance. Their spiritual experience is one of surface feeling rather than deep-rooted commitment. When the word costs "blood, sweat, or tears," it is abandoned. (3) Those to whom God conveys his word but who fall victim to the competition for the attention of other words. (4) Those who not only hear God communicating but allow that word to put down the roots required and to be nourished by God-implanted resources within. The resulting growth produced a great harvest.

Since the natural tendency is to think of persons other than themselves, you may have to encourage class members to ask of themselves: What kind of soil am I? What has happened within me to the new word that God wants to implant? In telling parables, Jesus wants each hearer to relate its meaning to herself or himself, not to someone else.

Another interesting form of growth-discussion is to ask whether the nature of the "soil" within us varies with the kind of word God gives us. To some of his words of truth and summons we are receptive, fertile soil. To some we become shallow, infertile soil. Some words from God we gladly let blow away. Why the difference?

Mark 4:10-12. The King James translation of this passage uses the word *mystery* for *secret* in verse 11. *Mystery* is a more literal translation because the Greek word here is *mysterion.* This Greek word, however, did not mean a mystery in the sense of a puzzle to be solved, but rather something not commonly understood but understandable to those "on the inside." Some organizations are named with initials that are meaningless to those outside the organization. The member, however, knows the meaning of those initials.

The parables of Jesus are also received like this. The casual observer may discover no meaning; but those who have entered into the "mind of Christ," who have developed by immersion into his Spirit a new sensitivity, see even the commonplace testifying to his word.

This passage is often viewed as one of the most difficult in the Gospels because it seems to suggest that the truth of God is deliberately coded to avoid its discovery and a new relationship with God from resulting. The roots of the passage are from Isaiah 6 describing the famous call of the prophet. We usually stop reading the Isaiah passage in verse 8 with the words, "Here am I. Send me!" Yet the passage goes on to call the prophet to preach even though the people do not respond. Remember that the Isaiah passage was written long after the actual event. Recalling the failure of the people to respond, in retrospect it seems that Isaiah was called to make a witness that would not be heard. Jesus borrows Isaiah's imagery to indicate that his experience might be the same. Yet he knows some persons do hear, understand, and respond. They are those who by circumstance or commitment have become open to new truth.

The passage is not meant to say that God shuts people out; but rather that, in spite of the potential obviousness of God's truth, people shut themselves out. The parable of the sower also illustrates this phenomenon.

Mark 4:15-19. Some receive the word but Satan carries off the word immediately after they hear it, so that the word has no lasting influence or permanence. Some receive the word with joy, but the joy is short-lived because the word's abode in them is short. Its influence and power last only through the period of exhilaration. The word is entertained only so long as it is entertaining; but when a price has to be paid through persecution or stressful fidelity to the gospel, the hearers of the word choose to drop the word and listen elsewhere for other words that offer more good feelings. In some the word is choked out by the luster of temporary gains such as material well-being. These priorities can pop up fast and choke the slow but steady growth toward spiritual growth.

Mark 4:21-32. Here we have four short parables. The story portion or picture is conveyed in one to three sentences. They are like a series of slides flashed on the screen, held there for just a moment for pondering and then quickly replaced by another. They are also more typical of the style of Mark than is the parable of the sower and seeds. Mark tends to be rapid-fire in form. He moves quickly from one event to another and from one teaching to another. The word pictures Mark recalls Jesus using are primarily brief and to the point. Most of them speak for themselves.

The third parable (verses 26-29), another parable about seeds, may have been a sequel to the earlier one in this chapter. It would be well to consider this parable along with verses 3-9 and 13-20. While the first parable emphasizes sowing, the second one emphasizes waiting. The first parable deals with doing the job; the second deals with letting the job go. The two rhythms are essential in responsible Christian discipleship—working and waiting—and trying to discover when to do which.

Helmut Thielicke, a German professor and pastor, in his book *The Waiting Father* (Harper & Row, 1959; pages 91-92) speaks of this twofold rhythm unveiled in this second parable:

> The fanatics who believe that man can "make" everything are really fools at bottom. They are not realistic at all, even though they have the cold, sober eyes of hardheaded men of fact. But the man who has grasped the mystery of the seed growing secretly and, like the farmer in the parable, goes out and does his part of the job and then commits the fields to God and lies down to sleep in his name—that man is doing not only the most godly thing but the wisest thing. For godliness and wisdom are far more closely related than our philosophy and the wisdom of the "managers" ever dream.

DIMENSION THREE: WHAT DOES THE BIBLE MEAN TO ME?

What Is the Purpose of Parables?

The parables of Jesus all have the same intent—to convey spiritual truth—but they do not all have the same specific purpose. At least three purposes are served by the use of parables: One purpose is to convey information or understanding. The parables of new patches on old garments and new wine in old wineskins previously studied (2:21-22) are examples of this intent, as well as that of the divided house (3:23-26). In this passage the parable of the sower and seed and that of the secret growth illustrate this purpose.

A second purpose of parables is to influence our feelings or attitudes. The second parable of the seed (4:26-29) calls us to an attitude of hopeful relinquishment of whatever we have done into the hands and power of God.

A third purpose of parables is to stimulate and mold our actions—to get us to do something. The parables of the lamp (4:21-22) and the measure of giving (4:24-25) stir us to be generous with our light of influence and our resources. We need to have a purpose for what we do with what we are and what we have.

Keep these purposes in mind as you encounter other parables in Mark. Continually ask, What is the purpose of this parable?

The common, traditional interpretation is that a parable is designed to teach one truth and one truth only. Personally, I have reservations about this concept. The concept may have originated out of a desire to distinguish between an allegory and a parable. In an allegory each component part represents something, while this is not necessarily true in a parable. Many parables do have only one primary message to convey. Yet I do not think the interpretations of parables have to be restricted to one meaning and one only.

Underlying all the parables is the remarkable ability of Jesus to perceive where the interests of his hearers are and what will communicate the greatest of truths to them in an understandable and thought-provoking way. His parables also give evidence of the sensitivity of Jesus to the ways of God that can be found in the lifestream that surrounds humanity. Jesus could hear God around him and hear the nature of persons. Jesus' psychological and spiritual receivers were finely tuned to hear God clearly all around Jesus and to unveil this to persons whose inner lives and needs he also knew so well.

We all should seek this spirit; we desperately need it. Yet it is not found as much through struggle as through relinquishment, as much through studious research as in pauses to hear what is readily available.

As you reflect on Mark 4:1-34 and the points made through the parables—with the parables of the sower, seed, and secret growth being the centerpiece—lead the class members to a moment of personal re-examination. As the group sits in quiet reflection, questions like these might be asked with a pause after each for them to ponder:

- If Jesus sat down with us today, what would he want to teach us?
- If he told us the story of the seed being sown, which type of soil are we?
- What word do we really not want to hear from Jesus, and which word have we already blocked out?
- What special light is needed for those around us right now but which we have hidden or even blown out?
- What have we *not* been willing to give and as a result have robbed ourselves of?
- Where do we need, having done all, to stop and wait expectantly for God to act?
- What little thing can we do for God's kingdom that God will multiply?

(These questions might also be copied in advance for the class members to take home after the session and to consider during the next week as a follow-up exercise.)

Who is this? Even the wind and the waves obey him (4:41b)!

4

The Miracle Worker

Mark 4:35–6:6

DIMENSION ONE:
WHAT DOES THE BIBLE SAY?

Answer these questions by reading Mark 4:35-41

1. Where is Jesus heading and with whom? (4:35-36)

   Jesus sets sail with the disciples with whom he has been meeting privately. They head for the other side of the Sea of Galilee.

2. What unexpected misfortune do they encounter? (4:37)

   A furious squall arises, and the waves break over the boat, so that the boat is nearly swamped.

3. Where is Jesus at this time? (4:38)

   Jesus is asleep on a cushion in the stern of the boat.

4. What do the disciples cry out to Jesus? (4:38)

   They shout in fear, "Teacher, don't you care if we drown?"

5. What does Jesus do? (4:39-40)

   He rebukes the winds and waves with the words, "Quiet! Be still!" The storm ceases and a calm occurs.

6. What is the reaction of the disciples? (4:41)

   They are filled with terror and awe.

Answer these questions by reading Mark 5

7. What is the shocking nature of the person Jesus meets on arriving at the other side of the lake? (5:2-5) What is this person's name? (5:9)

   A man with an "evil spirit" runs out of the tombs (or caves) where he has been living in exile from the community. He is crying aloud and is bruised from self-inflicted wounds and from chains that he has broken loose. He flings himself down in front of Jesus and says his name is "Legion."

8. What does this person shout out to Jesus? (5:7)

   Loudly, he shouts, "What do you want with me, Jesus, Son of the Most High God? Swear to God that you won't torture me!"

9. What does Jesus say to this tormented one? (5:8) What strange result takes place? (5:11-13)

   Jesus calls on the evil spirits to come out of the man. Then these spirits enter a herd of pigs nearby who stampede down the bank, falling into the lake, and drown.

10. When the people come to see what was happening, what do they see? (5:14-15) What are their reactions? (5:15, 17)

    They find the ill man sitting, dressed and in his right mind. So changed is he that they are afraid. They plead with Jesus to leave their area.

11. What is the healed man's request? (5:18)

    He begged Jesus to allow him to go with Jesus.

12. Instead, what different direction does Jesus give him? (5:19) What does the man do? (5:20)

    Jesus tells him to go to his own family at home and tell them what merciful things God has done for him. He does this, and he also spreads the news in the ten surrounding towns. (The Greek word for the ten towns is Decapolis.)

13. Who is Jairus, and what request does he make? (5:22-23)

   Jairus is a synagogue ruler. He comes in distress to report the serious illness of his daughter. He pleads with Jesus to come and lay his healing hands upon her to save her life.

14. How does Jesus respond? (5:24a)

   Jesus goes with Jairus toward his house.

15. What is the need of the next person among the crowd who seeks out Jesus? (5:25-26) Why does she turn to him? (5:27-28)

   A woman has been plagued for twelve years with bleeding that has not improved in spite of treatment by several physicians. She hears from others about Jesus' healing powers. She thinks if only she can touch his clothes, she can be cured.

16. What does she do, and what is the result? (5:27-29)

   She comes up behind Jesus and touches his cloak. She immediately knows she is freed from her suffering.

17. What question does Jesus ask? (5:30)

   Jesus turns around and, looking at the crowd, asks, "Who touched my clothes?"

18. What is the woman's feeling in response to his question? (5:33)

   Trembling with fear, she comes and falls at Jesus' feet, telling him all that has taken place.

19. What reassurance does Jesus give her? (5:34)

   He tells her that her faith has brought healing to her, which should forever free her from this illness. He encourages her to "go in peace."

20. What sad news comes from the ruler's house? (5:35)

   A messenger reports that Jairus's daughter has died.

21. What counsel does Jesus give? (5:36)

   He counsels Jairus, "Don't be afraid; just believe."

22. What is Jesus' reaction to the grief at the house of Jairus? (5:39)

   Jesus says, "Why all this commotion and wailing? The child is not dead but asleep."

23. What amazing event then takes place? (5:40-43)

   Jesus takes the parents and his own disciples into the room where the child is. After taking hold of the child's hand, he says, "Little girl, I say to you, get up!" To the overwhelming astonishment of those present, the little girl arises and walks around the room.

Answer these questions by reading Mark 6:1-6

24. Where do Jesus and the disciples go? (6:1)

   They return to Nazareth, "his hometown."

25. What is the synagogue congregation's reaction to Jesus? (6:2-3)

   They are amazed, perplexed, full of questions, and offended by him.

26. In this connection what does Jesus say about a prophet? (6:4)

   "Only in his hometown, among his relatives and in his own house is a prophet without honor."

27. What was the effect of their reaction on Jesus' ministry there? (6:5-6)

   While he helps a few persons who are sick, Jesus is unable to do miracles there. "He was amazed at their lack of faith."

DIMENSION TWO:
WHAT DOES THE BIBLE MEAN?

Just as Mark 4:1-34 focuses on Jesus as a teacher, Mark 4:35–6:6 focuses on Jesus as a miracle worker. Here are recorded events that brought amazed awe to the observers and elevated for them and for the readers the image of Jesus. Recall for your class members what was emphasized in the first lesson—Mark's theme as stated in 1:1. Mark wants us to know not just the biographical data about Jesus. He wants us to know the unique person that Jesus was—the Son of God!

Mark's account has already revealed a growing tension between who Jesus actually was and the suspicion and doubt some observers had about him. We have to admire Mark for his honesty in reporting. A recurring pattern in the presentation of material in Mark is the recognition of Jesus, the negative reaction to Jesus, and the validation by Jesus. In essence, Mark wants us to see Jesus, then to see the varying reactions to Jesus, and then convince us beyond the shadow of any doubt that Jesus is indeed the Son of God. Mark's method is admirable. He realized that among his ancient readers many, if not most, would be skeptical of the claims and the admiration for Jesus. He lets these readers identify with the skeptics and critics whom he describes confronting Jesus. They can find themselves reflected in the accounts. But after a while Mark comes through with a clear affirmation of the nature of Jesus as the Christ, trying to turn the tide of doubt forever for his readers.

So 4:35–6:6 is designed to tell us who Jesus is: a master teacher in the style of the greatest of rabbis, a miracle worker who excels even the prophets in the signs that come from God to affirm his ministry and his personhood.

As you begin this lesson ask the class members: What different opinions about Jesus have emerged thus far in Mark's account? Or you might ask: What might be your opinion of Jesus if all you knew of him was what you had read in Mark 1:1–4:34?

Mark 4:35-41. Note the description of the Sea (or Lake) of Galilee in the commentary on this section in the student book. If you have some class members who have traveled to Israel, invite them to bring a few slides or photos of the Sea of Galilee and the surrounding hills.

This dramatic account has several items worth identifying to class members. One is the contrast between the serenity of Jesus and the fear of the disciples. Jesus lies asleep in the midst of the storm. Was this simply physical weariness, or a profound trust in the "Ruler of wind and wave"?

The story also testifies to the mastery of Jesus over the physical elements of the universe. He *rebukes* the wind and the sea. Mark shows his readers that in Jesus you have divinity in action, for no one else could do these things. (See verse 41.)

The other item worth identifying to class members is faith. Faith can be perfected in discipleship. Faith is primarily a matter of trust in the acts of Jesus. This passage also was used by the early church to relate this story to many kinds of threats and dangers faced by Christians.

This story is the first of three boat scenes in Mark. (See 6:45-52; 8:14-21.) At the heart of the story is Jesus' question, "Why are you so afraid? Do you still have no faith?" (4:40). Questions for possible discussion by you and class members are the following: What is the role of faith in times of personal crisis? What should faith do for us? What should we not expect faith to do for us? Does faith overrule normal human feelings and fears, or does it help us confront and direct them? What is faith anyway?

Mark 5:1-20. In connection with this story you might recall an episode from Shakespeare's play, *Macbeth*. In Act V, Scene 3, Lady Macbeth has become the victim of mental illness. She imagines bloody spots that cannot be washed away and has wild and lonely conversations with herself. Macbeth inquires of the physician tending her,

"How does your patient, Doctor?"

He responds,

"Not so sick, my lord,
as she is troubled with thick-coming fancies
that keep her from her rest."

Macbeth insists,

"Cure her of that."

Then follows his famous question:

"Canst thou not minister to a mind diseased,
Pluck from the memory a rooted sorrow,
Raze out the written troubles of the brain,
And with some sweet oblivious antidote
Cleanse the stuffed bosom of that perilous stuff
Which weighs upon the heart?"

The physician responds,

"Therein the patient
Must minister to himself."

These seventeenth-century words also apply to the first century. Then, as now, an attitude of rejection leading to the isolation of persons with mental illness is common. Jesus comes to one who is stigmatized as being under the domination of an "evil spirit," whose treatment is a strait jacket ("chains") and exile to the tombs to be one of the living dead. The description of the man in this passage suggests an alienation from God, from the people of his community, and from himself. Tormented to the brink of suicide, no wonder he fears Jesus who comes to him. The only others who had come to him had come to ridicule or to hurt.

A study commissioned by the US Congress in 1961 to study the mental health needs of our nation included this observation among its discoveries: "It is a characteristic of the mentally ill that they behave in an irresponsible manner; it is a characteristic of society that we behave toward them in the same manner" (*Action for Mental Health*, Final Report of the Joint Commission on Mental Illness and Health, 1961; Basic Books, 1961; page 93). In spite of encouraging discoveries in medicine and science, public attitude sadly has not changed much throughout the years.

Jesus does not act this way, however. Not only do we see a man who was misunderstood, but we see a man who seeks to understand. Jesus dared to defy the traditional reaction to those who are emotionally ill. First of all, Jesus went to the man where he was. His situation was not only isolated but also considered ritually unclean for the Jews. The second thing Jesus did was to believe that the person actually could be helped, that the person possibly was curable. The third thing he did was to talk with the man, to identify with his needs, and to become aware of the fact of the multiplicity of causes within him. In advance of his day Jesus understood this interrelation of mind, body, and spirit, and was aware of exactly why this man was saying, "My name is Legion . . . we are many [persons]."

Is *Legion* a good name for each one of us? One mark of personal growth is when we have been able to accept and then recognize the several persons we are. For many years I kept on my desk this anonymously written poem:

Within my earthly temple there's a crowd
There's one that's humble, and one that's proud.
There's one that cares for naught but fame and self.
There's one who's broken-hearted for his sins.
There's one who, unrepentant, sits and grins.
From such perplexing care would I be free
If I could only once discover which is me.

Then Jesus walked with the man back into life again, helped him bridge the gap so that he might move back into society. Then that strange tragedy is compounded. The second tragedy is almost worse than the first. The first tragedy is the illness of the man and the results of the illness. The second tragedy is when he is sitting with Jesus, clothed, neat, in his right mind, rational, and the people come out to see what has happened. They see him sitting there, well, in his right mind, restored, under control; and they are afraid! They say to Jesus, "Please leave our territory," because Jesus dared to understand.

As a teenager I remember observing a long, high wall near downtown Columbia, South Carolina. That wall was about twice as high as the average person as I recall it. It extended for blocks. I used to wonder with youthful curiosity why the wall was there and what was on the other side. I later learned that on the other side of the wall was a state mental hospital. Several years ago the wall was torn down and made into a decorative, low wall. They took the bricks, which had formed the high wall by which people in society were separated from the sick and the sick were kept from moving into society, and used them to build a chapel on the campus of the state hospital. I see something symbolic there, symbolic of the nature of Christ, and something of what society is called to do and to be and to understand.

Mark 5:21-24, 35-43. The location of the synagogue whose ruler comes to Jesus is not given. In Mark 1, Jesus appeared in a synagogue in Capernaum, and while there cleansed a person of an evil spirit (1:21-28). Those in the synagogue were "amazed" and proclaimed that with authority "he even gives orders to evil spirits and they obey him." Possibly Jesus is heading back to Capernaum, which seems from Mark's perspective to have been the headquarters of Jesus' Galilean ministry. Jairus may have been the ruler (or president) of that synagogue in Capernaum and may have been present, even presiding, on that sabbath when the event took place described in Mark 1. This may explain why he turned to Jesus with such hope and expectancy.

Point out to class members that in telling the story Mark sets up every possible barrier to Jesus' achieving anything. First is the factor of distance—Jesus is distant from the sick child. Second, Jesus is delayed en route by the event of the healing of the woman with a chronic illness. Third, the child dies before Jesus arrives. Fourth, those at the bedside are skeptical not only of Jesus' power but even of his accurate understanding of what has taken place. "They laughed at him" (5:40).

Yet Jesus has the last laugh, the laughter of celebration! " 'Little girl, I say to you, get up.' Immediately the girl stood up and walked around" (4:41-42).

A new pattern by Jesus is introduced in this story. As they come to the ruler's house, Jesus allows no one to accompany him except Peter, James, and John. Thus the inner circle of disciples is established that will appear on some future occasions. No reasons are given in any of the Gospels for this reduction in the number of those to be with Jesus, or why these particular ones are chosen. Perhaps your class members might speculate on why Jesus chose an inner circle, and what it was about these persons that led them to be included in that circle. Was it on the basis of congeniality, need, potential, or merit?

Mark 5:25-34. This story tells of the healing of a chronic illness. Four "impossibles" for which nothing seemingly could be done were (1) physical calamity, (2) mental illness (demon-possession), (3) chronic illnesses, and (4) death. All society in Jesus' day accepted that these are tragic ultimates for which there was little, if any, relief. Yet Mark collects together these four episodes and through them testifies that Jesus as the Christ can deal with even the impossibles of life. The ultimates yield to his ministry. Thus Jesus must be the Son of God. The fact that one need only touch Jesus' garment brings the image of his power and potential for others one step nearer.

Mark 6:1-6. This section begins with a summary of the sense of reverence and awe given to Jesus. Part of that awe is perplexity, for Jesus has not announced who he is. Indeed, Mark wants us to know who Jesus is; it is privileged information known at this point only by us and the "evil spirits" (1:24; 5:7). This identification is the "messianic secret" to be revealed at the proper time in Jesus' perspective. Another source of perplexity is simply, How could someone of such common origins and humble background do what he has done? ("Isn't this the carpenter?" [6:3].) This type of questioning lays the foundation for Mark's thesis: The only explanation can be that God is in this person, for only God can do these things.

DIMENSION THREE: WHAT DOES THE BIBLE MEAN TO ME?

The class may discuss the following topic or use the material that is in the student book.

The Fear of the Uncontrollable

Although the intent of Mark in this section has been to clarify and affirm the nature of Jesus as the Son of God, we would miss something important if we did not notice some human issues that also run like a common thread through these episodes. Ask class members to look again at the disciples in the boat, Legion on the hillside, the woman on the roadway, and the ruler of the synagogue. Is there anything in common to all these different persons?

One unfortunate common trait to all of them is their fear of the uncontrollable. For the disciples it was the waves and winds. For Legion it was the tormenting spirits within and the tormenting persons around. For the woman it was the persistent, long-term loss of her vital bodily fluid. For Jairus it was the impending threat of death. All these persons were confronted by what seemed beyond control; and as a result, they were desperate.

So much of life today is haunted by this fear of the uncontrollable. Ask class members to list some of the elements in contemporary life that seem uncontrollable (competition, inflation, cancer, drug traffic, and so forth). In the midst of these besetting fears common to so many of us of all ages, we cry out for help.

To each of these desperate persons caught up in their various forms of fear of the uncontrollable, Jesus comes. He hears, he heeds, he helps, he hopes for, and he is with them, and he calls them to a new maturity of sustaining faith. Dr. Monroe Gilmour, an internist in Charlotte, North Carolina, and a committed Christian, once said in a lecture to his Presbytery, "If I am to help a patient, I must first discover what that person fears."

Jesus used the same therapeutic philosophy. When Jesus asks, "Do you still have no faith?" (4:40), he is asking two things. First, What is it that you fear so much that it dominates your attention and paralyzes your ability to respond? Second, In what form or content could you draw upon faith to help you find perspective and/or power to drain off the fear?

This exercise might be a way your class members can minister to one another. Give each person a number and ask each person to write that number on a piece of paper. Ask each person to write their greatest fear on the other side of the paper. Do not sign the paper. Each person should fold his or her paper and pass it to you. Use the material in one of two possible ways.

First, give each class member one slip of paper. Ask members to write on that paper how they would use the resources of faith to confront the fear they read there. Then have them fold the papers and give them to you. You will then return the papers to their original writers by the numbers on the sheets.

Another way would be to list on a large sheet of paper or chalkboard all the fears named on the sheets. Then invite the class members to discuss and share out of their own experience in what ways faith has enabled them to deal with each fear listed.

The passage studied ends with two pathetic commentaries. One is the famous statement about a prophet at home (6:4). The other is that Jesus "could not do any miracles there" due to their unbelief (6:5-6). Jesus stands on our threshold with his divine possibilities. He comes to us in whatever alienated or fearful state we may be, but he breaks no doors down. He stands ready with his divine resources to calm the troubled breast and to create new possibilities. Our faith opens the door.

5

Under Orders

Mark 6:7-56

DIMENSION ONE:
WHAT DOES THE BIBLE SAY?

Answer these questions by reading Mark 6:7-56

1. Whom does Jesus call? (6:7)

   He calls the twelve disciples to himself.

2. Why does Jesus call them? (6:7)

   He calls them to send them out two by two.

3. What authority does Jesus give them? (6:7)

   Jesus gives them authority over the evil spirits.

4. What are they to take? What are they to leave behind? (6:8-9)

   They are to take nothing for their journey except a "staff" (or walking stick), sandals, and one tunic. But Jesus specifically lists certain items not to be taken: no bread, no "bag" (either a pack with personal possessions or a container to receive collections), no money in their moneybelts, and no second tunic.

5. When are they to stay at a place? When are they to leave? (6:10-11)

   Whenever they are invited to stay in a home, that is the place where they are to reside as long as they are in that area. However, at any place where they are not received or the people refuse to listen to them, they are to leave and "shake the dust" off their feet as they leave.

6. What did they do and achieve on their first mission? (6:12-13)

   They preached a call for repentance. They drove out many demons (or destructive spirits) and, using the method of anointing the sick person with oil, brought about healing.

7. How does Herod hear of Jesus? (6:14a)

   King Herod heard about these things "for Jesus' name had become well known."

8. What are the rumors about Jesus? (6:14b-15)

   Some are saying Jesus is John the Baptist raised from the dead. Some say he is Elijah come back to earth because a tradition believed Elijah is to return to earth before the Messiah comes (Malachi 4:5). Many are saying Jesus is a "prophet" because, in many respects, he preaches and lives in the style of the Old Testament prophets. Also Jesus is seen as one who "spoke for" God, which is what the word prophet means and what Jesus does.

9. What is Herod's opinion of John? (6:16)

   Herod, on the basis of the rumors and descriptions of Jesus, has come to feel that he is indeed John the Baptist raised from the dead.

10. What had Herod first done to John the Baptist? Why? (6:17-18)

    Herod had arrested John because John had condemned Herod for marrying Herodias, his half-brother Philip's wife.

11. What role do Herodias and her daughter play in this tragedy? (6:19-25)

    Herodias also has a grudge against John the Baptist and would put him to death herself but does not have the power. However, she develops a plot to achieve her desire. On Herod's birthday he gives a banquet for military and political leaders. The daughter of Herodias (probably the child of Philip, Herod's half-brother) dances at the party and so delights Herod and his guests that Herod offers her any gift she wishes. Her mother tells her to ask for "the head of John the Baptist," which she did.

12. What is Herod's opinion of John the Baptist? (6:20) What is his personal feeling about Herodias's daughter's request? (6:26)

Herod has a fear of John, feeling he is a righteous and holy person. For this reason Herod tries to keep him safe. He was puzzled at much John said but still was open and interested in what John had to say.

When the request of the daughter of Herodias comes to Herod, he is distressed and sorry he had made this public offer to her.

13. What does Herod do about the request? (6:27) Why? (6:26)

Immediately Herod sends an executioner with orders to bring John's head. Herod does this because he has made his oaths and does not want to break his word.

14. What happens to the body of John the Baptist? (6:28-29)

The soldier brings back John's head on a platter, as promised by Herod, and gives it to the daughter who gives it to Herodias. The disciples of John come and take John's body away and bury it.

15. What invitation does Jesus convey to his disciples when they return from their mission? (6:30-31)

After they report to Jesus all they have done and taught, he suggests that they come away with him to a quiet place to rest.

16. What happens when they try to do this? (6:32-33)

They leave the crowd and set sail for a solitary place. However, many see them leave and go by land to their destination, arriving ahead of Jesus and his disciples.

17. What is Jesus' feeling about these people? (6:34)

Jesus has compassion for them, for to him they seem to be like "sheep without a shepherd." He begins to teach them.

18. What problem develops related to the crowd? (6:35-36)

Because it is a lonely place, and also because it was getting late, it becomes apparent that food for them would have to be found. The disciples bring this to the attention of Jesus with the suggestion that he send the people off to the nearby countryside and villages to find and buy food.

19. What suggestions does Jesus make? (6:37-38)

Jesus calls on the disciples to give them something to eat. They protest that they would have to pay a sizable sum to obtain enough bread. He then asks them to see how many loaves they have available.

20. What process does Jesus use to meet the need? (6:39-41)

He orders the people to sit in groups and rows on the grass, a hundred rows of fifty each. Taking the five loaves and two fish found by the disciples, Jesus offers thanks "to heaven." Then he gives the food to the disciples to distribute it to the crowd.

21. What are the results? (6:42-44, 52)

All are able to eat and are satisfied. Twelve basketfuls of bread and fish fragments then are collected. Five thousand men eat the food. The disciples, however, never really understand this episode because their "hearts were hardened."

22. Where does Jesus go? (6:45-46)

He sends the people away and the disciples to Bethsaida by boat. He then goes up into the nearby hills to pray.

23. When and where does Jesus next meet the disciples? (6:47-49)

The disciples have set sail as instructed but encountered strong headwinds. They are still struggling against these winds (as they had done before, 4:35-41) in the "fourth watch of the night" (between 3 and 6 A.M.). Jesus, who is alone on the hillside, perceives their trouble. He comes to them, walking on the water. He then appears to be passing them. The disciples think it is a ghost and cry out from fear.

24. What happens then? (6:50-52)

Jesus says to them immediately, "Take courage! It is I. Don't be afraid." Then he gets into the boat with them and the wind ceases. The disciples again are completely amazed.

25. Who are brought to Jesus, and what do they do? (6:53-56)

After coming ashore, Jesus is again recognized. From all regions people bring sick persons, even on stretchers (mats), to him wherever he is and in any public place he passes. They beg him to let them touch even the edge of his cloak. All who do touch him are healed.

DIMENSION TWO:
WHAT DOES THE BIBLE MEAN?

Up until now Jesus' ministry as reported by Mark has been essentially a solo ministry. Jesus has been carrying it out while others have been observers and learners, which you may wish to remind class members is the meaning of *disciple.* Now Jesus moved in the direction of expanding his ministry and involving others in his mission. The Scripture portion studied in this lesson introduces us to the *nature, price,* and *possibilities* of mission as God's servants in the world. These words could be written in large print and given to the class members before today's session. Then ask them to be on the lookout for what is to be discovered about these three things as you study together the remainder of Mark 6.

Mark 6:7-13. At the risk of seeing more than is supposed to be seen, let the class members ponder the interrelatedness of verses 5-6a, and 6b-7. One form of interpreting this relation is that of cause and effect. Confronted by sizable need and sizable unbelief, Jesus is unable to do successfully what is needed. Does he give up? No, he responds creatively. Jesus commits himself anew to teaching, but also he expands the circle of those carrying out similar responsibilities. Instruction and mission become Jesus' response to his own inability to lead all the people to believe. What types of response do we often give to the same frustrations?

Note again the prominent place Mark gives to the teaching role of Jesus (1:21; 2:13; 4:1-2; 6:2, 34). Jesus again involves himself in a teaching tour.

Having previously appointed twelve persons whom he would send out with special responsibilities, Jesus now outlines more specifically those responsibilities as he follows through on his intent to "send them out." (Remind class members that the word *apostle* means "one who is sent out.") Jesus carries out that intention. "Disciples" are to become "apostles." Those who have come to him and learned of him now move out in mission in his name and spirit.

Note the simplicity of their possessions and wardrobe that Jesus directs to be a part of their lifestyle while on mission. (Look at the information given in Dimension One on these items in the answer to Question 4.) The "staff" would be like a walking stick or shepherd's staff. Perhaps, symbolically, the staff might remind them of that aid that comes from beyond themselves in their mission—from God. "Your rod and your staff, they comfort me" (Psalm 23:4b). Carrying a staff also placed them in the tradition of those spiritual pioneers whose working staff had accidentally become the sign of their authority and pilgrimage (Jacob, in Genesis 32:10; the Jews leaving Egypt, in Exodus 12:11). These disciples, turning apostles, are also spiritual pioneers on pilgrimage.

By taking no bread, bag, money, or reserve clothing the disciples are being called on for absolute dependence on the providence of God. Jesus' directions to them are really a summons to be the opposite of the unbelief around them (verse 6:6a). There are echoes here of Jesus' counsel given in the Sermon on the Mount (Matthew 6:24-34). Class members might benefit from reading aloud that passage. You may also wish to express Jesus' directions in contemporary terms: "Bread" would be lunch box; the "bag" would be suitcase; the "money in their belt" would be their traveler's checks and credit cards; the "second coat," a raincoat or overcoat. They were called to mission without depending on what others would feel were essentials. Can class members recall individuals who have made their witness without dependence on such "essentials"? What are the implications of these directions for the lifestyle of us as Christians?

Time is to be important to the disciples. They are not to waste time where they can be of no effect. (Perhaps this direction is a reaction to what is described in verses 5-6a.)

The disciples' assignments are to preach (3:14) and to take authority over evil spirits (3:15; 6:7), that is, the destructive forces within persons that rob them of God's intent for them. Going out two by two in teams for mutual support, they succeed in their efforts—preaching repentance (6:12), driving out many demons, and bringing healing (6:13). Is there an interrelationship among these three facets, even for us?

Mark 6:14-29. The family name was Herod and members of this family ruled the Jewish population of Palestine from 33 B.C. to A.D. 70. The Herod who ruled under Roman auspices at the time of the birth of Jesus was Herod the Great, son of Antipater. He died in 4 B.C. His son, Archelaus, became king with his two brothers, Herod Philip and Herod Antipas, named tetrarchs, the title for a ruler of one fourth of the territory. Herod Antipas, tetrarch of Galilee and Perea, was the one who put John the Baptist to death. The Jewish historian Josephus gives the reason for this act as Herod's fear of rebellion. John the Baptist was, indeed, a rebel but not in the military-political sense. Perhaps Herod Antipas could not discern the difference.

Mark gives a different reason for John's execution. Herod Antipas divorced his wife so that he could marry Herodias, who was the wife of his half-brother Philip. Herodias and Philip had a daughter, Salome. These are the characters in this tragic drama.

John the Baptist is held in high esteem by friend and foe alike. Jesus said no prophet was greater than John the Baptist (Luke 7:28). Mark tells us the people flocked to hear John from distances (Mark 1:5). Even Herod holds him in awe and is fascinated with his preaching. This feeling of Herod's prevented Herodias from obtaining the death of John the Baptist earlier.

The development of events is easily understood, although distasteful to ponder. Your contribution at this point should not be to retell the story that almost everyone knows, but to unveil a hidden agenda that may have led Mark to include the story at this point in his narrative. Ask class members why they think the story appears at this point. The key word to the answer may well be the word *repentance.*

John the Baptist was preaching a call for repentance (1:4). Jesus identified himself with this calling (Luke 4:17-19) by using Isaiah's words to describe his mission. The Twelve have been sent on their own healing and teaching tour. Mark tells us that in fulfilling that mission they called for repentance (6:12). So far their results have been positive and encouraging. If, by chance, they went out with fear, they return with joy and the sense of success.

But at this point Mark brings in the tragic story of John the Baptist's death. Why? Of course, in the first verses the status of Jesus is elevated by the reporting of Herod's belief that Jesus was even John raised from the dead. This elevation of Jesus is a motif of Mark. Another special reason may be that John the Baptist, out of his deep commitment to the mission God had given him, preached repentance to everyone, from the lowest to the highest position. To Herod and Herodias, who had flaunted the biblical standards and sensitivity to persons in creating their marriage, John the Baptist called for repentance. The price for John's faithfulness to God's mission for him as he saw it was to receive resentment, ridicule, and death.

Whether looking at Jesus in his ministry or the Twelve in their mission, Mark wants us to know in the midst of any rejoicing that obedience to God's mission may not be encouraging and can be costly. Amid the initial achievements in ministry by a new breed of disciples, Mark recalls the "old-timer" and the price paid for true faithfulness to God's mission for him. We may be blessed or chastened as God's chosen for witness and service. By the material Mark includes in this chapter, Mark wishes us to sense this same understanding about the nature of being in mission.

Mark 6:32-44. The problem is the mix of so many people, an inadequate food supply, and the lateness of the hour. Does that not sound like today's headlines? The shepherd's heart makes Jesus and his followers aware and caring. This episode will be even more relevant if you lift up the similarity between their situation and our situation in terms of hunger. Indeed, raise the question in advance: What is the Christian mission in such a situation? Then together explore the passage seeking for part of the answer.

First, the disciples were sensitive enough to be aware of human need. Next, they were concerned enough to want something to be done. Jesus turns their concern around on them and tells them to do what they can do (verse 37). Then he tells them to discover what resources are available (verse 38), which involves initiative and research. Then Jesus instructs the disciples to become the means through which, and because of which, resources there are identified and shared. When they carry out these roles, blessed by Jesus, more is discovered and distributed than one could ask or even think.

Out of this event what do you think the disciples learned that should apply to their mission? Certainly among those things learned would be the importance of shepherds' sensitivity to need and of doing first what they could do, their potential helpfulness to so many through the strategies of enablement, and how much Jesus enables to take place through persons with this concept of mission.

Mark 6:45-52. You may want to contrast this story with the storm episode reported in Mark 4:35-41. This story takes place in "the fourth watch," between 3 and 6 A.M. when the night is darkest. The description of Jesus almost passing by the disciples suggests Jesus' urgency to get to the place of need. Again, the disciples are frightened but Jesus brings them words of hope. "Then, he climbed into the boat with them, and the wind died down" (verse 51). This story is the second of three boat scenes in Mark. (See 4:35-41; 8:14-21.)

Mark probably meant this passage to testify to Jesus' mastery over even the physical universe. However, in the light of the totality of Mark's Gospel, we can also see its possible meanings as an allegory. Indeed, I see a helpful beauty in the realization that Jesus does not pass us by. Instead, when we cry out to him, he not only encourages us with his presence but even gets into our fragile little human boat with us. Then the wind ceases.

Mark 6:53-56. Gennesaret was probably the land area near or next to Capernaum. Jesus is returning to his base of operations. Since at one time healing had come by touching Jesus (5:25-34), now many in need want simply to touch him.

Mark 6:30-31, 45-46. These verses are worth noting by themselves because they describe a certain rhythm that Jesus builds into his ministry (1:12, 35, 45; 2:13; 3:13; 4:10; 6:31, 45-46) and is commending to the Twelve in the midst of their mission. He is commending a pattern of involvement balanced with withdrawal; he is in the crowd, then away from the crowd. Hilltops and lakesides become oases for Jesus' thirsty spirit and weary body. His sense of who he is and why he is here is renewed. Like so many of us, Jesus had to struggle to find, or even preserve, these moments of retreat and replenishment.

Now Jesus invites his disciples to discover the value, even the necessity of such times as he invites them to come aside with him. In a real sense, Jesus says to his fledgling missioners that an important part of being in mission is knowing when not to be in mission. You might wish to point out these verses and thoughts briefly as the conclusion of today's lesson.

DIMENSION THREE:
WHAT DOES THE BIBLE MEAN TO ME?

Focusing on Mission

Look back at the first paragraph of Dimension Two here and in the student book. Note again that this passage helps inform us as to the *nature, price,* and *possibilities* of mission as God's faithful servants. Ponder together what each of the episodes tells us on these subject areas.

What about our call to mission? Have we discovered the nature of this for ourselves yet? What price may we have to pay? What price are we willing to pay?

These episodes tell us that even persons like ourselves can be used by God in mission. Our mission becomes the place where we (1) become part of deep human need, (2) enter into it to do what we can, (3) enable others to do what they can, (4) pause on occasion to refuel our intentions and refocus our purpose, and then (5) minister in companionship with the Master of all who models and enters into it (and into us) himself.

*And he said to them: "You have a fine way of setting aside the commands
of God in order to observe your traditions!" (7:9).*

— 6 —

Old Ways in a New Day

Mark 7

DIMENSION ONE:
WHAT DOES THE BIBLE SAY?

Answer these questions by reading Mark 7

1. Who are meeting with Jesus as this chapter begins? (7:1)

   The Pharisees and teachers of the law come from Jerusalem to confer with Jesus.

2. What do they observe? (7:2)

   They observe that some of the disciples eat with unwashed hands.

3. What customs does eating with unwashed hands violate? (7:3-4)

   All Jews have an inherited tradition of not eating without washing their hands first. This is especially true when they come from the marketplace. Washing their hands is a ritual act of purification, not then seen as a hygienic act. This ritual act also includes washing of the dishes used for cooking and eating.

4. What question do the Pharisees and teachers of the law ask? (7:5)

   They ask Jesus, "Why don't your disciples live according to the tradition of the elders instead of eating their food with 'unclean' hands?"

5. What does Jesus call these critics? (7:6)

   He calls them "hypocrites."

6. What Old Testament quotation does Jesus use in his response to these questioners? (7:6-7)

   He quotes from the prophet Isaiah: "These people honor me with their lips, / but their hearts are far from me. / They worship me in vain; / their teachings are but rules taught by men" (Isaiah 29:13).

7. What three accusations does Jesus make of them? (7:8-9, 13)

   First, "You have let go of the commands of God and are holding on to the traditions of men." Second, "You have a fine way of setting aside the commands of God in order to observe your own traditions!" Third, "You nullify the word of God by your tradition that you have handed down."

8. What illustration does Jesus give of their misuse of tradition? (7:10-12)

   He reminds them of the fifth commandment (Exodus 20:12; Deuteronomy 5:16) that calls for the honoring of father and mother and other commandments that warn against cursing parents (Exodus 21:17; Leviticus 20:9). Death is the penalty for disobedience. Yet if parents have a need that might be met by something the children have, but that has been offered in some ritual or offering to God, their tradition dictated they could not use it to meet their parents' need. Corban refers to an item or amount pledged to God as though it was already on the altar. Thus their tradition keeps them from fulfilling God's highest expectations of them. Tradition takes precedence over compassion.

9. What parable does Jesus tell his hearers? (7:14-15)

   He says to them that nothing outside a person can defile that person by entering in. Instead, the things that come out of a person make him or her "unclean."

10. How does Jesus explain this parable? (7:18-23)

Jesus distinguished between that which enters the body and passes into the stomach and that which enters the person and goes to the heart. The physical items received are discharged as waste from the body in some manner. But the attitudes and actions that are expressed by some persons can be harmful, even destructive, in a multitude of ways to one's self and others. The evil things come from inside a person rather than from outside.

11. What samples does Jesus name of the evils that can come from inside? (7:21-22)

His list includes evil thoughts, sexual immorality, theft, murder, adultery, greed, malice, deceit, lewdness, envy, slander, arrogance, and folly.

12. Where does Jesus go? (7:24)

He goes to the vicinity of Tyre (and Sidon).

13. What observation does Mark make about Jesus and the public? (7:24)

Jesus enters into a certain house without wanting anyone to know about it. Mark observes, "yet he could not keep his presence secret."

14. Who falls down at the feet of Jesus? (7:25-26)

A non-Jewish woman, born at Syrophoenicia (Syrian Phoenicia) in Greece, comes and falls down at his feet.

15. What is her request? (7:25-26)

She has a little daughter who is "possessed by an evil spirit." She begs Jesus to drive the demon out of her daughter.

16. What exchange of ideas takes place between Jesus and the woman? (7:27-29)

Jesus says to this Gentile mother that first the children (Israel) should be fed because "it is not right to take the children's bread and toss it to their dogs." However, she responds by reminding Jesus that "even the dogs under the table eat the children's crumbs." To this statement of determination and hope by the woman outside the circle of Jesus' own nationality and religious tradition, he responds by advising her that the demon has already left her daughter.

17. What does she find when she returns home? (7:30)

She finds the demon has gone and the child is lying peacefully in bed.

18. To what area does Jesus now move? (7:31)

He returns to the Sea of Galilee through the area of Decapolis.

19. What physical conditions does the person have who is brought to Jesus? (7:32)

The man brought to Jesus is deaf and can hardly talk.

20. What method does Jesus use to meet this man's need? (7:33-34)

Jesus first puts his fingers into the man's ears. Then he spits and touches the man's tongue with the spittle. Then, looking up to heaven, Jesus speaks to him the word Ephphatha.

21. What does *Ephphatha* mean? (7:34)

Ephphatha is an Aramaic word that means "be opened."

22. What happens to the man? (7:35)

He is enabled to hear and speak plainly.

23. What instructions does Jesus give to those present at this event? What do they do in response? (7:36)

Jesus commands them to tell no one of this healing; but the more he does so, the more they keep talking about it.

24. What is the reaction of those who hear their report? (7:37)

They are overwhelmed with amazement saying, "He has done everything well."

DIMENSION TWO: WHAT DOES THE BIBLE MEAN?

As Jesus moves more widely and deeply into his ministry, two important questions begin to occur in the minds of some of his observers: (1) Is Jesus seeking to replace the old religious tradition with something new? (2) What is the relation and relevance of Jesus to the non-Jewish or Gentile world? (*Gentile* is a Greek word used in the Septuagint version of the Old Testament to mean "foreigner." The word is used in the New Testament to refer to non-Jews.) In the past the Jews had held to their religious tradition as something precious and unique to Jews only. Is the intention of Jesus' ministry to create a new community under a new law? You might like to ask your class members these questions for discussion before examining Mark 7.

Mark 7:1-5. Here we are introduced to the Pharisees and teachers of the law (scribes). Jesus' previous conflict with them was over obedience to the laws concerning the sabbath. (See Mark 2:23–3:6.) Their initial plans were made then to undermine Jesus' ministry (3:6). This episode in Mark 7 is probably a result of their strategy.

Reacquaint class members with the Pharisees and teachers of the law who become increasingly important in Mark's narrative. Their roots go back to the time of the Exile when the law (Torah) was restored as the central focus of Jewish religious life. The task was supplemented by the Temple when it was rebuilt after the Exile. Part of the new Temple hierarchy of spiritual leadership were the priests who offered sacrifices and prayers and set religious policy. A body of lawyers, also called *scribes*, studied and taught the Torah and were advisers to the priests.

The word *Pharisee* appears to come from a word meaning "one who is separate." They sought to separate themselves from whatever was "unclean," namely whatever was not in accordance with the law. Josephus, an ancient Jewish historian, states that the Pharisees were noted for their strict accuracy in interpreting the Torah and their strict adherence to it. To achieve this strictness they developed an expansive set of legal commentaries and traditions (called the Talmud, meaning "to study" or "to learn") that more precisely defined and described the law and its practical implications. They were defenders of the law and sought for perfect obedience to the law. (For more information on scribes and Pharisees, look up the terms in a Bible dictionary.)

The phrase *tradition of the elders* (verses 3, 5) refers not just to the law or customs but to this expansion of the law called the Talmud. It had come to have almost as much authority as the law itself, especially to the Pharisees. From this source had come many of the requirements that the disciples had not obeyed.

Mark 7:6-13. Here Jesus, in response to the accusations of the Pharisees and scribes, uses the Old Testament tradition to do two things. One is to challenge the appropriateness of the charges against him and his disciples. The other is to point to the purpose, or heart, of the law that is beneath and beyond rigid guidelines for one's behavior. By quoting Isaiah, Jesus calls to their awareness the constant problem in Jewish religious history: the substitution of ritual acts for religious being and doing. This hypocrisy is not something new being identified by Jesus but something as old as the prophets and beyond.

To illustrate this point, Jesus refers to Moses' commandment for parental honor. To that important and simple commandment Jewish tradition has added refinements to state how the commandment is to be applied. For instance, if a commitment has been made of something to God, that thing cannot then be given instead to one's parents even if the parents develop a desperate need for it. Thus obedience to this scribal interpretation of the law to "honor" results in an action "dishonoring" parents. The law's interpretation becomes more important than persons. So the tradition voids God's original word or intention that persons be respected and sustained.

Mark 7:14-23. Jesus refers to the confrontation at the beginning of this chapter. Here again he challenges legal concepts that place more importance on things than persons. Note again the technique used by Jesus of answering a question with a question (verses 17-18).

Jesus' point is simply that food items enter and are then discharged in some way from our bodies. However, that which begins from within and is of a harmful or destructive nature is already a part of us, born out of our being. Since its origin is from within, it is harder to eliminate and potentially much more destructive. Jesus is implying that the purpose of the law is the enhancement of values and quality in persons. Food laws had that intent originally. They were to stress the worth of persons and what was for their spiritual and physical health. The tradition as it was developed missed that point and began to focus on dietary restrictions. The most important determinant to what a person becomes is not what that person eats but what that person is.

Note the parenthetical comment in verse 19. Mark understands Jesus' statements to mean dropping all religious dietary restrictions. These restrictions were a controversial issue in the early Christian church. Were Christians to obey the inherited Jewish food laws or not? (See Acts 10:9-16.) Since Mark's Gospel was written against the backdrop of the early Christian church, this comment was probably included to settle that question from Mark's perspective.

Mark 7:24-35. Jesus travels to the coastal towns of Tyre and Sidon (in ancient Phoenicia, which is now a part of Lebanon). When the Greek woman falls down at the feet of Jesus seeking his healing for her daughter, the issue becomes Jesus' relationship to non-Jewish persons. In Mark's account this event is Jesus' first occasion to respond to a request from a Gentile. Jesus was of Jewish ancestry and had begun his ministry of witness in Jewish synagogues. Most of his dialogues had been with Jewish inquirers and religious leaders. He was beginning to be seen as the promised Messiah to the Jews.

These facts underlie the response of Jesus to the woman in verse 27. However, just as Jesus did in his analysis of the law, so he does in his response to a person's request. The person is of more value in the eyes of God than customs of separateness or exclusiveness. Because she was obviously a person of need and faith, Jesus responds to her need and heals the child.

Jesus' repartee with the woman has been viewed in various ways. "Dogs" is an uncomplimentary reference to Gentiles, so it appears that Jesus is insulting the woman. Other commentators view it as humor; Jesus engaged in wordplay. He dangles the common characterization in front of her, perhaps to shame his hearers. When she responds with such an effective comeback, he does what we would have done anyway. He heals her daughter and uses the episode and an illustration against prejudice—the people see that the "dog" is worthy of Jesus' attention and compassion.

The healing episode in verses 31-34 reaffirm his concern for persons and their needs.

Mark 7:36-37. As he has done before (3:12; 5:43), Jesus again calls for silence about who he is and what he has done. Biblical scholars speak of this as the messianic secret. In his narrative Mark implies that Jesus was trying to prevent notoriety and retain until the proper time the disclosure of who he was. Of course, Jesus was largely unsuccessful as is illustrated by the response of this man who had regained his speech and hearing. Apparently, the more Jesus insisted on secrecy, the more publicly those who had received his ministry proclaimed who he was to them.

DIMENSION THREE:
WHAT DOES THE BIBLE MEAN TO ME?

Genuine Discipleship in Old Traditions

Mark 7, in large measure, opens up for us the question as to how we as followers of Jesus are to relate to the new—new ideas as well as new persons.

Our Christian tradition has always had a strange, but definite, tension between the old and the new. On the one hand, we are those who are part of a tradition. We have inherited Scriptures, creeds, doctrines, even forms of worship and organization from the past. We have often felt a primary concern to defend the faith and preserve the past. The church by nature is usually experienced as a conservative institution, if for no other reason than because it has seen it as its task to conserve what it has received and created.

Preserving the past is not necessarily bad. When you realize all the artistic creations, scholarly research, educational endeavors, and historical preservations that have taken place through the conserving role of the church, then you sense an immense feeling of indebtedness.

However, this story has another side, and herein lies the contradiction. As followers of Christ we are also pilgrims in the tradition of wilderness wanderers seeking for a city (Hebrews 11:8-10). In confrontation with new experiences, lands, and persons our spiritual forebears learned who God was and what God expected of them. In the new they found both sustenance (manna) and structure (law). Our first place of worship was a portable one (the Tabernacle), not a permanent one. Discoveries of God's providence, power, and truth were found in the new. The new, while sometimes feared, was full of hope because God would be there with God's next lessons and demonstrations.

Mark gives us a picture of Jesus mostly on the move, seeking the next chapter, ready for each new possibility. The followers of Jesus are literally that—they do not stay with Jesus but go with Jesus. In the Gospels new occasions teach new duties, and time makes the ancient good uncouth. God's textbook is not just the old but the new.

This idea is enhanced by our belief in the Holy Spirit. God is not dead—God is not a relic from the past. Through God's Spirit God still moves among us: convicting, interpreting, teaching, healing, enabling, comforting, loving. God is still in the "revealing" business. The Bible itself is a record of the continuing and increasing revelation of God and God's purposes for God's people over generations to all sorts and conditions of persons. The word keeps coming in new, different, and clearer forms until it even comes in the flesh (John 1:14) in the person of Jesus. But if we believe in the Holy Spirit, the last word still has not been spoken, the ultimate truth has not been completely discovered.

Now if this is true, how does an old tradition confront a new era wherein the footfalls of God may still be found? How do we as followers of Christ not withdraw with him into old enclaves, but follow him down new roadways to different towns, meeting different people? How can we hold the truth but be open to the truth at the same time? That's the essence of the dilemma being addressed by Jesus in his mind-wrestling matches with the scribes and Pharisees. They had taken a fresh revelation of God and put it into laws and codes as they attempted to hold onto it, fearful if they lost it, they might lose God in the process.

Jesus suggests another way. He suggests that we look at the heart of the matter of the tradition. What important concern did the traditions come into existence to address? What was the ultimate purpose of the traditions? What did the traditions try to achieve—or create? After discussing the traditions, we may ask whether God has a new, and possibly even better way to achieve the purpose of traditions. We must struggle to distinguish whether our inherited spiritual tradition is temporal or eternal. Otherwise, we block the road down which God's new lessons would reach us.

Explore your religious traditions with class members. Ask them, What new truths does God try to teach you? What different types of persons does God want to include in your fellowship? Since we tend to be more defensive than risk-taking in our discipleship, the discussion may not be easy. Still, the discussion is worth trying.

Another concern for the follower of Jesus is to fail as a disciple even with good intentions.

A sad fact of spiritual history tends to move rapidly toward codes and exclusiveness. Often we experience God's grace coming to us in some unexpected way. God's grace jumps over the hurdles and comes to us outside the circle. In some form God's grace comes even to us who do not expect or deserve it. Whatever the nature of our spiritual experience, God freshens and personalizes our faith. God comes to us, and we can begin a new life. We find a new freedom and a new commitment at the same time. Old things have passed away; all are made new.

What do we do with the new experience of grace? A new experience received from God freely can come to meet us wherever we are and no matter who we are. We begin to put one-two-threes on the new experience. We begin to structure how the new experience happens or must happen. In the next step we decide what must be the expectation of new spiritual experience. The next thing we know, we have taken a fresh spiritual experience that comes to us outside the norm (law), boxed it up with our rigid expectations, and tied it up with a new set of laws.

Amazingly, the greatest temptation Christians (who are supposed to be under grace, not under the law) have, is to move quickly toward a new legalism of grace. Moving toward a new legalism is a contradiction in terms. For example, why do some of us who have become followers of Jesus in response to his love become unloving persons toward those who are not exactly like we are? Why are Christians often judgmental? Jesus is aware of this tendency. Jesus keeps pushing persons who would approach the experience and expressions of faith through legalism to go back to basics—the worth and value of persons. Jesus teaches God's availability to everyone who is open to God's new truth, who has an honest understanding of who and what we really are, and who has a commitment with motion and growth to it.

Jesus keeps pushing the boundaries, especially the boundaries enfolding a person too closely, boundaries that have been created by a misuse of spiritual heritage. Invite the class members to ponder their spiritual pilgrimage. The invitation can either be in the form of sharing aloud or in the form of silent personal meditation guided by you. If the invitation is done in the form of guided meditation, it should not be done rapidly. Questions such as these might be asked:

• Do you recall a moment when you, like the Syrophoenician woman, desperately needed a ministry of God's grace, but because you were outside the circle of faith, you did not expect to receive it? Nevertheless, did you fall down before Jesus and receive it?
• What did you do with this experience of God's providential nearness in your life?
• Has this experience left you more aware of what God has done and opened your eyes to what God can do?
• Have you tended to make out of this new experience a pattern of one-two-three or to place this expectation on others without the freedom to encounter God's new truth in their own way?
• Do you measure or judge others on the basis of the convictions you have in common or on the differences among you?
• What new revelation has God brought you lately?

"But what about you?" he asked. "Who do you say I am?" Peter answered, "You are the Christ" (8:29).

7

The Tide Begins to Turn

Mark 8:1–9:1

DIMENSION ONE:
WHAT DOES THE BIBLE SAY?

Answer these questions by reading Mark 8:1–9:1

1. What is the problem faced by the crowd? (8:1)

   The crowd has nothing to eat.

2. What is the attitude of Jesus toward this crowd? (8:2-3)

   Jesus has compassion toward the people. He feels they may collapse on their way if he sends them home hungry. Some have traveled a long distance.

3. What do the disciples ask of Jesus? (8:4)

   The disciples ask, "But where in this remote place can anyone get enough bread to feed them?"

4. What does Jesus ask of the disciples in response? What is their answer? (8:5)

   Jesus asks, "How many loaves do you have?" They answer, "Seven."

5. Now what does Jesus do? (8:6-7)

   Jesus directs the crowd to sit on the ground. He takes the seven loaves and later a few small fish. Giving thanks, he breaks the bread and gives the food to his disciples to distribute to the crowd of people.

6. What is the result? (8:8)

   The crowd eats, and is satisfied. The disciples take up seven baskets of leftover pieces of food.

7. How many persons are present? (8:9)

   About four thousand men are present.

8. Where does Jesus go? (8:10)

   After sending the crowd away, Jesus gets into a boat with his disciples and goes to the region of Dalmanutha (an unknown location).

9. Who begins to question Jesus? Why? (8:11)

   The Pharisees begin to question Jesus. They want to test Jesus by asking of him for a sign from heaven.

10. What sign does Jesus give them? (8:12)

    Jesus gives them no sign.

11. What do the disciples forget to bring with them? (8:14)

    They forget to bring bread and have only one loaf with them.

12. What warning does Jesus give them? (8:15)

    Jesus warns, "Watch out for the yeast of the Pharisees and that of Herod."

13. What accusation does Jesus make of his disciples? (8:17-18)

    Jesus wonders whether their hearts have become hardened. He feels that they do not see with their eyes or hear with their ears, and do not remember what he has taught them earlier.

14. What episodes does Jesus have them recall? (8:19-20)

    By asking them questions about what happened, Jesus has his disciples recall the feeding of the five thousand and the four thousand.

15. Whom does Jesus meet next? What is his request? (8:22)

    Jesus meets a blind man who begs Jesus to touch him.

16. What does Jesus do? (8:23, 25)

Jesus takes the blind man by the hand, leading him out of the village. He spits on his hands and lays his hand twice on the blind man.

17. What are the results? (8:24-25)

The blind man finds his sight slowly returning. At first he sees persons looking like trees walking. After Jesus touches his eyes again, the man finds his sight restored and sees everything clearly.

18. Where does Jesus send the blind man after his sight is restored? (8:26)

Jesus sends him to his home with an instruction not to enter the village.

19. What questions does Jesus ask of his disciples? (8:27, 29)

Jesus asks, "Who do people say that I am?" and then asks "Who do you say I am?"

20. What are their responses? (8:28-29)

They respond that some say John the Baptist; others say Elijah; others say one of the prophets. Peter responds to Jesus' second question, "You are the Christ."

21. What new teaching about himself does Jesus offer his disciples? (8:31)

Jesus speaks of himself to his disciples as the "Son of Man." He says he must suffer many things; be rejected by the elders, the chief priests, and the teachers of the law; be killed; and after three days rise again.

22. What is Peter's reaction to this news? What is Jesus' reaction to Peter? (8:32-33)

Peter rebukes Jesus for Jesus' dire prediction. But Jesus rebukes Peter, "Get behind me, Satan! . . . You do not have in mind the things of God, but the things of men."

23. What invitation does Jesus extend to the multitude? What will result from accepting it? (8:34-37)

Jesus invites anyone to come after him by self-denial, taking up one's cross, and following Jesus. If one loses his life for the sake of Jesus and the gospel, that person will save his life. In contrast, if one saves his life, he will lose it. Indeed, one could gain the whole world yet forfeit his soul.

24. Of whom will the Son of man be ashamed? (8:38)

Jesus warns that when the Son of Man comes in his Father's glory, he will be ashamed of those who have been ashamed of him and his words in the midst of a sinful generation.

25. What prediction does Jesus make? (9:1)

Jesus states that some who are standing there with him will not die before they see the kingdom of God come with power.

DIMENSION TWO: WHAT DOES THE BIBLE MEAN?

Jesus continues to move successfully in ministry. Crowds are drawn to him, while the disciples still, at times, are puzzled by him. Yet as Jesus reaches the heights of achievement and acclaim, even being seen as the Messiah, the religious leaders against him become more intentional and obvious. Dark forebodings are shared by Jesus with his followers with the understanding that discipleship has a price.

Mark 8:1-9. Mark 8 begins with a second episode of the feeding of a large multitude that Jesus enabled to take place. It is striking to note that two such episodes are reported by Mark. Recall to class members that Mark is the shortest and most concise of all the Gospel narratives. Among all that Mark remembered and learned of Jesus' activities, he included what was to him most important and impressive. Since in his limited account Mark chose to report these two feeding events, they must have been very important and/or impressive to Mark.

The first feeding event appears, as we noted previously, in all four Gospels. However, this second event appears only in Mark and Matthew (15:32-38). Furthermore, while the accounts of the same event are usually briefer in Mark and expanded in the other Gospels, in the case of this event Mark's account is longer than Matthew's account.

Why do you think Mark and Matthew include two such similar stories? You and your class members might like to read through the two accounts side by side and compare specifically the developments in the two stories. For instance, both stories begin with a reference to the "compassion" of Jesus toward the people. Both events take place far from the homes of the persons present. In both events the disciples ask a question of Jesus; and Jesus responds by asking, "How many loaves do you have?" (7:38; 8:5). Both groups are told to be seated. Food is left over and collected both times. The number of loaves and the number fed vary.

One theory is that the first feeding took place primarily among Jews, and the second took place among Gentiles. This theory is based in part upon the fact that two different Greek words are used for "baskets" in the two accounts (7:43; 8:8). The first story used *kophinos,* a word for a type of food basket shaped like a water pot used by the Jews. The second story uses *spuris,* a basket much like a hamper. In this kind of basket Paul was lowered from the wall of Damascus (Acts 9:25). *Spuris* was a basket used by non-Jews. The region of the Decapolis (Ten Towns) was heavily populated with Gentiles.

Those who approach the two events from these perspectives see a significant symbolism in the two stories. The first occasion witnesses to Jesus as the bread of life, indeed the source to meet spiritual necessities and the enabler of true life for the Jews first. The second occasion witnesses to the same truth for non-Jews. In line with this interpretation, the wording in the dialogue between Jesus and the Gentile woman (7:24-30) becomes significant. Draw the attention of class members to the exact words they exchange (7:27-28) that refer to bread and who should be fed. This exchange could be the ideological hinge between the two stories. The first feeding had illustrated Jesus' words ("First let the children eat all they want . . . "). The second feeding illustrated Jesus' endorsements by his actions of the woman's words ("even the dogs under the table eat the children's crumbs").

In fairness let me point out that many scholars do not accept this interpretation as the reason for including the two similar events. No one knows if one event, verbal reports and recounting, became two, or if Mark himself was a personal witness to two such events. One thing is certain: Mark includes the two episodes to support his argument that underlies his whole book: "the gospel of Jesus Christ, the Son of God" (1:1).

Note the reference to "men" in verse 9. Of course, more persons were present than just men, as we discover in Matthew 15:38. However, this wording illustrates the male dominance in the society of Jesus' day. Family units were usually identified through the male figure (father, husband) of the household. Verse 9 does not imply that the only concern or intention was to feed the men. The men were responsible for their family units. The food would probably be divided among the men, who in turn would divide it among their family members.

The second feeding took place "in the region" of the Decapolis (7:31). Draw the attention of your class members to what occurred after the healing of Legion, the man who was mentally ill. Following Jesus' instructions, he went "to tell in the Decapolis how much Jesus had done for him" (5:20). After that episode, Jesus had left that area. Now he returns to that specific area for the first time since leaving. Could this be the explanation for the "great crowd" that gathered on this occasion? Might it be that one person's witness resulted in a multitude coming to Jesus and receiving his ministry? What might happen today as a result of a deeply felt witness by your class members?

Mark 8:10. This lesson might be an appropriate time to give a homework research assignment to a person who likes to study or produce maps. The assignment would be to trace on a map the movements of Jesus thus far in Mark's account. The basic map might be traced from a map of the Bible lands found in a Bible dictionary or atlas. Jesus' movements might then be plotted insofar as Mark provides locations. The later movements of Jesus could be added as later chapters are studied.

Thus far the trail should be as follows: Nazareth to the northern Jordan River (1:9); to the wilderness (desert) of Judea (1:12); to the west side of the Sea of Galilee (1:16); to Capernaum (1:21); through Galilee (1:39); back to Capernaum (2:1); to the seaside (2:13) and fields nearby (2:23); back to Capernaum (3:1); to the seaside (3:7); up into the nearby hills (3:13); to a town, probably Capernaum again (3:20); to the seaside (4:1); across the Sea of Galilee (4:35); to the northeast section near the country of the Gerasenes (5:1); across the sea to near Capernaum (5:21); to Nazareth (6:1); through the surrounding villages (6:7); back to the lake side across the sea to "a solitary place" (6:32); across the sea to Bethsaida (6:45); by sea to Gennesaret (on the west side) (6:53); to Tyre in Phoenicia (7:24); to Sidon (7:31); to the southeastern shore area of the Sea of Galilee called Decapolis (7:31).

Now Jesus goes to the area of Dalmanutha. This exact location is not known but it is thought to have been in the area of Magdala, on the western shore area of the Sea of Galilee.

Mark 8:11-13. Jesus' reputation as an insightful teacher and miracle worker is growing. The religious leaders become more fearful of his growing reputation and are more determined to counteract or undermine Jesus' appeal. Rather than initiate some radical act of condemnation or abuse at this stage, they hope they can trip up Jesus by their questions and implications. The religious leaders hope to discredit Jesus in the public eye. Now they come to Jesus seeking of him a "sign from heaven."

The idea of a sign to demonstrate or endorse one's credentials or abilities goes back to the Old Testament tradition. When Moses went before Pharaoh, he performed certain miraculous acts to convince Pharaoh that he spoke for God and in the power of God (Exodus 7–11; see especially 6:28–7:6). The prophets built on this model the expectation that God's anointed one, the Messiah, would come with and be identified by signs and wonders. Isaiah 7:10-14 presents a famous dialogue in which King Ahaz is invited to seek from God a sign as to whether the prophet's descriptions of future possibilities might be true. Ahaz responds that he will not put the Lord to the test by asking for a sign. Isaiah says that God will give a sign anyway in response to the impatience of the people with God's intentions. What is the sign? "The virgin will be with child and will give birth to a son, and will call him Immanuel" (Isaiah 7:14b).

In the well-known account of the conversation between Nicodemus and Jesus in John 3:1-21, Nicodemus speaks of what originally drew him to Jesus: "Rabbi, we know you are a teacher who has come from God. For no one could perform the miraculous signs you are doing if God were not with him" (John 3:2).

Out of this background the Pharisees come to Jesus seeking a sign that will prove who he is. Jesus, however, refuses to respond, stating instead that no sign would be given to this generation. Jesus refuses to allow himself to become a carnival performer, doing marvelous acts to win the applause of crowds. This refusal becomes more crucial in this context. By not responding to the Pharisees' request, and by not demonstrating through a marvelous act his divine credentials to this investigating body, he forfeited a major opportunity to turn the tide in his favor. Yet, Jesus will not take the compromising shortcut to personal acclaim. Jesus will not use the works of God simply to impress the power structure of his day.

Mark 8:14-21. This story is the last of three boat scenes. (See 4:35-41; 6:45–5:2.) This section is puzzling in the interrelatedness of its contents as well as its meaning. One school of thought feels that verses 14-15 are separate from what follows and belong with verses 11-13. The comment of Jesus is in reaction to the Pharisees' approach to him and their sinister intent. Thus Jesus is warning his disciples to beware of the Pharisees' destructive influence and power. Like yeast, the Pharisees' influence might be hidden but it would be strong enough to give rise to a change in their minds and natures if they became open and subject to it. The reference to the Pharisees is broadened here to include those close to Herod, the ruler, or of his frame of mind. (Recall Mark's previous account of Herod in 6:14-29.) Herod and/or his political companions were also becoming apprehensive and perhaps jealous of Jesus. The Pharisees and the Herodians were the sources of steadily increasing opposition to Jesus.

This comment on yeast seems coincidental to the conversation about bread. The initial discovery that they only had one loaf of bread may have triggered Jesus' comment about the Pharisees. As they sail, Jesus may be pondering this recent attempt by the Pharisees to undermine him. The mention of bread simply brings to Jesus' mind this figure of speech of yeast, for their influence can even influence the disciples. In contrast, however, the mind of the disciples is on their stomachs.

The exchange that takes place arises out of the disciples' anxiety over an inadequate food supply. Interestingly, this is the third time the disciples are concerned over the supply of food available (6:35-36 and 8:4). Perhaps you might ask your class members what this seems to suggest about the disciples. Also, are we similar to them in nature? Jesus recalls what has happened on the two previous occasions. In effect he is asking whether they have come to trust in the providence of God and the caring sensitivity of Jesus after having seen them occur in miraculous proportions. Jesus' words on this subject in the Sermon on the Mount (Matthew 6:24-34) can be applied to this attitude of frightful apprehension.

Mark 8:22-26. This story is similar to what is reported in 7:32-37. Ask class members: Why do you think that Matthew did not tell the second episode? John reports a similar experience but locates it in Jerusalem (John 9:1-7). Notice again that the blind man sought Jesus' touch on himself. Jesus' touch makes the difference. As a result the man's sight slowly returns, at first blurred wherein people "look like trees walking around." Then his vision clears.

As Jesus influences us by his touch on our lives, is this the process through which we pass? Do we immediately see persons and purposes clearly from God's new perspective? Or does it take time for his touch to really clear our vision and attitudes? As Jesus touches our lives, we change from seeing persons as things to seeing persons as persons.

Mark 8:27-33. This passage is one of the most famous events in the Gospels, known as Peter's confession. The passage comes right at the halfway point in Mark's narrative and divides it into two sections: Jesus' early ministry and Jesus' later ministry.

Jesus takes an inventory among his intimates as to their opinion of Jesus at this point. The disciples report to Jesus the rumors as to his identity (6:14-15). Then Peter affirms that Jesus is the Christ, the Messiah. (Previously only the insane Legion had publicly affirmed Jesus' messiahship in Mark 5:7.)

Peter, undoubtedly, was very surprised at Jesus' words in response. First, Jesus tells Peter to tell no one. Thus still the messianic secret holds. Second, to make it worse, Jesus reveals that not grandeur but tragedy is at the heart of the job description for the Christ. Peter would have expected just the opposite.

Jesus intentionally speaks of himself as the Son of man rather than "Christ" or "Son of God." This phrase has a long history behind it. This title was used in Daniel 7:13 for the exalted and triumphant emissary of God. "He was given authority, glory and sovereign power; all peoples, nations and men of every language worshiped him" (7:14). The title or description is echoed in Revelation 1:7, 13; 14:14. Although the title signifies triumph and honor, Jesus takes the title and gives it a new definition that is the opposite: suffering, rejection, death.

With horror Peter rebels at this notion. Then Jesus rebukes Peter because he has taken the typical human viewpoint that to be God's servant is to have all the advantages and successes. No, from God's perspective faithfulness to God's purposes for us is God's calling at whatever price we must pay.

DIMENSION THREE:
WHAT DOES THE BIBLE MEAN TO ME?

Mark 8:34–9:1—Triumph and Tragedy

In Dimension Two I did not discuss Mark 8:34–9:1. The reason is that this passage almost becomes the answer to our question and the challenge of the whole chapter.

Certain spiritual rhythms arise out of the events we have studied. First, there is the feeding of the four thousand that leaves us with an exalted picture of the Christ. The exaltation, however, comes not through a self-serving miracle but through a magnificent act of widely beneficial caring for persons and their needs. Second comes the temptation afforded by the Pharisees for Jesus to do something spectacular that would serve him well and impress others. Jesus reacts against this self-serving prospect. The dialogue with the disciples reinforces the warning not to be constantly focusing on what is impressive to others or simply self-serving.

The rhythm swings again to the exaltation of Jesus through the healing of the blind man and the titles of acclaim being given Jesus by his observers. Peter places the highest accolade on Jesus by affirming Jesus as the promised and long-sought Christ. Then immediately the rhythm reverts back to the subdued notes. Jesus, instead of capitalizing on their discovery and creating a movement of recognition and acclaim, wants no one told. Additionally, Jesus describes hurt and havoc to be his lot.

Peter wanted to change this alternating rhythm and so do we! Let exaltation continue and spread. Let everyone know who you are so that the triumphant acclaim predicted for the Son of man might be yours. Capitalize on who you are—make something for yourself out of it. Invite class members to consider whether such a perspective underlies some expressions of Christianity today. Do you see an attempt to get and have for the sake of Christ that which is the opposite of the style Jesus demonstrates and calls his disciples to practice (8:34-37)? If this is so, what has happened to bring about the new style for God's servant? What does the popularity of such messages say about us as listeners?

The new style for God's servants, to be demonstrated by the followers of Jesus, is not to be exalted but effaced, not to get but to give, not to serve one's self but to sacrifice for the gospel and for the sake of Christ. Following Christ does not mean to walk as the king's couriers into success, wealth, power, and acclaim. Instead, following Christ is to run the risk of losing all of these. We risk these losses when we hold as a priority using whatever we are or have for the sake of human need in faithfulness to the style of the Christ. God's opinion of us, now and in the future, is based not on what we have achieved but on what we have offered. The invitation is open, and the decision is left to each of us.

In this sense the kingdom of God can come in our lives. As we yield up ourselves as a living sacrifice to Jesus' mastery and Jesus' sacrificial lifestyle, then we know God's kingship that brings true life—life with quality, purpose, and meaning; life so worthwhile it never "tastes death"!

As they were coming down the mountain, Jesus gave them orders not to tell anyone what they had seen until the Son of Man had risen from the dead (9:9).

— 8 —

Down From the Mountain

Mark 9:2-50

DIMENSION ONE: WHAT DOES THE BIBLE SAY?

Answer these questions by reading Mark 9:2-50

1. Where does Jesus go? Whom does he take with him? (9:2)

   Jesus goes up to a high mountain. He takes only three of his disciples, Peter, James, and John, with him.

2. What happens there? Who also joins them? (9:2-4)

   Jesus is transfigured. His clothes become dazzling white. Elijah, traditionally regarded as the greatest (and one of the first) of the prophets, appears. Also Moses, the great lawgiver, appears. Together they talk with Jesus.

3. What is the reaction of these three disciples, especially Peter? (9:5-6)

   Peter is at first speechless and afraid, as are the other disciples. Then Peter bursts out with the suggestion that three shelters be built.

4. What event then takes place? (9:7)

   A cloud appears, enveloping them. A voice speaks out of the cloud saying, "This is my Son, whom I love. Listen to him!" As the three disciples look around, Elijah and Moses have gone and only Jesus remains.

5. What order does Jesus give the three disciples as they come down from the mountain? What do they do? (9:9-10)

   Jesus tells them to tell no one what they have seen until he has risen from the dead. They do this, while wondering among themselves what "rising from the dead" actually means.

6. As a follow-up to the Transfiguration experience, what question do these disciples ask Jesus? (9:11)

   The disciples ask Jesus, "Why do the teachers of the law say that Elijah must come first?" (before the Messiah comes).

7. What is Jesus' answer? (9:12-13)

   Jesus says that Elijah comes before the Messiah to restore all things. Yet, in spite of that, the Son of Man must suffer many things, including rejection.

8. On returning from the mountain, what do Jesus, Peter, James, and John find the rest of the disciples doing? (9:14-18)

   The disciples are in the midst of a large crowd where the teachers of the law (scribes) are arguing with them. Seeing Jesus, they are overwhelmed with wonder and run to greet him. When Jesus asks what they are arguing about, he learns that someone has brought to them a boy who is subject to destructive seizures that leave him collapsed, foaming at the mouth, gnashing his teeth, and rigid. The father has asked the disciples to cast out the destructive spirit. However, the disciples are unable to do so.

9. What does Jesus say? (9:19)

   He responds by speaking of them as an "unbelieving generation." He exclaims, "How long shall I stay with you? How long shall I put up with you?" Jesus invites them to bring the boy to him.

10. What request does the father of the ill boy make of Jesus? (9:21b-22)

    The father informs Jesus that his son has been a victim of this condition since childhood. The seizures have resulted in the boy falling into fires and into bodies of water where he might have been killed. The father asks Jesus if he can do anything—to have pity on them and help them if he can.

11. What promise does Jesus offer? What unusual prayer is offered by the father in response? (9:23-24)

Jesus affirms that all things are possible to anyone who believes. "Immediately the boy's father exclaimed, 'I do believe; help me overcome my unbelief!' "

12. What happens when Jesus seeks to eliminate the evil spirit? (9:25-27)

After Jesus rebuked the evil spirit to leave the boy forever, it shrieks and convulses the boy violently, then comes out, leaving the boy collapsed in a state like a "corpse." Observers think the boy is dead; but Jesus takes him by the hand, lifts him to his feet, and the boy stands up.

13. What question do the disciples ask of Jesus? What is his response? (9:28-29)

Privately, the disciples ask Jesus why they cannot cast out the evil spirit. Jesus answers, "This kind [of spirit] can come out only by prayer."

14. What teaching does Jesus repeat to his disciples that they still do not understand? (9:30-32)

As they journey, Jesus again reports that he will be delivered into the hands of enemies who will kill him, but after three days he will rise from the dead. Although the disciples do not understand this teaching, they are afraid to ask Jesus to explain it to them.

15. What do the disciples discuss together that they do not want to admit to Jesus? (9:33-34)

En route to Capernaum the disciples discuss who is the greatest.

16. What counsel does Jesus give them? (9:35)

Jesus tells his disciples that if anyone would be first, that person must be "the very last, and the servant of all."

17. How does a child enter the story at this point? (9:36-37)

Jesus takes a child and has him stand among them. Taking the child into his arms, he says, "Whoever welcomes one of these little children in my name welcomes me; and whoever welcomes me does not welcome me but the one who sent me."

18. What does John report to Jesus? (9:38)

John reports, "Teacher, we saw a man driving out demons in your name, and we told him to stop, because he was not one of us."

19. What new understanding does Jesus give the disciples? (9:39-40)

Jesus says, "Do not stop him. No one who does a miracle in my name can in the next moment say anything bad about me, for whoever is not against us is for us."

20. How does Jesus use a cup of water? (9:41)

Jesus states to the disciples, "I tell you the truth, anyone who gives you a cup of water in my name because you belong to Christ, will certainly not lose his reward."

21. What warning does Jesus give to anyone who causes "little ones" who believe in him to sin? (9:42)

Jesus warns that it would be better for that person if a huge millstone were tied around his neck and he be thrown into the sea.

22. What harsh advice does Jesus give? (9:43-48)

Jesus states that if one's hand or foot or eye causes a person to sin, that part should be cut off. He points out that it is better to be lacking a vital part of the body than to have that member cause a person to be thrown into hell where the fire never goes out.

23. How does Jesus use salt in his teaching? (9:50)

Jesus reminds his hearers of the value of salt. However, if salt loses its saltiness, then it cannot become salty again. He advises his followers to be as salt themselves and, as a result, be at peace with one another.

DIMENSION TWO: WHAT DOES THE BIBLE MEAN?

In Chapter 9 we come to the mountaintop experience. The experience is filled with drama and significance that defies our complete understanding. Yet part of the story is also a trip back, the blending of inspiration and perspiration, or heavenliness and earthliness. This experience is the pinnacle in the middle of Mark's story from which the journey into the valley of the shadow of death will take place.

Mark 9:2-8. The "after six days" reference by Mark could simply be informational. Mark's narrative does not usually leave a gap like this, however. Because of the nature of the experience to be described, it is also possible that "six days" is mentioned to imply the event took place on the seventh day, the sabbath.

For the second time (5:37) Jesus takes only the inner circle of disciples with him: Peter, James, and John. On both occasions they are invited to accompany him to a highly dramatic and unique experience. These three disciples were undoubtedly leaders in the early church when this narrative was written. Maybe their inclusion in the high moments of Jesus' life was part of establishing or confirming their credentials for church leadership. Also this inspiring event may be what Jesus was referring to in the statement just before this story in 9:1: "I tell you the truth, some who are standing here will not taste death before they see the kingdom of God come with power."

Tradition identifies a mountain just a short distance northwest of the Sea of Galilee as the Mount of Transfiguration. A small church is on its crest overlooking the sea. Adjoining the church is a lovely wooded garden area often used by pilgrims as a place of meditation and prayer. If any of the class members have visited Israel, they have probably been to this site and would have slides or pictures of it. Invite them to share any slides or photographs of these scenes with the rest of the class members. This Mount of Transfiguration may be the same place to which Jesus has withdrawn several times (1:35; 6:46).

In some way the appearance or form of Jesus seemed to change ("was transfigured").

The word translated "dazzling" is a word used for the brightness of the sun in its brilliance or of highly polished metal. The brilliance even saturates Jesus' garments with the untarnished whiteness of absolute purity.

Appearing with Jesus are Moses, the representative of the Law and the first lawgiver (Exodus 19:7), and Elijah, traditionally regarded as the first of the prophets. Law, prophecy, and gospel meet together upon the mountaintop. The personifications of the tradition that preceded Jesus appear with him—old covenant and new covenant. Patriarch, prophet, and the great high priest meet together on the mountaintop.

As if that is not enough, a voice with a tone of authority and authenticity speaks to the disciples, "This is my Son, whom I love. Listen to him!" Recall Mark's central theme as stated in 1:1. The Transfiguration becomes the climatic evidence of Jesus' divinity.

I see a parallel between Moses on Mount Sinai and Jesus on the Mount of Transfiguration. It is as if the writer of the Gospel would have us understand that a new Sinai had come to pass with the new Moses on the mountaintop. God spoke to Moses through a thick cloud (Exodus 19:9). On another occasion on Mount Sinai Moses catches a vision of the Lord with such brightness and glory that Moses cannot look at the Lord. Instead, Moses hides in the cleft of the rock and sees only the trail of God's glory passing by (Exodus 33:12-23). Recall also, that on Mount Sinai Moses receives his instructions from the Lord (Exodus 19:7-25; 34:1-28). Receiving the Law gave a new authenticity to Moses' leadership and to his role among the children of Israel. From that mountain he went back into the midst of the multitudes to find that they were essentially as he had left them, except more needful of his voice of leadership. Now a second Moses, Jesus, ascends the mountain and is confronted by the presence of the Lord with the same brilliance of light and glory and receives authenticity from his God.

The meaning of the Transfiguration for Peter, James, and John is clear in 9:7-8. The voice from the cloud declares that Jesus is the Son of God. And the passage adds, "Listen to him." The Son of God speaks with divine authority; the disciples must listen to Jesus.

Peter is thrilled—and terrified! He calls Jesus by the Hebrew word, *Rabbi* (meaning "master," verse 5), for the first time in Mark, again suggesting that the Transfiguration is a sabbath-day experience. Peter exclaims, "Let us put up three shelters." Shelters (or booths) are temporary shelters or shrines. Peter wants to hold on to what is taking place and not let it go away or have the disciples go away. But soon the three disciples look up and no one is there—no cloud—no Moses—no Elijah—just Jesus. Jesus beckons them to leave, and down the hill they go.

Mark 9:9-10. The messianic secret still prevails. In spite of this glorious revelation, Jesus' real identity is not to be published abroad by his disciples. In spite of the affirmation of Jesus as the Son of God, Jesus continues to speak of himself as the Son of man. In effect, Jesus is saying that his resurrection will be the ultimate testimony to all humanity as to who he is.

Still the disciples are puzzled. In Mark's account they are described as questioning among themselves what "rising from the dead" means. Mark alone reports this quandary. Perhaps since this was the earliest account, it was close enough in time to the events themselves that this bewilderment could be remembered and considered common. By the time Matthew and Luke wrote of this same conversation, the conviction about the meaning of the Resurrection had become so strong in the Christian community that they could not imagine persons close to Jesus not understanding what Jesus was saying.

Mark 9:11-13, 30-31. Once again there is a reference to Elijah and his coming (see also 6:14-15; 8:28). The disciples' question is clear but the answer as given in verses 12 and 13 is very unclear. The disciples want to know the purpose of the predicted coming of Elijah. Jesus says it is to "restore all things." However, from that point on the text becomes obscure. Some scholars feel that through the years some sentences may have gotten arranged in the wrong order. One rearrangement suggested by British scholar, C. H. Turner, is as follows: verses 10, 12b, 11, 12a, 13.

In Matthew's version of this story the question about Jesus' sufferings is turned around into an observation. That account (Matthew 17:10-11) is more logical in its form and more readily understandable. Perhaps Matthew intentionally corrected or clarified Mark's account.

Through his statements Jesus affirms that Elijah has come (probably in the person of John the Baptist) and did suffer. "Restoring all things" is not a task that brings glory and success, as the disciples think, but suffering and injustice. Justice must sometimes be advanced by being the recipient of injustice. Can class members find examples of justice being advanced in our time?

Obviously, the disciples still have trouble accepting the revised job description for the special servants of God as formulated by Jesus (Mark 8:31-33). Their preconceptions were so different. This lack of understanding becomes evident later in 9:31-32.

As they come down from the mountain, the disciples still cannot blend the exaltation of Jesus with the sufferings Jesus had foretold for himself. They were groping for some possible rationale to show it would not be true. Beneath their questioning was the meager hope that through Elijah's coming and achievements, what was described as inevitable might be altered. Indeed, perhaps what they had seen was evidence that things had changed. But to their deep disappointment, Jesus tells them in effect through his answers that the dark future remains the same. Inspiration does not alter facts, even though at times we like to pretend it does. Jesus tries to get this across in the first phase of the transition.

Mark 9:14-29. The transition from ecstasy to ordinary continues. The three disciples and Jesus are given no respite, no time for adjustment from the extraordinary to the commonplace or to pause for reverent reflection.

The second phase of the transition is circumstantial. Arguments and human inadequacy in the face of deep human need now greet them. Truly, now they are back home again. Paralyzed by controversy over who should do what, they let human need continue. Does this not sound all too familiar? People collapse on our personal and community and national thresholds, and we conduct seminars or debate methods. Ask class members to identify current crises to which a similar type of response is being given.

Jesus refuses to be drawn into this trap. Disregarding discussions and condemning their inactivity as faithlessness (verse 19), Jesus moves to meet the need.

The description of the boy suggests the symptoms of epilepsy. The sudden attacks result not only in convulsions but also in his falling into fires or into the lake from the water's edge, adding to the danger and hurt from his illness. The boy's evil spirit is described as "deaf and mute" (verse 25). Jesus rebukes the spirit and the boy, at first appearing to be dead, is lifted to his feet, healthy.

Face to face with a miraculous cure, we must decide how to react to all miraculous events recorded in the Gospels. Perhaps now is an appropriate time for class members to discuss how to interpret and understand the miracles. Differences of opinion should be encouraged and welcomed. A study group is valuable to the extent that it becomes open enough for participants to feel at home in expressing their convictions or doubts. Some people will tend to dismiss an event like this cure as impossible and feel it just did not happen. Other people will try to find some understandable process that could have happened

to bring the cure about. Perhaps the problem was emotional in cause and the underlying emotional conflict was resolved by Jesus' caring. Still other people will simply choose to accept such an event as a suspension of all natural laws and processes by God's power that enabled this healing to happen.

Regardless of differences at this point, we need to see why Mark included this healing and similar stories in his narrative. Knowing why these stories are here may be even more important than knowing what actually happened or how it happened. Mark wants the readers to know that Jesus is the Son of God, that he was divinity present and in action. It is almost as if Jesus wanted himself to be seen in his human aspect but Mark wants to be certain we see him in his divine aspect. To Mark "God was . . . in Christ" (2 Corinthians 5:19). That is what he wanted his readers to sense, discover, and know. So in the healing of the boy with epilepsy, something tremendous happened, so tremendous that we shall never know or understand it completely. But to Mark, and through him to us, the healing is a testimony to who Jesus is. Furthermore, this study is an invitation to discover what could happen if this same Jesus takes us by the hand and lifts us up.

Make a special note of Jesus' promise and the father's prayer in response (verses 23-24). The father hurts for and with his son. He wants, indeed, anything possible to be done to bring healing. Yet he has struggled a long time hoping for cures that never materialized. Now he is called on to hope again. He wants to, but is honest enough to recognize the difficulty and the fear in hoping again. Thus he prays, "I do believe; help me overcome my unbelief!" Have we not all felt this way and prayed this prayer? Perhaps class members might share times when they have felt this way. They might be helped by knowing that others feel this same need, and thus class members might become supportive of each other.

Another special note should be made of Jesus' answer to the disciples in verse 29—that they failed in their endeavors because only prayer can bring about the desired result. At the risk of reading more into his answer than belongs there, I seem to sense that Jesus was saying that they were relying on their abilities or seeking to do something for personal acclaim. But God's servants can only achieve when they know they are not able and must depend on God who enables them. Then the glory belongs to God and not to God's servant. How would class members relate these concepts to the stress today from many sources that say you can achieve success by a positive self-image and self-assurance?

Mark 9:33-37, 42-50. The lovely story of Jesus and the child is a part of the continuing effort by Jesus to overturn accustomed ways of determining values and priorities. He calls the disciples and us to entirely new perceptions. He shows the disciples that inspiration is not to be an escape, but an energizer to serve. He tells them that to be Son of God means being Son of Man through hurt and even death. He counsels them that spiritual achievement is not on the basis of reputation or ability but of such an awareness of inability that one yields to God's empowerment.

Now, Jesus finds the disciples embarrassed because they were discussing who is greatest. This discussion is perhaps prompted by the question as to whether those who were with Jesus on the Mount of Transfiguration now have a superior status. Maybe they feel they do. So Jesus uses an object lesson. A child is placed in their midst. The one who tends to be disregarded, the one who is powerless and generally considered unimportant, is identified as the most important. In the simple faith of a child one finds the example of dependence on God. Whatever attitude or neglect we have for the unnoticed ones, especially children, will bring our own judgment. We are to be the servant and the spiritual caretaker of the least-noticed and least-acclaimed. We are to be judged not by what we have done for the noticed ones, but for what we have done and for what evil we have prevented for the unnoticed ones.

Mark 9:38-41. Furthermore, Jesus wants his followers to know that they have no special or unique claim on God's powers to help and heal. God sometimes works through us; God sometimes works around us. This knowledge forever keeps us humble. To Jesus it is not so much the identity or credentials of who does the caring act, but that it is done. Jesus continues to attack the presumption that spiritual experience gives one superior status or greater ability. No, spiritual acquaintance should help us know our inadequacies and how God is present in persons and places where we never knew God to be.

DIMENSION THREE: WHAT DOES THE BIBLE MEAN TO ME?

The class may discuss the following topic or use the material in the student book.

"If You Can"

In Mark 9:14-27 the disciples have made the first attempt at healing a young boy who suffers from seizures, and they cannot do it. This may not seem so strange; Jesus is the one who is the Son of Man and who is the miracle worker in the group. Large crowds of people follow Jesus for the chance to be miraculously healed. They never went to the disciples for healing before the disciples began to travel with the Master.

Yet, Jesus expresses exasperation with them for not being able to drive out this evil spirit; they are part of an "unbelieving generation." Obviously this unbelief prohibits the power of healing. (Recall Mark 6:5-6.) When the boy's father petitions Jesus for his intervention, he prefaces his request by saying, "If you can do anything" (9:22). Jesus can, and he does.

Ask the class: What place do you think belief has in healing? If individual Christians have enough faith, can they heal the sick? If individual Christians have enough faith in prayer, will their illnesses be healed? Is the power of Christ limited by our lack of belief, or can we do anything we want in the name of God? How do we quantify how much faith is necessary to do God's will?

They were on their way up to Jerusalem, with Jesus leading the way, and the disciples were astonished, while those who followed were afraid (10:32).

9

On the Road Again

Mark 10

DIMENSION ONE:
WHAT DOES THE BIBLE SAY?

Answer these questions by reading Mark 10

1. Where does Jesus go now? What does he do there? (10:1)

   Jesus goes into the region of Judea and across the Jordan. In these places he again resumes teaching.

2. What questions do the Pharisees and Jesus ask of each other? (10:2-4)

   The Pharisees ask Jesus whether it is lawful for a man to divorce his wife. Jesus responds by asking what Moses, the lawgiver, has commanded. They answer that Moses has permitted divorce. A man writes a certificate of divorce and this makes it official (Deuteronomy 24:1-4).

3. What commentary does Jesus make about this law? (10:5-9)

   Jesus states that this law is only given as a concession to the hardness of heart of people who are not open to the higher intent of God for them. He recalls the Creation story (Genesis 1:27; 5:2) in which the making of persons into male and female is told. There it also provides that a man shall leave his own parents and be joined to his wife (Genesis 2:24). Thus the two become one. Jesus observes that since God has decreed that the two are one, persons should not separate what God has joined together.

4. What additional teaching on this subject does Jesus add later for his disciples? (10:10-12)

   Later in the house his disciples ask Jesus for more insight on this subject. Jesus then states that whoever divorces a spouse and marries another person commits adultery.

5. Who are brought to Jesus? What is the disciples' reaction? (10:13)

   The crowd bring children to Jesus so that Jesus might touch them, but the disciples rebuke them for doing so.

6. What feeling does Jesus have, and what does he say? (10:14-15)

   Jesus tells them to let the children come to him and not hinder them. He says that the kingdom of God belongs to children. He adds that whoever will not receive the kingdom of God like a little child shall not enter it.

7. What does Jesus do with the children? (10:16)

   Jesus takes these children into his arms and blesses them by putting his hands on them.

8. What question is asked by the man who runs to meet Jesus? (10:17)

   Addressing Jesus as "good teacher," he kneels before Jesus and asks, "What must I do to inherit eternal life?"

9. What answer does Jesus give? (10:18-19)

   Jesus first responds, "Why do you call me good?" Jesus affirms that "no one is good—except God alone." He then recalls some of the Ten Commandments (Exodus 20:12-16; Deuteronomy 5:16-20) because obedience to the Commandments is the way to life.

10. What is the man's reaction and Jesus' advice? (10:20-21)

    The man boasts that he has been observing these Commandments ever since he was a child. Jesus advises him that he lacks one thing: he needs to sell what he has, give to the poor, and follow Jesus. He will have treasure in heaven.

11. What are the inner feelings of the man and of Jesus? (10:21-22)

As he observes and hears him, Jesus loves this man. However, the man becomes disappointed with what Jesus tells him. He leaves saddened because he has many possessions that he does not want to lose.

12. What commentary does Jesus make about rich persons? (10:23-25)

Jesus says to his disciples that it will be very hard for those who have riches to enter the kingdom of God. It is easier for a camel to go through the eye of a needle than for a rich person to enter the kingdom of God.

13. How do the disciples react to this commentary? (10:24, 26)

They are amazed with this teaching. They become even more astonished and ask each other, "Who then can be saved?"

14. How does Jesus answer them? (10:27)

Jesus' answer to the disciples is, "With man this is impossible, but not with God; all things are possible with God."

15. What is Peter's testimony and Jesus' response? (10:28-31)

Peter begins to say that he has left everything to follow Jesus. Jesus promises that anyone who has left property or family members for his sake and the gospel may be persecuted, but will receive a hundred times as much in this life and eternal life in the age to come. However, Jesus cautions that many who appear to be first will actually be last, and those who appear to be last may actually be first.

16. Where does Jesus now head, leading the disciples? What is their feeling about it? (10:32)

Jesus goes toward Jerusalem with his disciples. They are amazed, and those who follow are afraid.

17. What does Jesus say awaits him in Jerusalem? (10:33-34)

Here Jesus restates with added details that he will be condemned to death in Jerusalem. He will be delivered to Gentiles who will mock him, spit on him, flog him, and finally kill him. He identifies the chief priests and teachers of the law as those who will initiate this tragic process. Jesus again predicts that three days after his death he will rise again.

18. What request do James and John make of Jesus? (10:35-37)

They first ask Jesus to do whatever they ask of him. Then they say to him, "Let one of us sit at your right and the other your left in your glory."

19. What question does Jesus ask them? What is their answer? (10:38-39a)

Feeling that the disciples do not really understand what they ask, Jesus asks them whether they are able to drink the cup he must drink or be baptized with the baptism he is receiving. They say, "We can."

20. How does Jesus respond to their answer? (10:39b-40)

Jesus predicts that they will drink the same cup he drinks and will be baptized with the same baptism. However, he cannot grant a position at his right or left. It is, rather, for those for whom it has been prepared.

21. After the other disciples become indignant with James and John, what insight does Jesus give them? (10:42-45).

Jesus points out that those who are supposed to rule over the Gentiles lord it over them, and their high officials exercise authority over them. But whoever would be great among you must be your servant, and whoever would be first among you must be slave of all.

22. To what town do they come? Whom do they meet there? (10:46-47)

They come to Jericho where there is a large crowd. As they are leaving Jericho, a blind beggar named Bartimaeus is sitting by the roadway and shouts, "Jesus, Son of David, have mercy on me!"

23. What is the reaction of the crowd and of Jesus to Bartimaeus? (10:48-49)

Many rebuke him, telling him to be quiet. Yet Bartimaeus shouts even more to Jesus. Jesus stops his journey and asks them to call him.

24. What does Jesus ask him? What is Bartimaeus's request? (10:51)

Jesus inquires about what Bartimaeus wants of him. Bartimaeus asks to be able to see.

DIMENSION TWO:
WHAT DOES THE BIBLE MEAN?

Mark 10 records the transition of the ministry of Jesus from the northern areas of Palestine to the southern areas. Chapter 10 tells of events that take place on the journey south. However, Chapter 10 is more than a change in place. Chapter 10 marks a change into a new phase of Jesus' ministry. Jerusalem, to which Jesus now heads, will be the place of supreme testing and final hours. Jesus knows this and those with him sense it.

Mark 10:1, 46. Now is an appropriate time to update our record of the movements of Jesus since they were summarized in Lesson 6. (See the commentary on 7:31.) These can be traced on your map, if class members have one available. From the region of the Decapolis on the southeastern shore of the Sea of Galilee, Jesus moves around the southern shore or across the sea on the western shore. Then by boat Jesus heads north over the sea to Bethsaida (8:22). Jesus continues directly north to Caesarea Philippi (8:27). Jesus moves up into a high mountain (9:2) that may have been between Caesarea Philippi and Mount Hermon to the northeast where such mountains are found. Or the high mountain may have been south near the Sea of Galilee at or near the traditional site of the Transfiguration.

Then Jesus moves into Galilee (9:30), the province on the western side of the sea. This trip to Galilee would be Jesus' last trip through his home area near Nazareth. The trip may well have been a sentimental journey home. After a circle through Galilee, he ends up at Capernaum that has been his "headquarters" during these years of ministry, for a final visit.

Now Jesus heads south with his disciples on their fateful trip. Jesus may have sailed across the sea to the southern point where the sea empties into the Jordan River. The Jordan River flows directly south for ninety miles, emptying into the Dead Sea as only a very shallow stream. After proceeding south about thirty miles on the west side of the Jordan, one comes to the provinces of Samaria and Judea stretching all the way west to the Mediterranean Sea, about fifty miles. (These places, along with Galilee, are in present-day Israel.) On the opposite, or east side of the Jordan, is the province of Perea (now part of Jordan), a very hilly mountainous area. This region was commonly spoken of as "beyond the Jordan."

Jesus heads south, probably in the vicinity of the Jordan River, visiting places on both sides in both provinces. Mark's report that "crowds of people came to him" again is especially interesting in this context. This territory is new for Jesus in large measure. Crowds gathering show how widely his reputation has spread and preceded him. Jesus will continue south along the Jordan until he comes to Jericho, five miles west of the Jordan. From Jericho an important road wound upward through the wilderness to Mount Zion and Jerusalem.

Mark 10:2-12. The Pharisees seem to be following Jesus closely, monitoring Jesus' moves and words. The Pharisees may be becoming apprehensive themselves as Jesus travels toward Jerusalem. What will happen there? Will he draw acclaim from the people? Will he be a threat to the religious authorities? In teaching this lesson it will stimulate interest if you underline or give expression to the dramatic circumstances of Jesus' movements toward Jerusalem and his dialogues with the Pharisees. Class members might enjoy using their imagination to create and roleplay one of the following:

- Two of the Pharisees discussing between themselves their opinions of Jesus and the implications of Jesus' trip to Jerusalem.

- Two or more disciples sitting around a campfire en route sharing their personal feelings about Jesus and this journey.

- Jesus and the Pharisees in dialogue together.

- Jesus musing with himself about what he sees and feels during his journey.

The issue raised with Jesus is that of divorce. Jesus refers back to the Mosaic law on divorce found in Deuteronomy 24:1-4. (Have someone read this passage aloud to the group.) This law was based on a patriarchal concept of society wherein the man made the decisions and women were subject to man's whim and will. If a husband disliked something about his wife, all he had to do was to write a bill of divorce and, in effect, to discharge her. (For a sample of the exact passage of this divorce certificate, see the commentary on Mark 10:5-9 in *The Interpreter's Bible*, Abingdon Press, 1979, Volume 7; page 796.)

Jesus interprets this permissive attitude in the law toward divorce as a concession to human weakness and indifference (hardness of heart) to God's purposes for marriage. Jesus goes back beyond this law to point to a more basic principle as stated in Genesis 1:27 and 5:2. Because Jesus sees a husband and a wife as one according to God's decree and creation, Jesus sees it as invalid for the husband to be able to discharge (put asunder) the wife.

Of course, this interpretation goes against what had become commonly accepted customs and practices. So the disciples ask Jesus more questions for clarification. The comments here (verses 11-12) are again in reaction to the other features of the Mosaic law just mentioned. That law provided that a second man might marry the divorced woman. If the second man divorced her, anyone else could still marry her except for the first husband. That was the only restriction against the marriage of a divorced person. Jesus here appears to extend even wider his concern and expectations regarding marriage commitments. Whereas earlier Jesus had attacked the concept in the law that allowed a husband to divorce his wife, now he attacks the part that allows the marriage of divorced women. His obvious intent was to have marriage looked on as a lifelong commitment, with equal respect and security for both partners. Jesus' teaching opposes the arbitrary right of the man and husband to treat as property his wife and elevates the woman and wife as meriting respect and care. (Note that Matthew adds a justifiable cause for divorce when he includes this teaching in 5:32.)

"Adultery" emerges out of a concept basic in the old Jewish tradition. The man or father was of prime importance. To have children was seen as the purpose of marriage. In that day of limited scientific understanding, the man was thought to produce the nucleus of that child that, through sexual intercourse, was placed in the mother's body to be nourished until birth took place. The mother's role was simply that of a custodian and nourisher of the growing infant until that baby emerged into the world. For the man's status, it was important to have a child who was his child. If sexual intercourse took place between the wife and someone else, then this might adulterate the line of descent. If a child was born, there would be uncertainty as to whose child it was.

Mark 10:13-16. You will want to recall the incident discussed in last week's lesson (9:36-37) where Jesus used children as an object lesson in teaching. Again Jesus refers to children in this passage. In the light of what Jesus told the disciples in the earlier incident, it is somewhat surprising that the disciples rebuke the parents for bringing their children to Jesus. However, as we have already noted several times in reading Mark's account, the disciples often appear slow to understand and act on what Jesus is teaching them.

The children had been brought to Jesus for his blessing ("to have him touch them"). Jewish parents would often bring their children to the rabbi for a blessing, especially a highly revered rabbi. The word translated *rebuke* has its roots in buying and selling a product. The word *rebuke* literally means "to mete out what was a due measure." In the negative sense this means "to censure or admonish." The word used for the feeling of Jesus in response (*indignant*) has its roots in the word for *grieving*. It describes a feeling of regret and resentment born out of a deep hurt.

In the earlier passage, Jesus pointed out that as the disciples received a child, the disciples received Jesus also. Now Jesus enlarges (or perhaps clarifies) that statement to say that as one receives a child, that person receives the kingdom of God. Implicit in this enlarged concept may be for the first time in Mark the identification of Jesus' coming into life and the Kingdom's coming into life as interrelated, if not identical.

This beautiful scene of Jesus taking the children up in his arms and blessing them will forever stand out as one of the loveliest scenes in all of the Gospels. Ask class members in advance to look for and bring to this session any artistic portrayals of this scene they can locate in books and children's Sunday school material. It might be interesting to see the different perspectives on the meaning of this occasion as conveyed through art.

Back to back, thus far in this chapter Jesus has testified to the value and sanctity of the family unit and each person in it: husband, wife, child.

Mark 10:17-31. The next stop on the way is an interruption by a man who seeks "to inherit eternal life." Perhaps Mark makes no connection with this story and the preceding story. A possible connection may be a response to Jesus' promise of the kingdom of God to children. If that is what children can receive, then the man, equating the kingdom with eternal life, wants to receive the same. This man is commonly identified as the rich young ruler because Matthew (and Matthew only) speaks of the man as a "young man" (19:22).

The deference to God alone being "good" expresses typical Jewish reverence for God. God was always seen as high and holy, deserving of profound reverence. When the word for God's name appeared in Holy Scripture, the word was not even pronounced; a substitute word was used. Thus only God was seen as truly good; all others were tainted by sin. Jesus reflects in his own attitudes an acceptance of this customary reverence for God. This comment about God alone being good is but one illustration. Have we lost this profound sense of respect and reverence for the name of God? Have we substituted a cheap, overly familiar concept of God that has resulted in the loss of reverence? How can we be intimate with God while still preserving reverence? Class members might profit by discussing these questions.

In answering the man's question, Jesus uses the traditional Jewish formulation of the way to life. The way to life is through obedience to the law. Psalm 119 celebrates this basic concept:

> If your law had not been my delight,
>   I would have perished in my affliction.
> I will never forget your precepts,
>   for by them you have preserved my life.
>   (Psalm 119:92-93)

The man's faithfulness to the law had not brought him life.

Jesus' attitude toward the man is impressive: "Jesus looked at him and loved him." Why do class members think Jesus loved the man? Could it be the man's willingness to go beyond traditional concepts and to be open to new possibilities? Could it be just for the man's willingness to do something about his deeply felt need?

The additional counsel of Jesus is that law must be translated into lifestyle. We are required to find life beyond having obedience—that is to have purpose and love. Giving allegiance is not enough; one must give one's self. Meaning is found not in living laws but in giving life. Jesus is the model of giving life for others. As we give, so do we receive. This spirit is found in the prophet Micah's famous insistence:

He has showed you, O man, what is good.
  And what does the LORD require of you?
To act justly and to love mercy
  and to walk humbly with your God.

  (Micah 6:8)

Once again Jesus has reversed the customary viewpoint. The man goes away sad because the cost of genuine spiritual life requires not more obedience to law but more sacrifice of self, a reversal of priorities. The disciples are amazed because again Jesus has challenged the customary concepts that accepted prosperity as a mark of God's blessings and the life for which all hoped and sought. *Life* had come to be seen as material blessedness. But the material blessedness is not the life of the Kingdom. If you plan to buy your way in, you will never make it!

Such sentiments create even more astonishment in the disciples, to the degree that they wonder whether anyone can be saved. Jesus stresses the point that the door to life is always opened by God to those in whom God's life and Spirit have entered. So God is the enabler for anyone's entrance to the Kingdom. God's Spirit within us, affecting the totality of our life including our use of our resources, is the key to the Kingdom.

The disciples are still groping for a means to show their spiritual attainments—that is, pride. If the key is not in what you have but in what you give, then Peter and the disciples can get merit and praise for their sacrifices. Jesus acknowledges that sacrifice will bring results and at times rewards. Yet in honesty he points out that it may also bring "persecutions" and a reversal of expectations. Self-sacrifice for the sake of the gospel is exactly that—for the sake of the gospel, not for some personal gain.

Mark 10:32-34. For the third time (8:31; 9:31) Jesus alerts his disciples to the sinister events that lie ahead. Perhaps Jesus intentionally states this passion prediction immediately after talking about what might bring pain not gain. In spite of this prospect and the disciples' dismay, Jesus walks on ahead of the disciples, as if to lead the way.

Mark 10:35-45. Perhaps sensing an impending climax to the story and still not understanding the nature of the life to which Jesus calls the disciples, James and John ask for special positions in Jesus' future state. James and John may have anticipated that the popularity of Jesus would turn the tide and Jesus would not suffer but be honored with high position. James and John want to be a part of that esteemed leadership team. Of course, the other way of looking at James and John's request is to feel they sense now the beginning of a final chapter. They do not want death to end it. In either event, James and John still are seeking for status while Jesus is talking about sacrifice.

James and John appear so eager to obtain status that they grandly state they can even "drink the cup" Jesus has to drink, little knowing its bitter depth. All this greatly frustrates and even irritates Jesus. Seemingly, James and

John will not listen, they will not understand, they will not do and become. So Jesus calls all the disciples together and makes it clear in unmistakable terms (verses 42-45). These statements sum up Jesus' ministry and his personhood.

Mark 10:46-52. This healing event at Jericho on the road to Jerusalem witnesses again to the fact that Jesus still has a concern for persons—their hurts and needs. The impending drama in Jesus' life does not prevent him from responding to persons in need along the roadway. Mark conveys to us a portrait of the greatness of Jesus—a greatness revealed through dramatic achievements and simple sensitivities. Such is the nature of what Mark's Gospel would show us to convince us Jesus is the Son of God—a new definition of divinity.

DIMENSION THREE: WHAT DOES THE BIBLE MEAN TO ME?

The New Road With Jesus

Chapter 10 begins with pronouncements by Jesus that fly in the face of much of what has become customary and acceptable regarding the impermanence of marriage in our era. Chapter 10 takes us down a roadway where we meet a person faithful to the commandments but spiritually empty, the self-seeking of disciples, spiritual and physical blinding, and a dark cloud ahead. Can this be put together in any way? I believe Chapter 10 teaches us two things about God. First, God is an understanding God, aware of our humanity, demonstrating this understanding by God's entrance into that humanity in Jesus and walking the common, hurtful road. Second, God is the God of the second chance. God is always there seeking to help us remake circumstances as they are or to create new circumstances through which redemption, grace, and renewal can be experienced. The awareness of our fallenness makes all of us stand in the need of grace. Though our marriages may be solid and stable, still there are areas of our lives in which we have known fallenness and in which we have desperately needed grace. Fallenness may be in our pride, in our self-seeking, in the habits that have hurt our health or hurt the health of others, or simply in the way in which we have pursued false priorities and idolatrous goals. Those of us who know we are fallen cannot bring ourselves to condemn others who have fallen in different ways, for we are all wrapped up together in fallenness. Yet we are all wrapped up together as recipients of God's grace that comes to us and helps us rebuild our relationships and our priorities.

Jesus is constantly humbling himself (hiding the fact of his messiahship, not wanting to be called good, using Son of Man rather than Son of God). At the same time the disciples are trying to exalt themselves. What does this reveal about, and say to, those of us in leadership positions in the service of Christ?

Those who went ahead and those who followed shouted, "Hosanna! / Blessed is he who comes in the name of the Lord!" (11:9).

— 10 —

Is This the Holy City?

Mark 11:1–12:12

DIMENSION ONE:
WHAT DOES THE BIBLE SAY?

Answer these questions by reading Mark 11:1-25

1. Where do Jesus and the disciples come? (11:1)

   They come to Bethphage and Bethany at the Mount of Olives.

2. What directions does Jesus give two of his disciples? (11:2-3)

   He tells them to go to the nearby village where they will find a colt tied on which no one has ever ridden. They are to untie it and bring it to Jesus. If anyone asks them about their actions, they are to say, "The Lord needs it and will send it back here shortly!"

3. What happens when the disciples go on their errand? (11:4-6)

   Everything takes place as Jesus has predicted.

4. What is done with the colt? (11:7-8)

   The disciples make a saddle out of their clothing, placing it on the colt. Then Jesus sits on it and moves down the road toward the city.

5. What do the crowds do? (11:8-10)

   Many place garments on the roadway and others place large, leafy branches to create a carpet. Those in front and behind him join together in shouting, "Hosanna! / Blessed is he who comes in the name of the Lord! / Blessed is the coming kingdom of our father David!"

6. What does Jesus do in Jerusalem? (11:11)

   Jesus goes into the Temple and looks around at everything there. Then, because it is late, he goes out with the disciples to the nearby village of Bethany.

7. What object does Jesus notice that prompts him to comment in an unusual fashion? (11:12-14)

   Being hungry, Jesus notices in the distance a fig tree with leaves but no fruit. Even though it is not the season for figs, Jesus says, "May no one ever eat fruit from you again."

8. What dramatic event takes place when Jesus returns to Jerusalem? (11:15-17)

   He drives out those buying and selling in the Temple. He overturns the tables of money changers and the benches of those selling doves. He forbids anyone to carry anything through the Temple. He accuses these persons of making the Temple a "den of robbers."

9. What Old Testament passage does Jesus quote? (11:17)

   Jesus quotes from the prophets (Isaiah 56:7; Jeremiah 7:11): " 'My house will be called a house of prayer for all nations.' But you have made it a 'den of robbers.' "

10. What is the reaction of the religious leaders? (11:18)

    The chief priests and the teachers of the law seek a way to kill Jesus. Yet they are cautious out of fear, because the whole crowd is amazed at his teaching.

11. What new discovery is made as the fig tree is seen again? (11:20-21)

    In passing the fig tree, they notice that it has withered from its roots. Peter calls Jesus' attention to this fact.

12. What counsel and promise does Jesus make? (11:22-23)

He calls on the disciples to have faith in God. He promises that even if one commands a mountain to be thrown into the sea, if that person "does not doubt in his heart, but believes that what he says will happen, it will be done for him."

13. What guidance does Jesus offer about prayer? (11:24-26)

Jesus counsels that whatever you ask for in prayer, believe that you have received it, and it will be yours. Also whenever you pray, forgive, if you have anything against anyone. In this way you may be like God who forgives your sins.

Answer these questions by reading Mark 11:27–12:12

14. Who are the religious leaders who approach Jesus? (11:27) What questions do they ask him? (11:28)

The chief priests, teachers of the law, and elders come to Jesus. They ask about the nature or source of his authority.

15. What question does Jesus ask in response? (11:30)

He asks if the baptism of John is from heaven or is of human origin.

16. What argument among them does Jesus' question create? (11:31-32)

Some feel that if they answer that John's baptism is from heaven, then Jesus will ask why they do not believe John. Others feel that if they answer it is of human origin, the sizable number of people who believe that John is God's prophet will strongly protest against them.

17. What does the discussion conclude? (11:33)

The religious leaders finally answer the question by saying, "We don't know." Jesus responds by saying that he will also not tell them by what authority he performs his deeds of ministry.

18. What form of teaching does Jesus use again? (12:1a)

Jesus begins "to speak to them in parables."

19. What does the owner of the vineyard do? (12:1b-2)

He plants the vineyard and puts a wall around it, adding a wine press and watchtower. He then rents it to some farmers to oversee and leaves on a journey. At harvest time the vineyard owner sends his servants to the tenants for some of the fruit.

20. What reception is given to these servants? (12:3-5)

As each of the first two servants arrive, they are physically abused and sent away wounded and empty-handed. The third servant who is sent is killed. Other servants are sent: some are beaten and others are killed.

21. What does the owner do? (12:6)

He sends the last representative he has, his own beloved son, thinking that surely the tenants will respect him.

22. What is the tenants' action? (12:7-8) What is the owner's reaction? (12:9)

The tenants look on the son as the heir. They feel if they kill the sole survivor of the owner's family, they will inherit the property. So they kill the son and throw his body out of the vineyard. Jesus then says that the owner will come himself and kill the tenants, giving the property to others.

23. What Old Testament passage does Jesus quote? (12:10-11)

He quotes from Psalm 118:22-23:
"The stone the builders rejected
*   has become the capstone;*
the LORD has done this,
*   and it is marvelous in our eyes."*

24. What do the religious leaders do? (12:12)

They look for a way to arrest him because they feel Jesus told the parable to accuse them of wrongdoing. However, for fear of the crowd, they leave Jesus for the time being.

DIMENSION TWO:
WHAT DOES THE BIBLE MEAN?

Humanity and divinity are reflected in the triumphal entry and what follows, both within and around Jesus. Indeed, divinity and humanity confront each other directly in the Holy City. This plot unfolds in Mark 11 and 12.

Mark 11:1. After climbing up the road from Jericho, Jesus approaches Jerusalem. Mark's account, along with Matthew, would lead us to believe that Jesus' trip to Jerusalem is his first visit to Jerusalem. Of course, Mark does not give detailed data of Jesus' travels. Perhaps Jesus had been in Jerusalem on other occasions. (See Luke 2:41-51.) Jesus' familiarity with the city and area around it that underlie his instructions to the disciples (11:2-3; 14:13-15) suggests he has been here before. Also Jesus' familiarity with persons in the Jerusalem area suggests this. In the Gospel of John Jesus is described as being in Jerusalem several times (2:13;

5:1; 7:10). Jesus' complete itinerary for his ministry may never be known.

Bethany is a suburban village near the old city walls of Jerusalem and adjacent to the road of Jericho. Pilgrims to Jerusalem, especially when the city was crowded at Passover, would often stay in Bethany. The location of Bethphage is not certain. It was probably another suburban village near Bethany. The Mount of Olives (named for the olive trees that grow there) is at Bethany and overlooks Jerusalem.

If a class member or your pastor has visited Jerusalem, invite that person to share slides and pictures of the sites and scenes that follow.

Mark 11:2-10. It is Sunday of Jesus' last week on earth. This section describes the physical arrangements being made for Jesus' entry into the city. The animal he plans to ride is a donkey colt. It is interesting to notice the immediate response of the colt's owner to the disciples' request to use the animal (verses 5-6). The owner must have been a great admirer or follower of Jesus, which suggests that Jesus and the disciples have already been in Jerusalem.

More important than the arrangements, however, is the significance of the choice by Jesus of this method of entering Jerusalem. Up to this point in Mark's narrative Jesus has refused to reveal or confirm in public his identity as the Messiah. Apparently Jesus' identity is to be unveiled in connection with Jesus' visit to Jerusalem and the events of this last week.

Three Old Testament passages should be noted in this connection. The first passage is Psalm 2, known as a royal psalm in celebration of the coming of God's anointed, later seen as referring to the Messiah. Ask a class member to read Psalm 2 aloud. Note especially verse 6: "I have installed my King / on Zion, my holy hill." (Mount Zion is the hill or small mountain on which Jerusalem is located.) You might look together at other ways in which Psalm 2 is descriptive of the experience of Jesus.

The second Old Testament passage is Isaiah 62:10-11a:

Pass through, pass through the gates!
    Prepare the way for the people.
Build up, build up the highway!
    Remove the stones.
    Raise a banner for the nations.
The LORD has made proclamation
    to the ends of the earth:
"Say to the Daughter of Zion,
    'See your Savior comes.' "

The third passage is from the prophet Zechariah (9:9):

Rejoice greatly, O Daughter of Zion!
    Shout, Daughter of Jerusalem!
See, your king comes to you;
    righteous and having salvation,
    gentle and riding on a donkey,
    on a colt the foal of a donkey.

This passage is quoted by Matthew (21:4-5) and John (12:14-15) in their narration of Jesus' entry into Jerusalem.

The three passages were well known to every Jew. They were frequently quoted in Jewish worship and served an important role in formulating pictures in the mind of the Messiah to come.

Apparently Jesus now is ready to confirm his identity as Messiah. However, if Jesus speaks about messiahship, that might result in immediate charges of blasphemy and destroy any possibility of completing the witness Jesus still wants to make. Rather than speak about messiahship, Jesus chooses instead to live it—to fulfill the scriptural imageries with which he feels at home, the humble servant rather than the mighty ruler or victorious soldier. Jesus goes "through the gates" down the cleared "highway," coming to the "Daughters of Zion and Jerusalem," "humble and riding on a donkey." Jesus uses this form of proclamation to announce who he is.

The spreading of garments and leafy branches on the roadway was a traditional form of tribute to a visiting ruler (much as we would roll out the red carpet). The word *hosanna* literally means, *O save!* or *Save now!* The shouts of the crowds were an echo of a Jewish hymn found in Psalm 118 and sung at the Passover Feast and the Feast of Tabernacles. Known as the *Hallel* (praise the Lord), its wording in the psalms in part is:

This is the day the LORD has made;
    let us rejoice and be glad in it.
O LORD save us [Hosanna];
    O LORD, grant us success.
Blessed is he who comes in the name of the LORD.
    From the house of the LORD we bless you.
                    (Psalm 118:24-26)

(In addition read Psalm 118:19-27, noting references to "entering through the gates" and the "festal procession" with branches. Later, in Mark 12:10-11, Jesus quotes from this psalm in relation to his situation.)

The reference to "the kingdom of our father David" (11:10) relates to two perspectives. David was regarded as the greatest of the kings and a spiritual standard-bearer for the future. The kingdom under David was seen as the greatest of all times. Thus to speak of the coming of the kingdom of David is to speak of the greatness of the Kingdom. Furthermore, the Messiah was to come from the line of descent from David. So to speak in the presence of Jesus of the kingdom of David is to rejoice in a kingdom brought by David's descendant, Jesus the Messiah.

Mark 11:11. It is Monday of Jesus' last week. Mark gives the impression that Jesus took an inventory of the Temple at this point: This inventory was either preparation for the cleansing of the Temple that would take place the next day or the reason for it. Matthew (21:12-13) and Luke (19:45-46) describe the cleansing of the Temple as taking place immediately after the triumphal entry.

Having completed the first day of this week, it might be helpful to survey the events of the week day by day as Mark records them:

Sunday (Palm Sunday): Entry into Jerusalem and return to Bethany (11:1-11)

Monday: Cursing the fig tree and cleansing the Temple (11:12-19)

Tuesday: Discourses [on the law and the future] (11:20–13:37)

Wednesday: Anointing in Bethany and Judas' betrayal (14:1-11)

Thursday: Preparation for the Passover, Last Supper, Gethsemane, arrest, trial before Sanhedrin (14:12-72)

Friday: Trial before Pilate, condemnation, Crucifixion, burial (15:1-47)

Saturday: Jesus in the tomb (15:42-47)

Sunday (Easter): Resurrection (16:1-8)

Mark 11:12-14, 20-25. These two passages are strange. The episode almost seems out of character for Jesus. The two parts of the story need to be examined together. In the first part Jesus goes to a fig tree that has leaves but no fruit. Even though it is not the season for fruit, Jesus curses the tree by wishing it may never have fruit for anyone. The next day, as Jesus returns to the city with his disciples, the disciples notice the tree has withered overnight. Whereupon, Jesus begins talking about having faith in God.

We wish we had Mark here with us to explain this event. Frankly, this story is so bizarre and puzzling that many scholars question its proper presence in the narrative. This story does have the flavor of some of the imaginative miracle stories about Jesus that appear in the New Testament Apocrypha. These were biographies of Jesus that were so fanciful and miraculous in their stories that they were not included in the official Scriptures (for example, *The Gospel of Peter*). Scholars feel the story was a later addition, which may even have been remembered or written wrongly.

Other scholars stretch hard to reach a meaning. Some think 11:12-14 may have been a take-off on the nearby town of Bethphage, which means "house of unripe figs." Perhaps this passage is a condemnation and warning to Bethphage for their lack of spiritual fruit.

Probably this event depicts Jesus conveying truth through a symbolic act in the style of some of the Old Testament prophets (for example, Jeremiah wearing a yoke in Jeremiah 27–28 and Hosea seeking his wife in Hosea 3). Israel had been referred to in the Scriptures as a tree bearing fruit, in the spirit and imagery of Psalm 1:3.

In their pronouncements of judgment, the prophets spoke of Israel's fruit withering or dying. (See Hosea 9:10-17; Ezekiel 15; 19:10-14.) A judgment is about to fall on Israel through the witness and ultimately the death of Jesus. The first part of this story occurs en route to the cleansing of the Temple. The second part occurs, according to Mark, the next day. Being hungry, Jesus goes to the tree, hoping at least for the early fruit that such trees did bear at that season. Finding none, Jesus deems the tree useless. Jesus condemns the fig tree because, in the hour of intense need of what it might provide, it provided nothing. Thus the fig tree had just as well die since the fig tree no longer served any purpose.

In the prophetic tradition Jesus has acted out a parable. Rather than verbalizing divine judgment on Israel at their distortion of God's purposes, their spiritual mismanagement, and their failure to sense their Messiah at hand, he acts out that judgment in a symbolic manner. The withering of the tree is a "sign" of the truth of Jesus' insight.

The Ezekiel passage (15:8) speaks of the destruction of the vine wood and surrounding desolation "because they have been unfaithful, declares the Sovereign LORD." The judgment on Israel was for the people of Israel's faithlessness. Jesus' symbolic act of judgment on Israel was for the same thing. Thus in response to the observation by the disciples of the tree's dying, Jesus begins to talk about faith. Jesus is not changing the subject but expanding the subject.

The death of the tree is both a warning and a calling to let faith come alive—to preserve life. As Jesus repeatedly revealed in the earlier episodes with persons of desperate need—physical, emotional, spiritual—faith can open the door to new and immense possibilities that God can enable to happen. The mountain moving into the sea is another variation on a theme Mark has helped us see. There is no limit to possibilities when faith's commitment is there; there is no value to life when faith's commitment is not there.

Interestingly, Jesus adds something to faith as an essential. That essential is the receiving and expressing of forgiveness. I see this as an intentional contrast to Jesus' attitude toward the fig tree. In condemning the fig tree Jesus was showing what Israel deserved and would have received under the old covenant. The new covenant is established upon grace and forgiveness. The new covenant through Jesus is an act of God's gracious forgiveness. So Jesus may be saying in effect, "Don't do as I did toward the fig tree, although the action might be deserved. Instead, do toward the faithless as I have done toward you—forgiving and accepting as they are for the sake of what God might enable them to be."

Mark 11:15-19. The fact that all four Gospel accounts include the story of the cleansing of the Temple (Matthew 21:12-13; Luke 19:45-46; John 2:14-16) suggests something of its importance to the writers. Shock waves resound all the way to the highest Jewish authority because of what takes place here.

The people who sold and bought in the Temple were persons selling animals, including doves, for altar sacrifices in worship. (Even today there is an animal market just outside the old city walls.) The money changers would be converting monies of the travelers from distant places into local coinage. (Money changing still takes place inside the old walls.) In both instances profit would be taken and probably corrupt and exploitative transactions would be commonplace. These transactions took place inside the Temple area itself that was built for worship and preparation for worship.

In a dramatic act of civil disobedience, made even more dramatic because it was not in character with the nature of Jesus as disclosed thus far in Mark, Jesus overthrows and casts out these operators of exploitative and profitable commerce within the Temple grounds. In the process of acting in the manner of some Old Testament prophets, Jesus quotes the prophets Isaiah (56:7) and Jeremiah (7:11) to justify his intentions and actions. The "house of prayer" quotation is from Isaiah and the "den of robbers" quotation from Jeremiah.

Let class members explore together what the implications of this act are for church life today. As for the implications in Jesus' day, they were grave. Now the chief priests and teachers of the law (who probably received a kickback from the Temple concessioners) "feared him" (verse 18) for a different reason, not because of Jesus' popularity among the people but because of Jesus' threat to the religious leaders' authority and livelihood. The crowd had seen and were startled—but were thinking anew.

Mark 11:27-33. It is now Tuesday of the last week. Jesus goes back to the Temple. Immediately, the Temple authorities come out to challenge Jesus. They question, probably in heated indignation, the source of Jesus' presumed authority. In the typical style of Mark, Jesus responds to a question with a question. Answering a question with a question was the rabbis' style.

Jesus turns the question of authority around as he asks the religious leaders' opinion of the validity of John's acts of baptism. Jesus seeks from them an authoritative ruling. Yet the religious leaders will not make an authoritative ruling because to answer either way, for or against John the Baptist, will create difficulties for them. They confess an inability to decide. So Jesus infers that if the religious leaders have authority but do not have the ability or willingness to think through and make an official opinion, then authority is really of no importance. Who cares who has what authority, if authority is revealed so poorly by them.

Mark 12:1-12. Jesus returns to his favorite method of teaching, the use of the parable. The happenings in the story speak clearly for themselves. For protection of vineyards that did not have fences around them in that day, the wall (probably a hedge) served as a fence to keep out stray animals. The "watchtower" served as a observation post also to guard against someone stealing or damaging the grapes. The story is a revision, with relevance to Jesus' circumstances of the prophetic song of the vineyard in Isaiah 5:1-7.

The relevance to Jesus is obvious. As this section in Mark began with the crowds shouting a portion of Psalm 118 in tribute to Jesus, so it now ends with Jesus quoting another part of the same psalm with a very different message (verse 22). Psalm 118:22 is Jesus' summary of the meaning of his parable.

This parable forms a conclusion to what has happened thus far in this last week and an introduction to what is yet to happen.

DIMENSION THREE: WHAT DOES THE BIBLE MEAN TO ME?

The class may discuss the following topic or use the material in the student book.

When Currents Collide

Off the coast of North Carolina two currents meet, one sweeping south and one sweeping north. Through the centuries in their meeting they have formed the famed and infamous Cape Hatteras. From the beach at the "point" you can see the spray tossed high in the air as the two streams collide. Unseen beneath the waves for miles outward a treacherous sandy shoal extends that has imperiled many a ship and sailor.

In the events recorded in the section of Mark studied in this lesson two currents are colliding. Ask class members to identify these two currents. One is the current of popular acclaim to the words of Psalm 118 offered by the crowd. The other is the current of jealous apprehension under the guise of legalism and tradition. In what forms do these currents exist today? The parable (12:1-9) illustrates what happens when the currents collide. Beneath the surface the shoals reach out unseen even farther, to the heart of the Temple, as illustrated by the cleansing, and to the whole of Israel, as illustrated by the fig tree.

Can the boat, with Jesus in it, sail safely over these stormy currents, as has been true earlier in Mark? Not without a lot of damage and loss of life. But there is hope beyond the whirlpool for those with God's purpose in their eyes and with faith in God's new possibilities in their heart.

What I say to you, I say to everyone: "Watch!" (13:37).

—11—

What Does the Future Hold?

Mark 12:13–13:37

DIMENSION ONE:
WHAT DOES THE BIBLE SAY?

Answer these questions by reading Mark 12:13-44

1. What new question do the Pharisees and the Herodians ask? (12:13-15a)

   They ask, "Is it right to pay taxes to Caesar or not?"

2. What does Jesus do and say in response? (12:15b-17)

   Jesus recognizes their real intention is to trap him. He asks for a denarius (a Roman coin) and asks whose portrait and inscription are stamped on it. They identify it as Caesar. Jesus says, "Give to Caesar what is Caesar's and to God what is God's."

3. What new group comes to Jesus? What question do they ask? (12:18-23)

   The Sadducees come to Jesus and refer to a law from Moses (Deuteronomy 25:5) known as the law of levirate marriage. This law provided that if a married man died with no children, the man's brother must take the widow and father children for his dead brother. In the Sadducees' question there are seven brothers. After the death of the first brother, each in turn took his wife until the death of each, but no children were born. Then the widow died. Their question is, "At the resurrection whose wife will she be, since the seven were married to her?"

4. What question does Jesus ask in response to their question? (12:24)

   Jesus asks, "Are you not in error because you do not know the Scriptures or the power of God?"

5. Then what answer does Jesus give? (12:25-27)

   He points out that in the resurrection there is no marriage but we are like "angels in heaven." Jesus then refers to the Old Testament episode of the burning bush (Exodus 3) when God spoke to Moses as the God of Abraham, Isaac, and Jacob. Jesus concludes that God is the God of the living, not the dead.

6. What question does a teacher of the law ask Jesus? (12:28)

   Favorably impressed with Jesus' previous answers, a teacher of the law asks him, "Of all the commandments, which is the most important?"

7. What two laws does Jesus identify in his answer? (12:29-31)

   As the most important law, Jesus identifies the first of the Ten Commandments known as the Shema (She-MAH) (Deuteronomy 6:4-5), which centers on the admonition to love God with all one's heart, soul, mind, and strength. Jesus then identifies as the law second in importance one that was not a part of the Ten Commandments. It is from Leviticus 19:18 calling for love of one's neighbor as one's self. Jesus adds that no other commandment is greater than these.

8. What reaction does the teacher of the law have to Jesus' answer? (12:32-33)

   The teacher of the law feels that Jesus answered the question correctly. He repeats what Jesus said. His opinion is that to love God in this way and to love one's neighbor as one's self is more important and valuable than "all burnt offerings and sacrifices."

9. What opinion does Jesus have of the teacher of the law? (12:34a)

   He feels the teacher of the law has given a wise response, and that he is not far from the kingdom of God.

10. What do the observers hesitate to do? (12:34b)

    No one dares ask Jesus any more questions.

11. What question does Jesus ask in the Temple? Why? (12:35-37)

He raises the question as to how the teacher of the law can say that Christ is the son of David when David himself (Psalm 110:1, regarded as written by David) spoke of the Messiah or God's special servant as his Lord rather than as his son.

12. What accusations and warning does Jesus include in his teaching? (12:38-40)

He accuses the teachers of the law of liking to wear flowing robes and to receive public recognition. He states that they want the best seats at synagogues and special places of honor at banquets. This takes place while they are foreclosing on widows' houses and making pretentious but insincere prayers. Jesus predicts that such persons will be severely punished and warns his hearers against them.

13. Where does Jesus sit down? Whom does he observe there? (12:41-42)

Jesus sits down across from the treasury at the Temple where persons are putting their offerings. He watches as many rich persons contribute large sums. Then he notices a poor widow who comes and deposits two copper coins, worth a fraction of a penny in that time.

14. What value does Jesus place on her contribution? (12:43-44)

He feels that she has contributed more than anyone else. The others had given out of a wealth of resources. The widow is poor and has given through her coins everything—"all she had to live on."

Answer these questions by reading Mark 13

15. What impresses one of the disciples? What shocking response does Jesus make? (13:1-2)

One of the disciples expresses admiration for the Temple buildings and their massive stones. Jesus predicts that these magnificent buildings will be demolished, stone by stone.

16. At the Mount of Olives, with whom does Jesus have a private conversation? What do they ask him? (13:3-4)

Jesus talks privately with Peter, James, John, and Andrew. They ask him about the destruction of the Temple, inquiring when this will happen and what will be the sign it is to take place.

WHAT DOES THE FUTURE HOLD?

17. As Jesus begins his answer, what warning does he give? (13:5-8)

He warns them not to be deceived by things they may hear. They will hear of persons coming in Jesus' name and claiming, "I am he!" who will deceive many persons. They will also hear of wars and rumors of wars. They should not be alarmed because this is not the end. War, earthquakes, and famines will not be the end but only the beginning of sufferings.

18. What unfortunate events await the disciples of Jesus? (13:9-13)

They will be questioned and punished by councils, they will be flogged in synagogues and summoned before rulers to defend their convictions. Family members will be against other family members because they are followers of Christ. This hatred will result in separations, betrayals, and even death. The disciples will be hated by all persons because of their devotion to Christ.

19. What consolations does Jesus offer? (13:10-13)

Even in the midst of suffering and disappointing circumstances, the gospel will be preached to all nations. Also, the disciples need not worry about what they shall say when arrested and brought to trial. The Holy Spirit will speak through them. Whoever stands firm to the end will be saved.

20. What event signifies a dangerous era? (13:14)

Jesus speaks of a time when "the abomination that causes desolation" will be standing where it does not belong.

21. What does Jesus say persons should do when this event does take place? (13:14-16)

He says that those who are in Judea should flee to the mountains. Those who are resting on their housetop should not go down into their house to try to save anything. One who is working in the field in work clothes should not return home to pick up a cloak.

22. How does Jesus describe this period? (13:17-20)

Jesus mourns for those who have children or infants during these destructive days. He urges prayer that it does not happen amidst the usual hardships of winter, because the days of distress will be unequaled from the time when God created the world. As a matter of fact, if God did not shorten the days, no human being would survive. God will curtail the length of the days of terror for the sake of his servants whom he has chosen.

23. What warning does Jesus give about false Christs? (13:21-23)

In these days of calamity possibly some will point to a person, identifying that individual as the Christ. They should not be believed because false Christs and prophets will be performing signs and miracles, seeking to confuse and deceive God's servants. Jesus wants his followers to know these things ahead of time so they will be on guard.

24. What will happen after this tribulation? (13:24-27)

Then the sun, moon, and stars will fail and the heavenly bodies will be shaken. At that time the Son of man will be seen coming in the clouds with great power and glory. He will send out the angels and gather in his elect servants from everywhere.

25. When will these things happen? (13:30-32)

Jesus states that all will take place before this generation passes away. The exact time, however, is not known by anyone, not even the angels or God's Son. God alone knows.

DIMENSION TWO: WHAT DOES THE BIBLE MEAN?

The scriptural material studied in this lesson divides into two sections. The first section (12:13-44) is another round of inquiries between the religious leaders and Jesus. In part the religious leaders asked out of curiosity about Jesus' answers to questions repeatedly discussed in Jewish religious circles. However, some questions are also asked with an intent to trap Jesus. By his answers to questions on controversial issues, they hope to obtain data on the basis of which legal accusations can be brought against Jesus immediately. The second section, Chapter 13, moves beyond the immediate moment to the distant future. Not just Jesus is to be tested; all humanity will ultimately be tested. Not just Jesus will go to trial; all his followers will experience trial in one way or another.

Mark 12:13-17. Note that two different groups come to Jesus, each with the same purpose—"to catch him in his words." These groups join in an unholy alliance in treachery. The Pharisees we have met several times previously. The Herodians, however, are new to us. They are not a religious sect or a distinct political group. They are influential Jews who, in great contrast to their other countrymen, were favorably disposed to the rule of Herod. (You may want to refer to the material on the Herod family's rule contained in Lesson 5—6:14-29.) Herod Antipas was the ruler of Galilee and Perea. Archelaus ruled over Judea and Samaria. However, his rule was so inept that he was deposed in A.D. 6. The Romans then made Judea an imperial province, ruling it directly through a procurator.

The Herodians wanted to see Herod Antipas (the Herod of Mark 6) become ruler of Judea also. Probably the Pharisees had enlisted the company of the Herodians, thinking that if they could not find legal charges against Jesus on religious grounds, they might be able to find charges against Jesus on political grounds. The Herodians could help this happen.

The statement of respect for Jesus in verse 14 is probably an insincere attempt to impress Jesus or to lead him to be less guarded in his response to their question. The question about "taxes to Caesar" goes back to the fact that since Judea was an imperial province, taxes were paid directly to Rome. As a matter of fact, the census that brought Mary and Joseph to Bethlehem (Luke 2:1-2) was to establish a census record for this taxation. The coin used, called a denarius, had Caesar's image on it (verse 16). For some Jews this taxation was an expression of subjection and they bitterly opposed it on religious grounds.

Jesus saw through what the questioners were attempting. If he advised that no taxes be paid, he would be in trouble with the Roman government. If he advised that taxes be paid, he would be in trouble with those who felt God's chosen people should not be compromised by subjection or tribute to any pagan regime. By his answer Jesus avoids both extremes, pointing to a dual obligation of every person and the necessity of each person to decide the nature of that obligation. Jesus had slipped out of their trap, and the Pharisees and Herodians "were amazed at him."

Mark 12:18-27. Here we meet the Sadducees, whom many trace back to Zadok the priest from whom their name may be derived. They were largely centered in Jerusalem and were supporters of the Jerusalem priesthood. They rejected the authority of teachers and the oral traditions of the interpretation of the law in contrast to the Pharisees. Instead of seeing Judaism as a religion, they tended to view it as a state. They tended to be well-to-do, old-line families. They saw the necessity of accommodating the powers that be for the sake of commerce and survival. They tended to be less rigid in judgments and more open to varying views. For instance, they did not believe in the resurrection of the body and were open to other concepts.

Ask class members to read aloud the Old Testament law in Deuteronomy 25:5 that is essential to seeing the validity of the plot. In essence, the response of Jesus is that in asking the question about the levirate marriage and heaven, they are misapplying earthly expectations to an entirely different type of being, which the "power of God" (verse 24) brings about. By quoting the famous self-identity statement of God first used to Moses in Exodus 3:6, Jesus implies that the realm of nearness to God is not limited by space, time, and customary earthly relationship. It is a new dimension of life, not subject to our limiting formulations.

Mark 2:28-34. At the beginning of the study of this passage, invite the class members to reread it to themselves. Then ask them to suggest ways in which this dialogue with a teacher of the law (scribe) differs from the previous dialogues with them in this chapter and earlier. For the responsibility of a teacher of the law, see the commentary on Mark 7:1-5 in Lesson 6. This time it appears that a teacher of the law approaches Jesus not out of hostility, but with a growing admiration. This attitude explains the striking difference between this exchange and the verbal exchanges with other questioners. Jesus does not answer this question with a question as he usually does. After all the previous arguments over the finer points of the law with other religious leaders, Jesus almost appears to welcome this question. Perhaps he welcomes the question because of the spirit of the questioner. Perhaps Jesus is also glad to respond to this question because it gives him a chance to express what is at the heart of his concept of life lived under God—and this concept can come right out of the law.

He first quotes the law the Jews know well from the Shema (Deuteronomy 6:4) as most important. Then quickly, instead of lifting up ritual observances or restrictive guidelines as normally a teacher might give as important consequences of that first law, Jesus picks up a rarely noted law (Leviticus 19:18) as the second greatest. All other laws and their expectations, such as those about which he had been questioned, are second to these (verse 31).

To the surprise, and probable dismay, of the other inquirers present, the teacher of the law agrees completely. He commends Jesus and even adds his own testimony to support the viewpoint of Jesus. Responding with obvious delight, Jesus tells the teacher of the law he is "not far from the kingdom of God." By this Jesus is saying that to understand these two laws and then by faithful commitment to live them out is the essence of Kingdom citizenship. This conversation, which turned the mood from confrontation to inspiration, left everyone silent with awe and personal reflection. No more questions are asked by the religious leaders in Mark's account.

Stress the importance of this passage in Mark. It probably is the basic truth Mark wants us to learn from his entire narrative of all that Jesus teaches and all that he does. This truth is the essence of the new insight that Jesus brings and models. If time permits, you might select random passages from earlier chapters and ask the class members to determine how that passage relates the truth summarized in this passage.

Mark 12:35-40. It appears that Jesus is very much aware of the difference between the teacher of the law with whom he has just talked and teacher of the laws in general. That difference leads him to comment about the teachers of the law as he usually has observed them. The first accusation is that of allowing their tradition to limit their vision. As an illustration, traditionally they spoke of the Messiah to come as the "son of David," implying a descent from David and a likeness in style to David. Yet Jesus uses the scriptural tradition itself (Psalm 110:1) to suggest that David looked on the Lord's anointed as his Lord and not simply as a human hero. So the scribes have let themselves become so narrow in their concepts that they cannot see God at their doorsteps.

Jesus adds that they have substituted ceremonial impressiveness for genuine servanthood to the very law they study. Most of the teachers of the law have missed the essence of the law in contrast to the previous teacher of the law who had found it.

Mark 12:41-44. This story of the poor widow and her sacrificial offering presents a contrast to the pretentiousness of the teachers of the law as just described. There is a movement from synthetic service of God to authentic devotion to God. This beautiful portrait also stands out in stark contrast to others whom Jesus observed in the Temple. (Read again 11:11, 15-17 and this passage and then ask class members to compare the two episodes as to the persons encountered and their lessons.) The poor widow's "two copper coins" were the smallest of Jewish coins.

Mark 13:1-37. This entire chapter is very different from anything so far encountered in Mark. Many scholars see it as a collection of materials already in existence that Mark borrowed to include at this point. The material is similar in nature to sayings attributed to Jesus in the Book of Revelation. It becomes almost like a farewell address or an unveiling of the future before Jesus' departure. Chapter 13 is in the style of the Old Testament prophets, a style we have already noted as having become more obvious in Jesus in his last days of ministry. This chapter is sometimes called the *apocalyptic discourse,* meaning the "uncovering" of the other side of history.

The construction of the great Temple was begun about 20 B.C. and was still under construction in Jesus' day. The Temple was regarded as a wonder of the world attracting curious visitors from all over the world. The Temple could clearly be seen atop Mount Zion from across the valley on the Mount of Olives. Jesus sits as he teaches, which was the style of a Jewish teacher.

The imagery of the chapter is deeply rooted in Old Testament prophecy. Underneath the entire passage is the concept of the day of the Lord, prominent in the preaching of the prophets. That day would be a day of God's punishment and reward, destruction, and preservation. Much in Chapter 13 of Mark is in the spirit and imagery of Isaiah, Joel, and Amos. The "abomination that causes desolation" (verse 14) originates in Daniel 9:27; 11:31; 12:11. This phrase is a figure of speech for a presence of evil that is so intense that it profanes the Temple and drives away God's people.

Note in verse 28 the reference to the fig tree. You may wish to review the two previous events concerning a fig tree (11:12-14, 20-24). Read the events again in connection with this present passage, also the commentary on them in Dimension Two of Lesson 10.

As you study this passage, you may be tempted to spend much time on each detailed event and figure of speech and then seek to apply them to some historical episode in recent generations. The figures of speech and succession of events are interesting. However, two things need to be clearly kept in mind. Much of what is contained here reflects, and is born out of, events that took place or were about to take place in the days of the destruction of the Temple by the Romans in A.D. 70 or the persecution of the church by the Romans in the latter half of the first century. The Gospel writer addresses this present situation in the context of a narrative about the past. Also, one can spend much time seeking to detect the exact reference in each phrase and still miss the greater and more important messages to be received from the entire passage. We shall look for these messages in Dimension Three.

DIMENSION THREE:
WHAT DOES THE BIBLE MEAN TO ME?

Watch Therefore

What is Jesus trying to say here on the Mount of Olives? First of all, he is honest enough to acknowledge the fact that life at times seems out of control. By virtue of that, life brings us the very things that we would just as soon not have. Indeed, societies, as well as individuals, are caught up in catastrophes from time to time. There are "wars and rumors of wars," loss of life, the unexplainable, that which seems to be unjust. In other words, life can never be shaped the way we want it, for there will always be that which is threatening, and which at the time seems to be unjust. Jesus frankly acknowledges this fact.

In Chapter 12 Jesus delivers some of the most critical statements that he has made in Mark. There we find sections in which he castigates the religious leaders. Then this episode at the beginning of Chapter 13 begins with a brief discussion about the impressiveness of the Temple. Yet Jesus responds: "Not one stone here will be left on another." What is the meaning of all of this?

What happened here is that all the things about which people built their concept of permanence and security were being threatened in Jesus' comments: the law and the Temple. What Jesus is saying in effect is that no one thing on which you can build a philosophy of life will bring more security. If you try to base your security on a certain set of rules, on a certain outlook, or relate it to a certain place, you will discover that all these are actually impermanent. Life cannot be structured with security based on things or places.

Furthermore, Jesus pushes home a point, which is an Old Testament lesson, that God moves in history as a God of judgment. This judgment can come in the events that overwhelm us. Those events may not be directly decreed by God; nevertheless, the justice and judgment of God work their way out through history and what happens in history.

TIME magazine reported a conversation with an eight-year-old in which she was asked, "What would you like to be when you grow up?" She responded, "Alive." That is where some of us find ourselves today amid the uncertainties of the future. But Jesus goes farther to say that you have to see beyond this future that will have its calamities and will indeed, at times, be the avenue of God's judgment on us. You must recognize that God stands on the other side of history. If you see God's coming as some ultimate event at the end of history, or if you see it in the way in which God comes to us day by day, whether his coming to us is an embarrassment or a consolation, whether it is potentially filled with condemnation or potentially filled with comfort, is really up to each of us. Whether God comes as Judge or as Savior, in the events of history or in the uncertainties of the future, is largely left up to us.

This uncertainty is why Jesus says, "Keep watch because you do not know when the owner of the house will come back." "Watch!" It is like the Boy Scout motto uttered over and over again with divine sanction: "Be prepared." It is a call to Christians to walk expectantly, though they walk uncertainly—to walk expecting Jesus' footfalls and to be ready to greet those footfalls with eager delight, not with embarrassed shame. Jesus' words give a comforting awareness that he will be there in history, he will be there at the end of history, and he will come to us.

What this watching means is that every moment brings meaning to Christians. We walk as those who always are watching, for we know not in what hour Jesus may come. We devote ourselves to his purposes, seek to copy his lifestyle, and seek to personify his nature because we are those who watch. Though history turns us upside down and destroys everything that we have embraced, we still know that Jesus stands there—that he comes—that he will be with us to the end—that he will be with us *through* the end. Knowing this, we find hope and our help.

What is it that Jesus is trying to say here on the Mount of Olives, as he tries to deal with the future? Read the call to watchfulness in Mark 13:33-37. Does the call to watchfulness only make sense if we believe Jesus is coming with clouds during our lifetime? Maybe there is some help for us in a sermon preached by a German preacher during World War II to his congregation who knew that the future looked uncertain, who had already known enough of catastrophe, who were linked up with a governmental structure that could hardly be called Christian, a setting similar to some of the things that Jesus described. Helmut Thielicke said: "This is no longer a mist-covered landscape into which I peer anxiously because of the sinister events which will dare befall me. Everything is now different. We do not know what will come. But we know who will come. And if the last hour belongs to us, we do not need to fear the next minute" (from *The Silence of God,* Eerdmans, 1962; page 9).

"My soul is overwhelmed with sorrow to the point of death," he said to them. "Stay here and keep watch" (14:34).

— 12 —

The Last Mile of the Way

Mark 14

DIMENSION ONE:
WHAT DOES THE BIBLE SAY?

Answer these questions by reading Mark 14

1. What is the Jewish season? What do the Jewish religious leaders decide about Jesus? (14:1-2)

   The time is two days before the Passover and the Feast of Unleavened Bread. The chief priests and teachers of the law are looking for some sly way to arrest Jesus and then kill him. However, to do so during the feast might result in a riot by his admirers. So they delay their intended actions.

2. What unusual act does a woman perform at the house of Simon the Leper? (14:3)

   As Jesus was dining, an unnamed woman comes with an alabaster jar of very expensive perfume made of pure nard and used for anointing. Breaking the jar, she pours it on (or anoints) Jesus' head.

3. What complaint is made about her act? (14:4-5)

   Some are indignant at her action, feeling the valuable perfume can be sold for more than a year's wages. This income can be used to help the poor.

4. How does Jesus respond to the complaint? (14:6-9)

   Jesus responds that she has done a beautiful thing, and he does not want to be bothered by those who object to her act. Jesus feels that opportunities to assist the poor are always present. Yet Jesus will not always be physically present with them. Jesus feels she has anointed his body in advance of his burial. He predicts that wherever the gospel is preached, her act of giving will be told in her memory.

5. What does Judas Iscariot do? (14:10-11)

Judas Iscariot goes to the chief priests to betray Jesus. The chief priests promise to pay Judas for this assistance. Judas begins to look for an opportunity to hand over Jesus.

6. What preparation do the disciples make for the Passover? (14:12-16)

   On the occasion of the first day of the Feast of Unleavened Bread, a Passover lamb is to be sacrificed and a special commemorative meal eaten. Jesus sends two of his disciples into the city of Jerusalem to prepare for the Passover meal. The disciples meet a man carrying a water jar whom they follow to a house. The disciples inquire about a room for the meal. The householder shows them a large upper room. They reserve this room and make preparations there for the evening meal.

7. What disturbing announcement does Jesus make at the outset of the meal? (14:17-18)

   He reveals that a person at the table will betray him.

8. How do the disciples react to this revelation? (14:19)

   They are saddened and each one asks, "Surely not I?"

9. How does Jesus identify the betrayer? (14:20-21)

   He says that the betrayer is the "one who dips bread into the bowl with me." He says that even though the Son of man will die as it is written in Scripture, it still would be better for the betrayer if he had never been born.

10. What symbolic acts does Jesus introduce at this meal? (14:22-25)

    He takes the unleavened bread, prays a prayer of thanks to God, and then breaks it and gives it to his disciples. He speaks of this bread as his body. Then Jesus takes a cup and prays a prayer of thanksgiving for it. He gives this to the disciples who all drink it. He speaks of this as "my blood of the covenant, which is poured out for many."

11. Where do Jesus and the disciples go after the meal? (14:26)

After concluding the meal by singing a hymn, they go out to the Mount of Olives.

12. What warning does Jesus give the disciples? How does Peter react? (14:27-29)

Jesus predicts that they will all fall away, quoting a verse from an Old Testament prophet (Zechariah 13:7) about the sheep scattering after the shepherd has been struck. However, Jesus also foretells that he will rise again and go ahead of them into Galilee. Peter protests that he will not fall away even if everyone else does.

13. What is Jesus' prediction to Peter, and what is Peter's reaction? (14:30-31)

Jesus tells Peter that during that very night he will deny Jesus three times. Peter reacts strongly, affirming that he will not deny Jesus even if he must die with Jesus. All the disciples join with Peter in this promise.

14. Where do they go next? (14:32) Who goes with Jesus? (14:33)

They go to the garden of Gethsemane at the foot of the Mount of Olives. Jesus leaves most of the disciples at the entrance, asking them to wait there while he prays. He takes Peter, James, and John into the inner garden area.

15. What is Jesus' feeling and his prayer? (14:34-36, 39, 41)

Jesus' "soul is overwhelmed with sorrow to the point of death." After asking Peter, James, and John to keep watch, he moves to a private place, falls on the ground, and prays that, if possible, the hour of trial and cup of suffering might pass from him. However, he adds, "Yet not what I will, but what you will." Three times Jesus prays the same prayer.

16. What are his three companions doing? (14:37-41)

Jesus finds the disciples sleeping. Jesus asks whether they cannot watch with him one hour. He urges them to watch and pray. However, they again fall asleep. Jesus describes it, "The spirit is willing, but the body is weak."

17. What sudden interruption takes place? (14:42-43)

Jesus senses that the hour of his betrayal has come. He awakens, then warns his disciples. While he is speaking to his disciples, Judas enters the garden with a crowd sent from the Jewish religious leaders. They are armed with swords and clubs.

18. How is Jesus betrayed? What is Jesus' response? (14:44-49)

Judas has agreed to identify Jesus to the chief priests by kissing him. Judas kisses Jesus, calling Jesus "Rabbi" (or "Master") as he does so. Immediately, the men seize Jesus. One of the disciples draws a sword and strikes off an ear of the high priest's servant. Jesus does not resist seizure. Jesus points out the strangeness of what is happening: They did not seize Jesus when he was easily accessible teaching in the Temple. Instead, they come at night with weapons.

19. What happens to the disciples? (14:50-54)

They desert Jesus and flee. One young follower of Jesus is seized by his linen garment. He drops his clothing and runs away.

20. What problem does the Sanhedrin have with witnesses against Jesus? (14:55-59)

After seeking persons with genuine accusations against Jesus, the religious leaders found none. Instead, they heard a series of persons who made false and contradictory accusations against Jesus. For example, some give testimony that Jesus had said he himself would destroy the Temple that was not hand-made. Yet other witnesses give a different testimony.

21. What questions does the high priest direct to Jesus? What is Jesus' response? (14:60-62)

The high priest asks if Jesus has his own answer to the testimonies about him. Jesus remains silent, making no response. Then the high priest asks Jesus if he is the Christ (Messiah). To this question Jesus responds that he is. He predicts that they will discover this to be true when they see the Son of man "coming on the clouds of heaven."

22. What symbolic act does the high priest perform? (14:63)

He tears his clothes. That is the traditional way of testifying that blasphemy (ideas about God that are irreverent and the opposite of truth) has been uttered in his presence.

23. What decision does the Sanhedrin render? (14:64)

The Sanhedrin condemns Jesus as worthy of death.

24. What accusations are made against Peter? (14:66-67, 69-70)

The high priest's servant girl accuses Peter, while he is in the courtyard, of having been with Jesus. Later she tells other bystanders that Peter is one of Jesus' followers. Then they confront Peter with the same accusation because they notice by his dialect or clothing that he is a Galilean. They know that Jesus came to Jerusalem from Galilee.

25. What is Peter's response? (14:68, 70-71)

To the maid's two accusations, Peter denies knowing Jesus. When the bystanders join in the accusation for the third time, Peter begins to curse and swear he does not even know Jesus.

26. When the rooster crows, what happens to Peter? (14:72)

A cock crows for the second time. Suddenly Peter remembers the warning Jesus had given him at the upper room meal. Jesus told Peter that Peter would deny him three times before the cock crows twice. And Peter breaks down and weeps.

DIMENSION TWO: WHAT DOES THE BIBLE MEAN?

Probably no chapter in the Bible is more filled with a variety of emotion than is Mark 14. We find here intense love and deep-seated hostility, secret conniving and open praise, close fellowship and intense loneliness, strong commitment and shameful betrayal, kisses and blows. Chapter 14 begins with plotting and ends with weeping. It seems that everyone in this drama feels strongly, whatever they feel. And now we shall feel it too.

Mark 14:1-2. It is now at least Wednesday. The Passover will be observed on Friday.

Today *Passover* is the term used among Jews to refer to the entire experience of commemorating their deliverance from Egypt. Originally, however, the entire celebration was usually referred to as the Feast of Unleavened Bread. Passover was the eve of the first day of the feast that lasted for seven days. Passover itself recalled that historic deliverance when the angel of death "passed over" or spared the dwelling of the Jewish slave families in Egypt where the Jewish people had sprinkled the blood of a sacrificial lamb on the doorposts, as directed by Moses (Exodus 12:21-27). Ask a class member to read aloud Deuteronomy 16:1-8 for the detailed instructions as to how the Passover and Feast of Unleavened Bread were to be observed.

Unleavened bread was eaten, as Moses instructed, as a part of their meal on the night of the death angel's visit. They were to continue eating unleavened bread for seven days. From this background the Feast of Unleavened Bread arose as an annual observance related to Passover (Exodus 12:8-14).

Passover and this feast were the highest festivals on the Jewish religious calendar. If a Jew could make only one pilgrimage to Jerusalem in a lifetime, that person would try to travel there at Passover. In time the Passover meal even ended with the parting expression, "Next year in Jerusalem." This is, in part, why Jesus was there with the disciples—as Jewish pilgrims to worship in the Temple during the feast.

Since the cleansing of the Temple (Mark 11:15-17) the chief priests and teachers of the law had decided Jesus must be destroyed. The chief priests and teachers of the law had been trying to trap Jesus with questions and even invited governmental leaders to join them in this intent. Now with the Passover near at hand and the city soon to be thronged with people, something must be done quickly. Yet because of the increasing number of people, it must be done privately lest a public uproar be created or Jesus obtain even more notoriety.

Mark 14:3-9. The home of Simon may be the place where Jesus has been staying all week (11:1, 11, 12). Of course, this Simon is not to be confused with Simon Peter. No one knows anything more about this Simon; but he may have been well-known to Mark's readers, perhaps as an early church leader.

Alabaster pots and jars are still handmade in the desert areas of the Middle East. "Nard" was an expensive perfumed ointment made from the roots and stems of an aromatic Indian herb. Its use as a perfume is mentioned twice in the Song of Songs (1:12; 4:13-14). The "years wages" was about three hundred denarii for a laborer.

The reference by Jesus to "the poor" was a paraphrase of Deuteronomy 15:11: "There will always be poor people in the land. Therefore I command you to be openhanded toward your brothers and toward the poor and needy in your land." This law is behind the protest expressed in verses 4-5 by some who are present.

Anointing the body (pouring on the head) was a practice used as a substitute in that day for the modern practice of embalming. The pleasant odor replaces the odors of bodily decay. As we shall later see, after the death of Jesus the women go to the tomb to "anoint Jesus' body." (16:1).

Jesus here places beyond valuation expressions of tribute and caring. Jesus sees this anointing as an example or memorial worthy of the world's note.

Mark 14:10-11. What the religious leaders needed (in keeping with their decision reported in verses 1-2) was someone on the inside who could tell them when Jesus might be seized away from public notice and who could identify Jesus, especially if it was dark, to the servants whom they would send to take Jesus. This identification was the form of "betrayal"; Judas became their man.

Mark 14:12-16. Because of the throngs in Jerusalem, it would be important for reservations to be made in advance for a place for the Passover meal, just as we would do if we were traveling to a busy city at a convention time. Jesus again suggests a familiarity with the city as Jesus instructs his disciples as to where to go and whom to see to make these arrangements.

Mark 14:17-26. The "table" would have been only about a foot to two feet high. Those dining were on cushions around the table in a half-sitting, half-reclining position.

No eating utensils were ordinarily used, just one's hands. As for the traditional menu for the Passover meal first would be the sacrificial lamb, returned by the priest after the blood and entrails were offered in the Temple sacrifice. Of course, they would have unleavened bread. The menu would include the fruit of the vine, used ceremonially four times during the meal. A bowl of salt water would remind them of the bitter tears shed by their ancestors while in slavery and/or the salty waters of the sea through which they passed. Bitter herbs would remind them of the bitterness of slavery. A pasty fruit sauce, called "harosheth," would remind them of the clay used to make bricks while the Hebrews were slaves in Egypt. The bread at Jesus' meal was probably being dipped in this sauce. (It would be an interesting experience for class members to have a Jewish rabbi or a member of an orthodox or conservative Jewish household to share with you the details of the preparation and observance of Passover.)

The sentence saying it would have been better if the betrayer "had not been born" uses a common proverbial figure of speech of that day.

Mark 14:22-26. Jesus uses simple illustrations to convey profound truths. Many of the images in his parables and teaching were commonplace: coins, fish, seeds, birds, lamps. At the meal, Jesus takes the most common of elements, bread and wine—staples of daily meals and absolutely necessary for life. By linking them with his body and blood, Jesus forms an image that can never be forgotten. Every day as they eat, they are to remember his fellowship and how he sacrificed himself so that they would have life. Though there is an abundance of food at the meal, Jesus' use of the simplest elements memorializes the event in a profound way.

As the Passover ended, usually the Hallel (praise the Lord, from which our word *hallelujah* comes), consisting of Psalms 113–118, were sung.

Mark 14:27-31. Amid the olive trees, perhaps in the grove of Jesus' host, Jesus and the disciples would find privacy. Jesus alerts the disciples of his fear for them, using Zechariah 13:7 to describe his feelings. In Mark and Matthew, Peter's famous affirmation takes place on the way to the Mount of Olives, rather than at the Last Supper, as most of us recall it. Tell class members that Peter has never wanted to come to grips with the grim realities. Whenever Jesus speaks to the grim realities, Peter reacts as if to change the prospect by his own intention (8:31-33; 10:24-28). The Greek word for *deny*, means to "refuse to recognize or ignore." Note especially that it is not just Peter who makes this promise; all disciples "said the same."

Mark 14:32-42. The English words used to translate the feelings evident in verses 33-34 are inadequate to convey the Greek meanings. *The Revised English Bible* comes closer to the feelings: "Horror and anguish overwhelmed him, and he said to them, 'My heart is ready to break with grief.'"

When Jesus "fell to the ground," it may not have been to assume a kneeling position as we picture Jesus, but a total collapse from the emotions Jesus feels.

When Jesus asks the disciples to "watch," Jesus really is asking the disciples to stay awake. Yet immediately after their affirmation that they will die with Jesus, the disciples cannot stay awake for Jesus. Perhaps the disciples, too, were exhausted from the emotional ordeals of the week.

Abba is the Aramaic word for "father." Jesus comes to God like a child in honest intimacy and deep need. The "cup" is now the cup of Jesus' blood, his death. Mark first introduced us to this concept in an earlier conversation with the disciples (10:38-39). Now the cup is at hand.

In spite of Jesus' urging the disciples to stay awake, they repeatedly fall asleep. Not knowing "what to say to him" means that they were too embarrassed and guilty to offer an explanation.

Mark 14:43-50. The unwelcome visitors come not just from the chief priests and teachers of the law but also from the elders. The entire governing body of the Jewish religious community, or at least their officers, have approved this action.

Leading the way is Judas who will identify Jesus for them in the dark. A kiss will be the mark of identification. There is note of protective concern for Jesus in the instructions from Judas to "lead him away under guard." The word used by Judas in greeting Jesus, *Rabbi* (master), is a title of respectful address that has only appeared twice before in Mark, both times by Peter: at the Transfiguration experience (9:5) and when viewing the withered fig tree (11:21). How strange that this term of high tribute is used now by the betrayer in the act of betrayal.

The reference to the "servant of the high priest" (verse 47) suggests that these were not soldiers as usually imagined but a hired crowd or servants in the employ of the Temple.

Mark 14:51-52. This strange report appears only in Mark and no one knows its real significance. This report may have some personal relationship to Mark himself. In Acts 12:12 we discover that Peter in Jerusalem visits the home of the mother of John Mark that apparently was used as a gathering place for Christians. Thus Mark must have lived nearby. Some even propose the Last Supper itself may have been in the upper room of Mark's home. Out of this speculation comes the possibility that Mark may have been this "young man" who, in the middle of the night, had heard trouble was afoot. Still wearing his bedclothes, the young man had come to see for himself. Mistaken in the dark for a disciple, the young man was at first seized but fled, leaving his clothes in an amazed captor's hands.

Mark 14:53-65. In Mark's account Jesus is taken directly to the assembly of the priests and elders. This place would have been the Sanhedrin, the supreme Jewish Council. The high priest served as the convener and president. The high priest's intent was to obtain a death sentence against Jesus from the Sanhedrin. Of course, only the Roman ruler could put someone to death. Yet the first step was for the Council members to find Jesus deserving of a death sentence.

Their intent, however, is about to be botched. First, the religious leaders could not find anyone who would testify against Jesus on their own volition. So the religious leaders secured persons who made up accusations against Jesus, undoubtedly for a price and with coaching from the priests. But this plan backfired because their various testimonies contradicted one another. The witnesses took the prediction of Jesus that the great Temple would be thrown down (13:2) and made it appear that Jesus had said that Jesus would destroy the Temple and build another.

In desperation the high priest confronts Jesus directly, who up to this point has remained silent. The high priest asks Jesus if Jesus is the Messiah ("the Christ, the Son of the Blessed One"). In Mark's account Jesus affirms that he is and will validate who he is by his status at God's right hand and his coming again. The high priest tore his garments, the traditional symbol of the religious leader on hearing blasphemy.

Now in the emotional furor the Sanhedrin is called on for a verdict. The verdict is that he deserves death, which means Jesus would have to be referred to the Roman governor for a hearing on this recommendation. Adding injury to insult, on adjournment some Council members spit on Jesus and mock him.

Mark 14:54, 66-72. To ward off the chill of the evening, Peter joins a group around a fire. The maid of the high priest may have seen Peter in the Temple earlier in the week. Thus she presumed Peter had been with Jesus and raises this possibility. Peter denies it and tries to move away. Peter's action gives her the feeling she is right. She reports her suspicion to others nearby, who then catch up with Peter just as he is going out the gate. They accuse Peter but he denies it. However, as Peter talks they detect a Galilean accent. This accent makes them more suspicious because they know Jesus was raised and ministered mostly in Galilee. At this point Peter explodes into profanity (that reflected more negatively on him than on those whom he was cursing—verse 71), emphasizing his denial.

The cock crows for the second time. Usually seldom noticed, this crowing is like a trumpet blast on this morning. Peter remembers (14:29-31) and weeps.

Ask class members why they think Peter became involved in these denials. Among those reasons would be for what seemed a good reason at the outset—to be close to Jesus. Then there were denials for comfort and to be at ease among the crowd. Denial then became a habit and a way out—until Peter discovered how far out he was.

DIMENSION THREE: WHAT DOES THE BIBLE MEAN TO ME?

Awareness of Neighbors' Bitter Struggles

In contrast to the divinity of Jesus as we saw it revealed so gloriously on the Mount of Transfiguration, we also face the humanity of Jesus, as Jesus knows it could lead him astray from God's purposes for himself. In Mark 14 humanity and divinity are in conflict because, on the one hand, Jesus sees his calling so high, so demanding, so rigorous, that it summons all his physical energies as well as all his will. Yet, on the other hand, Jesus sees the weakness of his disciples, and he cannot leave behind humanity. Whenever these two realities come into conflict within any one of us, it becomes an agonizing experience.

Indeed, the intensity of what Jesus is really saying is that he is not concerned in these moments about death on the cross; rather in the garden of Gethsemane he is struggling to accept God's will. The struggle of determining who you are and who you really want to be is perhaps more intense, if it is genuine, than any other struggle, even with illness or death. But this struggle was essential—this was the only way to adequately prepare for what was to happen. It had to be, for Jesus could not walk the Via Dolorosa (Jesus' route from Pilate's judgment hall to Golgotha) unless Jesus could walk in a calm, steadfast assurance based on a sure knowledge of who he was and what he wanted to do under God. No inspiring sham, no playing tricks with oneself about one's piety, no playing religious games could get Jesus down that road. Although it always brings agony, we still would dare to hope that every one of us sometime will find a Mount of Olives, where down beneath our pious surface and the superficialities of our faith, we will come to grips with who we are, why we are here, what we really want to be, and what redemption we wish to bring to the world. Then, and then only, can we genuinely make the commitment: "Your will be done."

"Don't be alarmed," he said. "You are looking for Jesus the Nazarene, who was crucified. He has risen! He is not here" (16:16).

13

From Darkness to Light

Mark 15:1–16:8

DIMENSION ONE:
WHAT DOES THE BIBLE SAY?

Answer these questions by reading Mark 15:1-20

1. Where is Jesus taken? (15:1)

   The chief priests, the elders, the teachers of the law, and the whole Sanhedrin hand over Jesus to Pilate.

2. What questions does Pilate ask of Jesus? What is Jesus' response? (15:2-5)

   Pilate asks Jesus whether he is "the king of the Jews." He replies, "Yes, it is as you say." But when the chief priests accuse him of many things, Jesus makes no answer, which amazes Pilate.

3. What custom does Pilate use as an attempt to free Jesus? (15:6-10)

   At the Feast of the Passover that celebrated the deliverance of the Jews from bondage, there was a custom that symbolized that deliverance. That was the custom of releasing a prisoner whom the people requested. Pilate had another prisoner, Barabbas, who had been involved in a murderous insurrection. Pilate thought that if he offered to release a prisoner of the crowd's choice, it would be Jesus.

4. How does the crowd respond to the offer? (15:11)

   They ask for the release of Barabbas, because the chief priests have stirred up the crowd.

5. What then does Pilate ask the people? How do they respond? (15:12-14)

   Pilate asks, "What shall I do, then, with the one you call the king of the Jews?" The people cry out for Jesus to be crucified! Pilate asks what crime Jesus has done to merit such punishment. Their only response is to cry louder for Jesus' crucifixion.

6. What do the soldiers do? (15:16-20)

   The soldiers take Jesus inside the palace from the outdoor area where Pilate conducted Jesus' hearing with the public. They invite all their whole company to join them in their acts of ridicule. Since Jesus had been called a king, they pretend in jest that he is a king to humiliate him. They put a purple robe on him to suggest a royal robe. They make a crown out of thorns and put it on his head as a painful diadem. Laughingly, they salute him as "king of the Jews." Taking a staff, they strike him with it, spit at him, and kneel down in mock homage. Then, replacing his own clothes, they lead him out to crucify him.

Answer these questions by reading Mark 15:21-41

7. What happens to the passerby? (15:21)

   Simon from Cyrene in North Africa is entering Jerusalem from the countryside. The soldiers force him to carry the cross for Jesus.

8. At the site of the Crucifixion, what happens first? (15:22-24)

   The site of the Crucifixion was known as Golgotha, a word that meant "The Place of the Skull." There the soldiers offer Jesus wine mingled with myrrh, but Jesus refuses it. Then, as they crucify him, the soldiers take his clothing and gamble for the items.

9. What time is Jesus crucified? (15:25)

   According to Mark, it is at the third hour after sunrise; that is, about 9 A.M.

10. What is the written charge against Jesus? (15:26)

    It reads simply, "THE KING OF THE JEWS."

11. Who were crucified at the same time as Jesus? (15:27)

Two robbers were crucified, one on each side.

12. What jeering comments were shouted at Jesus? (15:29-32)

Some made fun of the statement they understood Jesus had made about destroying the Temple and rebuilding it in three days. They taunted him to save himself by coming down from the cross. The religious leaders mocked him by saying that he claimed to save others, but cannot save himself. They suggested Jesus come down from the cross so that all might "see and believe." Mark adds that even those who were crucified with Jesus heaped insults on him.

13. What happens at the sixth and ninth hours? (15:33-34)

At the sixth hour (12 noon) there is darkness until the ninth hour (3 P.M.). Then Jesus cries out, "My God, my God, why have you forsaken me?"

14. What do bystanders do? (15:35-36)

Misunderstanding what Jesus says, they think Jesus is calling for Elijah. Since it is obvious to them that he is in pain and thirst from loss of bodily fluids, some seek to lift up to him a sponge with a moist sedative (wine vinegar). Others want to wait to see whether Elijah will actually come to free him.

15. What happens at the end? (15:37-39)

Jesus utters a loud cry and his breathing stops. In the Temple the curtain separating the Holy of Holies and the Holy Place was torn in two from top to bottom. Then the centurion who supervised the soldiers, seeing that Jesus had stopped breathing and how he died, exclaimed, "Surely this man was the Son of God!"

16. Who else is witnessing what is taking place? (15:40-41)

Among the women looking on from a distance are Mary Magdalene (Mary of Magdala); Mary, the mother of James; and Salome. Many other women who have journeyed with Jesus and the disciples to Jerusalem are also present.

Answer these questions by reading Mark 15:42–16:8

17. Who is Joseph of Arimathea? (15:42-43)

Joseph is a respected member of the Sanhedrin (Council) and a secret follower of Jesus.

18. What courageous deed does Joseph perform? (15:44-46)

He goes to Pilate and asks for the body of Jesus. After Pilate confirms that Jesus is really dead, Pilate grants Joseph's request. Joseph takes down the body of Jesus and wraps it with a linen shroud. Then he places the body of Jesus in a tomb. For protection, Joseph rolls a stone across the entrance to the tomb.

19. What action do the women take? (15:47–16:2)

Having seen where Jesus is buried, Mary Magdalene, Mary, and Salome return after the sabbath to bring spices to anoint the body of Jesus. They bring the spices on the first day of the week at sunrise.

20. En route, what concern do they have? (16:3)

Their concern is over who will roll away the huge stone that covers the tomb's entrance.

21. As they enter the tomb, whom do they meet? (16:5)

They see a young man dressed in a white robe seated on the right side of the tomb passageway. They are alarmed.

22. What does the messenger tell them? (16:6-7)

The young man tells the women not to be alarmed. Knowing they came seeking the crucified body of Jesus, the young man announces that Jesus is risen from the dead. The young man invites them to see this for themselves. Then he instructs them to go and tell the disciples of Jesus, especially Peter, that Jesus will be seen in Galilee where he has gone before them.

23. What is the reaction of the women? (16:8)

They flee from the tomb, trembling and bewildered. They keep this discovery to themselves because they are afraid.

DIMENSION TWO:
WHAT DOES THE BIBLE MEAN?

In a poem entitled, "Ash Wednesday," T. S. Eliot uses images of death, dying, and solitude to describe the feelings that Lent brings to him. These words also describe the mood of these two chapters in Mark. The prolonged processes that, slowly but surely, have led to the dying of Jesus reach their somber climax. The dreams seem dashed upon the rocks of hopelessness. But birth leads not simply to death. The Gospel of Mark teaches us that death can lead to birth—for Jesus and his church!

Mark 15:1-5. The seizure and first examination of Jesus had taken place during the night, probably in the very early

FROM DARKNESS TO LIGHT

hours of Friday morning. Time was of the essence because the sabbath would begin at sundown on Friday. Jesus could not, under Jewish custom, be put to death on the sabbath. Furthermore, the longer they waited, the more persons would learn of the sinister events and plans. There could be a massive public protest. So in the early morning the entire religious leadership consults together on how to implement their earlier decision that Jesus should die. For these reasons they decide to request of Pontius Pilate an immediate hearing. They bind Jesus so that there is no chance of him escaping and take him to Pilate.

Pontius Pilate was the Roman administrator (procurator) of Judea. In the absence of a "king," Judea was an imperial province governed by Rome directly through their official representative. Little is really known about Pilate outside the scriptural accounts and reports by Jewish historians. Pilate is presented as an insensitive Roman bureaucrat out for personal favor in Rome's eyes and as one who cared little for Jewish customs. The only time Pilate would stop doing anything he wanted to do was in the face of potential rebellion. Pilate was under a charge by Rome to keep things under control.

Pilate is probably not in a very good mood, having had his early morning interrupted by this unexpected task. Pilate hears the accusations and comes straight to the point with Jesus, asking Jesus if he is "the King of the Jews." Interestingly, from the charges leveled against Jesus by the Jews, Pilate focuses immediately on this particular one. (Ask class members why Pilate begins with this question.) To Pilate as Caesar's representative the potential threat of someone claiming to be the king of a large portion of the population merited immediate attention. The charges of blasphemy would be of little interest to Pilate.

Jesus answers in the affirmative. When it appears that Pilate is going to make a decision based on this one charge and knowing their case on this charge is weak, the chief priests quickly point out other charges. Jesus is silent, and Pilate is puzzled. (The three other charges are listed in Luke 23:2.)

Mark 16:6-15. The custom of releasing a prisoner appears only in the Gospels in ancient literature. However, it would not be surprising. Passover was the celebration of God's deliverance of the Jews from bondage. Thus it could well have been a custom to request an imprisoned Jew be freed, probably one unjustly imprisoned as the Jews were unjustly enslaved. This prisoner's release would be another symbolic act of deliverance.

No historical data is available on Barabbas (verse 7). Revolts by various partisans occurred with some frequency.

Pilate thus far is not swayed by emotion. Pilate already has perceived the real agenda of the religious leaders that led them to charge Jesus. Another possible way to translate the word for *envy* (verse 10) is "jealousy." Pilate was perhaps aware that the general Jewish populace, especially those from a distance, were not always supportive of the Jerusalem priesthood. Thus, sensing why Jesus had been charged,

Pilate sought to play off the crowd against the priests. Since Jesus obviously had many admirers, by offering to release Barabbas or Jesus, Pilate presumed they would ask for Jesus and the matter would end. But he had not counted on the shrewdness of experts in conniving to get their way. The priests arranged for the crowd to be infiltrated (verse 11) with those who would demand Barabbas be released, while a large number would simply not know what was going on or what to say.

Amazed at the crowd's reaction, Pilate then asks the crowd what to do with Jesus. Pilate may have thought they would call for him to be freed also. When Pilate sees they are insistent on Jesus being crucified, he asks for specific identification of a crime. By now, however, mob psychology has taken over and rational process has lost the day. (Can class members suggest other times this situation has been so and has resulted in tragic wrongdoing?)

As has been stated, Pilate was under orders to keep the peace. Threatened by the possibility of mob rebellion, Pilate approves the death sentence. However, first he has Jesus beaten with a rod ("flogging" or "scourging"), a common form of punishment. It may be, as Luke suggests (23:22), that he thought the bloodthirsty crowd might be satisfied with this brutal act alone. It was to no avail.

The word *crucify* comes from the Latin word for cross (*crux*). The word means "to put to death upon a cross."

Mark 15:16-20. What takes place here is related to the verbal exchange in verses 2-5. Pilate's focus in the entire episode, as Mark reports it, is on Jesus' "kingship." When Pilate questions Jesus, it is on this subject. When Pilate speaks about Jesus, it is with this title (verses 9, 12), perhaps in sarcasm. The soldiers pick up on this theme and use this theme as the motif for their mockery. These are the Roman soldiers, not the servants of the high priest who previously had Jesus in custody. They put a "purple robe" on him to be his royal cloak (purple symbolized royalty). They give him a crown (of thorns). They sarcastically salute him: "Hail, king of the Jews!" (verse 18). The staff is his scepter with which they also beat Jesus, and then they bow in mock homage before Jesus.

Mark 15:21. Cyrene was a town in north Africa where a number of Jews had settled. Simon (no relation to any other Simon in the Gospels) had traveled the long distance to be in Jerusalem for the Passover and Feast. As Simon is entering the city, the procession is heading out of the city. In a Roman province, the Romans could require any needed service out of a non-Roman. Thus Simon was pressed into service to carry the cross for Jesus, weakened by loss of sleep and bodily abuse. Mark introduces a different response from nowhere. The disciples are reluctant to take up the cross and follow Jesus. But Simon of Cyrene is forced to take up the cross. This act suggests the power of God to create discipleship.

Only Mark mentions Simon as the father of Alexander and Rufus. Obviously, to the first readers these names would have some special meaning. As Paul ends his Letter to the Romans, Paul sends greetings to "Rufus, chosen in the Lord, and his mother who has been a mother to me, too" (16:13). In Acts 13:1 a person named Simeon called Niger (meaning dark-skinned, such as was true of Africans) is a teacher in the church in Antioch that commissioned Paul to go out as a missionary. It is possible that Simon became a follower of Jesus out of this experience and led his whole family into Christian discipleship and leadership.

Mark 15:22-26. *Golgotha* was an Aramaic word meaning "skull." Golgotha probably referred to a nearby hill resembling a skull. (If a class member has visited Jerusalem, ask him or her to share pictures of Gordon's Calvary, a garden area a short distance outside the old city walls. This garden is one of two sites regarded as the possible place of crucifixion. At Gordon's Calvary you will see a hill with skull-like shapes in the rock precipice on the hillside.) The "wine mixed with myrrh" was probably intended to be a sedative before the pain of the cross, but Jesus refuses it. You will recall that in Matthew (2:11) myrrh is one of the three gifts presented to the young Jesus by the wise men. Myrrh has become symbolic of death.

The dividing of the clothing refers back to Psalm 22:18. Jesus has been carrying the crossbeam himself, until Simon had to take over. Now they will nail Jesus to that crossbeam, placing it atop an upright pole. The upright pole will have a little ledge to support his feet. And through lack of air, loss of blood and fluids (dehydration), and exposure, Jesus will die—in a manner used for slaves.

The "third hour" would be 9 A.M.

Mark 15:26-32. The inscription of the charge was placed by the Romans with the same focus that Pilate had: "THE KING OF THE JEWS." The cries at Jesus are jests and sarcasm. The one about destroying the Temple picks up on the accusation made against him by the false witnesses (14:58). The one about the "king" picks up on the sign nearby with this title on it. The two robbers also being crucified insulted (or reproached) Jesus.

Mark 15:33-36. The last hours of Jesus' life are on us. The "sixth hour" is noon. From 12 to 3 P.M. an unusual darkness covers "the whole land." (See Isaiah 60:2 for a picture that Mark may have had in mind.) In Aramaic Jesus cries out the words that begin Psalm 22. (Ask someone to read aloud Psalm 22. Note how the words speak for someone who senses the possibility of a tragic and unjust death.) Jesus must have felt a kinship with these feelings and thus made this old expression his own.

The word *Eloi* must have sounded to some like the name Elijah. Thus they think Jesus is calling for Elijah to come. Thinking pain or dehydration is affecting Jesus mentally, someone raises a sponge filled with fluid to his mouth, waiting to see if Elijah will really come. This act of offering vinegar is also based on a psalm (69:21).

The loud cry may have been, "It is finished" (John 19:30) or, "Father, into your hands I commit my spirit!" (Luke 23:46).

Mark 15:38-41. The curtain of the Temple was that partition that divided the section known as the Holy Place from the Holy of Holies, into which only the high priest could enter once each year on the Day of Atonement. In the Holy of Holies was the ark of the covenant. The splitting of the curtain could mean that now we have direct access into the holy place of God through Jesus and his sacrifice. An entirely different possibility is that this destruction of the curtain symbolized God's intent to destroy the Temple in judgment for what has taken place. A third explanation is based upon placing together 14:63 with 15:38. The high priest tore his garment in reaction to Jesus' "blasphemy." God tears the Temple curtain in reaction to Jesus' death as a valuation of who he is.

The centurion was a Roman officer, probably commander of the soldiers who put Jesus to death. What a difference these hours made in his feelings about Jesus. (An interesting activity for a class member would be to write down what the centurion might have been thinking as he watched and participated in the events of this day.)

These women have not been previously mentioned. They may be mentioned here as a later addition, or to serve as a backdrop for their role in 15:47–16:8. *Magdalene* means "from the town of Magdala" on the western side of the Sea of Galilee.

Mark 15:42-46. Again we must remember that the sabbath is close at hand. The burial must take place before the sabbath. Joseph is a member of the Sanhedrin ("Council"). The phrase "waiting for the kingdom of God" may mean he was a spiritual seeker, not until now an actual follower of Jesus. This description would help explain why he is not recorded as interceding in Jesus' behalf in the Council. The exact location of the town of Arimathea is not known, but it is thought to be twenty miles inland from Tel Aviv. To have had his own tomb would suggest that he was wealthy. Bodies of crucified criminals were often left for vultures to devour. Joseph's request of Pilate, who alone had authority to dispose of the body of Jesus, is a surprising and caring act.

Pilate's surprise at Jesus being dead may come from the sense of physical strength Pilate saw in Jesus. It may also reflect that often crucifixion could exact a day or more of suffering before the victim died. Jesus' crucifixion took about six hours, uncharacteristically quick.

Mark 15:47–16:8. Since the burial had also been quick, there had been no time to anoint the body. (See the commentary on 14:8.) The same three women mentioned in 15:40 make the trip to the tomb that had been carefully noted on Friday by the two Marys (15:47). They cannot come until the sabbath is ended, which would be Saturday at sundown. Then at night they could not see to carry out their caring task. So they come to the tomb at the first possible time early Sunday morning. (Christians worship not on the sabbath or the original seventh day of the week. Instead, we worship on Sunday, or the first day of the ancient week, as a weekly celebration of the Resurrection.)

Rolling a huge stone across the opening to a cave-like tomb was the means of sealing it and thus protecting it. No one person or even several persons, could push away the stone of the tomb (16:3-4). This stone had been put in place by Joseph and his servants on Friday.

On finding the stone rolled away, they meet a "young man." Some have speculated this person is the "young man" mentioned in 14:51. However, the traditional presumption is that this young man is an angelic being, the "white robe" seen as symbolic of this.

The women are told to tell the disciples that Jesus has risen and will go before the disciples into Galilee, which was the area of Jesus' early life and from which Jesus and the disciples had come to Jerusalem. In other words, the disciples will see Jesus again at home. Peter is singled out especially to receive this message. The reason may well be that Peter is brokenhearted over his failures to Christ and his broken promises. Mentioning Peter by name may be a way of sending him a desperately needed word of hope and caring.

Their mood in leaving the tomb is one of intense feeling; they are "trembling and bewildered." They are so afraid, in fact, that they do not say anything to anyone. Presumably, they are able to convey the message to the disciples.

SPECIAL NOTE

The oldest and most reliable of the ancient manuscripts of Mark end with verse 8. Other manuscripts have different endings. Some add one additional verse: "But they reported briefly to Peter and those with him all that they had been told. And after this, Jesus himself sent out by means of them, from east to west, the sacred and imperishable proclamation of eternal salvation."

Others add verses 9-20. It is generally believed these are a separate collection of Resurrection appearances that were in circulation and were added to Mark in the second century. This addition was probably made because Mark did not have any of these appearances in this narrative. They include an appearance to Mary Magdalene (verses 9-11), to two of his followers while they are traveling (verses 12-13), and to the remaining eleven disciples at a meal (verse 14). The Great Commission is given (verses 15-16) and promises of his enablement for them in their ministries (verses 17-18). This section ends with the account of Jesus' ascension into heaven (verse 19) and the going forth of the disciples to preach, supported by the Lord's presence and blessing (verse 20).

DIMENSION THREE: WHAT DOES THE BIBLE MEAN TO ME?

What Are New Discoveries of the Truth?

In a book I wrote for The Upper Room entitled *The Cross in 3-D* (1975), I told of an experience told by the late Lynn Harold Hough, Dean of the Divinity School of Yale University. He was vacationing in the Canadian Rockies. For diversion he was reading a Greek myth that tells of the love of the goddess, Artemis, for a human, Hyppolytus. When Hyppolytus was sick, Artemis came to his side out of love. But when the death rattle began in his throat, she exclaimed, "O Hyppolytus, I must leave for we on Mount Olympus cannot witness the corruption of physical death!" On reading this, Dean Hough lowered his book and looked at the distant mountains, pondering. He saw one that reminded him of a "green hill without a city wall," where, in contrast, Christ "tasted death" (Hebrews 2:9) for everyone.

This love is the vital essence of our Christian faith. Jesus, who out of love enters our humanity where we are to the point of death, leads with God's enabling power into new possibilities for life. This love is also the essence of Mark, who provided the essence for two other Gospel accounts. When we began, in Lesson 1, I suggested that when our series was completed, you might again discuss together why a New Testament scholar would call this work "the most important book ever written." Now is that time. Have you found some reasons?

Recall anew Mark's theme and purpose as stated in 1:1, "The beginning of the gospel about Jesus Christ, the Son of God." Never in this account does Jesus use these words of himself, but Mark wants us to know and believe that Jesus is the One. In this process, however, Mark wanted his Jewish readers to discover an entirely different image for what it means to be Son of God than what they had previously envisioned:

- One who challenges rather than commends religious legalism;
- One who ever looks beneath for lasting meanings rather than momentary forms;
- One who shuns rather than seeks notoriety;
- One who is open to those who are different;
- One who uses powers to meet others' needs rather than for personal acclaim;
- One who becomes humbly obedient unto death and is brought by God into life.

This is only the "beginning of the gospel about Jesus Christ, the Son of God." Now you and your class members must write the next chapters.

LUKE
Table of Contents

About the Writer

Horace R. Weaver is a retired editor of the former Department of Adult Publications, The United Methodist Publishing House. He has written nearly one thousand articles and lessons and two books.

You will be with child and give birth to a son, and you are to give him the name Jesus (1:31).

1

Preface, Jesus' Birth, and Boyhood

Luke 1–2

DIMENSION ONE:
WHAT DOES THE BIBLE SAY?

Answer these questions by reading Luke 1

1. Who is the writer who refers to himself as "me"? (1:3)

   The writer never reveals his name. Traditionally, the writer of this Gospel has been identified as Luke, a Gentile physician and traveling companion of Paul (Colossians 4:14).

2. What is the purpose of Luke's Gospel? (1:4)

   The purpose of Luke's Gospel is "that you may know the certainty of the things you have been taught."

3. What does Luke say is his method of writing? (1:1-3)

   Since many others have written narratives of the events of Jesus' life, "it seemed good also to me to write an orderly account."

4. What sources does Luke use in compiling his Gospel? (1:1-2)

   Luke's sources are "those who from the first were eyewitnesses and servants of the word."

5. How does Luke describe Herod, Zechariah, and Elizabeth? (1:5-7)

   Luke describes Herod as king of Judea, Zechariah as a priest, and his wife Elizabeth as a descendant of Aaron. Zechariah and Elizabeth "were upright in the sight of God. . . . Elizabeth was barren; and they were both well along in years."

6. What is Zechariah doing in the Temple? (1:8)

   He is "serving as priest before God" when his division is on duty.

7. How does Zechariah respond to the angel's promise of a prophetic son? (1:18, 22)

   Zechariah is skeptical of the promise, for "I am an old man and my wife is well along in years." When he comes out of the Temple, he cannot speak.

8. What words does Gabriel use to greet Mary? (1:28)

   "Greetings, you who are highly favored! The Lord is with you!"

9. Over what people does Gabriel say Jesus will reign? (1:32-33)

   God will give him the throne of his father David, and "he will reign over the house of Jacob forever."

10. What unique, divine event does Gabriel tell Mary will happen in her life? (1:35)

    "The Holy Spirit will come upon you, and the power of the Most High will overshadow you. So the holy one to be born will be called the Son of God."

11. What does Mary learn about her relative Elizabeth? (1:36)

    The angel tells Mary, "Even Elizabeth your relative is going to have a child in her old age."

12. What names does the angel tell Zechariah and Mary to give their sons? (1:13, 31)

    The angel tells Zechariah to name his son John and Mary to name her son Jesus.

13. In response to Elizabeth's warm greetings, how does Mary answer? (1:46-47)

    Mary says, "My soul praises the Lord, / and my spirit rejoices in God my Savior."

14. After staying three months with Elizabeth, where does Mary go? (1:56)

Mary returns home.

15. How does Zechariah confirm the naming of his son? (1:63)

Zechariah, still unable to speak, writes on a tablet, "His name is John."

16. One of Luke's special interests is the Holy Spirit. What does he say about the Holy Spirit and Mary, Elizabeth, and Zechariah? (1:35, 41, 67)

Luke says that the Holy Spirit will come upon Mary, Elizabeth is filled with the Holy Spirit, and Zechariah is filled with the Holy Spirit and prophesies.

17. About whom does Zechariah sing his praises? (1:68-79)

Zechariah blesses God, the child John, and Jesus.

Answer these questions by reading Luke 2

18. Why are Joseph and Mary going to Bethlehem? (2:1-5)

Caesar Augustus has ordered a census of the people, with each head of the house returning to his ancestral home. Since Joseph is of the house and lineage of David, he and Mary are going to Bethlehem, David's town.

19. What is the message of the heavenly host to the shepherds? (2:14)

"Glory to God in the highest, / and on earth peace to men on whom his favor rests."

20. What happens on the eighth day after Jesus' birth? (2:21)

At the end of eight days, the baby Jesus is circumcised and given his name.

21. What do Mary and Joseph offer as a sacrifice in their son's behalf? (2:22-24)

They offer, according to Jewish law, "a pair of doves or two young pigeons."

22. What do Joseph and Mary do after meeting the requirements of the law? (2:39)

They return "to their own town of Nazareth."

23. How often do Joseph and Mary visit Jerusalem? (2:41)

Joseph and Mary visit Jerusalem every year for the Feast of the Passover.

24. When Jesus is twelve, what is he doing at the Temple, after the Feast of the Passover? (2:42-49)

His parents find him "in the temple courts, sitting among the teachers, listening to them and asking them questions."

25. How does Luke describe Jesus' growth and development? (2:52)

"Jesus grew in wisdom and stature, and in favor with God and men."

DIMENSION TWO: WHAT DOES THE BIBLE MEAN?

The Gospel of Luke and the Acts of the Apostles make up one-fourth of the New Testament. These two books represent slightly less than all the thirteen letters of Paul plus the Letter to the Hebrews. But Luke and Acts represent much more than sheer bulk in the New Testament. They bring much that is new, such as Luke 9:51–18:14. They also show the compiler's (Luke's) use of many sources of information, such as Mark's Gospel (which became the basic outline for the Gospels of Luke and Matthew); the writings that only the Gospels of Luke and Matthew hold in common (known by scholars as *Q*); and the special and unique source that only Luke has (designated by scholars as the *L* source). A comparison of the Gospel of Luke with the Gospel of Mark shows how the writer felt free to correct, change, and grammatically improve sections used in Mark. Luke's editorial style is seen in such changes as the following:

Mark 1:32. "That evening after sunset the people brought . . ."

Luke 4:40. "When the sun was setting, the people . . ."

In the following comparison observe how Luke smooths out Mark's involved sentence structure:

Mark 3:7-8. "Jesus withdrew with his disciples to the lake, and a large crowd from Galilee followed. When they heard all he was doing, many people came to him from Judea, Jerusalem, Idumea, and the regions across the Jordan and around Tyre and Sidon."

Luke 6:17. "A large crowd of his disciples was there and a great number of people from all over Judea, from Jerusalem, and from the coast of Tyre and Sidon, who had come to hear him."

As is true of the other Gospel writers, Luke wrote in Greek and clearly used the Septuagint (Greek) translation of the Old Testament. He was a fine Greek scholar who knew his language well. Some of Luke's poems and descriptions are unexcelled in verbal beauty. (See 1:46-55, 68-79.)

The Scripture in this session is divided into six themes:

1. Preface: Writer's Purpose in Writing (1:1-4)
2. The Promise to Zechariah of the Birth of John (1:5-25)
3. The Promise to Mary of the Birth of Jesus (1:26-38) and Her Visit to Elizabeth (1:39-56)
4. The Birth of John (1:57-80)
5. The Birth of Jesus (2:1-20)
6. Jesus' Infancy and Childhood (2:21-52)

Luke 1:1-4. In no place throughout the Gospel of Luke does the writer identify himself. In Acts 1:1 the writer states, "In my former book, Theophilus, I wrote about all that Jesus began to do and teach." In Luke 1:3 we read, "It seemed good also to me." The early church fathers identified the *I* of Acts and the *me* of the Gospel with Luke the physician. If so, he is the physician named in Colossians 4:14.

In the Gospel and in Acts, Luke is writing to a person named Theophilus. The word *Theophilus* means "loved of God," so some have assumed that Luke wrote to anyone who loves God. But Luke seems to be writing to a friend, possibly a Roman or Greek benefactor, who is a person of considerable prestige—hence Luke's phrase "most excellent Theophilus."

Whoever it is, Luke writes for him an "orderly account." The purpose of the Gospel is "that you may know the certainty of the things you have been taught."

Luke's description of his method of writing the Gospel is valuable to us. He describes his method as one of research for information from as many sources as he could find—all around Palestine, the Near East (as in Ephesus, Antioch, Troas), and Europe (as in Athens, Corinth, Berea). Luke would have known of, heard, and observed the lifestyles and faith claims of Christians such as Peter, James, Lydia, Priscilla, Timothy, and Mary. Luke heard hundreds of witnesses to the person and teachings of Jesus while Luke worshiped at Corinth, Athens, Antioch, Caesarea, Ephesus, Philippi, Jerusalem, and Rome. Luke prayed with them. He witnessed with them. He knew how they interpreted the Old Testament in terms of the life and teachings of Jesus. Luke experienced the Holy Spirit at work in each of these churches. Yes, and he must have taken many notes for later use in his two volumes about Jesus and the disciples.

From scores of notes, written documents (such as the teachings of Jesus [an undiscovered document identified by scholars as Q] and the Gospel of Mark), and his memories of many witnesses and ministers of the word, the writer compiled his orderly account that we know as the Gospel of Luke.

Point out to class members that the authenticity of the Gospel of Luke depends on the authenticity of Luke's sources—of witnesses; of ministers of the word; and of persons he talked to, such as Peter, James, Mary, and many others. These kinds of questions are pertinent to our sincere quest for what the Bible means. Interpretation, exegesis, and commentary depend on the value given each source. To put it another way, Is every passage in the Bible—and in Luke—equally valid? Or were some sources more valid than others? Would the social, political, and religious conditions of A.D. 50 cause Christian interpreters to change or omit some of Jesus' sayings? For example, in Mark's Gospel, Jesus notes that the Temple is a house of prayer for people of all nations (Mark 11:17). But Luke omits the reference to people of all nations worshiping in the Temple. (See Luke 19:46.) Might Luke (who wrote in A.D. 80–85) have omitted such a reference because the Temple no longer existed, having been destroyed by the Romans in A.D. 70? Luke was a careful thinker, free of contradictions.

Luke 1:5-25. The author includes dates, rulers, and names of persons. In 1:5, Luke tells us that Herod was king of Judea. Theophilus would have known that Herod ruled Judea from 37 B.C.–4 B.C. and that the end of his reign (4 B.C.) was marked by the birth of two male infants, John and Jesus ("so that you may know the certainty of the things you have been taught"; 1:4). Luke then turns from a political event (the close of Herod's reign) to religious events (concerning an elderly priest and his wife and, in the next section, a carpenter and his young wife).

Zechariah was not the high priest or a chief priest; he was an "ordinary" priest of the division of Abijah. First Chronicles 24 describes the origin of the twenty-four-division system of priests. King David set the order of priests and Levites. Two groups of priests operated in the days of King David. They represented the sixteen priestly sons of Zadok and the eight priestly sons of Ithamar. Each of the twenty-four divisions was responsible, twice a year, for services in the Temple.

In Jesus' time one high priest (an appointee of Rome), two hundred chief priests who represented the elite of Jerusalem, and about seven thousand ordinary priests who lived outside Jerusalem served in the Temple. These ordinary priests were separated into twenty-four divisions. Their responsibility was to choose by lot several of their group who would serve at separate priestly tasks. Zechariah's task was attending to the offerings of incense and unleavened bread. Another priest would kill the sacrificial animals. Others were to light the sacred altar fires. The burning of incense was a symbolic act of offering prayer in behalf of all Israel. The placing of fresh goblets of wine and unleavened bread (the bread of the Presence) was symbolic of the communion between the believers and their Lord God. The priest's concluding action each day was to offer the ancient benediction found in Numbers 6:24-26, "The LORD bless you and keep you . . . ."

Zechariah was chosen by lot from the eighth of twenty-four divisions; his division was named Abijah. He served the Lord for a week, serving in the wonderful Holy Place. As a priest, he had to be a fully accredited descendant of Aaron.

Zechariah's wife had been barren throughout their long marriage. Perhaps at Elizabeth's urging, Zechariah, while renewing the bread of the Presence and offering the symbolic prayers for all Israel via incense, dares to pray for his wife. Somewhat like Moses who saw the "angel of the Lord" in the bush (Exodus 3:2), so Zechariah experiences "the angel" while he serves at the altar that day. *Fear* is an idiom for *awe* or religious experience. The angel tells the sincere priest that his wife will bear a son whom Zechariah is to name John.

Zechariah doubts that he and Elizabeth can have a child, since they are old. Because of Zechariah's doubts, he becomes speechless and remains so until eight days after John's birth.

Zechariah's inability to pronounce the benediction on all the worshipers must have disappointed him and them too. But by signs he indicates that he has experienced the living God in his life. The crowd understands that he has had a vision of God. Then Zechariah goes home to Elizabeth. She conceives and bears John.

Luke 1:26-56. When Elizabeth is six-months pregnant, Mary receives an announcement from God that she too will bear a male child, whose name will be Jesus. In Jesus, God has been and is with us, always. "The Word became flesh made his dwelling among us" (John 1:14). God became incarnate in Jesus.

Luke 1:35 calls to mind Genesis 1:2, where the Spirit of God hovers over the waters, bringing life into being. A child is being born of Mary who is set apart by God.

Mary leaves Nazareth to visit Elizabeth, her relative. On meeting, both know that each is bearing a son of great significance. Both Mary and Elizabeth know the experience of being "filled with the Holy Spirit." Mary and Elizabeth mark the beginning of God's new action in humanity's behalf.

Mary praises God. She breaks into song: "My soul glorifies the Lord." The song is known as the *Magnificat*, which comes from the first word in the Latin translation of this song. Mary, who is three-months pregnant, stays three months with Elizabeth, probably until the baby John is born.

Luke 1:57-80. Eight days after a Jewish boy is born, the parents mark their son as a son of Abraham by circumcision. At this time a Jewish boy also receives his name. This ritual was performed for John and for his cousin Jesus.

Many of Luke's sources probably go back to oral traditions that were perhaps written down later by loving persons for memorization by others. One could easily mix two independent and significant poems, especially eighty years after the event. Such seems to be the case with the words Zechariah quotes as prophecy: "He has raised up a horn of salvation for us / in the house of his servant David" (1:69).

Zechariah clearly is singing about the birth of Mary's son Jesus. (Jesus is descended from David; John is descended from Aaron.)

On the other hand, 1:76-77, 80 clearly refers to John, who will baptize thousands unto repentance and forgiveness of their sins. Luke 1:68-75, 78-79 refers to Jesus, who will bring light into the darkness of this world.

Luke 2:1-20. Luke likes order; so he gives dates, as well as names of significant persons and events. He states that Augustus Caesar (Roman emperor, 27 B.C.–4 B.C.) has given orders for a general enrollment of all persons in his empire. This enrollment took place, notes Luke, when Quirinius was governor of Syria. Against the background of royalty, Luke focuses on a simple carpenter and his wife—Joseph and Mary—the birth of whose baby is imminent. Finding no room in the inn, they go to a stable, where their son is born.

Read Exodus 33:14 aloud; then discuss how the shepherds fulfilled this experience that night. God has come very near; indeed they could say they had felt God's presence. God had been with them. Emmanuel! Had they not heard the angels sing, "Glory to God in the highest, / and on earth peace to men on whom his favor rests"?

Not long after, they kneel at the manger where the baby Jesus, the one to be Lord Jesus Christ, lies. The heartstrings of the shepherds vibrate with the frequencies of the harp strings of the heavenly host. "The shepherds returned, glorifying and praising God." And Mary treasures all these things, knowing that what she teaches Jesus will be spiritual muscle and sustenance as her little boy grows to manhood.

Luke 2:21-52. After Jesus' circumcision and naming, two other ceremonial rites are needed. The fortieth day after birth, he and Mary receive their ritual of purification (Leviticus 12:2-4). Then the parents present the baby to God, who ordered Moses to consecrate to God all the firstborn children and animals of all the people of Israel (Exodus 13:2). To this day, Orthodox Jews dedicate their first son to study the law from ages four to twenty-one. This dedication to studying the law may be bypassed by making an offering of redemption—a lamb if one is wealthy or two turtledoves or two young pigeons if one is poor, as were Mary and Joseph. The aged Simeon, who had yearned for the day when his eyes could see the long-awaited Messiah, ecstatically declares the words of Luke 2:29-32.

Luke knows of no trip to Egypt; so the Gospel states, "They returned to Galilee to their own town of Nazareth" (2:39). There the boy Jesus developed in many fine ways (2:40).

Luke states that "every year his parents went to Jerusalem for the Feast of the Passover" (2:41). Jesus, at twelve, probably has visited the Temple several times with his family and very likely has spent some time during these years with John, his cousin. They may have taken their bar mitzvahs together when they reached their thirteenth birthday. Each loved God and sought insights into the truths about Judaism and God's purposes for human life.

At their bar mitzvahs, they would naturally ask questions of the many priests in the Temple. Jesus' and John's purpose was to listen to the elders, not to try to tell them truths the elders had not yet heard.

When Mary and Joseph leave Jerusalem for Nazareth, they discover after several days' journey that Jesus is not with them. Returning to Jerusalem, they find him with the priests, whose duties include instruction in the law. Mary asks Jesus if he did not know that she and his father were looking for him anxiously? Jesus replies, "Didn't you know I had to be in my Father's house?"

Luke reports that the child "grew in wisdom and stature, and in favor with God and men" (2:52).

DIMENSION THREE:
WHAT DOES THE BIBLE MEAN TO ME?

The class may discuss the following topic or use the material in the student book.

Luke's Methodology of Writing

The first two chapters of Luke are a part of Luke's special contribution to Christianity. His Nativity scene is unique, differing from Matthew's. Let us seek several insights that this Gentile compiler and author offers us from the first several pages of his Gospel. His description in the preface of how his Gospel came into being is a major contribution to our understanding of the Bible. He states clearly that he sought various sources of information—written documents (such as the Gospel of Mark and a "booklet" of the teachings of Jesus), statements by witnesses who heard Jesus, and the testimony of various ministers of the word. From these varied sources he compiled his Gospel and the Book of Acts.

Without saying so, Luke assumed we would know that his Gospel would be as dependable and/or valid as his sources. Luke carefully collected, read, and often rewrote material he would print, as a good editor does today. He knew God needed persons to write. He knew God needed inspired persons through whom the divine Spirit could work.

Ask class members to discuss their attitude toward this Gentile physician for having told how he compiled the third Gospel.

Ask class members to think about the spirit of Christmas and the songs they hear. What makes for a true Christmas spirit? Write the answers on a chalkboard or on a large piece of paper.

What kind of questions would a confirmand of "just thirteen" ask at his bar mitzvah? What would Jesus and his cousin John be interested in asking?

The Spirit of the Lord is on me, because he has anointed me to preach good news (4:18a).

2

The Key to Jesus' Public Ministry

Luke 3:1–4:30

DIMENSION ONE:
WHAT DOES THE BIBLE SAY?

Answer these questions by reading Luke 3

1. What two sets of dates does Luke give us for dating the ministry of John (and therefore Jesus' ministry)? (3:1-2)

   Luke gives the political date, the fifteenth year of the reign of Tiberias Caesar, and the religious date, during the high priesthood of Annas and Caiaphas.

2. Where is John, the son of Zechariah, when the word of God comes to him? (3:2)

   John is in the desert.

3. Where does John go to preach? (3:3)

   John preaches in all the country around the Jordan.

4. What does John preach? (3:3)

   John preaches "a baptism of repentance for the forgiveness of sins."

5. What does John say to the crowds who come to him? (3:7-9)

   John tells them that only repentance and forgiveness of their sin can save them, not just being Jews—having "Abraham as our father."

6. What responses does John make to three different groups that come to him? (3:10-14)

   He tells the multitudes to learn to share with those who have nothing, the tax collectors to collect accurately, and the soldiers to refrain from extortion and false accusation and to be content with their pay.

7. How does John respond to those who think he is the Messiah, the Christ? (3:15-18)

   John says, "I baptize you with water. . . . He will baptize you with the Holy Spirit and with fire. His winnowing fork is in his hand . . . to gather the wheat into his barn."

8. Why does Herod the tetrarch imprison John? (3:19-20)

   John condemned the tetrarch's marriage to Herodias, his brother's wife, "and all the other evil things he [Herod] had done."

9. When John baptizes Jesus, at what point (before, during, or after) does Jesus experience heaven opening before him? (3:21)

   Jesus sees heaven open after he has been baptized and while he is praying.

10. To whom and for whose benefit does the voice from heaven declare that Jesus is his beloved Son? (3:22)

    The Holy Spirit (God) says to Jesus, "You are my Son, whom I love; with you I am well pleased."

11. How old is Jesus as he begins his ministry? (3:23)

    Jesus is about thirty years old.

Answer these questions by reading Luke 4:1-30

12. What leads Jesus in the desert? (4:1-2)

    Jesus is led by the Spirit for forty days.

13. After fasting forty days, Jesus is hungry and experiences three temptations. What are these temptations? (4:3-12)

Jesus is tempted (1) to turn stones into bread, (2) to assume authority and glory over all the kingdoms of the world, and (3) to jump from the highest point of the Temple to demonstrate his messianic power.

14. How does Jesus deal with these temptations? (4:4, 8, 12)

Jesus quotes passages from the Hebrew Scriptures, what Christians now call the Old Testament.

15. After the forty days in the desert, where does Jesus go? (4:14)

Jesus returns to Galilee.

16. Before going to Nazareth, where does Jesus teach? (4:15)

Jesus teaches in several synagogues in Galilee.

17. Where would Jesus normally be on the sabbath? (4:16)

Jesus usually would be found in the synagogue, "as was his custom."

18. What is the scroll from which Jesus reads? (4:17)

He reads from the scroll of the prophet Isaiah.

19. To what passage of Scripture does Jesus turn? (4:18-19)

Jesus turns to Isaiah 61:1-2: "The Spirit of the Lord is on me, / because he has anointed me / to preach good news to the poor. / He has sent me to proclaim freedom for the prisoners / and recovery of sight for the blind, / to release the oppressed, / to proclaim the year of the Lord's favor."

20. What does Jesus say that makes all speak well of him? (4:21)

Jesus says, "Today this scripture is fulfilled in your hearing."

21. What is the congregation expecting Jesus to do? (4:23)

They are interested, not so much in what Jesus says, but that he do what he "did in Capernaum."

22. How does Jesus deal with his friends' prejudices? (4:25-27)

Jesus reminds them of how God, during a long and severe famine, did not give help to any Jewish women but fed a widow

in the region of Sidon; also, God did not cure any Jewish leper, but he did cure a Syrian leper.

23. What do the worshipers do to Jesus? (4:28-29)

They drive him out of the town, take him to the brow of a hill, and try to throw him off the cliff to kill him.

24. How does Jesus escape? (4:30)

Jesus "walked right through the crowd and went on his way."

DIMENSION TWO: WHAT DOES THE BIBLE MEAN?

The Scripture for this lesson, the beginning of Jesus' Galilean ministry, is divided into four themes:

1. The Message of John the Baptist (3:1-20)
2. Jesus' Baptism and His Genealogy (3:21-38)
3. The Temptation of Jesus (4:1-13)
4. Jesus' Declaration of His Messiahship (4:14-30)

Luke 3:1-20. As we learned in Luke 2:1, Luke wants to be as precise as possible where events and dates are concerned. In these verses Luke gives two sets of dates, one based on the secular political leadership, the other based on religious leadership.

The dates based on the political leadership are drawn from three groups: the Roman emperor, the governor of Judea, and three tetrarchs (rulers of nearby regions). The first political leadership is the emperor, Tiberius Caesar (A.D. 14–37), who succeeded Augustus Caesar. During the fifteenth year of Tiberius's reign, John the Baptist begins his ministry.

The second political leadership is Pilate, who was governor of a province that included Judea, Samaria, and Idumea. Pilate held office from A.D. 26–36. The third political leadership is the three sons and successors of Herod the Great: Herod Antipas (tetrarch over Galilee), Philip (tetrarch of Iturea and Traconitis), and Lysanias (tetrarch of Abilene—a country west of Damascus). A tetrarch is one who rules one-fourth of a kingdom. You may want to point out these areas on a map of Palestine, showing their relation to Judea. Jesus was a political subject of Herod Antipas.

The religious set of dates refers to Annas and Caiaphas. Annas headed one of four powerful clans of high priests who were not descendants of Aaron but who purchased their position from Rome. The high priests were appointed by the Roman emperor. Annas had been high priest from A.D. 6 to 15. Caiaphas was appointed to serve as high priest from A.D. 18 to 36.

Luke notes that John, son of the priest Zechariah, is in the wilderness when the "word of God" comes to him. Some scholars assume John was at Qumran, in the southern part of the wilderness of Judah. If so, he may well have been a member of the Essenes, a dedicated priestly group who expected the kingdom of God to come suddenly at any time. The major expectation of this group was the coming of the long-awaited Messiah, who would come from the heavens with a great military force of angels to destroy the Roman military force of occupation and establish the kingdom of Israel, with the Messiah as king.

John "went into all the country around the Jordan, preaching a baptism of repentance for the forgiveness of sins." Both Mark and Luke refer to Isaiah 40:3-5. They identify John's ministry with the "voice of one calling in the desert / 'Prepare the way for the Lord.' " The original cry was from the prophet in Babylon, about 587 B.C.–539 B.C., who sought to revive his friends in exile and to ready them physically and spiritually to return home—The crooked shall be made straight, and the rough ways shall be made smooth. The prophet meant this literally, though John and Christians have taken it to mean becoming morally and spiritually straight. Truly, God is interested in that kind of reformation; for of such is the kingdom of God.

Class members might like to know that some scholars believe that verse 3:4b ought to read as follows:

The voice of one crying:
In the wilderness prepare the way of the Lord.

In this form, the verse more closely resembles Isaiah 40:3. Ask class members what difference this change makes. What was going on in John the Baptist's mind to make him address the crowds, "You brood of vipers! Who warned you to flee from the coming wrath?" The following scenario may help us understand John's strong feelings.

Luke 3:7-17 suggests the summer season when farmers are harvesting their grain. The crowds from Galilee and Judah have passed many such scenes as they walk toward the southern part of the Jordan River where John is preaching.

The travelers watch the process of harvest. Farmers have cleared circular areas on hilltops down to the solid limestone. The farmers place sheaves of barley or other grains inside the circle. If the farmer owns oxen, these animals move around the circle while pulling a small sledge with sharp spikes. The horn or rock spikes soon make a mass of chaff and grain. Next, the grain is separated from the chaff. Using a pitchfork, the chaff and grain is thrown into the air. The wind blows the chaff away. The grain falls to the ground and is swept into piles.

The chaff is swept into other piles and is eventually burned. At the burning, snakes and other vermin crawl out of the fiery pile, trying to escape. This scene may be behind John's harsh words (3:7-9). Kindness and subtle parables are missing.

Matthew 3:7 refers to the crowds of Luke 3:7 as Pharisees and Sadducees. They are the religious teachers who have come from Jerusalem to listen to the now-famous preacher. For these well read, ritualistic religious elite, John has harsh words. The harvesting scene seems appropriate:

They are like snakes trying to escape the fires that burn the chaff. They say to themselves, *Our lineage is right; we are sons of Abraham, and by that fact we will be saved.* But John shouts out, You are not saved by the roots but by the fruits of your life. Salvation comes, not by lineage, but by your style of life.

So John calls them to repent of their lack of justice, compassion, and mercy. He applies these categories to three groups that come to him. The crowds (possibly referring to overly zealous Pharisees and Sadducees) are to learn to share what they have with those who have not. Tax collectors (those who are at the customs offices) are to be just and not extort larger fees than the law permits. Soldiers in the army of occupation are to maintain peace and to abide by the legal and just use of power.

The Essenes had no deep concern for social ethics; they felt the world was so bad that only God could redeem it by cataclysmic action. John's responses to the three groups suggest a severe weakness in his social ethics. He envisions no great emotional thrust for justice in the new era. He does not rise above the past.

John, as did Elijah, wears the hairy camel's skin garment (Matthew 3:4)—the symbol of a prophet. Through John the word of God is being expressed anew, and a greater prophet than he will speak soon. When the Messiah comes, he will baptize, not just with water, but with the Holy Spirit and with fire (the symbol for judgment).

John's "good news" is very limited, for his message is extremely limited—mostly to getting commitments through fear of judgment rather than through love. Jesus recognized John's personal commitment yet considered him the least in the kingdom of God (the new era).

Luke 3:21-38. However, Jesus left Nazareth and sought John out so he could be baptized. Surely these cousins spent many an hour together prior to baptism; so John could sincerely say, "I need to be baptized by you, and do you come to me?" (Matthew 3:14).

Yet Jesus insisted and was baptized with the crowds. *After* Jesus was baptized and while he was still praying, "heaven was opened." Help class members see the significance of Jesus' praying: He experiences Immanuel—God is with us—and the kingdom of heaven is opened. It was at this time that Jesus heard a voice from the Spirit saying, "You are my Son, whom I love; with you I am well pleased" (3:22). Certainly this experience confirmed for Jesus that he was called of God to be the long-awaited Messiah (Christ).

Luke's genealogy of Jesus gives us the only statement as to his age: Jesus was about thirty when he began his ministry. It is interesting to know that priests had to be thirty before their ministry could begin.

Luke's genealogy differs considerably from that of Matthew. We note that Matthew goes from David through Solomon to Jacob the father of Joseph the husband of Mary. Luke reverses the order, stating that Jesus was "the son, so it was thought, of Joseph, the son [not of Jacob but] of Heli . . . to the son of Nathan, the Son of David . . . [and on to] Isaac, the son of Abraham . . . [on to] the son of Seth, the son of Adam, the son of God."

The two genealogies are in conflict, as has been known for some 1700 years. But their purpose is the same: to prove that Jesus was the Messiah, a descendant of David. Such was the popular expectation. Luke's list does not stop with David but goes to Adam, thus showing that God's interest is not just in the sons of Abraham (the Jews) but in all humankind. Thus Gentiles are included from the beginning of creation.

Luke 4:1-13. We have noted that after John had baptized Jesus and while Jesus was praying, Jesus heard God express extraordinary pleasure in him as God's Son. Jesus' mind and spirit must have been greatly stressed as he realized God had anointed him the Messiah through John's baptism. His mind would have worked like flashes of lightning as he quickly thought of the many concepts of the Messiah.

Undoubtedly, Jesus had already disavowed John's view; for John sought a redemption only through God's action, not through anything human beings might do—not even as collaborators. All redeeming actions would come from God alone, not by any dedication of human efforts. There was no thought of God and humankind working together. This view supported an apocalyptic concept of the coming kingdom of God in which the angels of heaven fight against the demons and against demonic persons on earth.

The opposite view of redemption was to omit divine activity altogether and to assume that dedicated human efforts in social redemption would save the world and the people within it. This view was held by Zealots who were ready to fight to the death in order to clear Judah from all foreigners and other impure things.

The Pharisees and teachers of the law (the scribes) were waiting for a Messiah who would require and achieve total obedience to both the written laws (Torah) and the unwritten laws (verbal traditions). Obedience to all laws would change the lives of every participant. Jesus knew such legalistic obedience never made bad lives good, however. This concept of the Messiah, too, must be set aside.

The Sadducees, the priests such as Zechariah, also expected a messianic age—with the anticipation of One who would achieve full loyalty and obedience to priestly concerns related to the Temple. The Messiah would emphasize and win full loyalty to observances of the three major religious festivals per year—the Feast of Tabernacles (Booths), Passover, and Atonement—plus sincere loyalty to minor duties such as making peace offerings, sin offerings, and paying various tithes. Jesus knew that the priestly kings of the Hasmonean period (immediately following the Maccabean wars, about 165 B.C.–163 B.C.) never achieved the kingdom of God. The priestly Essenes looked forward to One who would be prophet-priest-king.

In intuitive moments Jesus must have been aware that his mother Mary was touched, if not entered, by the Holy Spirit; the same was true of his relative Elizabeth (mother of John). Jesus experiences the Holy Spirit coming upon his life at baptism. This Spirit is now leading him into a forty-day wilderness retreat to meditate on his baptismal call to messiahship. John wore the prophetic mantle (hairy garment) symbolizing the prophet Elijah. God is speaking through John in a new way. Psalm 74 is shattered by the new activity of the Holy Spirit. Is John the one who is to come? No! It is Jesus who is filled with the Holy Spirit. It is he who will baptize with the Holy Spirit at Pentecost!

A new era has come indeed. What kind of Messiah did Jesus conclude that God, not various religious groups, sought? It seems inevitable that Jesus, who loved his Bible (what Christians now call the Old Testament), spiritually feasted on the servant passages (Isaiah 53 and 61:1-2) at his messianic banquet in the wilderness. How easily Jesus reads Isaiah 61:1-2 aloud at Nazareth. Here he explains what it meant to have the Spirit of the Lord upon him. You might want to read these passages (Isaiah 53 and 61:1-2) to the class at this time.

Many Jews wanted and expected a prosperity-creating Messiah who would redeem his (Jewish) people from poverty and hunger. Many Old Testament passages support this hope. Other passages support a view that the Messiah will free his people from political (Roman) oppression. Other passages suggest divine healings will be the signs of his having come. Thus Jesus is tempted both by human and biblical hopes. He decides that he will not administer a free food program; he will not turn stones into bread. (He knew that well-fed people do not necessarily make good people. People have a deeper hunger.) Jesus refuses to become a general of a military system that will coerce humankind to act with justice and righteousness. (Righteousness cannot be imposed by law, as Jeremiah learned.) Jesus refuses to obtain the accolades of humankind by performing miraculous acts. (People of all nations are easily won by astonishing feats, but these feats do not lead to spiritual conviction.)

Jesus quotes three passages from Deuteronomy (8:3; 6:13; 6:16), each of which nullifies his temptations, even though each might have contained some good. What each temptation proposes is good in itself, but it would keep Jesus from expressing and achieving his best. Jesus is loyal to the best, which he finds in Isaiah 53 and 61.

Luke 4:14-30. Luke begins this section by emphasizing the fresh activity of the Holy Spirit as Jesus goes to Capernaum and Nazareth. You might take time to point out on a map where these cities are located.

When Jesus speaks to his home congregation in the synagogue, the attending rabbi asks him to read the Scripture for the day and to address his friends. The rabbi would have followed the order of worship, which included singing a psalm, reciting the Shema (Deuteronomy 6:4-9), reciting the creed (of Deuteronomy 26:5-11), reading from the Torah and the Prophets (by a rabbi), sharing a psalm and a prayer, followed by the benediction (from Numbers 6:22-26). The reading that day was from the scroll of Isaiah. The attending rabbi hands Jesus the scroll, and he turns to

Isaiah and reads 61:1-2. After handing the scroll back to the attendant, Jesus sits down.

After looking at each male member of the small synagogue, Jesus then proclaims, "Today this scripture is fulfilled in your hearing." He read the Hebrew lesson well and with rhetorical feeling. "All spoke well of him and were amazed at the gracious words that came from his lips" (4:22).

Luke greatly abbreviates Jesus' sermon, so let me expand it somewhat. First, every male in the auditorium would have said his daily prayers that morning. The prayers (from the Siddur, prayer book) contain these sentences: "Blessed art thou, Lord, our God, King of the universe, who hast not made me a slave. Blessed art thou, Lord our God, King of the universe, who hast not made me a woman."

In his first sermon Jesus includes a condemnation of this kind of prayer in a way that no man can help but understand. Subtly he raises his point: In the time of Elijah (850 B.C.) many widows in Israel suffered from the three-and-a-half-year famine, yet God sent Elijah to a woman from Sidon (She was a Syrophoenician—a Gentile—and a woman at that.) to save her and her son from famine. Why should God have overlooked the Jewish widows? And Israel had many people with leprosy too, but God sent Elisha to heal the commanding officer of the Syrian army. Why did God overlook his real sons (of Abraham)? God healed Naaman, the commanding officer of the hated Syrian army. So how can you (Jews of Nazareth) thank God for not being a woman, and a Gentile woman at that? How can you thank God that you are not a Gentile (such as Naaman), and one with leprosy at that? Jesus' point is that God loves all persons—Gentile women as much as Jewish women and Israel's enemies (even lepers) as much as Jews.

Using the challenging verses of Isaiah 61:1-2, Jesus states how he knows the Holy Spirit is upon him: because he bears God's concerns for all persons. He is the Messiah because God has anointed him to preach good news to the poor, to proclaim release to all captives and recovery of sight to the blind, to set at liberty all those who are oppressed—and thus proclaim the new era, the kingdom of God. What a messianic mission!

Jesus' illustrations about God's concern for all persons shocks the congregation. Yet no person dares say it is not biblical. It is good news—if you can take it.

As a result, they take Jesus out of the city and lead him to the brow of a high hill where they intend to throw him to his death. As they move along, Jesus walks with the men, probably calling them by name. I wonder, since he was not permitted to give the benediction at the synagogue, if he might have done so to various ones individually as they walked toward the brow of the hill? Then something unique happens, for Jesus soon reverses his steps and "walked right through the crowd and went on his way." Were they ashamed? Encourage the class members to discuss this incident.

DIMENSION THREE: WHAT DOES THE BIBLE MEAN TO ME?

The class may discuss the following topic or use the material in the student book.

Seeing the Messiah

Matthew, Mark, and Luke state that Jesus spends forty days in the wilderness with the devil (Satan), who tempts him in various ways. What kind of being is a devil? I find the record of Peter's confession at Caesarea Philippi helpful. (See Matthew 16:13-23; Mark 8:27-33; Luke 9:18-22.) Jesus asks who men were saying he was. Some said John the Baptist, others Elijah. Peter was the first disciple to say, "The Christ of God" (Luke 9:20). Jesus honors Peter by saying, "On this rock [the faith that Jesus is the Messiah] I will build my church" (Matthew 16:18). Jesus begins to explain the implications of being the Messiah—that he must go to Jerusalem and suffer many things. Peter rebukes Jesus, tempting him to change his plans of being God's kind of Messiah to being something less than the best (Matthew 16:22). This temptation was one Jesus faced in the wilderness, and it was a temptation that Luke hinted at when he said the devil left him "until an opportune time" (Luke 4:13).

Peter and the disciples do not understand the kind of Messiah Jesus is. This fact is readily seen in Acts 1:3, 6, where Luke reports that after Jesus' resurrection, he teaches his disciples for forty days about the "kingdom of God." The disciples ask, "Lord, are you at this time going to restore the kingdom to Israel?" (1:6).

The disciples were still thinking in terms of a physical kingdom with its capital in Jerusalem, its throne built on the citadel of David, with armies, power, and authority. How can they be so blind? But they, as Peter, were not thinking the thoughts and ways of their Messiah. As such, they are devils. Jesus refers to Peter when he says, "Get behind me, Satan! . . . You do not have in mind the things of God, but the things of men" (Mark 8:33).

Many scholars assume Jesus used such a figure of speech to explain the psychological, moral, and religious stress under which he worked until he wholly dedicated himself to being God's Messiah, not a messiah dictated to or thought up by humans.

Jesus is dedicated to winning persons to the Father by persuasion, not by force; by love, not by fear; by strong and valid convictions, not by astonishing action on his part. In his loyalty to being God's Messiah, Jesus wins followers whose goals and mission in life are to fulfill those which Jesus adopted and shared with the people in Nazareth (Isaiah 61:1-2, in the spirit of the suffering servant of Isaiah 53).

Class members might value the opportunity to discuss private and church goals to see if they harmonize with those of our Messiah. If not, Jesus' charge to Peter may awaken us: "Get behind me, Satan!" This discussion could be the most important of our lives.

I have not come to call the righteous, but sinners to repentance (5:32).

3

Jesus' Galilean Ministry

Luke 4:31–6:49

DIMENSION ONE:
WHAT DOES THE BIBLE SAY?

Answer these questions by reading Luke 4:31-44

1. Where does Jesus go after he leaves Nazareth? (4:31)

   Jesus goes down to Capernaum, a city of Galilee.

2. While in the synagogue, a man verbally accosts Jesus. What is the man's problem? (4:33-34)

   The man was "possessed by a demon."

3. What does Jesus say to the demon? (4:35)

   "Be quiet! . . . Come out of him!"

4. Whose mother-in-law does Jesus cure, and what does she do after Jesus cures her? (4:38-39)

   Jesus cures Simeon's mother-in-law of a high fever; she immediately arises and serves them.

5. Whom does Jesus heal? (4:40-41)

   Jesus heals those sick with diseases and those under the influence of demons.

6. Where does Jesus go the next morning, and what does he say he must do? (4:42-43)

   Jesus goes to a lonely place. He says he must go to other cities to "preach the good news of the kingdom of God."

7. In what country is Jesus preaching? (4:44)

   Jesus is preaching in Judea.

Answer these questions by reading Luke 5:1-11

8. How many boats does Jesus see by the shore, and to whom do they belong? (5:2-3)

   Jesus sees two boats belonging to fishermen.

9. From whose boat does Jesus speak? (5:3)

   Jesus speaks from Simon's boat.

10. After teaching the people, what does Jesus tell Simon to do? (5:4)

    Jesus tells Simon, "Put out into deep waters, and let down the nets for a catch."

11. Why does Simon signal to his partners to bring their boat, and what are the results? (5:7)

    Simon's nets are breaking from their load of fish. He calls his partners for help. Soon both boats are filled with fish.

12. What does Simon Peter do? (5:8)

    Simon Peter falls at Jesus' knees and says to him, "Go away from me, Lord; I am a sinful man!"

13. Who are Jesus' first disciples? (5:10-11)

    Jesus' first disciples are Simon [Peter], James, and John.

Answer these questions by reading Luke 5:12–6:11

14. What does a person suffering from leprosy beg Jesus to do? (5:12)

    The leper begs Jesus to make him clean.

15. How does Jesus respond to the plea of the person suffering from leprosy? (5:13)

Jesus stretches out his hand and touches him.

16. What three things happen next? (5:13-14)

Immediately the leprosy leaves the man. Jesus charges him to tell no one but to "go, show" himself to the priest for proof of his healing.

17. Why does Jesus forgive the sins of the paralyzed man? (5:19-20)

Jesus forgives the man's sins because of his friends' faith.

18. Why do the teachers of the law and the Pharisees question Jesus' words? (5:21)

The teachers of the law and the Pharisees believe that only God can forgive sin. Therefore, Jesus' words are blasphemous.

19. Who becomes the next disciple, and what does he do to honor Jesus? (5:27-29)

Levi is the next disciple, and he gives a great feast in Jesus' honor.

20. What is Jesus' reply to the Pharisees and teachers of the law as to why he and his disciples do not fast? (5:33-34)

Jesus replies, "Can you make the guests of the bridegroom fast while he is with them?"

Answer these questions by reading Luke 6:12-49

21. After a night in prayer, Jesus called his disciples and "chose twelve of them, whom he also designated apostles." Who are the Twelve? (6:12-16)

The twelve disciples are Simon, Andrew (his brother), James, John, Philip, Bartholomew, Matthew, Thomas, James the son of Alphaeus, Simon the Zealot, Judas the son of James, and Judas Iscariot.

22. What are Luke's four Beatitudes? (6:20-22)

*"Blessed are you who are poor, / for yours is the kingdom of God.
"Blessed are you who hunger now, / for you will be satisfied.
"Blessed are you who weep now, / for you will laugh.
"Blessed are you when men hate you, / when they exclude you and insult you / and reject your name as evil, / because of the Son of Man."*

23. What does Jesus say about behavior toward enemies? (6:27-28)

Jesus says, "Love your enemies, do good to those who hate you, bless those who curse you, pray for those who mistreat you."

24. What is the reward for this behavior? (6:35)

The reward is that of being akin to God—"sons of the Most High."

25. What is Jesus' test of goodness? (6:43-45)

"Each tree is recognized by its own fruit," and "the good man brings good things out of the good stored up in his heart."

26. Everyone who hears and does Jesus' words is like a man who builds his house in a certain way. How does he build it? (6:48)

He digs deep and lays the foundation for the house upon rock.

DIMENSION TWO: WHAT DOES THE BIBLE MEAN?

The Scripture for this lesson is divided into four themes:

1. Healings in Capernaum, Time of Reflection (4:31-44)
2. Jesus Makes His First Disciples (5:1-11)
3. Healings and Confrontations (5:12–6:11)
4. The Great Sermon (6:12-49)

Luke 4:31-44. When Luke says Jesus "went down" to Capernaum, he is referring to the fact that Nazareth is 1,300 feet above sea level and Capernaum is below sea level.

Capernaum was a strategic center for Jesus' ministry. It was a toll collection point and a major trade route from Egypt to Syria—"the King's Highway." It was a port for trade across the Sea of Galilee to the eastern shore, where Decapolis (ten cities) and Perea are found.

Josephus, an early Jewish historian, states that a synagogue was built in Capernaum by a Roman officer about A.D. 250. Probably Jesus preached in the synagogue whose foundations were those of this later edifice. Here the man with the evil spirit accosts Jesus.

The "Ha!" (4:34) is a word of dismay: Oh me! The popular messianic hope of that day included healing of persons with both mental and physical illness.

We will face other exorcisms in this lesson. Notice the four characteristics of a typical exorcism story. First, the demon recognizes the exorcist and struggles to stay as he or she is. Second, the exorcist offers a command, which the demon seeks to evade. Third, the demon departs violently. Fourth, we receive a report on what happens to those who witness the freeing of the person who had been under the influence of the evil spirit. Now reread (meaningfully) 4:33-37. Perhaps you will want to remind class members of Jesus' experience in Nazareth where the worshipers wanted to hear what he had done in Capernaum (4:23).

Verses 38-39 refer to Jesus' going to Simon's home. According to Luke, Simon is not yet a disciple. In a sense, Jesus is alone in his ministry.

When Jesus and Simon enter the house, they find Simon's mother-in-law with a high fever. At Simon's request Jesus goes to her. (Mark says he took her by the hand.) Jesus, standing at the head of the bed, rebukes the fever; and she is made whole (shalom—well, at peace, calm, healed). She then does that which is against the law: She serves them (Simon and Jesus). Only men served meals to men on such occasions. Jesus does not argue the point. She is grateful and wants to do something for him.

Soon Simon will be called to be a disciple. We wonder if his wife went with him on his "missionary" journeys. Paul tells us that she did. (See 1 Corinthians 9:5.) We wish we knew the part the wives played in spreading the good news in many nations. Let class members consider possible roles the women played as they trudged the dirty roads for hundreds of miles.

Among Luke's many interests was Jesus' concern for women. Notice that the first miracle (4:31-37) was for a man; the second is for a woman (Simon's mother-in-law). Peter must have felt some obligation to teach her, as well as his wife, about the healer who would before long become his Lord.

At the close of the sabbath, sundown (6:00 P.M.) on Saturday, the physically sick and those under the influence of evil spirits or demons were brought to Jesus that their lives might be touched by the Master.

The next morning Jesus rises early and goes to a lonely place (Mark includes the words *where he prayed.*). Remind class members again that Jesus has no disciples yet. He has crowds of people interested in him, but no disciples. The people seek Jesus and try to keep him from leaving them, but he refuses. Jesus tells them that he "must preach the good news of the kingdom of God to the other towns also, because that is why I was sent."

Luke 4:44 ends with Jesus teaching in Judea—a difficult concept, since he was and is teaching in Galilee. Jesus is interested in outreach. His outreach includes all of Palestine and beyond. It is interesting to notice that Luke uses the word *Judea* for all Jewish lands: Samaria; Galilee; even Idumea; and broader yet, Gentile lands and people from Syrophoenicia. God's kingdom is boundless. If class members ask for specifics about Judea's representing Palestine, you might print the following references on a chalkboard or on a large piece of paper: 1:5; 6:17; 7:17; 23:5; Acts 10:37. Luke may have thought that Mark's picture of Jesus' ministry (in Galilee and Judea) was too restricted.

Luke 5:1-11. Recall two events for this section of study. First, Jesus knew Peter and Peter knew Jesus—since Jesus had been staying in Peter's house for a while. Up to this time Jesus had no confidante, but he needed companionship in those higher levels of his thought life. Second, John 1:35-36 tells us that John the Baptist is standing with two of his disciples when Jesus walks by. John says, "Look, the Lamb of God!" (that is, the Messiah). The two disciples follow Jesus and listen to Jesus throughout the day. Andrew, one of the disciples, goes to find his brother Simon and brings him to Jesus. Jesus thus knows both Andrew and Simon.

"One day as Jesus was standing by the Lake of Gennesaret [the Sea of Galilee]," people crowd around Jesus to hear him speak. Being by the shore of the Sea of Galilee, Jesus takes advantage of a boat he sees moored nearby. Getting into Simon's boat, Jesus asks Simon to push him out to sea a bit, from which point he teaches the crowd on the shore. After Jesus finishes, he asks Simon to row out into the deep. Simon does, and they let down their nets. To Simon's amazement his nets started to break with the huge catch of fish. He calls to his partners to bring their boat near and share in the catch. Both boats are filled with fish. (John 21:11 reports Simon caught 153 fish.)

Simon Peter falls down at Jesus' knees in amazement and, taking the role of a sinner, asks Jesus to leave him. Notice that Simon does not move from awe to proclaiming Jesus the Messiah. This proclamation occurs at Caesarea Philippi many months later. Simon does see Jesus as a master miracle worker, but astonishment (as Jesus well knew) does not win converts to the Kingdom.

Even so, Jesus calls Simon and the other fishermen to "catch men." Later they will be called to be apostles. The Codex Bezae (an ancient manuscript) translates verse 10, "Do not remain ordinary fishermen. Come and let me make you fishers of men!"

Luke 5:12–6:11. The Gospel of Luke records two stories of Jesus healing a leper. One of them is Luke 5:12-16. This description of being "covered with leprosy" suggests the disease was not Hansen's disease, which was loathed and feared, but some other skin ailment. Leviticus 13 describes "leprosy" in its many forms. The priests worked as health officers in these diagnoses, the isolation of victims, and checking their conditions. (You might want to study Leviticus 13 and report to class members the varied symptoms and descriptions of skin diseases.)

Years ago I visited a leper colony at the southern foot of the Mount of Olives and was horrified by cases of Hansen's disease (which today is controlled but not conquered). Jews were taught to fear it "for their life." Mothers hugged their babies and ran after their children if a person with leprosy came anywhere near, seeking food or clothing. Jesus had been taught from infancy to respond with fear and even disgust, for people with leprosy were thought to have sinned against God in some terrible way.

Now Jesus, in the early days of messiahship, is faced with a man with leprosy. It must have startled him and recalled fearful moments when his mother had held him tightly to protect him from the presence and contagion of this dread disease. Jesus quickly deals with the fact that he is expected by law to stay away from lepers. Now one of these persons comes to Jesus and piteously cries, "Lord, if you are willing, you can make me clean." Jesus (possibly feeling the tug of his mother's prejudices and fear) reaches out and touches him, saying, "I am willing. . . . Be clean!"; and the man becomes clean.

Jesus tells the cured man, as Leviticus requires, to report to a priest and be proved clean. I can imagine the shout of joy, for I have heard such joy from a group of people suffering from leprosy when they were given clean sheets, pillows, and covers for the first time in many years. How Jesus, and God, must have rejoiced in the man's courage of conviction that brought the master's healing touch. Interestingly, after healing the man, Jesus withdraws to the wilderness for prayer.

We now turn to the healing of the paralyzed man (5:17-26). Mark (2:1-12) has the setting in Capernaum, in Peter's home where Jesus lived during his Galilean ministry. You might like to describe (or ask a class member to roleplay) Peter's feelings as the scenario moves through the destruction of the roof of the house. The house was probably a one-room house with an outside staircase leading to the roof. The flat roof was thatched with branches and straw and then covered with mud.

Apparently a group of Pharisees and teachers of the law (scribes and priests—Sadducees) have come from a number of villages of Galilee and Judea to observe the teacher, Jesus of Nazareth (Luke 5:17). Men come carrying a man who is paralyzed, hoping he could touch or be touched by Jesus. But the large crowd in the small room is an impossible barrier. So they make a hole in the roof and lower their friend. Jesus marvels at the faith of the men; and he tells the man, "Friend, your sins are forgiven." The teachers of the law and Pharisees, unconcerned about healing, say, "Who is this fellow who speaks blasphemy? Who can forgive sins but God alone?" Jesus listens and soon speaks on their level: "That you may know that the Son of Man has authority on earth to forgive sins. . . . Get up, take your mat and go home." Which the previously paralyzed man does! Little wonder that amazement and awe seized them all; and they said, "We have seen remarkable things today."

You might want to write on a chalkboard or on a large piece of paper the categories of miracle stories in Luke: (1) Exorcism, (2) Healing Stories (such as the paralyzed man), (3) Resuscitations, and (4) Nature Miracles. We will refer various healings to these categories as we study Luke's Gospel. In the miracle story of the man who is paralyzed, we may well have an example of psychosomatic (body-mind) healing. Sometimes illness is caused, not by germs or a virus, but by selfishness, greed, hate, dishonesty, or uncontrolled passions. The sins of the mind cause debilitating illness as surely as do bacteria and germs. Jesus brings *shalom* (wholeness, health, peace) to those who respond to his offer of abundant life.

After leaving Simon's house, Jesus passes a tax collector named Levi (Matthew) sitting at his tax booth (5:27-32). Jesus calls him; and he follows Jesus, becoming one of the disciples. Levi invites Jesus and tax collector friends to dinner, and Jesus accepts. The Pharisees and teachers of the law complain and question why Jesus should eat with such trashy (ritually unclean) people (5:29-30). Jesus tells these religious leaders that he came, not "to call the righteous, but sinners to repentance."

The healing of the man with a shriveled hand (6:6-11) comes at the end of worship in a synagogue. Again, some Pharisees and teachers of the law watch, hoping to catch Jesus breaking their sacred traditions. Jesus knows their thought; malice is carved in their angry faces. In others Jesus can see and hear their yearnings to be clean and whole.

Luke 6:12-49. Luke 6:12-16 lists the names of the twelve disciples. Most of the Twelve are relatively unknown to us.

In the four Beatitudes (6:20-23) we have what Dante says of Luke, "this scribe of the gentleness of Christ."

1. "Blessed are you who are poor" (describing a basic characteristic of Christians, whose spiritual life is not determined by their material welfare), "for yours is the kingdom of God."

2. "Blessed are you who hunger now" (for a just and kind social order—right relationships), for your motives will set your mind in the paths toward justice.

3. "Blessed are you who weep now" over the painful consequences of uncontrolled sins (greed, hate, selfishness, dishonesty, inordinate passions), for you shall find enjoyment and relief from suffering.

4. "Blessed are you when men hate you" because of your stand for me and my way of life. Your reward is great in the spiritual life. Christians at the time of Luke's writing (about A.D. 80–85) faced the pain of being excluded from membership in many synagogues and of bearing the brunt of crude jokes and false statements.

What strategy can Christians employ to counter such evil persons? Jesus said, "Love your enemies, do good to those who hate you." (You might ask two class members to report on Mahatma Ghandi and Mother Teresa as outstanding persons whose lifestyles prove the validity of the strategy of love.)

Ask class members if they are ready to try an experiment. If so, state that Jesus' ethics reverse most ethical systems. Applying Jesus' ethics to our personal lives, ask class members to refer to specific situations that could illustrate one or two of Jesus' statements in 6:32-35.

Let the class members state in their own words the meaning of 6:35b. (For example, A Christian's character proves his or her kinship with the character of God; we are sons and daughters of God by imitating God's character.)

Ask if a person who is fundamentally ignorant of the valid directions of life (the "blind") can assume leadership in telling others the way to go; that is, "Can a blind man lead a blind man?" (6:39).

If a student, when fully trained, is like his or her teacher and the teacher is insensitive and opinionated, can his or her education be a success; or is it really a measure of the failure of both teacher and student?

On the other hand, a pupil (learner) who goes to Jesus and hears his words and does them is like a man who builds a house on a rock foundation; the house will never be shaken or destroyed by floods (6:47-49). A slight change of the metaphor would be, A person who builds his or her house of personality on the foundations of the Beatitudes and the love of God as seen in Jesus Christ has a structure that is everlasting; not even his or her death can destroy it.

DIMENSION THREE:
WHAT DOES THE BIBLE MEAN TO ME?

The class may discuss the following topic or use the material in the student book.

Luke 5:24—The Son of Man

We will consider one important issue: the meaning of the phrase *Son of Man*. *Son of Man* is the phrase that only Jesus used about himself (Luke 5:24). No other person in the Gospels refers to Jesus as Son of Man, yet Jesus himself uses it scores of times. What does the phrase *Son of Man* mean?

At the time of the Exile, the prophet Ezekiel used this phrase to refer to himself at least ninety times. As such, the phrase referred to Ezekiel himself as God's agent to take God's message to his people. In the later years, Ezekiel prophesied hope—especially through the vision of the Valley of Dry Bones (Ezekiel 37). The phrase, then, would have been quite meaningful to Jesus for its overtones in Daniel 7:13 in which "one like a son of man" appears in the clouds of heaven before the "Ancient of Days" and is given "authority, glory and sovereign power," representing the saints who will possess the Kingdom forever. The power of these references was very much alive in the thinking of the early church.

The healing in the home of Simon Peter of the man who was paralyzed (Luke 5:18-26) is the setting in which Jesus uses the phrase *Son of Man* for the first time. The phrase definitely has messianic overtones. Luke's two words, *amazed* and *awe* (verse 26) were also messianic terms.

The blind receive sight, the lame walk, those who have leprosy are cured, the deaf hear, the dead are raised, and the good news is preached to the poor (7:22).

4

Jesus: Messianic Teacher and Healer

Luke 7–8

DIMENSION ONE: WHAT DOES THE BIBLE SAY?

Answer these questions by reading Luke 7

1. Who owns a servant who is at the point of death? (7:2)

   A centurion had a servant "whom his master valued highly" who "was sick and about to die."

2. What does the centurion do to save the servant? (7:3)

   He sends elders of the Jews requesting Jesus "to come and heal his servant."

3. Why do the elders help the centurion? (7:4-5)

   They feel the centurion is deserving because he loves "our nation and has built our synagogue."

4. Why does the centurion send another delegation to Jesus, suggesting that he not come? (7:6)

   The centurion feels undeserving of having Jesus come to his house.

5. What does the centurion suggest instead? (7:7)

   The centurion says, "Say the word, and my servant will be healed."

6. What happens? (7:10)

   On returning home, those sent by the centurion to Jesus find the servant well.

7. As Jesus and a large crowd approach the city gates of Nain, what event is taking place? (7:11-12)

   They meet the funeral procession of a man who has died.

8. How does Jesus respond? (7:13-14)

   Jesus has compassion on the mother, a widow whose only son has died. Jesus touches the coffin; the bearers stand still; and Jesus says, "Young man, I say to you, get up!"

9. What does the crowd do and say after the man revives? (7:16)

   They are filled with awe and praise God, saying, "A great prophet has appeared among us."

10. What question does John the Baptist have two of his disciples ask Jesus? (7:19)

    "Are you the one [the Messiah] who was to come, or should we expect someone else?"

11. What happens "at that very time" that is a nonverbal answer to John's question? (7:21)

    "Jesus cured many who had diseases, sicknesses and evil spirits, and gave sight to many who were blind."

12. What is Jesus' verbal response to John? (7:22)

    Jesus says for the disciples to report to John what they have seen and heard about the persons who have been cured who were blind, lame, leprous, deaf, and about the raising of the dead and the preaching of the good news to the poor.

13. What is Jesus' conviction about the importance of John the Baptist? (7:28)

    Jesus says, "Among those born of women there is no one greater than John; yet the one who is least in the kingdom of God is greater than he."

14. What kind of woman comes to Jesus while he dines as the guest of a Pharisee? (7:37)

    She is "a woman who had lived a sinful life in that town."

15. What does she do that upsets the host? (7:38-39)

    She wets Jesus' feet with tears, wipes off his feet with her hair, kisses them, and pours perfume on them.

16. What does Jesus say in response to the woman's actions? (7:47)

    Jesus says, "Her many sins have been forgiven—for she loved much."

Answer these questions by reading Luke 8

17. What part do certain women play in the daily life of Jesus and his disciples? (8:1-3)

    These women help to support them financially "out of their own means."

18. In the parable of the sower, a sower sows his seed on four kinds of soil. What are these four kinds? (8:5-8)

    Some seeds fall along the path, some fall on rock, some fall among thorns, and some fall onto good soil.

19. Why does Jesus teach using parables? (8:9-10)

    Jesus says that the disciples are to know the secrets of the kingdom of God. For others he speaks in parables so that "though seeing they may not see; / though hearing, they may not understand."

20. What is the purpose of good soil? (8:15)

    The good soil refers to "those with a noble and good heart, who hear the word, retain it, and by persevering produce a crop."

21. What is the purpose of a lighted lamp? (8:16)

    The lamp is put "on a stand, so that those who come in can see the light."

22. Who does Jesus say are his real relatives? (8:19-21)

    Jesus says, "My mother and brothers are those who hear God's word and put it into practice."

23. When Jesus rebukes his disciples during a great storm on the Lake of Gennesaret (Sea of Galilee), what does he ask? (8:25)

    Jesus asks them, "Where is your faith?"

24. After Jesus cures the uncontrollable demon-possessed man, what do the townspeople find the healed man doing? (8:35b)

    They find the man "sitting at Jesus' feet, dressed and in his right mind."

25. What happens to Jairus's daughter? (8:40-42, 49-56)

    Jesus raises Jairus's daughter from the dead.

DIMENSION TWO:
WHAT DOES THE BIBLE MEAN?

The Scripture for this lesson about Jesus as a messianic teacher and healer is divided into four themes:

1. Jesus Gives Life to Two Persons (7:1-17)
2. Jesus and John the Baptist (7:18-35)
3. Jesus and a Penitent Sinner (7:36-50)
4. Jesus as Teacher and Miracle Worker (8:1-56)

Luke 7:1-17. Refresh your memory of Jesus' first sermon in Nazareth by rereading Luke 4:14-30 and the commentary on these verses on pages 150–151. This story gives a biblical background for Jesus' interest in responding to a Gentile army officer who seeks God's healing ministry. Jesus assured the worshipers in Nazareth that God is interested in the needs of all persons, including a commanding officer of the Syrian army (Naaman), and that God sent Naaman to Elisha to be cured. Since the centurion is a "god-fearer," he probably has heard the story of Naaman read in the synagogue. (See 2 Kings 5:1-14.)

The centurion concludes that God, through Jesus, might save his servant. So he sends a delegation of Jewish elders to Jesus, asking him to come and heal his servant.

The elders tell Jesus that the centurion is worthy of anything Jesus will do for him, that "he loves our nation and has built our synagogue." Not far from the house, a delegation of the centurion's "friends" meets Jesus. They report the centurion's view of himself as unworthy (the opposite of the elders' report to Jesus), which indicates that this man of great authority had a strong sense of humility. The friends state that the centurion admits that he, like Jesus, is a man of authority. (The title *centurion* implies that he has authority over one hundred men.) The centurion observes that he represents and wields authority. People obey him when he gives an order. So (by analogy) Jesus represents and wields the authority of God. The centurion's request to Jesus, then, is not for Jesus to come to his house but simply to "say the word," and his servant (who is at the point of death) will live. The centurion's faith in what God can do through Jesus' speaking the word amazes Jesus. Jesus' emotional response is, "I tell you, I have not found such great faith even in Israel."

The class members may notice an interesting omission: Jesus does not say anything, such as, "Be healed." Jesus simply admits that the man has more faith than any he has observed yet in Israel. Thus when his friends returned to the house, they "found the servant well." Luke's point is that Jesus' immediate presence is not required; he can heal from a distance equally well. But more important than distance and any spoken words is the *faith* of the centurion. The servant lives through faith in action. To have faith is to recognize that in Jesus the power of God is exercising its power.

The raising of the widow's son takes place at Nain (7:11-17), a small village near Nazareth. Only Luke tells this story. If possible, locate Nain on a map for class members.

As Jesus, his disciples, and a large crowd move toward the gate of the village, they meet a funeral procession. Luke focuses on the weeping mother, a widow, whose only son has died. Luke shows Jesus' compassion for the now child-less widow by comforting her with the words, "Don't cry." At some point Jesus "touched the coffin" (He reaches out and stops the procession.), and "those carrying it stood still." During this pause, Jesus addresses the young man and says, "Young man, I say to you, get up!" And the young man sits up and begins to speak.

The people who witness this miracle glorify God and shout, "A great prophet has appeared among us, . . . God has come to help his people." Point out that the statement "God has come to help his people" is significant. Now what they can see in Jesus' miraculous resurrection of the youth is a "great prophet." The Jews looked for a prophet "greater than Moses," the Messiah; yet they fail to recognize Jesus.

Luke 7:18-35. In Luke 7:18-23 we have a bit of uncertainty, if not rivalry, on the part of John's disciples as they compare themselves with Jesus' disciples. John's disciples tell John what Jesus is teaching and doing. They wonder if Jesus is the Messiah. John is uncertain himself, so he sends two of his disciples to Jesus to ask him to clarify his work and mission. "Are you the one who was to come, or should we expect someone else?"

Recall that John is in prison, so he cannot go to see Jesus himself. During a brief period of time ("at the very time") Jesus' ministry illustrates (for the benefit of John's disci-ples) whether he is the Messiah. Jesus heals all kinds of diseases and plagues, exorcises evil spirits from many, and helps the blind to see.

Then Luke summarizes the facts that prove Jesus is the long-awaited Messiah, referring to Isaiah 29:18-19; 35:5-6; and 61:1-2. Ask class members to find Isaiah 35:5-6 in their Bibles. Read the passage. Then read the messianic passage from Isaiah 61:1-2. This passage is the same one Jesus read in the synagogue at Nazareth to help the people under-stand that the Spirit of God was upon him and that he was called to this prophetic ministry of messiahship. Jesus tells John's disciples, "Go back and report to John what you have seen and heard." John and Jesus have different concepts of what it means to be the Messiah and of what the kingdom of God is.

Jesus understands the Messiah to be the One who will fulfill Isaiah 61:1-2. Jesus believes in living a life of mercy, kindness, and unselfish service. Jesus tries to clarify this mission through his teaching. John based his ministry on judgment and obedience to moral law. Jesus' messianic action is not what John expects the Messiah to be doing. John is looking for the destruction of the morally unfit; Jesus is looking for the restoration of the unfit to moral health.

Jesus' statement, "Blessed is the man who does not fall away on account of me," expresses his hope to John the Baptist and his disciples that they will not be offended by his (Jesus') lifestyle, his teachings, and his interpretation of what it means to be God's Messiah.

In Luke 7:24-35, Jesus (after the disciples of John leave) supports John's ministry. He asks some tough questions of those who had previously listened to John in the desert: "What did you go out into the desert to see? A reed swayed by the wind?" The reed movest according to any wind that blows. One hardly thinks of John as a tender reed moving with any wind that blows! He is no easygoing, pussyfooting man. He is a hardheaded, demanding prophet. He is not a kind and indulgent man.

Is John a man clothed in luxurious clothes? Such men appear only in the courts of kings. That is hardly what John was at the Jordan, nor what he is now in his imprisonment. John is a prophet, with the austerity and uncompromising courage of a prophet.

Jesus adds, John is more than a prophet; he is sent by God to be a herald of a new day, fulfilling what Malachi envisioned: "See, I will send my messenger, who will pre-pare the way before me" (Malachi 3:1). John the Baptist is the forerunner (herald) of the Messiah; he is not Elijah returned as the Messiah. (See John 1:19-21.) He is a voice shouting, "Prepare the way for the Lord" (Luke 3:4).

John had preached and baptized thousands of persons at the Jordan River. The common people especially responded to his ministry and were baptized. The Phari-sees and teachers of the law had heard John but refused to be baptized. Obviously, common people and religious leaders are in opposition. Many of the common people are for Jesus, and many Pharisees and teachers of the law are against Jesus.

It is possible that John has not thought of Jesus as Messiah until he hears about the impression Jesus makes. Two facts are obvious in the reading of this passage. John still has disciples, who remain aloof from the new move-ment of Jesus. And John does not preach the present kingdom that has arrived with Jesus. Therefore Jesus asks how he can compare these two groups of people. One group is happy and joyful; the other group is dour and sour, full of prejudice and empty of mercy. The two groups are like two groups of children: One group wants to play wedding and blow the flutes; the other group wants to play funeral and sing a dirge.

JESUS: MESSIANIC TEACHER AND HEALER

John's disciples prefer to play funeral hymns, fast, and drink no wine (7:33); but Jesus and his disciples are having a "wedding of a time," eating and drinking. Some call John too ascetic (austere, self-denying); some call Jesus a glutton, a drunkard, and a friend of tax collectors and sinners. What then shall we think of John?

Jesus says of John, "Among those born of women there is no one greater than John; yet the one who is least in the kingdom of God is greater than he" (7:28). John and his disciples live with judgment and fear; Jesus and his disciples experience the mercy of God and God's loving presence always.

Ask class members to read Acts 19 to see how Paul, when he went to Ephesus, found some disciples who had received "John's baptism." In what ways was this baptism incomplete?

In Luke 7:34, Jesus repeats a common criticism about himself when he says that he is "a friend of tax collectors and 'sinners.' " Apparently sinfulness is not a characteristic of eating and drinking as such. Some Jews find John too unsociable and Jesus too sociable.

Class members might profit from a discussion of the level of friendship that existed between John and Jesus. Both men were vitally interested in the kingdom of God. Yet they differed radically in their understanding of and approach to the Kingdom. Would they have spent much time talking together? Remind class members that John's message was not the gospel of his cousin Jesus. John held only to the Torah (the first five books of the Old Testament) as his Scripture. Jesus loved the writings of the prophets also, which he included in his Scriptures. John's major passage was from Deuteronomy 18:15—a greater prophet than Moses will come. Jesus loved especially the prophet Isaiah. John spent great amounts of time in the desert, a lonely, self-denying life. By contrast, Jesus loved to be with people and enjoyed friendships around the dinner table. Jesus tried to set people free. (You might ask two persons to roleplay the parts of John and Jesus, using the starter ideas suggested in this paragraph.)

Luke 7:36-50. These verses describe a story about Jesus, a Pharisee, and a woman who is probably a prostitute ("who had lived a sinful life"). The Pharisee invites Jesus to dinner as his guest. Hearing about the dinner, the woman determines to attend the party too in order to show gratitude for Jesus' interest in people like her. She apparently is wealthy, for she takes with her an alabaster jar of expensive perfume to pour on Jesus' feet. (Compare a similar story recorded in Matthew 26:6-13; Mark 14:3-9; John 12:1-8.) Suggest to class members that each person analyze the character of the Pharisee and the sinful woman. Then suggest that they analyze their own lives against those standards.

The Pharisee invites Jesus to dinner. Why? Out of friendship, out of gratitude, or out of a desire to be pompous and ingratiating? Why does he not greet Jesus with the usual kiss of a host, see that the dust is washed from his feet,

anoint his head with perfumed oil, extend the normal courtesies of a host? What is going on in his mind? Why is the woman from the street there? The story does not suggest that she uses words of repentance for having sinned. But certainly many of her actions imply it. She bathes Jesus' feet with her tears (of joy or repentance?), wipes them with her hair, kisses his feet, and anoints them with her precious perfume. Though she says not a word, her actions speak louder than words. Jesus understands and interprets her actions correctly. She is expressing her love of and appreciation for him.

The Pharisee totally misunderstands the situation because he sees only an unclean woman of the street. The woman says not a word, but the Pharisee's thoughts condemn him. "If this man were a prophet, he would know who is touching him and what kind of woman she is." Jesus says, "Simon, I have something to tell you."

Jesus then tells the parable of a moneylender who has two debtors, one owes five hundred denarii, the other fifty. When the time comes to pay the debts, neither man can do so. The moneylender forgives them both. The question is, Which of them loves him more? Simon answers, "The one who had the bigger debt canceled." Jesus approves Simon's answer and says, "Her many sins have been forgiven—for she loved much. But he who has been forgiven little loves little." Jesus turns to the woman and says, "Your sins are forgiven. . . .Your faith has saved you; go in peace."

Luke 8:1-56. As Jesus goes through the cities and villages, preaching and bringing the good news of the kingdom of God, he is accompanied not only by the disciples but also by some women—Mary (of the fishing town Magdala on the west coast of the Sea of Galilee); Joanna (the wife of Cuza, Herod Antipas's household manager); Susanna; and many other women. These other women may well have been the wives of the disciples, who apparently traveled with their husbands. (See 1 Corinthians 9:5.) "These women were helping to support them [the disciples and Jesus] out of their own means." That is, they financed them while on their journeys. Probably these women assumed responsibility for preparing meals and making housing arrangements at night.

Luke 8:4-8, a parable of different soils, is intended to tell Jesus' audience about the quality of different hearers. What persons in an audience may hear (in sermons, lectures, classes) depends on the moral and spiritual quality of their lives. The quality of a person's life determines how much attention can be given to specific teachings, the level of possible reception, and the will power to carry out the teachings.

The sower (the teacher or preacher) sows the seed. Some falls on hardened paths, is trampled on, and has no chance to grow. Some teachings fall on soil with a thin layer of dirt covering solid rock. Some teachings fall among thorns and are choked by those around them. And some teachings are sown in good soil (minds) and grow and yield a hundredfold. "He who has ears to hear, let him hear."

Luke 8:22-25 presents a nature miracle, the miraculous calming of a severe storm on the Lake of Gennesaret (Sea of Galilee). Equally important is that Jesus calms the fear in the hearts of seasoned fishermen and chides them for their lack of faith.

Luke 8:26-39 tells the story of another healing. The eastern shore of the Sea of Galilee is narrow and runs into very high and steep cliffs in the region of the Gerasenes. Here a frenzied man, who has been imprisoned and bound by chains from which he has escaped many times, apparently learns what has happened on the sea and in the boat. He hears that frightened men suddenly became calm and peaceful because one of their companions stood and spoke. That man spoke with authority to both storm and men. *Surely,* thought the frenzied man, *he can help me.*

Luke describes a fascinating scene. As Jesus steps out of the boat, "Legion" (who is naked and has been living in one of the tombs) meets Jesus. Jesus recognizes his mental disabilities and orders the evil influences to come out of him. The man responds, "What do you want with me, Jesus, Son of the Most High God?" Jesus asks him his name. He replies, "Legion." (*Legion* is a military word for a division of six thousand men.) His name symbolizes his problem: Whenever he tries to make a decision, many contradictory voices cry out in his mind, wanting their answers to dominate all the others. His mind is a mob. Legion needs an integrating, centralizing power in his life. He finds that power when Jesus, in his messianic role, sets the prisoner free.

When villagers hear what has happened to the demoniac, they come to see this miracle. They find him "sitting at Jesus' feet, dressed and in his right mind; and they were afraid."

The two concluding stories of Luke 8 deal with a girl of twelve who is dying and a woman who has been sick twelve years (8:40-48).

The father of the girl is Jairus, "a ruler of the synagogue." Judaism required at least ten men to form a synagogue. These ten men were known as the rulers of the synagogue. Jairus, having heard that Jesus is a healer, comes to request Jesus' healing power for his only daughter. "Please come and put your hands on her so that she will be healed and live" (Mark 5:23).

"As Jesus was on his way" to help Jairus's daughter, the crowd presses about Jesus. A woman in the crowd has suffered greatly because of a continual hemorrhage. This condition means she is ritually unclean, so she cannot worship in the Court of Women in the Temple and is not acceptable to her husband. She suffers the pain of humiliation and presumed guilt of sin, not to mention the physical problem itself. Perhaps because Luke is a physician, he omits what Mark says about the woman: "She had suffered a great deal under the care of many doctors and had spent all she had, yet instead of getting better she grew worse" (Mark 5:26). She is desperate.

Perhaps Jesus might remove her uncleanness and restore her to a healthy relationship with God in the Temple and with her husband, family, and friends. Twelve years of anguish force her to do what she certainly would not have done otherwise. She gets near the Master and touches his garment—perhaps only one of the four blue-and-white tassels (fringe) hanging from his outer cloak. (See Numbers 15:38-39; Deuteronomy 22:12.) She reaches out, touches a tassel of his garment, and is immediately healed.

Jesus stops short and asks, "Who touched me? . . . I know that power has gone out from me" (8:45-46). Trembling, the woman bows down at his feet and admits she has touched him. Jesus says, "Daughter, your faith has healed you. Go in peace."

While Jesus is still speaking, a man from the ruler's house comes and says, "Your daughter is dead." Jesus tells Jairus, "Don't be afraid; just believe, and she will be healed." Jesus goes to the house, and with Peter, James, and John, plus the father and mother, he enters and says, " 'My child, get up!' Her spirit returned, and at once she stood up." Again Jesus asks that they not tell others of this miracle. The time and the way of declaring his messiahship has not come.

DIMENSION THREE: WHAT DOES THE BIBLE MEAN TO ME?

Luke 8:9-10—Insiders

Luke 8:9-10 and Matthew 13:10-13 are based on Mark 4:10-12, which suggests that Jesus teaches in parables so only "insiders" (disciples) will understand and respond to the message. Surely teaching only insiders is not Jesus' intention. Luke 8:16-18 emphasizes that a lamp is ignited for the sole purpose of shedding light. You do not put a lamp in a jar or under a bed, since no light can be shed to find your way. So it is with parables. Jesus tells parables to illustrate and explain by stories and metaphors that which otherwise is difficult to understand.

The Old Testament, through the survivors of the house of Judah (Isaiah 37:30-32), teaches the doctrine of the remnant. Not everyone responds to the call of God for repentance and new life. Only a few do so. Isaiah 6:9-10 deals with the theological difficulty of why some persons respond, but most do not. Inasmuch as God is ultimately responsible for all things, God then must be responsible for persons who do not see the light and refuse to accept God's truth. But Jesus does not believe in this doctrine of predestination. He clearly recognizes the freedom of persons to determine their own fate by their own choices.

The purpose of all parables is to let the truth be known. Truth is never willfully hidden. Parables are not secretive, they enlighten all. Early church leaders applied the doctrine of the remnant incorrectly to the parables of Jesus. True, many refuse, but not because the parables are obscure. People refuse because their minds are obstinate. Jesus teaches in parables in order that hearers might hear and be transformed.

— 5 —

The Disciples Accept Jesus as Messiah

Luke 9:1-50

DIMENSION ONE:
WHAT DOES THE BIBLE SAY?

Answer these questions by reading Luke 9:1-17

1. Before Jesus sends "the Twelve" on their first mission, what does he give them? (9:1)

   Jesus gives his disciples "power and authority to drive out all demons and to cure diseases."

2. What does Jesus send them out to do? (9:2)

   Jesus sends the disciples out "to preach the kingdom of God and to heal the sick."

3. What rules does Jesus give for their journey? (9:3-5)

   They are to take nothing for their journey, to stay in one person's house, and to leave the town or house when they are not welcome.

4. What does Herod hear and think about these missions? (9:7)

   Herod hears of all that is done—healing and preaching; but he is perplexed as to who their leader is.

5. What political leader "tried to see" Jesus? (9:9)

   Herod, the tetrarch (ruler) of Galilee, wants to see Jesus.

6. After the disciples report to Jesus on their mission, where does Jesus take them? (9:10)

   Jesus withdraws with the disciples to a town called Bethsaida.

7. When the crowds search for and find Jesus at Bethsaida, where he and his disciples have withdrawn for a spiritual retreat, what does Jesus do? (9:11)

   He welcomes them, speaks to them of the kingdom of God, and heals their sick.

8. Late in the afternoon, what do the disciples ask Jesus to do? (9:12)

   They ask Jesus to send the crowd away so the people can find housing and food.

9. What does Jesus say to the Twelve? (9:13)

   Jesus tells them, "You give them something to eat."

10. After the disciples tell Jesus they have only five loaves and two fish, what does Jesus do? (9:14b-16)

    Jesus tells his disciples to divide the crowd into groups of fifty. He then takes the loaves and fish, looks up to heaven, and gives thanks for the food. Then Jesus gives the loaves and fish to the disciples to set before the crowd.

11. How many persons partake of this meal, and how much food is left over? (9:14a-17)

    Five thousand men (plus their wives and children) partake. Twelve baskets of broken pieces are left over.

Answer these questions by reading Luke 9:18-27

12. What responses does Jesus receive when he asks who people say he is? (9:18-19)

    Some people say John the Baptist; others say Elijah; still others say that one of the prophets has come back to life.

13. What response does Jesus receive when he asks, "Who do you say I am?" (9:20)

    Peter answers, "The Christ of God."

14. What command does Jesus then give the disciples? (9:21-22)

They are "not to tell this [that Jesus is the Christ] to anyone." Jesus tells them that "the Son of man must suffer many things and be rejected . . . and . . . be killed."

15. What must a person do to be Jesus' disciple? (9:23)

To be Jesus' disciple, a person must "deny himself and take up his cross daily and follow [Jesus]."

Answer these questions by reading Luke 9:28-43a

16. Eight days later, what happens to Jesus on the mountain, where he goes to pray? (9:28-30)

"The appearance of his face changed, and his clothes became as bright as a flash of lightning." Moses and Elijah appear "in glorious splendor" and speak with Jesus.

17. Who does Jesus take to the mountain with him? (9:28)

Jesus takes Peter, James, and John with him.

18. What proposal does Peter make to Jesus? (9:33)

Peter proposes to make three booths, "one for you [Jesus], one for Moses and one for Elijah."

19. What is the significance of the cloud? (9:34-35)

A voice speaks to the disciples from the cloud saying, "This is my Son, whom I have chosen; listen to him."

20. When the voice (of God) finishes speaking, who is left on the mountain? (9:36)

Jesus, Peter, James, and John are left alone on the mountain.

21. When Jesus, Peter, James, and John come down the mountain to the valley, who meets them? (9:37-39)

A large crowd and a father whose son has convulsions meet them.

22. Who has tried to heal the boy suffering from convulsions? (9:40)

The disciples have tried, but they cannot.

23. What does Jesus do? (9:42b)

Jesus rebukes the evil spirit, heals the boy, and gives him to his father.

Answer these questions by reading Luke 9:43b-50

24. While everyone is "marveling at all that Jesus did," what prediction does Jesus make of his Passion? (9:44)

Jesus says, "The Son of Man is going to be betrayed into the hands of men."

25. While Jesus tries to inform his disciples about his interpretation of the messianic hope, in what argument do the disciples engage? (9:46)

The disciples argue as to which of them would be the greatest.

DIMENSION TWO: WHAT DOES THE BIBLE MEAN?

The Scripture for this lesson, when, where, and how the twelve disciples finally accept Jesus as the Messiah (Christ), is divided into five themes:

1. Jesus Directs His Disciples in Mission (9:1-11)
2. The Feeding of the Five Thousand (9:12-17)
3. Peter's Confession and the First Prediction of Jesus' Passion (9:18-27)
4. The Transfiguration and Curing a Boy With Epilepsy (9:28-43a)
5. The Second Prediction of Jesus' Passion and a Pagan Exorcist (9:43b-50)

Luke 9:1-11. Inasmuch as Jesus is aware of his call by God to be the Messiah and inasmuch as he knows his Scripture very well, he cannot help but be influenced by Deuteronomy 18:15. This passage states that a prophet like Moses will come and that the people should listen to him. Jesus would have heard from childhood days how Moses served God yet was denied the right to enter the Promised Land. Jesus would have known the story of Moses' approaching death and how his successor (Joshua) was chosen and commissioned. (Read Numbers 27:15-20 to the class members. Ask if they think this passage may have influenced Jesus in the commissioning of his twelve disciples.)

Some facts from Numbers 27:15-20 that class members may want to know are these: (1) Moses asks God to "appoint a man over this community." (2) This man shall be a shepherd to Israel. (3) Joshua is called by God, for in him "is the spirit." He will be commissioned by Moses. (4) After Moses commissions Joshua as his spirit-led successor, Moses is to "give him some of [his] authority."

Joshua is told to take twelve men from the tribes of Israel, one from each tribe. These twelve will lead Israel in their campaigns to conquer and win the land. How similar is the commissioning of the Twelve Jesus chose? (Read Luke 9:1-2 to class members, which tells how Jesus called the Twelve, investing them with his power and authority.) Joshua called for leadership to lead in a war that would obtain the Promised Land. Jesus called for leadership that would win the minds and attitudes of all human beings. The methods of Joshua and Jesus were poles apart. Joshua did not go out to convert people to the kingdom of God; Jesus sought to win persons to the kingdom of God by persuasion, not by coercion. So Jesus calls, trains, and sends out twelve "missioners" who will seek by way of teaching, healing, and exorcism to set the captives free, to help persons who are blind to open their moral and spiritual eyes and see, to know the day of the Lord is upon them (Isaiah 61:1-2).

Though successful in teaching in Capernaum, Jesus apparently considers his work in Nazareth a failure. He leaves Nazareth and goes "around teaching from village to village" (Mark 6:6b). He would have gone to such villages as Nain (six miles southeast of Nazareth) and perhaps north to Sepphoris.

With the commissioning of the Twelve to represent Jesus' mission, we understand why he chose them and why Jesus prayed so earnestly in choosing them. Instead of being disciples who listen to his teachings, they now become preachers of his mission. His work becomes twelve times more effective.

Before commissioning the Twelve, Jesus gives them two important gifts: power (*dunamis*) and authority (*exousia*). The two Greek words, *dunamis* and *exousia*, also mean personal force and official right. The most effective leaders are those who possess both.

The commissioning includes five parts: (1) Jesus gives his own power and authority over all demons (evil spirits; Mark 6:7) and the power to cure diseases. (2) Jesus commissions them to preach. (3) Jesus gives them a rule for their journey: Travel light; take no staff, no suitcase, no bread, no money; take only one tunic (undershirt). Sandals were evidently allowed (Mark 6:9). (4) Choose the house (The inhabitants are likely to be converts.) and stay in that one place. (5) If the people (town or family) do not receive you well, when you leave, shake off the dust from your feet. This latter suggestion is a rabbinic custom. When returning from a trip to a foreign land, such as Samaria, the rabbi would shake off any dust as a symbol that he wanted nothing of paganism attached to him.

Apparently the ministry of the twelve disciples was very successful, for even Herod the tetrarch heard of "all that was going on." Ask class members what "all that was going on" might mean for Herod Antipas. (Consider specific healing miracles; unique teachings of and about Jesus; exorcisms by the disciples, such as setting people free from their mental and spiritual uncleanness; and so forth.)

Ask class members to suggest the ways in which Herod would have heard the gospel and ways he did not. For example, Herod lived in a time when there were no radios, no television sets, no satellite communication systems, no newspapers. He was totally dependent on oral (vocal) communication. Herod listened to those who either gossiped or had heard. (For example, do you think Cuza, husband of Joanna who helped finance Jesus, might have reported about his wife's experiences? Could Cuza have spoken plainly in an official meeting?)

Herod was "perplexed," in part because some had told him that Jesus was John resurrected—Herod's beheading of John had been on his conscience for some time. Herod had promised Salome (Herodias's daughter by Philip, Herod's half-brother) to grant any request she made. He obviously could not break his word. A promise is a promise—especially when the high-ranking military officers, mayors of villages and cities, and representatives from Rome have come for the birthday party. (Discuss this question: Is Herod unique in keeping promises that many persons hear but being unconcerned about keeping promises that are private?)

Since John the Baptist's beheading, Herod has been hearing great and grave reports about Jesus and his twelve disciples. Many have just finished a mission in several of his cities where they preached, healed diseases, and exorcised evil spirits in the name of their teacher, Jesus (9:6).

Herod's question "Who, then, is this I hear such things about?" is the question of the various episodes of this lesson. The man, Jesus, whom Herod hears about, sends disciples to preach throughout Herod's kingdom. Jesus feeds 5,000 men at one sitting. Three of his disciples (Peter, James, and John) hear Jesus admit for the first time that he is the long-awaited Messiah. These three men see Jesus transfigured on a high hill as he prays—and is ministered to by Moses and Elijah. He heals a boy from his seizures. He now moves toward Jerusalem. Herod has asked rightly, Who is this man? We will look more closely at the scenario.

Luke 9:12-17. Ask class members if Jesus knew and loved his Bible (what Christians now call the Old Testament). Must we not assume that he did? Jesus would have known well an experience in the life of the "sons of the prophets" during the terrible famine when Elisha was their head. One hundred prophets were without food. "A man came from Baal Shalishah, bringing the man of God [Elisha] twenty loaves of barley bread baked from the first ripe grain, along with some heads of new grain. 'Give it to the people to eat,' Elisha said. 'How am I to set this [little bit of food] before a hundred men?' his servant asked. But Elisha answered, 'Give it to the people to eat. For this is what the LORD says: "They will eat and have some left over." ' Then he set it before them, and they ate and had some left over, according to the word of the LORD" (2 Kings 4:42-44).

Jesus had referred to a miracle by Elisha when he preached in Nazareth, but the people refused to listen (Luke 4:16-30). Now Jesus addresses a similar question to his apostles, who have completed their mission throughout the villages of Galilee and have listened with five thousand men as Jesus taught all day. The day had been spent at Bethsaida, where Jesus had invited the Twelve to spend the day in sharing their new experiences as teachers and healers (their first mission). The crowd comes and interrupts Jesus' plans for spiritual renewal of his disciples. He never shows disappointment at this interruption of his personal plans. He welcomes the people.

The order Jesus gives to his disciples is this: "You give them something to eat." The disciples could only respond with despair: "We have only five loaves of bread and two fish." As with Elisha, how can you feed one hundred hungry men on twenty loaves? How do they feed five thousand men and their families on that which would be inadequate even for a man and his wife?

Jesus orders the disciples to divide the crowd into groups of approximately fifty each. After the inevitable commotion of dividing into groups, he made them all sit down.

Jesus takes the five loaves and the two fish; looks up toward heaven; and blesses (that is, praises God) and breaks them, giving them to the disciples. Then the disciples move among the groups, serving those who needed food. (You might ask which of the Synoptic Gospels states how Jesus multiplied the fish and loves to serve the great crowd. The answer, of course, is none; multiplication is not mentioned.) The people eat and are satisfied. And they (the disciples who served) take up what is left over, twelve baskets of broken pieces.

The early church's *Eucharist* (a Greek word meaning, even today, thanksgiving) had the same steps that a bishop or elder uses to administer Holy Communion, or the Lord's Supper. The people sit; the leader takes the bread, blesses and breaks it, gives it to the people, and takes up the broken pieces. Many biblical scholars assume that Luke's account is influenced by the way the Lord's Supper was served at the time Luke wrote his Gospel.

Your class members might like to know that drawings of bread and fish appear on frescoes in the catacombs symbolizing the Lord's Supper. It is interesting that Jesus is at Bethsaida, which means "house of fishing," when the dinner of fish and bread is served.

Describe the setting for the feeding of the five thousand. The crowd has come to the area of Bethsaida, where Jesus and his disciples had held a brief and interrupted retreat. Jesus welcomes the crowd and teaches them. Jesus always emphasizes the love of God with its overtones for moral action—sharing what you have with those who do not have, the meaning of Christlike human relationships based on justice and good intentions, the divine thrust in human lives urging us to yearn for and accept Jesus' lifestyle that would result in peace. (Perhaps you could let class members suggest a number of other emphases Jesus would normally raise.)

You may want to refer to what scholars call "the big omission" in Luke's Gospel. Between Luke 9:17 (the end of the account of the feeding of the five thousand) and 9:18 (the beginning of Peter's confession at Caesarea Philippi) are two large groups of material in both Matthew and Mark: Matthew 14:22–16:12 and Mark 6:45–8:26. We do not know why Luke omitted these episodes, unless he felt they would interrupt the pursuit of Herod's major point: Who is this man, Jesus?

Luke 9:18-27. Luke's choice of materials for this chapter concentrates on the identity of Jesus. Peter is the first of the Twelve to state forthrightly that Jesus is Christ. Both Mark and Matthew tell us that Jesus and his disciples go to Caesarea Philippi. Luke does not refer to Caesarea Philippi, perhaps thinking it does not matter where the great event takes place.

This Scripture passage introduces a new element in Jesus' ministry. At this point in Mark's Gospel, Jesus is no longer viewed as a public figure. Rather Mark portrays Jesus as the fulfillment of Isaiah's prophecy of the suffering servant. Jesus is portrayed as seeking to prepare his disciples for his Passion—for his abuse and his suffering on the cross. In Luke we shall see Jesus continuing his public ministry through what scholars call the Lukan Insertion (9:51–18:14).

Jesus and his disciples have been moving northward, in part to leave Galilee (ruled by Herod Antipas who has said he would like to see Jesus) and in part to be alone together as Jesus teaches them the meaning of messiahship. As Jesus prays in the hilly area of Caesarea Philippi, he turns to his disciples and asks them who the people say he is. Do they know his identity? The disciples answer that some people say he is "John the Baptist; others say Elijah; and still others, that one of the old prophets of long ago has come back to life." Now Jesus asks his disciples the question Herod has been asking: "But what about you? . . . Who do you say I am?" Peter answers, "The Christ of God."

Up to this point, when persons are healed or set free from unclean spirits and have declared that Jesus is the Holy One and the Son of God, Jesus asks them not to tell anyone. Now Jesus wants his disciples to recognize him as God's "beloved son," the Christ, the Messiah. Jesus accepts Peter's confession but declines to make it public. Jesus needs time to reinterpret the popular concept of Messiah (that most of his disciples hold) in terms of loving service, suffering, and sacrifice. His chosen men do not like this view.

Ask class members to discuss Jesus' command to his disciples at this time, to tell Jesus' identity to no one. What would it have hurt? Were the disciples free to discuss it? How long did Jesus want to wait and for what reason? (Jesus will wait until Palm Sunday when he will demonstrate Zechariah's understanding of one who would come riding on a lowly colt rather than a military stallion and " 'not by might nor by power, but by my Spirit,' says the LORD almighty" (Zechariah 4:6).

The significance of the phrase "the elders, chief priests and teachers of the law" lay in the fact that this group forms the Sanhedrin in Jerusalem. They are the final court of appeal for Jews in Jerusalem and throughout the land. Jesus now predicts, for the first time, that he, the Son of Man, will suffer many things, be rejected by the Sanhedrin, and after three days be raised from the dead.

Luke 9:28-43a. The key to understanding Peter, James, and John's experience of Jesus' transfiguration lies in the fact that Jesus wants his intimate friends to know with clear certainty that, in spite of the terrible fate that awaits him, he is nonetheless the Messiah, the Chosen One, God's beloved Son.

After eight days, following Peter's recognition of Jesus as the Christ, Jesus goes with three disciples to a high mountain (probably Mount Tabor). Jesus goes up to pray. While praying, Jesus' countenance is changed ("transfigured"), and his clothes become dazzling white ("as bright as a flash of lightning").

Luke tells us that two men are talking with Jesus, Moses and Elijah. They discuss with Jesus his departure (death) that will take place in Jerusalem. While talking, Peter, James, and John (who are half-awake) realize what is happening. They see Jesus' glory and Moses and Elijah with him. Ask class members to discuss why Peter's suggestion that they build three shelters on the mountain upsets Jesus.

A voice comes out of the cloud and says, "This is my Son, whom I have chosen; listen to him." The two phrases carry many Old Testament memories and emotions. The cloud, as in Old Testament times, symbolizes the presence of God. (See Exodus 24:15-18; 1 Kings 8:10.)

Interestingly, after the voice of God speaks (for the benefit of Peter, James, and John?), they find themselves alone. They tell "no one at that time what they had seen." (Why would the disciples tell no one of this great experience? Ask class members to venture guesses as to why.)

Luke 9:43b-50. Jesus tells his disciples a second time that "the Son of Man is going to be betrayed into the hands of men." The repetition probably means the disciples did not understand or believe it. Jesus uses strong words: "Listen carefully." And Jesus might have added that these words should sink into your minds or you will not understand my future and your relationship to it.

Ask class members to share their thoughts on the following: In what way would prayer for understanding of Jesus' interpretation of his messianic ministry help us mature in faith? Not to pray for continuing insights into the life and message of Jesus is to exclude our chances of an "at-one-ment" with the mind of Christ or of being transformed by his Spirit. The disciples could not vibrate with the inner life of Jesus until after Jesus' resurrection and the Pentecost experience. We cannot reach the top of the ladder until we have first climbed up each rung.

The disciples, perhaps with some jealousy, see a man casting out demons in the name of Jesus. He is not a follower of Christ, so the disciples forbid him to do so. Jesus says, "Whoever is not against you is for you." Suggest a brief discussion of denominationalism from this perspective.

DIMENSION THREE: WHAT DOES THE BIBLE MEAN TO ME?

The class may discuss the following topic or use the material in the student book.

Luke 9:9—Who Is This Man?

Luke 9 deals with Herod's question "Who, then, is this I hear such things about?" Today's Scripture suggests several responses, chief of which is that of Peter ("The Christ of God."). We would do well to ask ourselves Herod's question.

What does it really mean to be a follower of Jesus Christ? As Peter stated, it means to believe that Jesus is truly the long-awaited Messiah. It also means to know Jesus' mind (by way of parables, similes, and metaphors). We are so to love his lifestyle that we enjoy a wonderful "at-one-ment" with him and with his purposes. We are quick and alert to respond to all opportunities to participate in the kingdom of God.

A danger exists in our claims to know and to be dedicated to the person of Jesus. We may develop a pride in our achievements. This attitude is exemplified in the foolish dispute of the disciples (9:46-48) as to which one of them would (or, more probably, should be) the greatest. Perhaps they all seek positions that will make them closest to the "power of the throne." It is a selfish and inexcusable attitude. Jesus deals with it by taking a child, apparently in his arms as Mark 9:36 suggests. Jesus' point is not that a leader needs a childlike character to enter the kingdom of God but rather that to accept Jesus himself, a leader must be prepared to accept and honor even those persons of our society who are lowliest in mental alacrity and spiritual achievements. Jesus wants the disciples to see that he respects and associates himself with the smallest and least. Jesus never feels honored above others because he dines with the most educated or most intelligent person present. He loves all and yearns for his followers to love all in the same way.

Follow me (9:59a).

—6—

Jesus Sets His Face Toward Jerusalem

Luke 9:51–11:36

DIMENSION ONE:
WHAT DOES THE BIBLE SAY?

Answer these questions by reading Luke 9:51-62

1. To what city does Jesus "resolutely set out"? (9:51)

   Jesus sets out for Jerusalem.

2. Before going to a Samaritan village, what does Jesus do? (9:52)

   Jesus sends messengers ahead of him.

3. How does Jesus respond to James and John, who want to destroy the Samaritans who refuse to receive him? (9:55-56)

   Jesus rebukes them; they go on to another village.

4. When a man says, "I will follow you wherever you go" (9:57), what is Jesus' response? (9:58)

   Jesus responds, "Foxes have holes and birds of the air have nests, but the Son of Man has no place to lay his head."

5. Another man says, "Lord, first let me go and bury my father" (9:59). What is Jesus' response? (9:60)

   Jesus responds, "Let the dead bury their own dead, but you go and proclaim the kingdom of God."

6. A third man says, "First let me go back and say good-by to my family" (9:61). What is Jesus' response? (9:62)

   Jesus responds, "No one who puts his hand to the plow and looks back is fit for service in the kingdom of God."

Answer these questions by reading Luke 10

7. How many followers does Jesus appoint to send into every town and place? (10:1)

   Jesus appoints seventy-two followers.

8. If a town does not receive them, what are they to say? (10:11)

   They are to say, "Even the dust of your town that sticks to our feet we wipe off against you. Yet be sure of this: The kingdom of God is near."

9. What reports do the seventy-two make to Jesus? (10:17)

   The seventy-two return with joy, saying, "Lord, even the demons submit to us in your name."

10. What is Jesus' response to their joyful reports? (10:18)

    Jesus replies, "I saw Satan fall like lightning from heaven."

11. In Jesus' prayer, for what does he praise God? (10:21)

    He thanks God for having "hidden these things from the wise . . . and revealed them to little children."

12. How are Jesus' disciples blessed? (10:23-24)

    They are blessed with both sensitive eyes and ears.

13. What question prompts the telling of the parable of the good Samaritan? (10:25)

    An expert in the law asks, "Teacher, . . . what must I do to inherit eternal life?"

14. Who is "my neighbor"? (10:29, 36-37)

"My neighbor" is the person who is merciful in one's time of need.

15. Who receives Jesus into her house? (10:38)

Martha receives Jesus into her house.

16. How does Mary upset Martha? (10:39-40)

Mary sits at Jesus' feet listening to his teaching instead of helping Martha prepare the meal.

Answer these questions by reading Luke 11:1-13

17. What is Luke's version of the Lord's Prayer? (11:2-4)

Luke's version of the Lord's Prayer is, "Father, / hallowed be your name, / your kingdom come. / Give us each day our daily bread. Forgive us our sins, / for we also forgive everyone who sins against us. / And lead us not into temptation."

18. Why does the friend help his neighbor? (11:5-8)

The friend helps his neighbor because of his neighbor's persistence.

19. In order to receive, what must one do? (11:10)

One must ask in order to receive.

Answer these questions by reading Luke 11:14-28

20. When Jesus casts out a demon from a man who was mute, many are amazed. What do others say? (11:15)

Other people say, "By Beelzebub, the prince of demons, he is driving out demons."

21. What is Jesus' response? (11:17-20)

First, Jesus points out that a divided kingdom falls (therefore, would Satan cast out himself?). And second, Jesus affirms that it is by "the finger of God" that he drives out demons.

22. What happens when an evil spirit leaves a person? (11:24-26)

The evil spirit returns with seven other spirits more evil than himself.

23. What reply does Jesus make to the woman who says, "Blessed is the mother who gave you birth and nursed you"? (11:27-28)

Jesus replies, "Blessed rather are those who hear the word of God and obey it!"

DIMENSION TWO: WHAT DOES THE BIBLE MEAN?

In this lesson we begin a study of Jesus' journey from Galilee to Jerusalem, by way of Samaria. Luke provides a narrative framework in the form of a journey toward Jerusalem. The large literary work of Luke 9:51–19:27 is called the Lukan Insertion (into Mark's Gospel), or Luke's special section.

The geographical area covered in this Lukan Insertion is not clearly defined by Luke. But Jesus' travels are between the borders of Galilee and Judea. One Bible scholar remarks, "Once Jesus sets out on this lengthy journey, he seems to be no longer en route." That is, the teachings are more important than where he says them; so we are not informed as to specific places. In fact, we know very little about his location.

The Lukan Insertion (or special section) is a wonderful collection of Jesus' teachings: parables, legal and wisdom sayings, proverbs, critiques of sayings of his opponents, pronouncement teachings, and many miracle stories.

The Scripture is divided into five themes:

1. Conditions of Discipleship (9:51-62)
2. Mission of the Seventy-two (10:1-24)
3. Jesus Answers Questions (10:25-42)
4. Teachings About Prayer (11:1-13)
5. Casting Out Demons (11:14-28)

Luke 9:51-62. This section deals with Jesus' attitude toward Samaritans and people's readiness to follow Jesus. Jesus intentionally moves toward the place of religious authority, Jerusalem. "As the time approached for him to be taken up to heaven" (9:51) refers to Jesus' awareness of what lies in store for him. He knew the treatment that the prophets had received at the hands of the people. Jesus goes to Jerusalem to make his last appeal to the religious leaders of Israel.

Jesus sends messengers (from among his disciples) to visit various villages to prepare for his coming. Two messengers soon report rejection by Samaritans when the Samaritans learn that Jesus is on his way to Jerusalem. The Samaritans' temple on Mount Gerizim was destroyed by the Jewish leader John Hyrcanus about 128 B.C. The Samaritans still worshiped on Mount Gerizim and had their own festivals (the Feast of the Passover, Yom Kippur) and sacred Scripture (the Torah). Jews forbade Samaritans the right to worship in Jerusalem, but the Samaritans welcomed Jews at Mount Gerizim. Why should Jesus want to go to a temple built by the house of Herod? Why not worship at Gerizim?

James and John are angry at the Samaritans' apparent stubbornness and want to be rid of their kind. "Lord, do you want us to call fire down from heaven to destroy them?" The young men remember the story of a former prophet, Elijah, who said, "If I am a man of God, . . . may fire come down from heaven and consume you and your fifty men!" (2 Kings 1:12); and it did. How little these young fishermen understand Jesus' concept of the kingdom of God. The Kingdom was not to be coerced, nor was a curse put on those who rejected God's call. Did the Samaritans not receive God's judgment? Yes, but they received the kind of judgment that follows refusal of the good, the true, the attitudes and motives of the Lord God.

Ask class members to discuss Abraham Lincoln's response to the man who asked him why he was courteous to his enemies. Lincoln replied, "Do I not destroy my enemies when I make them my friends?" Similarly, Jesus turns and corrects his disciples. Then they go on to another village.

Luke 9:57-62 gives insight into Jesus' view of the nature of discipleship. Knowing his days are numbered, he welcomes those who want to become his followers. As they travel, several persons express interest in becoming his followers. One says, "I will follow you wherever you go." Jesus says to the aspirant, "Foxes have holes and birds of the air have nests, but the Son of Man has no place to lay his head." Jesus is on his way to Jerusalem to die. His only home is God's home. The aspirant to discipleship is warned to count the cost. Ask class members: What is Jesus trying to communicate?

As they walk, Jesus invites another aspirant to join him. The aspirant replies, "Lord, first let me go and bury my father." Jesus values filial ties. However, the man's presence implies that his father may be getting old but is not yet dead. The young man could easily lose many months between his initial commitment and his actual following. Jesus needs persons who can decide and act for the Kingdom now. Jesus tells the man to let the spiritually dead bury the physically dead.

A third person says, "I will follow you, Lord; but first let me go back and say good-by to my family." The price of discipleship includes being free of distractions, even loving ones. Looking back longingly and remembering fondly keeps our thoughts on the past. Jesus warns us to count the cost and to reckon with the conflict of loyalties that discipleship inevitably brings. Jesus probably remembers the story of Elijah who sought Elisha that he might put his prophetic mantle over his shoulders. Elijah found Elisha plowing with twelve yoke of oxen. He stopped Elisha in his work and placed his mantle over his shoulders. Elisha understood the symbol and begged Elijah to let him go home to kiss his father and mother good-by. Elijah permitted it. (See 1 Kings 19:19-20.) But Jesus demands undivided loyalty.

Luke 10:1-24. The sending out of the seventy-two (or seventy in the NRSV) is recorded by Luke alone. Why does Jesus choose this number? Perhaps because the Hebrew text of Genesis 10 lists seventy Gentile nations and the Greek translation sometimes lists seventy-two. Eventually, they will teach all nations.

The return of the seventy-two is a joyful occasion. While Jesus notes how he "saw Satan fall like lightning from heaven," the disciples proudly tell how they worked miracles in Jesus' name. "Even the demons submit to us in your name," they say. But Jesus says, "Do not rejoice that the spirits submit to you, but rejoice that your names are written in heaven."

Jesus pauses with the seventy-two and prays to God, thanking God for revealing hidden things to these persons. Jesus says to his rejoicing disciples, "Blessed are the eyes that see what you see." Many persons see only the obvious physical things around them. But the spiritually minded see where God has left identifying marks of God's presence.

How great it is to be with friends whose vision is not limited to only what the physical eyes see. And how exciting to talk with those who "see" the kingdom of God, which many hear about but never see.

Luke 10:25-37. An expert in the law asks Jesus a question to test Jesus' moral and spiritual fiber: "What must I do to inherit eternal life?" That is, what must I do to know I have salvation? Jesus asks the lawyer, "What is written in the Law [the Torah]?" The lawyer responds by uniting verses from Deuteronomy 6:5 and Leviticus 19:18: " 'Love the Lord your God with all your heart and with all your soul and with all your strength and with all your mind'; and, 'Love your neighbor as yourself.' " And Jesus says, "You have answered correctly. . . . Do this and you will live [be saved]."

Then the lawyer asks, "Who is my neighbor?" Jesus, instead of quoting outstanding rabbis or getting into a theological debate, tells a parable. As you read the parable, remember that for the Jew, a Samaritan is a half-breed descendant of the Israelites. In 721 B.C. the Assyrian king Sargon took thousands of Israelites from the Northern Kingdom (known as Samaria) as captives of war to Assyria. In an effort to denationalize the remaining Israelites, captives from other nations were moved to Samaria, where they eventually married the local Israelites. These marriages not only produced children of mixed heritage, they also produced a mixture of religious ideas and faith.

Read Luke 10:25-37 to the class and then discuss it. Notice the lawyer's significant question, "Who is my neighbor?" To answer this question, one must also know the answer to the question, Who is not my neighbor? Whom do we help and why? Where do we draw the line? Jews assumed that only Jews were their neighbors.

Second Chronicles 28:1-16 records an amazing story with a lovely ending. As background, tell the class that King Pekah of Israel (Samaria) and King Rezin of Syria have been trying to force King Ahaz (of Jerusalem, Judah) into

JESUS SETS HIS FACE TOWARD JERUSALEM

169

an alliance in order to stop the Assyrian forces from invading their lands. The two kings (of Samaria and Syria) invade Judah, leaving the people destitute.

Our concern focuses on Samaritan King Pekah whose armies slew one hundred twenty thousand Judean soldiers and took two hundred thousand captives. The Chronicler assumes a blood relationship between Samaritan and Jew; he states that the Samaritans "took captive from their kinsmen two hundred thousand wives, son, and daughters. They also took a great deal of plunder, which they carried back to Samaria" (28:8). Try to help class members visualize the terrible treatment the captives have received. They are naked, cold, abused, sick, weak, humiliated, beaten, and crippled.

Oded, a prophet, goes out to meet the victorious army and expresses strong opposition to their plans of enslaving their kinsfolk. "Aren't you also guilty of sins against the LORD your God?" he asks. "Now listen to me! Send back your fellow countrymen you have taken as prisoners." Four Samaritan chiefs stand up and support Oded against those who are coming from the war and say, "You must not bring those prisoners here." So the soldiers leave the captives and the spoil before the princes and all the assembly. The four chiefs "took the prisoners, and from the plunder they clothed all who were naked. They provided them with clothes and sandals, food and drink, and healing balm. All those who were weak they put on donkeys. So they took them back to their fellow countrymen at Jericho, the City of Palms, and returned to Samaria" (2 Chronicles 28:15). We might entitle this story *The Four Good Samaritans.*

Jesus' story involves a priest and a Levite, who are responsible for teaching and living the Torah. Their callousness stands in sharp contrast to the ideals over which they are the instructors and official guardians. They know the law but do not practice it.

In the story, the victim of a robber lies prostrate; three men come by. One is an ordinary priest who is on his way to Jerusalem to serve his required time in the Temple. He knows he will be ritually unclean if he touches a dead man. The victim is "half dead." After all, leadership in religious ceremonies and rituals is important! The second person, a Levite, sees the victim; and thinking of his important status that he must protect, he walks by on the other side. Then comes the Samaritan, who ministers to the victim. Jesus asks the Jewish lawyer which of these men really loved his neighbor, as God commanded. "The one who had mercy on him," is the reply. Jesus says, "Go and do likewise." The conversation between Jesus and the teacher of the law illustrates the difference between the ethics of law and the ethics of love.

Luke 10:38-42. Luke probably purposely placed the story of Mary and Martha in its present location. The good Samaritan was a doer of the word. In contrast, this story tells of the importance of faith attitudes. Martha has invited Jesus into her house. While she busily prepares a big meal—Is

that not what would please Jesus?—Mary sits at his feet intently listening.

Martha's mind is filled with ideas for food to please the Master—lentils, crushed peas, roast lamb with mint jelly, olives. Mary's mind is filled with Jesus' concerns—his ministry and mission.

Martha is getting tense because she needs help with the meal, and perhaps she is a bit jealous of the exclusive attention Mary is receiving from Jesus. She asks Jesus to instruct Mary to join her in her busy task of preparing the meal. But Jesus does just the opposite, though in a kind way. He says in effect, "Martha, I have other needs just as important as a good meal. Mary has chosen the good portion. I am grateful to both of you." How else might the situation have been handled? Encourage class members to make other suggestions.

"To sit at the feet" of a person is to be his or her student, or disciple. In Acts 22:3, Paul says he was trained under his teacher Gamaliel. Mary is learning of the kingdom of God. Mary chooses the good portion.

Luke 11:1-4. In Luke's Gospel, the Lord's Prayer is shorter than in Matthew (6:9-15) but probably is closer to Jesus' original prayer. It is a challenging and inspiring prayer. It is difficult to pray the Lord's Prayer honestly. It presupposes a desire to be Christlike in our attitudes, motives, and dispositions. It presupposes our desire to experience God and to know God's will for our individual and corporate lives. If we do not share that desire, we really cannot pray as Jesus did or as he taught.

When speaking to one's father, the Jew would say *Abba* and to God *Abi.* Jews felt one should not address God with the same word used to address one's parent—it was too familiar and intimate. So Jesus breaks the custom. When he prays, he says *Abba* (translated Father), which includes the emotional overtones of respect, affection, and love. Jesus teaches his disciples to do the same.

To hallow God's name is done supremely by so living and speaking that your style reminds others of the Christlike God. Jesus hallowed God's name in his living.

The kingdom of God is above all else. As we participate in the kingdom of God, we help fulfill the prayer "Your kingdom come." To permit hate, greed, jealousy, dishonesty, and unbridled passion to govern our lives denies our belief in and support of the kingdom of God.

The request "Give us each day our daily bread" implies that we are asking God to give us nourishment continually. Prayer includes the necessities of everyday life.

Ecclesiasticus (or Sirach) 28:2 explains the next petition about forgiveness of sins: "Forgive your neighbor the wrong he has done, / and then your sins will be pardoned when you pray." Jewish prayers insisted on the offender seeking forgiveness. Jesus insists that the injured person offer forgiveness. (Thus God can forgive.)

"Lead us not into temptation" presupposes the disciples' life in the world. They must learn to live in the context of the anxieties of the earthly life, and also they must learn to implore God for protection against the powerful attacks and temptations of the Evil One.

Luke 11:14-20. Jesus casts out a demon from a man who is mute without declaring that he is doing so in the name of God. For not saying by whose power he exorcised the "demon" of muteness, some said, "By Beelzebub, the prince of demons, he is driving out demons." *Beelzebub* was the name of the Philistine god of Ekron, whose name was mockingly distorted by the Jews in the times of Elijah (See 2 Kings 1:2-3.) to Baal-Zebub, which means "lord of the flies" as a corrupted form of "lord of the house." The Jews of Jesus' day know this distinction and are engaged in theological word play when they say Jesus healed through the power of Beelzebub, "the prince of demons." They are thinking of their "fathers" when they use the name *Beelzebub,* which in Aramaic means "lord of dung."

Jesus equates Beelzebub with Satan and says that Satan cannot maintain power and authority if he willfully destroys the things he stands for—such as demons. On the other hand, Jesus is healing to set persons free. The finger of God has left the divine marks of God's presence in the exorcism Jesus performs. The two kingdoms confront each other in a war.

DIMENSION THREE: WHAT DOES THE BIBLE MEAN TO ME?

The class may discuss the following topic or use the material in the student book.

Exorcism

The question of exorcism sometimes arises in our minds. How shall we understand and use it?

In postexilic and New Testament times, persons associated demons with disease and disabilities: blindness (Matthew 12:22), deafness (Mark 9:25), disorientation (Luke 8:30), epilepsy (Luke 9:39), and muteness (Luke 11:14).

Persons thought that demons lived in desert areas and that they were restless until they found their rest in human beings. To be free from demons, one participated in the annual exorcism of sin on the Day of Atonement. Leviticus 16:8-9, 20-22 describes actions of the chief priest, who chooses a goat at the same time he prepares a bull to sacrifice for the sins of all Jews. The priest puts his hands on the head of the goat, thereby transferring the sins of his people to the goat. When that is done, the goat is driven into the wilderness. Thus the goat is called the scapegoat because the peoples' sins have escaped them and have been put on an innocent sin-bearer, the goat. Though we do not offer scapegoats in our day, we practice the theory of it. How often is an innocent being (person) sacrificed to cover our own sin?

We exorcise demons of hate, greed, jealousy, irrational passions, dishonesty, and hypocrisy by sincerely repenting and seeking forgiveness of our sins. God absolves our sins by God's grace. Persons can be and are changed. We need to exorcise our own selves from demonic motives and thoughts. We do this by requesting power from the risen Lord, Jesus Christ. And that power is given and will be given.

You also must be ready, because the Son of Man will come at an hour when you do not expect him (12:40).

7

True Discipleship and Its Opponents

Luke 11:29–13:9

DIMENSION ONE:
WHAT DOES THE BIBLE SAY?

Answer these questions by reading Luke 11:29-36

1. What sign will this generation receive? (11:29)

    This generation will receive "the sign of Jonah."

2. Jesus says that he embodies something greater than the talents of two great biblical persons. Who are they, and what are their talents? (11:31-32)

    Jesus says he embodies that which is greater than the wisdom of Solomon and the preaching of Jonah.

3. After lighting a lamp, where does one put it, and why? (11:33)

    After lighting a lamp, one places it on a stand "so that those who come in may see the light."

4. What serves to light the body, and how does it function? (11:34)

    The eye is the lamp of the body; and if the eye is good, the whole body is full of light.

Answer these questions by reading Luke 11:37–12:1

5. When Jesus dines with a Pharisee, what astonishes the Pharisee? (11:37-38)

    The Pharisee is surprised that Jesus does not wash before dinner.

6. What name does Jesus call the Pharisees? (11:40)

    Jesus calls the Pharisees foolish people.

7. What does Jesus condemn in his three "woes" to the Pharisees? (11:42-44)

    The Pharisees neglect justice and the love of God, they love the most important seats in the synagogues and greetings in the marketplaces, and they are like unmarked graves.

8. What does Jesus condemn in his three "woes" to the experts in the law? (11:46-47, 52)

    The experts in the law load persons "with burdens they can hardly carry," they build tombs for prophets that their forefathers killed, and they "have taken away the key to knowledge."

9. What does Jesus first say to the thousands who gather to hear him? (12:1)

    Jesus says, "Be on your guard against the yeast of the Pharisees, which is hypocrisy."

Answer these questions by reading Luke 12:2-48

10. What does Jesus say to those followers who may and will face persecution? (12:4)

    Jesus says, "My friends, do not be afraid of those who kill the body. . . . Fear him who, after the killing of the body, has power to throw you into hell."

11. What is the unforgivable sin? (12:10)

    "Anyone who blasphemes against the Holy Spirit will not be forgiven."

12. What is more important than food and clothing? (12:23)

    Life is more important than food, and the body is more important than clothing.

172   LUKE

13. Why is it important that one invest in "a treasure in heaven that will not be exhausted"? (12:33-34)

"For where your treasure is, there your heart will be also."

14. In what condition does the master expect to find his servants? (12:36-37a)

The master expects to find his servants watching (alert).

15. What does the master do when he comes home? (12:37b)

He will dress himself and serve them as they recline at the table.

16. What is the key to the demands the master places upon his various servants? (12:48b)

"From everyone who has been given much, much will be demanded; and from the one who has been entrusted with much, much more will be asked."

Answer these questions by reading Luke 12:49–13:9

17. According to Jesus, does he come to bring peace or division? (12:51)

Jesus comes to bring division.

18. How will a family experience this division? (12:53)

A family will be divided, "father against son and son against father, mother against daughter and daughter against mother, mother-in-law against daughter-in-law and daughter-in-law against mother-in-law."

19. Why should persons attempt to settle their differences out of court? (12:57-58)

Persons should learn to judge for themselves what is right and try hard to be reconciled.

20. What question does Jesus ask in order to turn a political issue (Pilate's slaying of several Galileans in the Temple) into a religious issue? (13:2)

Jesus asks, "Do you think that these Galileans were worse sinners than all the other Galileans because they suffered this way?"

21. What is Jesus' response to this religious issue? (13:3)

Jesus says, "Unless you repent, you too will all perish."

22. What advice does the man give the person who took care of the vineyard about the fruitless fig tree? (13:8-9)

Leave it alone for a year, dig around it and fertilize it. Then, if it bears no fruit, cut it down.

DIMENSION TWO:
WHAT DOES THE BIBLE MEAN?

The Scripture is divided into four themes:

1. The Sign of Jonah and Two Parables (11:29-36)
2. Denunciation of Pharisees and Lawyers (11:37–12:1)
3. Responsibilities of Discipleship (12:2-48)
4. Reflections on Christ's Ministry (12:49–13:9)

Luke 11:29-36. Jesus discusses the people's need for a sign immediately after he heals a man who was mute. Jesus has demonstrated his power and authority over the demonic. What he does for people, he does in the power of God. The kingdom of God is in their midst. He is the king of that kingdom. Why can they not see this truth?

Yet, miracles do not prove who Jesus is. People should not be expected to conclude that a temple-jumping stunt person is the Messiah. Jesus is more than a miracle worker. His message is the most important part of his ministry.

The apostle Paul writes, "Jews demand miraculous signs and Greeks look for wisdom, but we preach Christ crucified: a stumbling block to Jews and foolishness to Gentiles" (1 Corinthians 1:22-23). Signs, signs, signs! How Luke must have valued Jesus' statement that "this is a wicked generation. It ask for a miraculous sign, but none will be given it except the sign of Jonah" (11:29). Jonah was a living sign of God's authority, proclaiming the judgment of God to the people of Nineveh. So Jesus, in his life, preaching, and deeds, is the supreme sign of God's presence and action. Through Jesus, something greater than the wisdom of Solomon and greater than the preaching of Jonah has come. Jesus himself is the wisdom of the Greeks and the sign of the Jews.

John would declare that Jesus is the light of the world. As such, this "lamp" of God sheds light on those dwelling in the darkness of emptiness, hopelessness, and despair. This lamp is not covered; it is placed on a stand where the light is seen by all. Some Old Testament passages that probably aided Jesus in his understanding of himself as the light might be these: "You O LORD, keep my lamp burning; / my God turns my darkness into light" (Psalm 18:28);

"The lamp of the LORD searches the spirit of a man; / it searches out his inmost being" (Proverbs 20:27); "Here is my servant, whom I uphold. . . . I will keep you and will make you / to be a covenant for the people / and a light for the Gentiles" (Isaiah 42:1, 6). You might ask three persons to look up these passages and read them aloud to the class.

Now read Luke 11:34-35 to class members. Ask class members to discuss its meaning. Since the eye is the "lamp" of the body, what does that suggest both for what we let ourselves see and for what can be seen through us? Do we have an eye for spiritual things? Do we entertain thoughts that make for darkness of the soul and body? How do we keep the eye sound, so that our bodies are full of light?

The apostle Paul introduced the word *conscience* to our Christian vocabulary. A person who has no conscience is spiritually blind. He or she misses some things in life, unable to see the light of the lamp of God.

Luke 11:37–12:1. Class members may have an interest in knowing who the Pharisees and teachers of the law (scribes) are—and how they differ. History does not supply us with the means of determining the precise period when the Pharisees and scribes appeared as religious groups. The religious emphases of both groups go back to the period of exile in Babylon (from 586 B.C. to 538 B.C.). Denied the use of the Temple, the rites and festivals were "memorialized"; that is, they were remembered but were not literally carried out. The exiles replaced the Temple with synagogues, which served as places of instruction in the Scriptures and prayer. Emphasis was placed on obedience to the laws of Moses and eventually to an elaborate system of oral tradition.

About 458 B.C., a number of Jews from Babylon returned to Judea, bringing with them the books of the Torah. After Ezra read the Torah (the first five books of the Bible) to the Judeans, it was adopted as the law and became the foundation of Judaism. The sacrificial system was restored with its powerful priests, who were still responsible for instruction in the law as well as oversight of Temple duties. But a new group of lay lawyers, called scribes, came into being. The scribes were not necessarily priests; they served more in the capacity of assistants.

Now the law, not the Temple, became the primary factor in Judaism (postexilic Jewish life). The scribes, the interpreters of the law, now became free to oppose the Temple. These lay scribes, lawyers trained in interpretation and application of the law, now became the religious leaders of Judaism.

The scribes formed the core of the group called Pharisees. The scribes were the learned members. The word *Pharisee* means "separated," a nickname for those who, in their meticulous observance of the law, "separated themselves" from the ritually unclean.

To assure ritual cleanliness, the scribes developed hundreds of oral laws that were applications made on the various Mosaic laws. These interpretations and applica-

tions are called "the traditions of the elders." The intent of the elders was good. Eventually, however, the oral (unwritten) traditions of the elders became more important than the original Mosaic law and the ethical claims of the prophets. The Pharisees and the scribes believed in immortality, with rewards or punishments according to the way a person has lived in this life. They also believed in resurrection. Politically, they were very powerful. They became the real administrators of public affairs. Jesus emphasizes this point in his parables.

While Jesus is teaching, a Pharisee invites Jesus to dine with him. Jesus accepts the invitation. When they sit down at the table, the Pharisee observes that Jesus has not washed his hands and therefore does not uphold one of the traditions of the elders. The question is not one of hygiene but of ritual.

What does this ritual washing before dinner involve? One day, while eating lunch in a restaurant in New York City, I witnessed a man "washing his hands" as he sat at his table before he ate lunch. He rolled up his sleeves to his elbows; held his hands slightly above the table top; and poured a small quantity of water over the tips of his fingers, letting the water run to his wrist. Then he cleaned the palm of each hand by rubbing the fist of the other into it. Lastly, he poured the remaining water over his hands, beginning with his wrist and running down to the fingertips. I sympathized with what I at first thought was a poor demented man until I suddenly realized what was taking place. He was a Hasidic Jew who was fulfilling one of the traditions of the elders by being ritually clean before eating.

The unwritten (oral) law requires a pious Jew to use at least a quarter of a log (enough to fill one and one-half egg shells) of water for this ceremony. The ritual is to be done in the order prescribed (noted in my illustration). To omit the slightest detail is to commit sin.

Jesus comments to his host, who noticed that "Jesus did not first wash before the meal," "You Pharisees clean the outside of the cup and dish, but inside you are full of greed and wickedness. You foolish people! Did not the one who made the outside make the inside also?" (11:39-40). Does not your inner life need cleansing too? Which is more important, to be clean within or without? You Pharisees are careful to give alms (coins) to the poor publicly, but you should learn to give gifts from within: Give hope, faith, love, and justice.

Jesus pronounces three woes to the Pharisees and three to the scribes. Ask class members to keep in mind that the scribes are the interpreters of the law; the Pharisees (with the exception of the scribal core) are those who are concerned with obedience to the law as interpreted.

"Woe to [in the sense of "Alas for"] you Pharisees," Jesus says, for your externalism, pride in legalistic religion, religious ostentation, and pious hypocrisy. We have already noted an example of externalism in their desire to wash their hands ceremoniously without cleansing their thoughts and attitudes. (See 11:37-40.) Jesus also rebuffs them for their legalistic religion. Jesus says, "You neglect justice and the love of God" (11:42).

Then Jesus adds the second woe: religious ostentation. Pharisees, in their pride of obeying all the laws the scribes could tally up, wanted recognition in their synagogues. They sat in the front seats. As they entered the synagogues, they were properly greeted and saluted by their peers and honored by persons of lesser qualifications in back of them. They were similarly welcomed when they went to the marketplaces and basked in the sunlight of their religiosity (11:43).

The third woe condemned the Pharisees for pious hypocrisy. Most persons assumed the Pharisees were as impeccable in morality and conduct as they were in their practice of religion. Jesus thinks of Numbers 19:16, which states that if a person is walking in a field and unknowingly touches a dead body or walks over a grave, he or she is unclean and cannot worship for seven days. Many Pharisees, by their inner corruption, make those around them unclean by their contact with them. They are "like unmarked graves, which men walk over without knowing it" (11:44). They could be likened to moral lepers who ought to say, "I'm unclean. Don't come near me; my sins are contagious."

Jesus also gives three woes to the scribes. (See 11:45-54). Luke, thinking of his Gentile readers, does not use the word *scribes*—for that would be interpreted as persons who write letters and documents. Instead, Luke substitutes *experts in the law*. Jesus condemns the lawyers (scribes), first of all, for loading down the average person with "burdens they can hardly carry." Behind this phrase are the thousand-and-one ways of breaking the Ten Commandments, according to the oral traditions of the elders. For several hundred years the teachers of the law had interpreted each of the Ten Commandments in terms of applications and illustrations. For example, a person could break the commandment "Remember the Sabbath day by keeping it holy" (Exodus 20:8) in 613 different ways. The scribes' job was to unlock the Scriptures.

To carry a burden on the sabbath is illegal, if you carry it in your usual manner. But if you carry it in an unusual manner, such as on the back of your hand; with your foot, your mouth, or your ear; or in your shoe, that is legal. Such petty interpretations of God's will infuriated Jesus. These interpretations portray God as unthinking and amoral in character. Also, the unwritten (oral) traditions become such a burden, the common people cannot do both their daily work and fulfill the (oral) laws of God. Jesus realized these interpretations and applications of the Mosaic law were replacing the true law (the Torah).

Jesus also condemns the scribes who honor only the dead prophets (such as Amos, Hosea, Isaiah, Jeremiah) and even built tombs honoring them. The scribes believe that God has spoken what God wants to speak in the law. They are not likely to listen to a new, living prophet. Their dedication to law makes the messages of the prophets secondary, whereas Jesus puts the prophets in first place.

(See 11:47-48.) The present generation must break with the past by repentance.

Jesus hurls his third woe at the experts in the law for having taken away "the key to knowledge," burying it in all the rules of the oral traditions of the elders. Thus the scribes are not the teachers of the law but a hindrance to God and his people. Woe to them! Instead of being guardians of the law, they have built fences that keep believers away from God. They obscure rather than clarify God's purposes, God's covenant, God's kingdom.

Naturally the lawyers and the Pharisees do not like Jesus' evaluation of their practices. So they "began to oppose him fiercely and to besiege him with questions, waiting to catch him in something he might say" (11:53-54). Little wonder that Jesus tells his disciples, "Be on your guard against the yeast of the Pharisees, which is hypocrisy" (12:1).

Luke 12:2-48. The rabbis' sermons were not logically developed as are those of most ministers of our time. The rabbis had several key points ("pearls of wisdom"), generally unrelated, that they wanted to make. We have several pearls in this section of the lesson.

One pearl assures the disciples not to be afraid of "those who kill the body." By implication, they are to fear the "yeast of the Pharisees" whose emphasis on obedience to oral laws stifles and eventually kills the soul. Therefore be loyal to Jesus' teachings, even if you must face martyrdom. Death cannot kill the spirit of the person whose body they killed. All persons die physically, but physical death does not have the last word. They should learn to "fear him [God] who, after the killing of the body, has power to throw you into hell" (12:5). God does not forget. Loyal ones will continue in eternal life because God values them as persons.

Another pearl of the jewels of the spirit is to give undivided loyalty, not to scribal laws, but to the person of Jesus Christ. (See 12:8-12.) Every person either acknowledges or denies spiritual kinship with Jesus Christ. The person who refuses commits the unpardonable sin. The unpardonable sin is the deliberate refusal to accept God's truth as it is made known to us through Jesus. Ernest Fremont Tittle once wrote, "The 'sin against the Holy Spirit' is not, of course, some one particular sin; it is a human will set deliberately and persistently against truth and right and love. No one who . . . truly desires the forgiveness of God has 'blasphemed' against the Holy Spirit" (*The Gospel According to Luke*; Harper & Row, 1951; page 134).

The unforgivable sin is simply to say no to God and never change that response. This sin is unforgivable because forgiveness comes in response to repentance. Jesus' preaching for repentance is his call to admit our folly, our stupidity, our sinful intent, and to experience the divine forgiveness of our sins.

Jesus' parable of the rich fool (12:13-21) is told in response to a man who is unhappy with his inheritance settlement. Perhaps Jesus recalls the time when Moses saw two brother Hebrews struggling together and he asked the man who did the wrong, "Why are you hitting your fellow Hebrew?" (Exodus 2:13). The Hebrew answered, "Who made you ruler and judge over us?" (Exodus 2:14). Jesus says to the younger brother, in the words of Moses, "Man, who appointed me a judge or an arbiter between you?"

Jesus sees the men as members of the same family, as worshipers in the same synagogue, readers of the same law and prophets. Jesus responds by telling a parable that might show the futility of covetousness. Ask a class member to read Luke 12:13-21 to the class. After the reading, you might reread verse 15 ("Watch out! Be on your guard against all kinds of greed; a man's life does not consist in the abundance of his possessions.") and verse 20 ("You fool! This very night your life will be demanded from you. Then who will get what you have prepared for yourself?"). So a person who lays up treasures for himself or herself is often poverty-stricken toward God. Discuss this statement: Today the chief end of many persons is to gain lots of money, regardless of consequences. Contrast this "chief end" with Jesus' statement, "Sell your possessions and give to the poor. Provide purses for yourselves that will not wear out" (12:33).

Luke 12:49–13:9. Jesus says he came "to bring fire on the earth." He brings disturbance and division by the nature of his teachings and his demand for decision. His teachings contradict and nullify the oral traditions of the elders, as taught by Pharisees and scribes. So they kindled fires to destroy his ministry. Jesus changed all persons with the warmth of God's love. Many brothers, sisters, parents, and children disliked the new person that conversion brought, and division and bitterness resulted. Even Jesus' own family thought he was out of his mind (Mark 3:21). Jesus had to ask, "Who are my mother and my brothers?" (Mark 3:33).

In Luke 13:1-9, Jesus deals with the political aspects of life. Pilate had killed some Galileans while they were preparing their sacrifices. Many Jews were urging Jesus to speak a message of revolt. Jesus, however, raises several theological questions: Did God cause these sinners to die? Was sin the issue? Might their deaths have been avoided if they had been warned? Are you not in constant danger from God's judgment? You are in danger. Beware!

The closing parable tells about "a man [who] had a fig tree, planted in his vineyard, and he went to look for fruit on it, but did not find any." A vineyard in Palestine would contain both vines and fruit trees. The owner comes to the fig tree and finds no fruit; it has not been fruitful for three years. So he suggests cutting down the tree, for it is using up the nutrients of the good earth. The person who took care of the vineyard recommends one more year with cultivation and fertilizer. If the tree produces no fruit next year, well and good, cut it down. The parable of the barren fig tree symbolizes the period of grace that the nation has been granted for repentance. So people are to be productive or repent and experience God's mercy for another try.

DIMENSION THREE: WHAT DOES THE BIBLE MEAN TO ME?

The class may discuss this topic or use the material in the student book.

"Pearls" of Insight

Luke preserves a beautiful "pearl" when he quotes Jesus' saying, "Provide purses for yourselves that will not wear out, a treasure in heaven that will not be exhausted, where no thief comes near and no moth destroys" (12:33b). To become rich in God's sight, one must begin with a repentant plea: "I am poor in spirit, poverty-stricken in soul. Give me faith, hope, love, and empathy for those living in substandard conditions." We must ask, Are we rich toward God or rich in things?

We find a second "pearl" of great price in 11:34: "When your eyes are good, your whole body also is full of light." We may ask ourselves, *Do we have an eye for spiritual things?*

Second Kings 6:11-23 tells of the king of Aram who tried to capture and kill Elisha, but somehow Elisha seemed to anticipate the king's every military strategy. Elisha's servant awoke and realized the Aramean army completely encircled him and Elisha. He awakened his master and cried, "Oh, my lord, what shall we do?" Elisha replied, "Don't be afraid. . . . Those who are with us are more than those who are with them." Elisha prayed, saying, "O Lord, open his eyes so he may see." And the young man could see that the mountains were full of horses and chariots of fire round about Elisha.

When the Arameans came toward them, Elisha prayed that they be struck blind; and he led the blinded army to Samaria. There he prayed, "Lord, open the eyes of these men so they can see." And the men could see the mess they were in. The king of Israel asked, "Shall I kill them?" Elisha responded, "Set food and water before them so that they may eat and drink and then go back to their master." So the king prepared a great feast for them; and when they had eaten and drunk, he sent them back to their master. "So the bands from Aram stopped raiding Israel's territory."

How attitudes determine what we can see! How is our spiritual sight? What do we see? What do we not see? What is the purpose of a parable? What should it mean to me? A parable calls for the hearer's participation and involvement. The involvement is not so much on the intellectual level as in the affective (emotional) domain. We are to "feel" for the lost, younger son and his father; for the rich man who never disciplined himself; for the widow who lost one of the few coins of her social security. Then suddenly we "feel" joy, exuberance, and boundless faith. In these varying moods our emotions listen to the good news Jesus brings. Then the mind understands the feelings; and we find wholeness, peace, and healing.

Make every effort to enter through the narrow door, because many, I tell you, will try to enter and will not be able to (13:24).

8

The Life of Discipleship

Luke 13:10–15:32

DIMENSION ONE: WHAT DOES THE BIBLE SAY?

Answer these questions by reading Luke 13:10-35

1. Where is Jesus when he cures a woman? (13:10-13)

   Jesus is in a synagogue.

2. Why is the ruler of the synagogue upset? (13:14)

   He is indignant because Jesus healed the woman on the sabbath.

3. What does the ruler say to the people? (13:14)

   He says, "There are six days for work. So come and be healed on those days, not on the Sabbath."

4. In essence, what does Jesus say to the ruler? (13:15-16)

   He says, "Doesn't each of you on the Sabbath untie his ox or donkey from the stall and lead it out to give it water? Then should not this woman . . . be set free on the Sabbath day from what bound her?"

5. Jesus compares the kingdom of God with what two things? (13:18-21)

   He compares the kingdom of God to a mustard seed and to yeast.

6. When someone asks how many will be saved (13:23), what is Jesus' reply? (13:24-30)

   He answers that "Abraham, Isaac and Jacob and all the prophets [and] . . . people . . . from east and west and north and south . . . will take their places at the feast in the kingdom of God." But "many . . . will try to enter and will not be able to."

7. When some Pharisees tell Jesus he should "leave this place and go somewhere else" because Herod wants to kill him, what does Jesus say? (13:31-33)

   Jesus says that he will continue to follow his planned schedule.

8. After Jesus laments over Jerusalem, when does he hint he will be there? (13:35b)

   "I tell you, you will not see me again until you say, 'Blessed is he who comes in the name of the Lord!' "

Answer these questions by reading Luke 14

9. One sabbath while dining with a ruler of the synagogue, what does Jesus do? (14:1-6)

   He heals a man who is suffering from dropsy.

10. What is Jesus' main point in the parable on choosing a seat at the wedding feast? (14:11)

    "For everyone who exalts himself will be humbled, and he who humbles himself will be exalted."

11. Whom does Jesus recommend you invite to a feast? (14:12-13)

    Do not invite those who can invite you in return; invite persons who are poor, crippled, lame, and blind.

12. Why will you be blessed for inviting these people? (14:14)

    You will be blessed because they cannot repay you.

13. What excuses do people make who are invited to a great banquet? (14:18-20)

    One person says, "I have just bought a field, and I must go and see it." Another says, "I have just bought five yoke of oxen, and I'm on my way to try them out." A third person says, "I just got married, so I can't come."

14. In anger the master tells his servant to go out and get some guests. Whom does he say to get? (14:21-23)

    He says to go out into the streets and alleys and "bring in the poor, the crippled, the blind and the lame." Then the servant is to go to the roads and country lanes and compel people to come in.

15. What four challenges does Jesus give to those who want to be his disciples? (14:26-35)

    1. You must learn to hate your father, mother, wife, child, brother, sister, even your own life.
    2. You must carry your own cross and follow him.
    3. You must count the cost.
    4. You must be "salty" persons.

16. To whom does Jesus say, "He who has ears to hear, let him hear"? (14:25, 35)

    Jesus makes this statement to the large crowds who are traveling with him.

Answer these questions by reading Luke 15

17. What is the cause of the muttering of the Pharisees and the teachers of the law? (15:2)

    The Pharisees and teachers of the law are muttering because Jesus welcomes tax collectors and sinners and eats with them.

18. Where does the shepherd who loses a sheep leave his ninety-nine other sheep while searching for the lost one? (15:4)

    He leaves them in the open country.

19. As a woman and her friends will rejoice in her finding a lost silver coin, who will rejoice over one sinner who repents? (15:10)

    "There is rejoicing in the presence of the angels of God over one sinner who repents."

20. What is the major sign of the younger son's degradation? (15:15-16)

    He becomes a herdsman for pigs and is so hungry he would gladly eat their food.

21. What does the younger son think his relationship to his father is? (15:19)

    He plans to tell his father, "I am no longer worthy to be called your son; make me like one of your hired men."

22. How does the father receive his lost son? (15:20-24)

    The father sees, has compassion for, runs toward, embraces, and kisses his son. Then the father orders clothes, a ring, and sandals for his son and prepares a feast to celebrate the son's return.

23. How does the elder son react to the younger son's return? (15:25-30)

    The elder son becomes angry because he has served his father well all these years and never has his father given a banquet for him and his friends.

DIMENSION TWO:
WHAT DOES THE BIBLE MEAN?

The Scripture for this lesson, "The Life of Discipleship," is divided into five themes:

1. Sabbath and God's New Creation (13:10-21)
2. Teachings During the Journey (13:22-35)
3. Table Talk in the House of a Pharisee (14:1-24)
4. The Conditions of Discipleship (14:25-35)
5. God's Love for the Lost (15:1-32)

Luke 13:10-21. Luke, a Gentile doctor, here tells of a woman who "was bent over and could not straighten up at all" (13:11). Luke is telling a story of God's healing of a Jewish woman who has suffered for eighteen years. And marvel of marvels, she is cured in a synagogue—an unheard of place for a woman even to be seen, let alone recognized—called to come to the front of the synagogue and to receive healing. How excited Luke is as he records the beautiful story. It must have been difficult for him not to use adjectives as he describes Jesus placing his hands on the woman, who is then immediately restored to standing straight.

This scene takes place in a synagogue—Luke's last recorded appearance of Jesus in a synagogue. The significance of this miracle comes with the objection in 13:14, answered by two counter questions (verses 15-16). Luke felt that something deeper lay behind this miracle. In a way, the healing of this woman points to the new era. Try to imagine Jesus seeing her behind the latticework in the back of the synagogue. Her eyes cry out to him for healing, and he calls her to come forward—to the seats of the Pharisees in the front row. Jesus puts his hands on her, she is healed, and she praises God.

What about the ruler of the synagogue? He does not praise God; he is indignant because Jesus has performed work on the sabbath. One of the works forbidden on the sabbath is to heal. You could put a bandage on a wound as long as you put no healing ointments on it. You could keep a sufferer from getting worse, but you were not allowed to better the person's condition. Jesus violates the law. The ruler of the synagogue calls for quiet and states his authoritative position: "There are six days for work. So come and be healed on those days, not on the Sabbath."

Jesus knows that religious leaders take their ox and donkey to water on the sabbath. He says, "You hypocrites! . . . Then should not this woman, a daughter of Abraham, whom Satan has kept bound for eighteen long years, be set free on the Sabbath day from what bound her?" (just as you loosen the bonds for the ox and the donkey on the sabbath day). The people are delighted; the religious leaders are humiliated. This is the focus of the text.

After such a healing and rejoicing, Jesus asks, "What is the kingdom of God like?" (13:18-21). The Kingdom starts in small ways, as with a mustard seed that grows until it can offer nesting to birds of all kinds in its branches. Also, the Kingdom is like yeast or leaven that likewise begins in small measure but when put in dough soon rises and changes the nature and taste of the bread. The kingdom of God has small beginnings in the lives of persons, families, and nations; but its potential is great.

Luke 13:22-35. This passage focuses entirely on Jerusalem. On their way to Jerusalem, many persons ask Jesus questions. One person asks, "Lord, are only a few people going to be saved?" Who will be saved? Pharisees and teachers of the law but few others? By what are persons saved, and from what are they saved? Is a person saved by being a son or daughter of David—automatic salvation because of place and family of birth? (In our day we might ask, Are we saved by our genes and chromosomes?) What does it mean to be saved?

At a new hotel on the shore of the Mediterranean, north of Tel Aviv, I met my classic illustration of what it means to be saved. We had just arrived, and I had put my suitcase in my room. In the hall was a woebegone, dejected, elderly man, an Orthodox Jew, all bedecked in his phylacteries (small containers with portions of Scripture inside them on left arm and head). He too had just arrived. He had saved for a lifetime to go to Israel in order to worship. He looked forward to the time he could touch the Holy Land and worship God in its sacred surroundings. But he discovered that no room in the hotel was reserved for worship. I felt sorry for him.

After several question-and-answer responses, I got to the heart of the issue. On being prodded by a Hasid (ultra-pious Jew), I asked the man if he was saved. He straightened, smiled, and nodded, saying, "Yes. I've been very careful all my life." I asked him, "By what margin are you saved?" He smiled and said, "Fifty-one percent. I keep close account of my observances of the (oral) law. But my wife is a good eighty-five percent; she has no anxieties." (Lord, will those who are saved be few?)

Jesus said, "Make every effort to enter through the narrow door, because many, I tell you, will try to enter and will not be able to" (13:24). Strive, not to be obedient to rules made by humankind, but to know and do the will of God. The prophets (such as Amos, Hosea, and Isaiah) struggled to know the will of God. They concluded, Act justly, love mercy, and walk humbly with your God (Micah 6:8). Striving to enter by the narrow door means agonizing over the will of God in prophetic stance until we identify with God's will as seen in the life and teachings of Jesus. Striving to enter by the narrow door means to know and strongly assert the will of God in all life. This striving is the meaning of, "Take up your cross."

Those who "enter by the narrow door" have agonized and sweated drops of blood, as it were, to know, accept, and assert God's will. Those who do not will hear the door close, seek to enter, and not be able to do so (13:24). Once outside, you knock and say, "Open to us. We ate church dinners in your presence, and you taught through your dedicated teachers in our classes and streets." But he will say, "I do not know you or where you come from."

What is the source of your faith? Is it the oral traditions of your admired ancestors? Is your faith a living well of water that quenches your thirst for the abundant life? Those who are workers of iniquity will weep and gnash their teeth—for you will "see Abraham, Isaac and Jacob and all the prophets in the kingdom of God, but you yourselves thrown out" (13:28). The meaning is getting all too clear, isn't it?

In Luke 13:31-33, Luke shares the news that not all Pharisees are against Jesus. Some Pharisees come to warn Jesus that Herod Antipas wants to kill him. Herod had killed Jesus' kinsman, John (son of Zechariah and Elizabeth), and apparently considered Jesus to be a revolutionary who might lead a revolt against Rome. So Herod wants to see and to talk with Jesus. Jesus knows Herod is as cunning and scheming as a fox. Jesus asks these friendly Pharisees to get word to Herod that he has a full schedule and will not change it just to see a king. In a short time Jesus will be in Jerusalem, where he wants to make his last appeal to the religious leadership of Judah.

Jesus' lament over Jerusalem follows the challenging statements in 13:32-34. "How often I have longed" presupposes Jesus' having been in Jerusalem a number of times. He even weeps over Jerusalem because the people do not know the style of life that makes for peace.

Many times Jesus would have thought of Deuteronomy 32:11, "Like an eagle that stirs up its nest / and hovers over its young, / that spreads its wings to catch them, / and carries them on its pinions" and of Psalm 36:7, "How priceless is your unfailing love! / Both high and low among men / find refuge in the shadow of your wings." Do you hear the cry of the Master, "O Jerusalem, Jerusalem, you who kill the prophets and stone those sent to you, how often I have longed to gather your children together, as a hen gathers her chicks under her wings, but you were not willing! Look, your house is left to you desolate" (Luke 13:34-35a)?

In 13:35 we may have a suggested date of Jesus' appearance in Jerusalem, Palm Sunday. Jesus says he will not see Jerusalem until they say, "Blessed is he who comes in the name of the Lord!" This verse is from Psalm 118:26, one of the six Hallel (praise the Lord) psalms sung at the Feast of the Passover. In Jesus' time the crowds observed Passover by singing the Hallel psalms and by waving the Hosanna palms. This occasion would be the great day of Jesus announcing publicly, for the first time, that he is the Messiah. Jerusalem would see him riding on a lowly donkey, the symbol of humility.

Luke 14:1-24. In Luke 14:1-6 we have Luke's account of Jesus' fourth healing on the sabbath. The first time, Jesus healed a man of an evil spirit in the synagogue at Capernaum (Luke 4:31-36). The second time, he healed a man with a shriveled right hand (6:6-11). The third time, he healed the woman who had been bent over for eighteen years (13:10-17). The fourth time, as Jesus dines in the home of a Pharisee (14:1-6), he cures a man who has dropsy. (Luke records two other times that Jesus was in the homes of Pharisees: Luke 7:36-50, when a woman poured expensive perfume on his feet; and Luke 11:37-44, when Jesus condemned the Pharisees for obeying the oral traditions of the elders rather than obeying the prophets.)

In 14:1-6, Jesus is again in the home of a ruler of a synagogue, where some Pharisees were watching him carefully. They apparently had planted a person in their midst who had dropsy. _Dropsy_ comes from the Greek word _hudropilos_, meaning "too much water." In English today the word used for this condition is _edema._ The old question came up again, Can we support working on the sabbath in the case of healing? Jesus heals the man of his edema, then asks the watching Pharisees, If you had a son or an ox that had fallen into a well, would you not immediately draw him out so that he will not drown? So if you have a man drowning in the water of his body (edema) on the sabbath, should we not save his life? Jesus challenges his host, exposing him to God's new creation. God's sabbath seeks to free the Pharisee, who bars the way to his suffering neighbor.

Perhaps Jesus was provoked that the Pharisees sought to prevent the healing of the man. In Greek, healing is also saving; and being saved is being healed. What better time to be healed/saved than when engaged in worship? Let the sabbath be known as the time when God's healing/saving is offered to all.

In Luke 14:7-14 we read of Jesus' teaching on humility. The purpose of the parable is to suggest appropriate responses to the offer of the kingdom of God. In the parable a man of relatively high standing arrives early and chooses a nice seat near the host. As others come, they seat themselves "below" him; soon the places are all taken. Then a person with considerable prestige arrives and is invited to the head of the table, to the very seat held by the man who arrived early. Of course he is asked to give his place to the man of honor—which, since all other seats are taken, puts him in the last seat. "Everyone who exalts himself will be humbled, and he who humbles himself will be exalted." Jesus has no concern for status.

Jesus, in the second part of the parable, says, if you give a party, do not always invite just your relatives and your close friends—people you feel close to and with whom you have a spiritual kinship. But see the needs of people who are poor, who have handicapping conditions, who are blind regarding spiritual fellowship and growth. They have no opportunity to rub shoulders with those who have great ideas and a life-giving faith. Feed the sinners with hope, faith, and charity. Some people sit at home, lonely and hungering for life. They look through their windows as the messianic feast is offered and wonder if there is bread for them, too. The reward for feeding bread of life to persons on the fringe of "respectability" will be yours as you see them in the Resurrection.

Closely related to the above is the parable of the great banquet (Luke 14:15-24). When one of the guests sitting near Jesus hears Jesus' first parable, he (looking around at all the guests, who are Pharisees) piously says to Jesus, "Blessed is the man who will eat at the feast in the kingdom of God!" The word _blessed_ may well have meant "O the happiness of those, like us, who will eat bread in the Kingdom." Remembering their obedience to legal traditions rather than to prophetic teachings, Jesus tells another parable—about a great banquet. Through the parable Jesus raises the question of motives and our basic loyalties.

The guests are invited; and when the feast is ready, the host sends his servants to those invited, telling them it is time to come. But many of the guests make excuses. One is a business excuse, the man has just purchased a field and yearns to see it. Another person has just purchased five yoke of oxen and wants to examine his ox-power. Still another man states he has just married and therefore cannot go. (This excuse is legally valid; for the law in Deuteronomy 24:5 says, "If a man has recently married, he must not be sent to war or have any other duty laid on him. For one year he is to be free to stay at home and bring happiness to the wife he has married.")

The parable lists excuses persons use for not giving full allegiance to the kingdom of God. The Jews had been waiting for centuries for the day of the Lord. Now it has come through the person of Jesus. But the people refuse to come to the greatest of all feasts, the messianic banquet, where the host is Jesus of Nazareth. In the parable Jesus portrays the host as angry and orders the servant to go to the city streets and alleys and invite the "poor, the crippled, the blind and the lame." To fill the still empty seats, the host orders the servant to call Gentiles to come (14:23). None of those who were invited first (the Pharisees and experts in the law) shall taste the banquet. The invitation goes far beyond all expectations. Those who were invited first have done nothing wrong; they have just failed to respond to the invitation.

Luke 14:25-35. Keep in mind the setting: Jesus is going through Samaria to Jerusalem and is facing possible crucifixion. He is paying a great price for accepting messiahship. What conditions might would-be followers expect to assume? Jesus tells of four conditions, which you might write on a chalkboard or on a large piece of paper: (1) Have no greater love than love for Christ. (2) Carry your own cross. (3) Count the cost of your commitment. (4) Be "salty" persons.

In the first condition for discipleship we find a difficult statement: "If anyone comes to me and does not hate his father and mother, his wife and children" (14:26). Jesus uses a Hebrew and Aramaic idiom ("hate") that is distorted if taken literally. The idiom means "loves less than." This idiom is illustrated in Genesis 29:30-31. Read the entire account in Genesis 29:21-31 to class members. Jacob fell in love with Rachel and thought he had married her—only to discover that Laban (his father-in-law) had substituted Leah, the older daughter. Jacob agrees to work seven years to "earn" Rachel, for "he loved Rachel more than Leah." Genesis 29:31 restates Jacob's love for Rachel by saying, in idiomatic form in Hebrew, "Leah was hated"; that is, Jacob loved Leah less than he loved Rachel.

So Jesus uses an idiom that all persons in his day understood but which, when taken literally, obliterates the intended meaning. Jesus is saying that primary allegiance must be made to God. You are expected to love God more than you love your family. If you cannot do this, do not ask to be a follower of Christ.

The second point Jesus makes is to carry your own cross, which means doing what you think God wants you to do regardless of the consequences.

The third point Jesus makes is to "count the cost," so you know what is needed and expected if you become a follower of Christ.

The fourth condition may need a comment: Be "salty" persons. That is, be persons who not only are preservatives for great values but also ones who give taste and zest to their relationships. No one wants to sit down to a dinner of salt. But a pinch of salt does wonders to a steak. Be a salty person. If you cannot measure up to this, do not become Jesus' disciple.

Luke 15:1-32. Luke presents us with one of his "twin" parables. Both have the same point. In this case the two parables are about a man (shepherd) who loses one of his sheep and a woman who loses one of ten silver coins. Friends, neighbors, and God rejoice when the lost are found.

Remind the class members again of Jesus' love of Scripture—the Law, the Prophets, and the Psalms. Many of his parables and teachings are based on biblical events, sayings, and idioms. The story of what we often call the good shepherd is one of these and reflects the two prophets Ezekiel and Isaiah. Ezekiel 34:15-16 says, "I myself will tend my sheep and have them lie down, declares the Sovereign LORD. I will search for the lost and bring back the strays. I will bind up the injured and strengthen the weak, but the sleek and the strong I will destroy." Isaiah 40:11 also describes the care of the shepherd for his sheep: "He tends his flock like a shepherd: / He gathers the lambs in his arms / and carries them close to his heart; / he gently leads those that have young."

Ask a class member to read the entire parable (Luke 15:3-7) aloud, perhaps after you have read the two prophetic passages from Ezekiel and Isaiah. Ask class members to discuss the question, What is unique about the Lord God in contrast to other deities? (You might want to list the differences on a chalkboard or on a large piece of paper.) One point you might want to include is that God is unique in that God seeks and searches for lost persons. God does not send angels after the lost; God seeks the lost, hoping to carry them over his shoulders or in his bosom to safety. The angels of heaven rejoice over even one sinner who repents.

So also the woman who loses one of her ten silver coins (a drachma)—meaning she loses a tenth of all she has—searches frantically until the lost coin is found and then calls in friends to celebrate. In the same way, there is great rejoicing in the kingdom of God when a person who was lost is found.

The concluding story of the lost son (15:11-32) is conditioned by Deuteronomy 21:17, which defines how one son (generally the older) receives the lion's share of the father's estate—two-thirds. The other gets one-third. In the parable the younger son asks for and is given his one-third of the estate prior to his father's death. The older son will inherit the remaining estate after the father's death. Read the parable aloud.

This parable is called "the greatest short story in the world." It beautifully describes how a "lost" son comes to his senses in a foreign land and returns to and is received by a caring, thoughtful father. The older son is just as lost as was the younger. He refuses even to refer to his brother as "my brother," preferring to say "this son of yours" to his father.

DIMENSION THREE: WHAT DOES THE BIBLE MEAN TO ME?

The class may discuss the following topic or use the material in the student book.

Luke 14:12-14—An Invitation to the Banquet

Luke 14:23 points out the importance of a word, as well as words, in "make them come in" to the banquet. Coercion does not work. Augustine demanded that the heretics called Donatists return to the Catholic church. Augustine forced people into the faith of the most powerful persons. Thus we have the origin of the terrible Inquisition, with its use of the rack, thumb screw, and other varied tortures to force theological uniformity. In Jesus' story the emphasis is on the consequences to those who freely and willfully chose not to attend the great banquet. At no time did Jesus coerce, force, or compel persons to accept his point of view. To the contrary, he told parables, hoping to win people to his way of life.

Jesus searches for persons who "make every effort to enter through the narrow door" (13:24). The action is not forced on possible converts but is the result of setting our priority in life and where it will lead us. Few consider the future to which their choices are leading them. The ancient proverb is so true, "What I am to be, I am now becoming." The amount of our agonizing determines which road we take and what our choices lead us to become.

Luke 13:30 quotes Jesus as saying, "Indeed there are those who are last who will be first, and first who will be last." The Pharisees loathed "the poor, the crippled, the blind and the lame" whose role is reversed in the kingdom of God. These last become first because they are the ones who hear and respond to the message of Jesus.

Whoever can be trusted with very little can also be trusted with much, and whoever is dishonest with very little will also be dishonest with much (16:10).

— 9 —

The Use and Abuse of Wealth

Luke 16–17

DIMENSION ONE:
WHAT DOES THE BIBLE SAY?

Answer these questions by reading Luke 16

1. To whom does Jesus tell the parable about a rich man who employs a dishonest manager? (16:1)

   Jesus tells the parable to his disciples.

2. What is the manager accused of doing? (16:1)

   He is accused of wasting his master's possessions.

3. On confronting his manager, what does the rich man order him to do? (16:2)

   The rich man orders the manager to turn in the account of his management, for he can no longer be manager.

4. Why does the scheming manager call in his master's debtors and discount their bills? (16:4)

   The scheming manager decides to discount the bills of his master's debtors so that people will receive him into their houses when he is unemployed and needy.

5. For what does the master commend the manager? (16:8)

   The master commends the manager for his shrewdness.

6. If a person is dishonest in a very little, what might one expect of that person in a larger capacity? (16:10)

   "Whoever is dishonest with very little will also be dishonest with much."

7. Into what two periods does Jesus divide time? (16:16)

   Jesus divides time into the time of the Law and Prophets until John and the time of the kingdom of God.

8. Who lies at the rich man's gate? (16:19-20)

   A beggar named Lazarus lies at the rich man's gate.

9. What happens when Lazarus dies? (16:22a)

   When Lazarus died, "the angels carried him to Abraham's side."

10. What happens when the rich man dies? (16:22b-23)

    The rich man dies, is buried, and goes to hell where he is tormented.

11. To whom does the rich man want Abraham to send Lazarus, and why? (16:27-28)

    The rich man wants Lazarus to go to his father's house to warn the man's five brothers so they can avoid the rich man's fate.

12. What is Abraham's response to the rich man? (16:31)

    Abraham says, "If they do not listen to Moses and the Prophets, they will not be convinced even if someone rises from the dead."

Answer these questions by reading Luke 17

13. What does Jesus say about the sin of causing others to sin? (17:2)

    Jesus says, "It would be better for him to be thrown into the sea with a millstone tied around his neck than for him to cause one of these little ones to sin."

14. If a brother sins against you seven times in the day and turns to you seven times and says, "I repent," what must you do? (17:4)

You must forgive him.

15. How do the disciples reply? (17:5)

The disciples reply, "Increase our faith!"

16. Why does one not thank a servant who does what he or she is told to do? (17:9-10)

One does not thank a servant for doing what is his legitimate labor.

17. As Jesus enters a village, he meets ten persons who had leprosy who ask for mercy. What does he tell them? (17:14)

Jesus tells the persons with leprosy, "Go, show yourselves to the priests."

18. As the persons who had leprosy go by, they are cleansed. Why does one person who had leprosy return and fall at Jesus' feet? (17:15-16)

He returns to give Jesus thanks.

19. Which one of the ten persons who had leprosy thanks Jesus? (17:16-18)

The man who is a foreigner, a Samaritan, thanks him.

20. What does Jesus say to Pharisees who ask when the kingdom of God is coming? (17:20-21)

Jesus says, "The kingdom of God is within you."

21. What warning does Jesus give his disciples about the false teachers who say the Kingdom is here, or the Kingdom is there? (17:22-23)

Jesus warns them, "Do not go running off after them."

22. What lesson can one learn from "the days of Noah" and "the days of Lot" with regard to "the day the Son of man is revealed"? (17:33)

"Whoever tries to keep his life will lose it, and whoever loses his life will preserve it."

DIMENSION TWO: WHAT DOES THE BIBLE MEAN?

The Scripture for this lesson is divided into four themes:
1. Faithfulness in Administration (16:1-15)
2. The Gospel and Wealth (16:16-31)
3. Forgiveness, Faith, Grace, and Ingratitude (17:1-19)
4. The Kingdom of God (17:20-37)

Luke 16:1-15. The parable of the unjust manager is one of the more difficult of Jesus' stories to interpret. In terms of Dimension Two, "What does this parable mean?" we are to think of administrators and managers (of estates) from a Christlike perspective. Obviously, some attitudes and actions are not acceptable. God cannot, by God's nature, support dishonest conduct of his managers. Or can he? Does the end justify the means? Does Christ approve immoral actions when the consequences seem to be good? Some interpreters during the centuries have assumed that Jesus supported the dishonest manager because he was a clever schemer. Let us look closely at the story.

Jesus speaks to his disciples. He tells them that a rich man placed his large estate of several farms in the hands of a manager (steward). The wealthy owner learns that his manager is spending his money "like mad." The owner calls his manager before him and asks, "What is this that I hear about you?" Apparently the manager admits by his silence the validity of the reports. So the owner orders him to turn in his various records. Still silent, but with a busy mind, the manager goes toward his home. He says to himself, *I know what to do so that those who owe my master will receive me joyfully in their homes when I am put out of my job as manager.*

The manager realizes he must act quickly before his debtors learn he has been fired. He summons his master's debtors one by one. He asks the first one, "How much do you owe my master?" He replies, "Eight hundred gallons of olive oil." The manager, wanting to win the debtor's gratitude, says, "Take your bill . . . and make it four hundred." (The debtor gets a windfall.) The manager asks the next farmer how much he owes for the large crop on his wheat field. He reports that he owes a thousand bushels of wheat. The manager says, "Take your bill and make it eight hundred."

The master, when he learns what his dishonest manager has done, commends him for his shrewdness. The master is in a difficult spot. If he calls his renters before him and admits that his manager has bested him, he will also have to admit that the debtors' enthusiastic acclaim of the manager's generosity and kindness is a fraudulent claim against his own character. At this point, the best course is to pretend to be the generous landlord who has reduced their rents. Meanwhile the scheming manager has won the favor of the farmers, since he pronounced the fine discounts.

By deliberately choosing a case from the field of human existence, Jesus addresses himself to human beings as they really are. Jesus cannot praise the dishonest manager for his immoral actions. He does acknowledge cleverness as a creditable attribute. Jesus says, "The people of this world are more shrewd in dealing with their own kind than are the people of the light" (16:8). The real point of this parable is about entering the kingdom of God. The coming of the kingdom of God remains wholly the act of God. The kingdom of God is a completely different world compared with all that is earthly, and in Jesus' view the kingdom of God is a gift of grace from God.

We all have heard people say, "He is a man of means." However, our concern focuses on worthy ends. Are the "means" (money, property, goods, things) being used for selfish purposes or for great and noble ends? We might ask, What makes for greatness? For the "people of the light," greatness is not judged by one's means but by the nobility of the ends.

Luke 16:14-15 gives a brief commentary about the Pharisees, whose major sin (as seen in the Gospels) is spiritual pride and religious arrogance. Little evidence exists to indicate that the Pharisees were dedicated to worshiping at the shrine of money. This charge could more readily be laid at the feet of the Sadducees, who were the truly wealthy and affluent Jews of Jesus' time. The Sadducees, the group of two hundred high priests of Jesus' time, all lived within the city of Jerusalem. They had beautiful homes of carved marble and enjoyed a fabulous income from taxes given to the Temple.

The Pharisees' sins were pride in their obedience to the oral traditions of the elders and pride in their ostentatious piety. (They prayed three times a day on busy street corners, and they prayed longer prayers than the law required.) Perhaps Luke remembers hearing the loud clatter of coins as Pharisees cast their gifts into the offering boxes at the Temple, contrasting with the almost silent tinkle of a widow's mite. Their love for money was subordinate to their love for recognition in pious giving to the Lord. Jesus said to them, "You are the ones who justify yourselves in the eyes of men, but God knows your hearts. What is highly valued among men is detestable in God's sight" (16:15).

Luke 16:16-31. The Gospel of Luke divides history into two parts (16:16). The giving of the Law and its varied interpretations, plus great covenants and promises of God made to, by, and through the prophets, occurs until John.

Jesus begins the second period by preaching the good news of the kingdom of God. And "every one is forcing his way into it" (16:16). Consider the feelings involved if your spouse, father or mother, or children put their love for Christ and God above their love for you. Consider the turmoil a pious Jew like Paul felt when he experienced the rending of his beloved law as the spirit of Christ led him to a much greater law—the law of love, faith, and hope in God as seen in the resurrected Jesus Christ. Many persons experience the turmoil and violence of rebirth.

An example of violence is noted in the pure and unadulterated irony of Jesus' words about those who are so dedicated to the written and unwritten (oral) law that "it is easier for heaven and earth to disappear than for [scribes and Pharisees to let] the least stroke of a pen to drop out of the Law" (16:17).

In the parable of the rich man and Lazarus (16:19-31), Jesus uses a personal name. The name *Lazarus* is the only proper name given in Jesus' parables. The rich man is clothed in purple and fine linen and feasts sumptuously every day. Ask class members to list what they know about Lazarus. (Work in small groups for five minutes; then share with the whole class. Write the suggestions on a chalkboard or on a large piece of paper.) Some ideas are these: He is a very poor man; he probably is an invalid, since he lies at the gate every day; his body is covered with sores that the dogs lick; his food is what falls from the rich man's table and is scooped up from the floor; and finally, he dies.

Contrast the deaths of the two men. Lazarus, the beggar, dies and is *carried by the angels to Abraham's side.* The rich man also dies and *is buried.* In hell the rich man, whose eyes had always focused on things on the earth, looks up and sees "Abraham far away, with Lazarus by his side." The rich man, who gave crumbs of mercy from his floor to Lazarus, now requests that Lazarus give mercy. He wants Lazarus to dip his finger in water and cool the rich man's tongue.

The parable has a poignant touch as the hearers recall that Sadducees do not believe in life after death. Perhaps this chasm is that to which Abraham refers when he says, "Between us and you a great chasm has been fixed, so that those who want to go from here to you cannot, nor can anyone cross over from there to us." The rich man then begs Abraham to send Lazarus to his five brothers to warn them, lest they too go to "this place of torment." The answer is this: "They have Moses and the Prophets; let them listen to them." That is, Read the Scripture! But the rich man pleads further, saying, "No, father Abraham, . . . but if someone from the dead goes to them, they will repent." Abraham's response is, "If they do not listen to Moses and the Prophets, they will not be convinced even if someone rises from the dead."

A class member may raise a question about life after death. In the Old Testament the Hebrew word *Sheol* is the name of the shadowy and gloomy place to which the spirits of persons go after death—as was the case with Samuel. (See 1 Samuel 28:8-19.)

The Jews began to think of Sheol (hell) as being divided into two distinct places: Gehenna and Paradise. Gehenna is the place that receives the unrighteous, such as the rich man in the above parable. In Gehenna those whose lives on earth were immoral and irreligious get their reward: everlasting punishment. In Paradise those whose lives were righteous and filled with faith are rewarded by being in a right relationship with Abraham, the founder of the faith, and, of course, with God. Persons on each side (Gehenna and Paradise) can see and hear one another, but they cannot cross over; for in between is a great chasm.

Mention to class members that people always want signs, the best of which (they say) is to see a person who has returned from the grave. Interestingly enough, Herod, who murdered John the Baptist, heard that Jesus was John the Baptist risen from the dead (9:7); yet Herod did not change his way of life.

Ask class members whether persons are redeemed by signs, by persuasive arguments that lead to decisions, or by either.

Another discussion possibility might be as follows: Was it foreordained that the rich man be condemned to Gehenna? What life choices might have changed his future? What determines our lot?

Luke 17:1-19. In this section we "string" four "pearls." In light of the above parable on rewards (Paradise or Gehenna), Jesus says it would be better for a person whose instructions lead one of these little ones to sin if a millstone was hung around his neck and he was thrown into the sea (17:2). The future life in Sheol is terribly bleak. What difference is there between the love of fine clothes and daily feasts and the search for truth? Help class members realize that raising questions about the meaning of parables is not a sin. We must raise questions; otherwise ignorance becomes the guide that misleads us.

If a brother or sister sins, we have several options we can pursue. We may (1) carry secret grudges; (2) complain to a third party; or (3), as Jesus suggests, lovingly rebuke him or her. If a person sins (particularly against us), we should help that person deal with the sin. For if sin is cultivated, it keeps persons from attaining the strongest, highest, and loveliest life. We sin if we do not help another deal with his or her sin.

If a person sins against us seven times a day and turns and says after each offense, "I repent," we must forgive him or her. Little wonder that the disciples turn in amazement and say, "Increase our faith!"

But how can we *forgive?* We must lay aside all claim to requital. We must pray for dissolution of our resentment. We must live with the offender in healing and creative love. As we forgive, the doors open; and love restores us to the abundant life.

Luke 17:7-10. In the parable of the servant and one's duty, Jesus makes the significant point that those who are truly committed to God always act out of the sense of "I ought." God does not owe us anything; we owe God. In formal ethics we might say that we act out of a dutiful will—with no room for pride or merit on our part: I ought to do this. "We are unworthy servants; we have only done our duty" (17:10).

Luke 17:11-19. Another "pearl" in our necklace of the jewels of the spirit is the parable of the grateful Samaritan.

To orient class members, give some background material by reporting on Leviticus 14:1-31, regarding the regulations for diseased persons at the time of ceremonial

cleansing. Make the report short, being sure to mention the use of a live bird to symbolize the leprosy that has flown away from the person who had leprosy. The life of a person with leprosy was exceedingly painful and humiliating. For priestly tests of leprosy and its cures, see Leviticus 13. Until the diseased person was cleansed, he was to cover his upper lip and cry out, "Unclean! Unclean!" The person with leprosy lived outside the camp. The isolation; the loneliness; and the physical, psychological, and theological pain were excruciating.

Luke, a Gentile physician, seems to enjoy telling about the (only) two healings of leprosy—and especially the one with the foreigner (Samaritan) who is the only one of ten who returns to thank Jesus. Nine of the ten persons with leprosy are Jews. It is this tenth one, the Samaritan, who returns to Jesus praising God. We assume the other nine find a priest who will pronounce them clean. What did the nine tell the priest at the Temple? Did they refer to Jesus as messiah, healer, or the unknown prophet? What do class members think? Did ingratitude warp the attitude toward Jesus of the nine persons cured from leprosy?

Suggest that we may find the ultimate meaning of this healing as we sympathize with the sufferers, especially with the foreigner, the Samaritan who praised God.

Luke 17:20-37. Apparently, some Pharisees are traveling with the disciples. Some may have marveled at the miracle of the healing, and perhaps the glory of the Samaritan's face stirs them to ask Jesus when the kingdom of God is coming. They are actually spectators already, but to "see" the King (Jesus Christ) of the Kingdom is beyond their spiritual abilities. Jesus again says the Kingdom does not come with observable signs (17:20). The specific signs in Nain and in Capernaum are all misleading. The only signs are those close at hand: The kingdom of God is in the midst of you: it is within you; it is among you. The yeast of the Kingdom is growing within and among persons. How easily we miss the meaning of this passage and substitute a search for fruitless signs. Jesus asks us not to waste our energies with such things. Jesus says, "The time is coming when you will long to see one of the days of the Son of Man, but you will not see it." He begs them, "Do not go running off after them." Accept Jesus.

DIMENSION THREE: WHAT DOES THE BIBLE MEAN TO ME?

The class may discuss the following topics or one or more of the topics in the student book.

Luke 17:11-19—Gratitude and Ingratitude

One of the major teachings of this lesson is the tragedy of ingratitude. When the Lord healed the ten men from their leprosy, his instructions were that they should go to the priest. When they left Jesus, they still had leprosy; it was while they were on their way that they were healed. Since the ritual cleansing was an important issue and since the men were already on their way doing just what Jesus had instructed, we may find it hard to blame the nine for ingratitude. Does not Jesus elsewhere criticize those who delay when they are told to follow his call? Yet the one returns for a word of thanks, and that is commendable.

Assuming the kingdom of God is in our midst—both within and among us— then we should occasionally thank Jesus for standing among us in his risen power. This apparently is what the Samaritan man could see.

Luke 17:3-5—Increase My Faith

A challenging word comes from 17:3-5 when Jesus responds to the disciples' amazement that their faith should be such that they can forgive a sinner seven times a day for the same sin—assuming real repentance. They say, "Increase our faith!" Jesus responds that it is not the quantity of your faith but the quality of your faith that makes the difference.

Who judges either the quality or the quantity of our faith? Is faith quantifiable? What are the signs of an "increased" faith?

What is impossible with men is possible with God (18:27).

— 10 —

The Kingdom of God

Luke 18:1–19:44

DIMENSION ONE:
WHAT DOES THE BIBLE SAY?

Answer these questions by reading Luke 18

1. In the parable of the unjust judge, how often does Jesus say they should pray? (18:1)

   "They should always pray and not give up."

2. What does the widow ask the judge to do? (18:3)

   She asks the judge to grant her justice against her adversary.

3. What word does Jesus use to describe the judge? (18:6)

   Jesus uses the word unjust *to describe the judge.*

4. Who are the two men who go into the Temple to pray? (18:10)

   One man was a Pharisee, and the other was a tax collector.

5. In his prayer, what kinds of people does the Pharisee say he is not like? (18:11)

   He says he is not like robbers, evildoers, adulterers, and tax collectors.

6. What does the Pharisee do? (18:12)

   He fasts twice a week and gives a tenth of all he gets.

7. How does the tax collector pray? (18:13)

   He stands at a distance and does not even look up to heaven and beats on his breast.

8. What does he ask God in his prayer? (18:13)

   The tax collector asks God to have mercy on him, a sinner.

9. What does Jesus say when the people bring infants to him? (18:16)

   Jesus says, "Let the little children come to me, and do not hinder them, for the kingdom of God belongs to such as these."

10. What does the ruler lack to inherit eternal life? (18:22)

    The ruler does not have treasure in heaven.

11. How does Jesus answer the question "Who then can be saved?" (18:27)

    Jesus says that "what is impossible with men is possible with God."

12. What will happen to Jesus? (18:32-33)

    Jesus will be mocked, insulted, and spat upon. They will flog him and kill him, and on the third day he will rise.

13. What does Jesus say to the blind man when he asks to have his sight restored? (18:42)

    Jesus tells him to receive his sight; his faith has healed him.

Answer these questions by reading Luke 19

14. Who tries to see Jesus in Jericho? (19:2-3)

    Zacchaeus tries to see Jesus.

15. What does he do so he can see Jesus? (19:4)

    He climbs into a sycamore-fig tree.

16. What does Jesus say to Zacchaeus when he says he will give half of his possessions to the poor? (19:9)

    Jesus says, "Today salvation has come to this house, because this man, too, is a son of Abraham."

17. What happens to the person who does not put the money in the bank to collect interest? (19:23-24)

The mina is taken from him and given to the one who has ten minas.

18. What does Jesus ask two disciples to do at Bethphage? (19:30)

Jesus asks them to find a colt, untie it, and bring it to him.

19. What are the disciples to say when someone asks them about taking the colt? (19:31)

They are to say that "the Lord needs it."

20. What does the crowd of disciples say as Jesus rides the colt down the Mount of Olives? (19:38)

They say, "Blessed is the king who comes in the name of the Lord! / Peace in heaven and glory in the highest!"

21. What does Jesus predict about Jerusalem? (19:44)

Jesus predicts that Jerusalem and its people will be destroyed because they did not recognize the time of God's coming.

DIMENSION TWO: WHAT DOES THE BIBLE MEAN?

The Scripture for this lesson is divided into four themes:

1. Parables on the Practice of Prayer (18:1-14)
2. Conditions of Entrance to the Kingdom (18:15-34)
3. Jesus in Jericho (18:35–19:27)
4. Jesus' Ministry in Jerusalem (19:28-44)

Luke 18:1-14. The key to the kingdom of God is prayer. However, we err when we assume that we can get anything we want if we only pray. Prayer is a way of learning the will of God, that we may then strongly assert it.

Jesus' parables sometimes use contrast rather than comparison. The parable of the widow and the judge is such a case. (See 18:1-8.) The judge is not interested in the widow's vindication. "Vindication" means to be cleared of suspicion, dishonor, or a charge of wrongdoing. The judge "neither feared God nor cared about men" (18:2). Again and again, the widow pesters him, attempting to "wear me out," as the judge says. He finally gives in, takes her case to court, and sees that she gets justice.

Notice the principle of contrast: If an irreligious and socially insensitive judge will respond to a woman's persistence in presenting her requests, how much more readily will the Father respond to a person who persists in prayer. Through persistence the "pray-er" can rethink, rephrase, and reshape the content of the prayer. Persistence includes opportunity to think.

The parable of the Pharisee and the publican deals with spiritual or religious pride. A quotation from a rabbi who lived at the time the Gospel of Mark was being written, about A.D. 70, states, "I thank thee, O Lord, my God, that thou hast given me a place among those who sit in the House of Study, and not among those who sit at the street corners; for I rise early and they rise early, but I rise early to study the words of the Law, and they rise early to engage in vain things; I labor and they labor, but I labor and receive a reward, and they labor and receive no reward; I live and they live, but I live for the life of the future world, and they live for the pit of destruction" (quoted by S. M. Gilmour, in *The Interpreter's Bible*, Volume 8; Abingdon Press, 1952; page 308).

Jesus tells this parable to "some who were confident of their own righteousness and looked down on everybody else" (18:9). Two men went up to Herod's Temple to pray, one a Pharisee and the other a publican (a tax collector for Rome). The Pharisee fasts twice a week—Mondays and Thursdays, though neither is required of him; and he tithes, not just of the produce of the land as required by the Torah, but "of all that I get." His prayer expresses gratitude for his virtues: "I thank you that I am not like other men—robbers, evildoers, adulterers—or [looking over at the publican] even like this [despicable] tax collector." The Pharisee's self-confidence and self-satisfaction oozed all over his countenance. But the tax collector, standing far off from the sacred altar, beats his breast in remorse and prays, "God, have mercy on me, a sinner." It was a shock to all the Pharisees and teachers of the law present to hear Jesus conclude that the kingdom of God requires reversal of values and therefore of judgments. The sinners are among the saved; the ostentatiously pious become the sinners in need of salvation.

By the second century A.D., many Christians fasted twice a week also—but on Wednesdays and Fridays! Their tithing habits often became legalistic too. They often fell into the same trap of self-righteousness. Keep in mind that *not all* Pharisees were self-righteous people. Many, as probably was Jesus' brother James, were sincere, loved God, and served people.

Luke 18:15-34. The Jews believed that the fathers (not the mothers) were responsible for teaching the faith to their children. (See Deuteronomy 6:4-12.) Obviously, many mothers assumed those responsibilities, however. On their children's first birthdays, fathers would take their offspring to an outstanding rabbi for his blessing of their infant. Luke states, "People were also bringing babies to Jesus to have him touch them" (18:15). The "touching" meant blessing them. Mark says "little children" were brought to Jesus, too (Mark 10:13). Jesus loved them; he embraced them and welcomed the children as those whom God would wish to have in the Kingdom. "Anyone who will not receive the kingdom of God like a little child will never enter it" (18:17). Trust is the absolute essential of faith.

In the parable of the rich ruler, Jesus admits that things of this world easily become barriers to a wholehearted devotion to the cause of God. The ruler is imprisoned by wealth. He says he is pious; he has honestly and earnestly obeyed all the written and oral laws of the Torah from his youth. Although he had mastered the letter of the Law, perhaps the import and the spirit of the Law had not yet mastered him, however. "Jesus looks at him and loved him" (Mark 10:21). But one thing he still lacks: Though wealthy, he has no treasure in heaven. Jesus tells him to sell all he has and distribute it to the poor. "Then come, follow me." But the rich ruler becomes sad, for he cannot part with his earthly treasures. You might ask class members: Does God require all persons to sell all they have and distribute it to the poor? How about Zacchaeus? (See Luke 19:1-10.) Jesus does not tell him to do this. What is the difference between the two men? Also ask: What does God demand of your commitments?

Jesus comments, "How hard it is for the rich to enter the kingdom of God! Indeed, it is easier for a camel to go through the eye of a needle than for a rich man to enter the kingdom of God." Some rich persons are saved—depending on their attitude toward and their devotion to the things they possess. Jesus says, "What is impossible with men is possible with God" (18:27).

Peter, understanding the young man's difficult choice, shares the experience he and his brother Andrew had when they left their comfortable homes. (Peter was rich. He owned a large house in Capernaum, where Jesus stayed for many months; and Peter operated a big fishing business.) "We have left all we had to follow you." Again call attention to Paul's statement in 1 Corinthians 9:5 that the disciples' wives accompanied them on their missions with Christ. Jesus must have felt it important for the men to have their wives with them. Some clearly do not have their wives or families with them, however. (See Luke 18:29.)

In verses 31-33, Jesus takes the Twelve aside and for the sixth time explains that they are going to Jerusalem where he must face physical, psychological, and spiritual pain. He will be mocked, spit on, flogged, and killed. But the sufferings are always told with the concluding word of confidence in Jesus' resurrection. You may want to write on a chalkboard or on a large piece of paper the six references to his expectation of what will happen to him in Jerusalem: 9:22; 9:44; 12:50; 13:33; 17:24-25; 18:31-33. You might assign six persons to read these passages aloud to the class.

Luke 18:35–19:27. Two events take place in the region of Jericho. As Jesus prepares to enter Jericho, a blind man stops him and asks for healing. And as Jesus prepares to leave Jericho, he sees Zacchaeus in a tree and invites himself to Zacchaeus's house.

This section of Scripture is a significant part of what is often called Luke's "Gospel of the Outcasts" (Chapters 15–19). The examples on the following list are either outcasts or a symbol of outcasts:

A stray sheep (15:3-7)
A lost coin (15:8-10)
A lost son (15:11-32)
A sick beggar (16:19-31)
A Samaritan man with leprosy (17:11-19)
A mistreated widow (18:1-8)
A despised publican (18:9-14)
A blind beggar (18:35-43)
A chief tax collector (19:1-10)

Ask for volunteers who will briefly review the passages as examples of "saved or found outcasts."

As Jesus enters and moves through Jericho, his mind focuses on anticipated events in Jerusalem within the next twenty-four hours. He teaches as he walks, with scores of followers seeking advantageous places from which to hear. Jesus would be talking loudly so all could hear.

The story of the blind man is very dramatic (18:35-43). The blind man is a beggar. He hears a multitude of people and the louder voice of a man teaching. He asks about what is happening. A friend says excitedly, "Jesus of Nazareth is passing by." Remembering stories he has heard of this amazing man, the blind man cries out loudly, "Jesus, Son of David, have mercy on me!" (This story is the only one in which both Luke and Mark [10:47-48] use the messianic title "Son of David.") The blind man wants to get Jesus' attention. Immediately, some people try to smother his voice, telling him to keep quiet. But he only cries louder, "Son of David, have mercy on me!"

Jesus stops his teaching and commands that the man be brought to him. Jesus asks what the beggar wants Jesus to do for him. The blind man says, "Lord, I want to see." Undoubtedly the phrase *Son of David* was meant to refer to the messianic dreams of great prophets such as Isaiah, who had said, " 'He will come with vengeance; / with divine retribution / he will come to save you.' / Then will the eyes of the blind be opened / and the ears of the deaf unstopped. / Then will the lame leap like a deer, / and the mute tongue shout for joy" (Isaiah 35:4b-6).

"Immediately he [the beggar] received his sight and followed Jesus, praising God" (18:43). What does it mean for this formerly blind man to follow Jesus? Well, he goes with Jesus to the home of Zacchaeus, then to Bethany and to Jerusalem.

Before leaving Jericho, "the city of palm trees"—a jewel given to Cleopatra by Mark Antony, the showplace of Judah with its beautiful gardens of roses, a huge gymnasium, and lovely stone palaces—Jesus goes to the house of a chief tax collector. Jericho is a great business center with caravans crossing the area for markets around the world. Taxes are high and in abundance in Jericho. It has a commissioner of taxes, Zacchaeus, who has a group of tax collectors under his authority.

Zacchaeus climbs a tree because he cannot see Jesus, Zacchaeus being a man of small stature (19:3). Zacchaeus becomes a follower. Unlike the rich ruler, he wants more than anything else to be a follower of Jesus. He gives, without being told to do so, half of his large estate to the poor and declares he will give fourfold to any person he has defrauded. He is a great man, though considered unclean because he is an employee of Rome. As a follower, he goes far beyond the requirements of the Torah. Jesus declares, "Today salvation has come to this house, because this man, too, is a son of Abraham."

Zacchaeus's name comes from a Hebrew word meaning "righteous." *Righteous* seems to be an ill-fitting name for a chief tax collector. Yet, after hearing Jesus, Zacchaeus probably joins the multitude of followers as they climb the steep hills to Jerusalem.

Luke 19:28-44. The followers climb seventeen miles upward to Jerusalem, first arriving at Bethany. Near Bethany, Jesus asks two of his disciples to help him prepare to enter Jerusalem (on what we call Palm Sunday). Some persons believe that Jesus arranged to have a colt tied at a specific spot in the small village of Bethphage. The two disciples then go and untie the colt. The owner asks, "Why are you untying the colt?" And the disciples respond with the agreed-upon reply, "The Lord needs it." If one accepts this interpretation, one realizes that Jesus had a plan for publicly declaring his messiahship. He would enter Jerusalem riding on a colt, the foal of a donkey, as Zechariah prophesied (Zechariah 9:9). Jesus would come as the king of the kingdom of God—a man of peace, not of war; humble, not proud; with love, not with swords loud clashing.

Behind this careful planning for a dramatic and symbolic expression of his messiahship is the element of surprise for tens of thousands. During Jesus' ministry in Galilee, Samaria, Perea, Syrophoenicia, and Judah, Jesus has told those he healed to tell no one. Some, such as Legion, declared quite readily that Jesus was the long-awaited Messiah. But on the whole, Jesus minimized these expressions. Jesus knew that current ideas of what the Messiah and the nature of his kingdom would be like were very different from Jesus' understanding and ministry. Now, on Palm Sunday, Jesus declares to all that God has appointed him to be the Messiah, the Savior.

As planned, multitudes of followers (19:35-38) parade around Jesus, placing their garments on the colt and on the road. The "whole crowd of disciples" probably includes the seventy-two missioners who participated in the work through Samaria, the Twelve who were always with Jesus, and the crowd from Nazareth who came to see what their neighborhood young prophet was doing and saying and to express their pride in him.

As Jesus moves on the old Roman road from Bethphage to the Kidron Valley, he can see the beautiful city of Jerusalem. To see the city makes him weep, for her people do not know the meaning of peace; they know not the things that make for peace: love, honesty, unselfishness, and loyalty to God's covenants. They know only the ways of war—selfishness, racial and religious discrimination, hate, and greed.

In preparation for the Feast of the Passover, the great hymns of the week are being sung. Six psalms were repeated again and again. The hymns were called the Hallel, which includes Psalms 113–118. Psalm 118:26 is the well-known verse, "Blessed be he who comes in the name of the LORD."

Obviously, Jesus chooses this day as the specific time to declare publicly his messiahship. Notice that Luke omits any reference to the supposed messianic tie to David. (See Matthew 21:9 and Mark 11:10.) Why would he do so? Was it intentional? Ask class members to discuss this question in terms of its omission in Luke 19:38 (as contrasted with Matthew 21:9 and Mark 11:10).

Discuss at length the difference between Acts 1:3—"After his suffering, he showed himself to these men and gave many convincing proofs that he was alive" and spoke of the kingdom of God—and what the disciples say in Acts 1:6: "Lord, are you at this time going to restore the kingdom to Israel?" Even the disciples, let alone all the followers, have not understood what Jesus is saying when he says he comes to bring in the kingdom of God—*not the kingdom of Israel.* Pontius Pilate is not the only one who cannot understand what Jesus means by the Kingdom. And perhaps thousands (or more) today to not know the difference.

One significant and beautiful sentence in this account is Luke's report of the disciples crying out, "Blessed is the king who comes in the name of the Lord! / Peace in heaven and glory in the highest." Luke begins his Gospel (Chapter 2) with the birth of Jesus in relationship to a decree from Caesar Augustus of Rome. Both the baby Jesus and Caesar Augustus have a special message concerning peace on earth and glory in the highest (2:14).

Luke associates the reign of Augustus (31 B.C.–A.D. 14) with the birth of Jesus in an unusually subtle way. Augustus brought an era of peace to the Roman Empire beyond anything seen previously. The Roman Senate ordered that an altar to Pax Augustus be erected and consecrated in the Campus Marius. Peoples in the eastern Mediterranean world hailed Augustus as god and "savior of the whole world." Rome celebrated the birthday of this famous man by declaring, "The birthday of the god was the beginning of the good news to the world on his account" (*The Interpreter's Dictionary of the Bible*, Volume A-D; Abingdon Press, 1962; page 319).

Luke associates the birth of Jesus, the Messiah of the world, with the famous emperor who brought peace to an empire. Luke writes to Theophilus that the real savior of the world, the real giver of peace to the world, is the babe born in Bethlehem. Jesus will be hailed, not as emperor, but as the King of the kingdom of God, the One who is to come in the name of the Lord. When all persons of all countries acknowledge that Kingdom, we will all know "peace in heaven and glory in the highest!" (19:38). Against that background Jesus predicts the destruction of Jerusalem (19:41-44) because its people have not learned the way that leads to peace.

DIMENSION THREE: WHAT DOES THE BIBLE MEAN TO ME?

The class may discuss the following topic or use the material in the student book.

Right Motivation

Religion that abuses the nature and character of God may become the most destructive force in a community. Jesus knew his people were religious and sincere. But pride and arrogance can destroy that which God has hallowed.

Faith is the thread of the woof that weaves the warp of life together into a brilliant and warm tapestry.

Jesus, after the Palm Sunday experience of declaring his messiahship publicly, goes to the Temple. Isaiah had said, "My house will be called / a house of prayer for all nations" (56:7). Jesus finds bawling cattle; a stench that stifles the smell of incense, myrrh, and frankincense; and a market for the greedy who hypocritically pretend to be serving those who seek absolution of their sins. Jesus, in a rare fit of anger, overturns the tables of the moneychangers, chases the beasts from the Temple area, and rebukes those who sold unblemished animals for the sins of others.

The stories of persons like Zacchaeus and the rich ruler remind us of the importance of motivation. Jesus does not intend to exclude from the kingdom of God such people as Zacchaeus and the rich ruler. For Jesus, the possession of property is not the obstacle; but wealth that becomes an idol is.

Heaven and earth will pass away, but my words will never pass away (21:33).

— 11 —

Jesus Responds to Difficult Questions

Luke 19:45–21:38

DIMENSION ONE:
WHAT DOES THE BIBLE SAY?

Answer these questions by reading Luke 19:45–20:18

1. Whom does Jesus drive out of the Temple? (19:45)

   Jesus drives out those who were selling sacrificial animals.

2. Who seeks to kill Jesus? (19:47)

   The chief priests, teachers of the law, and leaders among the people seek to kill Jesus.

3. What question do the chief priests, teachers of the law, and elders ask Jesus? (20:2)

   They ask, "Tell us by what authority you are doing these things? . . . Who gave you this authority?"

4. What question does Jesus ask them? (20:4)

   Jesus asks if the baptism of John was "from heaven, or from men."

5. In the allegory of the wicked tenants, what do the tenants do to the first servant? (20:10)

   The tenants beat the first servant and send him away empty-handed.

6. After sending the third servant to no avail, whom does the owner of the vineyard send? (20:13)

   The owner of the vineyard sends his son, whom he loves.

7. What do the tenants do to the beloved son? (20:15)

   The tenants throw the beloved son out of the vineyard and kill him.

8. What will the owner of the vineyard do? (20:16)

   The owner of the vineyard will kill the tenants and give the vineyard to others.

Answer these questions by reading Luke 20:19–21:4

9. What does Jesus say to those seeking to trap him on the issue of paying taxes to Caesar? (20:24-25)

   Jesus says, "Then give to Caesar what is Caesar's, and to God what is God's."

10. What question do the Sadducees ask Jesus about a woman who married seven brothers? (20:33)

    The Sadducees ask, "At the resurrection whose wife will she be?"

11. Why do the teachers of the law answer, "Well said, teacher!"? (20:39-40)

    Jesus' opponents could not come up with a response.

12. Of whom are the disciples to beware? (20:46)

    The disciples are to "beware of the teachers of the law."

13. Why does Jesus say the poor widow put more in the treasury "than all the others"? (21:4)

    Jesus says that the others contributed out of their wealth, but "she out of her poverty put in all she had to live on."

Answer these questions by reading Luke 21:5-38

14. When Jesus tells them that one day the Temple will be destroyed, what do the disciples ask? (21:7)

    They ask when these things will happen and what sign will indicate they are about to take place.

15. When will be the time for the disciples to be witnesses? (21:12-13)

   The disciples are to bear testimony when they are persecuted, imprisoned, and brought before kings and governors for Jesus' sake.

16. Why do they not need to worry before answering questions? (21:15)

   Jesus will give them words and wisdom that no one can resist or contradict.

17. How will they save their lives? (21:19)

   By standing firm, they will save themselves.

18. When they see Jerusalem surrounded by armies, what has come near? (21:20)

   Jerusalem's desolation has come near.

19. What is Jesus' prediction about Jerusalem and her people? (21:24)

   "They will fall by the sword and will be taken as prisoners to all the nations. Jerusalem will be trampled on by the Gentiles."

20. When the Son of Man returns, where will they see him? (21:27)

   "They will see the Son of Man coming in a cloud with power and great glory."

21. What will all the physical changes in the earth mean? (21:28)

   The physical changes in the earth will mean that redemption is drawing near.

22. When the trees sprout leaves, what will they know? (21:29-31)

   They will know "the kingdom of God is near."

23. What does Jesus say will not pass away? (21:33)

   Jesus says, "My words will never pass away."

24. What is Jesus doing during the day? (21:37)

   Every day he is teaching in the Temple.

DIMENSION TWO: WHAT DOES THE BIBLE MEAN?

The theme for this session deals with how Jesus responds to difficult questions. Jesus' answers to five basic questions show a brilliant logician, a masterful Bible student and theologian, and a man of unprecedented authority.

Jesus is first asked by what authority he teaches, heals, and interprets Scripture. The second question is clearly politically motivated: Should dedicated Jews pay their annual tax to Caesar? The third question asks if Jesus really believes in life after death, with its implications for marriage after the death of a spouse. The fourth question, raised by Jesus himself, deals with the relationship of the concept of the son of David with his understanding of the meaning of messiahship. The fifth question deals with how faith relates to prophetic ideas. You may want to list these five questions on a chalkboard or on a large piece of paper prior to the session.

The Scripture is divided into three themes:

1. Opposition of the Sanhedrin (19:45–20:18)
2. Three Basic Questions (20:19–21:4)
3. Events That Mark the End of the Age (21:5-38)

Luke 19:45–20:18. The Sanhedrin was furious at Jesus' cleansing of the Temple. This cleansing was particularly resented by the chief priests, who formed the largest group within the seventy-one members of the Sanhedrin. (Annas, an ex-chief priest, was a powerful member.) The chief priests were the authorities in matters of Temple ritual and worship. They validated animals brought to the religious festivals for sacrifice to God.

The house of Annas (whose son-in-law was the current chief priest, Caiaphas) owned all the booths that sold sacrificial animals. The priests were given the power to decide which animals were unblemished and worthy of being used as sacrifices to God. If a priest saw an animal that, for example, James and John (sons of Zebedee) of Galilee brought to Jerusalem, had a bit of black wool on his otherwise all-white body, he (always a male) was declared unworthy. The priest was glad to purchase the sacrificially worthless animal and substitute a perfect one from Annas's herd for a handsome profit. This practice extended to lambs, bullocks, pigeons, and goats.

Another lucrative business was the changing of coins from foreign countries into the coins of the Temple. Jews from throughout the world came to Jerusalem to worship. This worship involved offering sacrificial animals and changing the coins of their native land for the coins of the Temple in Jerusalem.

When Jesus drives out these persons who are gaining wealth through their monopoly on the sales of unblemished animals and when he overturns the tables of the moneychangers, he upsets the lucrative business of the priests. Jesus holds a view similar to the prophet Amos of

750 B.C. You might want to read Amos 5:21-24 aloud. These verses express Amos's anger toward those who place acts of worship (rituals, festivals, creeds) above a life of worship.

Jesus would readily agree with Amos that moral action rates higher than participation in religious holidays. Jesus' concern that persons accept and do the will of God in everyday life, even in the marketplace, and that they help others worship identifies him as a prophet. No wonder the priests wanted to get rid of Jesus, who was much too prophetic, not only in his thoughts but also in his actions.

In this highly emotional setting, we begin this lesson. Luke mentions that the chief priests, the teachers of the law, and leaders (the elders) of the people are trying to destroy Jesus. (See 19:47.) These three groups form the Sanhedrin. They hold not only religious power but also the money purses of Judaism. The Sanhedrin "could not find any way to do it, because all the people hung on his words."

So, the Sanhedrin, under the leadership of the priests whose purses were affected most, sought ways to trap this great teacher and concerned religious leader, Jesus of Nazareth. Apparently, a committee of the three groups comes to Jesus to entrap him. They say, "Tell us by what authority you are doing these things. . . . Who gave you this authority?" (20:2).

While in Galilee, Jesus is under the political authority of Herod Antipas. However, as a Jew, Jesus is under the religious authority of the Sanhedrin. While in Galilee, Herod had asked, "Who, then, is this [man]?" (Luke 9:9). Now the Sanhedrin asks a similar question, "Tell us by what authority you are doing these things. . . . Who gave you this authority?" (20:2). Ask class members to suggest ideas that fall under the category of "these things."

Some possible answers are as follows: healing miracles, such as the blind beggar, the persons with leprosy, or Zacchaeus who found a new wholeness when Jesus visited his home; Jesus' riding on a lowly donkey on Palm Sunday; the cleansing of the Temple to rid the sacred place of greed and the exploitation of the poor. No wonder members of the Sanhedrin met to plot the arrest and death of this political upstart, Jesus, the so-called Messiah.

By what authority does Jesus do "these things"? He does them by the same authority that John had when he baptized persons in the Jordan: by the authority of God. Jesus knows their minds, and he knows what motivates their question. Jesus employs an often-used method of rabbinical teaching by posing a counter question to the question. The answer to the counter question is often suggestive of the answer to the initial question. Jesus asks them if the baptism of John was from heaven or from men. Now the priests are trapped. If they say that John baptized because of a command from heaven (that is, from God), then they acknowledge that John's proclamation of the coming Messiah is true—and this may be he who stands before them. If they say John baptized by the authority of man, the people will stone them because the people believe John is a prophet. They talk together and finally answer that they do not know whence it was. Their failure to answer the

counter question enables Jesus to say, "Neither will I tell you by what authority I am doing these things" (21:8).

The Sanhedrin finds itself judged as invalid. The attack to paralyze Jesus' mission was itself paralyzed. But these unwholesome leaders are not yet finished. They remain in the crowd; and Jesus addresses his next story to them, which is in the form of an allegory. Allegories are stories with surface meanings that represent deeper truths. In this allegory (Luke 20:9-19), each object or person has a current counterpart. The owner represents God, the tenants are the Jewish leaders entrusted with God's work, the servants are the prophets, and the beloved son is Jesus. Even from Old Testament times, the vineyard itself is Israel. (See Isaiah 5:1-7.)

Jesus addresses the allegory to the members of the Sanhedrin who have just asked their impertinent question about authority. Now he tells them how disgusted God is with their leadership and that God will take their responsibilities away from them. They will be destroyed. With this in mind, you might want to tell or read the story. It goes like this:

Jesus tells the representatives of the Sanhedrin an allegory, which would apply directly to their own lives. A man (God) decides to leave the area for a long time. Not wanting to sell the land, the owner secures tenants (the religious leaders) who agree to pay him the customary amount. "At harvest time" (when the time came to collect his rent in kind—about five years according to Leviticus 19:23-25), the owner sends his servants (the prophets) for some of the fruit of his land. Three times he sends his servants; but each is beaten, treated shamefully, and sent away. Then the owner (God) sends his "son, whom I love" (Christ), hoping they will respect him. But the tenants plot and kill him, hoping to gain the inheritance. What will the owner of the vineyard do to the unworthy tenants? He will destroy them.

When the representatives of the Sanhedrin hear this, they say, "May this never be!" But Jesus looks at them and raises the question of God's judgment on them. He refers to Psalm 118:22 ("The stone the builders rejected / has become the capstone.") and Isaiah 8:14-15 ("And he will be . . . / a stone that causes men to stumble. . . . / Many of them will stumble; / they will fall and be broken.") Just so will judgment come to the immoral religious leaders of the Sanhedrin who do not accept Jesus as the Messiah.

Remember that the conditions indicated in this passage of Scripture reflect the period of time when Luke wrote. He is describing what the early church thought of the actions of the Sanhedrin against Jesus and how the early church soon accepted the rejected stone as the capstone of faith. (See Acts 4:11; 1 Peter 2:6-8.)

Luke 20:19–21:4. The teachers of the law and chief priests are aware that Jesus "had spoken this parable against them" (20:19). "Keeping a close watch on him, they sent spies, who pretended to be honest. They hoped to catch Jesus in something he said so that they might hand him over to the power and authority of the governor" (20:20). In 20:19, Luke observes that the teachers of the law and chief priests had "looked for a way to arrest him immediately. . . . But they were afraid of the people." Unable to arrest him, they want to take hold of what he said. What is the difference between arresting him and catching him in an incriminating remark? Perhaps class members would have some suggestions. Would Jesus have been aware of the two attitudes of these schemers from the Sanhedrin?

Both Matthew (22:16) and Mark (12:13) mention that the Sanhedrin included some Herodians in the group, who were sent to spy on Jesus. The Herodians were influential Jews who maintained good relations with the house of Herod. They feared revolt by messianic leaders, and they were concerned about the Sanhedrin's claims that Jesus was a revolutionary.

The spies from the Sanhedrin present their carefully worked out question to Jesus, "Is it right for us [Jews] to pay taxes to Caesar or not?" Explain to class members that an annual tax (tribute) was paid by every male from age fourteen to sixty-five and by women from age twelve to sixty-five. The tax was relatively low, a denarius, a day's wage for a laborer. The tax is less a matter of finance than of religion. For many Jews, paying the tribute to Caesar seemed to be an acknowledgment of a king other than the Lord God.

If Jesus answers, "Yes, pay the tax," many Jews would say that Jesus recognizes Caesar as his king, which contradicts their theological claim that only God is the king of the Jews. If Jesus answers, "No, do not pay the tax," then he can be accused of treason, of encouraging a revolt against Caesar.

Jesus asks for a coin that bears on one side the image of the reigning Caesar. Jesus says in effect, Give to Caesar what has Caesar's image on it and to God that which has God's image on it. (Ask a class member to read Genesis 1:27 aloud.)

Jesus uses logical argument. Jesus also deals with the issues; he does not avoid the questions. He says yes, pay the tax levied by and for Caesar; and give to the King of kings what he has demanded, a committed life. Primary allegiance belongs to God. Caesars, czars, and kaisers come and go; but God and his rule are forever.

The Sadducees (priests) raise another question in their attempt to catch Jesus in their net of words. Ask two persons to roleplay this event. Keep in mind that the Sadducees accepted only the Torah (the first five books of the Bible) and did not believe in the doctrine of life after death held by Pharisees. Perhaps the Sadducees address Jesus in scornful voice. They think they have the last word on doctrine, since Moses ordered them to teach the faith to all.

The conversation might go like this: The Sadducee speaks (with Genesis 38:8 and Deuteronomy 25:5-6 as background), "Teacher, Moses wrote that if a man's brother dies, leaving a wife but no children, the man must take the wife and raise up children for his brother. Now there were seven brothers; the first took a wife and died without children; and the second and the third brothers

took her, dying without children. Likewise all seven brothers were married to her, leaving no children. Afterward the woman also died. In the resurrection whose wife will the woman be?"

The modern disciple responding for Jesus might say, "How do you know all seven went to heaven?" Jesus replies, "The people of this age marry and are given in marriage. But those who are considered worthy of taking part in the resurrection from the dead will neither marry nor be given in marriage, and they can no longer die; for they are like the angels. They are God's children. In this age, marriage is necessary to multiply the human race but is no longer necessary when persons become like angels and do not die any more." Jesus goes on to say that the Sadducees err in thinking that life after death does not exist. "God is the God of the living. You Sadducees, even with your limited canon of Scripture, know that God said to Moses, 'I am the God of your father, the God of Abraham, the God of Isaac and the God of Jacob' " (Exodus 3:6). The present tense, *I am,* denies that God's concern is over those once loyal souls who are now dead; God's concern is those loyal servants who having died are with him now.

Once again, Jesus' understanding more than equals the teachings of the learned religious leaders of his day: "He [God] is not the God of the dead, but of the living, for to him all are alive" (20:38). No wonder some of the scribes say, "Well said, teacher!" Others no longer "dared to ask him any more questions" (20:40).

Jesus then raises a question with the Pharisees and Sadducees, both of whom honor and use the Psalms. The question deals with the identification of the Messiah with the son of David. In Luke 20:42, Jesus quotes Psalm 110:1.

In the Hebrew, the first line reads, "Yahweh [that is, the Lord God], says to Adonai [my liege, the king], sit at my right hand, till I make your enemies . . ." The poet has God talking to the Davidic king. For similar references of "my liege/my lord" (the king), see 1 Samuel 26:17; 1 Kings 1:13. The poet, writing a psalm for the enthronement of a new king, states that the king (of the Davidic dynasty) will be granted authority next to God. God will conquer his enemies, making them into a royal footstool. Judaism in the time of Jesus considered Psalm 110 a messianic psalm, as did early Christians—though it hardly matches the concept Jesus had of God's mission for the Messiah.

Luke wants to make it quite clear that Jesus the Christ is not a political leader. He is much more than the son of David, more than a descendant of the royal dynasty.

Jesus asks a difficult question of his hearers, "How is it that they [the teachers of the law and chief priests] say the Christ is the Son of David?" Jesus wants his hearers to know that he is indeed a descendant of David; but he wants to be known as the Son of God, a different kind of Messiah than David. Jesus is raising a significant question—not of genealogy, but of spiritual and moral sonship.

After these questions, Jesus apparently sits down on the Temple pavement to rest. He looks up and sees the rich putting their gifts into the treasury.

The priests were in charge of collecting, counting, and using the monetary gifts made at the Temple. The priests had thirteen basic items that made up their ongoing budget—such as costs for incense, wood for sacrifices, equipment for water, and so forth. So they developed a system of thirteen trumpet-shaped receptacles to receive the money. Each person put his or her gift in the receptacle of his or her choosing. Jesus watches the ostentation of the rich Sadducees (priests) and Pharisees as they loudly clang the trumpet-shaped receptacles with their metal coins. He also sees a poor widow who puts in two copper coins (leptons, worth one-tenth of a penny)—so small they can hardly be heard! Though small in size, her gift is of more value than all the gifts of the rich. "All these people gave their gifts out of their wealth; but she out of her poverty put in all she had to live on" (21:4). The greatest gift consists of that which costs the giver most and of the sacrificial generosity with which it is given.

Luke 21:5-38. You may want to write on a chalkboard or on a large piece of paper "Four theological/biblical concepts." The first theological concept is that Jesus predicted the destruction of the Temple (and Jerusalem).

Herod the Great began construction of the Temple in 20 B.C.; it was not finished when it was destroyed in A.D. 70 by Titus. The Temple was a beautiful building set in the center of a thirty-five-acre court. It was built of fitted white marble stones covered with huge plates of heavy gold. Golden spikes rose on all sides of the roof to a height of 165 feet. The back of a large porch had gold-covered doors, with Babylonian tapestry of purple, blue, crimson, and gold depicting the heavens. Above it was the symbol of Israel: a golden vine. On a bright morning, looking from Olivet, a person could not look at the Temple's beauty; for it reflected the sun.

During the past week, Jesus heard some people boasting of the Temple's beauty. He had previously wept over Jerusalem because its people knew not the things that make for peace. Now Jesus predicts its destruction. When Luke wrote his Gospel, the Temple had been destroyed for a little over a decade. (Luke wrote about A.D. 85–90.)

The second theological concept Jesus raises is the nature of time. Many Jews considered "the present age" evil and unredeemable (until God or his Messiah came). Eventually, "the day of the Lord" would come. (Read Isaiah 13:10-13 and Amos 5:18-20 to class members. These passages give us the imagery of the stars, the sun and moon, the shaking of the heavens and earth in the days of God's wrath.) These two prophets give background for several of Luke's verses (21:9, 11, 25-26). These events usher in "the age to come," the golden age of God's rule and Jewish supremacy.

The third concept is the second coming of Jesus in a "cloud," reminiscent of God's coming to Moses at the tent of meeting in the cloud of his presence. Luke 21:7-9, 27-28 includes many understandings of the day of the Lord.

The fourth concept deals with persecution. (See 21:12-19.) Luke probably thought of these verses as he recalled Peter and Paul's imprisonments. He includes their experiences in the Book of Acts.

DIMENSION THREE: WHAT DOES THE BIBLE MEAN TO ME?

Luke 20:41-44—The Son of David

Let us return to the question Jesus raises about Christ being David's son (Luke 20:41-44); that is, who is this man Jesus? Jesus raises this question because he wants his listeners (the group from the Sanhedrin) to acknowledge his divine appointment to messiahship. In the Fourth Gospel, Pilate states, "Here is the man!" (John 19:5) and "Here is your king" (John 19:14). In Matthew's Gospel, Pilate asks, "What shall I do, then, with Jesus who is called Christ?" (Matthew 27:22). Luke quotes Jesus as asking the disciples, "Why do you call me 'Lord, Lord,' and not do what I say?" (Luke 6:46).

The question is still very relevant: Who is this man of the genealogy of David (descended from David) whose views are often diametrically opposed to the beloved King David? Jesus was not the kind of king of Israel that the psalmist described in Psalm 110. Jesus asks the religious leadership of Jerusalem to rethink the meaning of the messianic hope, to reconsider his teachings and lifestyle cognitively, not emotionally. Does Jesus reflect God's Spirit? Is Jesus akin to God?

We have found this man subverting our nation. He opposes payment of taxes to Caesar and claims to be Christ, a king (23:2).

— 12 —

Jesus Faces His Disciples and Accusers

Luke 22:1–23:25

DIMENSION ONE:
WHAT DOES THE BIBLE SAY?

Answer these questions by reading Luke 22

1. As the Feast of the Passover draws near, what group of persons plot to get rid of Jesus? (22:2)

   The chief priests and the teachers of the law plot to get rid of Jesus.

2. To whom does Judas go to betray Jesus? (22:4)

   Judas goes to the chief priests and officers of the Temple guard to betray Jesus.

3. How do Peter and John know where Jesus and the disciples will observe the Passover meal? (22:10-12)

   They are to look for a man carrying a jar of water and to follow him to whatever house he enters. Then they are to ask the owner for the use of the guest room where the Teacher may eat the Passover with his disciples. The homeowner will show them a large upper room, furnished, where they are to make preparations.

4. After Jesus gives thanks for the wine, he says he will not drink wine until some great event occurs. What is this great event? (22:18)

   Jesus will not drink "of the fruit of the vine until the kingdom of God comes."

5. As they celebrate the Passover, where is Judas? (22:21)

   Judas sits at the table with all the disciples.

6. How does Jesus deal with the disciples' dispute about who is the greatest among them? (22:26)

   Jesus says, "The greatest among you should be like the youngest, and the one who rules like the one who serves."

7. What does Jesus tell Peter will happen before the rooster crows this day? (22:34)

   Peter will deny knowing Jesus three times.

8. What does Jesus ask of God in his prayer at Gethsemane? (22:42)

   Jesus prays that God will "take this cup" from him.

9. What does Jesus say when Judas draws near to kiss him? (22:48)

   Jesus says to Judas, "Judas, are you betraying the Son of Man with a kiss?"

10. What is Jesus' reaction when one of his disciples tries to protect him with a sword? (22:50-51)

    Jesus says, "No more of this!"

11. What does Jesus say to the chief priests, officers of the Temple guard, and elders? (22:52)

    Jesus asks them why they are coming after him with swords and clubs when he has been with them every day in the Temple courts—and they never laid a hand on him. He asserts that it must be because they were waiting for their hour—when darkness reigns.

12. Where do they take Jesus? (22:54)

    They lead Jesus to the high priest's house.

13. On what three occasions does Peter deny knowing Jesus? (22:56-60)

   1. A servant girl sees Peter as he sits in the light of the fire, and says, "This man also was with him." Peter denies it.
   2. Later someone else sees Peter and says, "You also are one of them." Peter denies it again.
   3. An hour later another says, "Certainly this fellow was with him, for he is a Galilean." Peter states emphatically, "I don't know what you are talking about." Then Peter hears the rooster crow.

14. When the rooster crows, who turns and looks at Peter? (22:61)

   The Lord turns and looks at Peter.

15. What do the men who hold Jesus in custody do to him? (22:63-65)

   The men mock him, beat him, and insult him. They also blindfold him and ask, "Prophesy! Who hit you?"

16. When day comes, where does the council of elders take Jesus? (22:66)

   At daybreak, the council of elders leads Jesus to their Council.

17. What does the Council ask of Jesus, and what is his reply? (22:67-69)

   The Council asks, "If you are the Christ, tell us." Jesus replies, "If I tell you, you will not believe me, and if I asked you, you would not answer."

18. With one voice they ask, "Are you then the Son of God?" What is Jesus' reply? (22:70)

   Jesus replies, "You are right in saying I am."

19. Where do the religious leaders take Jesus then? (23:1)

   The religious leaders take Jesus to Pilate.

20. What charges do the religious leaders bring to Pilate against Jesus? (23:2)

   They say that he is subverting the nation, opposing payment of taxes to Caesar, and claiming that he (Jesus) is Christ, a king.

21. What question does Pilate ask Jesus? What is Jesus' response? (23:3)

   Pilate asks, "Are you the king of the Jews?" Jesus responds, "Yes it is as you say."

22. Learning that Jesus is a Galilean, to whom does Pilate send Jesus? (23:6-7

   Learning that Jesus is a Galilean, Pilate sends Jesus to Herod, who is in Jerusalem at that time.

23. How do Herod and his soldiers treat Jesus? (23:11-12)

   Herod and his soldiers ridicule Jesus, mock him, dress him in an elegant robe, and send him back to Pilate.

24. Pilate offers to punish and release Jesus. For whose release does the crowd cry? (23:18-19)

   The crowd cries out, "Away with this man! Release Barabbas to us," an insurrectionist and a murderer.

DIMENSION TWO: WHAT DOES THE BIBLE MEAN?

The Scripture for this lesson is divided into four themes:

1. Jesus' Last Supper (22:1-23)
2. Jesus' Last Teachings to His Disciples (22:24-38)
3. Jesus in Gethsemane and His Arrest (22:39-65)
4. Jesus' Condemnation (22:66–23:25)

Luke 22:1-23. Today's Scripture is a part of the Passion narrative. The *Passion* generally refers to Jesus' sufferings prior to the cross, beginning with his arrest in Gethsemane. Luke 22:1-23 includes the Sanhedrin's conspiracy against Jesus, Judas's breach of faith, preparation for the Passover, and a portion of the Last Supper.

The Sanhedrin was the chief judicial council, or supreme court of the Jews. It had seventy-one members (see Numbers 11:16) and was chaired by the high priest. Originally this body was composed of priests and Levites. Under Herod the Great, many Pharisees—none of whom were priests, but laymen—became members of the Council.

The Pharisees represented a lay movement within the Council, and they were elected in parts. One person represented the legalistic party of Jesus' day (Shamai). He was paired off with a member of the liberal-thinking group (Hillel). The Pharisees' theological influence was tremendous, far exceeding that of the Sadducees.

Two days before the Feast of the Passover, some members of the Sanhedrin sought ways to arrest and kill Jesus. For fear of becoming ritually unclean and thus unable to participate in the Passover, they had decided to wait until after the Passover. Meanwhile they plotted as to how they could achieve their goal.

Class members might like to discuss the question, Were those members of the Sanhedrin who were plotting to kill Jesus surprised when Judas came and offered to betray him? Do you suppose they questioned whether the timing was right, with only two days remaining before the Feast of the Passover? And what about the question of the right psychological moment for arresting Jesus, a popular teacher?

The Synoptic Gospels assume that Jesus celebrates the Feast of the Passover with his disciples. Jesus reserves an upper room, possibly in the home of Mark in Jerusalem. Jesus explains to Peter and John that, when they see a man carrying a water jar, they should follow him into the house he enters. When they see the householder, they are to ask for the guest room where Jesus is to celebrate the Passover. Peter and John find the guest room and prepare for the meal.

The Passover meal included roast lamb, bitter herbs, unleavened bread, and cups of wine mixed with water. The twelve disciples would have arrived for the Feast prior to sunset, at which time the Feast begins. (If a class member asks when Passover falls, be aware that the Gospel of John gives a different date for the Passover—one day earlier than Matthew, Mark, and Luke. John "corrects" the Synoptic Gospels by saying Jesus was crucified on the day the paschal lamb was slain. If so, then Jesus could not have celebrated the Passover with his disciples. We are accepting the date the Synoptic Gospels give for our study.)

The last supper Jesus eats with his disciples includes the hallowing of the Feast—asking God's blessing on the home as the Feast is celebrated. This "hallowing of the sacred day" is called Kiddush. The leader takes bread in his hands and praises God. Later he takes the wine and also praises God. Jesus uses this basic ritual as he breaks bread with his disciples at Passover. He gives new meaning to the old Passover ritual by saying, after he blesses God for the wine, "Take this, and divide it among you." Then he takes bread, blesses God, and says, "This is my body." After supper he again takes the cup and says, "This cup is the new covenant in my blood, which is poured out for you."

Matthew and Mark write, "This is my blood of the covenant." Most Semites (such as Jews) of antiquity made covenants by smearing blood on the witnesses of or participants in the making of a covenant. (Refer to Exodus 24:6-8 where blood is used in making a covenant.) Perhaps Jesus had Jeremiah 31:31 in mind as he talked of his new covenant. The will of God will not be chiseled into tablets of stone, but into the hearts of persons. Remember that the heart (*lev*, in Hebrew) was considered the seat of motivation, will, and purpose. Asking Jesus to "come into my heart, Lord Jesus" means asking him to come into our motives, attitudes, dreams, and hopes. We move from low desires to the highest values in life when we permit the new covenant to become central in our lives. Such persons are witnessing with their "life's blood" on behalf of God's Messiah.

Paul is the earliest writer to describe the Lord's Supper (or Eucharist—meaning "thanks"). In 1 Corinthians 11:23-25 Paul adds, "Do this"—that is, perform or practice this. "Do this in remembrance of me." For Paul, the Lord's Supper is a time of remembering the Lord Jesus Christ. So

Paul emphasizes three aspects: (1) The covenant is a new covenant (Jeremiah 31:31); (2) The words *do this* make it a Christian institution; (3) It is a time for remembering.

Some class members may have read Mark 14:20 that refers to the one who "dips bread into the bowl with me." The Passover required use of rather hard, thin, unleavened bread. This unleavened bread was broken and dipped into the sauce. You might want to refer to John 13:27 that states Jesus gave Judas a piece of bread dipped in wine (a special sop). After taking the morsel, "Satan entered him." Judas, refusing Christ's love, became demonic. Perhaps class members might illustrate the point: How does rejection of God's and Christ's love warp a person's character until a demonic spirit controls his or her life? Did Jesus' love still surround Judas as he left to betray his Master?

Luke 22:24-38. Learning that one of them will betray Jesus, the disciples begin to question one another. Strangely, the questioning then moves to a dispute as to "which of them was to be regarded as the greatest." What would we think if a group of new bishops spent time debating among themselves as to who was the greatest?

Jesus' response to the question is, "The greatest among you should be like the youngest, and the one who rules like the one who serves." John's Gospel tells how Jesus takes a towel and a basin of water and washes his disciples' feet as a servant. The one who serves is greater than he or she who sits at table.

Jesus asks us to measure greatness, not by favors granted us, nor by merit earned, nor by position attained by self-seeking, but through our service to persons in Christlikeness. The model is the suffering servant who wins others to God by dedicated Christlike willingness to bear the burdens of others.

Luke 22:39-65. Luke, a Gentile, omits the last event in the observance of the Feast of the Passover: They sing a hymn. It would have been one of the six Hallel ("praise ye") psalms in the Old Testament, which was sung by all Jews as they celebrated the Passover that night. These psalms state God's mighty acts in Israel's behalf because of his steadfast love for Israel. Psalm 118 would reflect Jesus' immediate needs before God.

Surely the singing of the disciples bolstered Jesus. Perhaps they hummed as they left the upper room to go a few hundred yards to the garden of Gethsemane. Here Jesus leaves his disciples and goes to pray several yards farther up the terraced grove of olive trees. Jesus prays with the hope that God will "take this cup" from him. However, Jesus will follow God's will regardless of consequences. He would suffer the brutalities heaped upon the suffering servant (Isaiah 53) knowing that as he maintains good will, mercy, kindness, unselfishness, and hope, he will be God's man, living as God yearns for human beings to live. Jesus will demonstrate as never before what God wants human beings to be, even suffering and dying for sins he did not commit. He will die as he lived—a life that reflected the very life of God in attitudes, motives, disposition, thought-life, humility, mercy, and even judgment against evil.

Jesus prays to God in Gethsemane, not attempting to change God's will, but attempting to *know* God's will. When he knows God's will, he will assert it, even to the point of death. Gethsemane is a time, not so much of submission to the will of God, but of strong assertion of God's will. After Jesus concludes his prayer with a victorious conviction, he can take what will come to him, even betrayal by one of the Twelve and the eventual tortures of a cross.

You might want to discuss with class members the question: What did Jesus receive from prayer? Write answers on chalkboard or poster paper. Perhaps the most important thing Jesus received from prayer was God. Immanuel, God was with him. Nothing could separate him from the love and presence of God. And what did God receive from Jesus' prayer life? (Let class members make suggestions.) God got a man of God's own choosing, God's anointed Son, the Messiah.

Judas comes, guiding the captain of the Temple guards to the place where Jesus is. Luke says Judas starts to kiss him; but Jesus stops him with a question, "Judas, are you betraying the Son of Man with a kiss?"

The eleven disciples are ready to fight on Jesus' behalf. Jesus curtly responds to their militant attitudes and actions: Enough of this! And his would-be defenders soon leave him, not knowing what to do with a Messiah who will not fight for his rights. They are frustrated and are like sheep without a shepherd.

Jesus asks the chief priests, officers of the Temple, and elders why they come to him at night with swords and clubs. They have seen and listened to him teach the multitudes during the daytime, yet they had not laid a hand on him. "But this is your hour—when darkness reigns."

So they lead Jesus away from Gethsemane, across the Kidron Valley to the palace of Caiaphas in the south of Jerusalem. His various trials will soon begin.

Luke 22:66–23:25. You might want to explain the power structure of the chief priests, who play a great role in the Sanhedrin. Before Jesus' time, the high priest was chosen from the small but wealthy families who could trace their lineage back to Zadok, one of two chief priests appointed by David and the legitimate priest under Solomon. But in Jesus' time, Rome appointed the high priest and generally chose a man whose strain was not pure blood from Zadok.

Five powerful, wealthy families held the office of high priest in Jesus' time: the families of Boethus, Annas, Phabi, Camithus, and Cantheras. All were illegitimate priests. Annas headed up a strong clan. He was high priest from A.D. 6 to 14. Annas used his political power to see that five of his sons, his son-in-law Caiaphas, and later his grandson Jonathan held this powerful position of authority and wealth.

After Jesus' arrest in Gethsemane, the Temple officers take him to the home of the high priest Caiaphas, son-in-law of the powerful Annas. Caiaphas, as high priest, is the head of the Sanhedrin, some of whose members are plotting to kill Jesus. But it is not yet daybreak, so the Sanhedrin cannot meet. Meanwhile, Peter three times denies knowing Jesus, the Galilean. The men who are holding Jesus mock him and beat him. They blindfold him and ask him to "prophesy" who is striking him on the face.

At daybreak, the members of the Council meet, and Jesus is led into their session (22:66). Caiaphas probably opens the session, stating the name of the person who is on trial for alleged blasphemy. Everyone is interested in Jesus' answer to the following question: "If you are the Christ, tell us." Jesus does not answer yes or no. He says, "If I tell you, you will not believe me, and if I asked you, you would not answer." (So why should I answer anything?)

Jesus then says, "From now on the Son of Man [referring to himself] will be seated at the right hand of the mighty God." The logical conclusion leads to the final question, "Are you then the Son of God?" Jesus responds, "You are right in saying I am."

Jesus thus admits publicly that he is the long-awaited Messiah, the Christ. The Sanhedrin members ("the whole assembly," 23:1), then arise from their appointed seats in the Council and bring Jesus to Pilate for his judgment. Not all members of the Council draw the same conclusions. For example, Joseph of Arimathea is a secret disciple of Jesus. He later asks Pilate for Jesus' body to give it a proper burial, and Pilate agrees. After Jesus' death, "Nicodemus, the man who earlier had visited Jesus at night . . . brought a mixture of myrrh and aloes, about seventy-five pounds" (John 19:39). Paul knew some members of the Council, such as Gamaliel (Acts 5:34) who later cautions Council members that "you will only find yourselves fighting against God" (Acts 5:39). The ringleaders of the inner group who wanted to destroy Jesus include priests, Pharisees, and teachers of the law.

The plotters within the Sanhedrin want Pilate to condemn Jesus by confirming their decision of guilty (of blasphemy). They do not want Pilate to consider the case and decide by way of examination of the evidence. The plotters accuse Jesus, saying, "We found this man subverting our nation, and opposing payment of taxes to Caesar, and saying that he is Christ, a king." Pilate asks Jesus, "Are you the King of the Jews?" Jesus responds in the affirmative.

The witnesses generalize about Jesus' attitudes and his teachings, but no one names a specific Roman law he had violated. Pilate can find "no basis for a charge against this man" (23:4). The chief priests say that Jesus stirs people up with his teachings "all over Judea. . . . He started in Galilee and has come all the way here." Immediately, Pilate thinks of a way out—send Jesus to Herod Antipas, tetrarch of Galilee, who is in Jerusalem for the Feast of the Passover. Let Herod Antipas try Jesus and sentence Jesus, a citizen of Galilee.

So Herod Antipas faces Jesus. He knows many things Jesus is saying and is glad for this chance to see him. But Jesus does not respond to his governor's questions. Jesus gives no signs and works no miracles for Herod. The result is that Herod and his soldiers treat Jesus contemptuously and mock him. After Herod Antipas dresses Jesus in "an elegant robe," he sends this citizen of his own tetrarchy back to Pontius Pilate for him to deal with.

Pilate and Antipas, who have previously disagreed, become friends. On Jesus' return to the procurator's residence (the Tower of Antonia, just northwest of the Temple area), Pilate calls the plotters from the Sanhedrin and the people before him. Again Pilate declares Jesus innocent of all charges. He declares his decision to punish and release Jesus.

The frenzied crowd shouts for the release of an insurrectionist named Barabbas, who has committed murder. Pilate, apparently afraid of a mob scene, releases the insurrectionist, but "surrendered Jesus to their will" (23:25). Thus through the cowardice of a procurator of Judah and the hysteria of the populace created by some evil forces within the Sanhedrin, the Messiah (Christ) moves toward Golgotha.

DIMENSION THREE: WHAT DOES THE BIBLE MEAN TO ME?

The class may discuss the following topic or use the material in the student book.

Luke 22:13-30—The Last Supper and Greatness

Immediately after the Lord's Supper and before going to Gethsemane, a dispute arises among the disciples as to which of them is to be regarded as the greatest (22:24-30). Jesus sees the dangerous seduction of power. Following Jesus involves abandoning the good things of this world and enduring persecution when it is necessary to preach the kingdom of God. In the realm of morality, beauty, truth, and religious faith, the followers of Jesus will sit as persons of authority. They will help persons understand what is truly worthwhile and what is secondary in life.

Jesus' Last Supper has several meanings for Christians. One is Eucharist (The word *Eucharist* comes from a Greek word meaning thanksgiving.), which reminds us to take, eat, and be thankful. Another word is *sacrament,* which means a channel or means of grace. A third word comes from the Roman Catholic Church, *Mass.* It means "to be sent" (from the Lord's table into the world). A fourth word is *communion,* which emphasizes fellowship with Jesus Christ. Paul emphasized the fifth word, *memorial:* "Do this in remembrance of me" (1 Corinthians 11:24). Ask class members if we must choose only one meaning, or can we accept them all?

Father, into your hands I commit my spirit (23:46a).

— 13 —

Jesus Experiences Calvary and Resurrection

Luke 23:26—24:53

DIMENSION ONE:
WHAT DOES THE BIBLE SAY?

Answer these questions by reading Luke 23:26-56

1. Who carries Jesus' cross behind him? (23:26)

   Simon of Cyrene carries Jesus' cross.

2. What do the women who were in the large number of people who followed Jesus do? (23:27)

   They mourn and wail for Jesus.

3. What does Jesus say to them? (23:28)

   Jesus says, "Do not weep for me; weep for yourselves and for your children."

4. Why does Jesus say this? (23:29)

   They are to weep because a day will come when barren women who have never borne or nursed children will be considered more blessed than those who have.

5. How many other persons are led away with Jesus to be put to death? (23:32)

   They lead away two others, who are criminals, with Jesus to be put to death.

6. Where do they take the three men? (23:33)

   They take the three men "to the place called the Skull."

7. After they crucify the three men, what does Jesus say? (23:34)

   Jesus says, "Father, forgive them, for they do not know what they are doing."

8. Following Jesus' prayer, what do they do? (23:34b)

   They cast lots to divide up his clothes.

9. Who sneers at, mocks, and insults Jesus and what does each say? (23:35-39)

   1. *The rulers sneer, saying, "He saved others; let him save himself if he is the Christ of God, the Chosen One."*
   2. *The soldiers mock him, saying, "If you are the king of the Jews, save yourself."*
   3. *One of the criminals insults him, saying, "Aren't you the Christ? Save yourself and us!"*

10. Who defends Jesus? (23:40-41)

    The other criminal, hanging on his cross, says, "Don't you fear God, . . . since we are under the same sentence? We are punished justly, for we are getting what our deeds deserve. But this man has done nothing wrong."

11. What is Jesus' response to the man's request to remember him when "you come into your kingdom"? (23:42-43)

    "I tell you the truth, today you will be with me in paradise."

12. From the sixth until the ninth hours, what two major events take place? (23:44-45)

    Darkness comes over the land for three hours, and the curtain in the Temple is torn in two.

13. What are Jesus' last words on the cross? (23:46)

    Jesus' last words are, "Father, into your hands I commit my spirit."

14. When the centurion sees what has taken place, he praises God. What does the centurion say about this event? (23:47)

The centurion says, "Surely this was a righteous man."

15. What do the various people do at Jesus' death? (23:48-49)

The spectators return home, beating their breasts (that is, repentant). His acquaintances and the women who had followed him from Galilee stood at a distance, watching.

16. Who asks Pilate for Jesus' body? (23:50-52)

Joseph of Arimathea, "a member of the Council," asks Pilate for Jesus' body.

17. What do the women who have come with Jesus from Galilee do that afternoon? (23:54-56)

Sabbath was about to begin, so they followed Joseph to see the tomb and how Jesus' body had been laid there; then they returned home to prepare spices and perfumes to anoint Jesus' body for burial. Then they observed the sabbath.

Answer these questions by reading Luke 24

18. What do the women discover when they reach the tomb? (24:2-3)

They discover the stone rolled away from the tomb; but when they go in, they do not find the body.

19. What were the women wondering about, and who appears to them? (24:4-5)

They were wondering why the tomb was empty when two men in gleaming clothes stood by them. The men ask why they are looking "for the living among the dead."

20. What do the two men ask the women to remember? (24:6-7)

The men ask the women to remember what Jesus told them: "The Son of Man must be delivered into the hands of sinful men, be crucified and on the third day be raised again."

21. As two disciples walk toward Emmaus, who joins them? (24:13-15)

Jesus came up and walked with them.

22. After Cleopas and his companion summarize what has taken place in Jerusalem during the past three days, what does Jesus say? (24:25-26)

Jesus chides them for their foolishness and slowness of heart to believe what the prophets have spoken. "Did not the Christ have to suffer these things and then enter his glory?"

23. What opens the eyes of Cleopas and his companion to Jesus' identity? (24:30-31)

Jesus becomes known as he breaks the bread and gives thanks.

24. What happens when Cleopas and his companion tell the Eleven and those who are with them about their experience? (24:36)

Jesus himself stands among them with a word of peace.

DIMENSION TWO:
WHAT DOES THE BIBLE MEAN?

The Scripture for this lesson is divided into four themes:

1. From the Cross to the Burial (23:26-56)
2. Discovery of the Empty Tomb (24:1-12)
3. Jesus' Appearances After Resurrection (24:13-43)
4. Christ's Parting From His Disciples (24:44-53)

Luke 23:26-56. As the soldiers lead Jesus and the two criminals away to be crucified, they realize that Jesus cannot carry his cross after all the abuse he has experienced. The whole cross is not put on the back of the criminal, only the cross beam. The cross beam will be nailed to a pole, which will then be dropped into a hole. The soldiers seize Simon of Cyrene to carry Jesus' cross beam.

Mark 15:21 tells us that Simon is the father of Rufus and Alexander. Ancient tradition claims that his two sons became outstanding church leaders. We wonder if they were present with their father that day, preparing to celebrate the Passover. If so, what did they think of the demand placed on their father to carry the heavy cross beam? Would they experience rejection because their father carried a criminal's cross beam? Did they see something in their father's face when he returned? What happens to a person who, at first unwillingly, carries a cross in behalf of the Lord? What did Jesus say to Simon, or what did his eyes speak?

Simon was in Jerusalem to celebrate God's passing over Israel and thus bringing them freedom. Jesus also came to set people free. Simon would have heard the voices of the people and especially of the women who "mourned and wailed for [Jesus]." What did Simon think when he heard Jesus say, "Do not weep for me; weep for yourselves and for your children"? If they wept for a guiltless man, such as Jesus, how much more should they weep for the guilty persons who ruthlessly plotted and secured his death? Remember that Jesus also stopped and wept over the beautiful Jerusalem that knows not the thoughts, actions, and emotions that make for peace.

In A.D. 68, Titus (of Rome) would lead scores of military battalions to destroy Jerusalem and Judah. Women who were barren would thank God that they would not have to watch hunger, cruelty, and death befall their offspring. They would pray for death, that the mountains would fall on them and the hills cover them. (See 23:29-31.)

Luke 23:31 is a proverb: "For if men do these things when the tree is green, what will happen when it is dry?" If the innocent Jesus must suffer so greatly, what will be the fate of the guilty city?

The authorities lead the three men to the place of "the Skull." Whether it has that name because it looks like a skull or because the skulls of crucified persons are lying there, we do not know. Mark (15:22) and Matthew (27:33) call the place Golgotha, which is Aramaic for "The Place of the Skull." The Latin word for skull is *calvary*. The exact location of the Skull is not certain. We do know from Hebrews 13:12 that the place was outside the city gate.

Jesus is crucified between two criminals at the place called the Skull. Crucifixion was a method of Roman execution; the stoning of a person was the Jewish method. Either way was cruel and provided a spectacle for many. Crucifixion involved tying or nailing the outstretched arms of the victim to the cross beam while it lay on the ground. Then the cross beam was nailed or lashed to the upright beam, which was then dropped into the hole dug for it. Sometimes the body was supported by a kind of crude wooden saddle projecting from the pole. The feet were nailed or tied to the pole. The body was naked and exposed to sun, wind, flies, and the abuse of spectators. Death usually came by a combination of lack of air, exhaustion, and exposure. After death, the body was usually left to the dogs and buzzards.

Soon Jesus feels the excruciating pain in his nailed hands and feet as the pole drops into its hole with a thud. Jesus prays in anguish, "Father, forgive them; for they do not know what they are doing." What depth of love is required to outweigh the normal curse of pain. Then the soldiers cast lots for Jesus' garments (23:34).

Each of the four Gospels records the gambling for Jesus' garments—which seems to have been the right of those soldiers who carried out the Crucifixion. The major item of interest was his seamless robe. (See John 19:23-25.) Most robes were made by sewing together two long strips (about four feet wide) made of goat hair. Jesus' robe was one continuous cloth, which folded inward (about two feet), and was sewn together at the top. Two holes were made on the sides for sleeves. The robe acted as a cloak by day and a cover for the night.

The soldiers' gambling for the robe fulfills Psalm 22:18. Jesus spoke the opening words of this psalm from the cross, "My God, my God, why have you forsaken me?" (Psalm 22:1), which Matthew reports (Matthew 27:46).

Several groups verbally abuse Jesus. The rulers scoff at him, "He saved others; let him save himself if he is the Christ of God, the Chosen One." The soldiers and even one of the crucified criminals also mock Jesus in the same way. The other criminal replies to the first, "Don't you fear God? . . . We are punished justly. . . . But this man has done nothing wrong." Turning to Jesus, he says, "Jesus, remember me when you come into your kingdom." Jesus answers, "Today you will be with me in paradise."

Then Jesus, crying with a loud voice, says, "Father, into your hands I commit my spirit." Only Luke reports this statement from Psalm 31:5. Luke tells us the personal things that happen, especially to Mary. He writes about the annunciation to Mary. We now understand the words of Simeon to Mary, "A sword will pierce through your own soul too" (2:35). Mary, one of the women at the cross, hears her son's last words before death. They are the words she taught him as a small boy—his first prayer, which every loyal Jewish mother taught her child, "Into your hands I commit my spirit; / redeem me, O LORD, the God of truth" (Psalm 31:5). How Mary must have treasured his bedtime prayer! And now he prays it as his last words. Mary feels the sword piercing her soul.

We wish we knew the name of the centurion who witnessed Jesus' last words. Could it be his little girl whom Jesus healed at Capernaum? Whoever he was, he knew how to praise God; and he now states, "Surely this was a righteous man."

"When all the people who had gathered to witness this sight saw what took place, they beat their breasts and went away." The noncanonical "Gospel of Peter" says, "Then the Jews and the elders and the priests, perceiving what great evil they had done to themselves, began to lament and to say, 'Woe on our sins, the judgment and the end of Jerusalem is drawn nigh' " (7:25). And Jerusalem did fall and was destroyed in A.D. 70.

In contrast, scores of people who loved and valued Jesus' actions and words were petrified by his physical and mental pain. "All those who knew him, including the women who had followed him from Galilee, stood at a distance, watching these things" (Luke 23:49).

Ask class members to follow along in their Bibles as you read Luke 23:50-56. What can we learn about the man who buries Jesus? (1) His name is Joseph. (2) He is a Jew. (3) He lives in Arimathea. (4) He is a member of the Sanhedrin. (5) He did not consent to the purpose and deeds of the Council (Sanhedrin). (6) He is looking for the kingdom of God. (7) He goes to Pilate and asks for Jesus' body. (8) He takes the body down from the cross and wraps it in a linen shroud. (9) He lays the body in a rock-hewn tomb. The sabbath is just beginning.

The women from Galilee who had accompanied Jesus and had cared for his needs follow Joseph. They see the tomb and how his body is laid. As the sabbath (Friday evening) came, they "went home and prepared spices and perfumes" (23:56).

Luke 24:1-12. Mark's Gospel tells us that at the end of the sabbath, the women bought spices so they could anoint the body (Mark 16:1). The women include Mary, the mother of Jesus; Mary Magdalene; Mary, the mother of James the younger; and Salome, the mother of James and John. John probably accompanied Jesus' mother; since John received responsibility for her at the cross when Jesus thoughtfully said, "Dear woman, here is your son. . . . Here is your mother" (John 19:26-27).

This group of loyal persons goes to the tomb, taking the spices they have prepared. They find the stone rolled away; and upon entering, they do not find the body. However, two men in gleaming clothing stand by them. Frightened, the women bow low. The men say, "Why do you look for the living among the dead?" This statement is tremendous theologically. Jesus Christ cannot be found entombed, nor can he be entombed in creeds or rituals or traditional anthems. Christ was set free from all tombs and is alive throughout our world.

These Galilean woman are something to behold. They are actually the founders of our theological faith. They are the first to see, hear, and speak the good news: Christ is risen. The two radiant men say, "Remember how he [Jesus] told you, while he was still with you in Galilee: The Son of man must be delivered into the hands of sinful men, be crucified and on the third day be raised again." The women remember Jesus' words, and they return from the tomb telling all this to the Eleven and to all the rest.

Though the women witness to the disciples, the disciples doubt their words, which "seemed to them like nonsense." The noncanonical "Gospel of Peter" makes an interesting statement. The centurion and the soldiers report to Pilate that Jesus has left the tomb and that truly Jesus is the Son of God. Pilate answers, "I am clear from the blood of the son of God, but this thing seemed good to you." And they all came and asked and begged him to order the centurion and the soldiers to tell no one what they had seen. "For," they said, "it is better for us to incur the greatest sin before God, than to fall into the hands of the people of the Jews and be stoned." Pilate then ordered the centurion and the soldiers to say nothing (Peter 11:47-49).

Luke 24:13-43. Only in Luke do we find intimate experiences between the risen Lord and his disciples. For example, Luke tells the story of what happened on the road to Emmaus. Cleopas and his companion are going to a village named Emmaus. The question as to who Cleopas's companion is has been debated by scholars for many centuries. Eusebius, an early church historian, thinks it is Luke. John 19:25 implies it is Cleopas's wife. (John says Clopas, not Cleopas.) It may be that Cleopas is one of those sources (Luke 1:2) on whom Luke relied for this kind of story.

On Sunday morning, soon to be called "The Lord's Day" in honor of Jesus' resurrection, two followers of Christ are on their way from Jerusalem to Emmaus (probably about seven miles north). They are discussing the events of the past few days. While talking and discussing together, Jesus (unrecognized) joins them. He asks why they are so serious and sad. Then they tell their story. You might ask three persons to roleplay this scene. It can be quite effective. The actors are these: Jesus, Cleopas, and Cleopas's companion.

Cleopas responds to the stranger's question by saying, "Are you only a visitor to Jerusalem and do not know the things that have happened there in these days?" Jesus asks, "What things?" And they tell him of the plot of the Sanhedrin and how they condemned Jesus to death by crucifixion. They tell of their broken hopes that Jesus was the Messiah, come to redeem Israel. Furthermore, their hopes are dashed by his death and burial in a tomb. Some Galilean women say they went to the tomb where he was buried by order of Pilate, but his body was not there. The women say they saw two "angels" who stated emphatically that he is risen. Moreover, some of our Galilean men went to the tomb; and, truly, he was not there. Where is our Lord?

Soon Jesus interpreted the book of Moses (the Torah) and the prophets, helping Cleopas and his companion understand the relationship of Scripture to himself. He shows how the Christ must suffer (and undoubtedly referred to the suffering servant of Isaiah 53). Though their hearts burn within them, they do not recognize Jesus. You might discuss with class members: In what way are the eyes of Cleopas and his companion blinded? They do not see Jesus until the breaking of bread. Do we fail to see him too?

The point is significant: Cleopas and his companion recognize Jesus by the way Jesus prays. His blessings at mealtime reflect his nearness and at-one-ment with God. The style of a pray-er's prayer may reveal Christ's presence.

Cleopas and his companion return to Jerusalem immediately and share their experiences of being in the presence of the risen Lord. As they share, "Jesus himself stood among them." They know the Lord lives.

Luke 24:50-51. Jesus leads his disciples as far as Bethany, where he loved to spend some of his evenings in various homes. At Bethany he lifts up his hands and blesses them. While he was blessing them, he "left them." This parting is called the Ascension. Jesus "was taken up into heaven" from his friends in the sense of now being set free from the bonds of earth; he is no longer bound by the categories of time and space. The risen Lord is everywhere. Time is irrelevant.

DIMENSION THREE:
WHAT DOES THE BIBLE MEAN TO ME?

The class may discuss the following topic or use the material in the student book.

Luke 23:26-49—Christ on the Cross

One of the criminals on the cross turns to the guiltless Christ and says, "Jesus, remember me when you come into your kingdom." What a strange statement to say to a man suffering the tortures of the damned—hands and feet nailed to a scaffold; ridiculed and scoffed at by the religious leaders of the Holy City; the women of Jerusalem weeping at his pain, while the women of Galilee who had ministered to him for three years were in such agony they could only stand, with transfixed emotions and dulled minds, their hearts broken and their Christlike wills paralyzed.

Yet a kingly power reigned on the cross. And even as Jesus had come to set captives free, so his heavenly Father would set him free and raise him above all earthly powers as the King of kings and Lord of lords. He had a moral, aesthetic, righteous at-one-ment with God never known before. He was God's Chosen One through whom all people might know God. For God was revealed in the life, teachings, daily purposes, and death of Jesus of Nazareth, the Christ of God.

Luke states that while the sun's light failed from noon to three P.M., "the curtain of the temple was torn in two." The Holy of Holies was entered only once a year on the Day of Atonement by the high priest. A curtain separated the Holy Place from the Holy of Holies. The symbolism Luke conveys is that now, in Christ, all persons (not just the high priest) can offer prayer. "Anyone who has seen me has seen the Father" (John 14:9).

Especially at Lent we may ask about the seven last words (or sentences) Jesus uttered from the cross. They are drawn from all four Gospels in the New Testament. John has three that do not appear in the other three Gospels; Matthew and Mark have only one, and that does not appear in Luke or in John. Luke has three that do not appear in any other Gospel. Luke's three last words (or sentences) are found in Luke 23:34-46. They were probably remembered by the women from Galilee and became sources for Luke's Gospel. These last words are, "Father, forgive them; for they do not know what they are doing" (23:34); "I tell you the truth, today you will be with me in Paradise" (23:43); and "Father, into your hands I commit my spirit" (23:46).

A significant personal, as well as theological, concern is about the type of body we have after death. Paul argues strongly that the body Jesus had after his physical death was a spiritual body. (Read 1 Corinthians 15.) Jesus, and we ourselves, die. What we sow (the body) is perishable; what is raised is a spiritual body and therefore imperishable. The Christian lives in the kingdom of God—sometimes for a lifetime; some live there considerably less time. When a Christian dies and is already in the kingdom of God, her or his death is seen as the end of the physical life but the continuation of the spiritual life. The vision of the full abundant life now moves from hope to fulfillment.

JOHN
Table of Contents

About the Writer

At the time of writing this book, Dr. Woodrow A. Geier was a retired pastor and a retired editor of adult curriculum resources for The United Methodist Church. He is now deceased.

From the fullness of his grace we have all received one blessing after another (1:16).

— 1 —

The Good News—Fullness of His Grace

John 1:1–2:11

DIMENSION ONE:
WHAT DOES THE BIBLE SAY?

Answer these questions by reading John 1

1. What words of Genesis do the first three words of John's Gospel recall? (1:1; Genesis 1:1)

   John's Gospel and the Book of Genesis both open with the words "In the beginning."

2. What words of John suggest Jesus' divine nature? (1:2-4)

   John says that "In the beginning was the Word [Jesus], and the Word was with God"; that he was part of the creation of all things; and that "in him was life, and that life was the light of men."

3. What does John tell us about the relationship between life and light, light and darkness? (1:4-5)

   John tells us that light gives life and overcomes darkness.

4. Who is introduced into the Prologue of the Gospel in 1:6?

   "A man who was sent from God," named John, is introduced in verse 6.

5. What is John's purpose? (1:7-8)

   John's purpose is "to testify concerning that light, so that through him all men might believe." John is not that light.

6. To whom did the true light come? (1:11)

   "He came to that which was his own" and was not received.

7. What was given to those who believed and did receive him? (1:12-13)

   Those who believed received the right to became children of God.

8. What did the people ("we all") receive in the coming of the Son? (1:16-17)

   "We have all received one blessing after another. . . . grace and truth came through Jesus Christ."

9. How does John's Gospel describe John the Baptist? (1:23)

   John says of himself, "I am the voice of one calling in the desert."

10. Where is John baptizing? (1:28)

    John is baptizing "at Bethany on the other side of the Jordan."

11. How does John say that he recognized Jesus? (1:32)

    John says that he "saw the Spirit come down from heaven as a dove and remain on him."

12. Who are Jesus' first disciples, as listed by our writer? (1:40-51)

    Jesus' first disciples named in John are Andrew, Simon Peter, Philip, and Nathanael.

Answer these questions by reading John 2:1-11

13. Who attended the marriage feast at Cana of Galilee? (2:1-2)

    Jesus, his mother, and his disciples attended the marriage feast.

14. What did Jesus say to the servants? (2:7-8)

Jesus told the servants to "fill the jars with water" and to take some of the water to the master of the banquet.

15. What did the master of the banquet say about the wine? (2:10)

The master seemed surprised the good wine had been saved and served last.

16. What did Jesus achieve by the first of his "signs"? (2:11)

Jesus "revealed his glory, and his disciples put their faith in him."

DIMENSION TWO: WHAT DOES THE BIBLE MEAN?

Introduction. Most of us have been confronted by John's Gospel. In Sunday school we have heard stories from it. In worship services we have heard sermons based on it and have participated in the liturgy drawn from the Gospel. The words of John have comforted us at funerals and given courage in times of uncertainty, anxiety, disappointment, and stress. So John's Gospel is already a part of us, already a present help.

We shall approach the Gospel as a personal message of God—through the unknown author John—to the church and to us. We want to concentrate on bringing out the permanent values of John for us today.

Many studies of John begin by speculating on who wrote the book, whether it was from the hand of one author, when and where the book was written, the Hellenistic (Greek) and Jewish influences in the Gospel, and the relationship of John to the other Gospels. These are important questions, but they are not central to the present study. We do not want to approach the Gospel as a mysterious puzzle to be solved. We want to see it as a portrait of Jesus Christ and an account of what God is doing through him.

So when we read John's Gospel, we should be primarily concerned with what arises in our minds and hearts as we read, with what the Holy Spirit says to us through the printed page. The Word of God is not printed propositions. It is a living, personal Word that reaches us in the depths of our being.

The Word is Jesus Christ, God's personal self-communication to us. In this study, therefore, we should think of John's Gospel as a personal letter of God, telling us about Jesus Christ and his mission of love to us and to the whole earth. John's Gospel is God's Word already spoken to our desolation. It is the proclamation that in Christ the eternal God has triumphed over sin and death.

The study should help us get a sharp focus on the whole of the Gospel of John. You know what happens when a photographer simply and carelessly lifts a camera, randomly presses a button, and then develops the film. Because the photographer failed to study the whole setting and its light and shadows, the camera failed to get a picture that was worth the effort. Such picture taking may warn us of errors we may commit in the study of the Fourth Gospel.

To get to the heart of any literary composition we have to understand the author's purpose. The author of John makes his purpose clear: "Jesus did many other miraculous signs in the presence of his disciples, which are not recorded in this book. But these are written that you may believe that Jesus is the Christ, the Son of God, and that by believing you may have life in his name" (20:30-31).

John 1:1-18. We turn to the Prologue. If a class member is familiar with musical productions, ask that person to discuss the functions of the overture and its place in an opera or a symphony. Point out that an overture presents and repeats the musical themes from the rest of the production. An overture acts as a teaser, making the listener eager to hear more of the theme music as it is presented throughout the symphony or opera. Why is this term appropriate for the discussion of the Prologue to the Gospel of John?

John 1:1-18 is also like the lead paragraph of a journalistic article. It serves to hold the whole composition together. It suggests to the reader the direction the author is going. It defines the area of discussion.

Read John 1:1-18 aloud. This section of John is poetry—except for verses 6-8 and 15. Why would the author choose a poem to introduce the Gospel?

Poetry is a special way for writer and reader to share in truth. Poets deal in images and rhythms that evoke deep responses from readers. The poet *sees*. He or she cuts away humdrum language and conveys to us a sense of meaning and value in writing that otherwise might be meaningless. Poets stimulate deeper appreciations and perceptions of the reader. They do this through the beauty of their words. This beauty consists in fresh images, rhythm, and meter.

The poet's words create a power that is controlled and concentrated by the rhythm. The poet's words constitute a formula for us so that our minds are freed from dullness and distraction. The formula possesses power. The words become a part of us when they have been merged into a formula. A formula musters power because each word affects us strongly. Words that are metrically organized—such as you have just read in John's Gospel—develop an abiding hold on us. Consider these lines:

Do not let your hearts be troubled
and do not be afraid.

—John 14:27c

The rhythm of words is enhanced by firm control—as in the Psalms—through repetition, parallelism, refrain, or alliterative verse (using the same initial sound for words in the same line or at the beginning of each line). In our English poetry the rhythm is largely enhanced through rhyme.

True poetry is therefore the most imaginative, most forceful, and most effective way of saying something. We long remember such lines as we have quoted from the Prologue because they are the bearers of all the qualities of poetry.

Beautiful words are always the most powerful and creative words. So poetry provides the order, power, and simplification that enable us to understand a subject. Note the order, power, and simplification of the words of the Prologue.

The poetry of the Prologue is taken from Greek and Hebrew sources, but scholars think it is more a product of the latter. John has appropriated the Hebrew idea of cosmic wisdom that is beautifully described in Proverbs 8 and 9, especially in Proverbs 8. Read these two chapters in Proverbs to identify points at which John has taken the ideas of divine wisdom.

The chapters in Proverbs present the Hebrew concept of the preexistent divine Wisdom that has created the world. John's understanding of this reality parallels that of the apostle Paul: "Christ the power of God and the wisdom of God" (1 Corinthians 1:24). John and Paul want to affirm the continuity of the Old Testament revelation with that of the New Testament.

The Word in John's Prologue speaks to our universal and persisting human need for an ordered, coordinating principle that will hold the world together for us. We cannot live without some sense of relationship between things. We all need to make sense of existence. We do not like a disordered household or a world where machines run amuck. Our human nature seems to demand a principle and a power that governs all life. The doctrine of the Word speaks to this deep need of ours for order and dependability.

Discuss our human need for order and dependability. Give some examples of the lack of order and dependability. Ask class members for their reactions to a disorderly existence. Do they think the author of John is challenging readers to attain orderly minds? How?

Read and discuss Genesis 1:31. How does John reaffirm this verse? Why do you think the Prologue begins with the words, *In the beginning*?

Discuss the material in the student book on page 6 that begins "John also introduces. . . ." Why were Jesus' own people rejecting him?

Discuss John's words contrasting light and darkness. Why do you think John concentrates on the conflict be-

tween the two? Light brings life, enlightenment, knowledge, and healing. What else does light represent?

Summarize the material on rebirth in the middle of page 7 in the student book. What do you think *rebirth* means? (Make a note of class members' responses, and hold the notes for discussion of John 3:16 in the next lesson.)

The doctrine of the Word answers the deepest questions of the human heart. Who is this Jesus and what does he have to say to me? You know how it is to hear a knock on your door at midnight when the world is hushed and sleeping. Your first question of the intruder or friend is, "Who are you?" Everything then depends on the answer you get. Unless we know who Jesus is, we cannot know what he has to say to us. But when we know who Jesus is and receive him in faith (personal trust and obedience), we perceive that God is saying something special to us in Jesus. Our whole existence may be altered.

The doctrine of the Word tells us that Jesus Christ is both human and divine, "true God and true man," as the Christian creeds have reminded us over the centuries. This doctrine teaches us that the most important issue of our existence is wrapped up in God's coming to us as the Word—the Word made flesh. It is the good news of the Gospel—"one blessing after another."

Our God is not an impassive, unreachable deity who sits upon a throne afar off. God comes to us. So John's Gospel bears witness to the God whose steadfast love remains forever, the God who demonstrates love in the lowly form of our human existence. We have all received of God's fullness—"full of grace and truth."

Now the living Word has come. "For the law was given through Moses; grace and truth came through Jesus Christ" (1:17). Jesus reveals the God who is unseen. He does this, not only by teaching, but by his whole life poured out in love for the human race.

"We have seen his glory, the glory as of the One and Only, who came from the Father" (1:14b). The Jewish people held to a deep conviction that no one could see God's face directly and live. Exodus 33:18-23 gives us the classic treatment of this theme in the Old Testament. Here Moses says, "Now show me your glory." God replies that the divine face Moses cannot see, but that the divine glory will be present: "I will cause all my goodness to pass in front of you, and I will proclaim my name, the LORD, in your presence. I will have mercy on whom I will have mercy, and I will have compassion on whom I will have compassion."

The story of the Old Testament and the New Testament is the passing of God's redemptive mercy before us. God's glory is God's love in action, God's mighty deeds for our deliverance from sin. John 1:14-17 tells us that God's glory resided in the flesh (the human nature) of Jesus Christ. God's grace (God's love that redeems from evil) and God's truth (faithfulness to God's promises) are incarnate in Jesus Christ, who took on himself our human nature. These qualities are available to all people. They are the inexhaustible gift of God's fullness of grace that fulfills the law of Moses.

All this leads us to the conclusion that the main truth of the Christian faith is that the eternal Son of God has taken our humanity on himself. He bridges the gulf between the human and the divine. He is the mediator between God and us, the divine-human Redeemer. In Jesus Christ, God makes God's self known; God unites the human and the divine. In Jesus Christ, God meets us where we are; and God's revelation is God's search for us where we are. God does not simply wait for us to seek God. God seeks us.

Recall the story of Moses' encounter with the glory of God (Exodus 3:1-6). What does this story have to do with the words "we have seen his glory" (John 1:14)? How do you think Christ is the mediator between God and God's human children?

Close your discussion of John 1:1-18 with an examination of the meaning of *grace*.

John 1:19-34. In John's Gospel we are reminded quite forcefully that John the Baptist is not the light and that Jesus is far above John even before Jesus' name is mentioned. Nothing of John's ministry is reported, only his testimony concerning Jesus. When John sees Jesus approaching, he recognizes him immediately and says, "Look, the Lamb of God, who takes away the sin of the world! . . . I have seen and I testify that this is the Son of God" (1:29, 34). How does the Baptist figure in the mission of Jesus?

John 1:35-51. The account of Jesus calling his first disciples is different from the other Gospels' account of this event. (See Matthew 4:18-22; Mark 1:16-20; Luke 5:1-11.) Since these accounts cannot be reconciled, perhaps we can learn from them that the New Testament does not describe any specific way that a person has to react in order to become Jesus' follower. In John's Gospel some of Jesus' disciples come from being followers of John the Baptist. Some are introduced to Jesus by family or friends. Still others probably answered Jesus' direct call to them. What are some ways class members became Christian? How do persons today come to faith?

The writer of John ends Chapter 1 with these words of Jesus: "I tell you the truth, you shall see heaven open, and the angels of God ascending and descending on the Son of Man." Here the writer refers to the beautiful story of Jacob and the angels (Genesis 28:10-17). He also uses the term *Son of Man* to apply to Jesus' mission. Why does Jesus use the term *Son of Man* to apply to himself? This title is used often in John's Gospel. Here it means the disclosure of God's attributes in human form—the work of the Messiah.

Son of Man also represents the authority of Jesus to introduce into the present the judgment pronounced on all who accept or reject him who is in the world on God's mission.

John 2:1-11. The account of the wedding at Cana is a complete story in itself. The beginning of the account is "On the third day," which may be the writer's way of relating the account to the events just described—"On the third day" after calling Philip and Nathanael, which happened on "the next day" after Andrew and Peter were called (1:43). Or the writer may mean the third day of the wedding feast.

The story closes with a recognition that this work was "the first of his [Jesus'] miraculous signs" and that because of this manifestation of his glory, "his disciples put their faith in him" (2:11).

Read the story of the wedding feast aloud, and ask for class members' reaction to it. Why do Jesus' words to his mother seem harsh? What is Jesus' purpose?

DIMENSION THREE: WHAT DOES THE BIBLE MEAN TO ME?

The class members may discuss the following topics or use the material in the student book.

We Apply the Gospel to Ourselves

This closing section of the lesson should help class members find the meaning of the Scripture for their life. Make the atmosphere for your discussion informal; and encourage class members to question you, themselves, and one another.

How have class members been confronted by the Gospel of John? Ask them to quote some of their favorite verses from John. What do they think God is saying to them in these verses? How did verses from John help in times of stress and loss? What verses do we hear at funerals? What parts of John's Gospel do they use for their private devotions?

What does the Prologue mean to you? Point out the need we all have to find meaning and value for our life. How have class members found meaning and value in the passages in this lesson? Explore with them the purpose of the Prologue. What does this poem mean to them personally? Is it possible for men and women today to live creatively and constructively if they do not believe Genesis 1:31? What does the Prologue say to students about the nature of God? about the nature of the creation? about God's purposes for their life?

Explore with class members what it means to them to believe that Jesus is both human and divine. Recall the discussion of Jesus as the mediator. How have they found Christ to be the mediator in their life?

Explore what it means to "put their faith" in Jesus Christ. Lead class members to see that Jesus insists we go beyond mere acceptance of intellectual propositions about him. To believe faithfully means we commit ourself to Jesus Christ and what he wants in the world. Belief in Christ means having the whole weight of our love rightly directed.

God's Salvation Is at Hand

This lesson reminds us that the deepest-seated yearning of us all is for God. It centers on God in all God's infinite majesty and on the divine method of dealing with us in Jesus Christ.

This lesson goes to the heart of our search for meaning and value in life, for it challenges us to confront life's ultimate issues. It drives us to the center of the Christian revelation: the Word became flesh in Jesus Christ.

This lesson affirms the goodness of the creation and our involvement in it. A conflict between light and darkness, between good and evil exists in our world. In that conflict Christ has won the victory, and we may participate in his triumph. This lesson affirms that grace and truth have come to us in a person. The acceptance of this reality gives us confidence that God has not left us abandoned and alone on this earth.

Close by reading this quotation from *The Quest of the Historical Jesus*, by Albert Schweitzer:

He comes to us as One unknown, without a name, as of old, by the lake-side,s He came to those men who knew Him not. He speaks to us the same word: "Follow thou me!" and sets us to the tasks which He has to fulfill for our time. He commands. And to those who obey Him, whether they be wise or simple, He will reveal Himself in the toils, the conflicts, the sufferings which they shall pass through in His fellowship, and, as an ineffable mystery, they shall learn in their own experience Who He is.[1]

---

[1]From *The Quest of the Historical Jesus*, by Albert Schweitzer (A&C Black, Ltd., 1922), page 401.

For God so loved the world that he gave his one and only Son, that whoever believes in him shall not perish but have eternal life (3:16).

2

Jesus the Savior of the World

John 2:12–4:54

DIMENSION ONE:
WHAT DOES THE BIBLE SAY?

Answer these questions by reading John 2:12-25

1. During what great religious festival does Jesus go up to Jerusalem? (2:13)

   Jesus goes up to Jerusalem for the Passover.

2. Who was in the Temple, and what were they doing? (2:14)

   Men were selling cattle, sheep, and pigeons; others were sitting at tables exchanging money.

3. What does Jesus do and say in the Temple? (2:15-16)

   He makes a whip of cords and drives out the traders with their sheep and cattle. He says to "those who sold doves . . . , 'Get these out of here! How dare you turn my Father's house into a market!' "

4. What is the response of the Jews, and what is Jesus' answer to them? (2:18-20)

   They ask for a sign; but Jesus replies, "Destroy this temple, and I will raise it again in three days." The Jews reply that it had taken forty-six years to build the Temple, "and are you going to raise it in three days?"

5. What did the disciples finally conclude about the conversation between Jesus and the Jews? (2:21-22)

   After Jesus was raised from death, the disciples recalled what Jesus had said and "they believed the Scripture" and him.

6. Why does Jesus not trust himself to persons who believe in him because they see the signs that he does? (2:23-25)

   Jesus knows the human heart and mind ("all men"). He does not need to have anyone tell him what is in human nature.

Answer these questions by reading John 3

7. What does Nicodemus say first to Jesus? (3:1-2)

   He compliments Jesus as a teacher who has come from God and says no one can perform Jesus' miraculous signs unless God is with him.

8. What does Nicodemus find hard to believe about Jesus' answer? (3:3-4)

   Nicodemus does not understand Jesus' words that one must be "born again."

9. What is the heart of Jesus' message to Nicodemus? (3:16-21)

   God loved the world so much that God sent his one and only Son into the world, not to condemn the world, but that those who believe in him might be saved.

10. What is John the Baptist's testimony? (3:25-30)

    John testifies that the ministry of Jesus is the work of God ("what is given him from heaven"). John is the forerunner of the Christ, and John rejoices greatly in the ministry of Jesus.

Answer these questions by reading John 4

11. Who does Jesus meet at Jacob's well? (4:7)

    Jesus meets a Samaritan woman at Jacob's well.

JESUS THE SAVIOR OF THE WORLD

215

12. What does the Samaritan woman say when Jesus asks her for a drink? (4:9)

"You are a Jew and I am a Samaritan woman. How can you ask me for a drink?" (Jews had nothing to do with Samaritans.)

13. What does Jesus tell the woman about the water of life? (4:13-14)

The water of life that Jesus gives will quench one's thirst, because it will become "a spring of water welling up to eternal life."

14. What does Jesus say about true worship? (4:21-24)

Jesus answers that the time is coming "when the true worshipers will worship the Father in spirit and truth."

15. What is said about the Messiah in the conversation? (4:25-26)

The Samaritan woman says that when the Messiah comes, he will explain all things. Jesus replies that he is the Messiah.

16. What is the reaction of the disciples to Jesus' conversation with the woman? (4:27)

They are surprised to find him talking with a woman, but no one asks Jesus what he wanted or why he was talking to her.

17. Who believe in Jesus after the Samaritan woman's testimony? (4:39)

Many Samaritans believe in Jesus.

18. What is Jesus' second sign? (4:46-54)

Jesus heals a royal official's son.

DIMENSION TWO: WHAT DOES THE BIBLE MEAN?

If we are to grasp readily the meaning of the stories related in this lesson's Scripture passages, we should get the events described fresh in our minds. Review these events quickly. They may be grouped into these categories:

1. Jesus' cleansing of the Temple
2. Jesus' conversation with Nicodemus
3. John the Baptist's testimony about Jesus
4. Jesus' visit among the Samaritans
5. Jesus' talk with the woman at Jacob's well
6. Jesus' healing of the official's son

John 2:12-25. The problem with Temple worship lay in the use of religion for profit by some people. Outward observances and conformities to ancient rituals and practices were stressed, as though reverence for the forms could bring healing and reconciliation with God. As in the time of Amos, Hosea, and other Old Testament prophets, religion was used in this way. Jesus was following in the prophetic tradition when he denounced the buying and selling of animal sacrifices as a means of gaining God's favor. God is pleased by worship that springs from the heart and from pure motives. God delights in the worship of persons who seek to do the divine will—persons who are concerned with right relationships with God and with their neighbors. The prophets insisted that justice should "roll on like a river . . . like a never-failing stream" (Amos 5:24), that oppression of the poor must cease, and that peace be diligently sought. Jesus was severe in his condemnation of self-centered religion that would make the "Father's house into a market."

In driving the traders from the Temple, Jesus dealt with a problem that has persisted in every society, every religion, every Christian denomination. That problem is the exploitation of religious feelings and loyalties for worldly gain. The mixed-up religious and secular leaders of the Middle Ages did this when they launched crusades to wrest the tomb of Jesus from the "infidels." The buyers and sellers of indulgences in the day of Martin Luther did this when they presumed to forgive sins following payment of money. Ask class members to give examples of the exploitation of religion today: abuses by some leaders of the electronic church, cults, and others.

Jesus came proclaiming that faith is not a transaction but a relationship. The old abuses would have to give way to a new way in religion. He said the Temple of wood and stone—or material things given for salvation—is a false notion of what God requires of us. The old sacrifices are now replaced by the body of Jesus, the living sacrifice. His body, broken for the sins of the world—his body, that was to be raised in the Resurrection—is sufficient sacrifice.

The disciples and the Jews would like to have a sign that Jesus' message is authentic. But Jesus has already given a sign to them. Do they not see his mighty works every day? They stand beneath the rays of Jesus' sacrificial deeds, but they do not see them. They are like the man who stands inside a beautiful city and requests, "Show me a sign that this is a city." Or they are like the individual who, standing in the presence of God, says, "Prove to me that God exists." It is insulting to one in whose presence we stand when we presume to prove his or her existence. When taunted to prove God's existence, the early church pointed to Jesus Christ. What is our real proof of God? Many persons say Jesus Christ is the only proof we shall ever have or ever need.

One astute interpreter of events in the episode in which Jesus drove out the money changers and traders from the Temple has summed up the issue of the search for signs in this way:

One has a feeling of exasperation with these people bleating for a **sign**. It seems so silly. What need of a sign when no sign merely but the thing itself is there before their eyes? How can a prophet prove that he is a prophet except by doing the deeds of a prophet, by showing the zeal and passion for righteousness that makes a prophet, by arousing people's consciences to feel as intolerable things they had never noticed, or which they dully assumed to be inevitable and woven into the make-up of life? Yet when this unknown Galilean burst suddenly into Jerusalem, and temporarily at least swept away bodily a pollution that had desecrated the temple for years, and which must have jarred the consciences of many of the more spiritual worshipers, the authorities buzzed around him, asking inane and yet natural questions. By what right are you doing this? What evidence have you that you are really sent by God and are commissioned by him? Some of them, be sure, were angry. For no reform was ever carried through without arousing opposition, often from men quite good in other ways. So, no doubt, it was here. Vested interests, they felt, were being hurt. Worshipers from other countries found it a very real convenience to have the money-changers actually in the temple precincts, ready to make the payment of their dues much simpler and more expeditious; while many would just not have imagination enough to see anything unseemly in the established way of things, or why what had been there so long should not be altered. In all which there is a warning for us.[1]

John 3:1-21. Point out that the Pharisees were the best people of their day. They were the religious leaders, the elders, the most knowledgeable about Temple worship and the law of Moses. Nicodemus was a leader of these people, a man blameless in observance of the law. But Nicodemus had one problem. His righteousness was a righteousness of human beings, not the righteousness of God.

So Nicodemus, an honest seeker, comes to Jesus by night. Summarize for class members the conversation between Jesus and Nicodemus. What do they think happens in the new birth, or being born from above? How do they think the new birth affects one's goals in life? one's values? What does baptism have to do with the experience of the new birth?

The student book contains the idea that being reborn carries with it the idea of eternal life. Explore with class members what this term means in the New Testament. Christians stress their conviction that eternal life is God's gift. We do not have to die and be placed in the grave to participate in eternal life. Eternal life is a quality—God's own life—in which we participate in this life. Eternal life begins here on this earth on which we struggle. Eternal life is our sharing in God's own existence.

John's Gospel teaches us that we live in mystery. Note the conversation between Jesus and Nicodemus regarding the effects of the wind. It blows where it pleases. This blowing symbolizes the mystery that surrounds human life. We do not know how God's grace operates in the whole of our lives, but we can see its effects. All of us understand this phenomenon in our daily lives. We do not have to know all

about the ways a computer system operates in order to use and enjoy its benefits. We can watch a television show simply by pushing a button.

The experience of rebirth is not alone one of the intellect or of reason. The center of rebirth is the love of God extended to us in Jesus Christ and our response to that love. John's Gospel is talking about a dynamic that liberates all our powers. We sometimes ask ourselves, "What am I good for?" The correct answer is found by asking, not what we believe or hope, but what we love. The secret of Christian education lies in getting the weight of the learner's love rightly directed.

According to John's Gospel, what was the purpose of Jesus' coming down from heaven? Why can we claim that Jesus is the truth about God?

Read Numbers 21:4-9 and the paragraph in the student book on page 16 dealing with this passage. Why do you think Jesus applied this episode to his own role in the world? Why has the passage on Moses' lifting up the snake in the desert (John 3:14-15) become a key concept in our understanding of world salvation? Why would Martin Luther call John 3:16 "the gospel in miniature"? Why do many people today love "darkness instead of light"?

Discuss the two senses in which the word *world* is used in John. In the Prologue, the word means the created world: "the world was made through him," the world that is mentioned in Genesis 1:31. But the other use of the term means our human world, the existence of alienation where people do not know Christ. In rejecting Jesus the people are representatives of this estranged world. It is a world lost and hostile, but it is subject to God's redemption. Jesus saves this world at the same time he overcomes it.

John 3:22-36. John the Baptist had a movement all his own. He recruited and baptized disciples and preached repentance for sins. He could have been jealous of Jesus and considered Jesus an intruder into his territory. But John didn't. He rejoiced in Jesus' success, and he applauded the genuineness of Jesus' ministry. The Baptizer insisted that Jesus had come from God. John the Baptist set an example for future religious leaders to be open and gracious, supportive of genuine ministry that led people to God.

John 4:1-30, 39-42. The conversation between Jesus and a woman at Jacob's well serves to heighten the conviction that Jesus is the Savior of the world. The scene is Samaria, where the people are plagued with the disease of racial and religious prejudices and hostilities themselves and from the Jews toward them. Jesus defies the taboos and treats a Samaritan woman with compassion and respect. He goes even further in ignoring ancient prejudices against women. He listens to the woman's sad story, cutting through the prejudices against women that prevail in Samaritan and Jewish societies.

Read and summarize the discussion between Jesus and the Samaritan woman in the student book, pages 17–18 .

Why is the woman perplexed? What does "living water" mean to her at first? What do you think it meant to Jesus?

What does the discussion of worship have to do with the woman's life? How do we know Jesus is announcing a new day in religion? The Samaritans take from the ancient Jewish religion only what they want—the Pentateuch, another name for the first five books of our Old Testament. They affirm a partial truth at the expense of the whole truth. Do you observe among Christians today this tendency to take only what pleases us? Ask class members to give some examples. What happens to the Samaritan woman? How does she come to see herself as she really is? What do class members think causes us to see reality and to change our way of life?

What does the woman of Samaria do as a result of meeting Jesus? Why do you suppose the other Samaritans in that city believed this woman's words about Jesus?

John 4:31-38. Have you ever been absorbed so deeply in your work that you missed a meal? If so, you have a small inkling of Jesus' meaning when he tells the disciples that his food is to do the will of God ("him who sent me"). Jesus' concern for God's task is total, all absorbing. It sustains his life and purpose.

Ask class members what they think of Jesus' references to the harvest. Jesus is urging his followers to go out on God's mission. They may reap a rich harvest that others have sown. The disciples have entered into the labors of others. We benefit daily from the labors of people we have never seen. We share in their labors when we take upon ourselves the work of Christ. Ask class members to cite evidences of where they have reaped because others have sown.

John 4:43-54. This story moves Jesus into Galilee, "his own country." Perhaps after all the accolades he received in Jerusalem, Jesus wants to rest and recuperate where he is not so acclaimed. But his fame precedes him, and an official—probably a Roman and a Gentile—begs him to heal his son. Perhaps wearily, Jesus answers him, "Unless you people [all of his audience, not just the official] see miraculous signs and wonders you will never believe." The man asks for healing again, and Jesus grants it. The official does not rush away to check on the healing; he "took Jesus at his word."

Jews and Gentiles are involved in Jesus' ministry of healing. Jesus' signs—mighty works and miracles—always minister to human welfare. They are not given to cause a show.

DIMENSION THREE: WHAT DOES THE BIBLE MEAN TO ME?

A New Day in Religion

Discuss these questions with class members: What does John mean by "rebirth" and "born again"?

John's Gospel stresses the idea of rebirth, not a biological experience, but a transformation of the whole person. Along with this, the Gospel emphasizes the kingdom of God, a realm one cannot enter unless one is born from above, born again. In this whole experience the person is conscious of being the child of God, eternally loved and cherished by God.

The reality of being reborn carries the idea of eternal life. It is the reality of Jesus Christ taking charge of our affections, our wills, our lives. Through him we are reborn to new life. Through it, we are reborn, changed from self-centered creatures into persons who know our sins are forgiven and forgotten.

The symbol of all this is water (baptism), which represents cleansing. Baptism and the Holy Spirit signify the power of Christ in our lives, a power that gives victory over sin.

We then become citizens of the kingdom of God, children of God, who on this earth have life eternal—we participate in the very existence of God.

Jesus reacted in an unexpected way to the woman of Samaria. He treated her with respect and love. Are we able to treat all God's creation with this love? How do we treat those who are homeless? those who suffer from AIDS? those who have done us a wrong?

Jesus has planted the seed of this faith among us. Christians are left to reap the rich harvest. As God has sent Christ, so Christ sends us to proclaim the universal good news of God's love. Just as John the Baptist received humbly and magnificently the leadership of Jesus, so Christians today are called to serve God without pride and without jealousies, letting the credit fall where it may, but giving the final credit to God. How are you serving and giving the credit to God?

---

[1]From "The Gospel According to St. John's Exposition," by Arthur John Gossip, in *The Interpreter's Bible*, Volume 8; pages 499. Copyright renewal © 1980 by Abingdon. Used by permission.

Then Jesus declared, "I am the bread of life. He who comes to me will never go hungry, and he who believes in me will never be thirsty" (6:35).

3

Jesus the Bread of Life

John 5–6

DIMENSION ONE:
WHAT DOES THE BIBLE SAY?

Answer these questions by reading John 5

1. Where does Jesus attend the feast of the Jews? (5:1)

   Jesus attends a feast in Jerusalem.

2. What happens at the pool of Bethesda? (5:2-9)

   Jesus heals a man who is lame.

3. How do some Jews respond to Jesus' healing on the sabbath? (5:10, 16)

   They say it is unlawful to heal on the sabbath, and they persecute Jesus.

4. Why do "the Jews" seek all the harder to kill Jesus? (5:18)

   Jesus broke the sabbath and called "God his own Father, making himself equal with God."

5. How does Jesus answer his critics? (5:19-24)

   Jesus replies that his works have been approved by God and that those who believe in God who sent him have eternal life.

6. What does Jesus say about the coming age? (5:25)

   The coming age is already at hand and now has come in Jesus.

7. Why is Jesus' judgment just? (5:30)

   Jesus came not to do his own will; he seeks "not to please myself but him who sent me."

8. What does Jesus say about the witness of John the Baptist? (5:31-36)

   John's testimony about Jesus is true, but Jesus' witness is greater than John's.

9. What witness does Jesus have that he is sent of God? (5:36)

   The work that the Father has given him to finish, and which he is doing, is Jesus' witness.

Answer these questions by reading John 6

10. Why does a crowd follow Jesus? (6:2)

    "They saw the miraculous signs he had performed on the sick."

11. How do the people respond when they see the sign of the feeding of the five thousand? (6:14)

    They say of Jesus "surely this is the Prophet who is to come into the world!"

12. What does Jesus do when he perceives the people want to make him king? (6:15)

    Jesus withdraws to "a mountain" by himself.

13. What does Jesus say to his frightened disciples when they see him walking on the water? (6:20)

    Jesus says, "It is I; don't be afraid."

14. When the disciples find Jesus on the other side of the lake, what is his response to their questions? (6:26-40)

    "You are looking for me, not because you saw miraculous signs but because you ate the loaves and had your fill." Jesus tells them not to "work for food that spoils, but for food that endures to eternal life." Then he talks to them about the meaning of his claim: "I am the bread that came down from heaven."

JESUS THE BREAD OF LIFE

15. What is the response of "the Jews" to Jesus' words? (6:41-42)

They grumble about him and question his claim, thinking him only to be "Jesus, the son of Joseph, whose father and mother we know."

16. How does Jesus answer them? (6:43-51)

He interprets his role as "bread that came down from heaven," one who is sent by God.

17. What is the response of "the Jews" to Jesus' reiteration of his claim? (6:52)

They argue among themselves, asking how Jesus could give them his flesh to eat.

18. How does Jesus answer "the Jews"? (6:53-58)

He explains that to eat and drink of him is the means to eternal life; the living Father sent him and the one who feeds on him will live forever.

19. What do the disciples say about Jesus' words? (6:60)

They find his words are "a hard teaching" and difficult to accept.

20. What do many of Jesus' disciples do when they hear Jesus' words in verses 61-65? (6:66)

They turn away and no longer follow Jesus.

21. What is Peter's confession? (6:68-69)

He asks, "Lord, to whom shall we go? You have the words of eternal life." Peter says the disciples believe that Jesus is "the Holy One of God."

22. When does Jesus speak of Judas Iscariot? (6:70-71)

Jesus reminds the disciples that he had chosen them and that one of them is a devil.

DIMENSION TWO: WHAT DOES THE BIBLE MEAN?

John 5:1-18. Jesus plunges into the most desperate situation, a situation from which hope seems to have departed. Why does John's story concentrate on the one lame man? He wants to make clear the power of God in the situation. The lame man seems to have given up. He seems to be without hope. He needs a word from beyond himself and his sad plight. Jesus responds to the man's deeper need with the words, "Get up! Pick up your mat and walk."

The lame man has thought himself powerless and alone, but suddenly he finds himself able to walk. Jesus asks him whether he wants to be healed. In this question Jesus deals with the main issue: Would the man like to be made whole? Is he willing to drop the excuses that have hemmed him in and to face the possibility that God is working in his life? His fears and anxieties have been barriers to healing. These must be dealt with. These maladies in his existence have caused him to settle down with things as they are. The lame man has made himself comfortable with a second-best life, an accommodation to life as it is.

Jesus' dealing with the man breaks through this spirit of accommodation. Through a power not his own, the sick man is healed. He goes away without thanking the person who has been the instrument of his healing. He does not even learn Jesus' name. Later he learns who Jesus is and reports him to the authorities. When finally he recognizes Jesus, he is greeted with the words, "See, you are well again. Stop sinning or something worse may happen to you" (5:14). Jesus bids the man to avoid the greater enemy—sin.

What befits the sabbath? This question looms large after the healed man reports to the authorities that Jesus has healed him on the sabbath. The religious people should be asking, What goes on here? What is more important—a man's restoration to health or the observance of secondary rules? Instead, the response of the authorities is to focus on the breaking of the law.

In the moral codes of their day, the authorities had life fixed and regulated in a written code (like *Robert's Rules of Order*) that had an answer for every situation one faced. Jesus insisted that principles, not petty rules, should govern the conduct of his followers. Principles require that we think, that we see the possible consequences of values and make wise choices. We have standards to be applied reverently and wholesomely to the tough moral dilemmas that we face.

So Jesus applies principles to the matter of healing on the sabbath. One big principle: the sabbath is made for persons, not persons for the sabbath (Mark 2:27; 3:2-5). It is far better to do deeds of compassion and healing on the sabbath than to make minor rules central in our lives. Jesus tells the Jewish authorities, "My Father is always at his work to this very day, and I, too, am working" (John 5:17). The sabbath laws cannot apply to God. Jesus' work and God's work are one work. Jesus' followers are put on notice that their faith frees them from legalism that would give them little, simple rules for what they could or could not do in every situation. It is therefore fitting that persons do deeds of mercy and compassion on the sabbath, since God in Jesus' ministry is setting the example.

How do Christians decide on wholesome sabbath observance? Many businesses, especially retail and food service businesses are open on Sunday, and commerce seems to be brisk. Not only are stores open, we as customers keep them open. Yet we can find more biblical and faithful ways to observe the sabbath. How do we know it is better to visit patients in a hospital than to watch television on the sabbath?

John 5:19-29. Review the material in the student book (pages 24–25) dealing with the claims of Jesus.

In John 5:19-29, Jesus reaffirms his oneness with God. The authorities see Jesus' claims on the level of personal divine sonship that would set Jesus above God's laws. The claims remind them of the arrogance of pagan rulers of their times who claimed divinity for themselves.

For Jesus to speak of himself as the Messiah took extraordinary and unique courage; for he knew that his words were considered blasphemy by the orthodox Jewish leaders. Jesus' statements could only divide the Jews, for Jesus' position meant that people must accept Jesus for what he said he was or reject him as a blasphemer.

Jesus, however, does not make claims according to egotistical motives. With him, every claim points to God to whom he is obedient. God delegates authority to the Son and permits Jesus to confer "life to whom he is pleased to give it." As Son of God, Jesus should be honored as God is honored. When Jesus is doing the work God has sent him to do, he should be honored as God is honored. In human affairs we honor an ambassador from another country simply because of his or her mission.

Jesus is appointed by God to carry out the divine judgment. He has come to proclaim the future age. It is now. Judgment is present. Judgment is the crisis one encounters when Christ's message is submitted for belief or unbelief. If the person responds in faith (personal trust and obedience), the judgment is behind him or her, so that the person already lives in eternal life. Verses 28-29 apply to the future judgment and final resurrection. But the present and future aspects of judgment are present in the church.

Jesus Christ brings judgment, for a person's judgment depends on his or her response to Jesus Christ. To accept Jesus Christ is life, to reject him is death. When we accept the God of love who comes to us in Christ, we find a new relationship with God, with others, and with ourselves.

Jesus Christ raises the dead to life. This is his messianic claim. To be spiritually dead means to have given up in the struggle. Then we see ourselves as unable to overcome our faults and unable to become what we ought to be. We lose our feeling for higher things, our sensitivity to God's claims on us. We cease to repent daily—proof that we are spiritually dead. We lose our desire to learn, the challenge to use our minds, the desire to change.

In the presence of Christ we may triumph over all spiritual death. We then view with great seriousness the importance of this life, for it determines eternity. Here we choose life or death.

John 5:30-47. In these verses Jesus speaks of a number of witnesses who bear testimony to him. Who are these witnesses who confirm that Jesus has come from God? They are John the Baptist, Moses, the Scriptures, Jesus' works,

and God. These are witnesses the people can believe. Why did not more of the people believe? Many accepted these witnesses and even venerated them, and yet intellectual agreement was the extent of their "belief."

Take, for example, John the Baptist. Some who heard him described John as "a lamp that burned and gave light." They liked his preaching. They liked the sensation John had created. They applauded the movement that put John at the top of things—some would have even put John in competition with Jesus. John's role was to point to Jesus, and yet many of his admirers missed this reality.

Many of John's followers searched the Scriptures, so that the written word came to be an end in itself. The Scriptures did not point them to Jesus. Others held sacred the traditions of Moses but missed the truth to which the traditions should lead them.

Look around you and contemplate the mighty things that are happening in the name of Jesus Christ—the One whom God has sent, the One the enemies of Jesus do not believe.

The Jewish leaders clamor for absolute proof. God has given them the proof, but they will not believe the evidence before their very eyes. They are blind to the truth. Hence, they "diligently study the Scriptures." But they twist the Scriptures to prove trivial things—things that do not involve the central message of God. They pry into this and that, but they miss what God is really saying. God in the whole ministry of Jesus is trying to tell us something.

God is sending a message to us through the whole ministry of Jesus. In this ministry worldly success does not come to Jesus. He does not put stock in it: "I do not accept praise from men" (5:41). His glory is the glory of the "One and Only, who came from the Father" (1:14). The glory of the cross, the glory that turns the standards of this world upside down—that is the mark of the Messiah.

Verses 41-47 declare that Jesus will not be received by such people as One sent from God. And why? Jesus does not agree with them concerning the nature of God and what God is doing in the world. Many scholars say that verses 41-47 already are forecasting the shadows of the cross falling across Jesus' mission.

John 6:1-15. This miraculous feeding happens by the Sea of Galilee during Passover. Jesus feeds the physical hungers of the crowds, and yet he does more than that. He points beyond the bread to the Bread. Human beings are spiritual creatures, creatures of body, mind, and spirit, according to Christian views. They cannot be satisfied with the bread that will pass away. Like Moses, Jesus feeds the multitudes. But he does more than that; he ministers to the human yearning for God, for meaning, for full life.

The crowds, impressed by Jesus' miracles, fail to see them as signs of God's greater power. They try again to make Jesus king. He foils their efforts. What they need is not a ruler who will furnish bread and circuses. They need the abiding presence of God, a new relationship with God. Explore with class members the contrast between getting bread to satisfy daily hunger and being given the Bread of eternal life.

John 6:16-21. This passage speaks to our modern tendency to be frightened by Jesus' manifestation of his power to minister to our need. We miss the difference Jesus makes to our sense of calm and serenity. We cannot see that Jesus is in final command of the forces of nature. We live in a world where miracles have become quite ordinary, so we miss the sense of awe that the disciples experienced when they were confronted by the voice of Jesus. "It is I; don't be afraid." Therefore, we should question ourselves. Do we worship an ordinary Christ whose power is expressed only in commonplace ways? Or do we worship the Christ of the Prologue to John's Gospel? Have modern Christians lost the sense of awe? If so, how can we reclaim that sense of awe?

John 6:22-59. In this passage Jesus speaks to the human yearning and hunger for fuller life. He tells his hearers they seek him for the wrong reason. They want the loaves and fishes to continue, and they are concerned for immediate material satisfactions. Christianity is often welcomed as a means of getting material benefits in this world. It is rejected when it is understood as an absolute obedience to God. Jesus insists again that faith is a relationship with the eternal, not a transaction over the material things of life.

Yet his hearers ask Jesus a big question about this relationship: "What must we do to do the works God requires?" (6:28). They have been given tremendous gifts and powers. God has richly endowed them with all things necessary to life. Still, they may be wasting their time on secondary things, on trivial pursuits.

Jesus answers them: "The work of God is this: to believe in one he has sent" (6:29). Jesus' emphasis is more on being than on doing. What they are will be expressed through their doing. In John's Gospel "to believe," we remember, means to bet one's whole being on the Lord. But not everyone appreciates who the Lord is.

Jesus meets with opposition because he identifies himself with God instead of with Moses. The Jews are offended when he calls himself the bread they should eat. Eating flesh and drinking blood violated their whole tradition. Jesus' flesh and blood (the bread and wine of Holy Communion) are understood today as God's way of giving God's self to us. When we eat Christ's flesh and drink his blood, we have life by God's grace. Bread becomes more than bread—it is God's life given to us through Jesus Christ. This life is God's gift. Our salvation comes to us from above, as Jesus told Nicodemus. Faith is God's gift of sustaining power through time and eternity. Faith confers eternal life now and results in resurrection at the last day.

Why should Jesus' hearers believe in him? His coming in lowliness and love speaks to their depths. Jesus is different from all the other religious heroes they have known. He reveals the very grace and love of God. He comes

teaching, reconciling, healing, suffering, and dying because this is the way the eternal God must deal with sin.

In this way Jesus gives to humankind the true bread of life. This bread, this salvation, is for all. Jesus says, "He who comes to me will never go hungry, and he who believes in me will never be thirsty" (6:35). He promises his hearers that anyone who comes to him he will not cast out. Jesus declares that he is the living bread that came down from heaven. If anyone eats of this bread, that one shall live forever.

So the Christian feeds on Christ—participates in the strength of Christ, follows Christ's teaching, attains the mind of Christ, and makes his or her own the values that Christ wants in daily existence.

John 6:60-71. Not everyone is equipped and ready to follow. The disciples, hearing Jesus' proclamation, remark on how hard this teaching is to accept, and "from this time many of his disciples turned back and no longer followed him." In response, Peter makes a very early declaration of the holiness of Jesus. In sharp counterpoint to the affirmation of faith, Jesus ominously announces that one of the intimate circle will betray him. Is it at this point, perhaps, that Judas also "turned back and no longer followed" even though he remained for the time in the inner circle?

DIMENSION THREE: WHAT DOES THE BIBLE MEAN TO ME?

John 5:1-18—Do I Want to Be Well?

Review this passage again and then raise these questions. Do you need to be healed? Of what do you need to be healed? The tendency to give up? to flee from God's mercy? How does the lame man's illness differ from yours? Have you been guilty of evading a healing? What were your excuses? When have you experienced Christ's healing? Are you ready for change in your life? Are you, like the enemies of Jesus, holding on to a second-best in religion? What should be your attitude toward sabbath observance?

John 5:19-29—What Does the Messiah Mean to Me?

How might the disciples have heard all these comments about the dead hearing the voice of the Son of God and about the dead being raised? What kind of hope does that bring to you, if any, that believers are not condemned, but cross over from death to life? What do you think condemns a person?

John 6:1-5—What Does the Feeding of the Multitudes Mean to Me?

What does the story of the feeding of the five thousand say to your religious need today? What does this story say to the church today? What does your personal faith have to do with Jesus, the Bread of life?

John 6:16-21—Jesus Walking on the Water

What challenge does John 6:16-21 present to you? How do you find calm amid the storms of life? Do you really believe in the Christ who heals and commands the forces of nature?

John 6:22-71—What Does It Mean for Me to Live on the Bread of Life?

How is Christ the giver of the bread of life to you? When have you experienced him as the giver? as the bringer of judgment? What does it mean for you to live by Christ, the Bread of life?

When Jesus spoke again to the people, he said, "I am the light of the world. Whoever follows me will never walk in darkness, but will have the light of life" (8:12).

4

Jesus the Light of the World

John 7–8

DIMENSION ONE:
WHAT DOES THE BIBLE SAY?

Answer these questions by reading John 7

1. Why does Jesus go about in Galilee instead of Judea? (7:1)

   Jesus goes around Galilee because the Jews in Judea are waiting to take his life.

2. What do Jesus' brothers tell him to do? (7:3)

   His brothers tell him to leave Galilee and to go to Judea so that Jesus' disciples "may see the miracles you do."

3. When Jesus leaves for the feast and the Jews are looking for him, what do they say? (7:11-12)

   Some say he is a good man; others charge he is deceiving the people.

4. When Jesus goes into the Temple and teaches, what causes the Jews to be amazed? (7:15)

   The Jews are amazed at Jesus' learning. They ask how it is that Jesus has "such learning without having studied."

5. How does Jesus answer them? (7:16-24)

   He says his teaching is not his own but comes from God, whose honor he seeks. He reminds them that Moses had given them the Law, yet they do not keep it. Jesus asks why they seek to kill him and reminds them the Law of Moses condemns their desire to kill him. He asks, "If a child can be circumcised on the Sabbath so that the law of Moses may not be broken, why are you angry with me for healing the whole man on the Sabbath?"

6. How do some of the people of Jerusalem react? (7:25-27)

   The people of Jerusalem ask if Jesus is the man the authorities are trying to kill. They say he spoke publicly. Can it be that the authorities really know Jesus is the Christ? They say the possibility of Jesus' messiahship is denied because his origin is known.

7. What happens when the Pharisees hear the crowd whispering about Jesus? What is Jesus' response? (7:32-34)

   The chief priests (Sadducees) and Pharisees (bitter enemies of the Sadducees) unite in sending the Temple guards to arrest Jesus. Jesus speaks to them of his death and says that where he is going his enemies cannot come and find him.

8. What does Jesus do and say on the last day of the Feast? (7:37-39)

   He stands up and says loudly, "If anyone is thirsty, let him come to me and drink." Jesus asserts he is the water of life.

9. What happens when the people hear these words? (7:40-44)

   The people become divided over Jesus and his claims; some think he is a prophet, others the Christ. Some want to arrest him. But no one lays hands on him.

10. How is Nicodemus involved in the dispute? (7:50-52)

   Nicodemus intervenes when the Pharisees argue over the crowds who are supporting Jesus. Nicodemus says the Jewish law judges no man "without first hearing him to find out what he is doing."

Answer these questions by reading John 8

11. What happens when Jesus returns to the Temple? (8:1-11)

Jesus is faced with a woman caught in the act of adultery. Jesus resolves the conflict and the charge with the statement that he does not condemn the woman. He says for her to go and sin no more and for others who would condemn her to act only if they have not sinned themselves.

12. What happens after the incident of the woman taken in adultery? (8:12-30)

Jesus, proclaiming he is the light of the world and that he is doing the will of God, explains his mission again. The Jews dispute among themselves about the meaning of Jesus' claims. They miss his claims to oneness with God.

13. What does Jesus now say "to the Jews who had believed him"? (8:31-32)

He tells them that if they hold to his teaching, they are his true disciples. They will know the truth, and the truth will set them free.

14. How does Jesus answer their assertion that they are free by being "Abraham's descendants"? (8:34-47)

Jesus says, "Everyone who sins is a slave to sin." The freedom of sonship to God comes only through the Son. Though they insist that God is their father (verse 41), their murderous aim and resistance to the truth deny this and mark them as children of the devil.

15. How does Jesus answer their insults? (8:49-58)

He says God is judge and will confirm true believers in him with eternal life. Refusal to believe, he says, cuts them off from Abraham who rejoiced in the hope of the coming Messiah. Then Jesus says, "I tell you the truth, before Abraham was born, I am!" thus claiming a pre-existence and oneness with God.

16. How does this confrontation end? (8:59)

The crowd picks up stones to throw at Jesus, but Jesus hides himself away from them and slips out of the Temple.

DIMENSION TWO: WHAT DOES THE BIBLE MEAN?

John 7:1-13. Beginning on the fifteenth day of the seventh month (September-October) and lasting eight days, the Feast of Tabernacles commemorated the desert wanderings of the people of Israel. It was a time of thanksgiving, the celebration of rich traditions, the joys of feasting, and general merriment. By appealing to the popular fancies of the crowds, Jesus could have used the occasion to enhance his image. He had made what the crowds and the Pharisees viewed as fantastic claims for himself. Would he compromise his claims and seek the agreement and approval of the crowd?

Why did Jesus not agree to go up to Jerusalem when his brothers advised him to? His time, he said, had not come. By this he meant that the hour of God, the right opportunity, had not arrived. The time was still not right for a fuller demonstration of the divine. Perhaps Jesus was giving us a lesson in patience. We want so much to achieve our goals quickly, so we rush off without the necessary supports—prayer, discipline, study, an understanding of our problems, and a wise plan of action. We become more concerned with our public relations, with our image, than with the truth and the help of God.

When Jesus did go to Jerusalem *in private* what did he find? He met with much confusion. The Jews were searching for him, most of them not knowing whom they were seeking. Some people quickly agreed he was a good man. Others thought he was "Public Enemy Number 1." They should have asked: Is he the Christ, the self-communication of God to the world, the fulfillment of human hopes and dreams, the Word made flesh and living among us?

Even Jesus' enemies asked who he was. Who is Jesus? This is still the crucial question. Discuss the identity of Jesus with class members. Why does so much depend on who he is? What is God saying to us through him? Why is Jesus loved? Why is Jesus hated? What happens when we are indifferent to Jesus' claims?

John 7:14-24. We met much of the argument carried on here in Chapter 5. The enemies of Jesus do not believe in his person—that he is the One he claims to be. Therefore, they reject his mission. The situation regarding Jesus was similar to that of a well-known person today. You know how it is for people to say, "I don't like him or her. I'll oppose what he or she stands for." Jesus' foes said that he could not have come from God.

Jesus responded to these critics with his claim made at the beginning: His teaching was not his own; it came from God. Jesus was acting on God's authority. The people should judge him by the work he was doing, not by superficial appearances. Ask class members whether they think we judge Jesus by superficial appearances. Have the appearances of evil in our world so overwhelmed us that we miss the good in our world?

JESUS THE LIGHT OF THE WORLD

John 7:25-31. Some people were familiar with Jesus' family background. To them Jesus was merely a local boy; he could not be the fulfillment of the Scriptures. To them and to many others nothing good could come out of Nazareth. The writer of John does not mention Jesus' birthplace nor the expectation that the Messiah would be a descendant of King David. The Messiah would come in a highly dramatic way, not as a poor preacher and teacher.

Others believed on Jesus because his signs were in accord with what they understood of the Scriptures. They believed because in him they encountered God. Discuss the question, Why do we believe in Jesus?

John 7:32-52. The shadow of the cross now looms over the whole mission of Jesus. The authorities would gladly arrest him and put him to death, but they fear the people. They make another attempt to take him in, but they fail. Ordered to take Jesus captive, the Temple guards return empty-handed. This time they are overcome by awe in the face of Jesus' statements (7:46).

Jesus speaks according to the symbolism of the Feast of Tabernacles: Water stands for life. Without it we die. Without water life becomes impossible. Every Jew remembered the stories of how water had saved their people in the desert. Jesus now proclaims that he is the water of life, the very sustainer of the people's being, satisfying their deepest physical and spiritual needs.

What did the people say when they heard Jesus' promise that he is the water of life? Read verses 40-44. What would we have said?

Foiled in their attempt to arrest Jesus, the Pharisees began accusing the crowds. They expressed contempt for the crowd, showing that these people were not following the leadership of the Pharisees. They dismissed the people as an ignorant lot.

What attitude of the Pharisees have you seen in the church? Do you think Jesus approves of attitudes of contempt for the poor and the homeless? Ask class members to recall expressions of those attitudes they have seen in the newspapers or heard on radio and television.

John 7:53–8:11. Perhaps not a part of the original Gospel, this story about Jesus and his response to a helpless sinner was probably circulated in the early church. One important collection of manuscripts places this story after Luke 21:38. Many scholars think this position in Luke is the logical place for it. Read the concluding verses of Luke 21, and then read John 8:3-11. Does this story seem to fit in well? Now read John 7:45-52 and 8:12-20. Does anything seem to be missing in the sequence of events? The vocabulary of this story is different from John's, and the words used are more common to Luke's Gospel. Some editions of the Bible place John 7:53–8:11 in a footnote or identify it as a possible addition.

The important fact is that we have this precious story for our instruction. What does the story teach us?

1. *Beware of the callousness and ruthlessness of the Pharisees toward a person trapped in sin.* The religious leaders were quick to expose the woman to public disgrace. Acting from their own religious motives, they would gladly have stoned the woman to death. Their traditions and community attitudes approved their cruel intentions toward the unfortunate sinner.

2. *Beware of the temptation to use ancient law and custom to counter God's will for compassion toward sinners.* The Pharisees were locked into the past. They could not see that they and many others had a vested interest in the darkness and inequities of their time. They needed a weapon to discount Jesus, for he was a judgment on the status quo. They knew the demand for stern punishment of the woman would be popular in some circles. Yet they probably also knew Jesus was lifting a new standard against an ancient wrong.

3. *Beware of quick and unjust judgments.* The Pharisees came to Jesus evidencing quick temper and hostility. He was their real target. They wanted to trap him into an unjust judgment. But they had forgotten one thing: They too were sinners. The poor woman they had brought to Jesus was a member of the same human club as they. Jesus spoke to their consciences when he wrote in the sand and placed responsibility back on them.

4. *Be ready to open your minds to the compassion of God that hates the sin but loves and cares for the sinner.* When we forget the compassion advocated by Christ, we become capable of great wrongs against his creatures. Then we forget that we too will be brought to judgment. In this way they miss the reality of divine forgiveness toward others and toward ourselves.

John 8:12-20. Jesus picked the time of the first day of the feast to announce to the people that he is the light of the world: "Whoever follows me will never walk in darkness, but will have the light of life" (verse 12b). Jesus proclaimed himself as the light of God to the world. He called the people to follow him. To walk in Jesus' footsteps means, therefore, not to go wrong. It means to have Jesus' presence and support for our lives.

We have met the images of light and darkness in our previous study (see 1:5, 9; 3:19). The images of light and darkness are familiar in Judaism. In this faith many passages of Scripture speak of God, the Torah, and the people of Israel as light. Promises of light coming into this dark world pervade the Old Testament. Psalm 27:1 proclaims, "The LORD is my light and my salvation." Isaiah 60:19 promises, "The LORD will be your everlasting light." And Micah 7:8 assures us, "Though I sit in darkness, / the LORD will be my light."

In the passage from John's Gospel, however, the author connects light and judgment. Light gives life, as when a plant denied light suddenly receives light and begins to turn green. The light is not given to judge, however, but to save. Light gives us truth, and by that light we judge ourselves. We judge ourselves when we prefer darkness to

God's light. We judge ourselves by our response to the light.

So judgment comes on us when we choose darkness rather than light. To live in darkness means to lie to ourselves about our human situation. It means to refuse to hear the truth and to turn our backs on those who speak the truth.

When do we deny the light? We deny the light when we are complacent about conditions that maim human beings and make of life a dog-eat-dog existence. Darkness has overwhelmed us when we accept force, for example, as the final arbiter of human problems and disputes, when we meekly accept economic injustice in business and commerce. Darkness has taken over when we ignore prophetic voices all about us who would warn us of disasters to come.

The Gospel of John warns us against accommodating ourselves to darkness and piously calling it light. We live in a world where love is set against hatred, love is set against death, and truth stands against falsehood. By our choices we judge ourselves.

John 8:21-59. In these verses Jesus stresses the true nature of discipleship. He emphasizes the close relationship between doing and knowing the truth. Suppose a person sets out to know the truth. If, however, that person's life remains governed by greed or lust, that person is not continuing in Christ's way but in the broad way of death.

Discipleship means, then, that we base our beliefs firmly. We see how Jesus demonstrates God's love in the world, and we live our days according to God's example in Jesus Christ. We accept what Jesus teaches about God's love, about the dangers of sin, and about the purpose of our lives. Discipleship means hearing the word of God and learning it through commitment. Discipleship means that we study the word of God and build up dependable habits for our study. We do not become learners by random, haphazard approaches to faith.

Discipleship requires that we learn from Jesus—to see what he valued and how he met life's issues. Discipleship means asking ourselves, "What is God's purpose for my life?" Discipleship means coming to the point of saying, "I am not my own; I belong to Another." When we reach that point, the truth has released us from fear and set us free.

The Jews rejected Jesus' understanding of freedom. They had only a partial grasp of it. For them, to be free meant to claim the Jewish birthright and to share in the Jewish tradition and law that exempted the people of Israel from slavery. Freedom? Yes, indeed, said these Jews. We have it. We are not subject to the external controls of the Romans or the Greeks. We are no one's slaves.

The Jews were descendants of Abraham. They believed this fact protected them and made them free. Jesus countered their claim. The Jews, he said, could not live on Abraham's merit. Theirs was a false sense of security. Being descendants of Abraham would not save them. They could not live off the achievements of their ancestors.

Jesus transferred the argument to a higher level. Who are the true sons of Abraham? he asked. They are those who overcome sin through the power of God. Jesus told the people to act as Abraham acted, to make God's will central in their lives. Moral stamina and spiritual sensitivity make one the true child of Abraham.

Jesus clinched his statement when he pointed to the intention of his enemies to kill him. He said these people do the bidding of their father. And who is their father? He is the devil. Jews who claim to be true children of Abraham and do not make God's will central in their lives cannot be descendants of the ancient patriarch.

In Jesus, God is confronting the people. They are being judged on their response to God's appeal to them through Jesus. When these people hate the truth and try to destroy it, they are doing the devil's work.

The enemies of Jesus now accuse him of being a Samaritan—a hated enemy. Indeed, they view him as demon possessed and as mad with the madness of the evil one.

Jesus' assurance of who he was turned on the direct approval of God for his word and work. This word he affirmed when he said that anyone who kept his word would never see death. Jesus was here pointing to the mighty claim the whole new Testament makes: Christ is victor over our two chief enemies: sin and death.

DIMENSION THREE: WHAT DOES THE BIBLE MEAN TO ME?

Jesus and Our Picture of Him

Jesus caused varying reactions among his fellow Jews. His brothers, for instance, reacted in a teasing manner (7:1-5). They did not believe in him as the Messiah, but they persisted in egging him on to provoke him to react. This attitude of tolerant contempt is evident in our world. We may forget that Christianity is a matter of life and death.

Hatred was the reaction of the Pharisees and chief priests to Jesus. They hated Jesus for stirring up change—change that threatened their comfortable way of life. Sometimes we love our way of life more than we love God. We hesitate to follow the sacrificial way of Christ that would lead us into change.

Those who hated Jesus sought to arrest him (7:30, 32). They had to in order to protect themselves. Our choice, if we choose to follow Christ, is to continue doing as we always have done or to do what Christ shows us to do. If our choice is not to follow Christ's direction, we must get rid of him.

Some persons met Jesus with arrogant contempt (7:15, 47-49). He did not have the right credentials in their eyes; he was not an educated rabbi, so how could he explain the law to them? We need to take great care before rejecting Jesus' teaching and love just because they do not meet our preconceived ideas. Listen to Jesus' words with an open heart and mind and be prepared to receive his love.

The crowd in Jerusalem reacted to Jesus with interest (7:11) and discussion (7:12, 43). They were interested in learning about Jesus and his message. But some folks still wondered who Jesus was and where his authority came from. Their discussion sometimes became heated.

Do similar issues today divide people about Jesus? How can we help others clarify for themselves who Jesus is?

Jesus' claim "I am the light of the world" (8:12) was an astonishing claim. The rabbis taught that the name of the Messiah was *Light*. So Jesus' statement was incredible to the Jews.

What does Jesus' statement mean to us? What kinds of darkness does Jesus enlighten?

"I am the good shepherd; I know my sheep and my sheep know me . . . and I lay down my life for the sheep" (10:14-15).

—5—

Jesus the Good Shepherd

John 9–10

DIMENSION ONE:
WHAT DOES THE BIBLE SAY?

Answer these questions by reading John 9

1. What do Jesus' disciples ask him about the "man blind from birth"? (9:2)

   They ask Jesus why the man was born blind. Did his parents' sins cause the man's blindness?

2. How does Jesus answer them? (9:3-5)

   Jesus says that the man was born blind so that God's work might be displayed in his life. While time allows we must do the work of God, Jesus says; for the night comes when no one can work. He said, "While I am in the world, I am the light of the world."

3. What does Jesus do next? (9:6-7a)

   He spits on the ground, makes mud, and places the mud on the man's eyes. Then he tells the man to go and wash himself in the pool of Siloam.

4. What happens to the man born blind? (9:7b)

   The man does as he is told, and his blindness is healed.

5. What happens next? (9:13-16)

   The man is brought before the Pharisees. They question him, and he tells them what happened. The Pharisees are not satisfied with his answer and are divided over what is happening.

6. What do the Jews do? (9:18-29)

   They call the parents of the man who has received his sight and ask them about the man, but the parents say their son will have to speak for himself. The Pharisees call the man before them a second time. They question him. He cannot

answer all their questions, but he stands plainly on his statement: "One thing I do know. I was blind but now I see!" This response leads the Pharisees to insult the man, saying he is a disciple of Jesus.

7. How does the man answer? (9:30-33)

   The man defies the Pharisees' claim that he had been born in sin and witnesses to what Jesus has done for him.

8. How does Jesus answer all this? (9:35-38)

   He confirms the witness of the man, who says he is a believer in the Son of Man.

Answer these questions by reading John 10

9. What image does Jesus use to describe himself? (10:1-15)

   He declares he is the good shepherd (10:11) who lays down his life for the sheep in contrast to those who come as thieves and robbers.

10. What does Jesus say about other sheep? (10:16)

    He says that he has many sheep who "are not of this sheep pen" whom he must bring also.

11. Jesus' words cause what reaction? (10:19-21)

    His words again divide the Jews. Many of them say that Jesus has a demon; others ask if a demon could open the eyes of the blind.

12. What do the Jews ask Jesus in the Temple? What does Jesus reply? (10:22-30)

    The Jews ask Jesus to end their suspense: Is he or is he not the Christ? Jesus replies that the miracles he does in "my Father's name" speak for him, but the Jews do not believe. Jesus' sheep recognize his voice and follow him, and he gives them eternal life. No one can take them from him. Jesus and the Father are one.

13. How do the Jews respond to Jesus? (10:31)

They take up stones to stone Jesus.

14. What does Jesus say to them, and what is their answer? (10:32-33)

Jesus says that he has shown them many great miracles; for which deed will they stone him? They answer that they are stoning Jesus, not for his good works, but for blasphemy—that he, a mere man, was claiming to be God.

15. How does Jesus answer their charge? (10:34-38)

He points out that it was written in their own law: "You are gods." They are called gods to whom the word of God came. Jesus says he has been set apart as God's to go into the world, he is acting on God's behalf, and he and the Father are one. He asks them to accept the evidence of his miracles.

16. What happens then? (10:39-42)

The Jews try to seize Jesus, but he escapes across the Jordan to the place where John had been baptizing. The crowds come to Jesus, "and in that place many believed in Jesus."

DIMENSION TWO:
WHAT DOES THE BIBLE MEAN?

John 9:1-12. Read some Old Testament passages that express the belief that the sins of the fathers are visited upon the children: Exodus 20:5b; 34:7; Numbers 14:18; Deuteronomy 5:9.

Explore with class members any questions raised by the assumption that the sins of the parents result in the afflictions of their children. What picture of God do we get from these Old Testament verses? According to Jesus, how is God related to our physical calamities? How is God's power manifested in these afflictions? Jesus sees in these sufferings the opportunity for God's compassion and grace to be shown. He sees the healing of the man blind from birth as a sign of his own coming as the light of the world.

Ask: Does trouble draw from you a response of courage and a challenge to realize how God's work is manifested in your life?

Why do you think Jesus warns his followers to do the work of God while there is still time? Discuss our use of time. All of us have had the experience of knowing a person who died. Later we ask ourselves. Why didn't I tell this person how much I love him or her? Why didn't I ask this person the questions that he or she alone could answer? Business people sometimes place on the walls of their offices the word *NOW*. Jesus warns us to value the now and to learn its urgency. What changes should we make to give priority to the relationship between Jesus and us in our daily life?

Jesus' method of healing is part of his whole self-giving that expresses the very nature of God. Jesus shares our life and meets us on the level of our daily existence. Jesus comes to us in terms of the life we know.

This principle is illustrated in *The White Nile*, by Alan Moorehead, where the author discusses the way Jesus' method prompted Dr. David Livingstone in his efforts to preach Christ in Africa.[1] For thirty years Livingstone made unceasing efforts to evangelize the African people and to bring an end to the slave trade of central Africa. Livingstone explored the unknown regions of the continent, especially as he searched to discover the sources of the Nile. His description of the massacre of helpless people at Nyangwe raised worldwide concern over the slave traffic and forced the sultan of Zanzibar to shut down the slave market on that island off Africa's east coast.

Moorehead writes that Livingstone's mission began and ended in Africa. The world-renowned doctor lived with the Africans. He ate their food, slept in their huts, and suffered the diseases and hardships the Africans endured. Livingstone once wrote: "The strangest disease I have seen in this country seems really to be broken-heartedness, and it attacks free men who have been captured and made slaves."[2]

Livingstone never lost his determination to make life better for the Africans and to end their exploitation. Moorehead says Livingstone possessed a quality that the Arabs described as *baraka*, "the power of enhancing life and making it appear better than it was before." Livingstone's mere presence seemed to have conferred a blessing upon those who met him. Even the Arab slave traders felt his spiritual quality and helped Livingstone when they could.

John 9:13-23. Review the events recorded in John 5:1-18. What common themes do you and class members find in John 5:1-18 and John 9:13-23? Why do you think so much emphasis is placed on Jesus' healing on the sabbath?

Jesus had broken the sabbath law, and for this some Pharisees were merciless. In Jewish life a person was culpable if on the sabbath he or she put out a lamp to spare the lamp or put oil in the lamp to spare the wick. A person could not walk on the sabbath wearing sandals containing nails; for the weight of the nails was a burden, and burdens could not be carried on the sabbath. Healing was forbidden on the sabbath. One could give medical help only if a life was endangered. Jesus rose above the pettiness of these rules. He put human life above excessive regulations.

Discuss the attitude of the Pharisees. They, like many people, tended to condemn any religion or any religious observance that was different from theirs. Do we sometimes hold similar attitudes?

John 9:24-34. Why did the Pharisees expel the man cured of blindness from the synagogue? What testimony of the man could they not refute? The cured man had an experience that the Pharisees could not understand. It was outside their teachings. Though the man was not educated and could not speak in theological terms, still he knew what had happened to him, "One thing I do know. I was blind but now I see!" Though the Pharisees can see, they are blind to Jesus' power. What lesson do you think the incident of Jesus's healing teaches? What does it teach us about spiritual sight?

How do you think Jesus saves us from spiritual blindness? What is our role in this salvation? Describe times when new spiritual sight took the place of your blindness.

Such spiritual blindness may strike us all. Its presence may be so subtle that we are not aware of it. A writer who was discussing an English school said in a public speech: "Students learned much about Shakespeare and Milton there, but nothing about life." A thoughtful person might respond: Poor students—they lost sensitivity to the issues of good and evil and life and death. Shakespeare and Milton *are life*. How could students be so detached and parochial that they could not see that the masters of literature speak to every age?

Ask class members to recall Bible stories in which the lives of persons were turned around because new spiritual sight came to them. Jacob at Bethel (Genesis 28:10-17), the boy Samuel's call (1 Samuel 3:1-10), Isaiah in the Temple (Isaiah 6:1-8), Paul's conversion (Acts 9:1-19), Peter's vision of clean and unclean foods (Acts 10:9-16)—these and other stories may come to mind.

Think also of events in Christian history that changed a person's life. I can think of Saint Augustine's conversion in the Milanese garden, Saint Francis of Assisi's abandonment of the world to serve Christ, Martin Luther's discovery that the just shall live by faith, and John Wesley's experience in Aldersgate Street. In similar and less dramatic terms such experiences are still coming to persons all over the world.

How do you and class members think Jesus cures our blindness?

John 9:35-41. Jesus finds the healed man and challenges him to belief in the Son of Man. Commentators have often observed that God in Jesus Christ seeks out the man who was blind from birth. God is the seeking God who will reach us in all the events of our experience. That encounter may involve judgment, says Jesus. "For judgment I have come into this world, so that the blind will see and those who see will become blind."

We have met the idea of divine judgment several times already in John's Gospel. Here we might stress that divine judgment has its own way of correcting situations of evil: God allows the sinner to see for himself or herself the folly of shoddy relationships and conduct. The Pharisees were anxious to find out if Jesus were talking about them. "What?" many say indignantly, "Are we blind too?" They receive the disappointing answer, "If you were blind, you would not be guilty of sin; but now that you claim you can see, your guilt remains."

Many years ago a slumlord in Los Angeles was given a thirty-day sentence to live in one of his own slum properties. The apartment was rat-infested and roach-infested.

The judge decreed that the landlord should experience firsthand what it meant to live in his own building amid conditions that violated health, fire, and building code regulations.

Even without access to the details or merits of this case, it certainly seems to illustrate a principle of divine judgment. We have to live in the situations we have made for ourselves until in God's grace we are freed from them.

John 10:1-21. These verses present Jesus as the gate for the sheep. In the Middle East of Jesus' time, the sheepfolds on the hillsides were used to protect the sheep at night. The shepherd would lie down before the opening to the fold so that the sheep would have to go by him before they entered. The shepherd became the gate, for the sheep could neither enter nor go out without going over his body.

The "gate for the sheep"—this symbol pointed to the salvation of Jesus' own. Only through Jesus the gate could persons reach God. Jesus is the "way and the truth and the life"; no one can come to the Father except by him. If anyone enters through Jesus Christ, he or she will be saved. The ones who come advocating violence and trying to force their way into the fold are false leaders. These persons believe in murder and the exploitation of upheavals to gain advantages for themselves. Jesus' voice is the voice of peace, constructive reason, and compassion.

The author of John describes Jesus as the good shepherd. The Scriptures often depict us as lost sheep, and they portray Jesus as going out to seek us. The characteristic painting of this New Testament story presents God, not as one who sits upon a remote and impersonal throne, but as one who mixes in the common life we know. Jesus is the good shepherd reaching into the thorns on the wild hills to rescue the lost sheep. That is the picture of God we get from the New Testament.

Jesus knows his own—the humble ones who foster peace, love, and fullness of life. Jesus came not in war and bitter strife to bring in God's kingdom, not as the thief who seeks his own advantage.

The mark of the good shepherd is that he, unlike the hired hand, will give his life for his sheep.

Jesus' concern is not only for a small band of people of this fold. He is concerned for the world (John 3:16). The Gentiles must be brought into his Kingdom. His religion is universal—all people must be saved. First of all, Jesus comes to the house of Israel. Jesus makes clear that the revelation of God is intended for the Jews. But he is the Savior of all, one who will win the Gentiles. He speaks of one flock, who will hear his voice and for whom he will be one shepherd.

The Jews are offended and divided by Jesus' work. Some think he is mad. Others, reminded of his opening the eyes of the blind, ask whether his words can be those of an evil spirit.

How can Christians know Christ's voice in personal and social situations? Ask class members to name some attitudes and activities that Christ would disapprove. What attitudes would Christ approve? How is Jesus the gate of the sheepfold today? How can Christians distinguish between true and false leaders?

John 10:22-42. Why do you think Jesus made his claim to be the light of the world during the Festival of Lights?

The festival grew from Jewish experiences that went back to Antiochus IV Epiphanes, the king of Syria who ruled in the period 175–164 B.C. Antiochus came to his throne resolved to destroy Jewish culture and to introduce Greek thought and culture everywhere. Acting peacefully at first, he promoted Greek thought and lifestyles among the Jews. He urged the Jews to give up their religion and to become Greek in outlook. While some Jews went along with the tyrant, the people as a whole rejected Antiochus's campaign. Then the ruler attacked the Jewish people and sacked Jerusalem. According to reports of the time, some eighty thousand Jews were slain and an equal number were sold into slavery. Antiochus forbade Jews to own copies of the Law. He forbade Jewish women to circumcise their sons, and he crucified mothers who did so. Infants he slew, hanging them around the necks of their mothers.

Antiochus and his forces made the altar in the Temple an altar to Zeus, turned Temple rooms into brothels, and delivered the ultimate insult to the Jews: He offered up swine's flesh to the pagan divinities, a practice called to mind in the "desolating sacrilege."

These atrocities stirred the Jews to revolt. The war against Antiochus was led by the Maccabean brothers who threw off the tyrant's rule in 164 B.C. The Jews cleansed the Temple and rebuilt its altar. Then under Judas Maccabeus they set aside a time "of gladness and joy" in celebration of their victory. The festival was variously called the Festival of the Dedication of the Altar, the Memorial of the Purification, and the Festival of Lights. Huge lights in Jewish homes and in the Temple reminded the people of their hard-won freedom and that their faith had triumphed in a dark time.

Their successors, the faithful Hasidim, were the forerunners of the Pharisees.

Note that the conversation in this section of Scripture focuses on who Jesus is. What does it mean to us that Jesus Christ and the Father are one?

DIMENSION THREE: WHAT DOES THE BIBLE MEAN TO ME?

John 9 and 10—Guidance for Daily Life

Jesus used a common (for that day) method to heal the man blind from birth. Ancient people believed that spittle, especially the spittle from certain persons and fasting spittle, had great curative power. Even today we often put a burned or cut finger in our mouth almost without thinking. Healing, after all, depends to a great extent on the patient's faith in the treatment.

By his compassion and caring attitude, Jesus gained the man's confidence and was able to heal him. We can show the same compassion and caring for those in our world who are hurting and who are outcasts. How can we apply this love and care?

What are some ways that our eyes can be opened to situations around us that need our attention? How has this happened to you?

The image of a good shepherd is one of comfort and caring. A shepherd does everything for his sheep—directs them to sources of food and water, provides a safe place for them to sleep, and searches for them when they are lost. Jesus wants to be our good shepherd. In what ways is he our good shepherd?

[1]*The White Nile,* by Alan Moorehead (Harper and Brothers, 1960); pages 99–119.

[2]From *The White Nile,* page 100.

"I am the resurrection and the life. He who believes in me will live, even though he dies; and whoever lives and believes in me will never die" (11:25-26).

— 6 —

The Resurrection and the Life

John 11–12

DIMENSION ONE: WHAT DOES THE BIBLE SAY?

Answer these questions by reading John 11

1. What does Jesus say about the illness of Lazarus? (11:4)

    Jesus says that Lazarus's illness "will not end in death." The sickness is for manifesting the glory of God "so that God's Son may be glorified through it."

2. What do the disciples say to Jesus when he says they must go back to Judea? (11:8)

    They reply that the Jews have been trying to stone Jesus and question whether he should go to Judea again.

3. What does Jesus say about Lazarus's death? (11:11, 14-15)

    Lazarus, Jesus says, has fallen asleep. Then he says Lazarus is dead; and for the disciples' sake Jesus is glad he was not in Bethany when Lazarus died.

4. What do Martha and Mary do when Jesus arrives? (11:20)

    Martha goes out to meet Jesus, while Mary stays at home.

5. When Jesus sees Mary weeping, what does he say? (11:33-34)

    Jesus asks where Lazarus has been buried.

6. What does Jesus do next? (11:38-43)

    Jesus, deeply moved, goes to the tomb and says, "Take away the stone." He tells them if they will believe, they will see the glory of God. When they remove the stone, Jesus prays and calls out with a loud voice, "Lazarus, come out!"

7. What is the reaction of the crowd? (11:45-46)

    Many of crowd put their faith in Jesus. Others in the crowd go to the Pharisees and tell them what Jesus has done.

8. What does Caiaphas, the high priest, tell the Sanhedrin? (11:49-52)

    He predicts Jesus will die for the people. Jesus will die to save the whole nation from perishing. Jesus, he says, will not only die for the Jewish nation "but also for the scattered children of God, to bring them together and make them one."

9. What happens as a result of the Sanhedrin's meeting? (11:53)

    The authorities plot to take Jesus' life.

10. What happens next? (11:54-57)

    Jesus goes quietly "to a village called Ephraim" and stays with the disciples. Before the Passover the Jews come to Jerusalem for ceremonial cleansing before the feast. They ask questions and look for Jesus. Meanwhile, the chief priests and Pharisees issue orders for Jesus' arrest.

Answer these questions by reading John 12

11. What do Jesus' friends do for him when he comes to Bethany? (12:2-3)

    They prepare a dinner in his honor. Martha serves while Lazarus reclines at the table with Jesus. Mary anoints Jesus' feet and dries them with her hair. She pours over them a costly pint of pure nard.

12. What is Judas's question about Mary's act? (12:4-5)

    Judas wants to know why the perfume was not sold and the money given to the poor.

13. How does Jesus respond to Judas? (12:7-8)

Jesus tells Judas to leave her alone; it was meant that this perfume be used for his burial. There will always be poor persons, but Jesus would not always be with them.

14. What does the crowd do? (12:9)

The people gather to see Jesus and Lazarus, whom Jesus had raised from the dead.

15. What do the chief priests plan to do? (12:10-11)

They plan to kill Lazarus. On account of Lazarus many of the Jews are going over to Jesus and putting their faith in him.

16. What does the crowd do next? (12:12-13)

The people take palm branches and go out to meet Jesus as he approaches Jerusalem, shouting "Hosanna!" and hailing him as "the King of Israel."

17. What does Jesus do then? (12:14-15)

Jesus finds a young donkey, sits upon it, and quotes the Scripture that he fulfills: "Your king is coming, seated on a donkey's colt." (See Zechariah 9:9.)

18. What is Jesus' response to the questions of the Greeks? (12:23-26)

Jesus says the time has come for him to be glorified. He says, "Unless a kernel of wheat falls to the ground and dies, it remains only a single seed. But if it dies, it produces many seeds."

19. How do various ones, including Jesus, respond to the voice from heaven? (12:29-32)

The crowd standing by say it thundered. Others say that an angel spoke to Jesus. Jesus says the voice came for the people's benefit, not for his. He says his death will judge the world and defeat the devil ("the prince of this world"). When Jesus has been lifted up from the earth, he says he will draw all people to himself.

20. Why do many not believe in Jesus despite his signs? (12:37-41)

John points out that the unbelievers are confirming the words of Isaiah. As in Isaiah's day, the people are being blind and hard-hearted.

21. Why do others not express a belief in Jesus? (12:42-43)

They fear the authorities may put them out of the synagogue, and they love "praise from men more than praise from God."

DIMENSION TWO: WHAT DOES THE BIBLE MEAN?

John 11:1-16. The Resurrection is the central theme of the whole Gospel of John. Begin the session by asking class members why the discussion of the Resurrection recurs throughout the whole Gospel. Ask various class members to read aloud these verses from John: 5:25-29; 11:24-26. Then ask why they think John's discussion of the Resurrection is centered in the story of a single human being, a man named Lazarus, whose name means "God has helped." This individual is chosen for a great sign that points to the greater manifestation of God.

Share this summary of the New Testament teaching on the Resurrection with the class members.

> The New Testament assumes Jesus Christ's resurrection from the dead. The resurrection of Jesus was the work of God, confirmed in the lives of redeemed sinners and in the rise of the church to power and victory from the ashes of defeat.
>
> The earliest New Testament witness to Jesus Christ's resurrection may be the affirmation of 1 Corinthians 15. Here Paul related the resurrection of Christ to the resurrection of believers. The heart of the gospel is found in the great act of God in raising Jesus from the dead.
>
> To deny Jesus Christ's resurrection means to abandon the gospel. Stressing the corporate nature of our human existence, Paul believed that just as all persons share in the death of Adam, so those who live "in Christ" will share in the life of Christ eternally. The belief in our resurrection and God's act in raising Jesus Christ stand together.
>
> Paul discussed the kind of body we will have after our resurrection; he concluded that it will be a "spiritual body." In Paul's view, the body can be both physical and spiritual, a body of flesh and a body of spirit. Though the body of flesh dies, the body of spirit is raised to eternal life. Thus Paul believed the individuality and continuity of the person is preserved. Paul did not accept the Greek concept that a radical division exists between body and soul. He did not lose the uniqueness of the individual by submerging the person in some vague spirituality or some other impersonal essence. The resurrection of Jesus Christ affirms that the individual is raised up to share in eternal life with Christ.
>
> Jesus Christ's resurrection is a mystery. The Resurrection is God's mighty act for our salvation, an act that we cannot fully understand but something we can accept through faith in, personal trust of, and obedience to Christ. The Resurrection was Christ's victory over sin and death.[1]

The events recorded in John 11:1-16 have their basis in the Incarnation. These events are likewise based in God's eternal love, on God's mighty acts of redemption.

God "proves" God by doing what is true to the divine nature. Our modern habit is to look for the "proof" of God by looking to the immensities of space, the wonder of the stars, predictable sequences in nature, and the ordering of all things by God's foresight and power.

John 11:17-37. The friends of Jesus are grieving for Lazarus when Jesus arrives in Bethany. Jesus comes to them as the *final resurrection.* He brings the assurance that fellowship with God is possible here and now. Jesus tells them that eternal life, with an entirely new quality—a new hope—is possible now.

Life is dismal indeed when the Christian hope is lost. What do we miss when we no longer have the assurance of the Christian hope of eternal life? Theologian Emil Brunner has dealt with this question in his book *Eternal Hope.*[2] Among the consequences to us when hope in eternal life is lost are these:

1. *Panic fear of the end.* Having lost the peace that faith in eternal life gives, the individual seeks to find meaning in the scramble for material goods, for wealth, and for sensual gratification of immediate desires. Life becomes purposeless, so that the person asks: When the doors threaten to close and all seems over forever, why not lose oneself in immediate preoccupations? Life is aimless, and we have so little time. Let us eat, drink, and be merry while the rat race lasts.

2. *The tendency to nihilism. Nihilism* is the viewpoint that traditional values and beliefs are unfounded and that human life is senseless and useless. In society the idea takes hold that all morals and ethics are relative and that human society can find a substitute for hope in eternal life. So the idea emerges that belief in human progress can take the place of this hope—that belief in progress can take the place of the kingdom of God. Accordingly, the loss of the hope of eternity demolishes the value of the individual. Human life becomes very cheap if we do not believe there is a world beyond this present one. Often we make purely temporal ideas absolute, and our tendency is to ascribe an absolute value to the race, the tribe, the political and social system, in place of faith in God.

3. *The concealment of death.* When we no longer see the person as destined for eternal life—as one everlastingly precious to God—a great sense of emptiness steals into our lives. Death marks the end of the individual's life. So we deceive ourselves about death and its finality. Often death is reported in the newspapers in ways that try to soften its harsh reality. A person does not die; he or she passes away.

4. *The absolute valuation of natural vitality,* that is, "the brutal justification and operation of the *will in power.*" When the restraints on persons that belief in the afterlife gives are withdrawn, then people are ready for totalitarianisms of the worst sort. Sheer human power-grasping is recognized as permissible. It can "make itself absolute and unleash itself in boundless ferocity." Humanity took that step, Brunner says, in the absolutism of Marx, Lenin, and Stalin.

This then is Brunner's summary of the results of the loss of faith in eternal life. Ask class members why we become contemptuous of persons when our faith in eternal life is lost. Do they believe that life breaks up when people do not believe in eternal life anymore? How have they seen this break-up happen?

John 11:38-44. Jesus gave three directions at Lazarus's tomb: "Take away the stone," "Lazarus, come out," "Take off the grave clothes and let him go."

What are the stones that keep us entombed today? Guilt for past sins? Worries and cares? Fears? Lack of trust in God?

Jesus speaks to our dead selves. He becomes "the resurrection and the life" to us when we are dead in our sins and dead to God. The parable of Lazarus is for us all.

How would you describe the true environment of persons—the true home of the human spirit? What does it mean for us to be called to be human? How can we "come out to life"?

John 11:45-57. Jesus' sign of raising Lazarus from the dead causes people to take action. "Many of the Jews" believe in Jesus. They accept this sign as pointing to his messiahship. Other Jews, however, go directly to the Pharisees and tell them "what Jesus had done." Why did Jesus' words and actions produce divisions among the people? What are ways Jesus' words and the action of Christians produce divisions in our world?

Immediately the Sanhedrin is called together to decide what they shall do about Jesus. The Council members are afraid of losing their favored position of authority under the Romans. What was Caiaphas's prophecy?

The tension is thick in Jerusalem as the Jews gather for the Feast of the Passover. They look here and there for Jesus. "What do you think? Isn't he coming to the Feast at all?" This verse may have been used in the early church as preparation for celebrating Holy Communion. As often as we fail Christ, will he still come to our feast? Christ always remains faithful to us though we are faithless to him.

The danger is growing for Jesus. The chief priests and Pharisees are asking for anyone to inform them of Jesus' whereabouts "so that they might arrest him."

Why did all eyes turn toward Jerusalem at the time of the Passover? Read Exodus 12:1-28. This passage is an account of the Feasts of Passover and Unleavened Bread. The Jews valued these feasts very highly. The stories of the feasts can act for Christians as a parable of the whole existence of humankind. Of their own free will the Jews went down into Egypt. There the Jews became enslaved until God used Moses for their deliverance. Just as the Jews were delivered from slavery by Moses, so the human race is delivered from sin and death by Jesus Christ.

John 12:1-11. Focus now on the story of the anointing of Jesus' body for burial. Some persons still see Mary's act as impractical and wasteful. Jesus was able, however, to recognize and accept Mary's impulsive act as a spontaneous outpouring of her gratitude for all Jesus meant to her. To be able graciously to accept is a difficult thing for most of us to do. Yet Jesus saw beyond what we may see as an embarrassing moment to Mary's affectionate heart. In the Gospel of Matthew's account of this event, Jesus says, "She has done a beautiful thing" (Matthew 26:10).

Note in the Gospels of Matthew and of Mark (Mark 14:3-9, which is almost word for word the same) this person is identified simply as "a woman." No hint at all is given as to her character or where she came from. The Gospel of Luke (Luke 7:36-47) places the story very early in the text, uses the anointing story to set up an object lesson for the host about forgiveness, says nothing about the poor, and identifies her as "a woman who had lived a sinful life." Nowhere is this woman identified as Mary Magdalene, although tradition has suggested it was she. In fact, John has identified her as Mary, the sister of Martha and Lazarus; a fine, upstanding member of a very respected family. On one point all the Gospels agree—Jesus thinks the woman did a good and proper thing, and she has been immortalized for it.

The story may suggest to some persons the relationship between worship (Mary's act of anointing Jesus' feet) and Christian service (giving to the poor). How do you see that relationship working in your church? How does the Judas spirit make itself known today? Would the love that prompted Mary's deed ever neglect the needs of the poor?

John 12:12-19. Jesus enters Jerusalem riding on a young donkey, thus fulfilling the prophet Zechariah's prophecy that the Messiah will arrive "gentle and riding on a donkey" (Zechariah 9:9). Riding on a donkey indicates that Jesus comes in peace. (Riding a horse indicates the rider is bent on war.) Jesus is coming as the Prince of Peace, not as the warrior king most Jews are expecting.

Why do you think Jesus now shows himself dramatically as the Messiah? How does Jesus reverse the standards of this world? What do his actions imply for Christians today? What might our attitudes toward the values and institutions of contemporary culture be? Give some examples of how Christians are reversing the success and power standards of this world.

John 12:20-36a. Jesus' public ministry is drawing to a close. To the Greeks who come seeking Jesus, he speaks some hard words: One "who loves his life will lose it." Jesus is telling of his own death and of how his followers must approach life. Only because persons have been willing to face death have great ideas lived. Only when we bury personal ambitions can we serve God.

What kind of glorification does Jesus now face? Jesus' glorification will come at his crucifixion. Why would Jesus first pray to be saved from this hour? Most people do not want to die, especially when they see more challenges to be met in life. Obedience does not come without cost. Why must Jesus go to the cross? Jesus knows that his obedience in going to the cross will deal a deathblow to Satan. The sign of Jesus raised up on the cross will draw all people to Jesus.

John 12:36b-50. John quotes verses from the prophet Isaiah. These verses seem to say that our unbelief is due to God's action, that God has chosen some people to believe and others not to believe. Surely the God that Jesus taught about would not be so arbitrary.

William Barclay points out that a basic belief of the Jews was that God is behind everything. Nothing can happen outside the purpose of God. When a person does not accept God's message, God can still achieve God's purpose. God can use our unbelief for God's purposes.[3]

People find various reasons for not believing in God. Some of the Jews heard Jesus and believed him but would not confess it for fear of retaliation from the Pharisees, that "they would be put out of the synagogue; for they loved the praise from men more than praise from God" (12:42-43).

In his final words to the general public, Jesus repeats the claim that is basic to his life and teaching: In Jesus we are confronted with God. Jesus came into our world to save us. God's love sent Jesus, not God's wrath. Yet through Jesus' words we will be judged, the more so if we have heard his words and have not followed him.

DIMENSION THREE: WHAT DOES THE BIBLE MEAN TO ME?

The group may discuss the following topic or use the material in the student book.

The Resurrection and the Life

"I am the resurrection and the life. He who believes in me will live, even though he dies; and whoever lives and believes in me will never die" (11:25-26).

Jesus' words surely do not speak of our physical death; even Christians die physical deaths. Jesus was speaking of death to sin. In our selfishness we are dead to the needs of others. In our insensitivity we are dead to the feelings of others. In our petty dishonesties we are dead to honor. These deaths can be overcome, and we can receive new life when we hear Jesus' words and heed them.

Our new life brings us into a new relationship with God and with life. The new relationship with God brings us freedom. As we lose our fear and know absolutely that God is love, we are more open to live life as Jesus has commanded. Life becomes a lovely thing, and we have no fear of dying and going to live another life with God and Christ.

[1]Excerpt from "A Pauline Wordbook," by Woodrow A. Geier in *Paul: Leader's Guide,* pages 137–38. Copyright © 1987 by Graded Press.

[2]From *Eternal Hope,* by Emil Brunner, translated by Harold Knight (Westminster, 1954); pages 91–94.

[3]From *The Gospel of John,* Volume 2, revised edition, by William Barclay (Westminster, 1975); pages 132–33.

"Peace I leave with you; my peace I give you. . . . Do not let your hearts be troubled and do not be afraid" (14:27).

7

The Way and the Truth and the Life

John 13–14

DIMENSION ONE:
WHAT DOES THE BIBLE SAY?

Answer these questions by reading John 13

1. What does Jesus know that gives him the power and the will to wash the disciples' feet? (13:3)

   Jesus knows that God has put all things in his power, that he has come from God and is returning to God.

2. What does Jesus do before the Feast of the Passover? (13:4-5)

   He gets up from the supper table, prepares himself, and washes the disciples' feet.

3. What does Simon Peter say when Jesus comes to him? (13:6-9)

   Peter says that Jesus will never be allowed to wash his feet; but in response to Jesus' words, Peter asks Jesus to wash him all over.

4. How does Jesus answer Peter? (13:10)

   Jesus tells Peter that a person who has bathed is clean and "needs only to wash his feet."

5. What does Jesus say after he finishes the washing? (13:12-16)

   He resumes his place and tells the disciples he has just given them an example of how they should treat one another. "No servant," he says, "is greater than his master."

6. What does Jesus say about his disciples? (13:17-20)

   "Now that you know these things, you will be blessed if you do them." Jesus says he knows whom he has chosen and that "he who shares my bread has lifted up his heel against me" so that

the Scriptures may be fulfilled. Jesus says that when anyone receives a disciple, that person is receiving Jesus and the God who sent him.

7. How is the betrayal of Judas Iscariot presented? (13:21-30)

   Jesus is troubled after speaking with the disciples. He says one of them will betray him. "One of them, the disciple whom Jesus loved" (probably John) asks Jesus to tell who the betrayer is. Jesus replies that the one to whom he gives the piece of bread when it has been dipped is the betrayer. He gives the bread to Judas and tells him to do quickly what he will do.

8. What does Jesus say about the glorification of God and of himself? (3:31)

   "Now is the Son of Man glorified and God is glorified in him."

9. What counsel does Jesus give to his disciples? (13:33-35)

   "You will look for me. . . . Where I am going, you cannot come." Jesus gives them a new command to love one another. Their love should be founded on his love for them. They are Jesus' disciples if they have love for one another.

10. What does Simon Peter ask? (13:36a)

    Peter asks Jesus where he is going.

11. What is Jesus' reply? (13:36b)

    Jesus says Peter cannot come now but that later he can follow.

12. What does Jesus say to Peter when the disciple vows to lay down his life for Jesus? (13:38)

    Jesus tells Peter that the disciple will disown him three times before the rooster crows.

THE WAY AND THE TRUTH AND THE LIFE

13. What assurances does Jesus give to the disciples? (14:1-21)

"Do not let your hearts be troubled." "The words I say to you are not just my own. Rather, it is the Father, living in me, who is doing his work." Jesus speaks of the place he has prepared for them and that he will come back to take them there. Jesus says he is "the way and the truth and the life. No one comes to the Father except through me." He says he and the Father are one. Anyone who believes in Jesus will do the works that he does and even greater works. Jesus says the Spirit of truth will be in his followers: "I will not leave you as orphans; I will come to you." Anyone who keeps Jesus' commandments out of love will be loved by the Father.

14. What additional assurances does Jesus promise? (14:25-31)

God will send the Holy Spirit to be with the disciples. The Spirit will teach them all things and remind them of everything Jesus has said to them. Jesus will leave his followers with a peace that the world cannot give; so they should not be troubled or afraid. Jesus tells the disciples these things before they take place so that they may believe.

DIMENSION TWO: WHAT DOES THE BIBLE MEAN?

John 13:1-20. Chapter 12 describes the close of Jesus' public ministry. Now comes a lull in activity while Jesus is instructing his disciples about the meaning of his coming. He does this in the upper room and under serious threats against himself and his disciples. Jesus has shown the disciples that he is the way and the truth and the life; but now he wants to emphasize the meaning of these terms.

The disciples are at supper. During the meal, Jesus, who "knew that the Father had put all things under his power, and that he had come from God and was returning to God" (13:3), rose from the table, prepared for the washing, and began to wash the disciples' feet.

In the Gospel of Luke, a dispute arises among the disciples as they are traveling toward Jerusalem and this meal. "Also a dispute arose among them as to which of them was considered to be greatest" (Luke 22:24). Perhaps this dispute led to Jesus' actions at the meal.

Since the roads in Palestine were either dirty in dry weather or muddy in wet weather, most homes kept a jar of water and a towel near the door. The sandals people wore were merely a sole held on the foot by straps, giving little protection against the dust or mud. As each visitor to a home arrived, a servant or family member washed the visitor's feet. Perhaps the disciples were still so engrossed

in their dispute that no one would accept the duty of arranging for everyone's feet to be washed.

Here Jesus teaches the disciples and us a significant truth about ourselves. When we know where we come from, we are free persons. We are no longer orphans. We no longer feel lowborn. We no longer are under the evil power of the threat of being destroyed by insults and humiliations. We live in God's world, and we are free to serve God's creatures. We know from where we have come; we know to whom we shall return. Ours is no longer a craven existence.

Explore with class members the meaning of Christian freedom. Many counselors trace the spiritual maladies of individuals to an unawareness of who they are. We do not love God, nor do we love others, because we do not like ourselves. Our image of ourselves is distorted, faulty. We cannot cheerfully assume menial tasks for Christ.

Christianity speaks a message of true self-esteem. Christ is not concerned to buck up a false image of us. Left to ourselves, we are unlovely; but we share in the love of God. God values each of us with a love that is everlasting.

Who then is greatest in the kingdom of God? This question persists in the Gospels. In the upper room Jesus demonstrates the answer. To be eternally loved by God means to be free to serve: to be released from the slavish idea of competition, dominance, and superiority.

Simon Peter was at first enamored of worldly ideas of success and power. He vied for top recognition. Peter insisted on a total washing of himself, but he soon drew back from this possibility. Why did Peter change his attitude? What do you think about the total and deeper cleansing of baptism and participation in Jesus' movement? Are we Christians able to accept the baptism of Christ? What does that baptism involve? How do we respond when deep trouble comes? when we face hardships and sacrifices? Ask a class member to read aloud Mark 10:35-45. Then ask class members to give their views on true greatness.

John 13:21-30. When the disciples were told that one of them would betray Jesus, they began to look perplexedly at one another. "Who, me?" each said in effect.

Judas had been picked by Jesus for special honor, and yet Judas violated Jesus' trust and turned his Lord over to the authorities.

And it was night. The connection between Judas's deed and the fall of night makes for a powerful symbol. Is there something of Judas in each of us? When have we felt we have betrayed the truth?

What ultimately happened to Judas? Christians like to speculate about this question, but we do not have the answer. Matthew 27:3-5 and Acts 1:15-19 tell two different accounts of what happened to Judas. Review these passages along with others you have identified from the Gospel of John to get a composite picture of the kind of man John finds Judas to be. What does the Scripture tell us about Judas's plight? What kind of judgment falls on Judas? How does he suffer? What do you think about the solution to Judas's agony?

John 13:31-38. Now Jesus' hour has come. "Now is the Son of Man glorified." Jesus' glory comes at the cost of his life. The greatest glory comes from the greatest sacrifice. We remember Albert Schweitzer, not because he was a brilliant musician, theologian, or mathematician. We remember him because he sacrificed any success and fortune he may have gained in these fields to give his life to help people in Africa who did not have a doctor.

In Jesus, God is glorified. Through his complete obedience to God's will, Jesus gave supreme honor and glory to God.

Humans cannot know and love a Being who remains aloof and untouchable. Through the Incarnation and through Jesus' death on the cross God has shown God's glory in allowing us access to God. Now we know that God is love and understands our sorrow and pain.

God will also glorify Jesus. Though death on the cross was Jesus' glory, God demonstrated that glory in the Resurrection. Jesus' humiliation was changed to victory.

Even as he faced death, Jesus gave his disciples one last commandment: to love one another. Jesus' love for the disciples was selfless, sacrificial, understanding, and forgiving. Though they could not know all these facets of his love, Jesus held the disciples up to the best that they could be. He challenged them and us to follow his example and to love one another.

John 14:1-14. Why can we characterize this passage as the expression of calm in the midst of the gathering storm? Why can Jesus say, "Do not let your hearts be troubled"? Recall occasions when these words have been meaningful to you.

What kind of place has Jesus prepared for us? It is a place, not of separation, but where we realize divine love is incarnate in Christ. In this love Christians know that heaven is where Jesus is. It means that we enjoy even in the most bitter circumstances the assurance that Jesus' promises are true.

"No one comes to the Father, except through me." What is Jesus' answer to Thomas's question? How do we know the way? Do you think that events at the Last Supper tell us what the way is like?

What is Jesus' answer to Philip? How do you think experiences with Jesus help us to know God? We gain knowledge of God (verses 8-11) only through the person, work, and words of Jesus; and through prayer we may do even greater works than Jesus has done (verses 12-17).

Discuss Jesus' words, "You may ask me for anything in my name, and I will do it." Does this mean all prayer will be answered? What does it mean to ask for something *in the name of* another? What prevents some of our prayers from being answered? How do we know when our prayers are in Jesus' name?

John 14:15-31. From beginning to end, Jesus has sought to inspire courage in his followers. He who has loved these people to the end constantly reminds them that God is seeking deepened fellowship with God's children.

How will this be achieved? Jesus will pray to the Father, and God will send the Holy Spirit to live with the disciples and with us *forever*. The Spirit will be the prime reality for Christians, but the world will not be able to recognize his presence and his works among us and in the world. Why will the world be unable to recognize the work of the Holy Spirit?

Jesus recognized that the world could not see the Holy Spirit because the world was not equipped with the finer vision of God's love. We may illustrate this truth by referring to the vision of experts. A skilled medical doctor who works to heal persons who have dread diseases may spot trouble in a person's health that the layperson would miss. A skilled diamond cutter may see a precious jewel in a rough stone that a lay observer might miss.

Can you remember times when you did not recognize the Spirit? What attitudes must we have to recognize the Spirit?

Our fellowship with Christ depends on love that results in obedience (verses 25-27). The Spirit helps us understand Christ's teachings (verse 26) and brings peace to us (verse 27). Jesus promises that he will not leave us bereft or desolate. The Holy Spirit is a living presence with us always.

"Peace I leave with you; my peace I give you. I do not give to you as the world gives." What kind of peace does Christ's love give us? How does it differ from the peace of the world? The Hebrew word for peace, *shalom*, does not mean simply the absence of trouble. *Shalom* refers to all things that lead to our highest good. This peace we cannot lose; it is independent of outside influences.

DIMENSION THREE: WHAT DOES THE BIBLE MEAN TO ME?

John 13:1-20—Jesus as Servant

Jesus' example of servanthood is a strong picture. Just prior to their last meal together, the disciples had been arguing about who was the greatest among them. Status is very important to us, even from a young age. When teams are being picked on the playground at school, we want to be recognized as a good player by being picked first. We all strive for the more glamorous positions—pitcher, first base, catcher. No one wants to be a utility outfielder.

Even among church leaders pride of place, of status, is important. The mission of the church cannot be carried forth because a committee member did not get elected chairperson and refused to cooperate with the other committee members. A choir member does not get to sing a solo and refuses to sing at all. On an athletic team a player does not get to play the entire game and refuses to play at all. Jesus is teaching the lesson that only one kind of greatness exists—that of service.

John 13:21-30—Betrayal

No one among the disciples suspected that Judas planned to betray Jesus, although John apparently did not trust him (12:4-6). No one tried to stop Judas from leaving the meal on this last night. But Jesus knew. And even though Jesus knew what was in Judas's heart, he made appeal after appeal to Judas not to do this evil deed.

At the meal, Judas was placed on Jesus' left, the place of honor. In this place Jesus could talk intimately and privately with Judas without the other disciples overhearing. Jesus also offered Judas a special tidbit at the meal. In the Eastern world offering the first morsel at a meal was a special honor.

Nothing touched Judas's heart that night. He turned his back on Jesus, going out into the night. Following Christ is to walk in the light. To turn our back on him leads only into darkness. When have you walked in the darkness by denying Christ? How do you see the light when you are following Christ?

John 14:1-7—"The Way and the Truth and the Life"

In becoming our "way," Jesus does not just give us directions to follow—he walks with us, showing us the way to go. How can we find our way with Jesus?

Teaching the truth and being the truth are not the same thing. Most of us know what the truth is, but few of us are always truthful—little white lies to save someone's feelings or to smooth over a tense situation often pop out of our mouths. Only Jesus could say, "I am the truth." How can Jesus as the truth help us in meeting the moral questions of our life?

Jesus alone can show us how to make life worth living. We are searching for life, not knowledge about life, but that which will make life worth living. How does Jesus give our life this meaning?

John 14:27—"My Peace I Give to You"

The world offers us the peace of escape. This peace means the avoidance of conflict, the refusal to face things. Jesus offers us the peace of conquest. It is a permanent peace, not depending on events in the world. Nothing can separate us from Jesus' peace. How can we find this peace? How do we keep it?

"In this world you will have trouble. But take heart! I have overcome the world" (16:33).

— 8 —

Jesus the True Vine

John 15–16

DIMENSION ONE:
WHAT DOES THE BIBLE SAY?

Answer these questions by reading John 15

1. What images does Jesus use to begin Chapter 15? (15:1-6)

    He speaks of himself as the true vine; of God as the gardener (or vinedresser); of the Father's care for the vineyard so it will bear good fruit; of the disciples as the branches; of the unity that should exist among God, Jesus, and the life of faithful believers.

2. What happens to the branch that bears no fruit? (15:2, 6b)

    The gardener cuts off every branch that bears no fruit and burns it.

3. What happens to every branch that bears good fruit? (15:2)

    It is trimmed so it can bear more fruit.

4. What is the duty of the disciple? (15:4-7)

    The disciple's duty is to remain in Jesus and retain Jesus' words in himself.

5. What happens if the disciple keeps Jesus' command? (15:10)

    The disciple will remain in Jesus' love.

6. Why has Jesus spoken to his disciples of these things? (15:11)

    He has spoken of these things that his joy may be in them and that their joy may be complete.

7. What is Jesus' command? (15:12)

    Jesus commands the disciples to love each other as he has loved them.

8. When are the disciples called no longer servants but Jesus' friends? (15:14-15)

    The disciples become Jesus' friends when they do what he commands.

9. Why did Jesus choose the disciples? (15:16)

    Jesus chose the disciples so that they could bear fruit that will last.

10. Why does the world hate the disciples? (15:18-19)

    The world hates Jesus' disciples because the world hates Jesus, who has chosen them.

11. What will the Counselor do when he comes? (15:26)

    The Counselor will testify to Jesus.

Answer these questions by reading John 16

12. Why has Jesus told "all this"? (16:1)

    Jesus has told "all this" to keep the disciples from going astray.

13. What will happen to the disciples? (16:2)

    The disciples will be put out of the synagogues; they will be persecuted; and they will be killed.

14. Why will these frightful things be done to the disciples? (16:2b-3)

    These frightful things will happen because people will think they are offering service to God and because the world has not known the Father or Jesus.

15. Where is Jesus going? (16:5)

He will return to God who sent him to the world.

16. What will be the role of the Holy Spirit? (16:8-15)

The Holy Spirit will convict the world of guilt in regard to sin and righteousness, and of judgment. He will also guide the disciples into all truth and will glorify Jesus.

17. What does Jesus mean by the words "a little while"? (16:16-22)

Temporary sorrow over Jesus' death will yield to joy over Jesus' resurrection and abiding presence.

18. What will Jesus' pledge of triumph do? (16:25-33)

Jesus' pledge of triumph will make clear all Jesus' teachings, reveal the love of God, empower the disciples' prayers, and offer peace amid trouble.

DIMENSION TWO: WHAT DOES THE BIBLE MEAN?

John 15:1-17. List on a chalkboard or poster paper the images that Jesus uses to begin Chapter 15. Why do you think Jesus uses the figure of the vineyard that appears in various places in the Old Testament?

Ask class members to read Isaiah 5:1-7; Psalm 80:9-15; Jeremiah 2:21; Ezekiel 15; and Hosea 10:1.

In John 15:1, Jesus connects the church, the New Israel, with these images of the vineyard in the Old Testament. Jesus is now fulfilling the Old Testament promise of God's redeeming activity.

A healthy vine requires careful tending to promote wholesome, orderly growth. Often a gardener may turn his or her back on the vineyard for a while only to discover that the vines have grown wild. But in the case of the present vine, the New Israel, God is the gardener or vinedresser. Jesus is the vine. The disciples constitute the branches.

Discuss what it means to be branches of the vine, which is the source of life. What does Jesus mean when he says, "Remain in me"? How do we remain in Jesus? Like the branches of a lush vine, says Jesus, my followers must remain closely attached to the source of their life. They must always remember from where they have come and where they are going.

How is the church renewed? By private prayer and prayer groups? by public worship? by frequent celebration of Holy Communion? In many churches some members stay away from the service of Holy Communion. What do they miss in the Christian life? List the reasons for regular attendance at Holy Communion. By their nonattendance, how are Christians neglecting the central reality of their faith?

The church is renewed by faithful study of the Bible and books on the Christian faith. Does your church maintain an attractive library containing books essential for understanding the Christian faith? Is the library easily accessible to all? Discuss ways your group can improve the library and its use.

Jesus speaks of sending the disciples out to represent him in the world. So the church is renewed by serving others—visiting the sick, caring for widows and orphans, ministering to prisoners and to persons who are poor or homeless. Jesus sends us out to bear witness to him in society. Discuss ways Christians are witnessing to Christ today.

John 15:18-27. The Romans had a tremendous passion for discipline and order. They controlled a vast empire that stretched from the British Isles to the Euphrates River and from North Africa to Germany. The empire's lands included people of all kinds of races and religions. How could the Roman government hold the various elements together so that order could be attained? Without order nations cannot endure.

The Roman rulers were tolerant of religions so long as the religions could prove their beliefs and practices were not a threat to the state. The Romans could accept all gods. But Jewish monotheism and the Christianity that grew from it were suspect from the start. They were seen as troublemakers for the well-ordered state.

The Roman rulers needed a unifying force that would transcend the ambitions, loyalties, and conflicts of the various peoples subjected to Rome. They found this unifying force in emperor worship. This worship developed from the peoples of the empire themselves. The masses derived great benefits from Roman order. These people needed common symbols of meaning and patriotism that would hold the empire together. Caesar worship provided these symbols.

At first reluctant to be reverenced as gods, the rulers later found Caesar worship to be the force that could weld the empire into unity. Caesar worship could work to provide order, peace, and prosperity if all groups would acknowledge the emperors as gods. After all, the imperial rulers represented the spirit and the meaning of Rome. So emperor worship stood for the gratitude of various peoples for what Rome had done to achieve a peace that embraced the world. The Roman rulers allowed the various peoples to worship their own gods, but they insisted that all persons had to acknowledge Caesar as supreme. The Caesars eventually required every individual to burn incense to the emperor as a sign of loyalty to the state. Subjects of Rome were required to burn incense and to affirm, "Caesar is Lord."

The Christians refused to put the emperor above Christ. Christians, they declared, could not agree to worship what was human and finite. Not Caesar but Christ was their Lord.

The refusal of Christians to worship Caesar brought the serious charges of the Roman authorities. Christians were denounced as dangerous and unpatriotic. They were under suspicion of the Roman populace and the imperial powers. They were suspected of working to undermine the state.

What were some of the objections to the Christians? What were some atrocities charged to them? The populace of the Roman world readily accepted stories that accused Christians of cannibalism, a suspicion that sprang from the words of the Christian's private meal: "This is my body, which is for you" and "This cup is the new covenant in my blood" (1 Corinthians 11:24-25). Their enemies also accused the Christians of sexual immoralities growing out of the love feast or weekly meal. Christians greeted one another with "a holy kiss" or kiss of peace, and their foes read into their acts the charge that the Christians were engaging in immoral sexual practices.

The Christians were also charged with setting fires. Under the emperor Nero, they were charged with the terrible fires that ravaged Rome in A.D. 64.

To add to all these charges the public spread tales that the Christians were desecrating their marriage vows, breaking up families, and dividing homes. There was some truth in this last charge; for sometimes a child was rejected because he or she became a Christian, and sometimes half the members in a household became Christians while the other half remained in their pagan religion. All the divisions made for tension and disunity in the family.

William Barclay (in *The Gospel of John, Volume 2*; Westminster, 1975) sums up an excellent discussion of why the world hated the Christians by saying that the world suspects people who are different—the world keenly dislikes people whose lives condemn it. But the basic demand on the Christian is that he or she have the courage to be good.

Christians lived by higher standards than their neighbors around them. Their faith increasingly became a criticism of the low standards and conduct of the general population. Though Christians had the courage to be different, this courage would be punished. The world could not tolerate their idealism and their living on the basis of faith, hope, and love. Their admirable conduct was a constant criticism of their society.

In the upper room Jesus warned his followers that they would be persecuted, precisely because the world—a human society organized in disregard of God—was built of sin and would resent people who held to higher standards of living. Jesus represented the need for thorough cleansing from sin that only loyalty to God can bring about.

Jesus told his disciples that dire calamities would fall on them, but that he would not leave them bereft of help. He would send to them the help of the Holy Spirit or Counselor who would be a constant witness to God's love and care. They in turn would be required to witness to the world out of their personal experiences.

In *The Different Drum,* M. Scott Peck, a psychiatrist who speaks as a Christian, describes some means Christians adopt to "take matters that are properly related to each other and put them in airtight compartments." One example he cites is of the businessman who attends church services regularly on Sunday mornings, thinks he loves God, thinks he loves God's creation and his neighbors, but who has no problem with his company's dumping of toxic wastes into streams near his business. Here is the way Peck discusses the problem of integrity.

> *Integrity is never painless.* It requires that we let matters rub up against each other, that we fully experience the tension of conflicting needs, demands, and interests, that we even be emotionally torn apart by them. Take, for example, the fact that this country, on whose coinage is written the words "In God We Trust," is also the leading manufacturer and seller of weapons in the world. What are we to do with this? Should we be perfectly comfortable about it? Should we keep these matters in separate compartments? Or should we wonder if there is a conflict between them and agonize over the tension of trying to resolve that conflict? Should we consider, for instance, with integrity, changing the inscription on our coinage to read "In Weapons We Trust" or "In God We Partially Trust"?
>
> Since integrity is never painless, so community is never painless. It also requires itself to be fully open, vulnerable, to the tension of conflicting needs, demands, and interests of its members and of the community as a whole. It does not seek to avoid conflict but to reconcile it. And the essence of reconciliation is that painful, sacrificial process of emptying. Community always pushes its members to empty themselves sufficiently to make room for the other point of view, the new and different understanding. Community continually urges both itself and its individual members painfully, yet joyously, into even deeper levels of integrity.[1]

In his book *Training in Christianity,* Søren Kierkegaard, a Danish theologian, wrote about Christ drawing all persons to himself:

> *From on High He will draw all unto Himself.*
> *From on high*—for here upon earth He went about in lowliness, in the lowly form of a servant, in poverty and wretchedness, in suffering. This indeed was Christianity, not that a rich man makes the poor rich, but that the poorest of all makes all men rich, both the rich and the poor. And this indeed was Christianity, not that it is the happy man who comforts the afflicted, but that it is He who of all men is the most afflicted.—He will draw all to Himself—*draw* them to Himself, for He would *entice* no one. To draw to Himself truly, means in *one* sense to repel men. In thy nature and in mine and in that of every man there is something He would do away with; with respect to all this He repels men. Lowliness and humiliation are the stone of stumbling, the possibility of offence, and thou art situated between His humiliation which lies behind, and the exaltation—this is the reason why it is said that He draws to Himself. To entice is an untrue way of drawing to Himself, but He would entice no one; humiliation belongs to Him

just as essentially as exaltation. In case there was one who could love Him only in His exaltation—such a man's vision is confused, he knows not Christ, neither loves Him at all, but takes Him in vain. Christ was the truth [in His humiliation] and is the truth.[2]

John 16:1-21. Jesus' dealing with us shows a plan and a method. He knows our pace in learning, and he sets the method of teaching to fit with our possibilities. "I have much more to say to you, more than you can now bear." When we think back over our lives, we realize that some learnings we could not bear at the time. We have to master simple arithmetic and be at home with simple numbers and fractions before we can tackle the binomial theorem. Jesus teaches through experience, helping us comprehend his will and purpose as we are able. Christianity will engage us in constant growth, using all our powers and helping us become ever more mature disciples.

For our learning, Jesus will send the Holy Spirit who will instruct us in all things. The Spirit is not just for believers who receive his message. He will come to save and heal the whole world. The Spirit will "guide you into all the truth," glorify the Christ, and "will tell you what is yet to come." The Counselor will reprove the world of sin because it rejected the Christ. He will reprove the world of judgment. Convicting the world on these scores, the Counselor will contend with the world so that it will be challenged to repudiate its bad decision to crucify the Christ.

Evil will not have the last word; for the Crucifixion will be seen as victory over sin and death, not as the disgrace Jesus' enemies would label it. Jesus' passion, death, and resurrection will complete the revelation of the incarnate Word—a truth the disciples are now called upon to accept and proclaim to the world.

John 16:22-33. "Now is your time of grief, but I will see you again." I will see you again—We use these words in common everyday speech to say that our relationship with another person is not over. It will continue into the future. Jesus reminds us that no matter how sorrowful life may become, no matter how many personal sorrows and failures, no matter how obvious it would seem that evil has triumphed in the world, he will see us again.

Jesus is going to the cross, a journey that in the world's eyes will be a sorry end to his strange venture with the human race. But the cross is the way back to God, who sent Jesus on our behalf. Each of us can say now that Jesus the Christ will see us again. Because he sees us again, we can take joy in life; for it is redeemed by him. The joy is from inward to outward—that is why no one can take it from us. It will not be held captive by the world of change and threat.

"In that day you will no longer ask me anything." We are frustrated and sometimes embittered by the unanswered questions and unsolved problems that haunt us. These are here as divine challenges. We live in mystery, and the mystery prompts us to ask questions. But in Christ's kingdom we shall see God. We shall have full understanding.

"Ask and you will receive, and your joy will be complete." By going to the cross, Jesus has established for us a new relationship with God. In that relationship and in Christ's name, we are as children who are free to make our requests known. God will hear our requests. God will respond to them according to our needs and God's purposes for us. Always we should remember to pray, "Your will be done."

"I have been speaking figuratively." Jesus has used figures that are hard to understand, sayings that are veiled to the outside world, figures that prompt the Christian to think. Jesus has been speaking to us in figures—remember the bread of life, the water of life, the good shepherd, the light of the world, and others? But now Jesus speaks more plainly. We can now grasp the language of the cross in Jesus' words. This language is directed at us and at every human being. The language is clear; everyone can understand it; it is the language of sacrificial love. Certainly no one has ever spoken more clearly. Jesus is the personal expression of the love of God to us.

"Now you are speaking clearly and without figures of speech." Jesus has revealed to us the glory of God. God has sent to earth his very heart!

We believe God is speaking plainly in Jesus Christ, speaking in the call to us to be faithful to the Son of Man, the Son of God.

"You believe at last! . . . But a time is coming . . . when you will be scattered . . . [and] will leave me all alone. Yet I am not alone, for my Father is with me." Jesus bids us beware lest we desert him when the going gets tough. On that night in Jerusalem the disciples were put to the test. We are tested daily. Let us pray for divine aid that we may be faithful. We are prone to leave Jesus alone, to believe at the moment when it is popular and safe to believe. Is our faith strong enough to endure in times of upheaval and terror?

"I have told you these things, so that in me you may have peace." Jesus gives the peace of God, the peace that the world cannot give. The world wants the peace of selfishness, of conformity to its low ambitions and standards; but Jesus gives us another peace. His peace is like the peace that possessed the man who built his house on the rock. It will stand.

"In this world you will have trouble. But take heart! I have overcome the world." Jesus looks down into the future, knowing that in a world like ours tribulation will inevitably come. He sees disaster for the disciples, and at the same time he envisions the courage that he will send his own by the Holy Spirit. So his great gift to us is courage. We worship a Savior who promises he is more than a match for what evil can do to us.

"Take heart! I have overcome the world."

DIMENSION THREE: WHAT DOES THE BIBLE MEAN TO ME?

The group may discuss the following topics or use the material in the student book.

John 15:18-27—Jesus' Warnings of Persecution

The Christian life is a costly business. We should ask ourselves to what extent we are bearing the costs of Christ's witness. Few Christians in America are persecuted for their faith, but we should examine our attitudes and conduct to see whether the reason is because we are making compromises with the world. Would your neighbor recognize you as a Christian just by observing your day-to-day conduct?

Review the section on John 15:18-27 in the student book. Summarize Jesus' warning of persecution and his references to what was happening in the world ruled by Rome. How was the world's hatred of the Christians being expressed? How is it expressed today? How does the world express its hatred for God? In daily life it sometimes happens that men and women show contempt for God by mistreating God's children. How do you think Christians may be partly responsible for this mistreatment? How do we ignore Christ's people? What can we do to change these attitudes that hurt people?

Discuss the meaning of Jesus' words in Matthew 25 and how there he identifies with the unfortunate people of earth. Who are the "least of these" in our world? How are Christians ministering to them? Søren Kierkegaard wrote: "Everyone knows his neighbor at a distance, and yet it is impossible to see him at a distance; if you do not see him so close at hand that, before God, you see him conditionally in every man, then you do not see him at all."[3]

How do we see our neighbor "at a distance"? Seeing him or her at a distance may mean seeing him or her imperson-

ally as we would see an object, not a human being. Could seeing our neighbor "at a distance" mean also neglecting to bear witness against evils that maim our neighbor?

Discuss the relevance of emperor worship as it seeks to achieve purpose and meaning. Do modern people engage in "emperor worship"—making and giving ultimate allegiance to that which is human and finite? What are some of our modern gods? The state? patriotism? society? material gain?

Why must Christians refuse to put patriotism and loyalty to the state above their loyalty to Christ? How is the Christian faith a criticism of the society in which we live today? What are some areas of our nation's life in which Christians can bear witness for Christ? Unrestrained consumerism? sexual immorality? exploitation of sex and violence in the communications media? violence and corruption in commercial sports? pollution of the environment?

John 16:1-24—A Little While of Sorrow

Jesus stressed to his disciples that the persecutions would be severe, but that they would be a preface to the joy that would come to his own. Read to class members John 16:16-24. Discuss the nature of the consolation Jesus promises the disciples. Ask class members what they think Jesus is saying about our need for a comforting faith.

----

[1]From *The Different Drum*, by M. Scott Peck, M.D. (Simon and Schuster, 1987), page 235.

[2]From *Training in Christianity and the Edifying Discourse Which Accompanied It*, by Søren Kierkegaard; translated with an introduction and notes by Walter Lowrie (Princeton University Press, 1944), pages 153–54.

[3]From *Works of Love*, by Søren Kierkegaard (Princeton University Press, 1946), page 66.

— 9 —

Jesus' Prayer of Adoration and Thanksgiving

John 17

DIMENSION ONE:
WHAT DOES THE BIBLE SAY?

Answer these questions by reading John 17

1. What does Jesus do before the disciples leave the upper room? (17:1)

   Jesus prays what has become known as the high priestly prayer.

2. What is Jesus' first petition? (17:1)

   Jesus says, "Father, the time has come. Glorify your Son that your Son may glorify you."

3. Of what does glorification of the Father consist? (17:2)

   God's glorification consists in the giving of eternal life to all whom God has given Jesus.

4. Of what does eternal life consist? (17:3)

   Eternal life is found in the knowledge of the only true God and of Jesus Christ whom God has sent.

5. How has Jesus glorified God on earth? (17:4-6)

   Jesus has glorified God by doing the work God has sent him to do and by revealing God's name to the disciples whom God has given to Jesus.

6. Why does Jesus pray for the disciples? (17:9-11a)

   Jesus prays for the disciples for three reasons: (1) because they belong to God, (2) because Jesus is glorified in them, and (3) because the disciples will soon be left without the counsel and protection of Jesus when he returns to God.

7. What is Jesus' prayer to God on behalf of the disciples? (17:11b)

   Jesus prays that God will protect them by the power of God's name and that they will be one, as God and Jesus are one.

8. What has Jesus given the disciples? (17:14a)

   Jesus has given them the word of God.

9. Why has the world hated the disciples? (17:14b)

   The world has hated the disciples "because they are not of the world any more than I [Jesus] am of the world."

10. What more does Jesus pray for? (17:15-17)

    Jesus prays, not that God should keep the disciples out of the world, but that God should "protect them from the evil one." He prays that God will sanctify them in God's truth.

11. For whom does Jesus now pray? (17:20-23)

    Jesus prays for all those who will believe in him in the future that they may be brought to complete unity.

12. How does Chapter 17 close? (17:25-26)

    Chapter 17 closes with Jesus' words that the world has not recognized God, but that he and the disciples have known God who has sent Jesus into the world. Jesus also says that he has made known God's name, and that he will make it known. Finally, Jesus prays that the love with which God has loved Jesus will be in the disciples and that Jesus will be in them.

DIMENSION TWO:
WHAT DOES THE BIBLE MEAN?

John 17: An Overall View. Prayer was an essential part of Jesus' life. Though he rebuked mere formalized prayers (Matthew 6:5-8), he gave us the Lord's Prayer to use as a model (Matthew 6:9-13). Jesus' example to us shows how important prayer was to his life. He rose early for prayer (Mark 1:35). After feeding the five thousand Jesus went off alone to pray (Matthew 14:23). At his baptism Jesus was praying when the Holy Spirit "descended on him" (Luke 3:21-22). Jesus was in prayer all night before choosing his closest followers (Luke 6:12-13). In the Gospel of Luke we learn that Jesus was praying as the Transfiguration took place (Luke 9:28-29). It was prayer in the garden of Gethsemane that prepared Jesus for his suffering (Luke 22:41). And Jesus' last words from the cross were a prayer (Luke 23:46).

Fittingly, then, Jesus' last words to his disciples come in the form of a prayer. Ask class members to share their views on what prayer means to them.

In his classic book entitled *Prayer*, George A. Buttrick describes again and again Jesus' attitude toward prayer and his way of prayer. Jesus prayed, Dr. Buttrick says, in aloneness and in comradeship. He prayed "in the routine day" and "under provocation of crisis." Dr. Buttrick continues:

> Of the seven "Words of the Cross" three and perhaps four are prayers. The prayer of pardon, "Father, forgive them, for they know not what they do," leaves us "defenseless utterly." This vigil of prayer, never closely described in the Gospels, but repeatedly mentioned and reflected, is an ungainsayable testimony. He prayed and prayed—in the "great congregation" of the Temple, in the local friendship of the synagogue, in the circle of his friends, on the housetop under Syrian stars, in the fields outside Jerusalem, on the lonely mountainside, in the "inner chamber"—until prayer became the climate of his days. The saints said that "to work is to pray," and they believed profoundly that "to pray is to work." Jesus said in the language of deeds that "to live is to pray," and that "to pray is to live."
>
> We must not dogmatize about the limits of prayer, though we must recognize certain limits and try to trace them. For instance, we cannot too quickly conclude from Jesus that petitionary prayer has no place. Yet the fact remains that Jesus asked nothing for himself except daily bread, strength in the testing, and grace to reveal God to the world.[1]

This lesson is devoted to a single prayer of Jesus, a prayer that sums up his life and ministry. In this prayer Jesus prays for himself, but he asks nothing for himself (verses 1-5). He is concerned with the will of God alone. Jesus prays for his disciples (verses 6-19) that they be strengthened for God's tasks, that they remain faithful, and that they be kept in God's care and protected from the evil one. Jesus prays for the universal church and for us who belong to it (verses 20-26). Jesus wants his followers to be united with him.

Unity is the main theme of Jesus' discourses on the night of his arrest.

John 17:1-5. The great climax of God's redemptive purpose is at hand. The time for Jesus' glorification and for his glorification of God has arrived.

What does it mean to glorify something or someone? Our dictionaries can suggest common meanings: to make glorious by bestowing honor, praise, or admiration; to elevate to celestial glory; to shed radiance or splendor on (as a large chandelier glorifies the entire room); to cause to have great beauty, charm, or appeal; to give glory to (as in worship); and many other meanings.

In the Old Testament the "glory of God" is a term used to indicate that which the Jews can comprehend, by sight originally, of God's presence on earth. The idea goes back to Moses when God came down in the pillar of cloud and entered the Tent of Meeting to talk with him face to face, while the cloud stayed outside the door. The people saw the cloud as the visible sign of God's presence (Exodus 33:7-11), so that the cloud came to be a symbol of the divine presence. It was also seen as a veil to obscure the brilliance and power of the divine presence. Why was this so? Except in rare instances, the cloud veiled God's glory from human vision; for it was said that a human being could not endure the full light of God's presence and live.

The central meaning of divine glory is one of weight and substance that commands respect and honor. Glory stood for strength and power, brightness, wealth, honor, dignity, and noble bearing. For God's enemies the glory of God was a devouring fire. When the Jews began to look forward to the messianic age, the glory came to be thought of no longer as the actual or possible experience in this life but as a characteristic of the messianic age. Slowly the glory turned eschatological—that is, pointing to the end times.

In the New Testament the glory becomes an essential part of the kingdom of God. Present then, it was also expected in the future. Its eschatological factors converged dramatically in Jesus Christ. The glory of God shone around the shepherds when the angels sang at Jesus' birth. Jesus had made known the glory of God, for the people grasped the meaning of the divine glory through Christ. Christ is proclaimed as the glory of God available to all who have eyes to see. The Fourth Gospel stresses stronger than do other writings the full biblical content of the word *glory*: "We have seen his glory, the glory of the One and Only, who came from the Father" (John 1:14b).

In his miracles Jesus revealed his glory (2:11), a glory not of human beings but of God (5:41; 17:5). The high priestly prayer is dominated by the idea of God's glory. Jesus will go to the cross, not as a pathetic martyr, but as victorious sovereign over all life. Jesus' passion and resurrection reveal to the utmost the glory of God.

This brief summary of the concept of God's glory should help you grasp the deeper meaning of the glorification of Jesus and of God that we see centered in the high priestly prayer. Why is the cross central to Jesus' glory? How does it reveal God? How does the cross finish the work that Jesus was sent to do? Why does the cross appeal to many of us in the twentieth and twenty-first centuries?

The cross glorified God because it was suffered in obedience to God. Jesus could have evaded the cross, but he could not have glorified God by the evasion. Jesus honored God by obedience. Just as a child honors a parent by obedience or as a citizen honors his or her country by obedience, so Jesus honored God by doing God's will.

Examine the concept of Jesus to the effect that he was not of this world. Contrast worldly glory with that of the cross and the kingdom of God. What are the characteristics of the glory of this world? Money? fame? power? prestige? notoriety?

How did God answer Jesus' prayer that the Son be glorified? Why do we say the cross was Jesus' way back to God? The cross and the Resurrection freed Jesus from the limitations of time and space. He could now be present over the whole earth and be available to everyone.

John 17:6-19. "I have revealed you to those whom you gave me." Jesus has told us what God is like. To manifest his glory God dwells in lowliness. God comes to us in Jesus Christ. In "A Death in the Desert," a poem on John's Gospel, the English poet Robert Browning has described God's revelation this way:

> Though the whole earth should be in wickedness,
> We had the truth, might leave the rest to God.[2]

The Incarnation has made known clearer than anything else ever has that God is in the world that "the divine power first made."

> Is not his love at issue still with sin,
> Visibly when a wrong is done on earth?
> Love, wrong, and pain, what see I else around?
> Yea, and the Resurrection and Uprise
> To the right hand of the throne—what is it beside,
> When such truth, breaking bounds, o'erfloods my soul
> And, as I saw the sin and death, even so
> See I the need yet transiency of both,
> The good and glory consummated thence?
> I saw the power; I see the Love, once weak,
> Resume the Power; and in this word "I see,"
> Lo, there is recognized the Spirit of both
> That moving o'er the spirit of man, unblinds
> His eye and bids him look.[3]

Browning went so far as to say that the acknowledgment of God in Christ will solve all problems. He wrote:

> I say, the acknowledgment of God in Christ
> Accepted by thy reason, solves for thee
> All questions in the earth and out of it.[4]

There is much truth in what Browning says, but the Gospel of John stresses more than the acknowledgment of Jesus Christ by our reason. The revelation of God in Jesus Christ is directed to the whole person—mind, body, and soul. It grasps us in our total existence. Belief in Jesus Christ means commitment. Jesus not only tells us about the love of God, he imparts this love to us. What does it mean for Jesus to manifest the name of God? Do Christians today manifest God's name? How?

The Gospel of John says much about the unity of the church. This unity is grounded in our common love of God in Jesus Christ. It is strengthened by the realization that we are all *one*. God makes us *one* by God's work in creation and redemption.

What do class members think of Jesus' vision of the unity of humankind? What does the prayer tell us about Jesus' expectations for the future of his followers? Why does any person's death diminish us? How does Jesus expect us to be involved in humankind?

Jesus knew his disciples would face a hostile world when he left them, but he would send the Holy Spirit to be their counselor and guide.

Why did the world hate the disciples? Why are many Christians hated today? Why do you think Jesus would not pray that God take the disciples out of the world? What is the lesson for Christians and the church in this? How does a Christian witness to Jesus today? Ask class members to give some examples of Christian witness they have observed. What do they think is the most effective Christian witness?

What does it mean to be consecrated? Why did Jesus put emphasis on consecration (sanctification) of the disciples? How do you think Jesus Christ equips us for his witness today? Mention some persons you know—in the church and out—who are fitted with special skills for witnessing to God's love and justice today.

John 17:20-26. These verses that close Jesus' high priestly prayer show his complete faith and confidence in God and in the future for his followers. The immediate future is certainly grim for Jesus and his small band of followers. The next day Jesus is crucified. His followers become depressed and scatter around the country. Jesus looks beyond this grimness to a glorious future where many people will come to follow him.

Jesus' prayer for these latter-day followers (including us) is that they all will be one as he and God are one. The unity Jesus is praying for is a unity of personal relationship, not an administrative or organizational unity. Christians differ greatly in the ways they organize and administer their individual churches. But the love of God for each of them never changes. Jesus prays that this same love will be present in Christians' interpersonal relationships also. How are your class members working toward this unity of relationship with God and with other Christians?

Jesus ends his prayer by speaking of his coming glory. His glory will be the cross. By his perfect obedience to God's will, Jesus is glorified. We, too, can find glory in suffering for and being obedient to God's will. Why is being obedient to God's will often a difficult task? Why does our obedience sometimes lead to suffering?

DIMENSION THREE:
WHAT DOES THE BIBLE MEAN TO ME?

The class members may discuss the following topic before closing with using the meditation in the student book.

John 17
Jesus Prays for Us

Read John 17 aloud, perhaps in more than one Bible translation. Ask class members to list their feelings about the prayer as they listen to it, remembering these are Jesus' last words to his disciples. Do they agree that these are the best words Jesus could have left as his final message? Are there other messages Jesus could have left as his final message? Are there other messages Jesus could have left with the disciples? What are they?

Since most American Christians do not have to face the kinds of persecution that Jesus describes that his disciples will have to face, what meaning do these words have for us? How can contemporary Christians find comfort in Jesus' prayer?

Use the meditation in Dimension Three of the student book as your closing for this session.

[1]From *Prayer,* by George A. Buttrick (Abingdon Press, 1947), pages 36–37.
[2]"A Death in the Desert," by Robert Browning, in *The Complete Poetic and Dramatic Works of Robert Browning* (Houghton Mifflin, 1895), page 387.
[3]"A Death in the Desert," page 387.
[4]"A Death in the Desert," page 390.

"You are right in saying I am a king. In fact, for this reason I was born, and for this I came into the world, to testify to the truth" (18:37).

— 10 —

Jesus Is Arrested

John 18

DIMENSION ONE:
WHAT DOES THE BIBLE SAY?

Answer these questions by reading John 18

1. Where does Jesus go after he finishes the conversation with the disciples? (18:1)

   He goes with the disciples across the Kidron Valley, where there is an olive grove, which they all enter.

2. What does Judas do? (18:2-3)

   He goes to the grove with a detachment of soldiers and officials from the chief priests and the Pharisees.

3. How does Jesus respond to the coming of this detachment? (18:4)

   He steps forward and asks who they want.

4. What happens then? (18:5-8)

   When Jesus identifies himself, the crowd draws back and falls to the ground. Jews asks again, "Who is it you want?" They ask for Jesus of Nazareth and he tells the band, "I told you that I am he." He asks them to let his disciples go.

5. What does Simon Peter do? (18:10)

   Peter draws his sword and strikes Malchus, the high priest's servant, cutting off the man's right ear.

6. How does Jesus react to Peter's action? (18:11)

   He tells Peter to put away his sword and asks, "Shall I not drink the cup the Father has given me?"

7. What happens then? (18:12-14)

   The soldiers and officials seize Jesus, bind him, and lead him to Annas, the father-in-law of Caiaphas, the "high priest that year."

8. What does Simon Peter do now? (18:15-16a)

   He follows Jesus to the court of the high priest and stands outside the door of the court.

9. What does the girl on duty at the door say? (18:17)

   She asks Peter, "You are not another of his [Jesus'] disciples, are you?"

10. What does the high priest do? (18:19)

    He questions Jesus about his disciples and his teaching.

11. What does Jesus tell him? (18:20-21)

    Jesus says he had taught openly in the synagogues and in the Temple, where all Jews assembled. The high priest, Jesus says, should question those persons who had heard him.

12. What does one of the officials do after Jesus replies to the high priest? (18:22)

    He strikes Jesus in the face.

13. What does Annas do now? (18:24)

    He sends Jesus, bound, "to Caiaphas the high priest."

14. What happens to Peter, and how does he respond? (18:25-27)

    Twice more those in the high priest's courtyard accuse Peter of being a disciple of Jesus, and twice more he denies the charge.

15. Where do the soldiers and officials now take Jesus? (18:28)

They take Jesus to the praetorium (the governor's palace) to Pontius Pilate.

16. What does Pilate do and say? (18:29)

Pilate goes out to meet the band of accusers and asks, "What charges are you bringing against this man?"

17. How do they answer Pilate? (18:30)

They say they would not have brought Jesus to Pilate if Jesus had not been a criminal.

18. What is Pilate's response? (18:31a)

He tells them to take Jesus and judge him by their own law.

19. What do the Jews say to this? (18:31b)

They reply that they "have no right to execute anyone."

20. What now happens between Jesus and Pilate? (18:33-38a)

Pilate has Jesus brought before him. He asks Jesus if he is the king of the Jews. He also asks what Jesus had done that his own Jewish nation had brought him to trial. Jesus replies that his kingdom is not of this world. Pilate answers, "You are a king, then!" Jesus responds that Pilate is right in saying so. He has come into the world, Jesus says, to testify to the truth. Everyone who listens to him is on the side of the truth. Pilate asks, "What is truth?"

21. What does Pilate now tell the Jews? (18:38b-39)

He tells them that he finds no basis for a charge against Jesus, but that according to Jewish custom he can release one man to the Jews at the Passover. He asks if they want him to release Jesus.

22. What do the Jews say to this? (18:40)

The Jews shout out that they want Pilate to release not Jesus but Barabbas, who had taken part in a rebellion.

DIMENSION TWO:
WHAT DOES THE BIBLE MEAN?

The Passion Narrative. When we speak of the Passion narrative, we mean the events of the arrest, the trial and Crucifixion, the burial, the discovery of the empty tomb, and Jesus' appearances to the disciples. This narrative is recorded by Matthew, Mark, Luke, and John, who tell the same story but differ here and there in their use of episodes and descriptive details concerning Jesus. They all bear witness to the life, death, and resurrection of Jesus Christ. All agree that in Jesus the eternal God has said something very special to the human race. The Gospel writers also have their own individual concerns, and scholars generally agree that the Fourth Gospel's author is especially concerned with theology.

In *The Interpretation of the Fourth Gospel* (Cambridge University Press, 1965), a detailed study for scholars, C. H. Dodd discusses six traits of the Synoptic narratives (Matthew, Mark, and Luke) that are not included in the Fourth Gospel's Passion narrative (Chapters 18–21). They are listed here:

1. Generally, John's Passion narrative does not include the wonders occurring in nature that the others report. For example, the darkening of the sun in Mark's account (Mark 15:33); the earthquakes accompanying the Crucifixion and Resurrection in Matthew (Matthew 27:51b; 28:2); and the healing of the servant's ear as recorded in Luke (Luke 22:51).

2. John fails to give a eucharistic (Holy Communion) quality to the Last Supper, but that theme is included in the story of the feeding of the multitude (John 6:1-14).

3. John does not include the story of Jesus praying in Gethsemane.

4. John says nothing of the charge of blasphemy lodged against Jesus in the high priest's court or of Jesus' confession at the same occasion that he was the Messiah. These charges do appear in the section of John's Gospel describing Jesus' signs, however (John 10:30-39).

5. John does not include Mark's report that the cross was carried by Simon of Cyrene (Mark 15:21) but seems to question it (John 19:17).

6. John does not refer to mocking and reviling of Jesus on the cross. John omits Luke's account of expressions of sympathy from the women of Jerusalem and from one of the crucified robbers. John leaves out Jesus' cry of abandonment on the cross, a cry that Luke omits also.

Dodd also lists some fifteen instances where John includes details not given by Matthew, Mark, and Luke. Some examples are given here:

1. John stresses the voluntary character of Jesus' suffering. In the garden when the soldiers hesitate to arrest him, Jesus gives himself up—doing so on condition that his disciples be allowed to go free (18:7-8).

2. John lays greater emphasis on the political charge against Jesus by the Roman court. John de-emphasizes the importance of the hearing in the Jewish court.

3. John stresses the innocence of Jesus (18:38b; 19:4, 6b) more than Mark, but not more than Luke.

4. John includes the incident of the mother and the beloved disciple (John 19:26-27), which no other Gospel writer reports.

5. In chronicling the Crucifixion, John submits a different set of prophecies fulfilled. He cites "They divided my garments" (John 19:24), an episode to which the other

Gospels only allude. Other prophecies that do not appear in Matthew, Mark, and Luke are "I am thirsty" (19:28), "Not one of his bones will be broken" (19:36), and "They will look on the one they have pierced" (19:37).

6. John includes the detail that immediately upon the death of Jesus a thrust of a spear brought forth water and blood (19:34). He draws special attention to this incident. John wants to emphasize the idea that from Christ's broken body there flowed the life-giving stream—water that the Spirit had given to believers in Jesus (7:38-39). Jesus said that if one drank this water, one would never thirst again (4:14).

The list of details that John includes and the other Gospels do not is long. A few of them have been mentioned here because they will help you interpret the Fourth Gospel. You may want to emphasize the theological concerns of the Fourth Gospel writer. John's purpose was primarily theological—that his readers would believe, would accept Jesus Christ, and would have eternal life in his name.

As did the other Gospel writers, John used the details he deemed most essential to his purpose. The whole Gospel story is the richer and more meaningful because each writer wrote according to his own purpose. Some class members may remember that Matthew, Mark, and Luke differ at other points with John. Point out to them that John had a different purpose in writing his Gospel. This difference shows up especially in the Passion narrative.

John 18:1-11. In a matter of hours, Jesus will die. How will he endure the indignities and pains of humiliation and death? The writer of John's Gospel is concerned with the events of the Passion narrative, and he wants us to think about their meaning. He would have us probe beneath the surface of events to grasp the import of what is really happening.

One example of the author's deeper purpose is the dramatic contrast he draws between Jesus' calm and serenity and Peter's tendency to panic in threatening situations. Jesus represents the stability and courage that come when one's relationship with God is rightly directed. Peter represents the confusion and uncertainty that come when one's relationship to God and life is misdirected. Peter has fine intentions, but he feels the pressures of a world heedless of God. He has been taught time and time again about the kingdom of God and the courage that comes when one is assured that the Kingdom is built on right relationships. Had Peter not listened to Jesus' parables? Did he not know the teachings of the Sermon on the Mount? But Peter, a courageous but impulsive disciple, was caught up in the fast-moving chain of events surrounding Jesus' passion (suffering) and death. He is like many modern viewers of television and other media who become accustomed to communicating in "sound bites" rather than taking time to reflect on what it means to live.

Peter needed, as we all need, the discipline that comes with meditation and prayer. These were Jesus' sources of courage.

John's Gospel draws a subtle contrast between the steady courage of Jesus and the unsteadiness of Peter. This contrast is apparent in the story of Jesus' arrest in the olive grove. When the troops come to arrest him, Jesus immediately goes out and asks, "Who is it you want?" The soldiers and police say, "Jesus of Nazareth." Quickly, Jesus says, "I am he." Jesus had thought prayerfully about his response in advance of the encounter he knew was coming. Jesus could have hidden in one of the many caves around the quiet and peaceful garden. Knowing that his hour had come, however, he went out bravely to meet his enemies.

When Peter sees what is happening, he acts with courage; but his is a foolhardy courage, a courage that has failed to say its prayers. Peter might have known his own actions would be rash and futile if he had observed Jesus closely enough.

A parable within this incident of Jesus' arrest applies to all of us. Jesus here demonstrates how the love of God meets the hostility and brutality of the world. Jesus bids us to meditate on the divine will and to pray. He sets an example for Peter and for us. In the upper room Jesus prayed for Peter and for us all. Peter fails, as we often fail, to heed Jesus' example in the critical situation in the garden.

In the garden, Jesus not only showed his bravery, he also demonstrated his authority. His was the authority of one who knew what he was about, whom he represented, and what his purpose was. We all know how important authority is. We see daily that this person exercises the authority of a parent, of a teacher, of a traffic control officer, of the city government, of a secretary of state. In a decent society all authority comes ultimately from God.

For this reason the armed group recoiled, and some men fell to the ground when Jesus appeared before them. They were awed, overwhelmed by the majesty of the lowly Galilean. Peter apparently missed the meaning of their actions.

After Peter had struck out blindly, Jesus calmly asked him, "Shall I not drink the cup the Father has given me?" In other words, "Let's remember my commitment to the divine will regardless of the dangers. God is present in what I am doing here."

Do we overlook the symbolism of the cup? Psalm 75:8 may shed light on Jesus' question to Peter:

In the hand of the LORD is a cup
    full of foaming wine mixed with spices;
he pours it out, and all the wicked of the earth
    drink it down to its very dregs.

In Jesus' mind, moreover, may have been the words of Psalm 116:13:

I will lift up the cup of salvation
    and call on the name of the LORD.

Certainly, Jesus was reminding Simon Peter that he came to lift the cup of salvation (suffering) for the sins of the world. The bitter cup Jesus has chosen and now agonizes over in the garden of Gethsemane represents his decision and his alone. He freely decides on his sacrificial death.

What is the cup of salvation? Why would John use this term to describe the decision of Jesus?

John 18:12-27. Jesus was brought first to Annas, the powerful and corrupt former high priest. Annas was a member of a priestly dynasty in Jerusalem. He had held the politicized office of high priest in A.D. 6–15. His five sons succeeded him. Then Caiaphas, his son-in-law, held the office, which under Roman rule had become a political plum to be bought and sold.

The high priest's office brought great wealth to the family, thanks to the influence and power that Annas, in conjunction with Caiaphas, wielded. Annas grew rich through abuses of the sacrificial system of the Temple. His agents extorted money from the people by selling the sacrificial animals at outrageous prices. Outside the Temple, a pair of doves cost a few pennies; inside the Temple the agents of Annas could exact twenty times that amount for the same birds. Annas's agents acted like modern-day scalpers at athletic events. By managing shrewdly the system of traffic in sacred sacrifices, Annas and his family had amassed their wealth.

When Jesus drove the money changers from the Temple, he placed himself in direct opposition to Annas's vested interests. In Annas's eyes Jesus became a marked man. Annas wanted to destroy Jesus because this prophet threatened his system of exploiting the people.

Annas was one in a long line of exploiters of religious feelings and loyalties for personal profit. How are religious groups sometimes exploited today? What is being done to insure more responsible financial accounting for money raised for charitable and religious causes? What can individuals do to see that their money does not go for too much in administrative costs and into the pockets of the unscrupulous?

So Annas resolved to rid himself of an enemy who threatened to destroy his evil system. He resented Jesus' influence with the people. Annas ordered Jesus to be brought first to him. He set in motion the events that would lead to Jesus' death.

When Jesus appeared before Annas, Jesus' fate was already sealed. The hearing was brief, irregular, a sham, a violation of justice. Annas had already decided that Jesus should die. By failing to examine witnesses for Jesus, Annas violated the principles of Jewish justice (Deuteronomy 19:15). Jesus referred to this violation when he asked Annas why he didn't question some witnesses.

Annas sent Jesus on to Caiaphas. This leader in the Jewish religious hierarchy knew what was expected of him. He questioned Jesus briefly, took him to the Sanhedrin, and decided that Jesus was guilty of blasphemy. He knew the penalty of death by stoning was prescribed for this crime in the Jewish law. Caiaphas sent Jesus to Pilate.

A persisting theme in John's narrative is Simon Peter's reaction to the events of the trial. Peter presents us with a fascinating story. Three times he denies Jesus, and yet he stays close to Jesus during the court proceedings.

You may want to discuss the character of Peter that is sketched in John 18. Peter is cowardly and brave, loyal and disloyal, stable and unstable.

Commentators generally seem to have been unfair to Peter, but his story is one repeated in some fashion by all of us. Peter did not live up to our Lord's expectations, but he always had another chance. We should remember that the battle was not over when the rooster crowed. We should remember Peter's final triumph through God's grace was his missionary work described in the Book of Acts and the key role he played in the spread of Christianity. When we are inclined to judge Peter too harshly, we should recall his sermon at Pentecost (Acts 2:14-36) and the important part he played in the formation of the church. The Roman Catholic Church has taught that Peter is the rock upon which the church is built. Protestants stress the belief that Peter's *faith* is the rock upon which the church is founded. Peter's *faith* is the work of God in human hearts. A church tradition teaches that Peter was crucified upside down because he felt it unworthy to be crucified in the same fashion as his Lord.

A man who had been reading the Bible commented to his pastor, "What rascals we find in the Bible!" His pastor replied, "True! What wonders God has wrought through these rascals!" Peter would look back on his career and admit that he was a rascal in some critical situations, but his life is a study in what the grace of God can do with a person's life. Christianity is the religion of new beginnings.

John 18:28-38a. The full account of the proceedings before Pilate will be covered in the next lesson. This passage presents to us some important questions raised in Jesus' first encounter with the Roman governor.

Why did the Jews in the company that arrested Jesus refuse to enter the palace of Pilate? What was the charge the Jews brought against Jesus? What was Pilate's interest in the controversy surrounding Jesus? What did Pilate want to see accomplished in the trial of Jesus? Why could the Jewish authorities not put Jesus to death?

Why does John stress the idea that Jesus would be "lifted up from the earth"? Read John 12:32. John wants to emphasize the way an unbelieving world would kill the Messiah. He wants to stress the necessity of the cross for the salvation of the world. Jesus must be exalted by this execution so that all people can see his sacrificial death.

What was Pilate's attitude toward the Jews? What was Jesus' offense? Why would Pilate be moved by Jesus' claim to be the Son of God and the Messiah?

In what sense is Jesus the king of the Jews? What is his purpose? What is the source of his power? Recall the conversation between Jesus and Pilate concerning Jesus' claim that he came to testify to the truth. Do you think Pilate would not stay for an answer? Why would Pilate be ill-equipped to discuss Jesus' claim? The central question for Pilate was, What must I do with Jesus of Nazareth? Do you agree that that is the main question facing each of us? Why or why not?

John 18:38b-40. Pilate gave the crowd the choice of Jesus or Barabbas. Why do you think the crowd wanted Jesus to be slain? What part do you think hatred played in their choice? John presents in the story of the trial the devastating results of hatred. What were these results? Insensitivity to the claims of our common humanity? a warping of our judgment? loss of a sense of balance? blindness to the reality of God's judgment? to God's forgiveness? to God's love?

DIMENSION THREE:
WHAT DOES THE BIBLE MEAN TO ME?

Reflections on the Scripture

In Chapter 18 John confronts us with Jesus' calling of Peter to change. John does this by a subtle contrast between Jesus' calm command of the situation that goes before his death and Peter's nervous, hasty, and rash actions. Peter has many excellent qualities. He is sensitive, loyal, and brave. Peter remains to fight after all except "the other disciple" and himself have forsaken Jesus and fled. Yet Peter is quick-tempered, impulsive, weak in critical situations, and easily tempted to deny his loyalty to Jesus.

Peter had been called to the cause of Jesus many months before. He had responded eagerly; but now, long after-ward, Jesus is still converting Peter. Salvation began with Jesus' call of Peter to greatness, though Peter hardly knew all this call meant. Peter was among those Christians who are being converted. God's work of conversion in him was continuing in every episode that involved the apostle as Jesus' death neared. So it is with us. Daily we are being converted. Daily we are summoned by Christ to choose his way and grow. The question put to Peter is ours also: "You are not one of his disciples, are you?"

So Peter's call is a call to greatness, as is ours. We are called to serve Christ in our families, in the church, in the community, and in the world—to bear witness to Christ whatever our vocation, whatever the situation we meet. That means lives of becoming—becoming our best selves. Peter's temptation and ours is ever to take the easy way out, to refuse to take a stand against the evil that crushes God's children. But we are called to value Christ's values, to love and serve those he loved and served.

We face daily the question posed by Pilate: Jesus or Barabbas?

We also face daily the prior question posed by Jesus. "Who is it you want?" The troops surrounding Jesus unwittingly phrased the answer to the question the whole world is asking, "Jesus of Nazareth."

We are called daily to celebrate Jesus' call to the Christian life and to grow.

Lead class members in a discussion of ways you and they think John 18 confronts us with the need to change. Do we see Peter's failings and mistakes in ourselves? What do we mean by saying we are daily being converted? What does it mean to be a disciple of Jesus today?

When he had received the drink, Jesus said, "It is finished." With that, he bowed his head and gave up his spirit (19:30).

— 11 —

Christ Crucified: "It Is Finished"

John 19

DIMENSION ONE:
WHAT DOES THE BIBLE SAY?

Answer these questions by reading John 19

1. What does Pilate do after the crowd cries out, "No, not him! Give us Barabbas!"? (19:1)

   He takes Jesus and has him flogged.

2. How do the soldiers treat Jesus? (19:2-3)

   They twist together a crown of thorns and put it on Jesus' head. They dress him in a purple robe, hail him as the king of the Jews, and strike him in the face.

3. What happens then? (19:4-6)

   Pilate goes out of his palace again and tells the crowd he is bringing Jesus out to them so that they will know he found no reason to accuse Jesus. When Jesus comes out, Pilate says to the crowd, "Here is the man!" But when the priests and the officials see Jesus, they cry out, "Crucify! Crucify!" Again Pilate tells Jesus' enemies to take Jesus and crucify him, for Pilate can "find no basis for a charge against him."

4. How do the Jews respond to this? (19:7)

   They say they have a law and by that law Jesus ought to die, because Jesus has "claimed to be the Son of God."

5. What is Pilate's response to this charge, and what does he do and say? (19:8-9a)

   He is afraid and enters the palace again to ask Jesus a question, "Where do you come from?"

6. How does Jesus answer Pilate? (19:9b)

   Jesus does not reply to Pilate's question.

7. What does Pilate now say, and what does Jesus reply? (19:10-11)

   Pilate asks Jesus if he does not know Pilate has the power to release or to crucify him. Jesus says, "You would have no power over me if it were not given to you from above." Jesus says that those who have handed him over to Pilate's hands have the greater sin.

8. What does Pilate seek to do then, and what do the Jews say to this? (19:12)

   Pilate tries to set Jesus free, but the Jews keep shouting, "If you let this man go, you are no friend of Caesar."

9. What does Pilate do when he hears these words? (19:13-14)

   He brings Jesus out, and Pilate "sat down on the judge's seat." He says to the Jews, "Here is your king."

10. What do the Jews say to this? (19:15)

    They cry out, "Take him away! Take him away! Crucify him!"

11. What does Pilate do then? (19:16)

    Pilate hands Jesus over to the Jews to be crucified.

12. Where do the soldiers take Jesus for crucifixion? (19:17)

    The soldiers take Jesus to "The Place of the Skull," which in Aramaic is called Golgotha, to crucify him.

13. When they crucify Jesus, what does Pilate write for a title to be put on the cross? How do the Jews respond to the title? (19:19-21)

    Pilate writes in three languages—Aramaic, Latin, and Greek—the title "JESUS OF NAZARETH, THE KING OF THE JEWS." The Jews object, claiming the title should read, "This man claimed to be king of the Jews."

14. What do the soldiers do that fulfills the Scripture? (19:23-24)

   They divide Jesus' clothes into four shares and decide by lot who will get the seamless garment.

15. What does Jesus say from the cross to his mother and to the beloved disciple? (19:25-27)

   Jesus says to his mother, "Dear woman, here is your son." To the disciple Jesus says, "Here is your mother."

16. What are Jesus' next words from the cross, and what do the soldiers give him? (19:28-30)

   Jesus says, "I am thirsty," and the soldiers press to his mouth a sponge of wine vinegar fixed on a stalk of hyssop. After receiving the vinegar, Jesus says, "It is finished."

17. Who asks Pilate for the body of Jesus for burial? (19:38)

   Joseph of Arimathea, a disciple of Jesus in secret because of fear of the Jews, asks Pilate for Jesus' body.

18. How does Nicodemus figure in the burial of Jesus? (19:39)

   He brings to the tomb a mixture of myrrh and aloes, "about seventy-five pounds," for Jesus' burial.

19. When and where is Jesus buried? (19:41-42)

   On the Jewish day of Preparation, Jesus is buried near the place where he was crucified, in a tomb in a garden "in which no one had ever been laid."

DIMENSION TWO: WHAT DOES THE BIBLE MEAN?

Introduction. The dramatic encounter between Jesus and Pilate that began in Chapter 18 continues in Chapter 19. The story of the conflict reads something like a Greek tragedy, but it ends with Jesus' words of victory on the cross. "It is finished." Pilate's great dilemma—his tragic destiny—is expressed in the question: What shall I do with Jesus of Nazareth?

Jesus is sentenced to a criminal's death by the Roman ruler and goes to Golgotha, where he is crucified between two others. John tells the story of Jesus on the cross with short, powerful strokes. The soldiers gamble for Jesus' clothes; Jesus asks the beloved disciple to care for his mother and John then takes Mary into his own home. Jesus climaxes the drama with the words "I thirst" and "It is finished." Then he bows his head and yields to death. He who has lifted for all humankind the cup of salvation goes out with the taste of sour wine on his lips.

The Jews ask Pilate to authorize the breaking of the legs of the crucified ones, but when the soldiers come to Jesus, they find he is already dead. The rapidly approaching start of the sabbath necessitated hurrying along the process, so that Jesus' body could be handled without violating the proscription against work on the sabbath. Breaking the legs of the crucified men would force even more weight on their diaphragms. The greater pressure would reduce their breathing ability and hasten death.

Jesus' followers take his body away and bury it near the Crucifixion site in a garden—in a tomb where no one has ever been laid.

The calm of John's description of the burial contrasts sharply with the explosive fury of the crowd and Pilate's turmoil as he wrestles with his decision.

John will continue the story. In the quiet we shall await the Resurrection.

John 19:1-16. Pilate was procurator, governor, of Palestine from A.D. 26 to 35. Pilate had been appointed by Augustus Caesar to a post that was troubled by many problems. Resenting Roman rule, the Jewish people constantly threatened rebellion. We know little about Pilate's background; but we may assume he was a strong, successful administrator. A hard assignment like governing the area of Palestine would be reserved for a shrewd and able politician.

On going to his post, Pilate made a number of mistakes that turned the Jews against him. For example, he showed his contempt for their religion by refusing to remove the image of Caesar from his standard when he entered Jerusalem with his troops. Former governors had deferred to the religious feelings of the Jews by removing the metal image of Caesar from their standards. This image was official recognition that the emperor was a god.

Deploring the insensitivity of Pilate, the Jewish leaders begged him repeatedly to remove the graven image, but he refused to be swayed by what he regarded as Jewish superstition. The Jews persisted in their requests until the crafty ruler met with them in his amphitheatre to discuss his insult to their faith. Pilate brought in his soldiers and told the Jews that if they did not drop their requests, he would kill them all on the spot. Baring their necks, the Jews defied Pilate, daring the armed men to carry out Pilate's order.

Pilate did not want to cut down defenseless people, so he backed down and agreed to remove the image from his standard.

In another incident Pilate raided the Temple treasury in order to get money for building a much needed aqueduct for supplying Jerusalem with water. Pilate's actions set off rioting in the streets. The governor sent his soldiers, dressed in plain clothing and carrying concealed weapons, to mix with the crowds. At a given signal, the soldiers attacked the mob and clubbed and stabbed many Jews to death. The enraged populace threatened to retaliate against Pilate by demanding that the emperor remove the governor from office.

So when Pilate dealt with the Jews concerning what to do with Jesus, both sides had grievances. Behind the events of Jesus' trial stood a history of conflict and maneuvering for power. Many Jews were determined to "get Pilate" for what he had done to them and to their religion. The Jews had once before reported Pilate's injustices to Rome, and Pilate did not want them to do this again. He wanted to give the impression in Rome that he was master of the situation in Palestine. But his past actions came now to haunt him. Pilate knew the Jewish leaders could subject him to blackmail if he handled the trial of Jesus in a way that would displease them.

Most scholars, however, think Pilate did not want to send Jesus to his death. He wanted to compromise the issue so that Jesus would be punished enough to satisfy the Jewish leaders; but Pilate misjudged, at first at least, their hatred and intentions.

What did Pilate do with Jesus? First, he tried to get the Jews to take on his [Pilate's] responsibility. God was confronting Pilate in the man Jesus of Nazareth, and no human being could take on Pilate's responsibility for an answer to the question God raised. Every person must make his or her own decision concerning Jesus Christ, and it is the most important decision of one's life.

Pilate had Jesus flogged (brutally whipped) with the idea that this torture would cause the Jews to take pity on Jesus. His effort failed.

Pilate was a poor judge of ways to get along with the Jews. He expressed contempt for them and refused to be involved in Jewish disputes. He sensed in Jesus a splendor that fascinated him through all the controversy. He wanted to release Jesus, but he feared the Jews. He was curious about Jesus; so he was prompted to ask ultimate questions like Where are you from? and What is truth? Pilate may have sensed that Jesus was from God and that ultimate truth was being laid before him and his foes by the man of Galilee.

Pilate presided over the strangest trial of history. But he, not Jesus, was really on trial. Jesus was calm and straightforward in his testimony, but his kingdom was not this world of broken faith and moral and social corruption. Jesus came to bear witness to the truth—to live the truth before our eyes—to be the truth as the culminating revelation of God. Jesus was often silent, but his silence spoke the language of eternal life.

John 19:17-22. Pilate's defeat at the trial of Jesus is announced in the simple words of John 19:16: "Finally Pilate handed him over to them to be crucified." This was Pilate's confession that he was too cowardly to stand against the Jews. The governor delivered Jesus to the Roman soldiers for execution. The soldiers followed the usual method of crucifixion (see the student book, pages 92–93). They led Jesus out to the place of the Skull, a gaunt hill that likely got its name from its resemblance to a human skull.

John does not tell us that on the way to the Crucifixion Jesus found the cross too heavy to bear and that Simon of Cyrene was required to carry it for him (Mark 15:21). John stresses the idea that Jesus bears his cross for the redemption of the world, but we also are to take up our crosses and to follow him. We are not to call trivial inconveniences and irritations our crosses; our crosses can only be laid on us by Christ. These are accepted willingly, for we are to be Jesus' witnesses in the world. Christians die with Jesus Christ and rise with him to a transformed life.

The Gospel of John does not describe the dreadful details of the Crucifixion. He is more interested in the cosmic drama being enacted on the cross. Many of the hymns of the church capture the pathos of that event. Invite class members to look through the Passion hymns in your church's hymnal. How is the cross characterized? Many images come to mind: the "wondrous cross," "shameful tree," "faithful cross, sign of triumph," "noblest tree." The poets' words remind us of a need to see the cross in this broad, universal context that has profound meaning for each of us. Something world-shaking is going on here.

Over the cross, Pilate wrote, "JESUS OF NAZARETH, THE KING OF THE JEWS." These words were written in Aramaic, in Latin, and in Greek, three great languages of the ancient world, languages that have entered a thousand tongues of our world to proclaim the universal King and Savior. Pilate refused to change the words. They represent the record of his life and our own: "What I have written, I have written."

John 19:23-37. What are people doing while Jesus is on the cross? John gives us a vivid picture of some of the people who were nearby and witnessed the Crucifixion.

John pictures for us the soldiers gambling for Jesus' clothing. Here John symbolizes the world's indifference to Jesus' mission and death. Jesus came to tell people something by demonstrating the love of God in human life. But the soldiers, like many others, were engaged in a trivial pursuit in the midst of tragic events.

The indifference of the soldiers is like the indifference of many Christians during the Holocaust when Jews by the millions were sent to the gas chambers. The American folk hymn, "Were You There?" may be recalled by Christians to pierce the hard shell of our complacency over the evils that beset our nation.

> Were you there when they crucified my Lord? . . .
> Sometimes it causes me to tremble, tremble, tremble.

The words should startle us awake. Are we still stirred by the sacrifice of Jesus for our salvation? Do the lines of the hymn cause us to probe whether we may be indifferent when Jesus is bidding us from the cross to involve ourselves in the world's agonies?

Contrast the indifference shown by the soldiers with the response of the beloved disciple when Jesus says to him, "Here is your mother." The Gospel tells us that from that time John took Mary into his own home to care for her.

Literally one with the world on his shoulders, Jesus sees his mother and entrusts her care to the faithful disciple who stands near the cross. Here Jesus bids us remember that there is no conflict between our duty to the community (whether local or worldwide) and our duty to parents. In the hour of his death, Jesus repeats the lesson his whole life has taught—he suffers our real human woes. On the cross, he knows the pain of thirst.

John presents Jesus' answer to the religions and philosophies that were current in the early centuries of Christianity—systems that argued that spirit was wholly good and matter was wholly evil. This way of thinking was called *gnosticism.* It taught that God never would share in the contamination of the flesh that the Incarnation would involve. Matter is evil, the gnostics insisted. Gnosticism denied the Incarnation and the Prologue to the Gospel of John when it says, "The Word became flesh." Gnostics argued that Jesus did not have a real body that suffered the pains of the flesh. Jesus was understood as a pure spirit, and the gnostic religions were purely "spiritual" religions.

On the cross, Jesus refuted the gnostics' teachings of detachment from the world of matter. God has made human beings with body, mind, and spirit; and we are called to serve him in the marketplace and wherever else our duties take us.

"It is finished"—these were Jesus' last words on the cross. The mission he had been sent to accomplish was now completed. Jesus of Nazareth—he is our best proof of God. So the cry "It is finished" was a shout of victory that would be made plainer to the disciples on the morning of the Resurrection.

John continues his account of the "Word made flesh" with the act of the soldier in piercing Jesus' side with the spear. From Jesus' side there flowed blood and water. It was a strange phenomenon, a sign that attested to the reality that Jesus was a real man and had a real body. This event was another way of disproving the gnostics' belief that Jesus was not fully human.

John sees in the incident of the issuing of blood and water from Jesus' side a symbol of two church sacraments. One sacrament is based on water—namely, baptism. The other is based on blood; it is Holy Communion. In baptism the water is a sign of God's cleansing and healing mercy. In the fruit of the vine of the sacrament we have the sign of the cleansing blood of Jesus' sacrifice. The cross, therefore, speaks to us of the supreme love of God.

In his *Imitation of Christ,* Thomas à Kempis presents to us a summary of what the cross may mean for us:

In the Cross is salvation, in the Cross is life, in the Cross is protection against our enemies, in the Cross is infusion of heavenly sweetness, in the Cross is strength of mind, in the Cross joy of spirit, in the Cross the height of virtue, in the Cross the perfection of holiness. There is no salvation of the soul, nor hope of everlasting life, but in the Cross. Take up therefore thy Cross and follow Jesus, and thou shalt go into life everlasting. He went before, bearing His Cross, and died for thee on the Cross; that thou also mayest bear thy Cross and desire to die on the Cross. For if thou be dead with Him, thou shalt also in like manner live with Him. And if thou share His punishment, thou shalt also share His glory.

Behold! in the Cross all doth consist, and in our dying thereon all lieth; for there is no other way unto life, and unto true inward peace, but the way of the holy Cross, and of daily mortification. Walk where thou wilt, seek whatsoever thou wilt, thou shalt not find a higher way above, nor a safer way below, than the way of the holy Cross.[1]

John 19:38-42. After the death of Jesus, two members of the Sanhedrin came forward to arrange for his burial. Joseph of Arimathea, who was a secret disciple of Jesus because of fear of the Jews, went to Pilate and asked for the Lord's body. Then Nicodemus, also a secret disciple of Jesus, brought to the tomb sweet spices for the Lord's burial.

Both disciples held responsible positions in the Jewish power structure. Both risked disgrace and loss of influence if they became known as followers of Jesus. Both, however, suppressed their fears and paid tribute to the lowly Galilean.

Jesus taught that when he was lifted up, he would draw all human beings to himself. His cross drew these two members of the Sanhedrin to him. The cross made heroes of both men. So they buried Jesus in a new grave in the garden, in a tomb in which no one had ever been laid.

DIMENSION THREE: WHAT DOES THE BIBLE MEAN TO ME?

What Shall We Do With Jesus?

Lead the class members in a discussion and meditation on the section in the student book entitled, "What Shall We Do With Jesus?"

What mistakes did Pilate make that set the Jews against him before Jesus was brought to trial? How did Pilate try to evade responsibility for his decision concerning Jesus? Why may Christians conclude that Pilate lost the battle over Jesus?

In what ways do we evade making decisions about Jesus? How often in the past week have you spoken up for your faith? How often in the past week have you avoided taking a stand on an issue that would have identified you as a follower of Jesus?

Why can we say that Pilate wanted to be his own God? How do modern people show this same desire? Do we also desire to manipulate others, to wield power, and to be our God?

Read the definitions of a Christian in Dimension Three of the student book. What do you think is Christ's vision of the kingdom of God? Do we share it? What evidence do we put forth that we want what Christ wants? Do we, like Pilate, seek ways out of our responsibility? How?

Do you agree that Pilate was defeated in the encounter over whether Jesus should go to the cross? Why or why not? What do you think cross-bearing means in the Christian faith? What does it mean for Christians to die with Christ? Is this death always a physical dying? Is it, perhaps, harder to live for Christ than to die for him? Why or why not? Why do you think John does not describe the Crucifixion in detail?

What were the good and bad qualities in Pilate? What kind of record did Pilate write? What kind are we writing?

Why do you think Joseph and Nicodemus were willing to risk their prestige and fine community standing to bury Jesus' body? Why was the cross Jesus' supreme act of courage? How do you think this act affected Joseph and Nicodemus? How do you think Jesus' death on the cross can affect each of us?

---

[1]From *The Imitation of Christ,* revised translation, by Thomas à Kempis (Grosset and Dunlap, 1935), page 109.

Again Jesus said, "Peace be with you! As the Father has sent me, I am sending you" (20:21).

12

Christ Is Risen!

John 20

DIMENSION ONE:
WHAT DOES THE BIBLE SAY?

Answer these questions by reading John 20

1. When does Mary Magdalene come to the tomb early and see the stone had been removed from the entrance? (20:1)

   Mary comes "early on the first day of the week," while it was still dark.

2. When Mary runs from the tomb, whom does she meet? (20:2)

   Mary meets Simon Peter and the other disciple, "the one Jesus loved."

3. What does Mary say to them? (20:2)

   She tells them they have taken away the Lord from the tomb, and she does not know where they have put him.

4. Who outruns Peter to be the first disciple to reach the tomb? (20:4)

   The other disciple outruns Peter.

5. What do the other disciple and Peter see on reaching the tomb? (20:6-7)

   They see the strips of linen and the burial cloth that had been around Jesus' head.

6. What do the two disciples do? (20:8)

   They both enter the tomb. The "other disciple . . . saw and believed."

7. What does Mary do and see? (20:11-12)

   She stands outside the tomb crying, bends over to look into the tomb, and sees two angels in white sitting where Jesus' body had been.

8. What do the angels ask Mary, and what is Mary's reply? (20:13)

   They ask Mary why she is crying. She replies that she cries because Jesus has been taken away and she does not know where they have put him.

9. Whom does Mary now see, and what does he tell her? (20:14-17)

   She sees Jesus, but mistakes him for the gardener. Jesus calls Mary's name and tells her not to hold him for he has not yet ascended to the Father. He tells her to go to his brothers and to tell them that he is returning to his God and theirs.

10. What is Mary's message to the disciples? (20:18)

    Her message is that she has seen the Lord. Then she delivers the message Jesus gave her for them.

11. What happens on the evening of the first day? (20:19-20a)

    Jesus comes to the disciples who are behind locked doors. He greets them with the words, "Peace be with you!" and shows them his hands and his side. He says to them again, "Peace be with you! As the Father has sent me, I am sending you."

12. What is the response of the disciples to all this? (20:20b)

    The disciples are overjoyed.

13. What does Jesus do and say next? (20:22-23)

He breathes on the disciples and tells them to receive the Holy Spirit. He says if they forgive the sins of anyone, these persons would be forgiven; that if they do not forgive the sins of any they are not forgiven.

14. What do the disciples tell Thomas when he arrives? (20:25a)

They tell him that they had seen the Lord.

15. What is Thomas's reply? (20:25b)

He says he must see the mark of the nails and put his finger in their mark and also place his hand in Jesus' side before he will believe.

16. What happens a week later? (20:26-27)

Jesus comes among the disciples again. He told Thomas to touch him, to stop doubting, and to believe.

17. What is Thomas's response? (20:28)

He answers, "My Lord and my God!"

18. What does Jesus say? (20:29)

Jesus says that Thomas believes because he has seen, but that those who believe without seeing are blessed.

19. What was John's purpose in writing the Gospel? (20:31)

It was written so that "you may believe that Jesus is the Christ, the Son of God, and that by believing you may have life in his name."

DIMENSION TWO:
WHAT DOES THE BIBLE MEAN?

John 20:1-10. Mary Magdalene, the much forgiven sinner, came to the tomb first on Easter Day. Mary came early. As John's Gospel says, she came while it was "still dark."

The Fourth Evangelist does not mention the "other women" who were with Mary, but he implies their presence in the words, "They have taken the Lord out of the tomb, and we don't know where they have put him!" We turn to the Synoptics (Matthew, Mark, and Luke) for the information that with Mary Magdalene were Mary, the mother of James the younger, and Salome (Mark 15:40; Matthew 27:56) or Mary, the mother of James and Joanna (Luke 24:10).

In the early morning light Mary Magdalene was able to see that the stone has been taken from the entrance of the tomb. She ran to share this news with others, and she met Peter and the other disciple. She told them the tomb was empty. Mary announced a reality that she did not comprehend: the faith of Jesus is the faith of the empty tomb. This is the message the church must proclaim today. Christians worship not a grave but the living Lord. Jesus' body has been raised from death, so that he is present everywhere.

In the Fourth Evangelist's view, the material body of Jesus has been changed into a spiritual body. We do not understand all that this means, but Christians believe that our unique personalities are raised in the Resurrection. Flesh and blood, the bodies we now have, will not inherit life eternal; but in the mystery of God's grace we shall be given the spiritual bodies we need to live in the presence of him who dwells in eternal light.

Peter and the other disciple beheld a symbol of this reality when they saw the burial cloths of Jesus. The cloths were neatly folded and put away as a person who irons allows no wrinkle or disarray to mar his or her work. If thieves had come to steal Jesus' body, they would have taken him in his burial cloths. They would have left signs of haste.

The attentions of Peter and the beloved disciple were therefore centered on the neatly folded burial cloths and their meaning. Peter saw the cloths, but John was the first to see and believe. The beloved disciple was in a better position to believe in the Christ because he had great love for the Messiah. John saw and believed that Jesus had risen from the dead.

Countless Christians since the time of Mary Magdalene and the beloved disciple have also seen and believed. They have been convinced by what Christ has done in their lives. At Eastertide we sing the words of Martin Luther:

Christ Jesus lay in death's strong bands
    for our offenses given;
but now at God's right hand he stands,
    and brings us life from heaven;
    wherefore let us joyful be,
    and sing to God right thankfully
loud songs of Alleluia!
    Alleluia!

It was a strange and dreadful strife
    when life and death contended;
the victory remained with life;
    the reign of death was ended.
Stripped of power, no more he reigns,
    an empty form alone remains;
death's sting is lost forever!
    Alleluia!

John 20:11-18. Mary's Lord had been crucified between two thieves—"numbered with the transgressors" (Isaiah 53:12; Luke 22:37). As she cried Mary peeped into the tomb.

CHRIST IS RISEN!

Unlike Peter and John, she did not notice the burial cloths. Her eyes fixed on two angels in white, one sitting by the head and the other sitting by the feet where the body of Jesus had lain. By including the presence of the angels John wanted to emphasize that God was present in the events of the empty tomb. God was there to speak to the sorrow of Mary.

When the angels asked why Mary was weeping she said, "They have taken my Lord away, and I don't know where they have put him." Mary wanted to give Jesus' body an honored burial. When Jesus first spoke to Mary, she did not recognize his voice. Mistaking him for the gardener, she asked Jesus to tell her where the body lay so she could go find it and give it a proper burial.

Then Jesus spoke Mary's name, causing her to turn around and face him. Mary had an experience that is similar to our own. We know how we are affected when we hear our name called. Modern salespeople are taught that there is power in the calling of a person's name. The hearing of one's name shakes the person up and involves him or her in what is going on.

Mary was looking for Jesus among the dead, not looking for him as the living Savior. How many of us look for Christ among the tombs? We search the historic reports of his presence long ago, and that is well. We are ready to believe these accounts. But as record and history these reports do not touch us. A living Christ—one who confronts us at the office, in the home, in the school, in the business and political systems—that One puts us under obligation. Mary did not find Christ; for Christ found Mary, just as he finds us.

Our God is the God who seeks us. God pursues us unceasingly. When John wrote his Gospel, he was continuing the theme of God's search for the human being that we have chronicled in writings of the Pentateuch, the prophets, and the Wisdom Literature. The high points of the Old Testament come in the expressions of the love of God for Israel—as in Jeremiah 31:3: "I have loved you with an everlasting love; / I have drawn you with loving-kindness." The God who pursues us emerges most clearly in Psalm 139. (Read to class members the first twelve verses of this psalm.)

Mary sought Christ in the graveyard; but she did not recognize him when he appeared to her, just as we do not recognize him. He did not come to her in the expected way. He came in no thunderstorms or public fanfares. In her mixed disappointment and hope, Christ came to Mary tenderly.

So it is that in times of sorrow and loss, when everything seems to have collapsed for us, we may know that God's love does not fail us. That is the meaning of the Resurrection.

When Mary recognized Jesus, she tried to hold him, but he dissuaded her. Jesus, in effect, told Mary not to hold on to him in the flesh with its limitations. Instead, she should cling to him through his reunion with God

after the Ascension, which would be Jesus' last appearance on earth.

John 20:19-23. What are this individual's credentials? This question is often asked in our society. Candidates for political office and high court appointments are required to answer it. Physicians put their diplomas up on their walls. Teachers, mechanics, computer technicians, and nurses are required to furnish credentials. Young graduates of educational institutions are carefully coached on how to prepare résumés of their scholastic and work experiences so that prospective employers will be favorably impressed and will employ them. Writers, soldiers, and scientists earn their credentials by their performances. Feodor Dostoevski, the greatest of Russian novelists, was once taunted by a critic who demanded to know by what right he could speak for the Russian people. He simply pulled up his trouser cuffs and revealed the scars of Siberian chains.

What were Jesus' credentials? On Easter evening he came into the presence of his disciples and said to them, "Peace be with you!" Then he showed them his hands and his side that bore the wounds of the Crucifixion. The cross was his crown of glory, the sign by which he would be known throughout the world.

Jesus was preparing his disciples, a defeated and discouraged lot, to begin a ministry that would ultimately win the world to him. In the aftermath of the cross he brought courage to these disciples. The cross was once a symbol of humiliation and disgrace. Now it was the symbol of joy and victory.

Jesus' mission has been accomplished. His credentials will forever be the cross. He has been raised from the dead, thus conquering the two worst enemies of humankind: sin and death.

What does he do now? Jesus gives to the disciples the Holy Spirit, breathing on them to symbolize the giving of himself—the giving of new life. The Spirit would give power, imagination, and zeal to the disciples and the church.

Jesus gives this same Spirit to us, the same Spirit who works in every human situation, bringing good out of evil. Without the Holy Spirit, we can do nothing. With the Spirit, the church can preach the forgiveness of sins to the whole world and mediate the love of God to all people.

In the encounter with the disciples, then, Jesus gives us the selfsame message he gave to his first disciples: "As the Father has sent me, I am sending you." John's Gospel is a missionary book. It tells us and all humankind that love will triumph in the whole world because Christ is risen.

John 20:24-29. We have met Thomas in the study of 11:16 and 14:5. In the first passage Thomas, called Didymus (the Twin), challenges his fellow disciples to go with Jesus to Bethany where they could all die together. Thomas was willing to be a martyr for Jesus. In the second verse Thomas voices the skeptical statement, "Lord, we don't know where you are going, so how can we know the way?" Jesus replies, "I am the way and the truth and the life. No one comes to the Father, except through me."

Thomas knew the claim of Jesus that Jesus and the Father are one. He understood the consequences of being a disciple of Jesus. In the first verse cited about him, Thomas was courageous; but he was weak later when with the other disciples he forsook Jesus and fled.

After the Crucifixion, Thomas took time to think matters over. He wanted to see what would happen next. We might apply to Thomas the characterization that Charles Dickens gave of Joe Gargery: "He was a mild, good-natured, sweet-tempered, easy-going, foolish, dear fellow—a sort of Hercules in strength and also in weakness."[1] This description might be applied to many of us.

The disciples told Thomas the Lord had risen from the dead. For Thomas this claim was just too much. He would not believe the disciples' report until he could see for himself.

When Jesus came into the room where Thomas was, he challenged Thomas to examine his credentials: the wounds of the Crucifixion. These were the marks of Jesus' success! Thomas asked for tangible proof of the Resurrection. Jesus gave him proof of the Crucifixion. Jesus' presence was all the proof the disciple needed of the Resurrection. We prove our Lord by the encounter with him—by experience. This truth grasped Thomas and caused him to exclaim: "My Lord and my God!"

John 20:30-31. John wrote his work to win us to the belief that Jesus is the Christ, the Anointed One, the Son of God, and that believing in him we may have life in his name. John tells us of the God who demonstrates his love and care for us individually and for the world.

This story may help us in our meditations on that love and care:

A woman was driving alone through a very large American city. The traffic was congested and noisy—bumper to bumper at times—so that the woman became utterly confused. Having made three false turns, she lost the way. She finally managed to stop at a service station where she could ask for travel information. The woman got out of her car, went inside the station, and explained her predicament to an employee.

The service station attendant got down a map of the city, saying, "So you're lost. I don't know how you'll ever get to the interstate. There is much street construction along the way, and all the signs have been changed." The attendant scratched his head, pored over the map, and said, "You'll have to go back the way you came and take the right turns."

Said the woman, "I could never do that. I don't know how I got here in the first place."

Said the attendant: "You'll need to go southeast through the city. Let's see, you take a right on the boulevard, go past four traffic lights, turn left at the top of the hill, cross three traffic lights, and turn left at the river bridge. . . . No, that won't do. You'll run into road construction. Everything's torn up for six blocks. You can't get there from here."

After half an hour of the attendant's perplexity, another woman who had heard it all stepped forward and said to the other woman, "I'll show you the way. I'll lead you there. Just follow close to me. I'll drive slowly so the cars can't cut in between us."

The second woman put her small daughter in her car. Then she drove many miles through tortuous traffic, making many turns. Finally, she stopped her car at the entrance to the cloverleaf, got out, and walked back to give instructions about where to exit on the interstate. She laughed, wished the other woman well, and waved goodbye.

Here we have a parable of the journey of faith. Jesus came to show us the way and to help us reach our human destination.

DIMENSION THREE: WHAT DOES THE BIBLE MEAN TO ME?

The class members may discuss the following questions or use the meditation in the student book.

Searching for Jesus

Use the story above to begin discussing "What the Bible Means to Me."

Do we sometimes fail to recognize the Savior's voice when he speaks to us? How does Christ speak to us? How should we listen for his voice?

Christ is risen. So what? What does the Resurrection mean to us in these modern times? What did the Resurrection mean to Mary Magdalene? to Peter? to John? to Thomas? to other early Christians?

How are we like Thomas? Do we, like he did, wait for conclusive proof for our faith? Do we search for a firsthand religious experience that touches our minds as well as our hearts? What can Thomas's experience teach us about our faith?

---

[1]From *Great Expectations*, by Charles Dickens (Holt, Rhinehart and Winston, 1967), page 6.

13

Victory and Christ's Call

John 21

DIMENSION ONE:
WHAT DOES THE BIBLE SAY?

Answer these questions by reading John 21

1. To whom does Jesus reveal himself by the Sea of Tiberias? (21:1-2)

   He reveals himself to these disciples: Simon Peter, Thomas, Nathanael, the sons of Zebedee, and two other disciples.

2. What does Simon Peter say he is going to do, and what happens? (21:3)

   Peter says he is going fishing. Others join him; and they fish all night, catching nothing.

3. Who is standing on the shore early the next morning? (21:4)

   Jesus is standing on the shore, but the disciples do not recognize him.

4. When he asks the disciples if they had caught any fish and receives a negative reply, what does Jesus tell them to do? (21:5-6a)

   He tells the disciples to cast their net on the right side of the boat, "and you will find some [fish]."

5. What do the disciples do then, and what results from their action? (21:6b)

   They cast their net where Jesus had told them to. They are unable to haul in the large number of fish.

6. Who first recognizes Jesus, and what does he say? (21:7a)

   The "disciple whom Jesus loved" recognizes Jesus and says, "It is the Lord!"

7. What does Peter do when he hears this? (21:7b)

   He put on his clothes and "jumped into the water."

8. What do the other disciples do? (21:8)

   They bring in the boat, "towing the net full of fish."

9. What do the disciples see when they get to land, and what does Jesus say to them? (21:9-10)

   They see a charcoal fire "with fish on it, and some bread." Jesus says, "Bring some of the fish you have just caught."

10. What does Peter do then, and what does Jesus say to the disciples? (21:11-12)

    "Peter climbed aboard and dragged the net ashore." Jesus tells the disciples to come to breakfast.

11. What is said after they finish breakfast? (21:15-19)

    Jesus asks Peter three times if the disciple loves him. Peter replies three times that he loves Jesus. Each time Jesus tells Peter to care for his sheep. Jesus, suggesting the death by which Peter would die, says to Peter, "Follow me."

DIMENSION TWO:
WHAT DOES THE BIBLE MEAN?

The Epilogue. Many scholars maintain that John 21 is an appendix written by a different person than the one who wrote Chapters 1–20. They have strong reasons for questioning the conclusion that John the apostle (who is identified as the beloved disciple) wrote the final chapter. Detailed and comprehensive studies of the language and literary construction of the chapter lie behind their questioning. We do not know who wrote Chapter 21, but it is possible to suppose that a person who had been closely related to the apostolic author wrote it.

The questions of authorship, however, are secondary questions; for we should not let the problems of authorship take precedence over the primary question: Is the chapter true? The overwhelming evidence is that it is.

What is the concern of the author of Chapter 21? One purpose of the author was to remind the church that Peter, who had betrayed Jesus, had been forgiven and restored to his old status as natural leader of the apostles. The author also wanted to combat the false idea that Christ would come before the death of John, the last of the apostles.

Many scholars think the author of Chapter 21 also wrote to affirm the reality of the Resurrection. The risen Christ was no mere phantom, no mere vision cherished by the confused disciples. He was no hallucination, but a person of flesh and blood who had been raised from the tomb. Jesus indeed walked in the world and cooked and ate fish.

Chapter 21 indicates that a pure spirit probably would not concern itself with telling fishermen where the fishing would be best for a fine catch. A pure spirit would not build a fire by the sea and cook a meal to feed hungry fishermen.

Chapter 21, then, is in full harmony with the whole message of the Gospel. The Epilogue agrees with the Prologue: "The Word became flesh and made his dwelling among us." John's Gospel will never let us forget this reality. The characters of his drama get mixed up in the material world.

John 21:1-14. This section of Scripture is in accord with John's Gospel in the way it symbolizes truth. One example is indicated by the report that 153 fish were caught by the disciples. The writer does not describe the catch as a miracle or as a "sign," but he is concerned to bring concrete detail into his narrative; he wants to tell us the catch was a huge one and that Jesus knew where the fish could be caught. The writer wants us to see that the report of the catch has a deeper meaning.

Scholars have made many attempts to unravel John's hidden meaning regarding the catch of fish. Jerome has given us perhaps the best explanation. In an allegorical fashion Jerome declares that there were 153 different kinds of fish in the sea. The catch includes every kind of fish, and the number symbolizes the reality that in the future all nations will be gathered to Jesus Christ.

William Barclay has said that the whole catch of fish was placed in the net, and the net was not broken by the weight of the fish. The net symbolizes the church, and the church has room for persons of all nations. Again we have the clear note of universality affirmed in the Gospel. The Christian gospel excludes no one because of color, class, or nationality: and "the embrace of the Church," says Barclay, "is as universal as the love of God in Jesus Christ."[1]

At the heart of the Fourth Gospel is its author's resolve to show that in Jesus Christ we have the real Incarnation and the fulfillment of all human hopes. This is why Chapter 21 continues to combat the idea that Jesus Christ seemed to be something that he was not.

John took issue with the docetists, a heretical group of religionists who believed that Jesus Christ had no fleshly existence but came to earth in a human "semblance" without being corrupted by contact with the flesh and with the material existence. The docetists were part of the mixed and diverse system of thinkers, ideas, and writings that became known as gnosticism. The gnostics (from the Greek word *gnosis*, meaning knowledge) claimed that they possessed a knowledge that freed them from the fragmentary, the illusory, and the evil world. They said a rift existed between appearance and reality. Believing the fleshly existence was evil, they sought to shun it.

Gnosticism plagued the church for the first four centuries of its history; its downfall came with the work of Athanasius and other theologians who championed the faith that "God was reconciling the world to himself in Christ" (2 Corinthians 5:19) and that Christ was fully human and fully divine.

Gnostic ideas and attitudes have persisted in the modern church, however, and their persistence is what Amos N. Wilder calls the "false spirituality" of the church. Give some time to elaborate on evidences of this "false spirituality" in the church today. (See the student book, pages 108–110.)

What methods of escape from the pain and struggle of the world do Christians sometimes use? How do we locate religious experiences in "good feelings" rather than in the will? How do you think that false spirituality denies the Word made flesh? How does it disparage the world that God has created?

The Apostles' Creed reads: "I believe in the Holy Spirit, the holy catholic Church, the communion of saints, the forgiveness of sins, the resurrection of the body, and the life everlasting." Here is affirmed the work of the Holy Spirit in our lives, the universal church, the blessings of the Christian community, our forgiveness and a new start, the resurrection of the body, and the persistence of our individual personality into eternity. By the resurrection of the body we mean to affirm the unity of the person—body, mind, and spirit. The words symbolize the goodness of our material existence and the persistence by God's grace of the unique individual human being.

How have members of the class known the Word to reach them through their involvement with mundane and commonplace experience? How do they think the Holy Spirit meets us in the work place and the marketplace? Do you think the Holy Spirit gets mixed up with our political responsibilities?

Do you think the Holy Spirit brings joy to our work? How? Alfred North Whitehead has said that the world has more to gain from business people's joy in their work than it does from those who labor to endow hospitals.[2]

John 21:15-23. The questioning of Peter dominates the conversation here. Peter has come to the time of restoration following his cowardly refusal to be identified as a disciple of his Lord. Christ wants now to begin preparing Peter for the role he will play as the leader of the church.

"Do you truly love me more than these?" This key question is asked three times. The risen Lord asks us the same question. What stands in the way of our full commitment to him? We are called to give it up, as the rich young ruler was called to give up his possessions to follow Jesus.

Christ would have us remove the barriers to his love, the barriers that prevent our being fully human. Are we half-hearted in our allegiance to Christ? He would unify divided persons so that we can act with a single mind. Augustine said that the secret of Christian education is to get the weight of the learner's love rightly directed. This is precisely what Christ does with Peter and with us. He deals with the question of our chief love first. What do we love most? Can we love the Christ more than these? If so, Christ can restore us to our rightful place in his Kingdom.

When have we, like Simon Peter, turned our backs on Christ? When have we refused to follow him? Let us note that we are first asked to love the Lord—then by our love of the neighbor (anyone in need) Christ can know that we love him. Think of the most disreputable characters you know. Can you love them? Can you love all people—the hungry children across the world? the street people of our own towns? the men and women humiliated by unemployment? the people who are ill in body and mind and spirit?

When we consider the enormity of the problems of serving Christ's people today, many Christians are prone to despair. Human suffering is vast, and people of good will are often frustrated about what to do. Some Christians have been known to receive a dozen appeals for money in one day from church and philanthropic agencies.

What can we do? Ask class members to suggest creative and constructive ways of tending and feeding Christ's sheep. Not all of these needs involve money. These actions might point us in the direction of changing our attitudes. In Christian thinking the individual human being is of infinite, absolute value. Each bears the image of God, no matter how that image may have been defaced by sin. Can Christians be bitter and stingy toward the poor? the unfortunate and suffering? Do we need to rethink our giving? Do we know how our money for charities is managed? Do we require that agencies send us audited financial reports? What is our church doing to meet human need?

The needs are enormous in our home churches, in our local communities, in our nation, and throughout the world. Our efforts may seem feeble in view of the world's need. But the love of Christ supports us when we are inclined to underestimate ourselves and our efforts for those who are hungry, sick, homeless, and in prison. What we do may augment the services of innumerable others and prove that the victorious Christ is using us in making all things new. Christ requires only that we trust him and give ourselves for love of him so that no matter how hard the circumstances, we may serve the world he came to save.

Jesus said, "Follow me." Finally, Simon Peter got the message.

An old story that Christians have remembered across the centuries tells that Peter escaped from prison on the night before he was to be crucified. Peter was fleeing along the Appian Way when he met Jesus carrying a cross. "Lord, whither goest thou?" said Peter. And the reply came, "I am going to Rome to be crucified afresh." Peter returned to his cell. When the guards came for him the next day, Peter was there. Christ's love had made him captive.

Peter faced prison and martyrdom, but what of John?

We do not know if John the beloved disciple went to prison for his faith or if he was martyred. But we do know that John's vocation was to bear witness to the truth of the gospel of Christ. Peter wants to know what John's role and fate will be, and he asks Jesus a speculative question: "Lord, what about him?" Jesus tells Peter that the future of John is no concern of Peter's. His duty is to follow Christ. John has his own vocation, his own way of expressing his talents and gifts. He is to be a witness for the truth, following Christ above everything else.

John 21:24-25. The story has been told. It is a reliable witness to a story with reaches more vast, the unending account of what Christ is doing in the world.

He is alive, working within the church and within the world and in each of us to bring about the Kingdom that endures forever.

DIMENSION THREE:
WHAT DOES THE BIBLE MEAN TO ME?

The Christian Life Is a Victorious Life

In a scholarly book entitled *God Was in Christ: An Essay on Incarnation and Atonement*, British theologian D. M. Baillie has summed up what the New Testament says about human sin and Christ's victory over it. He sees the essence of sin as self-centeredness that destroys the individual and human community. Baillie gives a brief picture of our human life as it ought to be:

I would tell a tale of God calling His human children to form a great circle for the playing of His game. In that circle we ought all to be standing, linked together with lovingly joined hands, facing towards the Light in the centre, which is God ("the Love that moves the sun and the other stars"); seeing our fellow creatures all round the circle in the light of that central Love, which shines on them and beautifies their faces; and joining with them in the dance of God's great game, the rhythm of love universal. But instead of that, we have, each one, turned our backs upon God and the circle of our fellows, and faced the other way, so that we can see neither the Light at the centre nor the faces on the circumference. And indeed in that position it is difficult even to join hands with our fellows! Therefore instead of playing God's game we play, each one, our own selfish little game, like the perverse children Jesus saw in the market-place, who would not join in the dance with their companions. Each one of us wishes to be the centre, and there is blind confusion, and not even any true *knowledge* of God or of our neighbours. That is what is wrong with mankind. Of course a man is not really happy in that attitude and situation, since he was created for community with God and man.[3]

Baillie goes on to show how the resurrected Christ draws us out of ourselves into the life of unselfish community.

God has never given up on us. He has sent Jesus to live out amid a sinful humanity the life of love. Jesus taught, labored, suffered, and died at last on a cross, forsaken and alone. But God brought him through death, raising him up and giving him back to us in an unseen way, the Holy Spirit that made Jesus' followers into a community.

Now, looking back, we can know that all this was in fact the love of God dealing with our sin, offering us forgiveness and a new start. So God's love in Christ creates a new person, a new community everywhere it is accepted.

We come confessing: "Not I, but the grace of God." That reality of God's redemption shatters the barriers between persons and between nations; for it is "the new People of God, the new Israel, the *Ecclesia,* the Body of Christ, the Church."[4] In these the risen Christ says to us anew, "Take heart! I have overcome the world."

---

[1]From *The Gospel of John,* Volume 2, revised edition, by William Barclay (Westminster, 1975), page 284.

[2]From *The Aims of Education,* by Alfred North Whitehead (Free Press, 1967).

[3]From *God Was in Christ: An Essay on Incarnation and Atonement,* by D. M. Baillie (Charles Scribner's Sons, 1948), page 206.

[4]From *God Was in Christ,* page 208.

ACTS
Table of Contents

About the Writer

James F. Sargent is pastor of the Oxford United Methodist Church in Oxford, Ohio.

You will be my witnesses in Jerusalem, and in all Judea and Samaria, and to the ends of the earth (1:8).

— 1 —
The Mission to the World and Pentecost
Acts 1–2

DIMENSION ONE:
WHAT DOES THE BIBLE SAY?

Answer these questions by reading Acts 1

1. To whom is this book written? (1:1)

   Acts is written to Theophilus.

2. For how many days did Jesus appear to the apostles? (1:3)

   Jesus appeared to the apostles "over a period of forty days."

3. What are Jesus' instructions to the apostles? (1:4-5)

   Jesus instructs the apostles to return to Jerusalem and wait there for the coming of the Holy Spirit.

4. Who are the apostles, according to the list in Acts 1:13?

   The apostles are Peter, John, James, Andrew, Philip, Thomas, Bartholomew, Matthew, James the son of Alphaeus, Simon the Zealot, and Judas the son of James.

5. Who is the first preacher? (1:15)

   The first preacher is Peter.

6. How many people are numbered as Christian? (1:15)

   There were numbered about a hundred and twenty persons.

7. What are the requirements to be an apostle? (1:21-22; 24).

   To be an apostle one had to have accompanied Jesus during his earthly ministry, beginning with his baptism until "Jesus was taken up from us"—the Ascension. An apostle also had to be a witness to the Resurrection.

8. Who is selected as the twelfth apostle? (1:26)

   Matthias is selected as the twelfth apostle.

Answer these questions by reading Acts 2

9. When are the apostles "all together in one place"? (2:1)

   The apostles are all together on the day of Pentecost.

10. What charge is leveled against the apostles? (2:13)

    They are accused of being drunk.

11. Which Old Testament prophet does Peter quote? (2:17-21)

    Peter quotes the prophet Joel (2:28-32)

12. What does Peter recall from the life of Jesus? (2:22-24)

    Peter tells of Jesus' miracles, wonders, and signs; of his being handed over to the Jews by God's set purpose; of Jesus being crucified, and of God raising him from the dead.

13. How do the apostles know of the Resurrection? (2:32)

    They were all witnesses to the Resurrection.

14. What is the result of Peter's preaching? (2:37)

    "When the people heard this [Peter's preaching] they were cut to the heart, and said to Peter and the other apostles, 'Brothers, what shall we do?'"

15. To whom is the promise of forgiveness available? (2:39)

    The promise of forgiveness is available for all—you, your children, and all who are far off.

16. How many are baptized that first Pentecost? (2:41)

About three thousand persons are baptized that day.

17. To what do believers devote themselves? (2:42)

The believers devote themselves to the apostles' teaching, to fellowship, to breaking bread, and to prayer.

18. How does the writer of Acts characterize the Christian community? (2:44-46)

The people of the Christian community stay together, have all things in common, sell their possessions in order to help those in need, attend Temple worship together, and break bread in their homes.

19. How are Christians viewed by outsiders? (2:47)

The Christians have "the favor of all the people."

DIMENSION TWO: WHAT DOES THE BIBLE MEAN?

The earliest tradition of the post-apostolic age names Luke as writer of the Third Gospel (Luke) and the Book of Acts. Both books are addressed to *Theophilus*. The writer of Acts refers to a previous writing by himself about the life and teachings of Christ (1:1). The vocabulary and style of these two books are similar. Acts is the second volume of the two-volume work Luke-Acts.

While the writer does not name himself in either book, he uses the first person plural in certain parts of the account of Paul's journeys (the "we" sections, Acts 16:10-17; 20:5–21:18; 27:1–28:16) and by this suggests that he was Paul's companion.

Acts 1:1-5. Acts begins with a backward look—a sort of gathering up of the traditions about Jesus. "My former book," referred to in verse 1, is our Gospel of Luke (Luke 1:1-4). The first five verses in Acts thus serve as a sort of preface, a prelude to the continuing work of Jesus.

To whom was this book written? We can only guess. Perhaps the book was written for a patron of early Christianity who was sympathetic of the movement. *Theophilus* means "lover of God" and might possibly be a pseudonym for a Gentile Christian who held some official position under the Roman Empire and who needed to remain anonymous.

The Holy Spirit was already at work—before Pentecost. Jesus, in choosing the apostles and giving them commandments, had the help of the Holy Spirit. Election is God's choosing; being chosen by Jesus gives authority to the apostles and to the movement.

The apostles are eyewitnesses to the resurrected Jesus in their midst (preceding the Ascension) "over a period of forty days." Jesus speaks to them of the kingdom of God, which not only anticipates the question in verse 6, but gives it content and gives direction to the balance of the book. The Kingdom is mentioned several times in Acts (1:6; 8:12; 14:22; 19:8; 20:25; 28:23, 31).

The movement of Christianity from a sect within Jewish tradition to a worldwide movement that would be predominantly Gentile was not the work or design of humans. The movement was begun and sustained by Jesus.

Jesus tells the apostles to wait in Jerusalem for "the gift my Father promised," as if to suggest that the work he has in mind will be of such magnitude that they will not be able to do it on their own strength. They will need the very power and presence of God (Ephesians 1:13).

In contrast to the water baptism of John, which was characterized by repentance, the baptism of the Holy Spirit is the fuller release of power within and through those who are already Christians. However, the Spirit has already been at work. The Spirit has something to do with becoming Christian in the first place (John 3:5; 1 Corinthians 12:13).

The Holy Spirit does not depend on water baptism. In other settings in Acts the gift of the Spirit comes without water baptism (8:14-15; 10:44-48; 19:1-7).

Jesus' instruction is that the apostles should wait in Jerusalem. At the appropriate time the Spirit will gain a more complete possession of them for the purpose of spreading the kingdom of God.

Acts 1:6-11. The word *ascension* does not appear in the Scripture. However, *ascension* is used to describe the actual moment when Jesus left the earth.

The apostles are convinced that the coming of the Kingdom will be very soon. "Are you *at this time* . . . ?" The earliest Christians had hoped, as had Jews in general, that this outpouring of the Spirit would be a part of the end times. Therefore, the promised coming of the Holy Spirit held hope for many as the consummation of time with the promise of the establishment of the mighty order of God.

Jesus' response is to the question of timing, not to the issue of nation: "It is not for you to know times or dates the Father has set by his own authority" (1:7).

Luke here makes it clear that Christians cannot anticipate a quick return of Christ. Many Christians of Luke's generation were disappointed with the delayed return of Jesus Christ (2 Peter 3:3-4). Luke is telling the Christians that they will have to learn how to work within the world. At least part of the task facing Christians is the need to see the Kingdom not in nationalistic terms, but as a world mission.

Verse 8b has been suggested by some as an outline for the Book of Acts. However, many other territories and nations will receive the gospel that Acts will not deal with. Granted, geographical expansion is important to early Christians, but the geographical expansion is secondary to the religious, national, and racial boundaries that the gospel is to transcend.

Jesus tells the apostles they will receive the Holy Spirit (verse 8a). The Holy Spirit is the mediator of power. In many instances the Holy Spirit works wondrous miracles. In early Christianity, miracles were seen as signs that validated or made legitimate the ministry of Jesus and the apostles (2:22; 2 Corinthians 12:12). In Acts the Holy Spirit is absolutely essential both as director and sustainer of mission.

Immediately after his last word, Jesus is wrapped in a cloud and lifted up. The image recalls the Transfiguration (Mark 9:2-8; see also Revelation 11:12). The remarkable aspect of this description is the amount of reserve Luke shows.

The apostles continue gazing toward heaven only to be rebuked by two men (angels?) dressed in white. This rebuke (Acts 1:11) is reminiscent of the Resurrection as described in Luke (24:4-7). Here the apostles' attitude of expectation of a quick return is challenged. Yes, Christ will return. But the return will not be immediate. Luke here replaces hope for an imminent return with a new Christian hope that has to be content with the distant and with the not-yet-visible. The apostles were not to speculate about the end of the world and the coming of the Kingdom, but they were to devote themselves to the task of witnessing.

The Kingdom has already broken into history; it is not yet complete.

Acts 1:12-14. The apostles return from Mount Olivet where, according to Zechariah 14:4, the Messiah will return. The upper room's identity is a matter of conjecture. It could possibly be the same room in which Jesus' Last Supper was shared. Perhaps it was the home of John, Mark, or Mary (12:12).

A list of the disciples appears in three other locations (Matthew 10:2-4; Mark 3:16-19; Luke 6:14-16). Peter and John appear together in Acts 3:1 and 8:14. James's death is reported in 12:2. The rest of the disciples never appear again. The purpose of the Book of Acts then is clearly not the acts of all the disciples. Why are the names lost to obscurity? Some commentators think it is because they were never able as a whole to grow beyond a nationalistic and therefore restricted outlook.

The family of Jesus has caused much discussion. Were these people merely cousins? Were they sons of Joseph by a former marriage? Since names are mentioned in Mark 6:3, surely they were sons of Mary. Mary, mentioned only by John as present at the Crucifixion, is here named for the only time in Acts. Evidently, following Jesus along with the apostles, was another group, possibly wives and children. Certainly Luke shows concern for the women who supported Jesus (Luke 8:2; 23:49, 55; 24:10).

Acts 1:15-26. "In those days," that is, the days between the Ascension and Pentecost, the hundred and twenty believers in this Christian community, most of whom were Galileans, gathered at Jerusalem. These are not the only witnesses. Paul mentions an appearance to over five hundred (1 Corinthians 15:6), and there were witnesses in Palestine outside Jerusalem (Acts 9:31). Since Luke does not describe how Christian communities formed in other areas, it becomes clearer that his intent is not to describe the geographical expansion of Christianity.

Peter speaks to the community of Christians about Judas. He says, "Brothers, the Scripture had to be fulfilled" (1:16; see also Psalms 41:9; 69:26; 109:8). Luke emphasizes the fulfillment of Hebrew (Old Testament) Scriptures perhaps in part to recover the Hebrew tradition.

Judas was an apostle—one of the original Twelve who had witnessed the earthly life of Jesus. His falling away from the faith and his death required his replacement. No similar action is taken on the death of James, the son of Zebedee (12:2). Within Christian tradition there is debate over the death of Judas. In Matthew's Gospel (27:3-10), Judas hangs himself. Perhaps, as described in Acts, Judas bought a small farm, fell off the roof, and "his body burst open and all his intestines spilled out."

Whoever replaces Judas must meet three basic requirements: (1) be among those who followed Jesus from his baptism to the Ascension, who would therefore (2) be a witness to the Resurrection, and who must (3) be an appointment of the Lord himself. Two men meet these requirements—Joseph called Barnabas and Matthias.

Clearly the Christian movement cannot be understood apart from the fact of the Resurrection. Therefore, a successor to Judas who was an eyewitness to the resurrected Jesus had to be found. The need for men who had witnessed the earthly life of Jesus implies a corrective to those who were caught up in expectation of an imminent return by Christ. Also, in this apostolic witness subsequent Christians meet and are met by the living Christ.

The apostles pray together, displaying remarkable unity. They ask God to choose Judas's successor. "Show us which of these two you have chosen" (1:24). No mere democratic vote casting is done here.

With the selection of Matthias the circle of apostles is once again complete with twelve (1:26).

In Acts 1, the writer sets the stage for the phenomenal expansion of Christianity from a small sect within the Jewish tradition to a worldwide movement. Central to the whole enterprise is the apostolic witness to both the earthly ministry and life of Jesus as well as the Resurrection and Ascension. Luke's theological concern seems to focus on the resurrection of Jesus and the implications of that stupendous act. Now, what will happen when the very power of God enters into each believer and the community?

The Day of Pentecost. To Luke the presence of the Holy Spirit as the presence of God in power is the turning point for the Christian community. The Holy Spirit acts in guiding the mission of the church, especially in the first half of the Book of Acts. This miraculous event should never be construed as the first presence of the Spirit, however. The entire Old Testament gives witness to the activity of the Spirit in history.

In Luke's second volume (Acts) the coming of the Spirit parallels the coming of the Spirit as Jesus' baptism in the first volume (Luke 3:22).

Acts 2:1-13. On the fiftieth day following the Passover, the apostles are once again gathered together in Jerusalem for the Jewish feast of Pentecost. Pentecost had traditionally been a day that marked the end of the harvest (Leviticus 23:15-16; Deuteronomy 16:9-12).

Quite without warning, a phenomenon of sound, like that of violent wind, is heard. Then what was heard changed to what could be seen. The fiery tongue that came to rest on all of them gathered there gave evidence that the Spirit had been given to everyone. One note of caution: The phenomenon of sound and fiery tongues is temporary. The real importance is the continued presence of God's power within the Christian community. The inward presence of the Spirit should never be confused with the outward signs.

The effect of the mysteriously powerful presence causes discourse in other tongues, that is, other languages (verse 4). Perhaps no other verse in Acts has caused so much debate if not outright conflict through Christian history. Was that event *glossolalia*, speaking in utterances unintelligible to anyone? The evidence here suggests the opposite. People gathered from many nations, hearing the speech in their own languages. These Galilean followers of Christ could not have spoken clearly in many languages without the miracle of the presence of the Holy Spirit. The list of foreign nations in verses 8-11 further clarifies this utterance as something markedly different from a spirit language. The list of nations recalls the Diaspora, the Jews scattered and living outside Palestine.

What is the meaning of Pentecost? Some scholars have suggested two different sources: one historical, the other legendary. Others think of the event as having its origin in the first sermon, which then grew in repute through the years. Still others argue that the giving of the Spirit at Pentecost is the Christian parallel to the Hebrew tradition of the giving of the law at Sinai. Yet another interpretation is that, with foreigners able to understand the powerful word of God each in his own native language, the awful effect of Babel has been reversed. The work of Christ is that of healing the divisions of humankind (Isaiah 28:11).

Acts 2:14-36. In these verses, Luke tells us of Peter's Pentecost sermon. *Kerygma* is a Greek term meaning "proclamation" that has been used to refer to the preaching of the gospel, or good news that Jesus is the Christ and that we are saved by faith in him. *Kerygmatic* preaching contains many common elements that we will identify in the sermons presented in Acts.

Peter's message, in this earliest moment of the new movement, is addressed to a nationally and religiously Jewish audience. As yet, the Christian movement is a small group within Judaism. Peter quotes the prophet Joel (2:28-32)

in response to the largely negative estimate made by some observers (Acts 1:15-16).

The last days and the coming of the Spirit had long since been interrelated in the Jewish religious mind. Jews had hoped for generations that a triumphant Messiah would usher in the victorious new age of God's rule. In Peter's sermon this hope of triumph is challenged by the suffering Messiah—the crucified One.

Peter resumes with his own words in verse 22. The Christian message has always centered on the name of Jesus of Nazareth whose work is validated by wonders of all kinds performed by him. The miracles of Jesus are here presented as a single entity as they must have been generally known.

This Jesus is the person of historical reality and is the crucified One. For Luke, the Resurrection is the central point for the good news. God has overcome the power of death.

Early Christian interpreters perceived in Psalm 16 the resurrection of the Messiah. (See also Acts 13:35.) "You will not let your Holy One see decay." According to Luke, Jesus never felt abandoned. His Gospel does not include the cry of dereliction from the cross. Indeed, it is Luke's Gospel that contains the promise by Jesus to the penitent thief: "Today you will be with me in Paradise" (Luke 23:43).

The prophetic hope has now been fulfilled through Jesus of Nazareth. Here the Hebrew Scriptures are cited as proof of the Christian claim (Acts 2:31). This is one expression of kerygmatic preaching—scriptural fulfillment is a central element in early Christian preaching.

Acts 2:37-43. Now the recognition of guilt strikes to the heart of the hearers. Their response is, "What shall we do?" Peter answers, "Repent, and be baptized . . . in the name of Jesus Christ." Kerygmatic preaching always closes with a call for repentance (Acts 3:19, 26; 4:12; 5:31; 10:43).

One major difficulty arises from this Scripture. Verse 38 has often been used as evidence that baptism is a condition for forgiveness of sins. Such use of a single verse as proof text for a doctrinal position (baptism) is an inappropriate use of the Bible. The emphasis here is clearly on repentance and forgiveness. Moreover, in another sermon in Acts, only repentance is called for (3:19).

Also, the gift of the Spirit is not bound by the outward sign. Every Christian has the Spirit but not necessarily the outward sign of it. God has taken the initiative. The promise of forgiveness and of the Spirit is God's movement. The biblical notion of election is here well illustrated in God's movement. Election means God has chosen humankind, not the reverse.

Also, the promise is available to all. Here is evidence of a universal gospel that the apostles themselves were averse to accepting. The good news is for *all*. Luke's work will center on this impulse for a universal gospel that has its origin in the mind and intention of God.

So they were baptized—presumably following repentance. About three thousand were added to the community that day. The growth up to this point has been within the Jewish tradition. Clearly, the good news is addressed to Jews or Jewish proselytes, as Peter's entire sermon is based on accepted Hebrew scriptural texts—Joel and the Psalms. Not yet do we see the Christian movement breaking out of its Jewish surroundings. Doubtless the three thousand baptized were either Jews or converts to Judaism.

The Christian community shared in an exemplary life characterized by (1) listening to the teaching by the apostles, (2) sharing common meals, and (3) prayers. The breaking of bread has been variously interpreted as the fellowship meal (love feast) or the celebration of the Lord's Supper. The early Christians saw the Lord's Supper as a solemn event. But the celebration was a remembrance not only of the Last Supper but also of other meals shared with Jesus, especially after the Resurrection. Such meals as the one at Emmaus (Luke 24:30), with the Eleven (Luke 24:36-43), and at the sea (John 21:12-13) would surely be recalled. Given their Jewish roots the Christians would also recall the celebration of the Passover and the Exodus (Exodus 12).

Acts 2:44-47. Evidently at this early stage of the Christian movement no antagonism existed between either Christians and Jews or Romans and Christians. The life lived by Christians characterized by sharing of goods, attendance at Temple worship, and giving to the poor is called *koinonia* in Greek. This life is respected by outsiders.

Verses 42-47 serve as a means by which Luke separates Peter's speeches. This dividing scene gives a picture, our ideal picture, of the Christian life. The community shared deeply both in the need for the gospel—all were guilty—and in their common welfare. Cooperation alone is not the characteristic of the Christians. Only fellowship that comes from God essentially can be good.

The scene in Acts 2 closes with the good news that as yet knows no limits. All are impressed by the Christians' *koinonia.* Many are attracted to the distinctive life.

DIMENSION THREE: WHAT DOES THE BIBLE MEAN TO ME?

Our discussion suggestions will deal with the great themes with which Luke worked: (1) the Holy Spirit, (2) dealing with the future, and (3) recovery of Jewish heritage.

Pentecost and the Coming of the Spirit

Both the events and the meaning of Pentecost are often debated among Christians. As a means by which to determine something about both these issues, ask class members to do the following:
1. Tell the story of Pentecost from memory.
2. List the order of events and as many specific Scriptures as you can.

After completing the exercise, read the Pentecost section again (2:1-41). Which details were correct? Which details were incorrect or missing?

The "speaking in other tongues" of Pentecost is often thought to be the same as the utterances of unintelligible speech in 1 Corinthians 14:1-18. How do they compare?

The coming of the Spirit is often considered the birthday of the church. Pentecost has also been called the inauguration of a new age.

In August 1945, two atomic weapons were detonated over Hiroshima and Nagasaki, Japan. Ever since those awesome moments, human conflict has been forever changed. We simply cannot overlook the fact of the changes wrought by the advent of nuclear weapons, of chemical weapons, and the easy access to personal weapons which linger in the background as potential threats to personal, national, and international peace and security.

To early Christians the coming of the Holy Spirit changed the course of human history as well. The kingdom of God had broken into the realm of history and human experience. Discuss with class members which of the two earth-shattering changes seem most significant today. Is it the ability of persons and nations to arm themselves? Or is it the presence of the Holy Spirit? Reflect on this issue and make notes of your observations.

The Christian and the Future

What do Christians anticipate as inevitable? Throughout history some have tried to predict the date (specific time) of Christ's return. The emphasis by the writer of Acts challenges such a preoccupation. Indeed the writer of Acts asserts that Christians need to learn how to live with present reality.

The way we think and act is based in part on what we expect to be forthcoming reality. If we expect evil, then we prepare for evil. If we expect good, then we prepare for good. The ultimate question challenging a modern Christian, then, is what do we expect history leads toward? Will hell break loose on the morrow? Or will something else inevitably break loose?

To early Christians the kingdom of God was the inevitable reality. Indeed, the Kingdom had already begun its reign through the work and life of Jesus. Discuss with class members what various hopes, fears, and anticipations they have for what will inevitably break loose. Will it be evil? Or the Kingdom?

The Old Testament and the Christian

In the Pentecost sermon by Peter, the Old Testament is cited. This is the first of many references to the Hebrew Scriptures. At least one of the concerns of the writer is the recovery of Christianity's roots in Judaism.

Throughout the church's history that acknowledgement has been difficult. Among the earliest issues confronted by the church was the significance of the Old

Testament. In the middle of the second century, Marcion initiated a movement that survived until the mid-fourth century. His emphasis was that the Old Testament God could not possibly have been the father of Jesus Christ. The Old Testament God is a wrathful God who could not have been perfect. Therefore, Marcion rejected all Judaism, and of course the entire Hebrew Scriptures—what Christians call the Old Testament.

Marcion was declared a heretic. His teachings are not part of accepted Christian doctrine. While the church today may not have modern Marcionites, there is always the difficult issue of how the Old Testament is significant for the Christian.

How have you heard the Old Testament used? Was the usage a positive one? How often is the Old Testament included in worship as a lection reading or sermon text?

After they prayed . . . . they were all filled with the Holy Spirit and spoke the word of God boldly (4:31).

2

The Signs and Wonders of the Apostles

Acts 3–5

DIMENSION ONE:
WHAT DOES THE BIBLE SAY?

Answer these questions by reading Acts 3

1. Who goes to the Temple to pray? (3:1)

   Peter and John go to the Temple to pray.

2. In whose name is the man crippled from birth healed? (3:6)

   The man is healed in the name of Jesus Christ of Nazareth.

3. Peter declares that neither personal power nor piety healed the lame man. Who does Peter claim healed the man? (3:13, 16)

   "The God of Abraham, Isaac and of Jacob, the God of our fathers" through Jesus Christ healed the man.

4. What must the man have in order to be healed? (3:16)

   The man must have faith in the name of Jesus in order to be healed.

5. What does Peter ask of the people at the conclusion of his preaching? (3:19, 26)

   Peter asks people to repent, to turn to God from their wicked ways.

Answer these questions by reading Acts 4

6. Which group of Jewish leaders is disturbed by Peter's preaching? (4:1-2)

   The priests, the captain of the Temple guard, and the Sadducees are greatly disturbed by Peter's preaching.

7. Why are the leaders disturbed? (4:2)

   They are disturbed because Peter's proclamation contains the doctrine of "the resurrection of the dead."

8. What are the leaders' names? (4:6)

   The leaders' names are Annas the high priest, Caiaphas, John, and Alexander, "and the other men of the high priest's family."

9. What is the appearance of Peter and John? (4:13)

   Peter and John appear to be bold, "unschooled, ordinary men."

10. What do the authorities decide to tell the apostles? (4:18)

    The authorities command the apostles "not to speak or teach at all in the name of Jesus."

11. What is the apostles' response to the charge to remain silent? (4:19-20)

    The apostles reply: "Judge for yourselves whether is it right in God's sight to obey you rather than God. For we cannot help speaking about what we have seen and heard."

12. What occurs in the place where the apostles and their friends pray? (4:31)

    The place is shaken and the people were "all filled with the Holy Spirit and spoke the word of God boldly."

13. Who sells a field in order to share with the apostles? (4:36-37)

    Joseph, a Levite (also called Barnabas) sells a field in order to share with the apostles.

Answer these questions by reading Acts 5

14. Which two people sell a field and keep some of the proceeds for themselves? (5:1-2)

Ananais and Sapphira conspire to keep back part of the money for themselves.

15. What happens to the husband when Peter challenges him? (5:5)

Ananias fell and died.

16. What happens to the wife when she is confronted about the same matter? (5:10)

Sapphira suffers the same fate as her husband; she drops dead.

17. Which Jewish group rises up against the apostles? (5:17)

The Sadducees were filled with jealousy.

18. Who is the Pharisee in the Sanhedrin who speaks regarding the threat of the apostles? (5:34)

The Pharisee Gamaliel, "a teacher of the law," addresses the threat.

19. What is Gamaliel's counsel? (5:38-39)

Gamaliel's counsel is to leave the Christians alone. If the movement is of God, the Jews may be fighting God; if it is of human origin, it will fail on its own.

DIMENSION TWO:
WHAT DOES THE BIBLE MEAN?

Acts 3:1-10. The earliest Christian development occurs within the structures of Judaism. Here we learn that two disciples, Peter and John, go to the Temple about four o'clock one afternoon to pray.

In order to heighten the nature and extent of the miracle about to occur, the man's lameness is emphasized—he has been "crippled from birth." The man lies outside the Beautiful Gate of the Temple every day and begs the people entering the Temple for alms.

When the begging crippled man sees the two disciples, his attention shifts to them. (Luke uses an economy of acts in his drama. Only three men occupy center stage here. Throughout the Book of Acts, Luke uses a similar economy. Individuals and specific events are used to show through dynamic, dramatic stories how the Christian message is being spread.)

Expecting a gift of some kind, the man hears disappointing words. Money will not be forthcoming. But Peter offers something far greater. Peter speaks the name of Jesus Christ. The naming of the name has real power within it.

In addition to Peter's spoken word is his touch. Evidently there needs to be a channel through which this miraculous power can move. "Taking him by the right hand, he helped him up, and instantly the man's feet and ankles became strong. He jumped to his feet and began to walk" (verses 7-8; see also Isaiah 35:6.) To demonstrate the extent of the healing, the cured man now enters the Temple, "walking and jumping, and praising God."

All the observers are amazed. And well they should be, for a man who has been crippled all his life and who is well known to them has been healed. Since so many people witnessed the event, the authenticity of the healing is verified.

Acts 3:11-26. Peter, with the healed man still clinging to him, addresses the assembled crowd of worshipers. Apparently Solomon's Portico is a regular gathering place for the apostles (5:12). Peter tells the people that the power that has been made manifest is not the apostles' power. Nor is the power evoked by any special piety, practiced by the apostles. Rather, the power is God's, who is described in biblical terms that are familiar to the Jewish hearers (verse 13; see also Exodus 3:6, 15; Isaiah 52:13).

If the name of Jesus is to have any power, the individual listener must have faith. The preaching of the name brings about that faith. Thus preaching is no idle event. Preaching is the stirring up as well as the informing of faith and faithfulness.

With the use of the familiar *brothers,* Peter changes the tone of his sermon. No longer pointing an accusing finger; now he assumes a close relationship with his listeners. The implication is, of course, that there needs to be no separation because of religious barriers. The Jewish sin here is that of ignorance; they did not know (Luke 23:34). (This theme of ignorance will recur in Acts 13:27 and 17:30. For other references to the sin of ignorance, see Leviticus 22:14 and Numbers 15:22-31.)

Prophetic foretelling is an element of the *kerygma* (verse 18). In all classic kerygmatic preaching, also, a call to repentance is given. God and God alone is able to offer repentance. In Acts, repentance is not restricted to Jew alone. Repentance is available to Gentile (non-Jew) as well (2:38; 5:31; 11:18, 21; 14:15; 17:30; 20:21; 28:27).

Peter likens Jesus to the prophet Moses (Deuteronomy 18:15, 18), and says that anyone who "does not listen to him [Moses] will be completely cut off from among his people." Peter applies Moses' words to those who hear the Christians' preaching about Jesus. Anyone who rejects this preaching, this Jesus, will be excluded by God. By implication the new Christian movement is the true Israel (Leviticus 23:29).

All the prophets have pointed toward this hope of the true Israel. The hope of a Messiah, of course, is well known to these listeners whom Peter characterizes as "heirs of the prophets and of the covenant God made with your fathers" (verse 25; see also Genesis 12:3 and 22:18).

Acts 4:1-22. As the apostles are speaking, officials gather around them. The priests are those who perform official acts on behalf of the people. The captain of the Temple guard may have been the high priest's subordinate. The Sadducees are educated men, mostly wealthy and of good position. They were the high-cast nobility who did not support the Pharisaical movement of repentance and renewal. Here the Sadducees are in the role of authority.

The apostles are arrested because they are preaching the doctrine of "resurrection from the dead." The Sadducees reject the doctrine of resurrection outright (23:8).

Even with the arrest of the apostles, the Christian message has begun to spread. The number five thousand (verse 4) is probably a symbolic number. At this time Jerusalem had a population of approximately twenty-five to thirty thousand people. If the five thousand is accurate, then fully one-fifth of the city had become Christian. The conclusion therefore is that this number is not a statistic as much as a statement of hope.

The Sanhedrin consists, among others, of the high priest Annas, Caiaphas, John, and Alexander. All these men are of the higher, aristocratic, priestly family. Obviously this council holds great authority within Jewish circles. Luke presents the picture of two rather common men confronting the prominent and prestigious powers that be. Against this backdrop the apostles' courage shows as clearly as a ray of sunlight against a storm-blackened sky.

Peter is the spokesman for the apostles. John remains silent as he had during the preaching that led to the arrest. Luke describes Peter as "filled with the Holy Spirit" (verse 8). Here the action of the Spirit is not ecstatic speech nor miraculous healing. Rather, the Spirit now gives a special strength and courage in the face of hostile authority, and the promise of Luke 12:11-12 finds fulfillment.

The man who was crippled from birth has been healed by the name of Jesus, and Peter cites Scripture as proof. Psalm 118:22 suggests rejection. From the Christian perspective, the one denied is, of course, Jesus.

Evidently unschooled, ordinary men had never dared challenge the authority of the Sanhedrin. The officials are stunned. The men now confronting them were clearly associated with Jesus. What should their stance be? The man had been cured, there is no doubt about this, and the apostles have discernible wisdom and eloquence. The apostles are commanded not to speak or teach in the name of Jesus (verse 18).

Peter replies with the well-known statement that "we cannot help speaking about what we have seen and heard." (This statement will find a more refined expression in 5:29.) Therefore, the apostles will continue with their preaching.

Acts 4:23-31. The place trembles. To the ancient mind such an event indicated that the prayer had been heard. The Holy Spirit gives the apostles sufficient courage to preach the word even in the face of stark danger. Some scholars believe that the events of Acts 4:31 are a parallel account to the Pentecost events in Acts 2. The emphasis here, however, seems to be more to the point of how Christians react to the threat of persecution. Rather than shrink back from the challenge, the community prays for strength that is then forthcoming through the gift of the Holy Spirit.

Acts 4:32–5:11. The next two narratives present contrasting pictures of life within the early church. In one sense these stories interrupt the flow of the narrative of Peter and John, which resumes in 4:12. To some this interruption will seem strange. However, if the two stories represent evidence of an internal stress that mirrors the external stress affecting the church, then they make a good deal more sense.

Christians Sharing in Common. The remarkable fact is not that private property ceased to exist. Clearly private property was still owned. The Christians seem to have conceded their personal claims over it for the good of the entire community.

An Old Testament hope that there will be no poor among you (Deuteronomy 15:4), finds its fulfillment, even if only for a moment, in the early church's experience. The Barnabas episode may well have been included because it is a unique event.

Ananias and Sapphira. This terribly troubling story reflects internal stress. The story recalls the Achan episode in Joshua 7. There one man, against specific instructions, took for himself some of the devoted things of a vanquished city, bringing the wrath of God on the entire nation.

Peter speaks for the entire community first to ask why the deed had been done and second as to the source of evil. Ananias had done considerably more than attempt to conceal some of his proceeds from the sale of his property. He had lied to his Christian friends and to God. God executes a stern punishment.

Ananias's wife, Sapphira, apparently unaware of his death, appears. Peter discovers her complicity in the plan through two questions. Sapphira then suffers the same fate as her husband.

The story of duplicity and judgment is told in a straightforward manner without pity. The result of the deaths is to evoke great fear not only with the Christian community, but also within the non-Christian observers as well.

Scholars have suggested many different interpretations for the dreadful account. Some suggest this is a legendary treatment of the first deaths in the church. Perhaps by the time the story reached print the shock had worn off. Others have suggested this is a story by which to teach converts. Perhaps Ananias and Sapphira wanted to enter an elite group without paying an appropriate price.

In any event the story assumes that the Christians, filled with the Holy Spirit, can discern the thoughts of others' hearts (1 Corinthians 14:24-25). The emphasis is on God, not human beings.

Acts 5:12-16. Miraculous events are not restricted only to Peter and John. All the apostles perform miraculous signs and wonders. The Christians gather at Solomon's Colonnade in the Temple, apparently for regular worship. Evidently non-Christians hesitate to join the now well-known movement. Clearly the small Christian group stirs awe in observers. And while they would not join them, the outsiders hold the Christians in high regard.

Trusting in the power of Christians, both Christian and non-Christian Jews bring their sick to the apostles to be healed. The effect of Peter's shadow concerns scholars more than it seems to have concerned Luke. Evidently Luke (and others) expect to see such evidences of miraculous powers (19:12). The success stories spread beyond the confines of Jerusalem (verse 16).

Acts 5:17-42. The apostles are arrested and put "in the public jail." The Sadducees are still named as the challenging party. They are filled with jealousy at the increasing power of the Christians.

The motif of prison and miraculously opened doors occurs three times in Acts. Here Peter and John are imprisoned (5:17-21a). In 12:6-11, Peter is in jail, and in 16:26-34, Paul and Silas are imprisoned.

After their release, the apostles continue to preach the message of Jesus and the life and salvation available through him. The officers find that "at daybreak they [the apostles] entered the temple courts . . . and began to teach the people."

Remarkably the chief priest and other officials seem ignorant of the release. They send for the captives. The perplexed officials bring the apostles before the Sanhedrin.

With no reference to the release from prison, changes are leveled against the apostles. The ban of Acts 4:18 has been disregarded by the apostles. The council also seems concerned that the Christian preachers will require vengeance for the death of Jesus. Certainly the officials have been threatened by the preaching. Now the issue centers on the struggle for authority. The Sanhedrin has a traditional authority not questioned by many. The Christians on the other hand obey an internal authority and that evokes awe in observers. "We must obey God rather than men."

The apostles testify to Jesus who was crucified on a tree (Deuteronomy 21:22-23; Acts 10:39; and Galatians 3:13.) Jesus' life and the apostles' preaching lead to repentance and the remission of sins. Repentance is offered to Israel. By implication, repentance is offered to the officials as well.

Small wonder the officials are furious and want to kill the apostles (5:33). Without some sort of intervention the apostles are about to suffer a martyr's death at the hands of a group of men overwhelmed with anger and threat.

The Pharisee Gamaliel intervenes just in time. This teacher, held in high repute by everyone, speaks a wise word. Others in the past have come claiming authority: Theudas, who had about four hundred followers, and Judas the Galilean. They failed. Beware. Any movement based on purely human motive will fail of its own accord.

Surely a word must be said here on behalf of the beleaguered Jews. Sadducees have an argument with their Pharisaical brethren regarding resurrection, and they have an argument with the Christians. But up to this point the Pharisees are not antagonistic toward the Christians.

The apostles are flogged, which is no mean punishment. The Christians are instructed once again not to speak in the name of Jesus. In fact, the apostles will suffer because of the name of Jesus (9:16; 15:26; 21:13).

The chapter concludes with a description of the Christian community. Evidently, to this point the Christians are a small group still within the Jewish tradition, observing Jewish customs and yet preaching the life of the resurrected Messiah, Jesus.

DIMENSION THREE: WHAT DOES THE BIBLE MEAN TO ME?

Acts 4:5-21—The Action of the Holy Spirit

The action of the Holy Spirit is central in Luke's purpose. Earlier in the Pentecost event we saw the ecstatic infilling and the power that centers in Christian fellowship. When considering the Spirit, however, one must be careful not to limit its work to a particular manifestation, for example, ecstatic speech. In the stories of Acts 4 and 5, the apostles are brought before the highest Jewish authorities to make an accounting of their healing and preaching.

Ask class members for moments when they recall being challenged for their faith. How did they find sufficient courage to speak the truth of the gospel as they understood it? For instance, young people may recall the threat of peer pressure with respect to alcohol or drugs. Businessmen and businesswomen may recall threats by bosses who demanded questionable business or work practices. Others may recall times when they took a stand on one of the disturbing moral issues that defy simple answers and that require Christian insight.

Write these moments on a chalkboard or on poster paper. Then ask class members to say a short prayer to give thanks for the presence of the Spirit that gave them sufficient courage for that particular moment.

Acts 3:10; 4:21; 5:34-39—Relationship Between Christians and Jews

One of the biggest problems with which Christians must wrestle as they read the New Testament is the awful inclination toward anti-Jewish feelings. This look at Acts will have been a failure if class members end their study with little more than reinforced preconceptions about Jews and Judaism.

THE SIGNS AND WONDERS OF THE APOSTLES

A careful reading of Acts 3–5 indicates the only Jewish group to be offended, initially, is the Sadducees. The threat seems to have come in two forms. First of all, the Christians preached a doctrine with which the Sadducees disagreed. Second, the Christians did not show proper respect for the wishes of the offended Jews.

Begin a discussion by asking class members to state what the relationship ought to be (or is) between Christians and Jews. Then have them state precisely the relationship that seems to have existed between Christian Jews and non-Christian Jews in Acts. For instance, Christian Jews, in these chapters, are still keeping Jewish customs (Temple worship, daily prayer). The Christian Jews are held in high esteem by observers. Ask class members precisely where conflict with Jews occurs. What are the causes? Who is threatened? Why?

By way of concluding this discussion, mention the tragic element in the story. The tragedy is that the gospel of Christ that God intends for all will too often become a matter of contention rather than of healing and reconciliation. One might be sensitive to the tragedy but also might become adamant and triumphant prematurely and at the expense of the very gospel itself.

Acts 4:3-4; 5:17-26—A Gospel That Cannot Be Contained

In the first lesson we saw the apostles stunned and confused by the implication that the gospel would become universal (1:8). Throughout the Book of Acts various attempts will be made to, in some manner, contain the gospel of Jesus Christ. Acts 3–5 illustrates one such attempt.

Challenged by authorities, jailed, and then flogged, the apostles refuse to stop preaching. The Spirit intervenes both through miraculous means (the nighttime release from prison) and in unspectacular ways (an indwelling courage) to prevent the enclosure of the gospel.

Discuss with class members what it means to suggest that the gospel cannot be contained either by threat or imprisonment. Does this hold true for the gospel in a place where Christianity is unlawful (such as in some Islamic regions) or where Christians are persecuted? Ask class members whether they believe the gospel can be contained.

For the purposes of some image on which the balance of this study can be envisioned, imagine a pond. Most of us have at some time tossed a stone into the center of such a pond. After the first splash, did we not wonder at the way in which ripples would expand in ever-widening circles? Eventually every inch of the shoreline felt the effect of that single stone.

So with the gospel. The coming Jesus introduced the initial splash—what he began to do and preach (Acts 1:1). The Book of Acts presents the ripples that are the expression of the gospel.

Close this session by asking class members to list on the chalkboard or on a large piece of paper any new insights they may have.

So the word of God spread. The number of disciples in Jerusalem increased rapidly (6:7).

3

Stephen and Philip

Acts 6–8

DIMENSION ONE: WHAT DOES THE BIBLE SAY?

Answer these questions by reading Acts 6

1. Who are the people who are upset about suspected prejudice? (6:1)

   The Grecian Jews are disturbed "because their widows were being overlooked in the daily distribution of food."

2. Who are chosen as servers? (6:5)

   The chosen men are Stephen; Philip; Procorus; Nicanor; Timon; Parmenas; and Nicolaus, a convert from Antioch.

3. How are the servers authorized for their work? (6:6)

   The servers are authorized by prayer and the laying on of hands.

4. With whom does Stephen come into conflict? (6:9)

   Stephen conflicts with "members of the Synagogue of the Freedmen (as it was called)—Jews of Cyrene and Alexandria as well as the provinces of Cilicia and Asia."

5. What is the charge against Stephen? (6:14)

   Stephen is charged with saying that "Jesus of Nazareth will destroy this place [synagogue] and change the customs Moses handed down to us [the Law]."

6. How is Stephen's appearance described? (6:15)

   Stephen's face is like the face of an angel.

Answer these questions by reading Acts 7

7. Who begins the interrogation of Stephen? (7:1)

   The high priest begins the interrogation.

8. How does Stephen describe his listeners? (7:51)

   Stephen describes the listeners as stiff-necked, with uncircumcised hearts and ears, who always resist the Holy Spirit.

9. How do Stephen's listeners react to his charge, and what do they do to him? (7:54-58)

   They are furious and gnash their teeth at Stephen; then shouting at him, they drag him from the city and stone him.

10. Who is a witness to the death of Stephen? (7:58)

    Saul is a witness, giving approval to the death of Stephen.

11. What are Stephen's final words? (7:59-60)

    Stephen's final words are his prayers: "Lord Jesus, receive my spirit" and "Lord, do not hold this sin against them."

Answer these questions by reading Acts 8

12. Following Stephen's death what happens to the church? (8:1)

    A great persecution broke out against the church.

13. All Christians are scattered except for whom? (8:1)

    The apostles remain in Jerusalem.

14. Who is named as one of the worst persecutors of the church? (8:3)

    Saul is described as one who began to destroy the church, dragging men and women from their homes and putting them in prison.

15. Who goes to Samaria to preach? (8:5)

    Philip goes to Samaria to preach.

16. Who is the sorcerer with whom Philip comes into conflict? (8:9)

The sorcerer Simon is in Samaria when Philip arrives there.

17. How does Simon seek to obtain the Holy Spirit's presence and power? (8:18-19)

Simon attempts to purchase the Holy Spirit's power.

18. On his way back to Jerusalem, where is Philip told to go? (8:26)

Philip is told to go toward the south, to the desert road that goes to Gaza.

19. To whom does Philip interpret the Scripture? (8:27-35)

Philip interprets the Scripture to the Ethiopian eunuch.

20. What else does Philip do for the eunuch? (8:38)

Philip baptizes the eunuch.

DIMENSION TWO: WHAT DOES THE BIBLE MEAN?

Acts 6:1-6. To this point in Acts, Luke has presented the picture of Christians within the Jewish traditional structures of Temple and house. In Acts 6–8, the church comes under increasing stress, internally and externally, and it will begin to expand out of its traditional environment.

The followers of the new proclamation are increasing. Evidently the expansion has included Jews of the Diaspora. These Jews are people who, in an earlier era, were scattered throughout the Greek-speaking world. They are known as Hellenists (or Grecian Jews) as opposed to Hebrews or Aramaic-speaking Jews. In fact, the Hellenists have sufficient numbers to warrant their own synagogue (6:9). The evidence therefore indicates that the Christian movement sought for and gained converts from the Jewish congregations. Not surprisingly, conflicts arise because of economic disparity. The already established Jewish relief system is not an issue. What does appear is a strain on the relief work the Christian sect developed.

In order to relieve the conflict, "the Twelve gathered all the disciples together" (verse 2). A division of duties is recommended. Seven men of excellent reputation are to be selected by the community to wait on tables. The apostles will then have more time to concentrate on the tasks of prayer and preaching. The seven men are not appointed arbitrarily by the apostles. Rather, they are chosen by the church, the body of the disciples.

They choose "Stephen, a man full of faith and of the Holy Spirit; also Philip, and Procorus, Nicanor, Timon, Parmenas, and Nicolaus from Antioch, a convert to Judaism" (verse 5). The rest of our Scripture will focus on the impact Stephen and Philip have on the Christian movement. One note of irony—even though the apostles are now free from the menial tasks of serving tables, the server shows himself to have keen insights into the nature and implications of the gospel.

The laying on of hands implies a transfer of power as well as a visible sign of an authority granted. Note how prayer remains central in the life of the church. Not only during times of stress do the Christians pray; they pray as well at many moments of need.

Acts 6:7. Verse 7 is Luke's summary statement for the first major section of Acts. Christianity is still limited to the city of Jerusalem, though word about the apostles and their wonderful works has spread beyond the city. Up to this point the Christian movement has remained within the Jewish tradition and synagogue. Converts have been gained primarily through individual contact or as a result of the miracles worked by the apostles. No major resistance has yet erupted, with the exception of the Sadducees.

Acts 6:8-15. Luke begins the second major segment of Acts with the story of Stephen, the first-mentioned of the seven men chosen as servers. Stephen now performs miracles (verse 8). Stephen serves as the individual who begins the expansion of the Christian message out of its Jewish structures. He sees the universal meanings of the movement. Luke, in his economy of words and space, uses one person to represent a much larger phenomenon.

With their national and racial pride threatened, some Hellenistic Jews charge that Stephen spoke blasphemy against Moses and God. When mere words do not silence Stephen, a secret conspiracy is initiated. The authorities are told, by false witnesses, that Stephen constantly speaks blasphemy against the structures considered sacred to Judaism: the Temple and the Torah (Law).

Central to Stephen's preaching, of course, is Jesus of Nazareth. The charges brought against Stephen are similar to those leveled against Jesus (Matthew 26:61; Mark 14:58; John 2:19, 21; also Mark 2:23-28; 3:2-6).

Luke describes facial changes to indicate the presence of the Holy Spirit with Stephen: "His face was like the face of an angel" (verse 15).

Acts 7:1-53. The trial of Stephen intensifies the earlier efforts to silence the troublesome Christian preachers. Recall that earlier the Sanhedrin threatened the apostles (4:17, 21), then flogged them (5:40). The false witnesses and exaggerated charges against Stephen seem to parallel the trial of Jesus (Luke 23:2-16).

To the question "Are these charges true?" Stephen begins a long speech that both retells and reinterprets history. In effect, the speech does not answer the charges.

Stephen begins by referring to the patriarch Abraham (Genesis 11:27–12:4). The glory of God appeared to Abraham in Mesopotamia, a foreign land, before he entered the Promised Land. Though Abraham did not gain any land he could call his own, he did purchase the cave of Machpelah near Mamre as a tomb for his wife (Genesis 23:17-20). This detail is omitted in Stephen's speech.

Abraham was promised that his descendants would have this land as their own. God also gave Abraham "the covenant of circumcision" (verse 8). Stephen then lists the rest of the patriarchs and moves to Joseph's story.

Joseph's brothers were jealous of him (Genesis 37:11) and sold him into slavery (Genesis 37:28). But Joseph was not forsaken. God remained with him and rescued him (Genesis 41:39-46). Moreover due to the wisdom with which God blessed Joseph, Pharaoh made the lost brother governor over the nation and his personal home.

When famine swept over the lands of Egypt and Canaan, Joseph administered the division of stored grain. He was aware when his brothers came to Egypt to find food (Genesis 42:6-8). During their second visit, Joseph revealed his true identity to his brothers (Genesis 45:1-4) and invited all his father's family to journey to Egypt. In Egypt they settled and lived the rest of their lives.

Stephen's speech now turns to the story of Moses. The prophecy referred to in Acts 7:6 regarding the Hebrews being aliens in a foreign land is fulfilled in Moses' lifetime. Moses is described here as one "powerful in speech and action" (verse 22).

In the midst of his short story, Stephen makes the first allusion to the Hebrews' reluctance to heed the savior sent by God (verse 25). The added interpretation of Israel's refusal to hear the words of the man sent from God is what will enrage Stephen's listeners (verses 51-54).

Moses led the Hebrew people out of Egypt into the desert for "forty years." Stephen reminds his hearers that it was Moses who said, "God will send you a prophet like me from your own people" (verse 37). Even though Moses received God's word and transmitted it to the people of God, still the people rejected him.

David is described as finding favor in the sight of the Lord (verse 46).

The building of the Temple was, and remains, an act of apostasy. The Temple takes people away from the true service of God, for God does not dwell in a building (verses 47-50).

Earlier Stephen alluded to Israel's attitude in ancient days. Now the time changes. The speech becomes an indictment not of ancient Israelites but of contemporary Jews. As the ancients rejected Moses so now Jesus is rejected (Acts 3:13; Luke 24:21).

Acts 7:54–8:1a. The crowd is now worked up into a near frenzy by Stephen's reinterpretation of history as well as the scathing indictment made by the man who had been asked to answer a question himself.

Why does this speech cause such an uproar? Why is such a long speech included? In fact, this speech does not really answer the question that prompted it. Luke of course uses the speech to indicate the refusal of Jews historically to listen to the words of men sent by God. In effect, according to this argument, Jews have always resisted the Holy Spirit (7:51). Up to this time in Acts, we have seen a general popularity for the Christian movement. Now the attitude begins to change. Jews and Christians are becoming adamant antagonists. The angry crowd now begins to scream for Stephen's death. Stephen is dragged out of the city and stoned.

This setting provides Luke with the means by which to introduce a young man named Saul. Stephen kneels, prays, and asks for God to forgive his persecutors. He then dies.

Acts 8:1b-3. These verses provide the link between the persecution of Stephen and the story of Philip. They also further introduce Saul, a rabid persecutor of the Christians. Evidently all but the apostles are scattered by the outburst of persecution. Stephen has been condemned and killed by non-Christian Jews. Had all the Christians been gathered during the terror of Saul's activity (8:3), the movement might have been stopped; and Christianity would have become another footnote in history. The Hellenistic Jews who had been the source of persecution earlier now disappear. Saul replaces them. Not only does Saul lay waste to the church, violate personal privacy, and drag people off to prison, he forces them to blaspheme as well (26:11).

Acts 8:4-8. The attempted silencing of the Christians fails. Rather than eliminating the movement, the persecution provides the means by which Christianity spreads even more rapidly.

Philip, the second of the seven listed in 6:5, goes to Samaria. Thus the expansion described in 1:8 is well on its way. The preaching is accompanied by healings and exorcisms.

Acts 8:9-25. Simon the sorcerer made claims for himself. Magicians or sorcerers were not unusual (13:6-12; 19:11-20). The man had already had quite a career of dazzling the people of Samaria. Indeed in Samaria a movement sprang up that centered around Simon. For Luke, of course, the man is merely another wizard.

Philip's preaching, on the other hand, causes considerably more than mere amazement. Magicians and charlatans exist in every age. But the central issue has nothing to do with healings and magic. Much more to the point, the sorts of lives people have as a result of those remarkable events are significant.

The Samaritan wizard, amazed at what he sees, wants to have similar power. Incredibly, he offers to buy the Spirit! Peter, seeing that all Simon wants is another bit of effective magic, responds. "May your money perish with you, because you thought you could buy the gift of God with money!" The Spirit is not for sale. Simon is excluded from the Christian movement.

How can this story be interpreted? Why does Luke include this story? The genius of Christianity is in the superiority of the church over mere magic or false "miracles." The presence of the Holy Spirit is the church's great life. It cannot be bought, nor can it be overpowered. (The word *simony*, "buying or selling church pardons, offices, or other gifts," comes from this story.)

The Samaritan episode is brought to a conclusion with verse 25.

Acts 8:26-40. Philip is again the central character in a story about an outsider. Where Samaritans had formerly been the outsiders, now an Ethiopian eunuch is the object. The Christian movement continues its expansion beyond Jerusalem and beyond previously held restrictions to obsolete structures. The story begins with divine intervention of the Spirit (verse 29). While on the way to the designated place, Philip encounters an Ethiopian eunuch.

The Spirit directs Philip to intercept the chariot. Note here that the missionary ventures are not arbitrary. Rather the entire missionary expansion is under the guidance of God.

Many scholars see these verses as being important because it is the first time that the suffering servant image of Isaiah is combined with the Passion of Jesus. From the distinctively Christian perspective the Scripture interprets the life of Christ.

The eunuch is baptized. In terms that remind us of the Elijah story in the Old Testament, Philip is then caught up in the Spirit and he disappears (1 Kings 18:12; 2 Kings 2:16-18; Ezekiel 3:14; 8:3; 11:1, 2, 4; 2 Corinthians 12:2). For Luke the emphasis is clearly on the utter joy of the moment.

Philip reappears at Azotus, that is, Ashdad, from whence he preaches his way north along the coast to Caesarea. In the Old Testament this Palestine city was one of the five major cities in the region roughly halfway between Gaza and Joppa. During the Maccabean period it was taken by the Jews. Under the Roman governor Gabinius (governor 67–55 B.C.) it was rebuilt and populated as a Roman city (Joshua 13:3). Since Luke does not explain how Christian congregations are established at Lydda, Joppa, and Caesarea, perhaps Philip's preaching formed the initial congregations (Acts 9:32, 36; 10:48). From this story it is clear that Luke is not primarily concerned with how the gospel spread in a geographical sense. His concern is for how the gospel spread from its strictly Jewish origin and environment to the Gentiles.

The story of the Ethiopian eunuch poses many questions for interpretation. To begin with the eunuch could have been a Jew with the hope of Isaiah 56:3-5 replacing the admonition of Deuteronomy 23:1. Since Luke will later present Paul as missionary to the Gentiles, Philip cannot be the first missionary preacher to Gentiles. A clue to the significance of this story lies in its placement in the book. The conversion occurs between the Samaritan and Gentile mission. Thus, a different group of people is taken into the Christian movement.

The number of divine interventions makes this not just another conversion story. Remember that Luke is concerned to show that the growth of the Christian movement is not a matter of mere fluke or design by a few headstrong men. Theologically the church needs at its center the intervention and direction of God. To the ancient hearer and reader the divine intervention would serve to authorize and validate the work.

Since the Book of Acts has so many places mentioned and so many journeys taken, you may want to use maps to illustrate locations and directions.

DIMENSION THREE:
WHAT DOES THE BIBLE MEAN TO ME?

Acts 7:1-53
The Problem of History and National Pride

Among the most difficult challenges to the intentions of God has to be the force historians call *nationalism.* Harry Emerson Fosdick preached at one point that nationalism may well be one of Christianity's greatest enemies. But nationalism is not a new impulse in human affairs. The prejudice and pride of national experience runs long and deep in the flow of history.

Begin the class session by rereading the speech by Stephen. What are the key events mentioned? What are the key interpretations? What are the aspects that might well enrage the hearers? Point out the major reinterpretations Stephen asserts: God's mercy and deliverance have never been restricted to a specific land or place. God revealed Godself to Abraham in a foreign land, Mesopotamia. Abraham never owned land. Israel was freed from Egypt in order to worship. Jacob was buried in a despised foreign land. Moses was born in Egypt, a hated land of evil memory. Moses' wife was the daughter of a Midianite (Exodus 2:16-22). Sinai is in a foreign land. The building of the Temple violated God's intention.

In addition to these indictments, Stephen accuses the people of rejecting God's overture of the Holy Spirit.

Ask class members if they can think of any modern illustration in which a reinterpretation of American history may evoke a similar outcry. What might the reaction be if someone were to similarly indict the United States for rejecting God's overture through Martin Luther King, Jr.?

Acts 8:6-8—Miracles of Healing

Throughout Acts, the apostles and others work wonders of healing. People afflicted by lameness are cured, people possessed by demons are exorcised. Just as the apostles work what may be called legitimate wonders, so wizards and magicians attempt to dazzle crowds for a profit or at least a following.

Ask class members to share their own perceptions regarding the healings and wonders. Are the wonders believable? In what sense are they unbelievable? What should the attitude of a modern Christian be toward the scriptural miracles and the possibility of miracles in our own time?

The passage indicates that preaching and miracles are closely related. In both instances the preaching and wonder in and of themselves are not the ultimate concern. The ultimate concern is that hearers are moved to repentance and thus in a real sense to wholeness.

The miracles of the apostles are never performed as independent acts. They never dazzle without further purpose. Do people today perceive a strong relationship between miracles and moral behavior?

Acts 6:1-53—Preaching as an Event

To Luke the preaching event evidenced in Stephen and Philip is a radical event. Something is bound to happen as the result of Christian preaching. The message of Christianity is so radical—love enemies, turn the other cheek, visit the prisoner, spend your life for the gospel—that the gospel well proclaimed (and then taken seriously) must elicit a reaction.

Do contemporary church members think of preaching in similar terms? Clearly Stephen's preaching evokes remarkable response. The preaching of Philip evokes repentance and desire for baptism. What do modern church members expect from the preaching event? Have class members list on the chalkboard or a large piece of paper new insights they have gained from this lesson.

I now realize how true it is that God does not show favoritism but accepts men from every nation who fear him and do what is right (10:34-35).

4

The Conversion of Paul and Cornelius

Acts 9–10

DIMENSION ONE: WHAT DOES THE BIBLE SAY?

Answer these questions by reading Acts 9

1. Who continues his threats against the disciples of Jesus? (9:1)

   Saul is "still breathing out murderous threats against the Lord's disciples."

2. To which city does Saul travel? (9:2)

   Saul travels to the city of Damascus.

3. What happens on the road to Damascus? (9:3-6)

   A light from heaven flashes about Saul. When Saul falls to the ground, he hears a voice that questions his persecution and instructs him to go to the city and await further directions.

4. Who is instructed to find Saul? (9:10-12)

   Ananias, a Christian disciple in Damascus, is instructed to find Saul.

5. What is God's response to Ananias's objection? (9:15)

   God tells Ananias to go because Saul is God's chosen instrument to carry God's name "before the Gentiles and their kings and before the people of Israel."

6. What does Saul do when he hears of the conspiracy against him? (9:23-25)

   Saul escapes from the city by being lowered in a basket through an opening in the city wall.

7. Peter speaks the name of Jesus Christ in order to heal which man in Lydda? (9:34)

   Peter heals Aeneas in the name of Jesus Christ.

8. Whom does Peter revive at Joppa? (9:36-41)

   Peter revives Tabitha (which means Dorcas).

Answer these questions by reading Acts 10

9. Who is the centurion of the Italian Regiment in Caesarea? (10:1)

   The centurion of the Italian Regiment is Cornelius.

10. Who is lodging with Simon the tanner in Joppa? (10:5-6)

    Peter is staying with Simon the tanner.

11. What does Peter see in his vision? (10:10-12)

    Peter's vision is of a sheet suspended by four corners. In the sheet are all sorts of animals, reptiles, and birds.

12. What is God's answer to Peter's hesitancy? (10:15)

    The voice tells Peter that what God has made may not be called impure or unclean.

13. As Peter wonders about the meaning of the vision, who arrives? (10:17)

    Cornelius's messengers arrive from Caesarea.

14. What happens when Cornelius and Peter finally meet? (10:25-29)

    Cornelius falls at Peter's feet in an attempt to worship him. But Peter says, "Stand up. I am only a man myself." Peter then states the traditional relationship between Jesus and non-Jews (Gentiles), how it is unlawful for a Jew to associate with a Gentile. "But God has shown me that I should not call any man impure or unclean."

15. What is Peter's reason for associating with non-Jews? (10:34-35)

Peter says that he now understands that God shows no favoritism, but accepts anyone in any nation who does what is right and fears God.

16. In whose name are the Gentiles baptized? (10:48)

The Gentiles are baptized in the name of Jesus Christ.

DIMENSION TWO: WHAT DOES THE BIBLE MEAN?

In this lesson you will study Acts 9 and 10. Luke's purpose of showing the expansion of Christianity from its beginning to being a world force finds great expression in these two chapters. Up to this point the Christian Way has expanded to Samaritans and God-fearers. Now in what appears almost explosive in force is a persecutor of the church being converted by the action of Christ, and a reluctant Christian learns that God does not recognize racial and cultural boundaries.

Acts 9:1-9. Armed with writs of arrest, Saul proceeds to Damascus. In this city with a large Jewish population, Saul anticipates rounding up and arresting followers of the Way.

Light from heaven (22:6—bright light; 26:13—brighter than the sun) shines around Paul (22:6; 26:13—light shines on companions as well). Falling to the ground, Saul hears a voice asking, "Why do you persecute me?" The point, of course, is that whoever persecutes the church persecutes Christ.

Saul the powerful becomes Saul the weak. For Luke's first readers the implication would have been quite clear. The strength of the Spirit and the power of Christ are far more powerful than the mere power of religious authorities or any power directed against the church. Saul has been apprehended by the living Christ. The picture is one of dramatic irony: The "Terror of Christians" now stumbles blindly toward Damascus trusting solely in the guidance of the Spirit.

Acts 9:10-19a. The Lord speaks to Ananias, a Christian Jew living in Damascus, telling him to go to Saul. Saul has been praying and waiting for a man named Ananias to heal his blindness. Ananias protests against the instruction of the Lord. Though he does not know Saul personally, Ananias is well aware of Saul's reputation. From this we know that some time had elapsed between the outbreak of persecution in Jerusalem and Saul's effort toward Damascus. Here, as with earlier developments, determining exact time span is impossible. Suffice it to say that enough time passed during which Saul's reputation preceded him.

Regardless of Saul's former actions, God tells Ananias that Saul "is my chosen instrument to carry my name before the Gentiles and their kings and before the people of Israel." All this is capped ironically by the fact that Saul, who would have caused Damascan Christians suffering, will now suffer on behalf of Christ.

The powerful irony ends Ananias's protest. He enters the house in which Saul has been staying. Laying his hands on Saul, Ananias refers to the former persecutor by the Christian term *brother* and asks for the Holy Spirit. Healing occurs immediately, followed by baptism. Saul then eats and regains his strength.

Within a few verses, a drama that has captured imaginations and souls for centuries is played out. Luke's first readers would surely have been encouraged. Even the worst of enemies cannot withstand the power of the Holy Spirit. Now how will Saul carry out God's intention?

Acts 9:19b-25. Saul, with all the energy formerly poured into persecution, now begins his task of proclaiming the Christian message. Initially he seeks out synagogues to preach in, which he will continue to do throughout his travels.

Remaining in Damascus with his new Christian brothers, Saul preaches Jesus as the Son of God (Psalm 2:7; Mark 1:1, 11; 3:11; 5:7; 9:7; 12:6; 13:32; 14:61; 15:39; Acts 13:33). The effect of his preaching is immediate: People cannot believe that this is the same man who had breathed fire and death. Obviously observers had not yet come to terms with the overwhelming power of God. As he preaches Jesus as the Messiah, Saul gains more and more strength.

Against this new movement strong resistance comes to focus in a plot against Saul. Since the city gates are watched by conspirators, Saul escapes over the city walls in a woven basket. The hunter becomes the hunted.

Acts 9:26-31. Evidently the storm of persecution unleashed after Steven's death had calmed. The Christian community in Jerusalem survived and had emerged from hiding. Saul now goes to the community he formerly had persecuted. Small wonder, given the fact that bad news travels faster than good news, that the Jerusalem Christians are as hesitant as were Damascan Christians to receive Saul. Barnabas courageously trusts the conversion of Saul and takes him to meet the apostles. (Saul's relationship with Barnabas will develop into a close one until a final parting, 15:39.) The association with the Twelve is essential since it implies approval of Saul by the core of Christian authority. An open association with the apostles also indicates confession of faith in Jesus. Saul's preaching promotes disagreement with Hellenists, as had the preaching of Stephen. Another conspiracy develops against Saul. This time he is taken by Christians from Jerusalem to his native Tarsus by way of Caesarea.

This first visit of Saul to Jerusalem seems to contradict Galatians 1:15-18, which tells of a three-year lapse between his conversion and his visit to Jerusalem. The question of historical accuracy that dominates modern work was simply not a major concern for Luke and his readers. The purpose of this book includes the identification and encouragement of various Christian churches. The overall impact of the story just ended is of the power of God and the significance of Saul of Tarsus. Luke's purpose through this story is to show the Christian movement already established in Galilee, as well as Jerusalem, without concern for who established them. Since the dreadful persecution ended (verse 31), indeed the prominent persecutor converted, the Christian reader will perceive the work of the Holy Spirit.

Acts 9:32-43. This section consists of two stories about Peter. In preparation for the meeting between Cornelius and Peter at Caesarea, these stories serve to get Peter to that city. In Lydda, about twenty-five miles northwest of Jerusalem, Peter meets other Christians. Since Jerusalem is at a higher altitude than much of Israel, movement toward the city is referred to as "up to" and movement from Jerusalem is "down from." Peter travels "to visit the saints in Lydda."

There Peter meets a Christian who has been paralyzed and bedridden for eight years. When the name of Jesus is spoken, the man immediately is healed. Throughout Acts the real performer of miracles is Jesus. Those watching the event are astounded. Residents of Lydda and Sharon, Jews that is, are spurred to turn to the Lord.

Abruptly the scene shifts to Joppa (modern-day Jaffa). Tabitha (in Greek, Dorcas), a disciple known for "always doing good and helping the poor" and her donations of clothing (verses 36, 39), fell sick and died.

Peter's reputation has spread (recall the healing shadow in 5:15). Christians ask for his presence in Joppa with no mention of specific intention. When the garments are shown to Peter, the intent is to show Tabitha's work, certainly not as a means by which to purchase the apostle's work. After the miracle, Christians are summoned back to the room.

The result is that many Jews are moved to faith through the miraculous event of Peter's act. The chapter closes with Peter spending many days in Joppa with a tanner (Simon) who would have been considered an outcast by Jews who despised his work as unclean.

Luke has then accomplished two goals through these two stories. First, Jesus' power is shown. Second, the conversion of the area around Joppa and Lydda, that is in the western Jordan area north to Caesarea, has been accomplished. Peter has been guided by the Spirit and now awaits further directions.

Acts 10:1-8. Caesarea was built by Herod the Great on the site of an excellent harbor. Caesarea served as the seat of the Roman proconsul and also as a station to a Roman garrison.

Cornelius was a centurion. That is, he commanded a *century* made up of one hundred soldiers. Cornelius is described as "devout and Godfearing." This term is used to describe those non-Jews who admired the ethical integrity and monatheism of Judaism and who took part in syna-

gogue services. He is also a man of piety who gives generously to those in need.

At about 3:00 P.M. in broad daylight (the ninth hour of the day), Cornelius sees a vision of an angel. The vision terrifies Cornelius, but he says, "What is it, Lord?" God directs him to send messengers to bring Peter to Cornelius.

Now the importance of 9:43 becomes clear. Peter is not yet known to Cornelius. Indeed, the notion of a Gentile in any Jewish or Jewish-Christian community as anything but a welcome observer is beyond the realm of imagination. Neither Peter nor Cornelius has an inkling of what is about to happen. Luke's message is that both men are led equally by God.

The angelic presence leaves and Cornelius dispatches the messengers, as instructed. They begin the thirty-mile trip immediately and will complete it at noon the next day. With this image of two servants and a soldier making their way to Joppa, the first vision and scene of this dramatic action ends.

Acts 10:9-16. At the same time that Cornelius's messengers approach Simon's house, Peter goes to the flat rooftop to pray. Thus, scene two of the drama begins.

Peter becomes hungry and asks for food to be prepared. His hunger of course prepares the way for the second vision in this story. While the food is being prepared, Peter too enters into a trance in which something like a sheet containing all sorts of animals descends. A voice tells him to "kill and eat."

As a good Jew, Peter balks at the instruction, calling the animals "impure and unclean." The voice replies, "Do not call anything impure that God has made clean." The vision is of course not about kosher and nonkosher foods. Luke's first readers would have recognized this immediately. But Peter is confused and baffled. Even after the same pattern is repeated three times he remains confused and perplexed.

Acts 10:17-23a. Continuing to wonder about the meaning of the vision, Peter receives the three visitors who stand at the door calling for him. Since his perplexity is so profound Peter needs even more divine guidance (verses 19-20). Luke could hardly have stated his argument more forcefully. Through what appears almost comic, Peter's perplexity, Luke illustrates clearly that the notion of a Christian-Gentile joining was not the design or the intention of even the most outstanding apostle. The Gentile mission was not the invention of the church. The Gentile mission is God's intention and is led by the Spirit.

Acts 10:23b-33. Scene three opens with Peter on his way to Caesarea. The others from Joppa are Christian who will serve as witnesses to the remarkable events to follow (11:12).

Cornelius has been awaiting the messengers' return with Peter. He has gathered together family and friends to prepare an audience for Peter from which a Christian congregation might emerge. Incredibly, Cornelius throws himself at Peter's feet as if Peter were an angelic visitor. Showing an appropriate humility, the Christian apostle responds that he, too, is only a man.

Peter finally understands his vision. Food (clean and unclean animals) was not the issue at stake; racial prejudice was the central issue. Again, the association of Christian Jews with Gentiles, unprecedented as it is, is not the result of any one person's design. Much more to the point is Luke's concern that the Gentile mission in every form is the result of God's guidance.

Cornelius's recollection of the events of the preceding days confirms the divine guidance to which Peter has already alluded. Note that in this scene Luke presents to the readers a Gentile who can think and speak in biblical terms. This fact should not be terribly surprising as the centurion had seen Judaism at close range for some time.

Acts 10:34-43. Peter's speech is similar to those in Acts 2. Broadly stated, the outline is as follows: anyone is acceptable to God (verses 34-35), the good news of Jesus (*kerygma*, verses 36-41), scriptural proof (verse 43), and a summons to repentance (verses 42-43). Insofar as salvation is concerned, God will reject no one; God will permit no racial, cultural, or religious barriers to salvation.

Acts 10:44-48. Everyone who believes receives forgiveness of sins (10:43). The declaration of a universal gospel brings the speech to a stunning conclusion. Not only were the listeners stunned by the inclusion of all, but the Holy Spirit came upon them all. The decision of God that the whole world will be included in the saving gospel sets the tone and establishes the background for subsequent conflict and expansion.

Luke grasped the significance and the difficulty of the issue. Clearly the expansion of the Christian gospel to previously forbidden territory could not be the intent of one or two men. For such drastic and far-reaching effects a far greater authority must be involved. This does not mean to suggest that for Luke the Holy Spirit is but an attempt to secure authority for an otherwise troublesome development. To the contrary, the Holy Spirit has directed the movement from its beginning.

One of Luke's primary concerns is to present theologically sound reasons for the Gentile mission. Even with the Spirit's direction and authority, the issue is hardly conclusively decided. The struggle for a universal gospel continues throughout the Book of Acts. For the moment, however, the gospel has reached yet another element—the Gentiles. Recall the image of the splash in the pond. The concentric circles' steady expansion gives us an image not unlike the one presented by Luke—first a handful of followers, then the despised Samaritans, the previously unacceptable eunuch, then the God-fearers. We have now reached the point of the potential of Gentiles.

In order to make class members familiar with the major cities and regions named in these chapters, show them the route Paul took to Damascus and the cities mentioned in Peter's story. Point out the major geographical points in Palestine (Dead Sea, Sea of Galilee, Jordan River) and major cities in these stories (Jerusalem, Damascus, Lydda, Joppa, Caesarea). Use wall maps or a book of biblical maps.

DIMENSION THREE: WHAT DOES THE BIBLE MEAN TO ME?

Acts 9:1-9—Wrong Actions for Good Reasons

Among many questions raised by readers of Saul's conversion are those that cluster around his vehement persecution of the Christian movement. How could anyone act in such blind and destructive ways?

To begin with, we must recognize the potential of evil that lurks in the shadows of even our best intentions. Within each of us dwells the potential of great evil, a shadow side, especially when the deepest of our feelings are armed by or are in some manner linked to the religious impulse. What are some events that illustrate this problem? What of the persecution of Jews at any time in history? Is this persecution deliberate, intentional evil? Or in some sense is persecution the distortion of an honorable impulse?

A further note to this question has to do with the evil potential in the converted individual. One might wish that when anyone is converted by the life and presence of Christ the evil evaporates. Unfortunately, this is simply not the case. Always religious folk need to keep in mind that the entire being needs to be brought under the control not only of religion generally but of an ethic of love and compassion specifically, Paul's own fiery spirit was not stilled by conversion. Much more to the point, it was channeled into God's work.

Acts 9:10-19a, 26-29; 10:9-16, 47 God's Imperative and Our Reluctance

Christianity began as a small community within the structures and traditions of Judaism. Our study has shown several ways that the Spirit slowly but surely enlarged the circle of people who were included. Still Christians resisted. Lest the resistance to the Spirit's movement be considered only an ancient problem, we must ask ourselves what are the imperatives of the Spirit today in our churches? What are some of the barriers we see in our churches? Does racial prejudice and bigotry prevent the gospel from expanding? To what degree do we suffer from the same sin of racial and national pride? How can we discern the creative disturbance of the Spirit's presence in our lives? Is it when we are bothered by economic injustices to which the church turns a deaf ear? Or when national pride blinds us to our own evil?

List on a chalkboard or on a large piece of paper the areas in your church in which the Holy Spirit might be moving.

What are they? What issues does your church need to have with respect to God's intention for a universal gospel? How is your church resisting the Holy Spirit?

Acts 9:1-9—Conversions

Class members may want to discuss *conversion*. Luke's story of Saul's experience on the road to Damascus is packed with meaning and possibility. In order to begin a discussion use the following suggestion as to the process of conversion.

A moral issue is at stake. First a person must be aware that in the present circumstance there is a moral issue; for instance, Saul present at the stoning of Stephen. Was it the way Stephen died that first pricked Saul's conscience?

Past perceptions are not sufficient now. An illustration of this may be the time when parents realize that their child loves a person who, according to their prejudices, was previously unacceptable. If the family is to remain intact, the previous perception is insufficient.

The person is aware of the need for a different behavior or attitude. At this point the person knows what needs to be done.

The person acts on the new awareness/attitude. But how does a person find sufficient strength and courage to act on the new awareness? In Luke's presentation the implication is that the Christian community gives the support. Nothing will always be automatic, nor will it be easy. The support for conversion (not simply the demand for it) will be within the Christian fellowship.

Discuss the meanings of conversion with class members. When have they felt the need for conversion? How has the church served to support the conversion? Close the session by asking class members to share as a litany insights or disquieting feelings that came during this lesson. After each person shares have the entire class answer: "We thank you, O Lord." Close with silent prayer.

But the word of God continued to increase and spread (12:24).

— 5 —

The Mission to the Gentiles

Acts 11–12

DIMENSION ONE:
WHAT DOES THE BIBLE SAY?

Answer these questions by reading Acts 11

1. In which city are the apostles and the brothers gathered? (11:2)

   The apostles and brothers are gathered in Jerusalem.

2. What is the response to Peter's explanation of his vision and encounter with the Gentiles? (11:18)

   The hearers say, "God has even granted to the Gentiles repentance unto life."

3. To which cities and regions had Christians fled as a result of persecution? (11:19)

   Christians had fled to Phoenicia, Cyprus, and Antioch.

4. When the church in Jerusalem hears of the preaching to Gentiles, whom do they send to Antioch? (11:22)

   The apostles in Jerusalem send Barnabas to Antioch.

5. How is Barnabas described? (11:24)

   Barnabas is "a good man, full of the Holy Spirit and faith."

6. Where else does Barnabas go? (11:25)

   Barnabas goes to Tarsus to look for Saul.

7. What name is given for the first time to followers of Jesus in Antioch? (11:26)

   Followers of Jesus are called Christians for the first time in Antioch.

8. Which prophet predicts severe famine? (11:28)

   Agabus predicts famine.

9. What is the Christian response to the famine? (11:29)

   The Christian congregation determines "to provide help for the brothers living in Judea."

10. Who is entrusted with taking the collection to Jerusalem? (11:30)

    Barnabas and Saul take the collection to Judea.

Answer these questions by reading Acts 12

11. Who begins a new wave of persecution against the Christian movement? (12:1)

    King Herod begins persecuting "some who belonged to the church."

12. Which of the Twelve is killed during this persecution? (12:2)

    James the brother of John is killed.

13. Who is then arrested? (12:3)

    Peter is seized during the "Feast of Unleavened Bread" (Passover).

14. How is Peter rescued? (12:7-10)

    An angel of the Lord appears, and a light shines in the cell. The angel struck Peter on the side and woke him up. "The chains fell off Peter's wrists," and he is told how to dress. When wrapped in his cloak, Peter is led through miraculously opened doors out to the street.

15. What is the congregation's reaction to Peter's release? (12:12-16)

    The congregation thinks the servant girl, who answered Peter's knock at their door, is out of her mind; the knocking can only be caused by an angel. When they realize that Peter has actually escaped, they are astonished.

16. What does Herod do when he learns of the escape? (12:19)

Herod cross-examines the guards and then orders their execution. Then Herod goes to Caesarea and stays there a while.

17. How is Herod punished for his persecution and blasphemy? (12:20-23)

As punishment, an angel of the Lord strikes him down, and Herod is eaten by worms and dies.

18. What is Luke's conclusion as to the effect of this persecution? (12:24)

Though some Christians suffer, the church—the word of God—continues to increase.

19. Who travels with Barnabas and Saul? (12:25)

John, "also called Mark," accompanies them.

20. What are some turning points in Acts? Fill in the blanks.

Luke presents many turning points in Acts. The gospel is first preached within the ranks of "both JEWS and CONVERTS" (2:11). Then the gospel spreads to the formerly despised SAMARITANS (8:5) represented by SIMON (8:9). The next expansion took place with CORNELIUS (10:1-2). In Acts 11 and 12, the Christian movement finally begins to reach out to the GENTILES (11:1).

DIMENSION TWO:
WHAT DOES THE BIBLE MEAN?

In this session you will again study the Cornelius episode and the further work of Peter. You might be wondering why the Cornelius incident is repeated so soon. After all, the entire tenth chapter focused on the initial contact with Gentiles. Why repeat it in the verses immediately following? The conventions of historical writing that guide modern writers were simply not a part of the thinking that affected Luke and other writers of biblical materials. Luke simply wanted to speak of the burning questions challenging the Christian movement as a theologian trying to inform faith by means of stories, tradition, and speeches, as well as to advance the purposes of God as revealed in Christ. For this reason Luke tells the dramatic moment through Peter's reporting to the apostles and other Christians in Judea.

Acts 11:1-18. Word of Peter's encounter with Cornelius got back to the apostles and other Christians in Jerusalem. In the Jerusalem Christian community a staunchly conservative element was either already formed or was forming itself, here referred to as the "circumcised believers." Why should the conservative element be so concerned? To begin with, Luke presents the Cornelius episode as a single, self-contained unit. But, his economy is such that specific incidents serve as evidence of a much more widespread phenomenon. Therefore, not only Peter and Cornelius but in all likelihood other unnamed Christians and less well-known Gentiles have been in contact with each other.

These believers hold that converts to Christianity must come by way of Jewish tradition and practice as they did. Since this is being challenged, they have reason to be disturbed. Some of their oldest and most sacred traditions were giving way to a more inclusive and less law-oriented style of shared faith.

The conservative party questions not only the contact but the extended relationship of eating with Gentiles (verse 3). Note that to this point baptism is not the issue.

Luke has now set the scene. The conservative party has had sufficient time (since Peter and others stayed with Cornelius for some time) to work up their challenge. Peter, who had himself been slow to grasp the impulse of the Spirit, now presents his defense.

Peter's speech, while quite similar to the previous material, is not mere rote repetition. Compare Peter's defense speech to Luke's first telling (10:9-48). Through 11:11, the stories are the same. At verse 12, however, Peter indicates that six Jewish Christians were already present with him in the house when Cornelius's messengers arrive (10:17-19). In verse 14, Peter's defense indicates that not only did an angel appear to Cornelius, but that the angel told Cornelius the nature of what Peter would say (compare with 10:31). Peter then describes the coming of the Spirit.

Here the Spirit is said to have come as Peter preached (11:15) at the beginning of the incident. Chapter 10 implies the coming of the Spirit was delayed until nearer the end of the preaching (compare with 10:34-43, 44). Finally, Peter indicates that he remembered the Lord's word regarding baptism: John's baptism was one of water; Peter's would be one of the Holy Spirit (1:5).

Clearly Luke intended not only to reiterate Peter's defense to the conservative circumcision party. He intended to speak to the reader as well with the admonition: Remember. The baptism to which Peter and Luke refer is the same one spoken of and promised by Jesus.

The presence of the Spirit here refers to the relatively temporary gift of ecstatic speaking in tongues, not the permanent indwelling. But beware lest this presence be discounted, as it is still the authentic Spirit. Then Luke poses to the reader the question with which Peter challenges the conservative party. How can he, or by implication anyone, stand against God's intention?

Peter's defense seems to have been sufficient to silence the opponents (verse 18). Did Luke mean to imply that the other eleven apostles were opposed to Peter? We cannot be certain. We can be sure that if the other eleven did disagree, the entire church would have been stunned. A safe assumption is that a major element of the early Christian church opposed the new insight and direction proposed and carried out by Peter and others.

The question must now be asked, what did Luke accomplish through this second repetition of the Cornelius episode? For the Christian church, the central question from this time forward will be, How valid is the mission to Gentiles? Luke could hardly have stated his case more forcefully than a repetition along with the inclusion of such a powerful question. The issue has been clearly set. The resolution of the conflict, however, is not so easily achieved. Yes, the Christians conclude the scene with glorification of God because God has given to Gentiles "repentance unto life." But the issue does not die there.

Acts 11:19-26. The Jerusalem church had been brought back together (8:1b). The story of how the Christian Way spread into various areas now resumes, somewhat abruptly. Swept before the wave of persecution following Stephen's death (8:1), Christians traveled as far as Phoenicia, Cyprus, and Antioch. Who were these scattered Christians? They could easily have been members of the group of which Stephen had been the spokesman. They could even have been the Seven (6:5-6).

The areas to which the persecuted fled include the strip of land along the coast of the Mediterranean Sea. The major cities in this region include Tyre (21:3-4), Sidon (27:3), and Ptolemais (present-day Acre, 21:7). The city of Antioch is on the Orontes River, about fifteen miles upriver from the Mediterranean in Syria. This city was known as "the Third Metropolis of the Roman Empire" with a population of approximately five hundred thousand. Antioch served as the center for the legate of Syria.

Note that Luke is concerned only in passing with how the Christian faith spread so far. Hastening on, Luke addresses the basic problem at hand—mission to the Gentiles. The familiar figure of Barnabas appears again (verses 22-25). All that we know about Barnabas is found in Acts. Earlier he had sold a piece of property in order to help the destitute in the Jerusalem church (4:36-37). He was therefore a highly respected member of the Jerusalem congregation. He heads the list of prophets and teachers in Antioch (13:1).

Since the congregations prospered, Luke saw the approval of God on the enterprise. A great number of people turned to the Lord (11:26; see also 4:4; 6:7; 16:5). The notion that "the Lord's hand was with them" is also found in 2 Samuel 3:12. Nothing prospers without the presence of God.

At this time, Barnabas is sent by the Jerusalem church to Antioch. The purpose of his visit is not stated. However, the Christian leadership would surely have been concerned about how the sister congregation prospered.

Barnabas will in effect grant official approval by the Jerusalem church on the new mission. Barnabas preaches to the congregation. For Luke the sending of Barnabas by the Jerusalem church is not only the means by which the mission is granted approval. The approval most significant

to Luke is the presence of the Holy Spirit. The presence of the Spirit is responsible for the tremendous growth that takes place (2:41, 47; 8:12).

The story shifts quickly to Tarsus where, presumably, Saul has remained since his flight from a conspiracy to kill him (9:30). How long did Saul remain in Tarsus before being summoned again by Barnabas? Three years (Galatians 1:18)? fourteen years (Galatian 2:1)? Scholars are still trying to find out the number of visits, their duration, and their sequence. Perhaps Luke combined tradition or facts because Barnabas and Saul appear together in Antioch in 13:1.

In any event, Saul stays with Barnabas in Antioch for an entire year, which in Luke's scheme is quite a long time. In Antioch the disciples are first called by the name *Christian*. The distinctive name *Christian* was probably a term of derision. The Christians, however, saw the term in a positive light. Thus, a term intended as a curse was transformed into a blessing. More important to Luke and his readers, the distinction *Christian* signaled a break with Judaism. No longer could the Christian community expect protection that had been given by the state.

Acts 11:27-30. In those days, during the year of Saul's stay in Antioch (11:26) or very soon following, prophets arrived from Jerusalem. Agabus predicts a terrible famine. Later on Agabus predicts dire circumstances for Paul. Does this mean that in Acts' prediction of the future is a function of prophecy? Paul describes prophetic insight as that which can discern the thoughts (heart) of a man (1 Corinthians 14:24-25) of which Acts says nothing.

The disciples took this warning as opportunity for ministry. An offering is to be taken and the entire collection sent to Judea (verse 29).

The term *elders* appears with no explanation as to either its origin or what the office meant. From this incident it appears that elders performed both welfare and distribution roles. They could possibly have paralleled the work of the Hellenistic Seven (6:1-6). The collection is sent, according to Luke, by way of Saul and Barnabas to the elders in Jerusalem.

Acts 12:1-4. About that time Herod initiates another wave of persecution. This parallels 5:17-18.

The only one of the Twelve mentioned specifically is James, who is summarily executed. Luke's work has included persecution of the Christian community. Here, however, is the first mention of the violent death of one of the original twelve apostles.

Theologians tend to focus on two divergent points. On the one hand is the *theology of glory* or triumph. This view tends to focus on the victory of God and the triumphant protection of God's people. Much of Acts is of this slant. In many instances people are protected by interference by the Spirit.

The other theological view may be called the *theology of the cross.* Though Luke reports that Paul will suffer (9:16), the theology of the cross with its suffering motif and the anguish of an absent God is largely missing from Acts. In this short story, almost a prelude to another miracle story, the cross does cast its shadow across the life of the church. Luke thus implies to his readers that, in the midst of the triumphant flow of Christian expansion, the shadow side (martyrdom) is never completely removed from reality.

The death of James pleased the Jews. For the first time Luke uses the word *Jew* to describe all Jews as antagonistic to the Christian movement. Up to this point the conflict between Christians and Jews had been restricted to the Sadducees. Peter is arrested during the Feast of Unleavened Bread, that is, during the Passover season. In its timing Peter's arrest sounds similar to the arrest of Jesus.

The scene shifts from the prison to Peter's fellow believers in the congregation (verse 5). While he remains in prison, the congregation gathers to pray.

Acts 12:6-11. If there were any questions as to Peter's plight, the description of him bound by not one, but two chains and sleeping between two soldiers in prison, rules out any chance of Peter's escape. Luke then sets before the reader the absolute dependence of Peter in what is about to occur. In silence Peter awaits his fate. Luke does not even give him the responsibility of praying and singing that Paul and Silas will have at a later time (16:25). Luke could hardly have painted a more desperate picture.

During the night God sends "an angel of the Lord" to intervene. None of what happens is the result of Peter's work. The angel even assumes the responsibility of telling Peter how to get dressed! Peter wonders if this is a dream of some kind.

The angel leads Peter through the miraculously opened door past the sleeping guards. After reaching the safety and freedom of the city street, Peter comes to his senses. Now he understands what has occurred. Unlike his slowness to comprehend the vision in Joppa, he quickly grasps the significance of this event. The Lord has delivered him from certain death.

Acts 12:12-17. The scene following Peter's miraculous release is almost comic. The congregation had gathered to pray for Peter's life. What had they prayed? We have no idea and cannot possibly know. But they did pray. What did they expect to happen? Again we do not know, but we can discern through the ironic scene about to unfold that the Christians were totally taken by surprise when Peter is released.

Now free, Peter seeks out the home of Mary, the mother of John Mark. Seldom are persons identified in reference to their children. In this instance, of course, John Mark is the better known of the two. When Peter knocks on the door, Rhoda, the servant girl, answers. The young girl loses her wits; and leaving the recently delivered prisoner standing outside the gate, she runs to tell the congregation that their prayers have been heard. As if to suggest the congregation's expectations were not really that God would hear

their prayers, the congregation retorts, "You're out of your mind!" Meanwhile the apostle stands outside knocking at the door. Will his knocking arouse officials? Will he be caught again?

Gesturing for silence, Peter quiets the congregation. He then describes what happened. He must not delay. The congregation must tell James. Had James assumed leadership of the congregation? Peter then goes to an unnamed place.

Here ends the story of Peter's miraculous escape. Throughout the story, even in its comic element, Luke has skillfully shown the sheer helplessness of Peter and the titanic work of God.

Acts 12:18-19. As a sort of sequel to this miraculous event, the consequences for the persecutors are listed. That the soldiers were disturbed is no surprise. In the great commotion following the discovery, the soldiers could anticipate little more than death for dereliction of duty. Luke by the way indicates no ethical remorse for what will befall the unfortunate guards. The helplessness of Christian enemies is thus emphasized.

Acts 12:20-25. Herod's reaction is quite predictable—severe actions will be leveled against any people suspected of aiding the escapee. Reprisals are in order, possibly economic measures. With all sorts of regal pageantry, Herod prepares to issue the edict. Citizens thoroughly schooled in the politics of survival shout the party line, "The voice of a god, not of a man!" With scarcely a moment's interval, an angel of the Lord (the Holy Spirit?) strikes down Herod because he had not given glory to God. His fate is that his body is eaten by worms (verse 23).

The summary in verse 24 captures both the hope and promise of the Christian gospel. Though persecution raged against the core of Christian leadership, the movement could not be so easily quashed. To those Christians who wondered about the presence and providence of God either during this persecution or in subsequent persecutions, Luke's answer is a certain one. The Lord God will preserve the hope and promise of the gospel. In the confrontation and conflict between Herod (the threatened state) and Peter (the Christian movement) the Christian movement will, by God's power, prevail. Luke shows no remorse over Herod's or the soldiers' fate. Whoever stands in God's way will have to suffer the consequences.

Luke's lack of any remorse raises for some readers a terrible ethical problem. How can the Christian movement base its survival and subsequent life on the death of anyone? Furthermore, how can the church rejoice in the death of anyone? (See Ezekiel 13:32, "For I take no pleasure in the death of anyone, declares the Sovereign LORD. Repent and live!") Discuss with class members their perceptions of the moral dilemma(s) implicit in this story.

As a conclusion to the entire chapter, Luke points toward a continued relationship between the Jerusalem and Antioch Christian congregations. Barnabas and Saul return from Jerusalem. Had they already taken the collection to the church? Some authorities suggest the two are going to Jerusalem. In either event, Luke shows a solid relationship between the two congregations.

Verse 25 also serves to connect the previous events and the first missionary journey of Paul. Luke introduces John Mark into the story. Mark will play a major role in Paul's first missionary journey.

DIMENSION THREE: WHAT DOES THE BIBLE MEAN TO ME?

Luke's Literary Technique

Luke uses single illustrations to dramatize a widespread phenomenon. That is, the contact with Samaritans occurred more times than the one encounter of Philip with Simon of Samaria (8:5-13). By the same token, Christians contacted many people who for various reasons could not be included in traditional Judaism. Luke uses the story of the Ethiopian eunuch (8:26-36) to show this phenomenon.

By now you can see that Luke is not writing primarily to show how the gospel spread from Jerusalem, Judea, Samaria, and to the end of the earth. Had this been his central concern we would not read so often of Christian congregations in various cities and regions without any explanation as to how those communities were started. We can learn through stories and speeches that Luke's concern is on the expansion of the gospel past ethnic and cultural barriers of prejudice and bigotry.

With each turning point, each encounter, the gospel makes its inevitable way further into the whole range of cultural environment. The human dynamic of resistance, however, is just as inevitable. The intention of God bumps up not only against the oppressors of the movement or the pagans to whom the gospel is addressed. Throughout Acts, Luke cleverly and wisely illustrates the resistance to the implications of a universal gospel that issue from within the Christian community itself. Ask class members to share their feelings as they consider the reality of resistance to God's will by Christians themselves. Are people in any sense comforted by Luke's portrayal? Do they feel angry that Luke would dare reveal the shadow side of Christian human experience? Do your class members have any suggestions as to where your church may be as God's intention leads toward greater inclusiveness?

Acts 11:27-30
Human Need and the Opportunity for Ministry

The prophecy of Agabus regarding a terrible famine (11:26) prompts the disciples to take up an offering. Luke notes that the offering will come from "each one according to his ability." At least two issues can be raised from this short story.

First, human need—in this instance hunger due to famine—stirs the soul to, in some manner, help alleviate suffering and hardship. From the earliest moments of its life the church has always wanted to help where there is hurt and/or need.

Churches within a denomination and the ecumenical cooperation across denominational lines characterize what the body of Christ can do when individuals and churches unite to address human need. Where one church may have fallen on hard times, there is another congregation that has an offering to help with ministry. New churches need the support of the older, established congregations. Missionary work, both domestic and international, requires aid from local churches. Relief efforts after natural disasters profit immensely by the generosity of people of faith.

Discuss the implications of the collection taken by the Antioch church. How do members of the body of Christ unite for ministry? Do people see themselves in the great tradition of the Antioch church? Or do people resist the notion of ministry beyond the local church?

The second issue raised by the collection has to do with mission beyond the local church and the vitality of the church. The Antioch congregation thrives and becomes the center for missionary activity. The Jerusalem church, by way of contrast, appears hamstrung due to its internal discord between the conservative element and the most progressive element. For many reasons, no doubt, the Jerusalem church begins to fade out of the picture. Could part of the reason for its demise be that the Jerusalem congregation did not see mission as vital to its life? Luke never makes a statement to this effect. How do missions enliven the life of a congregation? In what sort of mission is your church involved?

Acts 12:6-17
Divine Initiative and Human Responsibility

Luke's picture of Peter's imprisonment and release shows Peter as entirely passive. Reread the story with class members. In what ways does Luke show Peter's plight? What is Peter's role during the actual rescue? How does the congregation react to Peter's escape? What is the relationship between divine intervention and human responsibility?

This difficult question gets to the heart of a major dilemma challenging all God's people. Luke's purpose seems to have been to show beyond any doubt that the work of the gospel cannot and indeed will not be stopped, even by the worst that would-be oppressors can fling at the church. But Peter nearly sleeps through the entire affair. Indeed, an angel has to poke him first to get up, then to tell him how to get dressed. Surely Luke does not mean to imply that in the course of faithful living we depend primarily on heavenly intervention with little if any daring response on our part.

To focus the question more sharply, let me suggest that religion is too often used as a means by which to escape or evade the task that makes us fully human. That central task is to know one's own responsibility for decision-making and courageous, faithful living in the world. Some religious perspectives contend that individuals ought to wait for the leading of the Holy Spirit and then to do exactly as instructed. For people of this inclination, personal assumption of responsibility is far from the center of one's life tasks.

A misuse of Peter's miraculous rescue would be to suggest that all we have to do in being faithful to Christianity is to await the divine intervention of God's Holy Spirit. To assume such an attitude is to hide behind religion and never live in the realm of daring and risk-taking. Equally as serious, however, is the notion that we do not need the presence or inspiration of the Spirit. Compared with Peter's escape is the arrogant assumption, by Herod, mindlessly parroted by the people, that when Herod speaks so has a god spoken. Clearly Luke's account shows that such assumptions are blasphemy.

Ask class members to think of issues with which they have wrestled. To what extent are they aware of hoping for more intervention than they have received?

Close this session by listing on the chalkboard or a large piece of paper issues and insight that class members found particularly interesting.

You may want to offer a prayer of thanksgiving for the continued presence of Christ who comforts and challenges us in our discipleship.

Set apart for me Barnabas and Saul for the work to which I have called them (13:2).

— 6 —

The First Missionary Journey

Acts 13–14

DIMENSION ONE:
WHAT DOES THE BIBLE SAY?

Answer these questions by reading Acts 13

1. Who are the prophets and teachers in Antioch? (13:1)

   The prophets and teachers are Barnabas; Simeon, called Niger; Lucius of Cyrene; Manaean, a member of Herod's court; and Saul.

2. Which two men are designated by the Holy Spirit for a special work? (13:2-3)

   Barnabas and Saul are set apart by the Spirit for special work.

3. Who directs the missionaries on their journey? (13:4)

   The Holy Spirit sends the missionaries on their journey.

4. Who summons Barnabas and Saul in order to hear the word of God? (13:7)

   The proconsul Sergius Paulus summons the two missionaries.

5. What happens to the false prophets Elymas (Bar-Jesus) when he tries to keep Sergius Paulus from the faith? (13:11)

   Paul curses him and the man is blinded temporarily.

6. Which missionary leaves Paul and the others in the middle of the journey? (13:13)

   John (John Mark) leaves the missionaries for Jerusalem.

7. Where and to whom does Paul address his proclamation? (13:14-16, 26)

   Paul goes to the synagogue in Pisidian Antioch. There he addresses the men of Israel and Gentiles who worship God.

8. What is the reaction to Paul's preaching? (13:42-44)

   The people ask for more preaching. On the following sabbath almost the whole city gathers to hear the word of God.

9. Why do Paul and Barnabas speak to the Gentiles? (13:45-46)

   The Jews, to whom the first message was addressed, rejected the word; now they turn to the Gentiles.

10. How do Paul and Barnabas react to the persecution stirred up against them? (13:50-52)

    Paul and Barnabas shake off the dust of the city in protest and go to Iconium. They are not discouraged as they are filled with joy and with the Holy Spirit.

Answer these questions by reading Acts 14

11. When the missionaries preach in the Iconium synagogue what is the result? (14:2-5)

    The missionaries' preaching at first converts a great number of Jews and Gentiles, but both unbelieving Jews and Gentiles stir up trouble. The city is divided and some plot to mistreat and stone the missionaries.

12. What is the reaction to Paul's healing of the man in Lystra who is lame? (14:11-13)

    The amazed people shout in their own language that the gods Zeus and Hermes have come down to them as men. The people want to offer sacrifices to the missionaries.

13. What happens when Jews from Antioch and Iconium arrive? (14:19)

    Paul is stoned and then dragged out of the city nearly dead.

14. After Paul recovers from the stoning, what does he do? (14:20-22)

Paul proceeds with Barnabas to Derbe. They then retrace their journey, encouraging and strengthening congregations along the way.

15. Through what must Christians pass in order to enter the kingdom of God? (14:22)

Christians must "go through many hardships" to enter the kingdom of God.

16. What do Paul and Barnabas tell the church? (14:27)

They tell the church all that God has done through them and how the door of faith has been opened to Gentiles.

17. Complete the following sketch of the first missionary journey:

From Antioch the missionaries go to SELEUCIA (13:4) from which they sail to CYPRUS (13:4). Upon arriving at SALAMIS (13:5) they preach to Jews in synagogues. Traveling west through Cyprus the missionaries arrive in PAPHOS (13:6). After the encounter with the magician Elymas, Paul and his company go to PERGA in Pamphylia (13:13). After John (Mark) departs, the balance of the company proceed to PISIDIAN ANTIOCH (13:14). Persecution drives the missionaries out of Antioch to ICONIUM (13:51). When the Christian missionaries learn of an impending persecution, they flee to LYSTRA and DERBE, cities of Lycaonia (14:6). After completing the mission, the men return to LYSTRA, ICONIUM, and ANTIOCH (14:21). The rest of the journey goes through PISIDIA and PAMPHYLIA (14:24). After preaching in PERGA (14:25) they go to ATTALIA (14:25). From here they sail back to ANTIOCH (14:26).

DIMENSION TWO: WHAT DOES THE BIBLE MEAN?

In this session you will study the first missionary journey, which will show the ever-widening circle of those affected by the gospel.

Acts 13:1-3. Luke begins Acts 13 by listing "the prophets and teachers" of the Antioch congregation. Barnabas of course is by now well-known. Simeon, called Niger (meaning "black"), and Lucius of Cyrene, which had a large Jewish colony, are unknown characters. Manaen was from the court of the tetrarch Herod Antipas and thus was a man of some note.

Two scenes describe the preparations for the mission. In the first, the Holy Spirit selects Barnabas and Saul. The subsequent journey is the responsibility of the Spirit. In the second scene the missionaries, after fasting and praying, are blessed by the congregation (see also 1 Timothy 4:14). The laying on of hands does not make the men apostles (Galatians 1:1); the Holy Spirit makes the men apostles.

Acts 13:4-12. With weighty importance given to the direction of the Spirit, Luke characterizes the missionaries as being sent on their way by the Spirit.

Seleucia was a harbor city, about fifteen miles west of Antioch, from which the men sailed. After landing at Salamis on Cyprus the men preach in synagogues. John Mark accompanies them. On the west side of Cyprus the town of Paphos is the backdrop for the only tradition Luke has regarding the entire mission in Cyprus.

Elymas the sorcerer opposes the missionaries. (Elymas, meaning "sorcerer" or "magician," is also called Bar-Jesus, which in Hebrew means "son of Jesus," perhaps Joshua). Luke characterizes him as a false prophet but not because he has no power. (The man possessed real power.) Rather, his falsehood has to do with the magical powers opposing the will of God. The story illustrates how the magical powers are subordinate to God's power as well. Luke shows that Christianity is unparalleled by any form of magic.

Cyprus was a senatorial province and therefore ruled by a proconsul. The false prophet, Elymas, tries to prevent the meeting of the proconsul and Saul. For this challenge Saul, "filled with the Holy Spirit" (verse 9), is prepared.

Saul, a Hebrew name and formerly used to indicate his full Jewishness, is now replaced by *Paul.* Could it be that since Paul will work primarily with Greeks and Gentiles Luke adopts the Roman form of his name?

Paul confronts the magician and performs a miracle, although one with negative overtones. The magician is temporarily blinded (verse 11). The teaching and miracle cause the proconsul to believe ("for he was amazed at the teaching about the Lord").

Acts 13:13-16a. Leaving from Paphos on the western end of Cyprus, Paul and the other missionaries set sail. Paul has, by implication, assumed leadership of the mission. With no explanation, John Mark departs for Jerusalem. Only later will the incident lead to controversy (15:37-39). The area to which the missionaries first go is to Perga, a seacoast town in Asia Minor.

Antioch in Pisidia, about one hundred miles north of Perga, is the missionaries' next stop.

The synagogues, and thus the Jews, are the first places Paul seeks out. The customary synagogue service includes the *Shema:* "Hear O Israel: The LORD our God, the LORD is one" (Deuteronomy 6:4-9); prayer; blessings; readings from the Law; and readings from the Prophets. Then followed pronouncements or a sermon.

Acts 13:17-41. Paul's speech is similar to that of Peter's at Pentecost (2:14-36) and that of Stephen's (7:2-53). Stephen's speech and Paul's sermon both reinterpret Israel's history. These sermons tell of Jesus dying at the hands of lawless men even though nothing could be found against him warranting death (13:28). But Jesus did not die as a victim drawn into a whirlpool of events stronger than he was. Rather, Jesus died as a part of God's plan and therefore with God's knowledge. Thus Scriptures are fulfilled (verses 32-33). God raised Jesus from the dead as promised.

The speech focuses on the fact of the Resurrection (3:15; 4:10). Central to the Christian faith is the vindication of Jesus' hope that Paul summarizes in this speech. The Resurrection is, of course, witnessed to by the apostles (verse 31) of which Paul considers himself one. The apostolic witness is that (1) Jesus is risen; (2) we are eyewitnesses; (3) thereby the promises of God are fulfilled. Ours is not an empty hope. (4) Our proclamation is founded in this central truth.

Note the Christological interpretation of Psalm 2:7 (verse 33).

Sharply contrasted with David, who when he died went the way of all flesh, Jesus knows no such corruption. Jesus' life is absolutely imperishable. Psalm 16:10, earlier used in Peter's Pentecost speech (2:25-28), is used again (verse 35).

Through this Jesus, "everyone who believes is justified from everything you could not be justified from by the law of Moses" (verse 39). Forgiveness, like faith, is a gift of grace.

Acts 13:42-52. Thrilled, and perhaps intrigued, the listeners beg for further proclamation on the following sabbath. Meanwhile, "many of the Jews and devout converts to Judaism" become believers (verse 43). These people continue urging Paul and Barnabas to preach.

In what must be an exaggerated image, nearly the entire city gathers to listen to Christian preaching (verse 44). For the first time, Luke represents Paul as a compelling orator.

As a result of Paul's preaching, the Christian movement gathers momentum in Antioch. Many Jews and non-Jews alike have been captured by the Christian proclamation and a new congregation begins to form around the preached word. Other Jews, clearly the majority of those who are threatened by the new movement, begin to stir up unrest (verse 45).

Paul always seeks the synagogues and Jews first. In Corinth the same pattern occurs (18:6). Now the full extent of the tragedy is stated. Though Paul seeks first the Jews, they exclude themselves from the gospel. For the first time in Acts, the mission to the Gentiles is openly declared (verse 46). This Gentile mission is now only in its initial stages and holds true only for Pisidian Antioch at this time. Cornelius, of course, had been characterized as a God-fearer. Therefore, with the exception of Sergius Paulus (13:7), nothing has been said of a specific Gentile mission.

Scripture (Isaiah 49:6) is cited as reason for the new direction (verse 47). Again, the use of Scripture in preaching is evident.

The Gentiles give thanks for participation in the Christian hope and life of the Resurrection. The preaching started by Paul and Barnabas spreads throughout the region.

Preaching not only spawns congregations, but resistance to the gospel develops as well. In this instance a specific group of Jews, the well-to-do, pious women and men, stir up persecution against Paul and Barnabas. Thus Paul and Barnabas are driven out of the region. The apostles leave the region using the image of shaking dust from their feet (Luke 9:5; 10:11) rather than a desperate flight from an enraged mob. The Christian community survives and will be visited later (Acts 14:24). The apostles then proceed to Iconium, an important junction in the plains region, several miles away. Luke then concludes the episode with a hopeful summary. A Christian congregation has been established in Antioch of Pisidia.

Acts 14:1-7. Iconium was a Roman city in Galatia in south-central Asia (2 Timothy 3:11). The first efforts in this new area are to the synagogue. We by now have come to anticipate the results of the preaching. On the one side are the converts to the Christian perspective that come from both Jewish and Greek ranks, on the other is the resistance to the gospel.

Because the preaching of the gospel causes significant response, the missionaries remain in Iconium for a long time. Part and parcel to the event of preaching is response. That response will not always be a positive one. But even a negative response is something. Along with this comes the insight that suffering and persecution are part of being Christian. The apostles trust God in the midst of a threatening circumstance.

The city is divided and another conspiracy develops (verse 4). When Paul and Barnabas hear of the plot, they flee to the region of Lycaonia. Within this region, (bounded to the south by the Taurus mountains, to the east by Cappadocia, to the north by Galatia, and to the west by Phrygia and Galatia), are two important cities, Lystra and Derbe. Luke's theological insight is that when the word is preached, something will happen and that even when persecution erupts, God will use the opportunity for the establishment of another Christian congregation.

Acts 14:8-18. Luke introduces the healing story with the customary formula: emphasizing the nature and severity of the ailment. As the man who is lame listens to Paul preach, Paul sees in the man faith, which is, along with the preaching, a precondition for healing. With a command reminiscent of Ezekiel 2:1, Paul instructs the man to stand.

Stunned by the miracle, the onlookers break into their native language, ready to make Paul and Barnabas into gods. Presumably the apostles did not understand the language because it is not until they see the priest of Zeus, the priest of the pagan religion of the area, approach with preparation for a sacrifice that the two are horror-struck. Paul and Barnabas refuse to allow worship of themselves. Paul's speech begins with the pagan orientation about the divine and moves toward the Christian gospel. Even though in the past the Gentiles received no revelation, they are not excused. Still God worked on their behalf (verses 15-17).

Acts 14:19-23. A new scene now opens, picking up from the event of 14:5. Paul is stoned, dragged out of the city, and left for dead. His enemies leave, and his friends gather around him. Paul is revived and reenters the city, but he leaves the next day for Derbe.

The impression Luke gives combines elements of suffering through persecution and triumph through miraculous power. Which of the two did he mean to emphasize in this short account? The story seems to emphasize the miraculous power more than the sufferings.

In one short verse Luke tells of the evangelization of Derbe (verse 21); no major event or person is mentioned.

On the return route (Lystra, Iconium, Antioch in Pisidia) Christian congregations are revisited. During the return trip the new Christians are told that "we must go through many hardships to enter the kingdom of God" (verse 22).

Elders are appointed, but Luke makes no attempt to describe the office or how it evolved.

Acts 14:24-28. Further missionary activity is limited to the preaching done in Perga with no mention of any results (verse 25). The missionaries arrive in Attalia, the port city from which they sail back to Antioch in Syria.

The entire journey had been initiated not by men and women, but by the Holy Spirit. This insight is the central theological element Luke wants his readers to grasp. God has opened the door to the Gentiles. God has given the Gentiles access to piety and to God.

Thus Luke brings to a conclusion the first missionary journey. The journey of no less than fourteen hundred miles in about A.D. 46–48 illustrates the remarkable tenacity of the missionaries, but more importantly, it illustrates the power and direction of the Holy Spirit.

DIMENSION THREE: WHAT DOES THE BIBLE MEAN TO ME?

Acts 13:16-50
Preaching and the Christian Congregation

Luke shows the Christian missionaries seeking out places in which to proclaim the Christian message. When the preaching concludes, something happens. Clearly the preaching event is one of potential and peril. Reread the stories of Acts 13 and 14. What are the results of preaching?

In Acts 13:48-52, converts are gained from both Jews and Greeks. Resistance also develops (13:50-51; 14:2-5). In 14:8, preaching stirs faith necessary for healing. In 14:21, a Christian congregation is born because of Christian preaching. The hope of Isaiah 55:11 is fulfilled:

So is my word that goes out from my mouth:
  It will not return to me empty,
but will accomplish what I desire
  and achieve the purpose for which I sent it.

Clearly, Luke intended to show the remarkable power of the preached word. But persecution never achieves its goal of eliminating the Christian message.

Discuss with class members what happens in the preaching event. Do class members see preaching as one of the central elements in the life of the church? Do they expect anything to happen as a result of preaching? Does the church need preaching today as it did in its formative years?

Can class members identify issues that, if addressed in preaching, might cause a healing response? What are some of the social, economic, spiritual, and moral questions that need to be addressed in preaching?

Acts 13:13-14; 14:8-18
The God of the Commonplace

Some readers are frustrated by the Book of Acts because in nearly every instance the events undertaken and experienced by the missionaries seem to be of an extraordinary nature. Major miracles of healing, superlative results from the preached word, spectacular results from large gatherings seem far removed from everyday life as we know and live it.

Why isn't much said about how the missionaries paid for boat trips or provisions for the journey? Were the missionaries required to work? A clue comes to us in Luke's presentations. As a rule the Christian preachers spoke on the sabbath in synagogues (13:5, 14, 44). Could it be that the day of rest and worship for Jews was also the only day of rest from daily labor for the missionaries as well?

Perhaps the readers of Acts should keep in mind the fact that Luke uses miracles and persecution to illustrate the power of the Holy Spirit. Perhaps in Luke's economy of witness the major part of gaining conversions through the word comes not through the spectacular but rather through the mundane and commonplace.

What are the implications for modern readers if indeed the daily lives of the missionaries were occupied with making a living and humbly sharing their witness to the action of God in Christ? Discuss with class members the implications that God can and will accomplish the expansion of the gospel through the commonplace.

Acts 14:21-25—Discipleship of a Sterner Sort

In the book *The Cost of Discipleship,* Dietrich Bonhoeffer states that when Christ calls on an individual, he bids that person come and die. Stern discipleship is not a central focus in Acts as it is for instance in the Gospel of Mark. But there are unmistakable indications that the Christian gospel will produce not only adulation and converts but opposition, and even persecution as well.

Have you ever heard the summons to Christian discipleship in these terms? Luke's implication is that not only for apostles and missionaries, but for any and all Christians, the means by which entry into the Kingdom is gained are trial and tribulation. Ask class members to list Christians whose witness brought on trial and persecution. Some names might be Martin Luther King, Jr., Bishop Desmond Tutu, and Dietrich Bonhoeffer. What are the implications of this understanding of the gospel? What would happen to our churches if this theology of the cross were more prevalent? Would our churches grow? Would churches shrink?

Conclude this session by listing on the chalkboard or a large piece of paper any new insights. If you feel any strong resistance or questions from class members, these might be listed as well, since they are legitimate responses to Scripture.

After both the insights and resistances are listed, close with a prayer giving thanks for the word of God that never returns void.

God, who knows the heart, showed that he accepted them by giving the Holy Spirit to them, just as he did to us (15:8).

7

The Jerusalem Council to the Gentiles

Acts 15:1–16:5

DIMENSION ONE:
WHAT DOES THE BIBLE SAY?

Answer these questions by reading Acts 15

1. What are the men from Judea teaching that Paul and Barnabas object to? (15:1-2)

   The men from Judea are teaching that unless a man is circumcised (becomes a Jew) he "cannot be saved" (become a Christian).

2. To which city do Paul and Barnabas, along with some others, then proceed? (15:2)

   They go to Jerusalem.

3. What is the initial response to the returning missionaries? (15:4)

   The returning missionaries are welcomed by the Jerusalem apostles and elders and the church.

4. What is the objection raised to the mission to the Gentiles? (15:5)

   Some believers in the Jerusalem church say, "The Gentiles must be circumcised and required to obey the law of Moses" (make the Gentiles Jews before they can become Christian).

5. Summarize Peter's argument. (15:7-11)

   The mission to the Gentiles was God's choice. God gave the Gentiles the Holy Spirit, thus making no distinction between Gentiles and Jews, having purified all hearts by faith. Therefore, we should not place more burden on the Gentiles than we ourselves can bear. Finally, all are saved through grace.

6. What is the assembly's response? (15:12a)

   The assembly is silenced by Peter's argument.

7. Who speaks after Peter? (15:12b)

   Paul and Barnabas speak after Peter, telling of the miracles done through them to Gentiles.

8. Summarize James's argument. (15:13-21)

   God first chose a people out of the Gentiles as the prophet Amos (9:11-12) had foretold. Therefore, we should not trouble any Gentiles who "are turning to God." We should send a letter to them recommending only that they "abstain from food polluted by idols, from sexual immorality, from the meat and blood of strangled animals."

9. When debate in the Jerusalem Council concludes, which men are sent to Antioch? (15:22)

   Paul, Barnabas, Judas called Barsabbas, and Silas are sent to Antioch.

10. Summarize the letter sent to Antioch. (15:23-29)

    From the apostles and elders in Jerusalem to Gentile believers in Antioch, Syria, and Cilicia: Unauthorized individuals have troubled you long enough. We have chosen to inform you of our decisions through Paul; Barnabas; and members of our congregation, Silas and Judas. By the authority of the Holy Spirit and of our assembly only these things need be observed: abstain from food sacrificed to idols, from the meat of strangled animals, and from sexual immorality.

11. What is the response to the compromise? (15:31)

    The congregations were glad for the encouraging message.

12. Which disciples remain preaching and teaching in Antioch? (15:35)

    Paul and Barnabas remain in Antioch.

13. Describe the conflict that arises between Paul and Barnabas. (15:37-40)

According to Luke's account, the conflict arises over the inclusion of John Mark in further missionary work because of John Mark's earlier desertion to Jerusalem.

14. Where do Paul and Silas go? (15:41)

Paul and Silas travel through Syria and Cilicia.

Answer these questions by reading Acts 16:1-5

15. Which disciple does Paul meet in Lystra? (16:1)

Paul meets Timothy.

16. What is done to Timothy before the journey continues? Why? (16:3)

Timothy is circumcised before the journey continues "because of the Jews who lived in that area."

17. What is reported to the cities along the journey? (16:4)

The decision of the Jerusalem Council is reported to the cities.

18. How does Luke summarize the beginning of the second missionary journey? (16:5)

Luke's summary is that churches are strengthened in faith and grew daily in numbers.

DIMENSION TWO:
WHAT DOES THE BIBLE MEAN?

The Christian movement that had begun as a small, unnoticed group within the environment of Judaism's Temple, worship, private piety, and strict ethical requirements had expanded rapidly by the time of the Jerusalem Council. The Twelve had preached with such fervor and the Holy Spirit had acted so powerfully that not only were Jews converted to the Christian faith but those formerly excluded were converted as well. Philip's work in Samaria with the magician Simon and the Ethiopian eunuch illustrated the initial conversions. The next group to which Christianity spread was the God-fearers, those non-Jews who had in a limited sense participated in Jewish worship and perspective. More recently in our study the gospel reached into the people neither Jewish nor God-fearers: the Gentiles.

Luke has also illustrated the resistances that developed to the gospel. Resistance to the movement first emerged from the Sadducean party of Judaism. Resistance seems to have developed due to differing theological assumptions about resurrection and about Jesus of Nazareth as the Christ—the Messiah. As the new movement gained momentum, resistance widened to include other Jews as well. Resistance from the authority of Roman rule also swings against Christians. Throughout Acts, Luke shows the superiority of the Christian faith and the inexorable will of God through the Holy Spirit mastering any and all resistance, even persecution.

In Acts 15:1–16:5, however, the Christian church and faith came up against something potentially far more damaging than resistance from outside sources. The Christian church will now have to deal with forces of resistance within itself. Signs of hesitancy have appeared earlier. When Philip's work was reported to the Jerusalem congregation (8:14-17), Peter and John were sent to endorse the work by invoking the presence of the Holy Spirit. We can sense a hesitancy with respect to the gospel's expansion away from the Jerusalem church.

Hesitancy and outright resistance to the Gentile mission is played out in the episode of Peter and Cornelius (Acts 10; 11:2-3). Even though Peter's vision included the insight that what God had made could not be unclean (10:15), Peter was slow in making the transfer from food restrictions to God's intending the gospel for everyone. By his own admission, Jews and presumably Jewish Christians were not to mingle with Gentiles (10:28). The insight that God recognizes neither racial nor cultural distinctions resounds with the force of a thunderclap (10:34-35). With the coming of the Spirit upon even Gentile baptism, inclusion in the fellowship of the Christian church cannot be denied anyone.

As the insight echoed, storm clouds of resistance gather. The circumcision party in the Jerusalem church raises the issue with Peter about eating meals with Gentiles (11:3). The authority of the Holy Spirit is claimed for the mission (11:17), thus carrying the hour. Even the conservative element cannot withstand the Spirit (11:18). But the final question of the extent of the Gentile mission has yet to be resolved.

The first missionary journey of Paul and Barnabas provide Luke with the series of events that will focus the question and thus lead to resolution of the problem. The vast sweep of the converted in Asia Minor (14:26-27) causes a good deal of dissension in the Jerusalem church (15:1-2). The storm finally breaks loose.

What was the nature of the conflict? Since some in the church were of a more conservative nature they could not imagine being Christian without first being Jewish. Being Jewish did not mean solely that males were circumcised. But it was around this specific issue that the conflict was fought out, since circumcision was a special sign of covenant with God for the Jews. Others in the church believed that new converts could be equally as Christian without undergoing the rite of circumcision. The question was, and in large measure remains, How much tolerance does the Christian church have for including people in its fellowship? To what extent do converts have to be like those already in the church? Should there be a Gentile mission?

For many today the conflict in Acts 15:1-4 may be shocking. Many Christians would like to somehow recover the church in her pristine state. Any attempt at such a recovery is doomed to frustration and failure, though, because such a pristine state never existed. Throughout the church's history conflict over conservative and liberal interpretation has always erupted, often to the church's embarrassment and always to the church's discomfort.

Luke presents the Jerusalem Council in five scenes. Scene One (15:1-5) opens with dissension among the church leaders. The apostles are sent to Jerusalem where they will debate with the conservative element. Scene Two (15:6-11) focuses on Peter's speech. In Scene Three (15:12-21) James speaks interestingly without reference to circumcision. In Scene Four (15:22-29) Judas, Barabbas, and Silas accompany Paul and Barnabas to Antioch (in Syria) with the letter of compromise. Scene Five (15:30-35) concludes the drama with victory for the Gentile mission.

The following verses, 15:36–16:5, are included in this lesson because they serve as a transition to the expanded Gentile mission.

Acts 15:1-5. Scene One opens with dissension among the church leaders. An unidentified group of men arrive in Antioch from Judea to teach the brothers. This arrival is not immediately after Paul and Barnabas return from the first journey. Luke points out that quite a long period of time elapses between the journey and the dispute (14:28). Earlier the problem had been about eating with Gentiles. Here the controversy centers on the question as to whether circumcision is essential for salvation.

The conflict will not be resolved in Antioch. Paul, Barnabas, and unnamed others go to Jerusalem. The apostles and elders will serve as something like a court of appeals. This episode will be the last time the Jerusalem church and its apostles will be the high authority for the Christian movement.

Passing through Phoenicia and Samaria, Paul and Barnabas report to Jewish-Christian congregations the success with the Gentiles. The news is received with great joy, giving evidence that the resistance to the Gentile mission is largely confined to a minority in the church.

The church, including the apostles and elders, welcomes the missionaries. Paul and Barnabas tell of the miracles and conversions of Gentiles, and Christians who are former Pharisees raise the issue of circumcision for the converted Gentiles with respect to the traditional law of Moses.

Acts 15:6-11. Scene Two begins with the apostles and elders gathered together. Where are the Christian Pharisees? Was it not the Pharisaical party that raised questions in the first place? Evidently the apostles and elders assumed leadership in the congregation.

Debate raged, no doubt fanned to a white-hot heat by the minority that had been replaced in leadership by the apostles and elders. The impression is one of great turmoil in the congregation. And then Peter stands to speak. In reminding the brothers of the earliest days, he implies that the issue is actually already decided—by God. The implication of course is that their responsibility is now to reaffirm God's choice.

God knows not the identity of an individual because of race, clan, or culture. Instead God knows what makes the individual (verses 8-9). To the Gentile, God has already given the Holy Spirit (10:44-47). Purity therefore does not depend primarily on adherence to the Mosaic law.

The conclusion is therefore beyond question. How can Christians demand more of Gentiles than God does? The demands of the Pharisaical party are too severe and beyond the capacity of anyone to fulfill. Luke subtly introduces Gentile freedom from the law and in doing so takes the position of the Gentile Christians.

Peter's speech closes with a gracious reversal. He could easily have patronized the Gentile Christians by suggesting they will be saved just as *we* are. Instead he reverses the assertion by placing the salvation of Gentile Christians before that of the Jewish Christians. Salvation for all comes through the grace of the Lord Jesus. Luke concludes the second scene with a gracious reaffirmation of the Gentile mission.

Acts 15:12-21. Scene Three opens as Peter's speech silences the assembly. Presumably the disturbance raised in verse 7 has been quieted. While the congregation remains silent, Paul and Barnabas relate the experiences of their missionary work. The "miraculous signs and wonders" give a visible evidence of God's intention. Thus, Peter's argument is underscored.

James steps forward (verse 13). Has he now assumed leadership in the congregation? Or will this speech propel him into the leadership role?

Using the Aramaic form of Peter's name, *Simon*, James carefully qualifies the previous argument. James performs two functions. First, he uses Scripture as evidence. Second, James suggests a resolution to the conflict. He draws careful distinction between Peter's statement that God had spoken through Peter to choose the Gentiles and the fact that God had first visited the nation to take a people for himself. Then James cites Amos 9:11-12 as his proof.

James's conclusion is therefore that the Christian church does not interfere with the law. Indeed, the Gentiles who want to become Christians should not be burdened with the law and its rites of passage. The net result of James's speech is as forceful as Peter's had been. James had not sided with the party of circumcision, and yet he avoids complete agreement with Peter. A compromise is suggested.

The conditions suggested (verses 20-21) are not legal impositions like circumcision. Rather, they are compromises that have primarily to do with the nature of relationships that must exist between Christians of different backgrounds and traditions. The new converts from the Gentile culture are not to eat meat that had been sacrificed to pagan gods. Gentile Christians must respect the marriage relationship (Leviticus 18:6-18). Gentile Christians must not eat flesh slaughtered in a nonritual manner. Finally, Gentile Christians must refrain from the pagan custom of drinking blood as a part of religious observance.

What is actually accomplished through the compromise offered by James? At stake is not only doctrinal integrity and maintenance of tradition. The fundamental issue is a relational one. How can Christians with Jewish heritage relate to Christians of Gentile culture? What is necessary in order to maintain, not merely tolerate, relationship?

Acts 15:22-29. Scene Four opens with the acceptance of James's compromise. A letter containing the decision is entrusted to Paul, Barnabas, Judas called Barsabbas, and Silas. Two dynamics are at work here. First, the authority of the Jerusalem Council is emphasized. Second, the congregation of Antioch is given a certain honor since men of high standing are given the responsibility of interpreting the decision to them.

The letter itself begins with a standard formula using the familiar greeting *brothers*. The churches addressed are Gentile churches in areas not yet mentioned in Acts (Syria and Cilicia). Again, Luke's concern is not with the geographical expansion of Christianity. The last barrier to a universal gospel has just dropped with the compromise measure suggested by James (verse 20).

Participants in the journeys and in the resolution of the conflict are to bring news of these events to the Gentile churches. These persons will be able, because of their personal experiences, to authenticate the issues at stake and the manner in which the final decisions were made.

Two sources of authority are mentioned (verse 28). First is the authority of the Holy Spirit, to whom the observance of ancient custom seemed an unnecessary burden.

Second, and not incidentally, is the authority of the church itself, for "It has seemed good to the Holy Spirit *and to us.* . . ." The authority of the church cannot be overlooked. Luke's implication is quite clear. The church has authority with respect to its corporate life and mission that may not be equivalent to that of the Holy Spirit, but certainly has great weight in monitoring Christian life.

Compromise makes the resolution of conflict and concludes Scene Four. The compromises are once again stated (verse 29), but not in a tone of legal requirement. The restrictions are more a statement of minimal expectations so that Christians of Jewish and Gentile heritage can share meals together. The whole question of how two different cultural traditions can live together in community is thus focused on the eating of meals. Note the sharp contrast

between the rigid requirement of circumcision and the openness and relative flexibility of these restrictions.

Acts 15:30-35. The final scene of the Jerusalem Council begins with the official delegation traveling to Antioch. Celebration breaks loose when the congregation hears that circumcision is not necessary in order to be fully Christian. The Gentile congregation does not resist the compromise measures.

Judas and Silas are characterized as prophets, with the capacity as well as the authority to exhort the congregation.

After an indefinite amount of time, the preachers are sent back to Jerusalem. What could easily have been the end of the tenuous beginnings of a universal gospel became instead the means by which Christians examined what the essential issues are. Clearly, the central issues are those of relationship and not those of ritual and custom.

Verse 35 ends the entire drama. Paul and Barnabas continue teaching and preaching together in Antioch before their final separation. Others are involved in the work as well. Therefore, when other journeys are begun, the congregation in Antioch is not in danger of collapsing through the loss of leadership.

Future missionary work by Paul and others is assured. The Gentile mission is both an accomplished fact and a future goal. The importance of the decision made as a result of the Jerusalem Council cannot be overestimated. Outside pressures and resistance will again break out against the Christian gospel. But outside resistance, like geographical boundaries, are not the gravest threats to the Christians. Not being able or willing to share the good news of Jesus Christ with everyone, Jew and Gentile, could easily have ended the Christian story in the first century.

Acts 15:36–16:5. These verses begin the second half of Acts. Paul, who had played a relatively minor role in the recently concluded conference, now assumes a major leadership function. The next missionary journey is his suggestion. The reason for the journey is to revisit those congregations that had been established on the earlier trip.

The conflict over John Mark may have stemmed from his departure (or desertion) from Pamphylia (13:13). Would Luke's readers sympathize with a missionary who did not want to take with him a companion of lesser courage or stamina?

Scholars do not agree as to what caused the final rift between Paul and Barnabas (verse 39). The obvious disagreement over the status of John Mark is often cited. The fact that Barnabas chooses to help John Mark is not held against him. Certainly Barnabas's stature in Acts does not suffer because of this intercession. Could the disagreement have centered on a much greater substantive issue, such as the eating together by Jews and Gentiles (Galatians 2:13)? Whether the separation was one of principle or preference (Acts 15:38-39), Luke's account implies the latter.

Barnabas and John Mark sail to Cyprus, Barnabas's homeland, and Barnabas is not heard of again in Acts. In 1 Corinthians 9:6, we learn that Paul assumes that Barnabas is still living. As Barnabas and John Mark leave, Paul and Silas, an important Jerusalemite (15:22), are given an official send-off. Luke underscores the importance of Paul's mission with this subtle detail.

Syria and Cilicia, mentioned in the apostolic decree (15:23), are now taken up by Luke. The decree had never been intended for particular usage in only the two areas mentioned. The decree has universal importance and will, therefore, be read in many churches.

Paul's relationship and dealings with Timothy raise many questions (16:1-3). The text deals with Paul, but many questions arise regarding Timothy. Evidently Timothy had been converted during the first missionary journey. He is mentioned many times in Acts (17:14-15; 18:5; 19:22; 20:4), and other references to him are numerous (Romans 16:21; 1 Corinthians 4:17; 16:10; Philippians 1:1; 2:19; 1 Thessalonians 1:1; 3:2, 6; 2 Thessalonians 1:1. Philemon 1). Timothy is the son of a Jewish mother, though not necessarily a strictly observant Jew since she married a heathen man (a Greek, presumed dead at this time).

Paul wanted the young man to be circumcised. Why would Paul insist on this rite so soon after the conflict that had forced the Council in Jerusalem? Paul himself staunchly refused to allow for circumcision to be a central issue in salvation (1 Corinthians 7:17-20). Perhaps part of the reason has to do with the desire to remain inoffensive to the Jews with whom they will come in contact during the upcoming journeys. Paul's freedom from the requirement of tradition did not necessarily mean he could only turn against it in a spiteful manner. He could in another place say that he may become like a Jew in order to win Jews (1 Corinthians 9:20). Paul remains a loyal Jew (Acts 18:18).

In every city along the route, the decree issued by the Jerusalem Council is read to Gentile churches. Luke ends the scene by saying that various Christian communities are strengthened in the faith and are gaining in numbers.

DIMENSION THREE:
WHAT DOES THE BIBLE MEAN TO ME?

Acts 15:1-21
The Jerusalem Council or The Peril of Prejudice

In order to help class members understand the importance of the Jerusalem Council, begin your session by listing on the chalkboard or on a large piece of paper the issues at stake. What were the issues raised by the conservative element? You may want to ask a class member to read about circumcision in a Bible dictionary and report to the rest of the class. Ask class members to state the issue in respect to the principle involved. Was the issue only that of circumcision for male Gentiles who desired to be included in the Christian community?

What was the moderate or compromise suggestion of James? Ask class members to look at how the prohibitions differ from the legal requirements of Jewish tradition. Do they read these prohibitions as compromise? Without compromise the early church would surely have been divided into splinter groups and been weakened.

Luke's placement of the Jerusalem Council gives a clue as to the importance he attaches to it. Coming exactly in the middle of the Book of Acts, the Council is the major turning point. From here to the end of the work, internal strife is absent. The struggle for an unhindered gospel became primarily a matter of a struggle against outside forces.

What are some internal forces that threaten to cripple the modern Christian church? Ask students to identify three of the hottest controversies in your church, denomination, or judicatory. What are the principle issues and arguments? (Identify them; this discussion is about what topics are, not about how you feel about the substance of the argument.) Do these hot topics revolve around the acceptance of certain persons, behaviors, attitudes, or beliefs? Is theology an issue? What is your church's stance on those questions and issues? Where does prejudice rear its head in the debates over these issues?

One caution with respect to teaching about the Council and about prejudices must be noted. Argument about problems is one of the most effective ways of avoiding one's own feelings and the feelings of others. For instance, if I argue with you about the historical problem of the identity or movement of John Mark or Barnabas in this chapter, then I do not have to come to terms with my own anxiety, about the substantive problems that not only challenged the ancient church but also challenge us. The prejudices of early Christians were as deeply ingrained as are present-day prejudices. How were the ancients able to work through to a more inclusive or universal gospel? How can we become more universal in our work and ministry?

Another way of saying this is that we must be careful lest our discussions become a subtle means by which to assign a problem to the dusty realm of ancient history, even though that ancient history is told in the Bible.

If this line of questioning is too strong for your class members, you may want to try a different approach. Every church has a certain personality to it. Therefore, almost without our noticing, the question is always asked about new members, "How will this person fit in our church?" Ask yourself and then ask class members to recall when they have asked this question. What was the major concern? Was the individual a minority voice with respect to social issues that you were not certain your church could tolerate? Perhaps the new member had a theological perspective that did not coincide with the general theological perceptions of your church. Did you wonder what might happen if this individual were to invite some of her or his friends to church? What if many persons of this different belief want to join?

You see, the issue with which the Jerusalem Council wrestled was the meaning of grace. For if grace means all are acceptable, then all must have equal access to life in the community. Any prejudice to some extent denies the grace of God.

Acts 15:36-41—Ruptured Relationships

The relationship between Paul and Barnabas had been a very close one dating from their first encounter. Each of them had learned to trust the other. During the first missionary journey they looked to each other for mutual support. Luke's account in Acts and Paul's reflection in Galatians 2:1-13 treat the final separation differently. Read Paul's account. Which seems to you to be more accurate?

You may want to prod class members' thinking with the following questions: Are there limits to friendship? Can friendships or even family relationships be ruptured due to matters of principle?

Have any class members ever had to end a friendship or working relationship due to matters of moral principle? Were they able to put theological meaning to the ended relationship?

What must I do to be saved? . . . . Believe in the Lord Jesus, and you will be saved (16:30-31).

8

The Second Missionary Journey

Acts 16:6–18:22

DIMENSION ONE:
WHAT DOES THE BIBLE SAY?

Answer these questions by reading Acts 16:6-40

1. Describe Paul's vision at Troas. (16:8-10)

   Paul has a vision at night. A Macedonian (a Greek) speaks to him asking him to come preach the gospel—"Come over to Macedonia and help us." Paul concludes that it is God's intention that the gospel be preached in Greece.

2. Where do the missionaries go to preach in Philippi? (16:13)

   The missionaries go "outside the city gate to the river" where people presumably have gathered for prayer.

3. What happens to Paul and Silas as a result of healing a slave girl? (16:19-24)

   The owners of the girl are enraged that the missionaries have harmed their trade. They charge Paul and Silas with advocating customs that are unlawful for Romans to accept or practice. Paul and Silas are then beaten, thrown into prison, and put in the stocks.

4. Why won't Paul simply leave the jail after his release? (16:37-39)

   Paul will not leave because he and other Roman citizens have been publicly humiliated. Therefore, Paul insists the officials must come to terms with their own violation of Roman citizens' rights.

Answer these questions by reading Acts 17

5. Where does Paul go to preach upon reaching Thessalonica? (17:1-2)

   Paul goes to the Jewish synagogue, as was his custom.

6. What is the result of Paul's preaching? (17:4-5)

   Some people, both Jews and Greeks, are persuaded by the preaching. Others are jealous and attempt to harm the missionaries.

7. What prompts Paul's speech in Athens? (17:16)

   Paul sees that the city is full of idols.

8. Paul's speech centers on the saying "to an unknown god." How does Paul suggest this god is a knowable god? (17:24-31)

   Paul begins with the world and everything in it as God's creation. All living things have life because of God. God cannot be represented by gold, silver, or stone. Rather we know God through the "man he has appointed" and whom God has raised from the dead.

Answer these questions by reading Acts 18:1-22

9. What trade does Paul practice with Aquila and Priscilla? (18:3)

   They were tentmakers.

10. What is the assurance Paul receives in his vision? (16:9-10)

    Paul is told not to be afraid for no harm will come to him. God has many people in the city.

11. What is the attitude of the Roman official toward the Jewish protests against Paul? (18:14-16)

    Gallio refuses to become involved in what appears to him to be an internal dispute. He will have no part of the conflict. The Jews are summarily ejected from the court.

12. When Paul preaches in Ephesus, where does he go to preach? (18:19)

   Paul goes to the synagogue to "reason with the Jews" (to preach).

13. Complete the following outline of Paul's second missionary journey.

   From Syrian Antioch, Paul goes through SYRIA and CILICIA strengthening churches (15:41). He travels west to DERBE and LYSTRA where he meets Timothy (16:1). Passing through the regions of PHRYGIA and GALATIA (16:6), he arrives at the place opposite Mysia where he is forbidden to pass over into Bithynia. Following his vision at TROAS (16:8-9), he seeks to go on to MACEDONIA (16:10).
   Sailing from Troas, Paul proceeds through SAMOTHRACE (16:11) and NEAPOLIS (16:11) to the city of PHILIPPI (16:12). There he meets LYDIA (16:14). In this city Paul performs an exorcism on the slave girl who had a spirit. After the miraculous release from jail, Paul and Silas proceed through AMPHIPOLIS and APOLLONIA (17:1) to the major city of THESSALONICA (17:1). After being hounded out of Thessalonica, the missionaries move on to BEREA (17:10). There they are received kindly. Silas and Timothy remain here when Paul sails for ATHENS (17:14-15).
   Following the success in Athens, Paul travels on to the isthmus city of CORINTH (18:1). Here he meets PRISCILLA and AQUILA (18:2). From this city the journey quickly concludes as Paul leaves for SYRIA by way of CENCHREA where he cuts his hair (18:18). Passing through EPHESUS (18:19), he proceeds to CAESAREA (18:22) and then to the home church in ANTIOCH (18:22).

DIMENSION TWO: WHAT DOES THE BIBLE MEAN?

In this lesson you will study Paul's second missionary journey. The journey is suggested by Paul with the intention of revisiting Christian churches to tell them the news of the decision at the Jerusalem Council.

Acts 16:6-10. Brief mention is made of the journey through the interior region of Asia Minor. Evidently Paul had intended to continue his missionary work there. However, he is forbidden by the Spirit in this effort (verses 6-7). Luke assumes that each turning point for the Christian mission centers on the action of the Spirit, that is guidance by and in some sort of revelation. Thus, the missionaries proceed past Mysia to Troas.

In another direct intervention through revelation, Paul has a nighttime vision. On the far shore stood a Macedonian summoning Paul to Europe. Some interpreters have seen this event as the beginning of the Christian enterprise in Europe. Luke's early readers, however, would have been much more concerned with the dramatic encounters between Christianity and rival religions than they would have with geographical expansion.

Paul concludes that the overwhelming importance of God's instruction cannot be ignored. He, therefore, proceeds to the Roman province that includes the cities of Philippi, Thessalonica, and Berea.

Acts 6:11-15. Travel begins immediately for the missionaries from Troas to Samothrace, an island approximately halfway between Troas and the Macedonian coast. A mountain on the island over five thousand feet high made it a landmark for seagoing ships. Neapolis is on the Strymonian Gulf, and at this time was second only to Thessalonica in importance as a seaport. Philippi is a leading city but not the capital of the Roman district of Macedonia. Here the missionaries stay for a few days.

Verse 10 begins the "we" passages in Acts. Interpretation of these verses varies among scholars. They cannot be Paul's own words, obviously. Whose are they? Who is speaking? Since Silas and Timothy are both mentioned in close relationship with the missionary journeys (15:4; 16:3), perhaps the passages are one or both of their reflections on the experience. Other suggestions include the possibility of an eyewitness account, which would indicate that the eyewitness is the author of the book (Luke?).

We simply cannot conclude beyond a doubt who "we" refers to. One fact does overshadow the entire question of identity. The "we" passages perform the remarkable literary function of including the reader in the dramatic action. In some sense, the reader or listener when seeing or hearing *we* feels a close relationship to the stalwart souls en route to far-flung regions. The hope, dream, and peril of the undertaking is then part of the reader's life due to the literary usage of *we*.

On the sabbath Paul proceeds to what is presumed to be the place of prayer. Whether it is a synagogue or merely a gathering place is uncertain. In either case Paul goes first to Jews.

Lydia, a seller of luxury items for wealthy people, hears the preaching. Almost hurriedly the story shifts to a baptism scene. Lydia becomes a Christian through her baptism. Christian missionaries now have a sound base from which to continue their work. Paul will revisit Lydia later (16:40).

Acts 16:16-22. During a subsequent visit to the same place of prayer, the missionaries meet a slave girl who has the spirit of divination. Her owners used her gift of clairvoyance for profit from the pagan population. Luke is showing here the larger drama of the confrontation between the claims of God through Christ and the lesser claims of pagan mystery cults and religions.

The scene pictures the slave girl following after Paul screaming at him with her owners and many others watching. The demon identifies itself so that not only Paul but the Gentile listeners will understand the challenge. The true meaning of the Christian mission is in this manner announced.

After many days Paul performs an exorcism, invoking the name of Jesus Christ. The spirit is immediately expelled from the young woman. Predictably the girl's owners are irate at the loss of income. Paul and Silas are dragged into the public marketplace and charged with disturbing the peace. Paul and Silas are imprisoned.

Acts 16:23-34. In this jail scene Luke presents an account similar to that of Peter's jailing and miraculous rescue in 12:6-11. Paul and Silas are shackled in instruments of torture, kept in the innermost part of the prison, and heavily guarded. Nonetheless, Paul and Silas sing hymns and pray through the night. Such peculiar and yet courageous behavior attracts the attention of other prisoners as well.

Quite without warning, an earthquake shakes the structure (verse 26). Doors fly open, fetters fall loose, and the prisoners are miraculously free. The jailer, assuming the prisoners have fled and knowing the punishment for letting prisoners escape, is prepared to kill himself. But Paul cries out to him, "Don't harm yourself! We are all here!" Then the jailer calls for torches and hurries into the prison. The terrified jailer asks about his own salvation.

Paul's answer is directed to the jailer, his family, and his retinue of servants. "Believe in the Lord Jesus, and you will be saved—you and your household" (verse 31). The missionaries then speak to all the jailer's family. In the middle of the night, perhaps 1:00 A.M., the jailer takes the men to his home, where their wounds are washed. Baptism for the entire household follows. Without regard for what his superiors may say or do as a result of the escape, the jailer rejoices in his newfound faith.

Acts 16:35-40. As if completely unaware of both earthquake and escape, the authorities on the next morning decide that a flogging plus one night in prison is sufficient punishment: Paul and Silas are to be released.

Surrounded by hostile authorities, Paul will not allow for an underhanded, almost secret dismissal. A Roman citizen's rights have been violated by means of public scourging and jailing without any legal proceedings. Paul insists that the authorities themselves escort the wronged man out of the city. As the magistrates had not known of Paul's citizenship, the notion of such a violation troubles them greatly. Even though an apology is given, Paul is still asked to leave the city.

As the missionaries leave, they revisit the recently established Christian congregation in Lydia's home (verse 40). Note that once again persecution does not eradicate Christian churches. Even as the missionaries leave, there remains a significant Christian presence in that city.

Acts 17:1-9. Paul continues the journey, through Amphipolis and Apollonia. Little if any missionary activity occurs at these places. Presumably, the missionaries proceed to Thessalonica in order to preach in the synagogue. Thessalonica was the capital city of another district of the province of Macedonia and was the residence of the proconsul.

For three weeks Paul argues for the Christian interpretation of Scriptures in the context of the Jewish worship service. From the Christian perspective the Messiah must suffer, die, and be raised from the dead (verse 3).

Luke makes a point of showing that the Christian faith appealed to a wide range of the social order (verse 4). Even the influential women who are attracted to the movement cannot stem persecution. Not surprisingly the success of the Christian preachers threatens a number of Jews.

Riot is instigated by a handful of rabblerousers. They attack Jason's house. Jason's identity is difficult to establish. He had opened his home to the missionaries and is accused of harboring dissidents in opposition to Caesar (verse 7). Not only are the city authorities disturbed but the entire city is concerned. Civil disturbance could easily bring military or police action.

Acts 17:10-15. With the momentary lull, the Christian community quickly sends Paul and Silas to Berea, some twenty-two miles away. Similar to their efforts in Thessalonica, Paul and Silas seek the synagogue in Berea.

Daily study and teaching occupy the missionaries' time in what appears to be a much more congenial atmosphere. Again converts are gained from Greeks and from women of much influence as well as from the ranks of men in the area. Sopater (20:4) is from this city, which suggests a continuity of the Christian congregation in an otherwise obscure place.

Word of the Christian successes spreads back to Thessalonica. Here the "word of God" means Christian preaching. Jews from Thessalonica come to Berea to set up the crowds against Paul.

For the first time since 16:3, Timothy appears with Paul and Silas (verse 14) with no explanation as to why or how he arrived on the scene. Paul is set to sail while Silas and Timothy remain in Berea, presumably to continue sustaining the Christian congregation and to withstand the threat posed by malcontent Thessalonians. Silas and Timothy will meet Paul again in Corinth (18:5).

Acts 17:16-34. Athens would have contained five thousand citizens at this time. The center of Greek culture, with its remarkable artistic and architectural beauty, causes no comment from Paul, except that the religious imagery he saw around him is little more than idolatry. Paul's soul is vexed, so he seeks out the synagogue in which he continues to present the Christian message. During the week, Paul seeks people in the marketplace.

For the first time Greek philosophies are introduced (verse 18). Luke often uses two groups to illustrate the struggle Christianity has against its environment. Usually one group shows interest and the other shows little concern (2:12-13; 14:4; 23:6; 28:25). Epicureans were practical atheists and materialists. To them Paul is little more than a babbler. In the Greek, the word *babbler* is a play on words that brings up the image of one who, like a bird in the marketplace, snatches up every scrap indiscriminately, snaps at ideas without any idea of their meaning. The Stoics on the other hand represent the Athenians (Greeks) as a whole. Again the Resurrection is central, though the Greeks cannot understand it.

What happens next is somewhat muddled. Paul is either arrested and brought before the authorities or he is brought out of the near riot to the relative quiet of Mars' Hill (the Areopagus). Some interpreters picture Paul standing in the center of a semicircle addressing the crowd. Others think that Paul is kept away from the hearing of the crowd. Perhaps he is talking with an internal gathering of philosophers.

Paul assumes the posture of an orator (verse 22). His speech does not begin condescendingly, but rather with the observation that the people are very religious. Indeed, the speech has been triggered by an inscription Paul had seen earlier, "TO AN UNKNOWN GOD." Paul's task is a complex one. He addresses people familiar with many gods and who have many forms of worship. However, they know little about the God of biblical revelation. Paul must therefore explain the biblical God to the listeners. Where can he start?

Citing Isaiah 42:5, Paul begins his speech with the biblical account of creation. From the beginning God's continuing lordship is amplified. The God of creation does not reside in temples created by the hands of men. Sacrifices do not honor God either. God has given life to all and sustains all life (verses 24-25).

Having established the link between all creation and God, Paul continues with the human task to be at home on the earth and to seek God. God, in contrast to the inscription's assertion, is not distant and unknown. Rather, God is near with respect to the relationship with all humans (verse 27).

In sharp contrast to Romans 1, Paul says that ignorance has been overlooked by God. Now repentance is proclaimed and the formerly unknown God now becomes very well knowable.

Judgment exists in relation to a specific day that has been established by God. Ignorance is no longer valid. The anticipated judgment will be carried out by a "man he [God] has appointed." The speech concludes with the resounding affirmation of Christianity's central truth, the Resurrection (verse 31). When the Resurrection is mentioned, the listeners are stunned. (See also verse 18.) Many scoff at the notion; others ask for time to consider and comprehend.

Against the apparent failure of the preaching to the crowd, a few names are mentioned of those who are in fact converted (verse 34). These names may indicate that a Christian congregation does indeed survive after Paul's departure, though they do not appear in the list of 1 Corinthians 16:15. By Paul's witness the "house of Stephen" are the first converts of Achaia.

The Christian missionaries have now left the relative security of the customs and traditions of the Jewish synagogue. Just how much the expansion will have to endure as it moves increasingly into pagan environments is yet to be seen. Clearly, no matter what the setting, be it Jewish or Gentile, the doctrine of resurrection will prove to be a constant stumbling block.

Acts 18:1-17. Unlike earlier episodes where Paul had been hounded out of cities, he appears to leave Athens without undue stress. He proceeds to Corinth, the capital city of the Roman province of Achaia. This commercial city with two sea fronts had a reputation of being one of the most notorious cities in the entire ancient world. A saying among sailors captures the hedonism rife in the city of Aphrodite's temple and its one thousand cult prostitutes: "Not every man can afford a trip to Corinth." For Paul's own account of the establishment of the Christian congregation at Corinth, see 1 Corinthians 1–4.

Aquila, a Jew, is in Corinth because of Claudius's decree that banished Jews from Rome. Aquila and his wife Priscilla seem to have had a small church in their home. However, they did not begin the Christian mission in Corinth.

Timothy and Silas reappear rather suddenly and without the slightest word of preparation by Luke. In 17:15, they had been instructed to proceed to Athens when notified by Paul. Were the helpers to bring a gift from the Philippian congregation? (Philippians 4:15-16). Paul is now occupied full-time with his preaching.

Preaching brings conversion and reticence. When Jews refuse to accept Jesus as the Christ, Paul's patience wears thin. Exasperated, Paul shakes out his garments, a symbolic act (Nehemiah 5:13). Luke's account shows the Jews refusing salvation through Christ, not Paul giving up on the Jews.

Paul takes the refusal of Jews as sufficient reason to seek other arenas in which to preach. The Gentiles mission is opened.

Some scholars identify Titius Justus as Titus, even though Titus is not mentioned in Acts. Other scholars identify him as the Gaius of Romans 16:23.

Crispus is one of the few persons that Paul personally baptized. Because he is the chief leader of the synagogue, his conversion impresses the God-fearers and will lead to further conversions.

Missionary work in an alien and hostile environment is not an easy task. Paul's anxiety is eased by another nighttime vision of Christ (verses 9-10). The image recalls the Elijah story of 1 Kings 19:1-8. When Elijah thought that he and he alone struggled to maintain the presence of the Eternal, he was assured that seven thousand others also had not yet succumbed to the powers of evil or heathenism. So Paul is assured that even in Corinth, God has people who have not lost hope. Paul's work in Corinth continues for a year and a half.

Gallio, proconsul of Achaia, seems to be neutral to the new Christian movement. When Jews bring charges of sedition against Paul the charges are summarily dismissed. Thus Luke uses a specific individual to represent the official Roman attitude toward the emerging church. Christianity is not a hostile or revolutionary movement bent on usurping Roman rule. Christianity is in no manner a violent movement.

From the Roman perspective the squabble has to do with little more than names and obscure Jewish law. Though not violently opposed to Christianity the Roman authorities do exhibit a measure of anti-Semitism: the Jews are driven away from the court.

Frustrated by Roman inaction the Jews seize Sosthenes (possibly the man named in 1 Corinthians 1:1) and beat him. Luke seems disinterested in the violence unleashed on an apparently innocent victim as well as the lack of concern expressed by Roman authorities. Luke is not concerned with the ethical problem of the apparent injustice. Could this be another of those unimportant details to which Luke attaches no particular significance? Or is this evidence of the matter-of-factness of arbitrary and not infrequent injustice of this time?

Acts 18:18-22. Paul sets sail for Syria, taking with him Priscilla and Aquila.

Why did Priscilla, Aquila, and Paul proceed to Ephesus, the capital of the Roman province of Asia? Perhaps the business is moved to a more lucrative location. Are Paul's fellow workers left behind at Ephesus in order to provide reason for a return visit? In any event, Paul soon leaves.

Arrival in Caesarea marks the end of the second journey (verse 22). This verse raises many critical issues, not the least of which is whether Paul visits Jerusalem. If he does, which church does he visit? Could the apostolic council have occurred at this time rather than earlier, as Luke presents the sequence of events? Answers to these questions vary and to a degree are a matter of scholarly conjecture.

Paul's second missionary journey, of some twenty-eight hundred miles, comes to an end with new Christian congregations established in Europe (Greece). Though Luke gives little chronological information, the journey could have lasted as long as three, perhaps three and a half years.

DIMENSION THREE:
WHAT DOES THE BIBLE MEAN TO ME?

Acts 18:9-10—The Elijah Syndrome

The peril of any preacher, missionary, or other conscientious Christian is that of feeling alone in the struggle of the Christian gospel against an environment that may be lethargic or hostile. Paul suffered the pangs of loneliness and anxiety as he worked in Corinth.

Begin a discussion by asking class members to recall moments when they felt alone in the struggle. Ask them what kept them at their work. What gave them sufficient courage to remain steadfast to their hope? To whom did they look for encouragement? What sort of encouragement did they get?

Acts 17:2-3—The Stone of Stumbling

The entire Gospel narrative, with its inevitable conclusion that the Messiah suffers, dies, and is raised from the dead, would offended us. But because of our familiarity with it, we are not offended by such a preposterous notion. Surely God's intention is for something different from suffering and death.

To begin a discussion ask class members to describe popular conceptions of what Jesus does to help our lives. To which interpretation do we give more authority? That which gives us a pleasant savior or one that is stouthearted and makes equal demand on us to share in the suffering?

Ask class members where they see the opportunity for sharing in the suffering of this world. Do they perceive the opportunity as a means of grace? Where is your church shouldering the burden of the world's hurts as a means by which to share in the hurt? Are people attracted to Christ through our hope for resurrection, or something else?

Acts 16:13-15, 40; 17:34; 18:19-21
The Subtle Work of the Holy Spirit

One danger in reading stories with exciting elements (rescues and miraculous escapes, exorcisms and healings, wonderful visions, and remarkable supernatural intervention) is that of identifying the work of the Spirit solely in such dramatic terms and by such spectacular actions. Glossolalia, waking of the dead, and words of a nocturnal visit by Christ are not the only means by which the early church is sustained.

In strategic moments, Luke indicates almost matter-of-factly the conversions and continuity of Christian congregations throughout the areas visited by well-known and by anonymous preachers. The Spirit continues the work central to the church: conversion and church-growing.

Ask class members to list the times when they have seen the working of the Spirit through a conversion. How is the work of conversion the work of the Spirit? Can there be conversion without the presence of the Holy Spirit? What of church growth? Can the church grow without the movement and continued presence of the Spirit?

What are the implications of this subtle work of the Holy Spirit? Will such an outlook make the Spirit more available to otherwise resistant and anxious members? Sometimes the more dramatic phenomena threaten otherwise interested and yearning Christians. Perhaps a more down-to-earth perspective will open up new vistas for the work of the Spirit.

Close this session by asking a class member to list on the chalkboard or a large piece of paper insights gained in this lesson. Then, offer prayer for the unnamed, anonymous persons through whom God is working right now in the midst of your community. God uses the unnamed as he uses the people we know and with whom we are comfortable.

In this way the word of the Lord spread widely and grew in power (19:20).

9

The Third Missionary Journey

Acts 18:23–20:38

DIMENSION ONE: WHAT DOES THE BIBLE SAY?

Answer these questions by reading Acts 18:23-28

1. Who comes to Ephesus proclaiming the baptism of John? (18:24-25)

   Apollos, a native of Alexandria, "a learned man, with a thorough knowledge of the Scriptures," comes to Ephesus to preach the baptism of John.

2. Which Christian followers correct his preaching? (18:26)

   Aquila and Priscilla teach Apollos "the way of God more adequately."

Answer these questions by reading Acts 19

3. What does Paul ask the Christians in Ephesus when he arrives there? (19:2-3)

   Paul asks the Christians if they have received the Holy Spirit. They reply, "No, we have not even heard that there is a Holy Spirit," having only received the baptism of John.

4. What happens when the Christians are baptized in the name of the Lord Jesus? (19:5-6)

   The Holy Spirit comes upon these Christians as they are baptized.

5. How long does Paul preach in Ephesus? (19:8-10)

   Paul preaches in Ephesus for more than two years.

6. What sort of powers are accorded to Paul? (19:11-12)

   Paul performs extraordinary miracles of healing and exorcism. Even pieces of his clothing can transmit this power to others.

7. At the conclusion of his successful ministry in Ephesus, where does Paul want to go? (19:21)

   Paul decides to visit Macedonia, Achaia, and Jerusalem after which he wants to visit Rome.

8. Describe the conflict that develops between Demetrius and Paul. (19:23-27)

   Craftsmen who make religious images for the Temple of Artemis, led by Demetrius a silversmith, feel threatened with economic disruption if not ruin by the Christian message. Not only is economic ruin possible; the entire cult of Artemis is threatened.

9. A riot is narrowly averted due to the city clerk's intervention. What is his argument? (19:40)

   Riot will bring the wrath of the higher authorities down on the town.

Answer these questions by reading Acts 20

10. Why does Paul change his travel plans? (20:2-3)

    A plot is made against Paul by the Jews, just as he is about to sail, forcing Paul on an overland route rather than a sea voyage.

11. Which people go with Paul on the journey? (20:4)

    The company is made up of Sopater of Berea, the son of Phyrrhus; Thessalonians named Aristarchus and Secundus; Gaius of Derby; Timothy; and Asians Tychicus and Trophimus; as well as the narrator ("us" in verse 5).

12. Why does Paul avoid landfall while on the way to Jerusalem? (20:16)

    Paul does not land at Ephesus because he was in a hurry to arrive in Jerusalem by Pentecost.

13. According to Paul's farewell in Miletus, what awaits him in Jerusalem? (20:23)

The Spirit that compels Paul to return to Jerusalem warns him in every city that imprisonment and hardships are facing him.

14. What is Paul's attitude toward his life? (20:24)

Paul is unconcerned about his life as long as he can accomplish the mission on which the Holy Spirit has sent him, namely testifying "to the gospel of God's grace."

15. What perils are in the future for the Christian congregations? (20:29-30)

Paul sees a day when fierce opposition (savage wolves) will come in among the "flock." Worse yet, some of their own members may arise and distort the truth and divide the congregation.

16. To whom does Paul commend the care of each Christian and Christian congregation? (20:32)

Paul commits the Ephesian Christians to God and to the word of God's grace, which can build them up.

17. How does Paul conclude his time with the Christians? (20:36-38)

Paul kneels down and prays with all the assembled Christians. After all weep, embrace, and share the peace, they accompany Paul to his ship.

DIMENSION TWO: WHAT DOES THE BIBLE MEAN?

In this lesson, you will study the third and final missionary journey of Paul. Two items are contrasted to each other throughout this account. The first is the brilliance of the apostle Paul. Luke pictures the apostle at the apex of his career. This image is the one most often recalled in church history. Second, the shadow of the cross darkens the apostle's life and work. For the last time Paul will exercise his ministry freely. What begins as a story of glory and magnificent Christian success will change to a drama of epic proportions of Christianity's struggles against the might of empire and threat of internal heresy.

Acts 18:23-28. Paul begins his journey by going through Galatia and Phrygia, visiting Christians along the way. In Ephesus, where Paul had known success earlier, another preacher is preaching the gospel message to the people. Apollos is an Alexandrian, well educated in the Hebrew Scriptures and in knowledge of the Christian Way. As to where he had been educated, we do not know. Luke describes him as fervent in spirit, which could describe either a volatile temper or a gift of the Holy Spirit (Romans 12:11). All that he taught is accurate, except that he knows only the baptism of John the Baptist.

Priscilla and Aquila correct the teaching of Apollos, presumably with emphasis on the baptism of the Holy Spirit. In spite of his incomplete gospel, Apollos is a powerful preacher who uses Scripture effectively to present Jesus as the Christ.

Acts 19:1-7. When Paul returns to Ephesus, he finds a group within the church made up of John the Baptist's followers. Many modern readers often think that the beliefs in the early church were not complex and consistent in every locale. Many a church member wrestles with the hope that somehow we can recover doctrinal and communal purity like that which was found in the earliest Christian church. A careful reading of this account reveals that even the earliest Christian communities had members with differing beliefs and theological perspectives, causing strife.

The "interior" country (19:1) is the Asia Minor uplands, Galatia, and the region of Phrygia (18:23). Does Paul doubt the genuineness of the disciples' Christianity? He determines its authenticity by asking about the Holy Spirit. These disciples have heard only of John's repentance.

The disciples are baptized in the name of Jesus. Because they had only received John's baptism, this second baptism is not rebaptism. Some scholars maintain that Aquila did the baptizing since Paul had refused to baptize many. As hands are laid on the disciples, the Holy Spirit comes upon them and they begin to speak in tongues and to prophesy (verse 6).

Glossolalia (speaking in tongues) and prophecy are different gifts (1 Corinthians 14). This incident is remarkably similar to the account of Peter in Acts 8:14-17. Acts 10:44, 46 also tells of the Spirit being dispensed through Peter.

Luke's readers would no doubt observe the central position that Paul occupies in these two Ephesian stories. In the first story Paul's friends correct Apollos; in the second story Paul himself confronts the Apollos group.

Acts 19:8-20. Paul's ministry in Ephesus continues for over two years (compare with 20:31). While Paul is in Ephesus he writes the letters to the church at Corinth, First and Second Corinthians. The Pauline letters reveal an apostle under fire from discontent Christians. The portrait painted by Luke in Acts suggests a man fairly striding through the worst of opposition.

Paul begins with Jews in the synagogue (18:19). Some hearers "publicly maligned the Way"; others follow Paul away from the synagogue to "the hall of Tyrannus." This hall was probably a lecture hall, perhaps used as a school most of the time. The identity of Tyrannus cannot be determined. He may have been a schoolmaster or a teacher.

The two years mentioned in verse 10 should be extended to include the three months in verse 8 and maybe more (20:31). "All the Jews and Greeks who lived in the province of Asia" would include Mysians, Lydians, and Carfans. With Ephesus as the base, further Christian churches were founded in Colossae, Laodicea, and Hierapolis. Luke implies that Paul's authority is enormous.

In addition to Paul's preaching, miracles occur by his hands (verse 11). The statement of verse 11 sounds similar to Acts 5:15. Here, linen cloths used to mop the brow are vehicles of power. In 5:15, the mere shadow of the apostle Peter is sufficient to transmit power.

Because magic is so thoroughly debunked, magicians (or sorcerers) gather in Ephesus to confess their evil deeds. Parchments of papyrus leaves on which "Ephesian writings" (magic) had been written are burned in a public book burning.

Luke uses a familiar phrase to conclude this episode. The Christian church continues growing in Ephesus.

Acts 19:21-22. An interlude gives Luke an opportunity to indicate for the first time where Paul's final destination will be. Some question arises over Paul's resolution to go to Rome. Is the decision compelled by his first resolve or by direction of the Holy Spirit? The trip to Jerusalem is mentioned with no explanation. What of the collection that is so important in Paul's own writings? (Acts 24:17-21; Romans 15:26; 1 Corinthians 16:1-4; 2 Corinthians 9:1-5.)

According to 1 Corinthians 16:5-8, Paul wants to remain in Ephesus until Pentecost and then travel to Corinth by way of Macedonia. However, 2 Corinthians 1:15-16 indicates another itinerary: Corinth, Macedonia, Corinth for a second time, and finally, on to Jerusalem. Luke is less concerned with the specific facts of historical sequence than he is with the overwhelming successes Christianity has against pagan and Jewish resistance.

Timothy plays a minor role in Luke's account. In Paul's correspondence, Timothy plays a much larger role (Romans 16:21, 1 Corinthians 4:17; 16:10-11; 2 Corinthians 1:1; Philippians 1:1; 2:19-23). Erastus is listed in Romans 16:23.

Acts 19:23-41. The riot in Ephesus occurs after some time passes: "He stayed in the province of Asia a little longer" (19:22).

A mid-first century inscription has been found in Ephesus with Demetrius's name on it. Miniature temples have not been found. Demetrius acts as the spokesperson for what is obviously a great industry, whipping up threatened craftsmen into a frenzy.

As Paul had already done in another city, once again he draws people away from idols (19:26; 17:29). Worse yet in Ephesus and the entire region a religious change will bring with it economic disruption.

Demetrius also charges that Paul's teaching will put their local temple and goddess into disrepute. The Temple of Artemis was one of the seven wonders of the ancient world.

Demetrius's speech brings forth what sounds like the cry of a religious slogan. One wonders whether the craftsmen really understand the issues at stake or whether they are simply parroting a slogan that seems to fit their mood of intense fear.

The mood turns vicious. The theater in Ephesus held twenty-four thousand people and was therefore an excellent place for mass assemblies. To that site Paul's companions Gaius from Derbe, (20:4) and Aristarchus from Thessalonica (20:4; 27:2; Colossians 4:10; Philemon 24) are taken.

"Disciples" prevent Paul from entering the theater. No motive is suggested. Could it have been a matter of conscience? Or perhaps the issue of Roman citizenship emerged again. In addition, officials of the province (Asiarchs) who are friends of Paul warn him not to go. Asiarchs were influential people appointed from the towns in Asia to conduct annual celebrations to honor the Roman emperor. Local rulers often used this network in order to maintain loyalty to Rome.

Luke's picture shows a mob scene of absolute chaos and gross ignorance (verse 32). A crass and ugly feeling of anti-Semitism runs through the enraged mob. Jews feel threatened, and one of the Jews, Alexander, tries to offer a defense. He is shouted down.

Finally some order is established by the town clerk (verse 35), the man who would have been responsible for the executive branch of the community's decision. Cities and people were occasionally characterized as "guardian of the temple" to a god.

The city's reputation is of sufficient authority that the relatively minor threat posed by Christianity should not create near panic. Demetrius's shortsighted accusation must be dismissed. The men, Aristarchus and Gaius, are neither robbers nor blasphemers.

With the echoes of an enraged mob only recently quieted, Demetrius is told of the legal system and regular meetings of the popular assembly or court (that met three times a month according to one ancient authority).

Paul utters not a single word throughout the entire riot account. We hear of Paul's power and authority through the threat and anger of Demetrius. Clearly Paul's preaching did threaten the religious cult of Artemis. No better evidence could be presented than the witness of those whose livelihood depended in large measure on the life of the cult. Luke skillfully keeps Paul at the center of the drama, even as the two traveling companions stand mute before the unruly crowd.

Acts 20:1-6. In other places Paul had to flee for his life, hounded out of cities by irate or plotting men. His departure from Ephesus, in contrast, seems quite deliberate.

Macedonia includes the cities of Philippi, Thessalonica, Berea, and Corinth. Almost impatiently Luke describes the route Paul takes with its final destination of Jerusalem and Rome. The period of three months (verse 3) is probably a guess. The planned sea voyage has to be abandoned in the face of another Jewish plot. An overland route through Macedonia must be taken. Could Paul and the other travelers be carrying with them the collection for the relief of Jerusalem? (Acts 24:17; Romans 15:25-27; 1 Corinthians 16:1-4; 2 Corinthians 8:23.)

Paul's companions (verse 4) are sent on ahead to Troas "after the Feast of Unleavened Bread (Passover)."

As with the earliest chapters of Acts, the passage of time is difficult to figure. How long a period of time does 20:1-6 occupy? As much as a year some estimate. The passage of time, however, is not of the greatest importance. Luke is now beginning to build toward the final crescendo of Acts.

Acts 20:7-12. The first day of the week is Sunday. Paul gathers with other Christians. Some may wonder why the detail of lamps is included in verse 8. Vapors from the lamps may have been part of the reason the young man, Eutychus, falls asleep. Another suggestion is that the account is intended in part to show that Christianity is not a mystery cult that prospers only in the dark.

After the young man is revived, the Eucharist (Communion) is shared, then Paul continues preaching until dawn.

The story is reminiscent of Peter's raising of Tabitha (9:36-43), however the two scenes are not merely parallels. Paul's effort comes at the conclusion of a remarkably successful mission and serves as an underscoring of this tremendous power and authority.

Acts 20:13-16. The "we" motif reappears with the departure of the missionaries from Troas to Miletus. Paul had arranged for an overland route. Why? As a means of personal solitude perhaps.

The image Luke presents is that Paul, always the pious Jew, wants to be in Jerusalem for Pentecost.

The offering for Jerusalem's relief is not given as a reason for the journey.

Acts 20:17-38. Miletus was at this time an important port on the Menander River, a few miles south of Ephesus. Paul asked the elders from the church at Ephesus to join him at Miletus.

Paul's farewell speech is made up of four sections. The speech (1) reflects on the past, (2) addresses the present, (3) anticipates the future, and (4) concludes with blessings and instructions. Interpretation of the speech varies. Some interpreters see in this an autobiographical reflection by Paul. Others see the speech as Luke's witness to the apostle.

The speech itself is the only speech in Acts that is addressed primarily to "the elders of the church."

The first section (verses 18-21) reflects on the past. Paul's reference to Asia (verse 18) obviously includes the time he spent in Ephesus. By way of preparing the elders for what will follow, Paul emphasizes his way of life as well as his religious attitude—humility, tears, and severe testing.

Publicly and privately, Paul has preached an accurate and authentic gospel. Major elements in the kerygma include both repentance and faith in one Lord, Jesus Christ. The reason for reemphasizing the true apostolic tradition will be made clearer in later verses. Such emphasis implies the peril of internal weakness or heresy.

The second section of the farewell speech (verses 22-24) addresses the present by focusing on present stresses and directions. Paul's journeys and duties are by direction of the Spirit, and Paul cannot contradict or defy them. The exact nature of what will happen to Paul is unknown, but the Spirit has prepared him for "prison and hardships." Even as the clouds of affliction gather, Paul still shines as one ready to give his life in behalf of the gospel.

The third section (verses 25-31) anticipates the future of the church and Paul. Clearly the writer believes Paul will not be seen again either by Ephesians or by other congregations.

The whole counsel of God has always been included in Paul's preaching. Evidently other interpretations have begun to achieve fairly widespread circulation and authority. In short, heresy now threatens the church from within. Ironically, the threat of heresy appears at the moment Paul can no longer exercise his authority due to the need to travel to Jerusalem and then Rome.

Paul reminds the elders of their role and responsibility by referring to the shepherd image. What had been implicit now is expressed openly; internal strife will erupt in the church (verse 30). Paul cannot be responsible for failures of churches to adhere to doctrinal integrity. The elders also are reminded to remember Paul's work and gospel.

The speech concludes (verses 32-35) with blessings and instructions to care for the needy. All congregations are commended to the care of the Lord. Paul's concern with respect to how he ministered goes beyond mere concern for doctrine. He, and Luke as well, want to assure congregations that he has not robbed them of wealth. Paul did not covet wealth and did support himself (1 Corinthians 4:12; 2 Corinthians 11:9; 1 Thessalonians 2:9; 2 Thessalonians 3:8). The implication is clearly that Christian leaders should not live at the expense of the church.

The words Paul attributes to Jesus (verse 35) do not occur in any of the Gospels.

At the end of Paul's speech, the Christians kneel for prayer. The final departure is a scene of sorrow and of great affection. Christians share the kiss of peace, remembering Paul's prediction: this departure is final; Paul will not be seen again.

DIMENSION THREE:
WHAT DOES THE BIBLE MEAN TO ME?

Acts 19:11-19—The Liability of Secondhand Faith

The confrontation with the itinerant exorcists is serious and comic. Its seriousness rests on the real threat that evil presents to any person or society. Its comic element is apparent when the overwhelmed exorcists run naked through the street. Thus with a marvelous literary flair, Luke triggers our imaginations and causes us to think as well.

Exorcism may not be the task we want to learn. We may, however, want to apply the power and authority of the Christian faith to certain issues, such as hunger, peace, social justice, economic equity, the horrendous evils of drug abuse, and the like. But we will never effectively deal with evil if all we can do is parrot words given to us by someone else. Nor will we be able to confront any evil by merely mimicking programs suggested by higher authorities.

Ask class members if they have ever tried to use another's words or ideas without really understanding them. What was the result? Did they feel as if they had effectively tackled the issue? Did they feel like running from the situation?

Most denominations will have national programs and perhaps mandates that congregations are expected to follow and curriculum and other resources to support various ministries. To what extent do class members feel as if some of the programs are not really theirs, but someone else's? If this is the case, what are some of the specific issues that demand your church's own design in order to more effectively tackle problems?

Acts 19:23-41—When Christianity Goes From Preaching to Meddling

Paul's preaching had some impact: the entire region is affected. Even the economic lives of some are adversely affected. Small wonder that a riot erupts in Ephesus.

Sooner or later Christianity changes from a doctrinal understanding to a moral imperative. You may want to discuss ways in which the Christian faith might threaten our economic order. What for instance might the effect be if one were to take Christianity into the military defense contract industries? Could members whose livelihood depends on such work defend the Christian faith? Or would they find themselves threatened by their beliefs?

Perhaps a previous question needs to be asked: When is the Christian faith a threat to the economic, social, or political order? Quite often popular religion is interwoven with the status quo; and therefore, any suggestion with respect to changing the economy carries with it necessary changes in religious perspective. To what extent does our religious orientation require "things as usual" in our economy, society, and political structures?

Close your session by asking each person to consider the impact Christianity has had on his or her use of money and other resources. You may want to list on the chalkboard or on a large piece of paper fresh or disturbing insights that have come as a result of this session's work. Close with a prayer asking for God's strength to act on the basis of the new insight or understanding.

You will be his witness to all men of what you have seen and heard (22:15).

— 10 —

The Arrest of Paul

Acts 21:1–22:29

DIMENSION ONE:
WHAT DOES THE BIBLE SAY?

Answer these questions by reading Acts 21

1. What do the Christians in Tyre try to tell Paul? (21:4)

   The Christian disciples in Tyre try to prevent Paul from going to Jerusalem.

2. How is Paul sent off from Tyre? (21:5-6)

   The Christians with their entire families gather with Paul near his ship. There they kneel on the beach, pray, and then bid Paul farewell.

3. To whose house do the missionaries go in Caesarea? (21:8)

   Paul and the other missionaries go to the home of Philip the evangelist.

4. What symbolic act does Agabus perform? (21:11)

   Agabus takes Paul's belt, ties his own hands and feet with it, and prophesies Paul's arrest and persecution in Jerusalem.

5. What is Paul's attitude regarding the prospect of suffering? (21:13-14)

   Paul seems unconcerned and wants only to do the will of the Lord.

6. Why is Paul cautioned by Christian Jews in Jerusalem? (21:20-22)

   Many Jews suspect Paul of apostasy and turning away from the law of Moses. When Paul's presence becomes known, trouble is bound to develop.

7. What advice is given to Paul? (21:23-25)

   Paul is advised to make a conciliatory gesture. He is to take a temporary Nazirite vow.

8. When the Jews do see Paul, what changes are leveled against him? (21:28-29)

   Paul is charged with blasphemy ("teaches all men everywhere against . . . the law") and with desecrating the Temple through bringing a Greek within the walls of the holy place.

9. The Roman authorities seem initially to confuse Paul with whom? (21:38)

   The Roman soldiers seem to think Paul is a rebellious and militant nationalist terrorist ("the Egyptian . . . who started a revolt").

Answer these questions by reading Acts 22:1-29

10. In what language does Paul address the mob? (22:2)

    Paul addresses the mob in Aramaic.

11. What biographical information does Paul reveal to the mob? (22:3)

    Paul is a Jew, born in Tarsus. He had been trained in the law in Jerusalem by no less a rabbi than Gamaliel.

12. As Paul tells of his conversion experience, how does his account differ from the one in Acts 9? Who hears the voice? (22:9; see 9:7)

    According to this account, Paul alone hears the voice. His companions do see the bright light.

13. The role of Ananias is increased somewhat in this story. What does Luke show here about Ananias? (22:12-16; see 9:10-17)

In this report Ananias is shown to be an exemplary Jewish man, devout, highly respected, using traditional Jewish language to express longstanding Jewish hope.

14. What triggers renewed anger among the Jews? (22:21-22)

Paul's defense of his mission to the Gentiles triggers another uproar.

15. How is Paul able to avoid torture? (22:25)

Paul is a Roman citizen and therefore cannot be tortured.

16. According to this account, Roman citizenship could be purchased, as the soldier obviously had done. How does Paul say he has Roman citizenship? (22:28)

Paul was born a Roman citizen.

17. What is the response of the Roman commander when he finds out that Paul is a Roman citizen? (22:29)

The soldier is alarmed because it is against the law to torture a Roman citizen.

18. Complete the following outline of Paul's third journey by reading Acts 18:23–21:17.

Starting in ANTIOCH in Syria (18:23), Paul travels through GALATIA and PHRYGIA (18:23) to the city of EPHESUS (18:24). The mission in Ephesus continues for more than TWO YEARS (19:8, 10). After this successful mission, Paul moves through MACEDONIA and GREECE (20:1-2). After three months he had to move on due to a plot against him. Paul alters his route to pass through Macedonia to TROAS (20:5).

The final leg of the journey begins with the farewell at MILETUS (20:17). In what appears almost an impatient listing of itinerary, Paul completes the journey by traveling through COS, RHODES, and PATARA (21:1). On the trip to Phoenicia the missionaries pass close to CYPRUS (21:3). From there they sail on to SYRIA (21:3) and land at TYRE (21:3).

Against the desire of Christians along his route, Paul continues his journey to Jerusalem through PTOLEMAIS (21:7) and CAESAREA (21:8). The journey ends in JERU-SALEM (21:15).

DIMENSION TWO: WHAT DOES THE BIBLE MEAN?

In this lesson you will study the rest of Paul's third missionary journey. Luke devotes a remarkable amount of time and space to the final scenes of Paul's ministry. Travels are detailed, incidents are numerous, and the Christian gospel is always pictured as expanding inexorably toward Rome.

Acts 21:1-6. From Miletus the entire party sails directly to Cos in a single day's journey. On the following day Rhodes is the destination. The third day finds the missionaries in the Lycian harbor of Patara. According to some authorities, the third day's destination was Myra. Presumably the entire party travels together as Luke mentions no departures of Paul or any others.

The group boards another vessel, a cargo ship (verse 3), for the rest of the trip. Passage is made on a direct course to Phoenicia. Traveling to the south of Cyprus, the cargo ship proceeds to Syria and lands at Tyre where cargo is unloaded.

For one week the Christian missionaries remain with the unnamed Christians at Tyre. Even though Paul seems to have some knowledge of his destination (20:22-23), the Christian disciples in Tyre warn Paul not to go to Jerusalem. This apparent contradiction—the Spirit giving different directions to Paul and to the disciples—will recur with the incident of Agabus (21:10-11). Luke's readers will have immediately recognized two parallels between Jesus' Passion and Paul's pilgrimage. Both Jesus and Paul are admonished to avoid the peril of Jerusalem, and they are both compelled to journey to Jerusalem even though the consequence is suffering.

The departure from Tyre is similar to the earlier departure from Miletus. Christian disciples accompany the missionaries to the ship. There they kneel and pray (20:36-38).

Acts 21:7-16. The journey continues to Ptolemais, modern-day Acre, near Haifa. There the missionaries meet with another Christian congregation.

Leaving Ptolemais, they travel to Caesarea, the home of Philip, one of the original Seven (6:5). Luke, showing an interest in the men and women who greeted and housed Paul, tells of four prophesying daughters (verse 9). However, no comment is made with respect to the content of their utterances. If they have any insight as to Paul's future, nothing is said.

Agabus, whom we met in Antioch earlier (11:28), reappears. He arrives from Judea. Caesarea belonged to the administrative district of Judea. Acting in the manner of an Old Testament prophet (Isaiah 20:2-6; Jeremiah 13:1-11), Agabus performs a symbolic gesture. The belt (verse 11) is a long cloth wound several times around the waist.

Jerusalem is for Paul the place of possible imprisonment and death, as it had been for his Lord (Luke 9:51). Paul's resolve subdues any opposition to his intentions. "The Lord's will be done" (Acts 21:14; Luke 22:42).

At the end of what must have been more than a single day's journey, Paul arrives in Jerusalem. Thus the third missionary journey comes to an end. The journey of approximately twenty-eight hundred miles lasted roughly four years.

Mnason, who may have been an early disciple of Stephen and a native of Cyprus (as was Barnabus, 4:36), offers his home to the missionaries (verse 16).

Acts 21:17-26. Paul's time in Jerusalem begins on a happy note: he is welcomed "warmly." The "we" segments end here and do not reappear until 27:1. A glimpse into the Christian community is provided by the careful wording in verse 18. James, who had played a major role in the Jerusalem Council (15:13-21) is mentioned only by name. Nothing is said of the apostle Peter, nor is John mentioned (Galatians 2:9). The story then focuses on Paul.

Paul, fresh from the mission field, tells the events of the journey (verse 19). In this detailed report no mention is made regarding the collection. The claim of thousands of Jewish converts implies a very strong Jewish-Christian group in the city.

Much concern exists among the legalists and/or conservatives with respect to Paul's teaching (verses 21-22). Even with the success of Christianity among Jews and Gentiles alike, some people are preoccupied with the threat Paul and his perspective pose to tradition. Not surprisingly the issue centers on circumcision again. Jewish Christians in Antioch do not feel compelled to observe the traditions regarding food (Galatians 2:12). Thus Paul did have an impact there. But Paul had, after all, circumcised Timothy (16:3; 1 Corinthians 9:20). Will another major controversy erupt when word circulates that Paul has returned?

In order to avoid sharp controversy, Paul is advised to take a Nazirite vow (Numbers 6:1-21). Already four men have undertaken just such a discipline. If Paul consents, then he effectively illustrates his conformity to Jewish custom and Levitical purity.

The compromise restrictions of the Jerusalem Council are again listed (15:22) as if Paul knew nothing about them. Perhaps Luke is using this inclusion as a means to speak directly to his original audience.

Paul consents to the suggestion. The vow is complete when a sacrifice is offered for each. Paul had by his conciliatory action become "like a Jew" (1 Corinthians 9:20).

Acts 21:27-36. Since the season is the Pentecost season, Jews from all around the empire (those living outside Palestine) have gathered in Jerusalem. (Recall the first Pentecost, Acts 2.) The prediction that Paul's presence cannot be kept secret proves accurate (verse 27). "The Jews from the province of Asia" precipitate a riot by attacking Paul. Grossly overstating their objections they accuse Paul of utter apostasy. Worse yet, Paul is accused of bringing a Greek into the Temple, which is a capital offense. Evidently these people had seen Paul with an Ephesian, a Greek named Trophimus (20:4).

As to whether the entire city erupts into an uproar, some question exists. Luke uses overstatement to illustrate the point. However, sufficient chaos breaks out to arouse the Roman garrison. As soon as Paul is dragged out of the Temple, the gates are locked shut.

Luke deftly shows the attitude of the Romans through their role in protecting the threatened Christian apostle. The Roman troops stationed in Jerusalem consisted at this time of one cohort, approximately seven hundred and sixty infantry with one other squadron of some two hundred and forty men. The entire corps were housed in the Tower of Antonia adjacent to the Temple.

With Jerusalem in riot, the troops are mustered and come to Paul's aid. The prediction of 21:11 is fulfilled: Paul is chained. Paul, already beaten, and now chained, is interrogated. Because of the noisy mob outside, the Roman commander orders Paul taken into the fortress. "The violence of the mob was so great he had to be carried by the soldiers" (verse 35). Frustrated because Paul has been rescued from their grasp, the lynch mob explodes.

Acts 21:37-40. Incredibly, even as the mob yells, Paul addresses the commander with sophisticated politeness. The picture of Paul, recently beaten and presumably now chained, speaking in any way intelligibly strains the imagination. Luke, however, is using the account as a means by which Paul can present his own justification to the Jerusalem crowd.

Paul confesses that he is not one of the Sicarii, that is assassins who had, about A.D. 50–70, carried out political terrorism (verse 39). These assassins stabbed their victims with daggers (*sica*) thus they were known by their weapons.

Militant nationalists chafed under Roman occupation. (Read about Theudas in 5:36.) In one incident, nearly thirty thousand Sicarii moved toward the Mount of Olives intending to seize Jerusalem. Paul, and therefore Christianity, poses no threat to the Roman state.

Identifying himself as a Jew from Tarsus (something he does not do in Philippians 3:5), Paul asks permission to speak. Given permission, he assumes an orator's stance and motions for the people to be quiet.

Acts 22:1-21. Paul's speech, addressed to Jews and in Aramaic (sometimes mentioned as Hebrew), is addressed to "brothers and fathers" (see Stephen's speech, 7:2). Always concerned for the continuous relationship with Jews, Paul is pictured as conciliatory. Neither the Sanhedrin nor the high priest are present. They will appear later (23:2).

The Aramaic language performs two functions. First, it quiets the crowd. Second, using Aramaic implies strong ties with Judaism.

The information already given to the tribune is repeated. Note that Paul uses the present tense: "I *am* a Jew." More biographical material is then added. Born in Tarsus, Paul grew up in Jerusalem. The term "under Gamaliel" refers to the practice of students sitting on the ground at the feet of their teacher. Gamaliel served as the rabbi about A.D. 25–50.

Paul recollects his sordid and brutal past (9:2; 26:10), his remarkable experience on the road to Damascus, and the direction in which his life has gone ever since.

Paul refers to the time of day of the conversion experience (verse 6). Evidently the light was even brighter than the sun.

In the conversion account in Acts 9, Paul's companions hear the voice but do not see anyone (9:7). Here Paul says, "My companions saw the light, but they did not understand the voice of him who was speaking to me."

Paul describes Ananias as a good Jew, in high standing with other Jews. Ananias's use of "the God of our fathers" and "the Righteous One" carries with it a strong attachment to the Jewish tradition.

Paul gives no indication of a tardy or detoured return to Jerusalem from Damascus. The fact that he received the revelation in the Temple (verse 17) is a further indication of his loyalty to the Jewish tradition. It was to the pious Jew that Jesus appeared.

The speech comes to an end as Paul tells his audience that Jesus himself sent him to the Gentiles (verse 21).

Paul's speech raises many questions. Why doesn't he address the charges that have been brought against him? His arrest occurred because he had taken a Greek into the Temple, but not a word is addressed to that indictment (though the charge will be mentioned again in 24:6). What then is the purpose of the speech?

Luke uses this incident to show the tension that exists between Christianity and Judaism. What is the relationship? Was the question pertinent only to Paul's listeners, or is the question one with which Luke's first readers would have had to contend as well? Two themes are interwoven in the speech. The first has to do with Paul's identity with the Jews and as a Jew. He uses the present tense to describe himself as a Jew. Throughout, he takes pains to illustrate the extent to which he had maintained his Jewishness. However, Paul refuses to concede preeminence to Jewish nationalism or the Temple religion.

The larger issue is that of the entire Gentile mission. Paul's listeners and Luke's first readers all wrestled with whether Gentiles could be included within the faith. The Christian perspective, of course, contends that anyone can become Christian through baptism (verse 16). Does the mission with the Gentile Christian congregations, spawned by the movement, in some way maintain an essential continuity with the traditions and faith of Judaism?

Acts 22:22-29. As Paul asserts the basic continuity of Judaism in this movement and contends the validity of the Gentile mission, the mob that had been unusually quiet, explodes in fury, demanding death for the apostate. Renewed anger bursts out. Immediately the scene reverts to the ugliness of 21:36.

Graphic expressions of outrage and anguish are made in response to the suggested blasphemy by "throwing off their cloaks and flinging dust into the air" (verse 23).

The drama reaches an intense moment of suspense. The screaming mob, calling for death, forces the Roman authorities to seize control of the situation before it gets completely out of hand. The accused (Paul), already battered, is taken inside the barracks. The scourging is not so much punishment as it is a form of torture used to force information out of prisoners. Torture however was not to be forced on Roman citizens. Its use was restricted to non-Romans and slaves. As Paul is stretched out to the flogging post he asks about his rights as a Roman citizen— and as an uncondemned one as well (verse 25).

The claim of Roman citizenship stuns the soldiers. One ancient saying contended, "To bind a Roman citizen is a crime; to strike him, an offense; to kill him, murder!" Small wonder the soldiers are near panic. Citizenship could be purchased; in contrast, Paul's claim of citizenship by birth is especially powerful and authoritative (verse 28).

Paul's Roman citizenship saves him from torture: the soldiers "withdrew immediately."

The scene of threatened flogging shows the inability of the Romans to gather any hard evidence against Paul. Therefore, Luke is saying, Rome can find nothing in Christianity to warrant persecution (23:28-29; 24:22; 25:20, 26). Luke's specific purposes seem to shift in their emphasis. Here quite clearly the interest in an apologetic to the Romans is critical. Indeed, the remarkable amount of space Luke uses to show Paul's arrest, trial, and subsequent travel to Rome (21:32–28:31) gives strong evidence that one of Luke's primary concerns is precisely the relationship between Christianity and Roman authority.

DIMENSION THREE:
WHAT DOES THE BIBLE MEAN TO ME?

Acts 21:27-36—An Exercise in Historical Imagination

A sense of historical imagination helps when reading a passage such as the one in Acts 21:27-36 (the arrest of Paul). One way to begin is to ask class members to list in order the events of the upheaval and arrest. Ask the following questions:

Who are the antagonists?
What is the reason for the upheaval?
What images occur to you? What are the sights and sounds in the story?
What is the dramatic action?
What feelings are aroused in you as you read this story?

After exploring the text with imagination, then you can go to work with the issues raised and the questions the Scripture asks.

Acts 22:1-21—An Unresolved Question

Luke's intentions in Paul's arrest and speech are more than merely telling the historical circumstance and detail. The speech serves as a means by which Luke can address his audience, the first people who read or heard his work. The question with which Luke challenges his readers is the question of spreading the Christian gospel to everyone—Jew and Gentile—or keeping it within Judaism.

Evidently the decisions of the Jerusalem Council had not entirely quashed the impulse within many Jewish Christian groups to keep Gentiles out of the church. The problem of unresolved questions is still a vital one in our churches today. Whether we like it or not, there are theological, racial, political in some instances, and economic influences that define who will or will not be welcome in a specific church.

Are there certain expectations unwritten but nonetheless real with respect to the theological perspective that your church has for members? Are theological perspectives a major consideration in regard to church membership? Are there expectations or tacit restrictions with respect to social standing or economic status?

Your discussion may be difficult because we are not pleased when our prejudices are pointed out. In a hundred ways we can defend ourselves and our preferences while at the same time preventing the full extension of God's grace.

Acts 22:17-21
Personal Preference or Jesus' Prerogative?

Paul's speech contains many indications that Paul did not go into the missionary field on the basis of his own preference. Instead Paul had been sent by Jesus. When Luke's first readers read these allusions to Jesus' prerogative, they too wondered about the direction of their ministries.

Ask class members to list on the chalkboard or a large piece of paper ministries to which they have been averse. Do they center around any specific people? or class? or issues? Do your class members avoid certain ministries or instances due to the probable cost to reputation? economic well-being? community prestige?

Paul's witness is that he went not as a blind man, but rather as a person fully aware of the consequences. What ministries have you attempted even though personal cost was involved? What gave the first missionaries enough strength and courage to follow Jesus' prerogative over their own preference?

Sing or meditate on a hymn about Jesus' call to disciples.

Paul looked straight at the Sanhedrin and said, "My brothers, I have fulfilled my duty to God in all good conscience to this day" (23:1).

11

Paul on Trial

Acts 22:30–24:27

DIMENSION ONE:
WHAT DOES THE BIBLE SAY?

Answer these questions by reading Acts 22:30–23:35

1. Why is Paul brought before the Jewish authorities? (22:30)

   Paul is brought before the Sanhedrin because the Roman authorities want to know more exactly what the conflict is between Paul and the Jews.

2. What happens to Paul after he declares his clear conscience? (23:2)

   The high priest Ananias orders those standing near Paul (his servants) to slap Paul for his statement.

3. Does Paul recognize the high priest? (23:5)

   Paul does not recognize the high priest or else he would not have spoken so harshly.

4. Which theological supposition does Paul center on when talking with the Sanhedrin? (23:6-8)

   Paul speaks of the hope of resurrection that Pharisees believed and Sadducees did not.

5. Why do the Roman authorities become involved? (23:10)

   The Romans fear an outbreak of violence. Their intervention has nothing to do with religious issues.

6. How is Paul encouraged during his first night in the Roman jail? (23:11)

   Paul has a vision of Christ who assures him that Paul will be able to witness for Christ in Rome: "As you have testified about me in Jerusalem, so you must also testify in Rome."

7. Who conspires to kill Paul? (23:12-15)

   Over forty Jews "bound themselves with an oath" to kill Paul. Some members of the Sanhedrin also join the conspiracy.

8. Describe the precautions taken by the Roman authorities to protect Paul. (23:23-24)

   The commander secures two hundred soldiers, seventy horsemen, and two hundred spearmen or bodyguards to take Paul to Caesarea by night.

9. According to the letter sent to Felix, what are the charges against Paul? (23:26-30)

   Claudius Lysias can find nothing for which Paul should be tried. The problem is an internal Jewish problem.

10. Where is Paul kept while in Caesarea? (23:35)

    Paul is kept under guard in Herod's palace.

Answer these questions by reading Acts 24

11. Who speaks for the delegation from Jerusalem? (24:1-2)

    Tertullus, a lawyer, presents the case for the delegation from Jerusalem.

12. What is the first charge brought against Paul? (24:5)

    Paul is charged with civil disturbance as a leader of the sect of Nazarenes.

13. What is the second reason for Paul's arrest? (24:6)

    Paul is accused of trying to desecrate the Temple.

14. Paul discounts the possibility of spreading rebellion since he has only been in Jerusalem for a short time. How long has he been in Jerusalem? (24:11)

Paul has been in Jerusalem for only twelve days.

15. Why has Paul come to Jerusalem? (24:11)

Paul has come to Jerusalem on a pilgrimage to worship.

16. How does Paul link the Jewish tradition and faith with the Christian faith? (24:14-15)

Paul links the two faiths through the patriarchs, the observance of Law and Prophets, and finally, the belief in the resurrection.

17. Which of the charges is the real problem according to Paul? (24:21)

The difference of belief between Pharisees and Sadducees on the issue of resurrection is the real problem.

18. Why does Felix delay judgment and put Paul in jail? (24:22)

Felix delays judgment until the commander Lysias can arrive in Caesarea.

19. What is the real reason for Paul's imprisonment? (24:26)

Felix hopes to receive a substantial bribe in return for Paul's release.

DIMENSION TWO:
WHAT DOES THE BIBLE MEAN?

This lesson's material centers on Paul's trial. Recreating an exact representation of the historical event will be difficult. Therefore, we will work with the event and Luke's purpose in presenting the event.

Luke is a historian to a degree, but he is also a theologian trying always to interpret the meaning of events from the perspective of God's intention and the realities of Christian struggles in a real world. The task of biblical interpretation is to know the events as well as the meaning of those events to the Christian narrator and his audience.

Acts 22:30–23:5. The story picks up with the morning following Paul's tumultuous arrest. The guard wants to know exactly why Paul is the focal point of such a demonstration as occurred near the Temple (21:34). Technically the Roman tribune did not have the authority to summon the Sanhedrin and chief priests. Nonetheless, the Council meets and Paul makes his defense.

Unbowed by persecution and unaffected by the authorities, Paul declares his lack of fear since he has a clear conscience. The scene turns to one of ugly rancor. The high priest Ananias's servants strike Paul. Though surrounded by hostile authority, Paul is not intimidated. He hurls the curse of Deuteronomy 28:22 back at the high priest. The allusion to a whitewashed wall may refer to Jesus' words to the Pharisees in Matthew 25:27.

Whether Paul had spoken without recognizing the high priest is not clear. The words seem to imply a serious statement rather than sarcasm (verse 5).

Acts 23:6-10. Sadducees have, throughout all Acts, opposed any notion of resurrection. Paul seizes this moment to drive a wedge between his opponents. He appeals to the Pharisees as brothers. Paul's ploy shatters the image of a unified Jewish resistance. Instead, the rival parties erupt into theological debate. Pharisaism with its beliefs regarding resurrection, spirit, and angels shares a great deal with Christianity. Therefore, Christianity is not a breakaway sect from Judaism but rather a continuation of Judaism.

Luke's early readers would immediately perceive his purpose. Christianity and Judaism are not by their nature antagonists. The two share a great deal and, therefore, can maintain amicable relations. Indeed, this account shows Pharisees defending the Christian Paul.

Fearing more violence, the Roman commander seizes control. He has Paul taken away to jail (protective custody?). While in jail, Paul experiences a renewed burst of courage through a vision of Christ (verse 11). Paul is assured that he "must also testify in Rome."

Acts 23:12-15. Since the story of Paul's hearing shows Pharisees sympathetic toward Paul, the notion that all Jews mount a conspiracy is ill-founded. Clearly a conspiracy is devised among over forty Jews who vow to kill Paul. (The killing cannot be done in the tower jail due to the heavy Roman presence there.)

Co-conspirators seem to be high Jewish authorities. They are to get Paul out of the protective custody of the Roman garrison under the pretext of more questioning.

Inside the barracks Paul gives the orders to the commander, who then carries them out. Paul's nephew (who appears in verse 16) explains the rumored conspiracy to the commander. Sometime in the afternoon, as Paul is being moved, the assassins will strike. Fully aware of the danger, the commander dismisses the young man.

Before continuing, we need to ask why the narrator spends such a large amount of time with this story. The key lies with the Roman attitude. Luke's purpose includes that of showing Roman authority as benign toward Christianity. Each detail of this story shows the Roman garrison, along with its leaders, interested solely in the maintenance of order in the city. When a plot to kill Paul becomes known to the commander, he arranges to protect Paul.

Acts 23:23-30. A sizable contingent of troops is mustered: two hundred soldiers, seventy horsemen, and another two hundred identified as spearmen, who are perhaps bodyguards. The entire force will leave at about nine P.M. Paul will ride as well.

Antonius Felix, procurator (governor) of Judea from A.D. 52–60, was the brother of a powerful Roman. Cruel and tyrannical, the man was accused by Jews of wrongdoing. Claudius Lysias, the tribune, was a Greek and was not born a Roman citizen (22:28).

The letter is here reported in summary. In the letter, Claudius Lysias takes the Sanhedrin's role and charges seriously. Most commentators point out that the commander portrays himself in better light than actual fact reveals. The narrator gives the impression that all the Roman authorities have treated Paul with respect from the outset. Once Paul's citizenship became the issue, the Romans protected Paul in three instances: at the Temple (21:32); from the Sanhedrin (23:10); and from the plot to kill him (23:12-24).

The letter summarizes what happened in 21:31–22:29, with the exception of Paul's speech. Then the commander tells what he understands to be the issue—a matter of theological dispute within Judaism. Once the plot has been uncovered, secrecy is necessary. The conspirators will make an accounting another time (verse 35).

A nighttime march is undertaken to Antipatris, a distance of approximately forty miles. The next morning, the foot soldiers must march back to Jerusalem. Horsemen accompany Paul to Caesarea, another twenty-five miles further on. Both the explanatory letter and the apostle are presented to the governor.

Felix is pictured as an impartial governor who begins making appropriate arrangements for legal hearings, all of which will take place when Paul's accusers arrive. According to Roman law, hearings could be held in the accused's home province (Paul's was Cilicia); the province in which the incident or issue took place; or the province in which the accused has been captured.

Acts 24:1-9. After an interval of five days Paul's accusers arrive. Tertullus, the spokesman, is familiar with both Jewish and Roman law. He begins with gracious words for the Roman governor. Felix had executed many nationalists in order to put down a possible upheaval. He also introduced some reforms. However, Tertullus's tone sounds either like that of a sycophant or a cynic. Without modesty, Tertullus overstates the honor in classic rhetorical style.

Tertullus's speech attacks Christianity as a sect of Nazarenes (verse 5). The charges would no doubt have reminded Luke's early readers of the charges against Jesus (Luke 23:2) and the entire Passion event. Could Luke be implying that just as events went for Jesus so they will proceed for the apostle Paul as well? The charges conjure up images of political revolution with Paul as the leader. The charge of desecrating the Temple is reserved almost as an afterthought. Further examination by the governor will confirm the accusations.

Acts 24:10-21. Paul presents his defense. The image is of the single, stouthearted apostle in a hostile environment, charged with sedition by authorities, amidst the trappings of Roman imperial rule. The situation calls for great courage to remain faithful and still be calm.

Paul accounts for twelve days in Jerusalem (verse 11), possibly with the following schedule: day 1, arrival in Jerusalem (21:17); day 2, with James and the elders (21:18); days 3-9, days of the vow (21:27); day 10, appearance before the Council (22:30); day 11, the conspiracy is discovered (23:12); and day 12, transfer to Caesarea (23:31). The overall impression is of Paul, the prisoner Jew, going to Jerusalem to worship.

Paul answers the charge in verse 5. Tertullus's charges cannot be proved. The Way (9:2), condescendingly known as a "sect," is linked with the ancient tradition of Judaism: the patriarchs, the Law and the Prophets (verse 14). Note Luke's continuation of the Jewish-Christian relationship through Paul's speech. The hope shared by both Jews and Christians is the hope of the Resurrection for both the just and the unjust. No mention is made of the Messiah or the even more inflammatory identity of Jesus as the Messiah. Judgment is always bound with resurrection. Therefore, Paul proclaims his own clear conscience.

At long last the collection for the relief of Jerusalem congregations is mentioned (verse 17). Paul refers to it as gifts for the poor.

Paul claims no responsibility for the riot. He accuses "some Jews from the province of Asia" instead. Since they are not present, the charges cannot be proved. Furthermore, the men who are present can only bring charges with respect to theological differences.

The alleged desecration of the Temple is effectively refuted by the image of Paul as the pious pilgrim on his way, with alms no less.

Acts 24:22-23. Felix is characterized as having a thorough knowledge of the Christian Way. How he learned of the Way is in no manner indicated. The Account does show that a Roman who knew of Christianity does not immediately launch into oppression and persecution. Felix suggests adjournment of the present proceedings and then postpones a verdict.

Paul remains a prisoner, though one with certain freedoms. Paul's friends, Christians perhaps, can visit and serve him. Roman authority is presented as a benevolent power with respect to Christianity.

Paul defends himself in a dialogical style. First Paul is accused and then he speaks in his own defense. This dialogic defense of a position is called *apologetic.*

The speech itself is an apology (defense) that touches only briefly on the charges of sedition, which would have been of primary importance to the Romans. The major elements in the apology are theological in nature and stress the continuity between Christianity and Judaism. Scholars contend, therefore, that Paul's speech is intended for Luke's early readers, since a burning question for them as well as for us, is the nature of the relationship between Judaism and Christianity. From Luke's perspective (Paul's as well) the new movement is not a complete breakaway from the past. The anticipation of the Messiah and resurrection holds Christianity and Judaism in an unbreakable embrace. The Sadducees may disagree, but theirs is little more than an internal problem.

Acts 24:24-27. Felix arrives with his wife Drusilla. Drusilla is the daughter of Herod Agrippa I. The sister of Agrippa II and Bernice (25:13), Drusilla had first been engaged to Epiphanes of Commagene and later married to King Azizus of Emesa. Felix and Drusilla share an apparent interest in the Christian faith.

Paul interprets the central laments of all post-apostolic preaching: justice, that is, righteousness; self-control; and the future judgment, that is, the coming judgment. Felix is visibly disturbed. Paul's behavior parallels that of John the Baptist's with Herod Antipas (Matthew 14:3-14; Mark 6:17-19). Interestingly, Luke's Gospel does not tell of this incident. Was Luke trying to edit his earlier material so as not to offend any Roman sensitivities? Both Herod Antipas and Felix got their wives due to breaches in previous marriages, both clearly reprehensible actions in the Jewish-Christian perspective. Felix is not converted.

Paul is sent back to prison, Felix still hoping for a substantial bribe. But where would Paul be able to raise a large sum of money? Many commentators suggest that he could use the collection at this time (24:17). One commentator contends that Paul is being served by his family plus two slaves. Another suggests that Paul has a sizable inheritance at his disposal. Doubtless, Luke's early readers would have known that bribery was so widespread as to be a common practice. Therefore, he gives no further comment or explanation.

Felix, not wanting to antagonize the Jews, imprisons Paul for another two years. The sentence continues past Felix's tenure into the reign of Porcius Festus.

DIMENSION THREE: WHAT DOES THE BIBLE MEAN TO ME?

Acts 24:1-21—An Exercise in Historical Imagination

Reread the narrative of Tertullus's accusation and Paul's apology in Acts 24:1-21. What does the scene look like? Who are the antagonists? How do they look at each other? What tones of voice do you hear? What sorts of gestures are made? How do the observers react to what Tertullus says? to what Paul says? What emotions are triggered by the story? Do you feel any emotions from it?

Acts 24:10-21—What Holds Us Together?

In Luke's account of Paul's defense, Paul's apology contains elements of history and theology that hold both Judaism and Christianity together. List the three major themes that are shared by the two faiths: the stories and traditions of the fathers (the patriarchs, Genesis 12–50), the Law and the Prophets, and the hope of resurrection. Note that Luke includes no mention of Jesus of Nazareth in Paul's apology. Could it be that Luke was more concerned with maintaining relations with Jews than with dividing the two faiths because of Jesus? In Paul's earlier speech at the Areopagus (17:22-31), no mention is made about Jesus either. Luke's intention, therefore, seems to be to continue a strong relationship between Christianity and all people, especially Jews, because so much belief and tradition is shared. Jews and Christians share a common belief that the universe has a moral God at the center of it. This moral God demands moral behavior from the creation. Certain moral expectations are part of being the people of God.

Ask class members to consider their understandings of the relationship between themselves as Christians and Jews. Is Jesus the sole reason for the antagonism between the two faiths? Is there an area within which the two faiths can and indeed must maintain relationship?

One possible interpretation of the Christian expansion and subsequent antagonism between Christianity and Judaism is that at the same time the Christian movement experiences triumph, the Jews exclude themselves from God's message of salvation. There is simply no need to further exaggerate the tragedy by increasing antagonisms among God's people.

Acts 23:1-11—The Authority of a Higher Calling

Luke's portrayal of Paul is one of great courage and stamina. Surrounded by hostile authorities Paul steadfastly continues to hold to his convictions. Readers will no doubt wonder at what gives Paul the resources to withstand such virulent attacks without losing heart.

Your class members will no doubt recall moments when they too have been sorely pressed when trying to maintain a Christian stance and character in difficult situations. Ask them to tell what the problem seemed to be. Then ask them to describe what gave them sufficient strength to continue.

Paul holds fast to the gospel even when challenged by what the majority of people would see as the authority that needs to be obeyed. Namely, Paul challenges synagogue officials, governmental authority, and traditional interpretation of the Scriptures. Ask class members to think of moments when similar challenges in our time are appropriate. What are moments when church officials might well be challenged? When might government authority be challenged due to Christian convictions? Ask class members to consider the resistance to the military expense portion of tax payment as one area in which Christian witness is demonstrated. What of social spending? domestic needs? foreign policy?

Conclude by listing on a chalkboard or a large piece of paper fresh insights that have come from these chapters.

And now it is because of my hope in what God has promised our fathers that I am on trial today (26:6).

— 12 —

Paul's Defense

Acts 25–26

DIMENSION ONE:
WHAT DOES THE BIBLE SAY?

Answer these questions by reading Acts 25

1. Which Roman official arrives in his new province? (25:1)

   Festus arrives in Caesarea and travels "up from Caesarea to Jerusalem."

2. Which people bring charges against Paul? (25:2)

   Charges are reported to Festus by the chief priests and Jewish leaders of the community.

3. Paul defends himself on which three grounds? (25:8)

   Paul says he has done nothing against the law of the Jews, has not profaned the Temple, and has not stirred up civil strife against Roman authority.

4. According to this account, why does Paul appeal to Caesar? (25:10-11)

   Paul has done nothing against Roman law. Since the Jews can find nothing for which to try him, Paul keeps the proceedings within Roman authority by appealing to Caesar.

5. Who arrives in Caesarea to greet Festus? (25:13)

   King Agrippa and Bernice arrive in Caesarea.

6. According to Roman thinking, what seems to be the problem between Paul and the Jews? (25:18-21)

   Festus can make little sense out of what appears to him little more than superstition. Paul claims that Jesus, a dead man, is yet alive.

7. Why is Paul brought before Agrippa? (25:22, 24-27)

   Not only has Agrippa indicated he wants to see the apostle, but Agrippa seems to be the expert with respect to Roman law. Festus has been unable to find any offense sufficiently gross as to warrant death. In fact, he can hardly find enough to write any sort of charges to be sent to Rome.

Answer these questions by reading Acts 26

8. Based on Paul's introductory remarks, what is Agrippa's religious tradition? (26:2-3)

   Agrippa is of the Jewish tradition and is therefore familiar with Jewish customs and controversies.

9. According to Paul, what is the great hope promised to the ancient patriarchs? (26:6-8)

   The great hope promised by God is the hope of resurrection.

10. How severely had Paul persecuted the followers of the Christian Way? (26:9-11)

   First, Paul opposed Christians and put them to death in Jerusalem. Then, Paul "tried to force them to blaspheme" and in his "obsession against them" even "went to foreign cities to persecute them."

11. Describe the events on the road to Damascus according to this account. (26:13-18)

   While traveling toward Damascus, Paul and his companions are enveloped in a light brighter than the sun itself. Everyone in the company falls to the ground, but only Paul hears a voice speaking in Aramaic. Paul also hears an explanation of the mission to which the Lord is calling him.

12. According to Paul's defense, why are the Jews now prosecuting him? (26:19-21)

Paul obeys the heavenly command to preach to people in Damascus, Jerusalem, Judea, and also to Gentiles. The appeal to Gentiles to repent and to live lives of repentance offends the Jews.

13. According to Paul's interpretation of Scripture, what must happen to the Messiah? (26:22-23)

Paul, interpreting the prophets and Moses, says "that the Christ would suffer and, as the first to rise from the dead, would proclaim light to his own people and to the Gentiles."

14. What is Festus's initial response to Paul's defense? (26:24)

Festus interrupts Paul and shouts at him that he must be out of his mind, driven insane by his great learning.

15. What seems to be Paul's greatest wish? (26:29)

He hopes that all who hear him accept Christ and follow the Way.

16. What is the Roman opinion at the conclusion of Paul's defense? (26:30-32)

The king, the governor, Bernice, and the other Roman officials agree that Paul has done nothing to warrant death. Had Paul not appealed to Caesar the entire affair would be dropped.

DIMENSION TWO: WHAT DOES THE BIBLE MEAN?

The continuing drama of Paul's trial and defense fills Acts 25 and 26. Four events over a period of maybe a month, and covering a distance of about sixty-four miles, are described in these two chapters. Luke's earlier stories covered vast distances and a myriad of places in similar-length chapters. Paul's first journey of hundreds of miles is covered in two chapters (13:1–14:25). The second journey (15:41–18:22) spans four years and some twenty-eight hundred miles. The third journey (18:23–21:6) also covers several years and many hundreds of miles.

Acts 21:17-40 sets the stage for an extended exchange between Paul and the Roman authorities. The confrontation ends in a draw (22:1–24:47). Acts 25–26 presents yet another elaborately staged dramatic exchange between Roman authority and Paul. Why? What is the narrator's purpose? Some scholars treat the trial scene as a set of courtroom minutes, including first-person speech in what sounds like an eyewitness account. Other scholars see the drama as a story of extended suspense. The question left at the conclusion of Acts 24, "What will happen to Paul?"

is still not answered. The effect is that Paul's trial dominates the action of the last section of Acts 21–28, nearly a quarter of the book.

What then of Luke's earlier emphasis on the Holy Spirit? Has the story deleted the action of the Spirit? Not altogether, though the role of the Spirit in Acts 16–28 is markedly less than in Acts 1–14. Evidently the narrator's purpose in the latter half of Acts has more to do with the relationships between Christianity and Judaism and Christianity and Rome. Certainly with Paul's trials, speeches, and Roman authority, the story focuses on Christianity and Rome. Our present account continues the motif of Roman good will toward Paul and, by implication, toward Christianity as a whole.

Acts 25:1-12. After two years, Paul is finally given further hearing. Festus (Porcius Festus) became procurator (governor) of Judea in A.D. 60 and ruled probably only until A.D. 62. The new governor visits Jerusalem at a convenient time early in his tenure, thus setting the trial and hearings into motion again. We must remember that Festus could liberate Paul, but he was in a difficult position. Paul's case was held over from Felix's administration. He would want to know why Felix had not freed him. Furthermore, Paul was accused by the highest authorities among the Jews as an enemy of the state.

"The chief priests and Jewish leaders" present their accusation against Paul. Still intent on the execution of Paul, the Jewish leaders revive the plot to ambush him (verse 3).

Whether Festus can discern the intentions of the Jews is left ambiguous. Perhaps he wanted to visit another area of his realm. In either event, he declines. Festus will go to Caesarea, and the accusers will have to travel to Caesarea in order to press their charges. Only then will Paul be judged.

Within eight or ten days, Festus travels to Caesarea. To free Paul without a thorough investigation of charges would imperil his relations with his new subjects. Paul is brought before the court, and charges are brought against him (verses 6-7). Festus naturally is anxious to get off to a good start in his new position.

Paul defends himself against all charges. He says he has not violated Jewish law, profaned the Temple, or stirred up revolt against Caesar. The mention of Caesar (Roman authority) is a new charge. Had Paul been charged with civil disorder (other than disturbing the peace)?

What occurs next (verses 9-11) is interpreted in different ways. Does Festus, previously concerned about Paul, abruptly change his attitude? Does the offer of a change of venue afford Paul the opportunity to secure more witnesses? Perhaps Festus had already decided to avoid making any decision in the case. Finally, could Festus be giving in to the demands of the Jews? Paul insists on a trial according to official Roman law.

Paul chooses a trial by Roman law. The entire scene may have struck him as a subtle conspiracy between the Jewish and Roman authorities. Many questions have been raised by interpreters. When was an appeal allowed? Here Festus refers to his council. Was the appeal allowed only after sentencing had taken place (25:11)? Was release in any way possible after an appeal had been made (26:32)? In any event, Paul appeals his case under what must have been extremely stressful conditions. He will go to Caesar.

Acts 25:13-27. Some time passes. Herod Agrippa II (great-grandson of Herod the Great) and his sister Bernice arrive in Caesarea, and Festus presents the case against Paul. Why would Luke repeat the entire charge for his readers? The reason seems to be to illustrate how Roman authority treated the prisoner (and therefore Christianity) with respect and appropriate legal care. In no manner could Christian or Roman readers interpret this account as an inflammatory, anti-government polemic aimed at stirring up civil strife.

The events that had taken place much earlier in Jerusalem are retold (verse 15). The effect is to intensify the drama or to heighten the suspense. In this version the entire assemblage of Jewish authority appears to want Paul condemned from the very first. But the Roman authority would have nothing to do with summary execution (verse 16).

In verse 17, Festus seems to imply by his words that "justice delayed is justice denied." But contrast verse 17 with Festus's's actions in 24:22 and 25:6.

Regardless of the Jewish intensity, the Romans simply cannot fathom the conflict. From the Roman view no real offense has been committed; this conflict is merely over theological or religious internal questions. The Christian doctrine of resurrection completely escapes the Roman imagination (26:24).

Unable to deal with the complex issue, Festus posed the question of venue to Paul. The appeal (25:11) is self-evident and does not need to be repeated. A complete factual report of the entire case is to the Romans impossible. The whole conflict seems at once both incomprehensible and frivolous. Luke's account suggests a benignly ignorant Festus.

Agrippa wants to meet Paul. The suspense continues. What will happen during the upcoming meeting?

With an economy of words, a scene of incredibly ornate and dazzling ceremony is portrayed (verse 23). Luke's earliest readers would have no difficulty imagining the scene of Paul, the single prisoner, surrounded by the pomp and pageantry of imperial Roman rule. What chance has Christianity in such a setting? Luke seems to draw the Christian predicament into an almost unbearable focus, and in the middle of it all stands Paul.

Festus now describes the charges as coming from the entire Jewish people. Never in earlier scenes in Acts have all the Jewish people been against Paul and Christianity. Entire theories of anti-Jewish thought could emerge from the questionable words of Festus.

As far as the Romans are concerned, Paul has done nothing wrong. The entire conflict between Paul and the Jews is once again described as nothing more than troublesome internal squabblings. Luke could hardly have stated his perspective on Roman reaction more forcefully. With no charge to write that would make any sense to other Romans, the present hearing must be held, presumably to find out if some sort of resolution can be made of the matter. To send any prisoner to the emperor without charges is tantamount to utter foolishness if not a travesty of law (verse 27).

How can we interpret this glittering scene? Many readers will see a historical event. Others will see an implication that in Christianity a force has been set loose in the world—the power of God through the Holy Spirit—to which some will react violently as did many Jews. Others will react in a kind of ignorant stupor that can make no sense out of Christianity at all. However, in either response one can see Christianity as an undeniable power with an undeniable importance. Thus at least one of Luke's concerns finds further expression. Namely, the gospel of Christ will not be hindered either by oppression or by tolerance. Paul's bonds contribute to the advancement of the gospel. First Festus and his counselors, and then Agrippa II, his sister Bernice, the military tributes, and the leading men of Caesarea heard the good news of salvation from Paul. This trial and defense gives Paul an opportunity to preach for a verdict.

Acts 26:1-23. Paul is given the opportunity to speak in his own defense by Agrippa, who appears to be the real expert and authority with respect to the law. Luke pictures Paul in the stance of an orator; but how can he? Is he not chained to soldiers? (26:29).

With elegant rhetoric, Paul defends himself. Paul is answering the charges of an internal Jewish-Christian controversy and not the large indictment of sedition. The central idea of Paul's defense is that he is guilty of no crime but that of being a good, loyal Jew, a Jew after God's own heart. Festus, remember, had seen no evidence of crime against the state (25:25). Paul assumes, as does the narrator, that Agrippa is familiar with Jewish customs. Agrippa was not a practicing Jew, however.

Luke's concern with Christianity's Jewish roots appears again. This Christian apostle standing before Agrippa is no less than a Pharisee from no less a city than Jerusalem. Paul omits any reference to either Tarsus or to his Roman citizenship.

The hope and promise God has had for Jews always centered on either nation or the land. Paul refers to neither. Instead Paul establishes God's hope firmly in the shared theological belief of resurrection. Thus, the link with Judaism is repeated. The resurrection of Jesus is obviously the fulfillment of the messianic hope.

The Resurrection, so long hoped for and so manifestly real through Jesus, is still the stone of stumbling for all Jews (assuming Paul addresses Agrippa as a Jew) and certainly all Romans (who can at best call such hope *religion* if not mere *superstition*) (verse 8).

The theme of Christianity's continuity with Judaism has been stressed up to this point. The speech now changes to Paul's own behavior toward the Christian movement. From his strict background, Paul had felt compelled to resist the new movement that centered around Jesus of Nazareth. In Jerusalem, the same city from which current indictments come, Paul had sought out many Christians (verse 10), Paul's role in those terrible persecutions finds its sharpest expression in verse 11. In contrast to 8:1, where Paul is pictured as consenting to the death of Stephen, here Paul's role is more as the leader of persecution. Evidently, Paul actually took part in the deaths of Christian people.

Here again the event is intensified (verses 13-18; compare 9:3-6; 22:6-10). In 9:4, only Paul falls to the ground while the companions see no one. Acts 22:6 shows Paul alone being struck. In Acts 26, both blindness and the intermediary role of Ananias are omitted. The impression left on both Roman authority and for the third time on Luke's readers is that Paul is entirely caught by the power of Jesus.

The image of opening eyes is of course a reference to the servant's summons in Isaiah 42:7, 16. Here Jesus' words to Paul come to an end (verse 18).

Paul continues addressing King Agrippa, telling him that the missionary work upon which Paul set out could not be resisted. This is also another strong affirmation of the Gentile mission. Paul's mission began first through preaching in Damascus and in Jerusalem. Paul's Christian preaching contained the classic call for repentance and change (verse 21). Presumably the preaching of Paul caused Jewish authorities to seize him in the Temple. No further mention is made regarding profaning the Temple. Is the narrator trying to illustrate the emptiness of Jewish charges against Paul?

The promised help of God (26:17) had indeed been forthcoming. Paul has gratefully received God's help. Moreover, the work to which Paul has been called and to which he continues to give witness is nothing less than the continuation of what Moses and the prophets had said would be inevitable. (Again Paul and the narrator show the strong link between Judaism and Christianity.)

The specific point of departure between Judaism and Christianity is the Messiah (verse 23). By Christian interpretation, the Old Testament states that the Messiah will suffer. Christians for instance see the suffering of Jesus anticipated in the suffering servant of Isaiah 53. Jews still read that utterance only as the servant of the Lord.

The Messiah who suffered and died is raised from the grave so that he may continue to proclaim the light to the world. The proclamation of light occurs through the Resurrection to both Jews and Gentiles.

Acts 26:24-32. Paul's words are interrupted by Festus. Remember that Festus had already declared the Resurrection to be impossible (25:19). Therefore, the problem, as Festus sees it, is that Paul has finally lost his mental balance due to too much study. Notice the skill of the narrator. Festus's interruption forces the reader to reexamine the Resurrection as a central element in Christian doctrine.

The sober truth, that is works of both truth and prudence, expresses a truth that is neither in need of Festus's assent nor contingent upon Paul's assent. The truth is in some sense objective and can therefore be understood. Also Christianity has been spread openly, this "was not done in a corner" (verse 26). Agrippa, a Jew, although a nonpracticing one, is asked to be a witness.

Paul cleverly works with Agrippa's Jewish past. Had Agrippa read the prophets? Then he would have to believe also in the death and resurrection of the Messiah. Paul brings the argument around so that Agrippa will have to consider the Christian interpretation of the Scriptures and, of course, Jesus.

Agrippa's response is a marvelously inviting and yet ambiguous one. Many scholars see in his statement a near conversion. Others see a shrewd sidestepping of the theological content while at the same time granting Paul a tacit assent. In either case the stature of Paul remains a towering presence. Even the Roman king must acknowledge the great power of Paul.

Luke uses a beautiful literary technique. The reader, heretofore an observer of the great dramatic confrontation, is now included by Paul's own words. Norman Rockwell's paintings often contained a similar invitation into the scene. Most of the characters are involved in the specific event being portrayed. But Rockwell would often paint one character looking directly at the viewer. The result is that the audience feels a closer affinity to the scene. Luke's story does the same thing. Clearly the plea is for *all* to be Christian, including the readers.

The final word is Paul's. All the Roman authorities can do is confess their own conviction that Paul cannot be found guilty. Indeed, Paul could be set free had he not earlier appealed to Caesar.

The purpose of the story becomes quite clear. The Roman authorities can find no punishable offense in Paul nor, by implication, in Christianity. Christianity has been shown to be a powerful movement and a force that has been loosed within the empire. No resistance either subtle or stark can silence the witness of men, women, apostles, and anonymous others to the messiahship of Jesus, the will of God, or the inevitable victory of the Holy Spirit.

Christians, by the time of Luke's writing, would have to be prepared to live out their faith in the empire. The towering figure of Paul under extreme duress would afford Christians an excellent example of how Christianity will prevail. And the Roman authorities would not have to fear the intentions of Christians. The movement is firmly rooted in a long-accepted, even if not completely understood, Jewish tradition. Christianity has no intention of stirring up civil strife and disobedience.

DIMENSION THREE:
WHAT DOES THE BIBLE MEAN TO ME?

Acts 26:16—Appointed to Serve

God's words to Paul remind us of Ezekiel being told to stand on his feet (Ezekiel 2:1, 3). Without a doubt, God summoned these two men for courageous ministries to reluctant and recalcitrant peoples. We may be inclined to read of such majestic heroes with little or no thought as to how God continues to summon men and women to the still-vital task of proclaiming the claims of God in our time.

Ask your class members to think of tasks to which God may be calling them. Is anyone in your class moved to declare the claim of God with respect to social issues? to racial prejudice? to civil rights? to increased violence? Then ask them to identify just how they came to the awareness of the tasks to which they feel called. Did they feel something twitch inside? Did they hear the call of God through the moans of the hungry? the cries of the dispossessed? the anguish of the poor? Ask them how, when resistance grew strongest, they managed to continue without growing either discouraged or distressed.

Be sure to point out that for both the prophet and the apostle, an awareness of the continued presence of God helped them fulfill their tasks.

Acts 26:19-28
The Plight of Theology in a Cynical World

Paul's assertion of a suffering Messiah and resurrection strikes the Romans as absurd or at least incomprehensible. Yet, Paul continued to present the gospel as he understood it even if such affirmations caused people to think him crazy.

We live in an age when many church people want not only the opportunity to present the gospel, but they want the gospel to triumph over any and all opposition. Luke's presentation of Paul in Rome suggests that the appropriate Christian posture is that of courageous proclamation even in an environment where cynicism prevails. The accounts of Paul's hearings illustrate stout courage and a certain gospel message. But they do not suggest that Paul and Christianity emerge victorious and superior over all culture.

Ask class members what they believe is the legitimate hope of the church's task. Do we as Christians really expect to triumph over all resistance? Must we have the majority opinion in culture? Or can we in some sense be satisfied to have the opportunity of proclaiming our message?

Luke's account suggests a certain patience on the part of the apostle. Paul does not need to win in order to effectively carry out his ministry. Even the cynical Roman king is intrigued by the Christian message. Would we be satisfied with the interest our gospel stirs in our hearers?

Acts 26:23—The Gospel of Resurrection

Throughout the Book of Acts, the notion of resurrection provides both the thread that holds the Jewish faith and Christian movement together and is the source of great bewilderment for scoffers.

Death may represent the single most important event in the drama of human experience. Does death represent an annihilation of everything? Or does death bring about a transition from something we can see, touch, taste, and smell to something that is essentially mystery but at the same time is essentially good?

Furthermore, resurrection implies that the death of one or even many does not invalidate nor kill the hope and intention of God. From the Christian perspective, death is not the final answer in any context. The gospel cannot be forever buried. The victory of God is inevitable.

Ask class members to discuss why the Resurrection is so incomprehensible to some observers. In what sense do class members share the resurrection hope that the purposes of God cannot be contained, not even by death itself?

— 13 —

Paul's Journey to Rome

Acts 27–28

DIMENSION ONE:
WHAT DOES THE BIBLE SAY?

Answer these questions by reading Acts 27

1. Who is responsible for Paul's travel to Rome? (27:1)

   A centurion of the Imperial Regiment, Julius, is responsible for Paul.

2. In addition to Paul and the narrator, who goes with the company? (27:2)

   Aristarchus, a man from Macedonia, goes with the prisoners.

3. What does Paul predict about the rest of the journey from Fair Havens? (27:8-10)

   Paul predicts disaster including loss of cargo and loss of life.

4. What is the hope Paul offers to the ship and its crew? What gives them that hope? (27:22-25)

   Paul assures the crew and others that no harm will come to them since a vision of an angel (Christ) has assured him that the Christian missionary journey to Rome must be successfully carried out.

5. How long does the vessel drift in the Adriatic (Sea of Adria)? (27:27)

   The vessel is adrift for two weeks.

6. How are Paul and other prisoners saved form death? (27:42-43)

   The centurion stops the guards from killing the prisoners to prevent escape. The centurion ordered all who could swim to jump overboard and get to land. By protecting Paul, he saves all the prisoners.

Answer these questions by reading Acts 28

7. Where does the ship's company land? (28:1)

   The ship beaches on the island of Malta.

8. How do the islanders show kindness toward the ship-wrecked company? (28:2)

   The islanders build a fire, around which those suffering from exposure can dry and warm themselves.

9. What happens to Paul? (28:3-6)

   While gathering firewood, a viper bites Paul on the hand. The islanders, based on their superstitions, assume Paul to be a murderer who is getting his justice after all. But Paul survives with no ill effects.

10. Whom does Paul heal? (28:7-8)

    Paul heals the father of Publius, the chief official of the island.

11. Whom does Paul first look for in Rome? (28:17)

    Paul looks for leaders of the Jewish community.

12. According to this account, why did Paul make his appeal to Caesar? (28:19)

    Paul appealed to Caesar because of Jewish resistance to him.

13. How long does Paul continue to preach the gospel in Rome? (28:30)

    Paul remains in Rome, "in his own rented house" for two years.

14. Complete the following outline of Paul's journey to Rome.

Paul and other prisoners are turned over to the centurion JULIUS (27:1). Intending to sail along the coast of Asia Minor, the ship sails to SIDON (27:3). Next the ship sails on the lee side of CYPRUS (27:4), arriving at MYRA (27:5). Boarding a different ship, the company continues with some difficulty to CNIDUS (27:7) and then under the lee of CRETE (27:7), near the port of SALMONE (27:7). They sailed along the coast to FAIR HAVENS, near the city of LASEA (27:8).

Midwinter voyages are perilous affairs at best. Paul predicts a terrible outcome. Nonetheless, the voyage continues toward PHOENIX, a Cretan harbor (27:12). A storm forces the voyage off course. Sailing to the south of CAUDA (27:16), the ship's crew desperately tries to avoid the shoals of Syrtis. As the storm increases in its ferocity the ship is driven for two weeks across the ADRIATIC SEA (27:27). Landfall is finally made on the island of MALTA (28:1).

Three months later, after Paul's miraculous survival of being bitten by a poisonous snake (28:3-6) and healing of Publius's father (28:7-8), the journey continues. The first port of call is SYRACUSE (28:12) where the travelers stay for three days. From there the company continues to RHEGIUM (28:13) and PUTEOLI (28:13). Along the way the travelers stop at two well-known resting areas: FORUM OF APPIUS and THREE TAVERNS (28:15). Finally Paul arrives in Rome.

DIMENSION TWO:
WHAT DOES THE BIBLE MEAN?

In this lesson you will study the final journey of Paul. Paul's earlier journeys have been missionary journeys. These two chapters contain one long story of great adventure, as the heroic apostle makes his way toward Rome.

Acts 27:1-12. The story begins with the appearance of another "we" section. Paul is being sent to Rome because of his appeal to Caesar. Perhaps some of Paul's friends can accompany him on the journey (this would account for the *we* section). Paul, however, is included in a group of prisoners. Julius, a centurion of the Imperial Regiment, is responsible for the prisoners. (A corps of this description was stationed in Syria during the first century.)

The ship in which the voyage is to be made is from the port of Adramyttium, southeast of Troas and northwest of Pergamum. Presumably prisoners traveled on ships used for other purposes as well as the transport of cargo. Aristarchus is mentioned during the demonstration of the Ephesian silversmiths (19:29), then as a participant in the journey to Jerusalem with the collection (20:4).

Following the northerly current along the Syrian coast, the first leg of the journey takes one day (approximately seventy miles). Paul is treated kindly by the Roman centurion and is allowed to see some friends (verse 3).

The term *to the lee* (also translated *under* or *under the lee*, verse 4) is a nautical reference to the leeward or east side of Cyprus, thus protecting the vessel from strong westerlies prevalent during the late summer months.

When they arrive at Myra the centurion has to find another ship. The ship from Alexandria (verse 6) may well have been a cargo ship carrying grain to Rome.

Cargo vessels of this time had but one large sail. The design of the vessel prohibited any sailing except directly with the wind or with the wind from the side. Tacking, or working one's way slightly into the wind, was impossible. The route would therefore have been from Myra to Rhodes, south to Crete by the lee of Crete (to the southeast of the island) by Cape Salmone. Near the city of Lasea the vessel stops in a bay opening to the east called either Fair Havens or Good Harbor.

The notion that much time had been lost (verse 9) implies a voyage that had already taken more time than had been expected. Thus the ship, the crew, and passengers are in great peril if the journey continues. Sea voyages in any season were perilous. But during the late fall they became markedly worse and ceased altogether between mid-November and mid-March.

Paul, the tentmaker, whose seagoing experience has been limited to a handful of voyages, announces a terrible prediction: "Our voyage is going to be disastrous and bring great loss to ship and cargo, and to our own lives also" (verse 10). Luke's purpose, however, is not to show Paul as the traveler with great knowledge. To keep Paul in the center of the action, Luke does two things. First, he portrays Paul as one with great prophetic foresight. Second, to make this description possible, the centurion appears to have much more authority than in actual fact he could have had. A centurion would have no seafaring expertise. The centurion's only task would have been to secure space to the transport of prisoners.

Acts 27:13-26. When a south wind picks up allowing the vessel to change harbors, they sail close to the shore and make the day's journey uneventfully.

The gentle, favorable breezes change into tempestuous northeasters that strike as the ship clears the edge of the island. The ship is driven before the wind into the open sea where a real storm whips up. Because the ship cannot come about, that is turn away from the wind in order to adjust the sails, it could only continue making way as best as it could. To do otherwise would have left the ship foundering and subsequently beaten to pieces by the angry sea. The ship may well have been making way with only the smaller sail set on the bow.

Sailing in the lee of a small island called Cauda, the ship's crew and passengers have a momentary respite from the severe buffeting they have been enduring. Evidently the crew took this moment to check the smaller lifeboat being towed behind (verses 16-17).

Here the biblical storyteller's art is wonderfully illustrated. The reader can almost see the heavy, ponderous cargo vessel driven by raging winds and buffeted by crashing waves. Sailors scurry about on deck hauling lines and sail in order to secure what can be saved in the momentary calm. Heavier lines were placed lengthwise along the ship and tightened with a winch. Perhaps the crew and ship may survive the storm yet.

Syrtis is an especially treacherous area with sandbanks that could easily ground a vessel. Sails have already been reefed in order to preserve them from being tattered by the wind (verse 17).

As the storm continues raging, the ship is now threatened with sinking. Extra tackle, line, and spare parts are thrown overboard.

Finally, the narrator pictures storm-tossed seas with clouds scudding over a foundering vessel. By his own admission any hope of survival is lost amid the screeching winds and crashing seas. The picture is one of utter hopelessness (verse 20).

In the midst of this scene of darkening despair, Paul assumes the role of orator! Anyone familiar with trying to maintain balance on board a ship will smile at this image. Keeping one's balance is difficult enough. To assume an orator's stance is ludicrous, unless one keeps Luke's purpose in mind. Seasick sailors assemble to listen to their prisoner-passenger.

The appearance of an angel (verse 23) would be accepted by both Jew and Gentile without question. Luke's Christian readers would understand immediately the import of Paul's vision.

The crew need not worry. Because Paul has been destined to witness before Caesar, all the people on the ship will be saved as well. The narrator thus shows why the entire ship's company of crew, guards, and prisoners are not lost at sea.

Paul promises hope to the terrified men. Luke's purpose of placing Paul in the incongruous position of orator amid wind and waves is to show Paul's utter faith in God.

Paul declares, even as bearings are impossible due to clouds, that the ship will strike land (verse 26). The only island in two hundred and fifty miles of open sea between Tunisia and Sicily is Malta.

Acts 27:27-32. The story resumes from verse 20. After two weeks adrift, as much as four hundred and seventy miles in the raging Adriatic, the sailors sense landfall. How could they know? The roar of breakers on the island of Malta would have warned them.

Depths are read; first twenty fathoms (one hundred twenty feet), then fifteen fathoms (ninety feet). Due to the short interval between readings, the sailors know they are approaching land very quickly. They are in danger of running aground. Anchors are lowered to try to slow the ships's approach. The four anchors would keep the ship stern-to-the-waves, thus preventing a broadside to the breakers.

The events that follow are extremely muddled (verses 30-32). Surely the captain would have noticed peculiar

behavior by the sailors. Sailors themselves would have been well aware of the relative security of the larger vessel in a dangerous shoal, especially in the darkness of night. Soldiers, accustomed only to land maneuvers and nearly panicky about the prospects of death at sea, would have misunderstood any effort to use the lifeboat. Perhaps the sailors tried to use the lifeboat to take an anchor at some distance to be lowered. Incredibly the soldiers cut loose the smaller lifeboat. Now the larger cargo vessel will have to be beached.

Acts 27:33-38. Two weeks with absolutely no food would have made everyone practically useless due to exhaustion and hunger. The image is one of effect to show the desperate plight of everyone. Against the backdrop of disaster Paul again reassures the men (verse 34)

The image of Paul breaking bread and giving thanks reminds us of the Eucharist (Communion). Here Paul uses only part of the ritual—the bread before the meal.

After seeing Paul eat, the rest of the crew and company, some 276 people, eat. Strengthened by eating, the crew sets about preparing the ship for beaching.

Acts 27:39-44. This section could easily have followed verse 32 without interrupting the flow of the story. Luke's purpose, however, requires the image of Paul's trust and the Eucharist amid dire circumstances. In what is now called Saint Paul's Bay, the crew plans to beach the ship. Anchor lines are cut, tillers loosened, and a small sail is set in the bow's small mast. The ship can now be steered toward a safe landing. Instead the ship runs aground on a sandbar and is torn asunder by the massive waves (verse 41).

The soldiers intend to execute all prisoners lest there be an escape during the disaster. But God's purpose of Paul witnessing in Rome is helped by the centurion. Again note the manner in which Luke shows the lack of Roman hostility toward Paul and the Christian movement. Because the centurion saves one, all are rescued. Thus the promise of verse 24 is fulfilled.

Acts 28:1-10. The promise of 27:26 is fulfilled. The ship lands at the only possible landfall within hundreds of miles. Again, the *we* passages appear.

Malta had been settled by some Romans and veterans of Caesar's armies as well as natives. The narrator does not say whether the entire 276 survivors cluster around the fire. In all likelihood the narrator wants to show the small band of Christians ("we") around the fire. The huddled group, suffering from exposure and sitting around the blaze, sets the stage for the next scene.

As Paul busies himself helping the shivering group, he is bitten by a viper. According to the natives such an event means that justice has finally caught up with Paul. To the utter amazement of onlookers, Paul shakes the reptile off into the fire and "suffered no ill effects." Paul's miraculous survival prompts the natives to call him a god or at least to say he is favored by the gods. Note that in this instance Paul makes no effort to protest as he had earlier in Lystra (14:11-18).

The narrator also tells another story in which Paul is the central focus. Publius is the chief official who is aided by the apostle. Even at this late time Paul is still described as the worker of miracles.

The healing is accomplished through the laying on of hands and prayers (verse 8).

The gifts presented to the Christian could possibly have been fees, though in all probability they were more like honors (verse 10).

Acts 28:11-22. After a three-month midwinter delay, the journey continues. The wreck occurred sometime in November and therefore the journey resumes in February. Another ship from Alexandria had successfully wintered in the bay. The Alexandrian vessel is adorned by the figureheads of Castor and Pollux ("the Twin gods"), both of whom are worshiped by sailors.

Perhaps because of wind conditions or the need to unload cargo, three days are spent in Syracuse on the island of Sicily. Traveling in a circuit the company passes through Rhegium (modern-day Reggio Calabria). After a one-day stay they continue to Puteoli on the north side of the Gulf of Naples. The journey then continues to Rome along the Appian Way (some five days' travel). The Forum of Appius and Three Taverns were well-known stopping places along the Appian Way (verse 15).

Scholars have tried to explain what appears to be two arrivals in Rome. Verse 14 indicates that the travelers have arrived in Rome. However, verse 16 makes a similar claim. The centurion already has orders to hasten the prisoner to Rome as many delays have already retarded their movement (27:9). The delay en route allows time for Paul's arrival to be announced. The twofold repetition sounds much like the journey to Jerusalem motif (21:15-17).

After three days, Paul summons the Jewish leaders. He addresses them with the familiar greeting *Brothers*, implying closeness. By Paul's own witness he has done nothing against Jews or the traditions of the patriarchs. Still, he had been turned over as a prisoner to the Romans. Luke uses the speech to show the parallel between what happened to Jesus in his trial in Jerusalem and what happens to Paul in Rome.

The Romans appear to want the release of Paul. Here Paul says that the Jewish outcry compelled his appeal to Caesar. The case is stated differently than in 25:10-11. Indeed, Paul's anxiety about the efforts of the Sanhedrin to have him idled is not even suggested in this account.

Paul now, at the crowning point in his missionary career, attempts to clarify exactly what his stance has been (23:6; 24:15; 26:6-7). Luke uses the final moments of the drama to state for the final time the Christian hope. The hope is of course the messianic hope, which for Paul, Luke, and the balance of the Christian community is the Resurrection hope of Jesus Christ.

Acts 28:23-29. Large numbers of Jewish leaders assemble to hear Paul's presentation and interpretation. In order to show Paul's intensity Luke describes the proceedings as occupying a full day's time. Evidently Paul, though still a prisoner and bound with chains (verse 20), had privileges enough to secure a room in which to entertain a large group of Jewish leaders.

Paul's presentation correlates the kingdom of God and the life, death, and resurrection of Jesus. Scriptural evidence is central in Paul's interpretation, especially as the messiahship of Jesus is concerned. The Christian proclamation is firmly rooted in the Hebrew Scriptures, what Christians now call the Old Testament.

The response to Paul's interpretation is by now quite as expected. A handful of listeners are persuaded but the large majority reject the Christian interpretation outright (verse 24). The entire scene of Paul seeking out Jews with whom to share the Christian interpretation and hope is reminiscent of other similar encounters in Acts. In Pisidian Antioch the Jews rejected the gospel (13:46). In Greece, Jews of Corinth rejected the gospel (18:6). Now finally in Rome, Jews again reject Christianity.

Luke puts into Paul's words the Christian understanding as to why the Jews continually reject the gospel. Isaiah 6:9-10 is often used to describe the rejection of Christian interpretation (Matthew 13:14-15; Mark 4:12; John 12:40). Isaiah 6:9-10 is cited to assess responsibility of guilt on the stubborn people who refuse the gospel. Therefore, salvation by the authority of the Holy Spirit will be sent to the Gentiles (verse 28). The mission to the Gentiles has been forced by the Jews rejecting the gospel.

The image of Paul here is one of great authority. This image contrasts sharply with Paul's own description (2 Corinthians 10:10). Luke's purpose has been to show the apostle as a towering figure, a powerful preacher, and a Christian par excellence, confronting any and all challenges graciously yet courageously.

Acts 28:30-31. For two years Paul's ministry continues. According to verse 30, *all* were allowed access to him. Paul's dying a martyr's death is assumed through the vision in 27:24 and also the prediction in the farewell speech at Miletus (20:25, 36). The manner in which Paul dies is not described.

Luke ends the book with preaching and teaching about the Lord Jesus Christ continuing openly and unhindered.

The Christian movement has endured many trials, struggled with strong opposition, and wrestled mightily with dissension within and oppression from without. Yet, through it all, the gospel has emerged victorious and still moving on toward its universal application. No rejection will make the gospel void. No opposition will defeat it. No amount of persecution will drain it of its power.

DIMENSION THREE:
WHAT DOES THE BIBLE MEAN TO ME?

Acts 28:31—A Concluding Hope

Luke brings his work to a hopeful conclusion, but his story does not end here. The conclusion is more a suggestion of a continued mission by the apostle and, by implication, the church as a whole.

The Christian movement began as a relatively obscure movement within the province of Judea. Within two generations the gospel had spread throughout the entire Roman Empire. Within two hundred years, the Christian church had its center in Rome itself. For the next millennium, the Catholic church held the stretched fabric of society together.

Our own century confronts the gospel with challenges and opposition. If Luke were writing today, would he conclude the story on a hopeful note? Is the church challenged today with continuing to proclaim the gospel in what may appear to be an alien and hostile environment?

Can the Christian gospel hold together what appears to be increasingly fractured? Ask class members to point to hopeful signs of where the church functions as a strength that holds life together.

Acts 28:31—The Struggle for an Unhindered Gospel

Luke ends the Book of Acts by describing Paul preaching "boldly and without hindrance." The peculiar ending prompts one to consider the manner in which the action continues. Against oppression and persecution, the gospel had struggled successfully. With the peril of internal discord and heresy the gospel wrestled successfully. Against the prejudice of racial and cultural bigotry the gospel fought mightily. And in each of these areas the struggle continues.

Ask class members to list on a chalkboard or poster paper areas in which the gospel continues to struggle to be unhindered. Are our churches unbiased with respect to membership? to ministers and members of racial or ethnic groups different from the majority? to women? Do we really believe in the means of grace for everyone, or do we still resist the inclusion of particular types or classes of people?

You will want to conclude this study by listing insights that have begun to take shape. Ask class members to add to the list. Some of the insights may be disturbing. List them as well.

Then close with a prayer giving thanks for the ever-living word of God.